PRINCIPLES

OF

CRIMINAL

PROCEDURE

Fourth Edition

By

Russell L. Weaver

Professor of Law & Distinguished University Scholar
University of Lousiville
Louis D. Brandeis School of Law

Leslie W. Abramson

Professor of Law
University of Louisville
Louis D. Brandeis School of Law

John M. Burkoff

Professor of Law
University of Pittsburgh
School of Law

Catherine Hancock

Professor of Law
Tulane University
School of Law

CONCISE HORNBOOK SERIES®

WEST.

A Thomson Reuters business

Mat #41173727

© West, a Thomson business, 2004, 2007
© 2008 Thomson/West
© 2012 Thomson Reuters

       610 Opperman Drive
       St. Paul, MN 55123
       1-800-313-9378

Printed in the United States of America

ISBN: 978-0-314-27666-7

To Ben and Kate, with love, RLW

For Lisa, Same, Shel & Will, LWA

Dedicated, with love, to Nancy,
Amy & Sean, David & Emmy,
Emma, Molly, Hannah & Cyrus, JMB

For Elizabeth, Caitlin & Margeret, CH

Preface

This fourth edition of Principles of Criminal Procedure brings the book up-do-date through the 2010–2011 United States Supreme Court term. Otherwise the book continues to analyze criminal procedure case and concepts, and presents them in a concise and easy to understand way. The book includes all leading United States Supreme Court Cases and some important state court decisions, as well as commentary on those decisions.

In order to facilitate learning, each chapter beings with "focal points" designed to introduce students to the topic, and ends with "points to remember" designed to reinforce the concepts presented. These "focal points" and "points to remember" are designed to enhance understanding and learning.

In an effort to save space, this book does not include any footnotes. Rather than trying to create a treatise or encyclopedia, our goal was to create a student friendly book that is easy-to-use. For those students who might want to look up a case that we discuss, the book does include "U.S." citations to United States Supreme Court decisions and relevant state citations. However, it does not include parallel cites.

RLW, LWA, JMB, & CH

Summary of Contents

Table of Contents

PRINCIPLES
OF
CRIMINAL
PROCEDURE
Fourth Edition

Chapter 1

INTRODUCTION

Focal Points for Introductory Chapter

- Sources of defendants' rights.

- Prosecution systems.

- The roles of prosecutors and defense counsel.

- Pre-arrest investigation stage.

- The arrest stage.

- The booking and jailing stage.

- The post-arrest investigation stage.

- The decision to bring formal charges through a complaint.

- The defendant's first appearance in court.

- The preliminary hearing or grand jury stage.

- The arraignment stage.

- The pre-trial motions stage.

- The trial stage.

- The sentencing stage.

- The appeal stage.

- The post-appeal stage and post-conviction remedies.

Lawyers who work in the criminal justice system rely on many sources of law, including the constitutional case law of the United States Supreme Court. These famous federal precedents are part of the bedrock knowledge of defense counsel and prosecutors who practice in municipal, state and federal courts, and roughly a dozen precedents are produced by the Court every year. This case law is the primary source for most criminal procedure casebooks, but the significance of the Court's rulings can be difficult to understand in context, because of the narrow doctrinal focus exhibited in a single case. The Court's opinions rarely describe the procedures and lawyering activities that occurred before a case was briefed and argued in the rarified forum of the Court's chambers. Each opinion usually gives the reader only a tiny glimpse of the large backdrop of law, custom, and practice that surrounds each case. This chapter provides a brief overview of that backdrop, which practicing lawyers take for granted as a frame of reference for understanding the Court's precedents.

A. Sources of Law That Create Legal Rights for Criminal Defendants and Regulate the Procedures of the Criminal Justice System

Certain federal constitutional rights are available to all defendants who are charged with crimes. These rights are established in particular provisions of the Bill of Rights, such as the Fourth, Fifth, Sixth, and Eighth Amendments, and by the Due Process and Equal Protection Clauses of the Fourteenth Amendment. A defendant in a federal prosecution is also entitled to rights that are provided by federal statutes, such as the Federal Code of Criminal Procedure. A defendant in a state prosecution is entitled to invoke not only federal constitutional rights, but also rights provided by state statutes, such as state codes of criminal procedure.

Most importantly, state defendants also have state constitutional rights that may provide greater protections than federal constitutional rights. Most state constitutions have provisions that are similar to the Bill of Rights, and each state supreme court is the final authority on the meaning of these provisions. From a state supreme court's point of view, federal Supreme Court interpretations of a particular right provide a model for interpretation of the state constitutional version of that right. However, the federal model may be rejected by state courts that choose to provide greater protections for state court defendants. While many rulings by the United States Supreme Court are borrowed by state supreme courts as interpretations of parallel state constitutional provisions, some rulings are rejected by state courts that choose to take an independent course. In effect, the federal constitution creates a "floor" that establishes the minimum rights that must be recognized in all criminal prosecutions, but the state courts are free to establish their own "ceilings" that establish the maximum rights that will be enforced in state prosecutions. These ceilings may be expressed in state constitutional case law, in rulings based on interpretations of state statutes, or in rulings based on other legal sources. From a defense counsel's perspective, representation of a client in a particular state court requires a bedrock knowledge of that state's constitutional and statutory law, in order to raise all relevant state-law claims in tandem with arguments based on the federal constitution. State prosecutors also possess the same bedrock knowledge, which enables them to respond to all these claims.

In addition to constitutional and statutory law, there are other sources of law that create rights for criminal defendants or regulate the criminal justice process in important ways. One case-law source is the body of judge-made rules that derive from a court's "supervisory" authority over the criminal court system and its evidentiary rules. One statutory source is the rules of court adopted by judges to govern procedure in particular courts. These sources exist in both federal and state jurisdictions. There are also "local" sources of law that create rights and regulate criminal procedure, such as city ordinances and municipal court rules.

Occasionally, it may be unclear whether a person is charged with a "crime," or only with a "civil" offense that does not entitle her to state and federal constitutional and statutory rights reserved for criminal defendants. When the Congress or a state legislature labels a sanction as criminal, courts recognize this as sufficient to allow a defendant to invoke such rights. However, if the legislature labels a sanction as civil, this does not end the inquiry. The Supreme Court has ruled that it is theoretically possible for a defendant to persuade a court to treat a proceeding as criminal despite its legislative classification as civil. However, it is usually very difficult for defense counsel to win such an argument, without strong evidence that the statutory scheme is punitive in purpose or effect.

While the Supreme Court's federal constitutional precedents have been likened to a "code" of criminal procedure, they are neither as systematic nor as comprehensive as a legislative code. Instead, they reveal the Court's historical preoccupations with particular issues that raise fundamental questions about fairness in the treatment of people who are charged with crime, and about the needs of law enforcement officers to prosecute crimes effectively. For example, the Prohibition era provided the setting for the Court's early development of Fourth Amendment law defining police powers to perform searches and seizures, and the focus on the prosecution of drug crimes in recent decades has provoked the Court to establish many new Fourth Amendment precedents. Moreover, the Court's precedents are concentrated in particular fields of criminal procedure, so that some fields are heavily influenced by them and other fields are not. Even in fields where many precedents exist, the Court's decisions often provide sketchy guidance for lower courts that must attempt to interpret and enforce these holdings. Thus, in most fields of criminal procedure, the Court's decisions provide a starting point for analyzing some issues, and create a limited degree of legal uniformity in the decisions produced by state and federal courts.

When state legislatures and courts consider the need to define or interpret statutory codes governing criminal procedure, they are often influenced by the Federal Rules of Criminal Procedure and other federal statutes, and by the American Bar Association Standards for Criminal Justice. They also may be influenced by the American Law Institute's Model Code of Pre–Arraignment Procedure. However, there is little pressure for the "nationalization" of criminal procedure doctrine and practice, in part because of the long history of state and local autonomy and diversity in this field. In fact, the politicization of "law and order" issues in recent decades has created the opposite kind of pressure for constant local experimentation with criminal procedure rules. Public criticism of the weaknesses of the criminal justice system is a permanent feature of the modern legal landscape, and political calls for reform of the system have affected many aspects of criminal procedure, ranging from the election of state supreme court justices based on their doctrinal views to legislative attempts to repeal or restrict various criminal procedure rules that protect defendants, such as the writ of habeas corpus and exclusionary rules of evidence.

B. Prosecution Systems

1. Multiple Jurisdictions, Major and Minor Crimes

When a person does a criminal act, he may violate simultaneously the criminal law of multiple jurisdictions, such as federal and state laws, or state laws and municipal ordinances. According to the Court's Double Jeopardy doctrine, multiple prosecutions for the same act by different "sovereign" governments are not prohibited by the constitution. Therefore, if an act violates state and federal law, for example, it is up to the prosecutors in each jurisdiction to decide how to coordinate the two potential prosecutions. It is possible that a statute of limitations may bar prosecution in one jurisdiction, or that prosecution in one jurisdiction is particularly advantageous because of the penalty, the procedural rules, or some other reason. Or, some prosecutors may lack resources that other prosecutors possess, and this difference may influence the timing and outcome of decisions to prosecute in only one or both jurisdictions.

In federal and state jurisdictions, most prosecutions are for minor crimes. While the definition of a "minor" crime is not uniform among the states, in most states a misdemeanor cannot be punished for more than one year in prison. Fewer than one tenth of state prosecutions are for felonies. By contrast, about one third of federal prosecutions are for felonies. Not surprisingly states have established different procedures to deal with the almost 12 million minor-crime prosecutions that occur every year. For example, a defendant who is charged with a misdemeanor may not be entitled to a preliminary hearing, grand jury review, pretrial discovery, or a jury trial. Also, prosecutions for minor crimes may be tried in municipal court before a magistrate who may not be a lawyer.

2. *The Gap Between Law and Practice*

When lawyers practice criminal law, they find that the criminal procedure rules "on the books" may not be reflected in reality, and that a defendant's rights may be rarely invoked or enforced. This may be the result of defense counsel's advice to waive these rights, as when a defendant pleads guilty and thereby waives the right to trial by jury and the privilege against self-incrimination, among others. Or, it may be that a defense counsel lacks the resources to pursue all potential legal arguments available to an indigent defendant, or that such counsel is incompetent under A.B.A. standards (but not provably "ineffective" under federal constitutional standards). It may be that a defense counsel lacks evidence that will persuade a judge or prosecutor to accept a defendant's claim, as when a judge credits a police officer's testimony concerning an event and rejects the defendant's testimony. Even when a defendant has a good claim, it may be that she has no right to the assistance of appointed counsel to pursue such a claim. According to Supreme Court precedents, the Sixth Amendment guarantees trial counsel for indigent federal defendants in all criminal prosecutions, but guarantees trial counsel for an indigent state defendant only when she will receive a jail sentence. For appeals, the Fourteenth Amendment guarantees indigent defendants a right to counsel only for the first appeal. Defendants who seek to pursue claims in other circumstances have no federal constitutional right to counsel, although they may have such rights based on state constitutional or statutory law.

The gap between law and practice also is created by the decentralized nature of prosecution systems. The federal system is the most centralized institution, because police and prosecutors both answer to a single prosecutorial authority, the Department of Justice (DOJ). The DOJ attempts to create some uniformity among its agents through the promulgation of policy positions to be followed by all United States Attorneys and, for example, all Drug Enforcement Administration officers. By contrast, in state prosecution systems, police and prosecutors work for different authorities, so that police actions may not be authorized by prosecutors, but authorized only by the police department. Typically, state prosecutors have "territorial" jurisdiction over a particular county (which often overlaps with the jurisdiction of certain local prosecutors or city attorneys), and a variety of police departments also have overlapping jurisdictions within the same territory. This collection of autonomous groups in the prosecution system makes it difficult for uniform policies or practices to be implemented without the cooperation of all the agents in the system.

Finally, both police and prosecutors are vested with considerable discretion, which further widens the gap between law and practice. For example, the police have some discretion to ignore criminal acts, or to arrest one person for certain crimes but not others. Prosecutors have discretion in their charging decisions, and in plea bargaining. When there are no legal consequences for particular actions by these prosecuting agents, their discretion allows for discriminatory law enforcement. Some of the Supreme Court's remedies for constitutional violations by police and prosecutors are assumed to be necessary in order to create incentives for these prosecuting agents to adhere to constitutional requirements. Yet even the existence of incentives cannot guarantee the enforcement of constitutional rights on the streets or in court.

C. The Roles of Prosecutors and Defense Counsel in Various Stages of a Criminal Prosecution

1. The Pre–Arrest Investigation Stage

One goal of most pre-arrest investigations, whether conducted by police or by prosecutors working together with police, is to obtain evidence that will satisfy the "probable cause" standard required both for arrest and for judicial validation of any decision to charge a person with a crime. This standard does not require as much evidence as the "preponderance" (more likely than not) standard for proving liability in a typical civil case. But the probable cause standard requires more proof than the lower "reasonable suspicion" standard that allows police to stop, question, frisk, and briefly detain people during pre-arrest investigations. A second goal of most pre-arrest investigations is to obtain sufficient evidence to satisfy the "beyond a reasonable doubt" standard required for conviction at trial or for a guilty plea. If this kind of evidence cannot be obtained before an arrest is made, then police and prosecutors will attempt to obtain it by using a variety of investigatory techniques after the arrest.

A prosecutor's first contact with a case usually occurs after police have engaged in some investigative procedures following the report of a crime, or after police have arrested a person following such a report and investigation. Police may not be able to make a crime-scene arrest, but they usually will interview the victim and any witnesses and collect evidence, in order to effectively preserve a record for later prosecution. Unlike the police activities portrayed in television dramas, investigations for most crimes do not go beyond these simple activities.

When further investigation is called for, prosecutors sometimes may be asked to participate in police efforts to obtain a warrant for searches and seizures of a person's home, or in interviews of witnesses or interrogations of a person who is a possible suspect but not in custody. Occasionally, a prosecutor must participate in investigations of unreported crimes. They may help to supervise "sting" operations, for example, or to advise the police concerning the use of undercover police agents or informants, or the use of police surveillance techniques such as electronic monitoring. Prosecutors may also investigate crimes through the use of grand jury proceedings, and rely on subpoenas to compel witnesses to testify and provide evidence to grand juries.

A defense counsel usually will not play a role in most pre-arrest investigative activities by prosecutors and police, unless called upon to do so by a client. For example, a person with retained counsel may ask for advice concerning the advisability of agreeing to a police interview, and may decide to agree to the interview only in the presence of counsel. A witness who is required to appear before a grand jury may consult retained counsel during breaks in the course of the grand jury proceedings. A person who believes he may be the "target" of the grand jury investigation may also employ retained counsel to communicate with prosecutors concerning the case, in order to protect his interests or to attempt to influence the ultimate charging decision.

2. The Arrest Stage

There are two different kinds of arrests: the non-custodial "citation" arrest and the "full-custody" arrest. Both require probable cause, but the citation arrest is used typically only for minor offenses such as traffic crimes. Many states and municipalities authorize police to issue an arrest citation for such crimes, in their discretion, and to release the arrested person after giving her the citation. The arrestee has the obligation to respond to the citation, either by pleading guilty and paying a fine, or by appearing in court to contest guilt. Even for minor offenses, however, police may retain the discretion to perform a full-custody arrest, and usually they will follow this practice when arresting a person for a serious crime. After forcibly detaining the arrestee, the police will take him to the police station for "booking," and then the arrestee will be jailed or possibly released to await the outcome of the prosecutor's review and decision to charge.

Most arrests are made without warrants, as authorized by the Supreme Court's precedents establishing a variety of exceptions to the Fourth Amendment's warrant requirement. Thus, police will seek an arrest warrant from a magistrate only when this is required by law, or when there is some practical reason to do so. Prosecutors may work together with police in preparing the documents to present to a magistrate. The request for a warrant must be supported by sworn affidavits describing the investigation that led the police to believe there is probable cause that a crime has been committed by a particular person. The magistrate's hearing on the police request for an arrest warrant is *ex parte,* so that defense counsel usually has no role to play in this procedure.

The power to make a full-custody arrest carries with it other powers. It entitles police to perform a full search of the arrestee's person at the scene of arrest, and to search the compartment of a car when arresting a driver. Once a person is in custody, more intrusive searches may be allowed for arrestees who are going to be jailed. Even though these searches may be made without probable cause, a warrantless arrest must be based upon probable cause that will be reviewed by a magistrate at a hearing after the arrest. The Supreme Court's precedents establish 48 hours as the normal deadline for such a hearing, but some states have a 24–hour deadline.

3. The Booking and Jailing Stage

People who have undergone a full-custody arrest will also undergo the booking process, which usually occurs at the police station or jail. The purpose of booking is to allow the police to keep a record of arrests, and to obtain photographs and fingerprints of arrestees. There is no connection between booking and the formal "charging" process, which occurs sometime later. During booking, the arrestee is asked to supply biographical information, such as name and address, but may not be asked questions about the crime. After booking, police may allow people who are arrested for minor crimes to post "bail" immediately, and to be released on their own recognizance, pending the outcome of later decisions to bring a formal charge against them. However, people who lack the money to pay such bail will be jailed, as will people who are charged with serious crimes. Someone who is jailed may be subjected to a thorough search of his person, and a complete inventory of his possessions may be performed. State or local law, or police custom or practice may allow him to telephone a lawyer or a friend at this stage, but if no such calls are allowed, an arrested person who is indigent may not have any contact with defense counsel until the arraignment stage.

4. The Post–Arrest Investigation Stage

After an arrest, a prosecutor may participate in the same kinds of investigative activity that precede an arrest, such as witness interviews or interrogations, and the procuring of search warrants. Additionally, a prosecutor may participate in activities that usually occur after arrest, such as a "lineup." An indigent arrestee has no *per se* right to have appointed counsel present during the lineup, where police require the arrestee to stand with a group of people who roughly resemble her, and ask a witness to attempt to identify the person who committed the crime. Not until the initiation of formal "adversarial judicial proceedings" does such a right to counsel exist. Nor does the arrestee have a right to have appointed counsel present at a photographic "showup," where police show a witness an "array" of photographs which includes a picture of the defendant, and ask the witness to attempt to identify the guilty party. A prosecutor also may participate in the interrogation of an arrested person, who is now entitled to *Miranda* rights because of the existence of "custodial" interrogation. While the arrestee has no right to the presence of defense counsel at this interrogation, the arrestee may invoke the right to counsel by asking for a lawyer, and thereby preclude further interrogation in the absence of counsel.

5. The Decision to Bring a Formal Charge by Filing a Complaint

When a person is arrested, the police have, in a sense, informally "charged" that person with committing a crime. But the prosecution does not begin until a "complaint" is filed, either by the prosecutor or by the police. Many arrests do not result in the filing of complaint. In some cases, a supervising police officer will decide that the charge should not be pursued. In many jurisdictions, a prosecutor will make this decision, although it is possible that the decision to drop a case may not be made until after the defendant's "first appearance," or even later, after the filing of an information or issuance of an indictment. When a prosecutor decides to drop a charge, it is most often because of insufficient evidence, or because of the unavailability of witnesses whose testimony is believed to be necessary for conviction. In making charging decisions, a prosecutor also may decide to change the original charge, or to add additional charges. It is common for a prosecutor to review all felony arrests before deciding which charges to pursue by filing a complaint, and to allow police to file a complaint for most misdemeanor charges without a prosecutor's review.

When a complaint is filed either by a prosecutor or by police, it is filed in a magistrate's court. At this point, the arrestee is now a "defendant." The complaint usually sets forth a description of the crime and a citation to the criminal code concerning the offense being charged. Either the police or the victim will sign the complaint, and swear to the truth of its allegations. The act of filing the complaint is not necessarily accompanied by other immediate formal judicial proceedings. However, this filing sets other procedures in motion under state or local law, such as the requirement that a defendant must make a "first appearance" in court within a certain time period. If the defendant is not in jail, there may be a time lapse of several days before this hearing, but any defendant in jail must be brought "promptly" before a magistrate. Further, if a defendant was arrested without a warrant, the validity of probable cause for the arrest must also be determined promptly by a magistrate.

If the crime is a misdemeanor, the complaint will remain the "charging instrument" for the prosecutor, and the case usually will be tried in the magistrate's court. However, if the crime is a felony, the complaint will be replaced with a different instrument after proceedings in the magistrate's court are finished, and the case proceeds to the court where the trial will occur. In cases where the grand jury is involved, that instrument will be the indictment, and in other cases, that instrument will be a document called the "information." Defense counsel usually do not play a role at the charging stage, unless they have been retained by a client to communicate with the prosecutor and to attempt to negotiate the disposition of the charge.

6. The Defendant's First Appearance in Court

The defendant's first appearance occurs after the complaint is filed. This initial hearing before the magistrate may occur as early as a few hours after arrest, or as late as several days after the arrest, depending on the defendant's custodial status and the nature of the arrest. Usually, the hearing has three purposes. First, the magistrate informs the defendant of the charges set forth in the complaint, and typically describes the defendant's various rights, such as the right to remain silent and the right to counsel. Second, the magistrate must determine whether the defendant is indigent, and ask an indigent defendant whether he wishes to be represented by appointed counsel. Most defendants are indigent. Most often, these defendants will be represented by attorneys who are employed by a state or local public defender agency. However, some jurisdictions continue to use a system of appointing attorneys from the private bar. A few jurisdictions allow a private law firm or other group to have a contract for representation of indigents. The magistrate is supposed to take whatever steps are necessary to begin the process of having counsel appointed in a particular jurisdiction. Finally, the magistrate sets bail for the defendant at this hearing, assuming that this is necessary because the defendant is in custody. The magistrate may require the defendant to post cash or a bond that is secured from a professional bonding agency. In the alternative, the magistrate may decide to release a defendant, but impose conditions on that release. Some states allow the magistrate to perform a fourth function at this hearing, which is to review the grounds for probable cause for a warrantless arrest. For misdemeanor cases triable in the magistrate's court, a fifth function of the first appearance is to ask for the defendant's plea on the record. It is possible for a misdemeanor defendant to plead guilty, assuming that any right to counsel and other rights are properly waived. The magistrate's acceptance of a guilty plea is regulated by standards set forth in constitutional precedents as well as statutory law. In felony cases, the defendant's plea on the record will occur at the arraignment. While indigent defendants will not be represented by appointed counsel at the first appearance, retained defense counsel may participate in the hearing.

7. The Preliminary Hearing or Grand Jury Stage

The preliminary hearing usually will be the first stage where an indigent defendant will have representation by appointed counsel, and thus for most defendants, it will be the first proceeding where the prosecutor and the defense counsel meet formally as adversaries. However, a preliminary hearing may not occur for a variety of reasons. A prosecutor may decide not to pursue the charge and file a *nolle prosequi* motion in order to have the complaint dismissed. A defense counsel may advise a client to plead guilty, and to waive the preliminary hearing in anticipation of the plea. Or, a prosecutor may decide to avoid the disadvantages of a preliminary hearing by seeking an indictment from a grand jury.

The primary disadvantage of a hearing, from a prosecutor's point of view, is that it provides advantages to defense counsel. Specifically, it allows defense counsel to cross-examine the "probable cause" witnesses who will testify at the hearing, and thereby to obtain a record that may be used for impeachment of these witnesses at trial. Defense counsel may also discover a prosecutor's evidence or strategy that would otherwise be difficult to learn about before trial. Typically, the defense does not present evidence at a preliminary hearing, in order to avoid the very disadvantages that may provoke a prosecutor to avoid such a hearing. By taking the same witnesses to a secret grand jury proceeding where defense counsel is absent, the prosecutor may obtain a finding of probable cause, and avoid the need for a magistrate to make this determination at a preliminary hearing.

• In any event, even if the prosecutor does decide to go forward with a preliminary hearing, and to minimize the exposure of witnesses by presenting a small amount of evidence, it is the rare case where a magistrate rejects a complaint for lack of probable cause. After all, another magistrate has determined that probable cause existed for the arrest, and unless other evidence casts doubt upon that determination, the result of this second probable cause determination will be the same. Once this decision is made, there are two possible routes that the prosecution will take, depending on the requirements of state law. In a majority of states, the defendant must be bound over to the trial court, where the prosecutor will file an "information" which will supplant the complaint. In the other states, and in federal prosecutions, the defendant must be "bound over" to the grand jury, so that an indictment may issue from that body, and supplant the complaint. In states where a prosecutor has the options of using the grand jury or filing an information, the latter procedure is typically used. If the grand jury option must be used, this group of people is required to make an independent determination of probable cause, based on a prosecutor's marshalling of the evidence. Defense counsel do not have access to these secret proceedings. It is the rare case where a grand jury refuses to indict a defendant, whether or not the grand jury's proceeding was preceded by a preliminary hearing.

Once an indictment is issued or an information is filed, Supreme Court precedents create some limitations for a prosecutor's investigative activities. For example, if secret police agents deliberately elicit incriminating statements from a defendant at this stage, such statements are not admissible at trial on the charged offense. If a prosecutor wishes to conduct a lineup, and does so in the absence of counsel, any identification obtained at the lineup is likewise inadmissible.

8. The Arraignment Stage

The arraignment has two functions. It is a hearing in the trial court where the judge will inform the defendant of the felony charges in the indictment or information, and where the defendant will be asked to enter a plea to the charges on the record. Most defendants will enter a plea of not guilty, and the judge will then set the case for trial. An indigent defendant is entitled to representation by appointed counsel at arraignment. If counsel has not been appointed and a defendant asks for counsel, this will operate as a bar to further police interrogation about the charged crime, but not necessarily other crimes.

Once the arraignment occurs, plea negotiations will begin, although in some cases they may occur earlier. A defense counsel may advise a defendant to plead guilty because of the benefits offered by a prosecutor in exchange for a plea, whether in the form of an agreement to reduce charges or to recommend a lower sentence. However, a prosecutor may refuse to offer such benefits, especially for serious charges. Most cases are resolved by guilty plea, but the rate of pleas varies among jurisdictions and among crimes. If no guilty plea occurs, a prosecutor may either dismiss the charges as in earlier stages, or continue to investigate the case and prepare for trial. The prosecutor will seek discovery material from the defense as permitted by statutory law, such as a list of trial witnesses. In some jurisdictions, the defense must give the prosecution notice of the intent to raise certain defenses at trial, such as insanity. The prosecutor may also rely on expert witnesses to assist with forensic evidence, or with preparation for rebuttal of certain defenses.

Ideally, if a defense counsel has the resources and time to investigate a case thoroughly, she will hire a private investigator to assist in interviewing witnesses and collecting evidence. She will interview the defendant, examine the police report, and seek discovery of exculpatory material from the prosecutor, as well as other discovery material allowed by state or federal law, such as a list of trial witnesses. She may seek to have an expert appointed for an indigent defendant to assist in trial preparation of crucial issues. She will attempt to follow the A.B.A. Standards concerning the proper representation of the defendant. There are especially complex duties of preparation required by the A.B.A. Standards for capital cases. However, appointed defense counsel are sometimes burdened with large case loads and have few or no resources for investigating a case thoroughly. In some jurisdictions, there are caps on the maximum fees that appointed counsel may receive, such as $1,000 for all the work involved in preparing and trying a capital case. In a few jurisdictions, these caps have been challenged on constitutional grounds, and legislative and judicial responses to these challenges have created some changes in the kinds of resources available to defense counsel.

9. The Pre–Trial Motions Stage

As part of a defense counsel's investigation of a case, certain pre-trial motions may be filed, such as a motion to compel disclosure of evidence, or for the appointment of expert witnesses to testify at trial concerning a mental state defense. Other motions will be made in order to pursue a defendant's claims that the police or prosecutor violated the federal or state constitutions or statutory law. These motions include a motion to exclude inadmissible evidence at trial, usually referred to as a "motion to suppress" evidence. Other standard motions include a motion to quash the indictment because of particular defects, a motion for reduction of bail, and a motion *in limine* to limit the prosecutor's examination of witnesses in some way.

Most motions to suppress are filed in order to exclude materials seized in illegal searches, incriminating statements by the defendants obtained in illegal interrogations, or pre-trial identifications by witnesses obtained in an illegal manner. In the small percentage of cases where a motion to suppress is granted, this ruling may result in a prosecutor's filing a *nolle prosequi* motion to dismiss, because the prosecutor now believes there is insufficient evidence of proof of guilt "beyond a reasonable doubt" to obtain a conviction at trial. However, the prosecutor may obtain more evidence later and proceed with the same charge against the same defendant again, because the protection of the Double Jeopardy Clause does not attach until the jury is sworn at trial.

10. The Trial Stage

Defendants are guaranteed the right to a speedy trial, and some defendants will receive a trial within the time limits set by federal or state statutes, which often require that the trial occur within six months of the indictment. However, a defense counsel may advise a defendant to waive the right to a speedy trial, and if not, a case may fall within a statutory exemption to the required deadline.

A defense counsel and a prosecutor will conduct *voir dire* of the jury in most states, although in some state courts and the federal courts the judge conducts *voir dire*. Based on the information obtained from juror questionnaires and the answers obtained from jurors during *voir dire* questioning, the prosecutor and defense counsel will challenge jurors "for cause" and with "peremptory challenges." This process is regulated by Supreme Court precedents governing jury selection, as well as by statutory laws that define the grounds for challenges and limit each side to a certain number of peremptory challenges.

Most cases are tried to a jury, although a defense counsel will advise the defendant to waive the right to a jury trial in some cases. Only a small percentage of trials end in a mistrial because the jury cannot agree on a verdict. Supreme Court precedents limit the right to jury trial to cases where the maximum sentence is more than six months in prison, but some states provide for this right in other cases. Most states require that the jury verdict be unanimous, although Supreme Court precedents allow for non-unanimous verdicts. Most states also require a jury of twelve for serious felonies and capital cases, and some states use six-person juries for misdemeanors or less serious felonies. The Court's precedents hold that a unanimous jury of six is the smallest size that can be used for a criminal trial. Most trials end in conviction, and the conviction rates vary significantly for different crimes.

11. The Sentencing Stage

In most states, a convicted defendant in a non-capital case will be sentenced by the trial judge, but in a small number of states the jury will sentence the defendant. In a capital case, the jury has the responsibility of choosing between life and death. Some states have adopted complex sentencing guidelines for non-capital cases, modeled on the federal sentencing guidelines. These guidelines, or the existence of statutory "mandatory minimum" sentences, may sharply limit the discretion of a sentencing judge.

An indigent defendant is entitled to representation by appointed counsel at a non-capital sentencing hearing, which is usually held some weeks after the trial so that the probation department may prepare a presentence report for the judge. This report will contain information about the defendant's history that the probation officer believes is relevant to sentencing. At the hearing, the defense counsel may try to challenge information in the report, and may produce new information for the judge's consideration. Usually, however, the role of a defense counsel and prosecutor is confined to argument concerning the appropriate exercise of judicial discretion, based on the facts in the presentence report. Most defendants convicted of misdemeanors receive a fine or community service, or both, instead of a jail sentence, but most defendants convicted of serious felonies receive a substantial prison sentence. Once a sentence is imposed, the state corrections system takes on the responsibility for administering it. The availability of parole and "good time" may mean that a defendant will not serve the same time as the sentence that is imposed by the judge.

12. The Appeal Stage

When a defendant appeals a conviction, Supreme Court precedents hold that this action constitutes a waiver of double jeopardy rights, so the defendant may be tried again in the event that the conviction is reversed. The Court's precedents also hold that an indigent defendant is entitled to appointed counsel to pursue the first appeal "of right." While there is no federal constitutional right to such an appeal, all states have a long tradition of providing this right. For a state defendant, this appeal lies in the intermediate appellate court, or in the state supreme court of a state that has no such courts. For a federal defendant, the appeal lies in the federal circuit court. In most states with intermediate appellate courts, once the defendant loses the first appeal of right, a further appeal to the state supreme court will be heard only if that court exercises its discretion and decides to hear the case. Supreme Court precedents do not establish a right to appointed counsel for indigent defendants for this second appeal, or for the later stages, such as the pursuit of a writ of certiorari from the Supreme Court, or of subsequent avenues of judicial review. Only after the appeal process is exhausted will the conviction be termed "final," and then an indigent defendant must pursue the inaptly named "post-conviction remedies" that are available in state and federal court.

13. The Post–Appeal Stage of "Post–Conviction" Remedies

Once a conviction is final, a state defendant usually must pursue his claims by filing a petition in the state trial court, seeking state "habeas" or "*coram nobis*" relief. A defendant may seek an evidentiary hearing on such claims, and some states provide that indigents have a right to appointed counsel at this stage. Even in states that do not provide counsel automatically at this stage, a trial court may decide to appoint counsel in a particular case, in order to have the merits of the case briefed and argued, or in order to provide representation at the evidentiary hearing. Most requests for evidentiary hearings are not granted. If the hearing is granted, it will be conducted as a civil proceeding. The losing party may appeal to the intermediate appellate court, and then to the state supreme court. At this point, a losing defendant usually will have "exhausted" his available post-conviction remedies in state court, and may file a petition for a writ of habeas corpus in federal district court, in order to pursue federal constitutional claims. A federal defendant begins the post-conviction process by filing that petition at the outset in federal district court. In non-capital cases, post-conviction relief is granted in a small percentage of cases. In capital cases, however, there is a higher percentage of cases where relief is granted, especially in some federal circuits.

POINTS TO REMEMBER

- Defendants have rights under the Bill of Rights, the Due Process and Equal Protection Clauses of the Fourteenth Amendment, various statutes, and state and federal codes of criminal procedure.

- Defendants also have rights under state constitutions.

- The federal constitution creates a "floor" that establishes the minimum rights that must be recognized in all criminal prosecutions, but state courts are free to establish their own "ceilings" that establish the maximum rights that will be enforced in state prosecutions.

- There are judge-made rules that derive from a court's "supervisory" authority over the criminal court system and its evidentiary rules.

- Most prosecutions are for minor crimes. While the definition of a "minor" crime is not uniform among the states, in most states a misdemeanor cannot be punished for more than one year in prison.

- One goal of most pre-arrest investigations, whether conducted by police or by prosecutors working together with police, is to obtain evidence that will satisfy the "probable cause" standard required both for arrest and for judicial validation of any decision to charge a person with a crime.

- There are two different kinds of arrests: the non-custodial "citation" arrest and the "full-custody" arrest. Both require probable cause, but the citation arrest is used typically only for minor offenses such as traffic crimes.

- Most arrests are permissible without warrants.

- People who have undergone a full-custody arrest will also undergo the booking process which allows the police to keep a record of arrests, and to obtain photographs and fingerprints of arrestees.

- After an arrest, a prosecutor may participate in the same kinds of investigative activity that precede an arrest, such as witness interviews & interrogations force a suspect to, and the procuring of search warrants. Additionally, a prosecutor may force a suspect to participate in activities that usually occur after arrest, such as a "lineup."

- When a person is arrested, the police have, in a sense, "charged" that person with committing a crime. But the prosecution does not begin until a "complaint" is filed, either by the prosecutor or by the police.

- When a complaint is filed either by a prosecutor or by police, it is filed in a magistrate's court. At this point, the arrestee is now a "defendant."

The complaint usually sets forth a description of the crime and a citation to the criminal code concerning the offense being charged.

- If the crime is a felony, the complaint will be replaced with a different instrument after proceedings in the magistrate's court are finished. That instrument will be the indictment, and in other cases, that instrument will be a document called the "information."

- The defendant's first appearance in court has three purposes. First, the magistrate informs the defendant of the charges set forth in the complaint, and typically describes the defendant's various rights. Second, the magistrate must determine whether the defendant is indigent, and ask an indigent defendant whether he wishes to be represented by appointed counsel. Finally, assuming an appropriate case, the magistrate sets bail for the defendant.

- The preliminary hearing usually will be the first stage where an indigent defendant will have representation by appointed counsel, and thus for most defendants, it will be the first proceeding where the prosecutor and the defense counsel meet formally as adversaries.

- The arraignment has two functions. It is a hearing in the trial court where the judge will inform the defendant of the felony charges in the indictment or information, and where the defendant will be asked to enter a plea to the charges on the record.

- Defense counsel may file certain pre-trial motions such as a motion to compel disclosure of evidence, or for the appointment of expert witnesses to testify at trial concerning a mental state defense.

- Most cases are tried to a jury, although a defense counsel will advise the defendant to waive the right to a jury trial in some cases.

- In most states, a convicted defendant in a non-capital case will be sentenced by the trial judge, but in a small number of states the jury will sentence the defendant.

- Only after the appeal process is exhausted will the conviction be termed "final," and then an indigent defendant must pursue the "post-conviction remedies" that are available in state and federal court.

- Once a conviction is final, a state defendant usually must pursue his claims by filing a petition in the state trial court, seeking state "habeas" or "*coram nobis*" relief. A defendant may seek an evidentiary hearing on such claims, and some states provide that indigents have a right to appointed counsel at this stage.

Chapter 2

INCORPORATION & RETROACTIVITY

Focal Points for Chapter 2

- Selective incorporation.

- Retroactivity not automatic.

- Bag and baggage.

- Pending appeals.

- Collateral review.

A. Incorporation

The constitutional rights included in the first ten amendments to the United States Constitution—the "Bill of Rights"—do not apply in and of themselves to the states. The Bill of Rights applies only to the federal government. *McDonald v. City of Chicago, Illinois*, 130 S.Ct. 3020, 3028 (2010); *Barron v. Baltimore*, 32 U.S. (7 Pet.) 243 (1833). As a result, absent some legal or doctrinal mechanism serving to "carry over" the rights (and prohibitions) to the states, individuals do not have any entitlement to the familiar panoply of rights guaranteed to them by the Bill of Rights (e.g. freedom of speech, right not to be subjected to unreasonable searches or seizures, right against self-incrimination, right to counsel, etc.) against state or local governments.

State constitutions do apply to the actions of the states. But the states are not required to possess any particular constitutional right, prohibition, or entitlement in their constitutions. More to the point, the states are not required to—and do not—guarantee to their citizens the same rights and protections contained in the Bill of Rights under analogous provisions set out in their state constitutions. Again, without some legal or doctrinal mechanism serving to "carry over" these federal rights (and prohibitions) to the states, the various states would only end up providing to their citizens a patchwork of civil and criminal rights and liberties that might well be significantly different from the rights and liberties guaranteed by the United States Constitution.

But you already know "the end of this story," i.e. you know that today you *do* have the right to free speech and the right against unreasonable searches and seizures and the right to counsel and a right to a criminal jury in the states, so the question becomes: how did that happen? And, secondarily but equally significant, is there any difference between an individual's Bill-of-Rights protections as against the federal and the state governments? The answers to these questions revolve around interpretation and application of part of one of the Civil War amendments, the Fourteenth Amendment Due Process Clause ("nor shall any State deprive any person of life, liberty, or property, without due process of law"), as discussed below.

1. Fundamental Rights

When faced with questions about the applicability of Bill-of-Rights-type rights to the states, decisions handed down by the Supreme Court in the first half of the Twentieth Century resolved these questions by determining on a case-by-case basis whether or not the asserted rights alleged to have been violated in each case involved "fundamental rights." If these rights were deemed to be fundamental, then the Court held that they applied to the States under the authority of the Fourteenth Amendment Due Process Clause.

But the tests utilized by the Court to determine whether such rights were so fundamental as to be applied to the States were exceedingly demanding and difficult to satisfy. In a leading 1937 decision, for example, Justice Cardozo explained for the Supreme Court that, to be deemed fundamental in this regard, the rights in question had to be: "implicit in the concept of ordered liberty"; "of the very essence of a scheme of ordered liberty"; "[t]o abolish them [would be] to violate a 'principle of justice so rooted in the traditions and conscience of our people as to be ranked as fundamental' "; "a fair and enlightened system of justice would be impossible without them"; "so acute and shocking that our policy will not endure it"; and "violat[ive of] those 'fundamental principles of liberty and justice which lie at the base of all our civil and political institutions'." *Palko v. Connecticut*, 302 U.S. 319, 325, 328 (1937). *See also, e.g., Snyder v. Massachusetts*, 291 U.S. 97, 105 (1934) (to satisfy this test, an asserted right must "offend[] some principle of justice so rooted in the traditions and conscience of our people as to be ranked as fundamental."); *Twining v. New Jersey*, 211 U.S. 78, 107 (1908) ("Is it a fundamental principle of liberty and justice which inheres in the very idea of free government and is the inalienable right of a citizen of such a government? If it is, and if it is of a nature that pertains to process of law, this court has declared it to be essential to due process of law.").

Once again, such tests were not, to put it mildly, easy to satisfy, and some critics suggested that they reflected an inappropriately grudging attitude toward those individual rights the States were constitutionally bound to respect.

Moreover, application of these exacting tests for determining fundamental-rights status by the Supreme Court sometimes appeared to be overly subjective and unstructured. In *Rochin v. California*, 342 U.S. 165 (1952), for example, the Supreme Court held that an individual had a fundamental right (protected, accordingly, by the Fourteenth Amendment Due Process Clause) not to have his stomach pumped forcibly by the police to look for drugs. Applying a variant of the *Palko* tests set out above and asking whether this conduct "offend[ed] those canons of decency and fairness which express the notions of justice of English-speaking peoples," Justice Frankfurter, speaking for the *Rochin* Court, decided that the Court was "compelled" to conclude that this police conduct "do[es] more than offend some fastidious squeamishness or private sentimentalism about combatting [sic] crime too energetically. *This is conduct that shocks the conscience.* Illegally breaking into the privacy of the petitioner, the struggle to open his mouth and remove what was there, the forcible extraction of his stomach's contents—this course of proceeding by agents of government to obtain evidence is bound to offend even hardened sensibilities. They are methods too close to the rack and the screw to permit of constitutional differentiation."

But, although stomach-pumping was not OK, warrantless eavesdropping on bedroom conversations was okay . . . 5–to–4. In *Irvine v. California*, 347 U.S. 128 (1954), a bare majority of the Supreme Court ruled that an individual did not have a fundamental right to exclude evidence obtained by the police unlawfully when they made a warrantless entry into his home and hid a microphone in his bedroom to record all that transpired. The majority found that this police conduct was not as or more shocking than in *Rochin*, while the dissenters either disagreed or proposed that this whole fundamental rights approach be replaced (a position that ultimately prevailed).

As a result of concerns about the appropriateness of the use of this fundamental-rights approach to determining the applicability of rights to the States, including concern about the arguable subjectivity of its application, the Court ultimately discarded that test.

2. Total Incorporation & Total Incorporation Plus

Some justices—none of them currently sitting on the Court— argued that a better (than the fundamental rights approach) and more objective approach to determining the applicability of rights like those found in the federal Bill of Rights to the states would be to simply apply *all* of those rights to the States, i.e. to "totally in- corporate" them as a matter of Fourteenth Amendment due process. *See, e.g., Adamson v. California*, 332 U.S. 46, 71–72 (1947) (Black, J., diss'g) ("My study of the historical events that culminated in the Fourteenth Amendment, and the expressions of those who spon- sored and favored, as well as those who opposed its submission and passage, persuades me that one of the chief objects that the provi- sions of the Amendment's first section, separately, and as a whole, were intended to accomplish was to make the Bill of Rights, appli- cable to the states.").

But a majority of the Supreme Court rejected the total incorpo- ration approach, concluding that it neither reflected a proper inter- pretation of the legislative history of the drafting of the Fourteenth Amendment, nor did it permit appropriate experimentation in the States as to what and how liberties should be protected, *see, e.g., Adamson v. California*, 332 U.S. 46, 67 (1947) (Frankfurter, J., conc'g) ("A construction which gives to due process no independent function but turns it into a summary of the specific provisions of the Bill of Rights would, as has been noted, tear up by the roots much of the fabric of law in the several States, and would deprive the States of opportunity for reforms in legal process designed for extending the area of freedom."), and it never became the law of the land. *McDonald v. City of Chicago, Illinois*, 130 S.Ct. 3020, 3033 (2010) ("the Court never has embraced Justice Black's 'total incorporation' theory").

Nor did the "total incorporation plus" approach, a variant on total incorporation espoused by a few individual Justices, ever suc- cessfully garner majority approval from the Court. Under this ap- proach, it was argued that the Fourteenth Amendment Due Process Clause not only incorporated all of the rights contained in the Bill of Rights, but also any additional rights (not included expressly in the Bill of Rights) that the Court deemed to be fundamental.

3. Selective Incorporation

Ultimately, the Supreme Court adopted an approach that re- flected doctrinal aspects of all three of these earlier approaches to this issue: the fundamental-rights approach; the total-incorporation approach; and the total-incorporation-plus approach. The Supreme Court concluded that the Fourteenth Amendment Due Process

Clause "selectively incorporated" those particular rights contained in the Bill of Rights the Court deemed to be sufficiently fundamental to merit application to the States.

As Justice White observed for the Court in *Duncan v. Louisiana*, 391 U.S. 145 (1968), a leading selective-incorporation decision that incorporated the Sixth Amendment right to a jury trial (through the Fourteenth Amendment Due Process Clause) to the States, the Court had used a number of tests to determine whether or not a right should be selectively incorporated, "[t]he question has been asked whether a right is among those 'fundamental principles of liberty and justice which lie at the base of all our civil and political institutions,'; whether it is 'basic in our system of jurisprudence,'; and whether it is 'a fundamental right, essential to a fair trial.' " Duncan, 391 U.S. at 148–49, quoting *Powell v. State of Alabama*, 287 U.S. 45, 67 (1932).

In *Duncan*, the Supreme Court ruled that "[b]ecause we believe that trial by jury in criminal cases is fundamental to the American scheme of justice, we hold that the Fourteenth Amendment guarantees a right of jury trial in all criminal cases which—were they to be tried in a federal court—would come within the Sixth Amendment's guarantee."

The Court in *Duncan* stressed, however, that the "fundamentalness" test used to determine whether a right contained in the Bill of Rights should be incorporated so as to apply to the States was different from the tests used to assess whether a "fundamental right" existed in the pre-incorporation days. As the Court explained this difference, "[e]arlier the Court can be seen as having asked, when inquiring into whether some particular procedural safeguard was required of a State, if a civilized system could be imagined that would not accord the particular protection. [The] recent [selective-incorporation] cases, on the other hand, have proceeded upon the valid assumption that state criminal processes are not imaginary and theoretical schemes but actual systems bearing virtually every characteristic of the common-law system that has been developing contemporaneously in England and in this country. The question thus is whether given this kind of system a particular procedure is fundamental—whether, that is, a procedure is necessary to an Anglo–American regime of ordered liberty. [Of] each ... determination[] that a constitutional provision originally written to bind the Federal Government should bind the States as well it might be said that the limitation in question is not necessarily fundamental to fairness in every criminal system that might be imagined but is fundamental in the context of the criminal processes maintained by the American States."

This difference in approach was deemed by the Court to be quite significant. Again, as Justice White explained for the Court, "[w]hen the inquiry is approached in this way the question whether the States can impose criminal punishment without granting a jury trial appears quite different from the way it appeared in the older cases opining that States might abolish jury trial. A criminal process which was fair and equitable but used no juries is easy to imagine. It would make use of alternative guarantees and protections which would serve the purposes that the jury serves in the English and American systems. Yet no American State has undertaken to construct such a system. Instead, every American State, including Louisiana, uses the jury extensively, and imposes very serious punishments only after a trial at which the defendant has a right to a jury's verdict. In every State, including Louisiana, the structure and style of the criminal process—the supporting framework and the subsidiary procedures—are of the sort that naturally complement jury trial, and have developed in connection with and in reliance upon jury trial."

Ultimately, using the "new" selective-incorporation approach, as described above, the Supreme Court selectively incorporated almost every right contained in the Bill of Rights though the Fourteenth Amendment Due Process Clause to the States. Most recently, although not necessarily a "criminal right," the Supreme Court has ruled that the Second Amendment "right to keep and bear arms" is selectively incorporated. *McDonald v. City of Chicago, Illinois*, 130 S.Ct. 3020, 3042 (2010) ("it is clear that the Framers and ratifiers of the Fourteenth Amendment counted the right to keep and bear arms among those fundamental rights necessary to our system of ordered liberty"). The only "criminal rights" not (or not explicitly) selectively incorporated are the Fifth Amendment right to indictment by a Grand Jury in felony cases and the Eighth Amendment prohibition against excessive bail. *See id.* at 3035 n.14.

4. *"Bag and Baggage"*

When the Supreme Court selectively incorporated the Sixth Amendment jury-trial right to the States (through the Fourteenth Amendment Due Process Clause), it held that "[b]ecause we believe that trial by jury in criminal cases is fundamental to the American scheme of justice, we hold that the Fourteenth Amendment guarantees a right of jury trial in all criminal cases which—*were they to be tried in a federal court*—would come within the Sixth Amendment's guarantee." Duncan, 391 U.S. at 149 (emphasis added). The emphasized language—"*were they to be tried in a federal court*"—reflects the understanding of a majority of the Supreme Court in *Duncan* (and other decisions) that when a right was selectively incorporated, its incorporation implied carrying through to the States not just the right itself, but all of the accompanying "baggage" of interpretative decisional law relating to the application of that right applicable in the federal setting. *McDonald v. City of Chicago, Illinois*, 130 S.Ct. 3020, 3035 (2010) ("[T]he Court decisively held that incorporated Bill of Rights protections 'are all to be enforced against the States under the Fourteenth Amendment according to the same standards that protect those personal rights against federal encroachment.'").

Although this "baggage" point has commanded (and continues to command) the support of a significant majority of the Court, it is nonetheless significant that not every Justice has agreed with it. In *Duncan*, for example, Justice Harlan, in dissent, argued against the selective incorporation approach entirely, but he also argued that, even if a right were to be incorporated in this fashion, it should not be incorporated so as to include necessarily "the sometimes trivial accompanying *baggage* of judicial interpretation in federal contexts." His argument was that a majority of the Court had simply and inappropriately "assumed that the question before us is whether the Jury Trial Clause of the Sixth Amendment should be incorporated into the Fourteenth, *jot-for-jot and case-for-case*, or ignored." *See also id.* at 171 (Fortas, J., conc'g) (emphasis added) ("There is no reason whatever for us to conclude that . . . we are bound slavishly to follow not only the Sixth Amendment but all of its *bag and baggage*, however securely or insecurely affixed they may be by law and precedent to federal proceedings."). In other words, some Justices argued that even after a right was selectively incorporated, it could—and should—apply differently to the States than it does to the federal government.

Since this is a dissenting position, why is it significant enough to discuss? The answer is that even though the baggage issue has now been long decided by a majority of the Court, this dissenting argument—that a right incorporated so as to apply to the States need not carry precisely the same interpretative baggage—ended up influencing the Court's interpretation of the scope of some constitutional rights. The best example of this influence is found in the companion cases of *Apodaca v. Oregon*, 406 U.S. 404 (1972), and *Johnson v. Louisiana*, 406 U.S. 356 (1972). The issue before the Court in these cases was whether states could constitutionally convict accused individuals with less-than-unanimous, criminal-trial juries. Oregon's Constitution permitted 10–to–2 criminal convictions; Louisiana's permitted 9–to–3 convictions; convictions in the two cases before the Court were obtained on votes of 11–1 and 10–2, respectively. In answering this question, the Court necessarily had to look at the Sixth Amendment jury-trial right which had been selectively incorporated to the States in *Duncan*, as discussed above, and answer this question: Did the Sixth Amendment jury-trial right permit the federal government to convict a criminal accused on the basis of a non-unanimous jury-trial verdict?

Four of the nine Justices concluded that it did, i.e. that the Sixth Amendment jury-trial right *did* permit non-unanimous, criminal, jury-trial verdict. Four other Justices concluded just the opposite, that the Sixth Amendment jury-trial right *did not* permit non-unanimous, criminal, jury-trial verdicts. But all eight of these Justices did agree on one thing, namely that the Court's baggage point applied, meaning that whatever the rule was for federal courts, it should be the same for the States.

But Justice Powell, the ninth Justice and the deciding vote in this 4–to–4 deadlock, taking the same position that Justice Harlan took in dissent in *Duncan*, disagreed with the baggage conclusion, arguing instead that "in holding that the Fourteenth Amendment has incorporated 'jot-for-jot and case-for-case' every element of the Sixth Amendment, the Court derogates principles of federalism that are basic to our system. In the name of uniform application of high standards of due process, the Court has embarked upon a course of constitutional interpretation that deprives the States of freedom to experiment with adjudicatory processes different from the federal model. [There] is no sound basis for interpreting the Fourteenth Amendment to require blind adherence by the States to all details of the federal Sixth Amendment standards." Johnson, 406 U.S. at 375 (Powell, J., conc'g) (footnotes omitted), *quoting* Duncan, 391 U.S. at 181 (Harlan, J., diss'g).

Moreover, because Justice Powell then concluded that the Sixth Amendment criminal jury-trial right required verdict unanimity in the federal courts, but not in the state courts, and because Justice Powell's opinion also provided the fifth—and, hence, the deciding—vote on both the federal and state court holdings, the Supreme Court judgment in these cases was that federal criminal juries must be unanimous, but that state criminal juries need not be. Ironically, this was a position taken by only one member of the Court, and it was based upon a legal theory (rejection of the baggage point) accepted (then) by only one member of the Court. *See* Johnson, 406 U.S. at 395–96 (Brennan, J., diss'g) (footnote omitted) ("Readers of today's opinions may be understandably puzzled why convictions by 11–1 and 10–2 jury votes are affirmed . . . when a majority of the Court agrees that the Sixth Amendment requires a unanimous verdict in federal criminal jury trials, and a majority also agrees that the right to jury trial guaranteed by the Sixth Amendment is to be enforced against the States according to the same standards that protect that right against federal encroachment. The reason is that while my Brother Powell agrees that a unanimous verdict is required in federal criminal trials, he does not agree that the Sixth Amendment right to a jury trial is to be applied in the same way to State and Federal Governments. [In] any event, [this result] must not obscure that the majority of the Court remains of the view that, as in the case of every specific of the Bill of Rights that extends to the States, the Sixth Amendment's jury trial guarantee, however it is to be construed, has identical application against both State and Federal Governments."). Nonetheless, this position taken by only one Justice became (and continues to be) the law of the land.

Subsequent to the *Apodaca* and *Johnson* decisions, Chief Justice Burger and then-Justice Rehnquist appeared to accept Justice Powell's (and formerly Justice Harlan's) minority position on the baggage issue, but this position, while still important to bear in mind as was demonstrated in *Apodaca* and *Johnson*, has not commanded and still does not command a majority of the Court. *See McDonald v. City of Chicago, Illinois*, 130 S.Ct. 3020, 3046 (2010) (plurality opinion of Alito, J.) ("There is nothing new in the argument that, in order to respect federalism and allow useful state experimentation, a federal constitutional right should not be fully binding on the States. This argument was made repeatedly and eloquently by Members of this Court who rejected the concept of incorporation and urged retention of the two-track approach to incorporation. . . Time and again, however, those pleas failed. Unless we turn back the clock [,this] argument must be rejected.").

B. Retroactivity

1. Case–by–Case Analysis

Traditionally, the prevailing litigant in a case wherein the Supreme Court establishes a new constitutional rule has been deemed to be entitled personally to the benefit of that new rule. But what about other accused persons and/or already-convicted defendants whose cases involve the same issue as that decided in a case handing down a new constitutional rule? What rule applies to them . . . the old or the new one?

In 1965, the Supreme Court, in the leading case of *Linkletter v. Walker*, 381 U.S. 618 (1965), rejected the prevailing common-law rule (what it called the "Blackstonian" theory, referring to the famous Blackstone's *Commentaries* on the common law) that a new constitutional ruling simply restates what the law always was (or should have been) and, hence, always applies retrospectively. The *Linkletter* Court, held instead that "the Constitution neither prohibits nor requires retrospective effect." *Id.* at 629. The Court then added that "[o]nce the premise is accepted that we are neither required to apply, nor prohibited from applying, a decision retrospectively, *we must then weigh the merits and demerits in each case by looking to the prior history of the rule in question, its purpose and effect, and whether retrospective operation will further or retard its operation.*" *Id.* (emphasis added).

Applying this case-by-case, balancing approach (sometimes called the "*Linkletter* Doctrine"), the *Linkletter* Court concluded that *Mapp v. Ohio*, 367 U.S. 643 (1961), the landmark decision overruling prior Supreme Court precedent and applying the exclusionary rule to the States, did not apply retroactively. By that holding, the Court indicated that *Mapp* did not apply to any cases that had been finally decided prior to the date when the *Mapp* decision was handed down. As the *Linkletter* majority explained the basis for its conclusion, "[t]he misconduct of the police prior to *Mapp* has already occurred and will not be corrected by releasing the prisoners involved. [The] ruptured privacy of the victims' homes and effects cannot be restored. Reparation comes too late. [Finally,] there are interests in the administration of justice and the integrity of the judicial process to consider. To make the rule of *Mapp* retrospective would tax the administration of justice to the utmost. Hearings would have to be held on the excludability of evidence long since destroyed, misplaced or deteriorated. [To] thus legitimate such an extraordinary procedural weapon that has no bearing on guilt would seriously disrupt the administration of justice."

Subsequently, in *Stovall v. Denno*, 388 U.S. 293, 297 (1967), the Supreme Court fleshed out the *Linkletter* retroactivity test by declaring further that "[t]he criteria guiding resolution of the question [whether a new constitutional ruling is to be applied retroactively] implicates (a) the purpose to be served by the new standards, (b) the extent of the reliance by law enforcement authorities on the old standards, and (c) the effect on the administration of justice of a retroactive application of the new standards."

The Supreme Court has also indicated that the related question of from what specific date a new constitutional ruling is to apply when the Court has ruled that it is to apply prospectively only (e.g., from the date of the decision? from the date of the police conduct in question?), is up to the Court to decide; as with retroactivity analysis generally, the Constitution does not dictate a particular rule.

Between 1965 and 1982, the Supreme Court applied the *Linkletter* Doctrine (as construed in *Stovall*) to more than twenty cases.

But, because so much discretion and policy analysis was involved in determining whether or not a new constitutional ruling should be made retroactive, the Supreme Court decisions making these determinations have often been criticized as lacking a unifying theme and producing inconsistent results. As a result, it became extremely difficult to predict with any precision how the Supreme Court would apply the *Linkletter* and *Stovall* tests to new constitutional rulings in particular cases. Indeed, as the Court itself admitted in 1989, "[b]ecause the balance of the three *Stovall* factors inevitably has shifted from case to case, it is hardly surprising that, for some, 'the subsequent course of *Linkletter* became almost as difficult to follow as the tracks made by a beast of prey in search of its intended victim.' " *United States v. Johnson*, 457 U.S. 537 (1982), *quoting Mackey v. United States*, 401 U.S. 667, 675 (1971) (separate opinion of Harlan, J.). *See also Davis v. United States*, 131 S.Ct. 2419, 2430 (2011); *Danforth v. Minnesota*, 552 U.S. 264, 273 (2008) ("application of the *Linkletter* standard produced strikingly divergent results").

2. Cases Pending & Not Yet Final

The Supreme Court has, however, provided some additional clarity to retroactivity analysis by focusing upon the question whether a particular case was pending or was, instead, "final" at the time that a new constitutional ruling was handed down. By "final," the Court has explained that it means "a case in which a judgment of conviction has been rendered, the availability of appeal exhausted, and the time for a petition for certiorari elapsed or a petition for certiorari finally denied." *Griffith v. Kentucky*, 479 U.S. 314, 321 n.6 (1987). A case is final even though it is theoretically possible that a state court might, as a discretionary matter, decline to enforce a procedural bar to raising an issue and choose to apply a new rule of law. *Beard v. Banks*, 542 U.S. 406, 412 (2004).

In a 1969 decision, *Desist v. United States*, 394 U.S. 244, 253 (1969), the Supreme Court opined that it did not see "any distinction between final convictions and those still pending on review." But Justice Harlan, in dissent in *Desist*, argued that there is—and should be—a significant difference in retroactivity analysis between cases still pending on review when a new constitutional ruling is handed down (which should ordinarily receive the benefit of the new ruling) and cases that were final on that date which come before the court only on collateral (habeas corpus) review (which should not ordinarily receive the benefit of the new ruling). Although Justice Harlan made this argument in dissent in *Desist*, his views on this point were subsequently adopted—to a significant extent—by a majority of the Court twenty years later in *United States v. Johnson*, 457 U.S. 537 (1982).

In *Johnson*, the Court was faced with the question of the retroactivity of *Payton v. New York*, 445 U.S. 573 (1980), the decision in which the Supreme Court had (newly) ruled that the Fourth Amendment prohibits the police from making a warrantless and nonconsensual entry into a suspect's home in order to make a routine felony arrest. The *Johnson* Court, describing the different (and arguably inconsistent) approaches used by the Court in its post-*Linkletter* retroactivity decisions, decided to "rethink" the law relating to retroactivity altogether. As a product of that rethinking, the Court reasoned that "[a]n approach that resolved all nonfinal convictions under the same rule of law would lessen the possibility that this Court might mete out different constitutional protection to defendants simultaneously subjected to identical police conduct." Accordingly, the Court ruled that, except in those situations that would be clearly controlled by existing retroactivity precedents that hold directly to the contrary, "a decision of this Court construing the Fourth Amendment is to be applied retroactively to all convictions that were not yet final at the time the decision was rendered." On that basis, since Johnson's case was pending on direct appeal on that date when *Payton* was decided, the Supreme Court concluded that *Payton did* apply retroactively to it.

The *Johnson* rule, limited on its face to Fourth Amendment rulings, was extended to Fifth Amendment rulings in 1985. *Shea v. Louisiana*, 470 U.S. 51, 59 (1985) ("There is nothing about a Fourth Amendment rule that suggests that in this context it should be given greater retroactive effect than a Fifth Amendment rule.").

a. Rejection of the "Clear Break" Exception

The Court in *Johnson* expressly excepted from the retroactivity rule set out above situations where a new rule is a "clear break" with past precedent. Johnson, 457 U.S. at 549 ("where the Court has expressly declared a rule of criminal procedure to be 'a clear break with the past,' it almost invariably has gone on to find such a newly minted principle nonretroactive."). As the Court in *Griffith v. Kentucky*, 479 U.S. 314, 325 (1987), subsequently explained the resultant *Johnson* rule, "[u]nder this ["clear break"] exception, a new constitutional rule was not applied retroactively, even to cases on direct review, if the new rule explicitly overruled a past precedent of this Court, or disapproved a practice this Court had arguably sanctioned in prior cases, or overturned a longstanding practice that lower courts had uniformly approved."

The *Griffith* Court, however, re-examined the *Johnson* Court's rationale for the "clear break exception" and found it wanting. In the *Griffith* Court's view, "the 'clear break' exception, derived from the *Stovall* factors, reintroduces precisely the type of case-specific analysis that Justice Harlan rejected [in *Desist*] as inappropriate for cases pending on direct review. [And] the use of a 'clear break' exception creates the same problem of not treating similarly situated defendants the same. [The] fact that the new rule may constitute a clear break with the past has no bearing on the 'actual inequity that results' when only one of many similarly situated defendants receives the benefit of the new rule." Griffith, 479 U.S. at 327–28, *quoting United States v. Johnson*, 457 U.S. at 556 n.16.

Accordingly, the Supreme Court concluded, "[w]e therefore hold that a new rule for the conduct of criminal prosecutions is to be applied retroactively to all cases, state or federal, pending on direct review or not yet final, with no exception for cases in which the new rule constitutes a 'clear break' with the past." *Id.* at 328.

In *Griffith*, the Supreme Court, applying its latest approach to retroactivity analysis (rejecting the "clear break" exception), concluded that its new constitutional ruling in *Batson v. Kentucky*, 476 U.S. 79 (1986), holding that a defendant in a state criminal trial could establish a prima facie case of racial discrimination violative of the Fourteenth Amendment based on the prosecution's use of peremptory challenges to strike members of the defendant's race from the jury venire, should be applied retroactively, even though it was a "clear break" with the Court's past precedent. *See also Davis v. United States*, 2011 WL 2369583 (2011) (new rule on searches of cars incident to recent occupant's arrest held retroactive, but good-faith exception to exclusionary rule applied).

b. "New Rules"

Retroactivity or prospectivity only becomes an issue when a court announces a *new* constitutional rule. *Schriro v. Summerlin*, 542 U.S. 348, 351 (2004); *but see Fiore v. White*, 531 U.S. 225, 228 (2001) (a mere "clarification" of the law is not a new ruling). It is not always easy, however, to figure out whether a new Supreme Court decision has stated a new constitutional rule or, instead, whether it was simply applying an existing rule to new and different circumstances.

In 1989, the Supreme Court, while prefacing its comments with the concession and disclaimer that "[i]t is admittedly often difficult to determine when a case announces a new rule, and we do not attempt to define the spectrum of what may or may not constitute a new rule for retroactivity purposes," nonetheless observed that "[i]n general, . . . a case announces a new rule when it breaks new ground or imposes a new obligation on the States or the Federal Government. To put it differently, a case announces a new rule if the result was not *dictated* by precedent existing at the time the defendant's conviction became final." *Teague v. Lane*, 489 U.S. 288, 301 (1989); *see also Danforth v. Minnesota*, 552 U.S. 264, 270 (2008)*; Whorton v. Bockting*, 549 U.S. 406, 416 (2007).

3. Collateral Review

In contrast to the application of new rulings to cases still pending on direct appeal when a new constitutional ruling is handed down (i.e. not "final"), once again following Justice Harlan's dissenting opinion in *Desist*, discussed above, a majority of the Supreme Court concluded in 1989 that "[u]nless they fall within an exception to the general rule, *new constitutional rules of criminal procedure will not be applicable to those cases which have become final before the new rules are announced.*" *Teague v. Lane*, 489 U.S. 288, 310 (1989); *id.* at 316 (White, J., conc'g) (emphasis added). *See also Danforth v. Minnesota*, 552 U.S. 264, 274-75 (2008).

Two exceptions exist to this general rule: (1) "a new rule should be applied retroactively if it places 'certain kinds of primary, private individual conduct beyond the power of the criminal law-making authority to proscribe' "; and (2) "watershed rules of criminal procedure: . . . those new procedures without which the likelihood of an accurate conviction is seriously diminished." *Teague,* at 311, 313 (Op. of O'Connor, J.); *id.* at 317 (White, J., conc'g). *See also Danforth v. Minnesota*, 552 U.S. 264, 266 (2008) ("New constitutional rules announced by this Court that place certain kinds of primary individual conduct beyond the power of the States to proscribe, as well as 'watershed' rules of criminal procedure, must be applied in all future trials, all cases pending on direct review, and all federal habeas corpus proceedings. All other new rules of criminal procedure must be applied in future trials and in cases pending on direct review, but may not provide the basis for a federal collateral attack on a state-court conviction.").

a. Forbidden Punishment Exception

As to the first *Teague* exception, the Supreme Court has termed this rule "substantive" (as opposed to "procedural"), *Whorton v. Bockting*, 549 U.S. 406, 415 (2007), adding that it "cover[s] not only rules forbidding criminal punishment of certain primary conduct but also rules prohibiting a certain category of punishment for a class of defendants because of their status or offense." *Penry v. Lynaugh*, 492 U.S. 302, 330, 314 (1989).

b. Watershed Rules of Criminal Procedure Exception

To fall within the second *Teague* exception, the Court has concluded that "a new rule must meet two requirements: Infringement of the rule must 'seriously diminish the likelihood of obtaining an accurate conviction,' and the rule must 'alter our understanding of the *bedrock procedural elements*' essential to the fairness of a proceeding." *Tyler v. Cain*, 533 U.S. 656, 665 (2001), *quoting Sawyer v. Smith*, 497 U.S. 227, 242 (1990).

As the Court has added, " '[w]hatever the precise scope of this [second] exception, it is clearly meant to apply only to a small core of rules requiring observance of those procedures that . . . are implicit in the concept of ordered liberty.' " *O'Dell v. Netherland*, 521 U.S. 151 (1997), *quoting Graham v. Collins*, 506 U.S. 461, 478 (1993). More recently, the Court has cautioned, "[t]his class of rules is extremely narrow. . ." *Schriro v. Summerlin*, 542 U.S. 348, 352 (2004) (holding that the Court's prior decision that a sentencing judge sitting without a jury could not find an aggravating circumstance necessary for the imposition of the death penalty was not a "watershed" rule requiring retroactivity to cases already final on direct review); *see also Beard v. Banks*, 542 U.S. 406, 418 (2004) (watershed rule must be "sweeping and fundamental").

In fact, since *Teague* was decided in 1989, the Supreme Court has "rejected every claim that a new rule satisfied the requirements for watershed status." *Whorton v. Bockting*, 549 U.S. 406, 418 (2007) (holding that a decision that testimony of an absent witness is admissible only where the declarant is unavailable and defendant had an opportunity to cross-examine *not* to be a watershed rule).

However, the Supreme Court has added that state courts have the authority to give broader effect to new rules of criminal procedure than is required of federal courts exercising habeas corpus jurisdiction by the *Teague* decision. *Danforth v. Minnesota*, 552 U.S. 264 (2008) (permitting Minnesota Supreme Court to apply *Crawford* confrontation right ruling broadly). As the *Danforth* Court explained, "[s]ince *Teague* is based on statutory authority that extends only to federal courts applying a federal statute, it cannot be read as imposing a binding obligation on state courts. ... *Teague* speaks only to the context of federal habeas," *id.* at 278-79, 281.

c. The Retroactivity Inquiry Process

The Supreme Court has concluded that a federal district court applying *Teague* in a retroactivity inquiry in habeas corpus proceedings, should follow the following three steps: "First, the date on which the defendant's conviction became final is determined. Next, the habeas court considers whether ' "a state court considering [the defendant's] claim at the time his conviction became final would have felt compelled by existing precedent to conclude that the rule [he] seeks was required by the Constitution." ' If not, then the rule is new. If the rule is determined to be new, the final step in the *Teague* analysis requires the court to determine whether the rule nonetheless falls within one of the two narrow exceptions to the *Teague* doctrine." *O'Dell v. Netherland*, 521 U.S. 151, 156–57 (1997), *quoting Lambrix v. Singletary*, 520 U.S. 518, 527 (1997); *see also Beard v. Banks*, 542 U.S. 406, 411 (2004) ("First, the court must determine when the defendant's conviction became final. Second, it must ascertain . . . whether the rule is actually 'new.' Finally, if the rule is new, the court must consider whether it falls within either of the two exceptions to nonretroactivity.").

POINTS TO REMEMBER

- The federal Bill of Rights does not apply to the states in and of itself.

- Most Bill of Rights protections, including most recently the right to keep and bear arms, have been "selectively incorporated" through the Fourteenth Amendment Due Process Clause to apply to the states.

- The Supreme Court is not required to apply a new constitutional ruling retroactively or prospectively, but looks on a case-by-case basis at the merits and demerits in each case to determine retroactivity or from what point it will apply.

- A Supreme Court decision construing the Fourth or Fifth Amendment is to be applied retroactively to all convictions that were not yet final at the time the decision was rendered.

- Unless they fall within an exception to the general rule, new constitutional rules of criminal procedure will not be applicable to those cases which have become final before the new rules are announced.

Chapter 3

RIGHT TO COUNSEL

Focal Points for Chapter 3

- Indigent right to counsel under the Sixth Amendment.

- Right to proceed pro se.

- Ineffective assistance test: performance & prejudice.

- Conflicts of interest.

- Griffin–Douglas Doctrine.

A. Scope of the Constitutional Right

1. Appointed Counsel for Indigents

a. Source of the Constitutional Right

In 1938, the Supreme Court held that *federal* criminal defendants who could not afford an attorney had a constitutional right to have criminal defense counsel appointed for them under the Sixth Amendment. Justice Hugo Black, writing for a majority of the Court, explained that "[t]he Sixth Amendment stands as a constant admonition that if the constitutional safeguards it provides be lost, justice will not 'still be done.' It embodies a realistic recognition of the obvious truth that the average defendant does not have the professional legal skills to protect himself when brought before a tribunal with power to take his life or liberty, wherein the prosecution is represented by experienced and learned counsel. That which is simple, orderly, and necessary to the lawyer—to the untrained layman—may appear intricate, complex, and mysterious. [The] Sixth Amendment withholds from federal courts, in all criminal proceedings, the power and authority to deprive an accused of his life or liberty unless he has or waives the assistance of counsel." *Johnson v. Zerbst*, 304 U.S. 458, 462–63 (1938).

It was not until 1963, however, that the Supreme Court held, in *Gideon v. Wainwright*, 372 U.S. 335 (1963), that this same Sixth Amendment right to appointed criminal defense counsel also applies to criminal defendants in *state* court criminal proceedings. In

Gideon, Justice Black, once again writing for the Court, concluded that

> reason and reflection require us to recognize that in our adversary system of criminal justice, any person haled into court, who is too poor to hire a lawyer, cannot be assured a fair trial unless counsel is provided for him. This seems to us to be an obvious truth. Governments, both state and federal, quite properly spend vast sums of money to establish machinery to try defendants accused of crime. Lawyers to prosecute are everywhere deemed essential to protect the public's interest in an orderly society. Similarly, there are few defendants charged with crime, few indeed, who fail to hire the best lawyers they can get to prepare and present their defenses. That government hires lawyers to prosecute and defendants who have the money hire lawyers to defend are the strongest indications of the wide-spread belief that lawyers in criminal courts are necessities, not luxuries. The right of one charged with crime to counsel may not be deemed fundamental and essential to fair trials in some countries, but it is in ours. From the very beginning, our state and national constitutions and laws have laid great emphasis on procedural and substantive safeguards designed to assure fair trials before impartial tribunals in which every defendant stands equal before the law. This noble ideal cannot be realized if the poor man charged with crime has to face his accusers without a lawyer to assist him.

b. The Meaning & Consequences of "Indigency"

Who is sufficiently poor to have counsel appointed? The Supreme Court has never defined the meaning of "indigency" for these Sixth Amendment purposes. As a result, each and every jurisdiction defines this constitutional entitlement, usually by statute or court rule, in its own way.

Representation of the literally millions of indigent criminal defendants charged in state and federal courts each year is provided through a number of different types of service-delivery systems: public-defender programs; contract-attorney programs; or simply by means of an appropriate judge or judicial officer assigning the indigent's defense to a private attorney by order of appointment. Unfortunately, however, skyrocketing dockets and caseloads combined with inadequate funding for indigent-defense programs has too often led to poor representation.

c. Choice of Appointed Counsel

Indigent defendants do *not* have the right under the Sixth Amendment to actually choose the defense attorney who will be appointed to represent them. The Supreme Court has explained that "the essential aim of the [Sixth] Amendment is to guarantee an effective advocate for each criminal defendant rather than to insure that a defendant will inexorably be represented by the lawyer whom he prefers. [An indigent] defendant may not insist on representation by an attorney he cannot afford or who for other reasons declines to represent the defendant." *Wheat v. United States*, 486 U.S. 153, 159 (1988).

Nonetheless, a judge may (or may not), in the exercise of judicial discretion, appoint the particular attorney desired by an indigent defendant, if that attorney is available, if he or she is willing to accept the appointment, and if he or she is also agreeable to accepting the (typically low) compensation that is made available for provision of such appointed services.

d. When the Right Attaches

The Supreme Court has, in a number of decisions, ruled on the question of *when* the Sixth Amendment right to counsel attaches so as to entitle an indigent to the appointment of counsel. Because the Sixth Amendment text applies to "all criminal *prosecutions*," not simply to "all criminal *trials*," the Supreme Court has held that the right to appointed counsel attaches prior to trial, at any "critical stage of the criminal prosecution" after the "initiation of adversary judicial criminal proceedings—whether by way of formal charge, preliminary hearing, indictment, information, or arraignment." *Kirby v. Illinois*, 406 U.S. 682, 683, 689 (1972). *See also Iowa v. Tovar*, 541 U.S. 77, 80–81 (2004) ("The Sixth Amendment secures to a defendant who faces incarceration the right to counsel at all 'critical stages' of the criminal process.").

The Supreme Court has, moreover, deemed a proceeding to be such a critical stage of a criminal prosecution when "potential substantial prejudice to the defendant's rights inheres in the particular confrontation," and "the ability of counsel [can] help avoid that prejudice." *United States v. Wade,* 388 U.S. 218, 227 (1967). In application to specific proceedings, the Court has found the right to counsel to apply, for example, when a criminal defendant appears at his or her preliminary hearing, at a guilty-plea hearing, and at a sentencing proceeding.

e. "Day in Jail" Rule

In the 1972 decision of *Argersinger v. Hamlin*, 407 U.S. 25 (1972), the Supreme Court ruled that an indigent defendant cannot be imprisoned in jail or prison for any period of time—even a single day—unless he or she had been given the opportunity to have counsel appointed for his or her defense. The *Argersinger* rule also applies, requiring appointment of counsel, to defendants who receive suspended sentences rather than actual, immediate incarceration as such a sentence may ultimately result in incarceration. *Alabama v. Shelton*, 535 U.S. 654 (2002).

This so-called "day in jail" rule does *not* mean, however, that an indigent defendant has a right to counsel when he or she is charged with an offense conviction of which could result in *potential* imprisonment. *Scott v. Illinois*, 440 U.S. 367 (1979). What it means instead is that a judge cannot sentence an indigent defendant to jail or prison (even if the sentence is suspended) if that defendant had not been previously afforded the right to counsel. As the *Argersinger* Court explained, "every judge will know when the trial of a misdemeanor starts that no imprisonment may be imposed, even though local law permits it, unless the accused is represented by counsel. He will have a measure of the seriousness and gravity of the offense and therefore know when to name a lawyer to represent the accused before the trial starts."

A misdemeanor conviction of an indigent defendant who was not appointed counsel (as the defendant was, for example, sentenced to no jail time) can still be used, however, to enhance a subsequent criminal conviction under an appropriate state sentencing-enhancement statute which includes such misdemeanors.

2. Retained Counsel

In contrast to indigent defendants, a criminal defendant who possesses sufficient financial resources to retain his or her own private criminal defense counsel has the right to be represented at trial by any criminal defense attorney he or she chooses to employ. *United States v. Gonzalez–Lopez*, 548 U.S. 140 (2006).

However, such retained counsel must be admitted to practice law in the jurisdiction in which the criminal proceedings are to take place, unless the trial court exercises its discretion to grant counsel special admission to the Bar of that jurisdiction for purposes of representing the defendant in that criminal proceeding only ("*pro hac vice* admission"). The Supreme Court has concluded that "the Constitution does not require that because a lawyer has been admitted to the bar of one State, he or she must be allowed to practice in another." *Leis v. Flynt*, 439 U.S. 438, 443 (1979).

B. Waiver of the Right to Counsel

1. Knowing & Intelligent Waivers

A criminal defendant may waive his or her Sixth Amendment right to counsel, provided that such waiver is made knowingly and intelligently.

The Supreme Court has been very protective of a defendant's right to counsel and has declined to recognize a waiver of that right as sufficient unless careful precautions are taken by the trial court. As the Court has explained, "[t]he constitutional right of an accused to be represented by counsel invokes, of itself, the protection of a trial court, in which the accused—whose life or liberty is at stake—is without counsel. This protecting duty imposes the serious and weighty responsibility upon the trial judge of determining whether there is an intelligent and competent waiver by the accused. . . If the accused . . . is not represented by counsel and has not competently and intelligently waived his constitutional right, the Sixth Amendment stands as a jurisdictional bar to a valid conviction and sentence depriving him of his life or his liberty." *Johnson v. Zerbst*, 304 U.S. 458, 465, 468 (1938). Accordingly, trial courts should not accept a waiver of counsel unless and until they obtain the defendant's assurances on the record that he or she fully understands the significance and consequences of such a waiver.

Indeed, a four-justice plurality (but not a majority) of the Supreme Court argued in a 1948 decision, referring to federal district court judges acting under the Sixth Amendment, that

> [i]t is the solemn duty of a [judge] before whom a defendant appears without counsel to make a thorough inquiry and to take all steps necessary to insure the fullest protection of this constitutional right at every stage of the proceedings. This duty cannot be discharged as though it were a mere procedural formality. [To] discharge this duty properly in light of the strong presumption against waiver of the constitutional right to counsel, a judge must investigate as long and as thoroughly as the circumstances of the case before him demand. The fact that an accused may tell him that he is informed of his right to counsel and desires to waive this right does not automatically end the judge's responsibility. To be valid such waiver must be made with an apprehension of the nature of the charges, the statutory offenses included within them, the range of allowable punishments thereunder, possible defenses to the charges and

circumstances in mitigation thereof, and all other facts essential to a broad understanding of the whole matter. A judge can make certain that an accused's professed waiver of counsel is understandingly and wisely made only from a penetrating and comprehensive examination of all of the circumstances under which such a plea is tendered.

Von Moltke v. Gillies, 332 U.S. 708, 722–24 (1948) (Opinion of Black, J.).

However, the detail required by the *Von Moltke* plurality approach is clearly not required by the Court today. In 2004, the Supreme Court concluded that a defendant seeking to waive counsel in order to plead guilty is *not* required to be advised "specifically: (1) [that] 'waiving the assistance of counsel in deciding whether to plead guilty [entails] the risk that a viable defense will be overlooked'; and (2) * * * 'that by waiving his right to an attorney he will lose the opportunity to obtain an independent opinion on whether, under the facts and applicable law, it is wise to plead guilty.' " *Iowa v. Tovar*, 541 U.S. 77, 81 (2004). Instead, the Court concluded simply that

[w]e have described a waiver of counsel as intelligent when the defendant "knows what he is doing and his choice is made with eyes open." We have not, however, prescribed any formula or script to be read to a defendant who states that he elects to proceed without counsel. The information a defendant must possess in order to make an intelligent election [will] depend on a range of case-specific factors, including the defendant's education or sophistication, the complex or easily grasped nature of the charge, and the stage of the proceeding.

Id. at 88.

2. Representing Oneself

a. Right to Proceed Pro Se

Despite the "strong presumption" against defendants' waivers of the Sixth Amendment right to counsel, and despite the Supreme Court's admonition that such waivers can only be accepted if made knowingly and intelligently, the Court has nonetheless permitted defendants to waive counsel and represent themselves (commonly called proceeding or appearing "*pro se*") in appropriate circumstances.

In 1942, the Supreme Court ruled that a defendant in a federal criminal proceeding possesses the right to proceed *pro se* as "the

Constitution does not force a lawyer upon a defendant. He may waive his Constitutional right to assistance of counsel if he knows what he is doing and his choice is made with eyes open." *Adams v. United States ex rel. McCann*, 317 U.S. 269, 279 (1942). Subsequently, in *Faretta v. California*, the Supreme Court extended the right to proceed *pro se* to criminal defendants being tried in state court criminal proceedings. *Faretta v. California*, 422 U.S. 806 (1975). The Court reasoned that, despite our paternalistic desire to assist such defendants, assigned counsel cannot ordinarily be forced upon accused persons who do not want them. As the Court explained:

> There can be no blinking the fact that the right of an accused to conduct his own defense seems to cut against the grain of this Court's decisions holding that the Constitution requires that no accused can be convicted and imprisoned unless he has been accorded the right to the assistance of counsel. For it is surely true that the basic thesis of those decisions is that the help of a lawyer is essential to assure the defendant a fair trial. . . But it is one thing to hold that every defendant, rich or poor, has the right to the assistance of counsel, and quite another to say that a State may compel a defendant to accept a lawyer he does not want. The value of state-appointed counsel was not unappreciated by the Founders, yet the notion of compulsory counsel was utterly foreign to them. . . It is undeniable that in most criminal prosecutions defendants could better defend with counsel's guidance than by their own unskilled efforts. But where the defendant will not voluntarily accept representation by counsel, the potential advantage of a lawyer's training and experience can be realized, if at all, only imperfectly. To force a lawyer on a defendant can only lead him to believe that the law contrives against him.

The *Faretta* Court also made clear, however, a further consequence of a defendant's decision to proceed *pro se*, namely that "whatever else may or may not be open to him on appeal, a defendant who elects to represent himself cannot thereafter complain that the quality of his own defense amounted to a denial of 'effective assistance of counsel.' " Justice Blackmun, dissenting in *Faretta*, pointed to another supposed adverse consequence of *pro se* representation, when he opined that "[i]f there is any truth to the old proverb that 'one who is his own lawyer has a fool for a client,' the Court by its opinion today now bestows a constitutional right on one to make a fool of himself."

In any event, the trial court must assure itself that a defendant who seeks to waive his or her right to counsel and proceed *pro se* is mentally competent to make such a decision.

b. Standby Counsel

In a footnote in its *Faretta* decision, the Supreme Court acknowledged parenthetically that "[o]f course, a State may—even over objection by the accused—appoint a 'standby counsel' to aid the accused if and when the accused requests help, and to be available to represent the accused in the event that termination of the defendant's self-representation is necessary." Since the Court's decision in *Faretta* was handed down, many trial courts have availed themselves of this option, appointing "standby counsel" either to advise a *pro se* defendant who is undertaking his or her own defense and/or simply for the purpose of having counsel available to take over the defense should the defendant decide at some point not to continue proceeding *pro se*.

Subsequently, in *McKaskle v. Wiggins*, 465 U.S. 168 (1984), the Supreme Court offered further guidance on the proper role of standby counsel. In *McKaskle*, defendant's two standby criminal defense attorneys engaged in numerous acts of unsolicited (by defendant) involvement in defendant's robbery trial, including significant participation in making motions and argument, questioning witnesses, and colloquies with the judge, to which defendant often (but not invariably) objected. Although the Supreme Court in *McKaskle* upheld the defendant's conviction and his life sentence, it nonetheless recognized that "the *Faretta* right must impose some limits on the extent of standby counsel's unsolicited participation," those limits being described as follows:

First, the *pro se* defendant is entitled to preserve actual control over the case he chooses to present to the jury. This is the core of the *Faretta* right. If standby counsel's participation over the defendant's objection effectively allows counsel to make or substantially interfere with any significant tactical decisions, or to control the questioning of witnesses, or to speak *instead* of the defendant on any matter of importance, the *Faretta* right is eroded.

Second, participation by standby counsel without the defendant's consent should not be allowed to destroy the jury's perception that the defendant is representing himself. The defendant's appearance in the status of one conducting his own defense is important in a criminal trial, since the right to appear *pro se* exists to affirm the accused's individual dignity and autonomy. . . From the jury's perspective, the message conveyed by the defense may depend as much on the messenger as on the message itself. From the defendant's own point of view, the right to appear *pro se* can lose much of its importance if only the lawyers in the courtroom know that the right is being exercised.

Put another way, as the *McKaskle* Court explained metaphorically: "We recognize that a *pro se* defendant may wish to dance a solo, not a *pas de deux*. Standby counsel must generally respect that preference. But counsel need not be excluded altogether, especially when the participation is outside the presence of the jury or is with the defendant's express or tacit consent."

C. Ineffective Assistance of Counsel

In 1932, the Supreme Court concluded that a criminal defendant's Sixth Amendment right to counsel includes necessarily the right to the "effective" assistance of counsel. *Powell v. Alabama*, 287 U.S. 45 (1932). But the Court did not establish a constitutional test by which to measure such effectiveness (or ineffectiveness) under the Sixth Amendment until 1984. Prior to 1984, these determinations were made by the Supreme Court on an essentially *ad hoc* basis, and state courts developed their own idiosyncratic tests to evaluate the constitutionality of criminal defense counsel's performance.

1. Extrinsic Ineffectiveness

The question that is raised when a criminal defendant claims that his or her defense counsel was guilty of "extrinsic ineffectiveness" is whether some factor or factors *extrinsic* to counsel's *actual* performance created a permissible inference of Sixth Amendment ineffectiveness. Such claims focus commonly, for example, on counsel's age (too young or too old), his or her inexperience (overall or simply in criminal cases), disability, personal or emotional problems, alcoholism or substance abuse problems, problems with the law (*e.g.*, he or she is under indictment), lack of sufficient preparation time, or status in the Bar (*e.g.*, disbarred or suspended or facing such charges).

In 1984, in its decision in *United States v. Cronic*, the Supreme Court unanimously established criteria for evaluating when claims of extrinsic ineffectiveness suffice to establish ineffective assistance of counsel. *United States v. Cronic*, 466 U.S. 648 (1984). Significantly, these criteria make it exceedingly difficult—almost impossible— for a criminal defendant to successfully make such a claim.

In *Cronic*, defense counsel was appointed belatedly, after defendant Cronic's retained counsel had already withdrawn. This was a complicated federal mail-fraud prosecution. The new, appointed attorney was very young, a real-estate practitioner, had never practiced criminal law before, had never tried a case to a jury, and was given only twenty-five days to prepare a case that the prosecution had investigated for four and one-half years, a case that involved many thousands of documents, including hundreds of checks. After a trial in which Cronic was convicted and sentenced to twenty-five years in prison, he argued on appeal, *inter alia*, that his young counsel's lack of preparation, his inexperience, and all of the extrinsic factors listed previously created an inference that Cronic had received ineffective assistance of counsel. The Supreme Court disagreed.

The problem with Cronic's argument (and the difficulty in making such extrinsic claims of ineffectiveness) was that Cronic was not pointing to some *actual* deficiencies in his counsel's representation as the basis for his Sixth Amendment claim. Rather, he was arguing that the Court should *infer* ineffectiveness from the types of extrinsic and apparently problematic factors listed previously. The Supreme Court refused to accept such a hypothetical basis for finding ineffectiveness, concluding instead that, ordinarily, a defendant can "make out a claim of ineffective assistance only by pointing to specific errors made by trial counsel."

The Court explained its decision on these specific facts by noting that "the period of 25 days [is] not so short that it even arguably justifies a presumption that no lawyer could provide the respondent with the effective assistance of counsel required by the Constitution." And, the Court added,

> [t]hat conclusion is not undermined by the fact that [Cronic's] lawyer was young, that his principal practice was in real estate, or that this was his first jury trial. Every experienced criminal defense attorney once tried his first criminal case. Moreover, a lawyer's experience with real estate transactions might be more useful in preparing to try a criminal case involving financial transactions than would prior experience in handling, for example, armed robbery prosecutions. The character of a particular lawyer's experience may shed light in an evaluation of his actual performance, but it does not justify a presumption of ineffectiveness in the absence of such an evaluation.

[T]he gravity of the charge, the complexity of the case, and the accessibility of witnesses[,] are all matters that may affect what a reasonably competent attorney could be expected to have done under the circumstances, but none identifies circumstances that in themselves make it unlikely that [Cronic] received the effective assistance of counsel.

The *Cronic* Court did recognize that exceptions to this general rule (*i.e.*, that ineffectiveness cannot ordinarily be established extrinsically) *do* exist. "There are," the Court acknowledged, "circumstances that are so likely to prejudice the accused that the cost of litigating their effect in a particular case is unjustified." The Court explained the nature of such highly unusual cases,

> [m]ost obvious, of course, is the complete denial of counsel. The presumption that counsel's assistance is essential requires us to conclude that a trial is unfair if the accused is denied counsel at a critical stage of his trial. Similarly, if counsel entirely fails to subject the prosecution's case to a meaningful adversarial testing, then there has been a denial of Sixth Amendment rights that makes the adversary process itself presumptively unreliable. No specific showing of prejudice was required in *Davis v. Alaska*, 415 U.S. 308 (1974), because the petitioner had been "denied the right of effective cross-examination" which " 'would be constitutional error of the first magnitude and no amount of showing of want of prejudice would cure it.' ". . . [Such c]ircumstances . . . may [also] be present on some occasions when although counsel is available to assist the accused during trial, the likelihood that any lawyer, even a fully competent one, could provide effective assistance is so small that a presumption of prejudice is appropriate without inquiry into the actual conduct of the trial.

Nonetheless, despite this list of exceptions, it is extremely rare for an appellate court to reverse a defendant's criminal conviction on the basis of a finding of extrinsic ineffectiveness. Subsequent to its decision in *Cronic*, the Supreme Court has ruled, for example, that extrinsic ineffectiveness did not exist simply because defense counsel conceded his client's guilt of the murder with which he was charged as "concession of . . . guilt does not rank as a 'fail[ure] to function in any meaningful sense as the Government's adversary.' " *Florida v. Nixon*, 543 U.S. 175, 190 (2004)(quoting *Cronic*). Once again, as the *Cronic* Court counseled, referring to the exceptions to the rule set out in the quotation above, "[a]part from circumstances of that magnitude, . . . there is generally no basis for finding a Sixth Amendment violation unless the accused can show how specific errors of counsel undermined the reliability of the finding of guilt."

Moreover, the Supreme Court has stressed that "[w]hen we spoke in *Cronic* of the possibility of presuming prejudice based on an attorney's failure to test the prosecutor's case, we indicated that the attorney's failure must be *complete*." *Bell v. Cone*, 535 U.S. 685 (2002) (emphasis added). Bearing this condition in mind, the Court held that defense counsel's alleged failures of performance at specific points during defendant's capital sentencing hearing might raise issues of *actual* ineffectiveness under *Strickland*, but not under *Cronic*. As the Court noted, "[t]he aspects of counsel's performance challenged by [defendant]—the failure to adduce mitigating evidence and the waiver of closing argument—are plainly of the same ilk as other specific attorney errors we have held subject to *Strickland's* performance and prejudice components."

Similarly, the Court has held that a trial court's order denying a defendant the opportunity to consult with his attorney during a fifteen-minute recess taken while the defendant was continuing to testify was not extrinsic ineffective assistance of counsel as the order did not amount to " '[a]ctual or constructive denial of the assistance of counsel altogether.' " *Perry v. Leeke*, 488 U.S. 272, 280 (1989), *quoting Strickland v. Washington*, 466 U.S. 668, 686 (1984).

2. Actual Ineffectiveness

In a companion case to the *Cronic* decision, *Strickland v. Washington*, 466 U.S. 668 (1984), the Supreme Court handed down the seminal and leading decision establishing the criteria for establishing effective (or ineffective) assistance of counsel when claims of *actual* episodes of ineffectiveness are alleged.

In *Strickland*, defendant Washington confessed to having committed a series of grisly crimes, including three murders. Ignoring his defense counsel's advice to him, Washington waived his right to a jury trial, and pleaded guilty to all of the offenses for which he was indicted, including three counts of first-degree murder. During Washington's guilty-plea colloquy, he "stated . . . that he accepted responsibility for the crimes." The trial judge, significantly, responded by telling Washington in open court that he (the judge) "had 'a great deal of respect for people who are willing to step forward and admit their responsibility' but that he was making no statement at all about his likely sentencing decision." (In fact, the trial judge ultimately sentenced Washington to death at his capital sentencing hearing.)

As the Supreme Court described it, Washington contended on appeal that his defense counsel was ineffective at the sentencing hearing in six different respects: "He asserted that counsel was ineffective because he failed to move for a continuance to prepare for sentencing, to request a psychiatric report, to investigate and present character witnesses, to seek a presentence investigation report, to present meaningful arguments to the sentencing judge, and to investigate the medical examiner's reports or cross-examine the medical experts. In support of the claim, [Washington] submitted 14 affidavits from friends, neighbors, and relatives stating that they would have testified if asked to do so. He also submitted one psychiatric report and one psychological report stating that respondent, though not under the influence of extreme mental or emotional disturbance, was 'chronically frustrated and depressed because of his economic dilemma' at the time of his crimes."

Indeed, Washington's counsel conceded that he had done little preparation for the capital sentencing hearing. Again, in the Court's words, "counsel spoke with [Washington] about his background. He also spoke on the telephone with [Washington]'s wife and mother, though he did not follow up on the one unsuccessful effort to meet with them. He did not otherwise seek out character witnesses for respondent. Nor did he request a psychiatric examination, since his conversations with his client gave no indication that respondent had psychological problems."

The Supreme Court explained the reason that counsel apparently decided—intentionally—to do nothing more in the way of preparation than this small amount:

That decision reflected trial counsel's sense of hopelessness about overcoming the evidentiary effect of respondent's confessions to the gruesome crimes. It also reflected the judgment that it was advisable to rely on the plea colloquy for evidence about respondent's background and about his claim of emotional stress: the plea colloquy communicated sufficient information about these subjects, and by forgoing the opportunity to present new evidence on these subjects, counsel prevented the State from cross-examining respondent on his claim and from putting on psychiatric evidence of its own.

Counsel also excluded from the sentencing hearing other evidence he thought was potentially damaging. He successfully moved to exclude respondent's "rap sheet." Because he judged that a presentence report might prove more detrimental than helpful, as it would have included respondent's criminal history and thereby would have undermined the claim of no significant history of criminal activity, he did not request that one be prepared.

At the sentencing hearing, counsel's strategy was based primarily on the trial judge's remarks at the plea colloquy as well as on his reputation as a sentencing judge who thought it important for a convicted defendant to own up to his crime. Counsel argued that respondent's remorse and acceptance of responsibility justified sparing him from the death penalty. Counsel also argued that [Washington] had no history of criminal activity and that [Washington] committed the crimes under extreme mental or emotional disturbance, thus coming within the statutory list of mitigating circumstances. He further argued that [Washington] should be spared death because he had surrendered, confessed, and offered to testify against a codefendant and because [Washington] was fundamentally a good person who had briefly gone badly wrong in extremely stressful circumstances. The State put on evidence and witnesses largely for the purpose of describing the details of the crimes. Counsel did not cross-examine the medical experts who testified about the manner of death of [Washington]'s victims.

At the end of Washington's sentencing hearing, the trial judge sentenced Washington to death on each of the three counts of first-degree murder, finding several aggravating circumstances to have existed with respect to the murders, counterbalanced by a relatively insignificant mitigating circumstance (no significant history of prior criminal activity). And, on this factual record, the Supreme Court concluded that Washington had *not* made out a case for ineffective assistance of counsel.

In order to assess whether or not defense counsel had provided the constitutionally-requisite effective assistance of counsel, the Court in *Strickland* fashioned a two-pronged test for gauging the ineffective assistance of counsel:

> A convicted defendant's claim that counsel's assistance was so defective as to require reversal of a conviction or death sentence has two components. First, the defendant must show that counsel's performance was deficient. This requires showing that counsel made errors so serious that counsel was not functioning as the "counsel" guaranteed the defendant by the Sixth Amendment. Second, the defendant must show that the deficient performance prejudiced the defense. This requires showing that counsel's errors were so serious as to deprive the defendant of a fair trial, a trial whose result is reliable. Unless a defendant makes both showings, it cannot be said that the conviction or death sentence resulted from a breakdown in the adversary process that renders the result unreliable.

These two prongs are independent of one another, i.e. to establish ineffective assistance of counsel, a defendant must show *both* that his or her defense counsel performed deficiently *and* that the deficient performance actually prejudiced his or her defense.

Moreover, as the *Strickland* Court pointed out, "there is no reason for a court deciding an ineffective assistance claim to approach the [two-pronged] inquiry in [a certain] order or even to address both components of the inquiry if the defendant makes an insufficient showing on one. In particular, a court need not determine whether counsel's performance was deficient before examining the prejudice suffered by the defendant as a result of the alleged deficiencies. The object of an ineffectiveness claim is not to grade counsel's performance. If it is easier to dispose of an ineffectiveness claim on the ground of lack of sufficient prejudice, which we expect will often be so, that course should be followed."

a. The Performance Prong

Three points should be borne in mind in applying the "performance" prong of the *Strickland* Court's two-pronged ineffectiveness test. *First*, there is no one (or more) specific task that defense counsel must do or not do in order to be deemed effective. Indeed, the Court flatly rejected an ineffectiveness approach using a "checklist [of counsel's basic duties or obligations] for judicial evaluation of attorney performance." Instead, as the *Strickland* Court stressed, "the proper standard for attorney performance is that of *reasonably effective assistance*."

Second, "[j]udicial scrutiny of counsel's performance must be highly deferential. It is all too tempting for a defendant to second-guess counsel's assistance after conviction or adverse sentence, and it is all too easy for a court, examining counsel's defense after it has proved unsuccessful, to conclude that a particular act or omission of counsel was unreasonable. A fair assessment of attorney performance requires that every effort be made to eliminate the distorting effects of hindsight, to reconstruct the circumstances of counsel's challenged conduct, and to evaluate the conduct from counsel's perspective at the time." Indeed, "[b]ecause of the difficulties inherent in making th[is] evaluation [of ineffectiveness]," the Court added, a reviewing appellate court "must indulge a *strong presumption* that counsel's conduct falls within the wide range of reasonable professional assistance; that is, the defendant must overcome the presumption that, under the circumstances, the challenged action 'might be considered sound trial strategy.' There are countless ways to provide effective assistance in any given case. Even the best criminal defense attorneys would not defend a particular client in the same way."

And, *third*, "[w]hen a convicted defendant complains of the ineffectiveness of counsel's assistance, the defendant must show that counsel's representation fell below an *objective standard* of reasonableness."

Putting these three points together, in order to establish the performance prong of the Court's ineffectiveness test, a convicted defendant has the difficult task of overcoming the strong presumption that his or her defense counsel acted in an objectively reasonable fashion.

The Supreme Court has, for example, concluded that defense counsel was *not* ineffective in a case where counsel conceded his client's guilt of the murder with which he was charged as the evidence of guilt was so clear that counsel decided to concentrate his defense instead on establishing, at the penalty phase, cause for sparing his client's life. *Florida v. Nixon*, 543 U.S. 175 (2004). As the Court explained, defense counsel's "concession of Nixon's guilt does not rank as a 'fail[ure] to function in any meaningful sense as the Government's adversary.' Although such a concession in a run-of-the-mine trial might present a closer question, the gravity of the potential sentence in a capital trial and the proceeding's two-phase structure vitally affect counsel's strategic calculus. Attorneys representing capital defendants face daunting challenges in developing trial strategies, not least because the defendant's guilt is often clear. Prosecutors are more likely to seek the death penalty, and to refuse to accept a plea to a life sentence, when the evidence is overwhelming and the crime heinous. In such cases, 'avoiding execution [may be] the best and only realistic result possible.' "

As the *Nixon* decision illustrates, "[a]s is obvious, *Strickland's* standard, although by no means insurmountable, is highly demanding." *Kimmelman v. Morrison*, 477 U.S. 365, 382 (1986). That may be an understatement. Some justices have been less charitable about *Strickland's* effect. *See, e.g., McFarland v. Scott*, 512 U.S. 1256 (1994) (Blackmun, J., diss'g from denial of writ of cert.) ("Ten years after the articulation of [the *Strickland*] standard, practical experience establishes that the *Strickland* test, in application, has failed to protect a defendant's right to be represented by something more than a 'person who happens to be a lawyer.' ").

Although the *Strickland* test might sound rather general and open-ended, that sort of pragmatic flexibility is precisely what the Supreme Court intended. "More specific guidelines are not appropriate," the Court concluded, as "[t]he Sixth Amendment refers simply to 'counsel,' not specifying particular requirements of effective assistance." Indeed, as the Court added, "[a] number of practical considerations are important for the application of the standards we have outlined. Most important, in adjudicating a claim of actual ineffectiveness of counsel, a court should keep in mind that the principles we have stated do not establish mechanical rules. Although those principles should guide the process of decision, the ultimate focus of inquiry must be on the fundamental fairness of the proceeding whose result is being challenged. In every case the court should be concerned with whether, despite the strong presumption of reliability, the result of the particular proceeding is unreliable because of a breakdown in the adversarial process that our system counts on to produce just results."

In determining what constitutes effective assistance of counsel for Sixth Amendment purposes, moreover, the *Strickland* Court eschewed specifically reliance (for constitutional purposes) upon professional codes for lawyers, explaining that "[p]revailing norms of practice as reflected in American Bar Association standards and the like, e.g., ABA Standards for Criminal Justice * * * ('The Defense Function'), are guides to determining what is reasonable, but they are only guides. No particular set of detailed rules for counsel's conduct can satisfactorily take account of the variety of circumstances faced by defense counsel or the range of legitimate decisions regarding how best to represent a criminal defendant. Any such set of rules would interfere with the constitutionally protected independence of counsel and restrict the wide latitude counsel must have in making tactical decisions. Indeed, the existence of detailed guidelines for representation could distract counsel from the overriding mission of vigorous advocacy of the defendant's cause. Moreover, the purpose of the effective assistance guarantee of the Sixth Amendment is not to improve the quality of legal representation, although that is a goal of considerable importance to the legal system. The purpose is simply to ensure that criminal defendants receive a fair trial."

The Supreme Court subsequently expanded upon this point in a 1986 decision, explaining that "[u]nder the *Strickland* standard, breach of an ethical standard does not necessarily make out a denial of the Sixth Amendment guarantee of assistance of counsel. When examining attorney conduct, a court must be careful not to narrow the wide range of conduct acceptable under the Sixth Amendment so restrictively as to constitutionalize particular standards of professional conduct and thereby intrude into the state's proper authority to define and apply the standards of professional conduct applicable to those it admits to practice in its courts." *Nix v. Whiteside*, 475 U.S. 157 (1986).

Despite these repeated warnings about the lack of necessary and specific tasks that criminal defense counsel *must* undertake, it is important to bear in mind that defending a client effectively nonetheless does, as the *Strickland* Court put it, "entail[] certain basic duties." Expounding upon this point, the Court emphasized that "[c]ounsel's function is to assist the defendant, and hence counsel owes the client a duty of loyalty, a duty to avoid conflicts of interest. From counsel's function as assistant to the defendant derive the overarching duty to advocate the defendant's cause and the more particular duties to consult with the defendant on important decisions and to keep the defendant informed of important developments in the course of the prosecution. Counsel also has a duty to bring to bear such skill and knowledge as will render the trial a reliable adversarial testing process."

In the *Strickland* case itself, the Court found that application of this newly-crafted performance prong to the facts of that case was simply "not difficult[.] The facts [make] clear that the conduct of [Washington]'s counsel at and before [Washington]'s sentencing proceeding cannot be found unreasonable." As the Court explained:

> [T]he record shows that [Washington]'s counsel made a strategic choice to argue for the extreme emotional distress mitigating circumstance and to rely as fully as possible on [Washington]'s acceptance of responsibility for his crimes. Although counsel understandably felt hopeless about respondent's prospects, nothing in the record indicates [that] counsel's sense of hopelessness distorted his professional judgment. Counsel's strategy choice was well within the range of professionally reasonable judgments, and the decision not to seek more character or psychological evidence than was already in hand was likewise reasonable.

The trial judge's views on the importance of owning up to one's crimes were well known to counsel. The aggravating circumstances were utterly overwhelming. Trial counsel could reasonably surmise from his conversations with [Washington] that character and psychological evidence would be of little help. [Washington] had already been able to mention at the plea colloquy the substance of what there was to know about his financial and emotional troubles. Restricting testimony on [Washington]'s character to what had come in at the plea colloquy ensured that contrary character and psychological evidence and [Washington]'s criminal history, which counsel had successfully moved to exclude, would not come in. On these facts, there can be little question, even without application of the presumption of adequate performance, that trial counsel's defense, though unsuccessful, was the result of reasonable professional judgment.

The *Strickland* decision does *not* mean that the Supreme Court has implied that defense counsel may (constitutionally) ignore investigation of his or her client's case. In a subsequent decision, for example, the Supreme Court held that the *Strickland* performance prong had not been met where defense counsel failed to discover before trial that the State had in its possession critical evidence which counsel could have moved to suppress. *Kimmelman v. Morrison*, 477 U.S. 365 (1986). Although the Supreme Court reaffirmed its view that it is important to look at the whole picture of defense counsel's conduct, including counsel's "overall performance" in assessing ineffectiveness, the Court nonetheless added that

> [i]n this case, however, we deal with a total failure to conduct pre-trial discovery, and one as to which counsel offered only implausible explanations. Counsel's performance at trial, while generally creditable enough, suggests no better explanation for this *apparent and pervasive failure to "make reasonable investigations or to make a reasonable decision that makes particular investigations unnecessary."* [At] the time [defendant]'s lawyer decided not to request any discovery, he did not—and, because he did not ask, could not—know what the State's case would be. While the relative importance of witness credibility [and] related expert testimony is pertinent to the determination whether respondent was prejudiced by his attorney's incompetence, it sheds no light on the reasonableness of counsel's decision not to request any discovery. We therefore agree with the District Court and the Court of Appeals that the assistance rendered respondent by his trial counsel was constitutionally deficient.

Similarly, a majority of the Court in *Rompilla v. Beard*, 545 U.S. 374 (2005), held that defense counsel in a capital case was ineffective for failing to make reasonable efforts to obtain and review critical material relating to a prior conviction that counsel knew the prosecution would probably rely on as evidence of aggravation at the sentencing phase of trial (where there was a reasonable probability that if counsel had obtained that file and used the information contained therein, the sentencing jury might not have sentenced the defendant to death). The Court made clear that this holding did *not* serve to create, however,

> a "rigid, per se" rule that requires defense counsel to do a complete review of the file on any prior conviction introduced[.] Counsel fell short here because they failed to make reasonable efforts to review the prior conviction file, despite knowing that the prosecution intended to introduce Rompilla's prior conviction not merely by entering a notice of conviction into evidence

but by quoting damaging testimony of the rape victim in that case. The unreasonableness of attempting no more than they did was heightened by the easy availability of the file at the trial courthouse, and the great risk that testimony about a similar violent crime would hamstring counsel's chosen defense of residual doubt. It is owing to these circumstances that the state courts were objectively unreasonable in concluding that counsel could reasonably decline to make any effort to review the file. Other situations, where a defense lawyer is not charged with knowledge that the prosecutor intends to use a prior conviction in this way, might well warrant a different assessment.

See also Sears v. Upton, 130 S.Ct. 3259 (2010) (finding ineffectiveness in another shoddy capital murder sentencing mitigation investigation); *Porter v. McCollum*, 130 S.Ct. 447 (2009) (same).

More recently, the Supreme Court in *Padilla v. Kentucky*, 130 S.Ct. 1473 (2010), concluded that defense counsel engaged in deficient performance under *Strickland* by failing to advise a defendant that his plea of guilty made him subject to automatic deportation. "This is not a hard case in which to find deficiency," the majority ruled, "[t]he consequences of Padilla's plea could easily be determined from reading the removal statute, his deportation was presumptively mandatory, and his counsel's advice was incorrect." *Id.* at 1483.

b. The Prejudice Prong

The Supreme Court in *Strickland* ruled that to establish ineffective assistance of counsel, a defendant must show *both* that his or her defense counsel performed deficiently *and* that the deficient performance actually *prejudiced* the defense: "Conflict of interest claims aside, actual ineffectiveness claims alleging a deficiency in attorney performance are subject to a general requirement that the defendant affirmatively prove prejudice."

As the Supreme Court explained subsequently, "the 'prejudice' component of the *Strickland* test [focuses] on the question whether counsel's deficient performance renders the result of the trial unreliable or the proceeding fundamentally unfair. Unreliability or unfairness does not result if the ineffectiveness of counsel does not deprive the defendant of any substantive or procedural right to which the law entitles him." *Lockhart v. Fretwell,* 506 U.S. 364, 372 (1993). The Court has also added that "an [ineffectiveness] analysis focusing solely on mere outcome determination, without attention to whether the result of the proceeding was fundamentally unfair or unreliable, is defective."

But, the Supreme Court has also concluded—more recently—that defense counsel's deficient performance in failing to object to a legal error that affected the calculation of a prison sentence, an error resulting in additional incarceration—however short—is *clearly* prejudicial to a defendant: "Authority does not suggest that a minimal amount of additional time in prison cannot constitute prejudice. Quite to the contrary, our jurisprudence suggests that any amount of actual jail time has Sixth Amendment significance." *Glover v. United States*, 531 U.S. 198, 202 (2001).

In *Strickland*, the Supreme Court also established the precise nature of the prejudice showing that a defendant must make in order to prove ineffectiveness (assuming an independent showing of performance deficiency also exists): "The defendant must show that there is a *reasonable probability* that, but for counsel's unprofessional errors, the result of the proceeding would have been different. A reasonable probability is a probability sufficient to undermine confidence in the outcome."

Or, as the Court made the same point in another way: "When a defendant challenges a conviction, the question is whether there is a reasonable probability that, absent the errors, the factfinder would have had a reasonable doubt respecting guilt. When a defendant challenges a death sentence such as the one at issue in this case, the question is whether there is a reasonable probability that, absent the errors, the sentencer—including an appellate court, to the extent it independently reweighs the evidence—would have concluded that the balance of aggravating and mitigating circumstances did not warrant death."

As with the performance-prong inquiry, the *Strickland* Court stressed the commonsensical nature of this analysis and established a presumption against a finding of prejudice. As the Supreme Court explained:

> In making the determination whether the specified errors resulted in the required prejudice, a court should presume, absent challenge to the judgment on grounds of evidentiary insufficiency, that the judge or jury acted according to law. An assessment of the likelihood of a result more favorable to the defendant must exclude the possibility of arbitrariness, whimsy, caprice, "nullification," and the like. A defendant has no entitlement to the luck of a lawless decisionmaker, even if a lawless decision cannot be reviewed. The assessment of prejudice

should proceed on the assumption that the decisionmaker is reasonably, conscientiously, and impartially applying the standards that govern the decision. It should not depend on the idiosyncracies of the particular decisionmaker, such as unusual propensities toward harshness or leniency. Although these factors may actually have entered into counsel's selection of strategies and, to that limited extent, may thus affect the performance inquiry, they are irrelevant to the prejudice inquiry. Thus, evidence about the actual process of decision, if not part of the record of the proceeding under review, and evidence about, for example, a particular judge's sentencing practices, should not be considered in the prejudice determination.

In the *Strickland* decision itself, the Court concluded that defendant Washington had not in fact been prejudiced by his counsel's conduct. The Court explained that "[t]he evidence that [Washington] says his trial counsel should have offered at the sentencing hearing would barely have altered the sentencing profile presented to the sentencing judge. As the state courts and District Court found, at most this evidence shows that numerous people who knew [Washington] thought he was generally a good person and that a psychiatrist and a psychologist believed he was under considerable emotional stress that did not rise to the level of extreme disturbance. Given the overwhelming aggravating factors, there is no reasonable probability that the omitted evidence would have changed the conclusion that the aggravating circumstances outweighed the mitigating circumstances and, hence, the sentence imposed."

In separate decisions handed down subsequent to *Strickland*, the Supreme Court has found no prejudice to exist for Sixth Amendment purposes where defense counsel threatened to withdraw if his client perjured himself at trial, *Nix v. Whiteside*, 475 U.S. 157 (1986), where defense counsel failed to make an objection in a capital sentencing hearing that would have (then) been supported by a decision that was subsequently overruled, *Lockhart v. Fretwell*, 506 U.S. 364, 372 (1993), and where defense counsel had misinformed his client of his parole eligibility date in explaining to him the consequences of his contemplated guilty plea, *Hill v. Lockhart*, 474 U.S. 52 (1985).

In the latter decision, the Court elaborated in a helpful fashion on how prejudice should be assessed in cases where a defendant has decided to plead guilty and subsequently claims that his or her criminal defense attorney performed in an ineffective fashion:

> In many guilty plea cases, the "prejudice" inquiry will closely resemble the inquiry engaged in by courts reviewing ineffec-

tive-assistance challenges to convictions obtained through a trial. For example, where the alleged error of counsel is a failure to investigate or discover potentially exculpatory evidence, the determination whether the error "prejudiced" the defendant by causing him to plead guilty rather than go to trial will depend on the likelihood that discovery of the evidence would have led counsel to change his recommendation as to the plea. This assessment, in turn, will depend in large part on a prediction whether the evidence likely would have changed the outcome of a trial. Similarly, where the alleged error of counsel is a failure to advise the defendant of a potential affirmative defense to the crime charged, the resolution of the "prejudice" inquiry will depend largely on whether the affirmative defense likely would have succeeded at trial.

3. Ineffective Assistance Analysis in Federal Habeas Corpus Proceedings

In 1996, Congress enacted the Antiterrorism & Effective Death Penalty Act of 1996 ("AEDPA"). Both before and after adoption of the AEDPA, the decision whether or not to grant an evidentiary hearing to raise ineffectiveness claims was a matter left to the discretion of district courts. If the record refutes the applicant's factual allegations or otherwise precludes habeas relief, the court is not required to hold a hearing. *Schriro v. Landrigan*, 550 U.S. 465 (2007) (holding 5–to–4 that district court did not abuse its discretion in not holding a hearing because applicant could never have established prejudice under *Strickland* due to his refusal to allow his counsel to present mitigating evidence at sentencing).

However, when a hearing is held, the AEDPA changed the standards for granting habeas corpus relief, providing, *inter alia*, that "[a]n application for a writ of habeas corpus on behalf of a person in custody pursuant to the judgment of a State court shall not be granted with respect to any claim that was adjudicated on the merits in State court proceedings unless the adjudication of the claim * * * resulted in a decision that was contrary to, or involved an unreasonable application of, clearly established Federal law, as determined by the Supreme Court of the United States." 28 U.S.C. § 2254(d)(1).

A 5–to–4 majority of the Supreme Court ruled, in a 2000 decision, *Williams v. Taylor*, 529 U.S. 362 (2000), that this AEDPA provision "places a new constraint on the power of a federal habeas court to grant a state prisoner's application for a writ of habeas corpus with respect to claims adjudicated on the merits in state court."

More particularly, the Court held, under this new provision,

the writ may issue only if one of the following two conditions is satisfied—the state-court adjudication resulted in a decision that (1) "was contrary to . . . clearly established Federal law, as determined by the Supreme Court of the United States," or (2) "involved an unreasonable application of . . . clearly established Federal law, as determined by the Supreme Court of the United States." Under the "contrary to" clause, a federal habeas court may grant the writ if the state court arrives at a conclusion opposite to that reached by this Court on a question of law or if the state court decides a case differently than this Court has on a set of materially indistinguishable facts. Under the "unreasonable application" clause, a federal habeas court may grant the writ if the state court identifies the correct governing legal principle from this Court's decisions but unreasonably applies that principle to the facts of the prisoner's case.

Significantly for purposes of evaluating Sixth Amendment claims of defense counsel's ineffectiveness, the fact that a state court may have made an *incorrect* constitutional ruling on an ineffectiveness inquiry no longer suffices—under this AEDPA provision—to entitle a defendant to habeas corpus relief. As the majority in *Williams* stressed, "the most important point is that an *unreasonable* application of federal law is different from an *incorrect* application of federal law. [In this AEDPA provision], Congress specifically used the word 'unreasonable,' and not a term like 'erroneous' or 'incorrect.' Under [the] 'unreasonable application' clause, then, a federal habeas court may not issue the writ simply because that court concludes in its independent judgment that the relevant state-court decision applied clearly established federal law erroneously or incorrectly. Rather, that application must also be unreasonable."

In a subsequent decision, the Supreme Court once again pointed to the distinction between an *unreasonable* and an *incorrect* state-court decision. In *Woodford v. Visciotti*, 537 U.S. 19 (2002), the Supreme Court stressed that "[u]nder [the] 'unreasonable application' clause, a federal habeas court may not issue the writ simply because that court concludes in its independent judgment that the state-court decision applied *Strickland* incorrectly. . . . Rather, it is the habeas applicant's burden to show that the state court applied *Strickland* to the facts of his case in an objectively unreasonable manner."

The *Woodford* Court concluded that while the California Supreme Court may have *incorrectly* concluded that a capital defendant whose defense counsel failed to introduce available mitigating evidence was not prejudiced given the severity of the aggravating factors also in evidence, such a conclusion was not *unreasonable*. As the Court explained, "[t]he federal habeas scheme leaves primary responsibility with the state courts for these judgments, and authorizes federal-court intervention only when a state-court decision is objectively unreasonable. It is not that here."

Similarly, in *Bell v. Cone*, 535 U.S. 685, 702 (2002), the Supreme Court concluded that the Tennessee Court of Appeals had not acted *unreasonably* in concluding that defense counsel at a capital sentencing hearing was not ineffective (1) for failing to present sufficient mitigating evidence, and (2) by waiving final argument. In both instances, the Court concluded that the Tennessee Court of Appeals' decision that there were valid tactical reasons for defense counsel to have behaved in this fashion was not "objectively unreasonable." Again, it would not have mattered if the Tennessee court had been wrong or had applied the law incorrectly, as long as its conclusions were not so inappropriate as to be objectively unreasonable.

Moreover, the Supreme Court has made clear that "whether a state court's decision resulted from an unreasonable legal or factual conclusion does not require that there be an opinion from the state court explaining the state court's reasoning. . . .. Where a state court's decision is unaccompanied by an explanation, the habeas petitioner's burden still must be met by showing there was no reasonable basis for the state court to deny relief." *Harrington v. Richter*, 131 S.Ct. 770, 784, 785 (2011).

But the Supreme Court has not always justified incorrect state court decisions relating to ineffective assistance of counsel as nonetheless reasonable (in actual fact, not "unreasonable") for AEDPA purposes. In *Rompilla v. Beard*, 545 U.S. 374 (2005), for example, the Court found that the Pennsylvania Supreme Court had acted incorrectly and objectively unreasonably in concluding that defense counsel in a capital case were not ineffective when they failed to make reasonable efforts to obtain and review critical material relating to a prior conviction that counsel knew the prosecution would probably rely upon as evidence of aggravation at the sentencing phase of trial.

Significantly, the Supreme Court ruled in a 2011 decision, *Cullen v. Pinholster*, 131 S.Ct. 1388 (2011), that a §2254(d)(1) ineffectiveness inquiry is limited to the record that was before the state court that adjudicated the claim on the merits; evidence that was presented to the federal habeas court may not be considered. The *Cullen* majority conceded that "[t]his [test] is . . . 'difficult to meet,'

... and [it is a] 'highly deferential standard for evaluating state-court rulings, which demands that state-court decisions be given the benefit of the doubt[.]'" *Id.*

4. When Ineffective Assistance Claims Can Be Brought

In *Massaro v. United States*, 538 U.S. 500 (2003), the Supreme Court unanimously concluded that "an ineffective-assistance-of-counsel claim may be brought in a collateral proceeding under § 2255, whether or not the petitioner could have raised the claim on direct appeal."

Resolving a conflict in the lower federal courts, the Supreme Court ruled that the procedural-default rule that is usually applied when an appellant fails to raise an issue on appeal should not—and does not—apply to ineffective assistance of counsel claims. The Court concluded that "[a]pplying the usual procedural-default rule to ineffective-assistance claims would . . . creat[e] the risk that defendants would feel compelled to raise the issue before there has been an opportunity fully to develop the factual predicate for the claim."

It is important to add, however, that a federal defendant need not wait to bring a § 2255 motion in order to raise the issue of ineffectiveness. To the contrary, the *Massaro* Court ruled expressly that "[w]e do not hold that ineffective-assistance claims must be reserved for collateral review."

The same rule the Supreme Court adopted, namely that an ineffective-assistance-of-counsel claim may be brought in a collateral proceeding whether or not the defendant could have raised the claim on direct appeal, is the majority rule in the states as well.

D. Conflicts of Interest

1. Constitutional Right

The Supreme Court first ruled in 1942 that a criminal defense attorney's conflict of interest in representing a criminal accused can amount to ineffective assistance of counsel under the Sixth Amendment. *Glasser v. United States*, 315 U.S. 60 (1942). As the Court explained at that time, "[e]ven as we have held that the right to the assistance of counsel is so fundamental that the denial by a state court of a reasonable time to allow the selection of counsel of one's own choosing, and the failure of that court to make an effective appointment of counsel, may so offend our concept of the basic requirements of a fair hearing as to amount to a denial of due process of law contrary to the Fourteenth Amendment, so are we clear that the 'Assistance of Counsel' guaranteed by the Sixth Amendment contemplates that such assistance be untrammeled and unimpaired by a court order requiring that one lawyer shall simultaneously represent conflicting interests. If the right to the assistance of counsel means less than this, a valued constitutional safeguard is substantially impaired."

Subsequent and more recent Supreme Court decisions have reaffirmed strongly every criminal defendant's Sixth Amendment right to be represented by conflict-free defense counsel. As the Supreme Court pointed out in a 1978 decision, "in a case of * * * conflicting interests the evil—it bears repeating—is in what the advocate finds himself compelled to *refrain* from doing, not only at trial but also as to possible pretrial plea negotiations and in the sentencing process." *Holloway v. Arkansas*, 435 U.S. 475, 490 (1978) (emphasis in original).

2. Conflicts Raised Prior to or During Trial

In *Holloway v. Arkansas*, 435 U.S. 475 (1978), the Supreme Court first addressed the issue of when allegations of a potential conflict of interest unsuccessfully raised by criminal defense counsel in the joint representation of multiple criminal defendants give rise to ineffective assistance of counsel under the Sixth Amendment.

Trial counsel in *Holloway*, a public defender, was appointed to jointly represent three co-defendants, each of whom was charged with one count of robbery and two counts of rape, all arising out of the same criminal episode. Both prior to and during trial, counsel moved for the appointment of separate counsel for the three co-defendants; these motions were denied. Although counsel protested that he would not be able to cross-examine the co-defendants on behalf of other co-defendants when they testified due to his conflict of interest, the court instructed him to simply put his clients on the stand and let each tell his story without any questioning at all. That is exactly what defense counsel did and, on appeal, the Supreme Court reversed. The *Holloway* Court agreed fully with counsel's objections to his multiple representation and held that each of the defendants' Sixth Amendment rights to conflict-free counsel was violated.

Significantly, that does *not* mean, the Court stressed, that criminal defense counsel can never engage in joint representation of more than one criminal accused charged with the same crimes. To the contrary, as the Court made crystal clear, "[r]equiring or permitting a single attorney to represent codefendants, often referred to as joint representation, is not *per se* violative of constitutional guarantees of effective assistance of counsel. This principle recognizes that in some cases multiple defendants can appropriately be represented by one attorney; indeed, in some cases, certain advantages might accrue from joint representation. In Justice Frankfurter's view: 'Joint representation is a means of insuring against reciprocal recrimination. A common defense often gives strength against a common attack.' " *Id.* at 482–83, *quoting Glasser, supra,* 315 U.S. at 92 (Frankfurter, J., diss'g).

However, the Supreme Court concluded, where trial counsel timely identifies and alerts the trial court to the risk of a conflict of interest as trial counsel did in that case, the trial judge *must* "either [appoint] separate counsel or [take] adequate steps to ascertain whether the risk was too remote to warrant separate counsel."

As this quoted language indicates, when faced with the possibility of a conflict, a court can hold a remoteness-of-risk hearing to determine whether or not the risk of conflict is real. Such a hearing cannot be perfunctory in nature, however; it must include a thorough and meaningful inquiry into any and all potentiality for conflict. Given the searching nature of this inquiry, and, further, given the fact that defense counsel may well be prohibited by applicable ethical rules (and the attorney-client privilege) from revealing any confidential information which (usually) gives rise to the potential for conflict, *see, e.g.,* American Bar Association, Model Rules of Professional Conduct Rule 1.6(a) ("A lawyer shall not reveal information relating to the representation of a client unless the client gives informed consent. . .") (2006 amended ed.; exceptions omitted), trial courts may be best advised simply to appoint separate counsel in response to current counsel's request without holding such a hearing. That is, indeed, often what happens.

Where counsel has brought the issue of potential conflict to the trial court's attention and the trial court fails properly to respond to the motion, e.g. by failing to either grant the motion or to ascertain the potentiality of a conflict at an appropriate hearing, it is important to note that, in contrast to ordinary ineffectiveness inquiries, reversal of a defendant's conviction is "automatic," *even in the absence of a demonstration of prejudice. Holloway,* 435 U.S. at 489. As the Supreme Court has more recently reiterated this rule: "*Holloway* [creates] an automatic reversal rule [where] defense counsel is forced to represent codefendants over his timely objection, unless the trial court has determined that there is no conflict." *Mickens v. Taylor,* 535 U.S. 162 (2002).

3. Conflicts Raised After Trial

In a 1980 decision, *Cuyler v. Sullivan*, 446 U.S. 335 (1980), the Supreme Court addressed the issue left open two years earlier in *Holloway v. Arkansas* of when an alleged conflict of interest *not* raised prior to or during trial could and should amount to ineffective assistance of counsel. In *Cuyler*, three co-defendants in separate first-degree murder prosecutions arising out of the same incident were jointly represented by two privately-retained criminal defense counsel. One of the three co-defendants, Sullivan, came to trial first and was convicted. His two co-defendants were tried subsequently and acquitted.

Sullivan argued in collateral relief proceedings that he had received ineffective assistance of counsel, *inter alia*, because his counsel possessed a conflict of interest in their representation of the three co-defendants. As the Supreme Court noted, one of Sullivan's lawyers conceded that the reason he had decided to rest Sullivan's case without presenting any evidence on his behalf was because "he had not 'want[ed] the defense to go on because I thought we would only be exposing the [defense] witnesses for the other two trials that were coming up.' "

Significantly, unlike the *Holloway* case, neither of Sullivan's trial counsel had raised the possibility of a conflict of interest. The Supreme Court in *Cuyler* concluded that the fact that the issue had not been raised at or before trial dictated a different approach than that taken in *Holloway*. "In order to establish a violation of the Sixth Amendment," the Supreme Court ruled, "a defendant who raised no objection at trial must demonstrate that an actual conflict of interest adversely affected his lawyer's performance." In contrast, in *Holloway*, the Court had concluded that a trial court's failure to adequately respond to defense counsel's motion for separate counsel automatically required a reversal of the defendant's conviction, i.e. without demonstrating, as *Cuyler* requires, the necessity of establishing that "an actual conflict of interest" existed which "adversely affected [the defendant's] lawyer's performance."

The *Cuyler* Court did reaffirm the proposition that "unconstitutional multiple representation is *never* harmless error." Accordingly, "a defendant who shows that a conflict of interest actually affected the adequacy of his representation need not demonstrate prejudice in order to obtain relief. But," the Court continued, "until a defendant shows that his counsel actively represented conflicting interests, he has not established the constitutional predicate for his claim of ineffective assistance." In the *Cuyler* case itself, as a result, the Supreme Court remanded for a lower court determination whether or not Sullivan had been adversely affected in fact by an actual conflict of interest.

4. Waiver

All lawyers' ethics codes contain provisions which permit clients to waive conflicts of interest in most situations, assuming they are fully informed of the consequences of such a waiver. However, in *Wheat v. United States*, 486 U.S. 153 (1988), the Supreme Court concluded that trial courts possess broad discretion to decide whether or not to permit criminal defendants to accept such a waiver under the Sixth Amendment as

> a district court must pass on the issue whether or not to allow a waiver of a conflict of interest by a criminal defendant not with the wisdom of hindsight after the trial has taken place, but in the murkier pre-trial context when relationships between parties are seen through a glass, darkly. The likelihood and dimensions of nascent conflicts of interest are notoriously hard to predict, even for those thoroughly familiar with criminal trials. It is a rare attorney who will be fortunate enough to learn the entire truth from his own client, much less be fully apprised before trial of what each of the Government's witnesses will say on the stand. A few bits of unforeseen testimony or a single previously unknown or unnoticed document may significantly shift the relationship between multiple defendants. These imponderables are difficult enough for a lawyer to assess, and even more difficult to convey by way of explanation to a criminal defendant untutored in the niceties of legal ethics. Nor is it amiss to observe that the willingness of an attorney to obtain such waivers from his clients may bear an inverse relation to the care with which he conveys all the necessary information to them.

For these reasons we think the district court must be allowed substantial latitude in refusing waivers of conflicts of interest not only in those rare cases where an actual conflict may be demonstrated before trial, but in the more common cases where a potential for conflict exists which may or may not burgeon into an actual conflict as the trial progresses.

E. The Griffin–Douglas Doctrine

In *Griffin v. Illinois*, 351 U.S. 12 (1956), a majority of the Supreme Court concluded that an indigent prisoner appealing from his conviction in state court had a Fourteenth Amendment right (under both the due process and equal protection clauses) to a free transcript of his trial where such transcripts were often a practical necessity for success on appeal. A plurality of the Court explained that "to deny adequate review to the poor means that many of them may lose their life, liberty or property because of unjust convictions which appellate courts would set aside. Many States have recognized this and provided aid for convicted defendants who have a right to appeal and need a transcript but are unable to pay for it. A few have not. Such a denial is a misfit in a country dedicated to affording equal justice to all and special privileges to none in the administration of its criminal law. *There can be no equal justice where the kind of trial a man gets depends on the amount of money he has.* Destitute defendants must be afforded as adequate appellate review as defendants who have money enough to buy transcripts."

Subsequently, in *Douglas v. California*, 372 U.S. 353 (1963), a companion case to *Gideon v. Wainwright*, 372 U.S. 335 (1963), wherein the Supreme Court established the right to appointed counsel for indigents in the states, the Court followed the *Griffin* reasoning by concluding that indigent defendants convicted at trial have a Fourteenth Amendment right (again, under both the due process and equal protection clauses) to the assistance of counsel on a first appeal where the state has granted them the right to appeal (as opposed to those instances where entitlement to appeal is only discretionary). The Court ruled that "[a]bsolute equality is not required; lines can be and are drawn and we often sustain them. *But where the merits of the one and only appeal an indigent has as of right are decided without benefit of counsel, we think an unconstitutional line has been drawn between rich and poor.*"

However, in a 1974 decision, *Ross v. Moffitt*, 417 U.S. 600 (1974), the Supreme Court changed the focus of this so-called *"Griffin–Douglas* Doctrine." Instead of focusing upon the question of whether or not an indigent defendant could obtain the same sort of services that a non-indigent defendant could or would receive, the Court concluded instead that "[t]he duty of the State under our cases is not to duplicate the legal arsenal that may be privately retained by a criminal defendant in a continuing effort to reverse his conviction, but only to assure the indigent defendant *an adequate opportunity to present his claims fairly.*"

Applying this less-demanding test, the *Ross* Court ruled that indigents undertaking state *discretionary* appeals (as opposed to appeals as of right) and appeals to the United States Supreme Court (which are also discretionary and not of right) are *not* entitled to the appointment of counsel, even though a non-indigent would have the resources and, hence, could retain such appellate counsel. The Court conceded that, under this new test, "[a]n indigent defendant seeking review in [a state supreme court] is therefore somewhat handicapped in comparison with a wealthy defendant who has counsel assisting him in every conceivable manner at every stage in the proceeding." However, as a majority of the Court explained, "[t]he fact that an appeal has been provided does not automatically mean that a State then acts unfairly by refusing to provide counsel to indigent defendants at every stage of the way. Unfairness results only if indigents are singled out by the State and denied *meaningful access* to the appellate system because of their poverty."

Despite this more grudging approach to *Griffin–Douglas* analysis, the Supreme Court has nonetheless recently ruled that a state may *not* cut off the constitutional entitlement to appointed counsel on an appeal as of right simply because a convicted defendant has pleaded guilty or *nolo contendere* in the trial court. *Halbert v. Michigan*, 545 U.S. 605 (2005). As the Court acknowledged, "Halbert's case is framed by [these] two prior decisions of this Court concerning state-funded appellate counsel, *Douglas* and *Ross*. The question before us is essentially one of classification: With which of those decisions should the instant case be aligned? We hold that *Douglas* provides the controlling instruction. Two aspects of the Michigan Court of Appeals' process following plea-based convictions lead us to that conclusion. First, in determining how to dispose of an application for leave to appeal, Michigan's intermediate appellate court looks to the merits of the claims made in the application. Second, indigent defendants pursuing first-tier review in the Court of Appeals are generally ill equipped to represent themselves."

Other post-*Ross* Supreme Court decisions raising *Griffin-Douglas* Doctrine issues have focused on answering the question of to what a defendant should be entitled in order to insure "meaningful access to justice." In *Ake v. Oklahoma*, 470 U.S. 68 (1985), for example, using this approach, a majority of the Court held that an accused was entitled to have access to a psychiatrist and a psychiatric examination when raising an insanity defense, as such services are, in the Court's view, a "basic tool" and might well be a "substantial factor" when the issue of sanity is raised at trial or sentencing. Hence, indigent defendants possess this entitlement to expert services under the *Griffin-Douglas* Doctrine in order to have "an adequate opportunity to present their claims fairly within the adversary system."

POINTS TO REMEMBER

- Indigent defendants in federal and state cases have a right under the Sixth Amendment to appointed defense counsel at critical stages of the prosecution.

- Indigent defendants cannot receive even a "day in jail," whether or not their sentence is suspended, if they did not receive or waive their right to counsel.

- Waivers of the right to counsel must be "knowing and intelligent" but need not follow a formula or script in order to be effective.

- Competent defendants may waive their right to counsel and proceed pro se.

- Defendants have a right to the effective assistance of counsel.

- To establish ineffective assistance of counsel, a defendant must establish ordinarily that counsel committed actual, specific errors.

- Ineffective assistance of counsel is established by using a two-part test that assesses the reasonableness of counsel's performance and whether or not defendant was prejudiced by that performance.

- For a federal habeas-corpus petitioner to establish ineffective assistance of counsel arising out of a state conviction after 1996, a state court must not only have applied the Sixth Amendment incorrectly or erroneously, but "unreasonably" as well on the basis of the record that was before the court.

- Where counsel's alleged ineffectiveness is based on a conflict of interest, prejudice does not have to be demonstrated.

- Indigent defendants must receive at government expense the basic tools necessary to assure that they have meaningful access to justice at trial and on appeal.

Chapter 4

SEARCH AND SEIZURE

Focal Points for Chapter 4(A)

- Historical importance of warrants.

- Warrant Requirement.

- Probable cause test: fair probability.

- Probable cause test: totality of the circumstances.

- Staleness.

- Franks hearing.

- Particularity requirement.

- Knock & announce doctrine, but no federal exclusionary rule.

- "Plain-view" seizures.

A. Search Warrants

1. The Significance of Using a Search Warrant

a. Warrant History

The Warrant Clause of the Fourth Amendment requires expressly that "no Warrants shall issue, but upon probable cause, supported by Oath or affirmation, and particularly describing the place to be searched, and the persons or things to be seized."

This clause was included in the Fourth Amendment as a result of the American colonists' experience with the use by the English colonial authorities of "writs of assistance." Writs of assistance were a form of "general warrant," legal documents that permitted the English officials to search colonists' homes and persons whenever and wherever they wanted (i.e. "generally" rather than specifically targeting a particular place and particular evidence of criminal activity). The debate (and the anger) in the American colonies about the arbitrary use of these writs of assistance by the English "was perhaps the most prominent event which inaugurated the resistance of the colonies to the oppressions of the mother country. . . [This debate] and the events which took place in England immediately following the argument about writs of assistance in [the colonies] were fresh in the memories of those who achieved our independence and established our form of government." *Boyd v. United States,* 116 U.S. 616, 625 (1886).

Indeed, "[t]he driving force behind the adoption of the [Fourth] Amendment . . . was widespread hostility among the former Colonists to the issuance of writs of assistance. . . [T]he purpose of the Fourth Amendment was to protect the people of the United States against arbitrary action by their own Government. . ." *United States v. Verdugo–Urquidez,* 494 U.S. 259, 266 (1990).

The significance of this constitutional history to the use of warrants today was made clear by Justice Felix Frankfurter in 1950 when he cautioned that "[i]t is true . . . of journeys in the law that the place you reach depends on the direction you are taking. And so, where one comes out in a case depends on where one goes in. . . It makes all the difference in the world whether one recognizes the central fact about the Fourth Amendment, namely, that it was a safeguard against recurrence of abuses so deeply felt by the colonies as to be one of the potent causes of the Revolution, or one thinks of it as merely a requirement for a piece of paper." *United States v. Rabinowitz,* 339 U.S. 56, 69 (1950).

b. The "Warrant Preference"

The Supreme Court has made it clear on many occasions that because we would prefer that law enforcement officers not engage in warrantless searches, but rather that they search only *after* they have obtained a search warrant, thus subjecting their probable-cause determination to the neutral and detached scrutiny of a magistrate, "[t]he Fourth Amendment demonstrates a 'strong preference for searches conducted pursuant to a warrant.' " *Ornelas v. United States,* 517 U.S. 690, 699 (1996), *quoting Illinois v. Gates,* 462 U.S. 213, 236 (1983). The implication of this constitutional preference (albeit perhaps more in theory than in actual practice) is that in "close cases," e.g. situations where it is a close question whether or not probable cause exists, courts should lean toward upholding ("preferring") searches based upon warrants and lean against upholding (not "preferring") warrantless searches.

As the Supreme Court has explained, "[b]ecause a search warrant 'provides the detached scrutiny of a neutral magistrate, which is a more reliable safeguard against improper searches than the hurried judgment of a law enforcement officer "engaged in the often competitive enterprise of ferreting out crime," . . . we have expressed a strong preference for warrants and declared that "in a doubtful or marginal case a search under a warrant may be sustainable where without one it would fail." ' " *United States v. Leon*, 468 U.S. 897, 913–14 (1984), *quoting United States v. Chadwick*, 433 U.S. 1, 9 (1977) quoting *Johnson v. United States*, 333 U.S. 10, 14 (1948) and *United States v. Ventresca*, 380 U.S. 102, 106 (1965).

c. The "Warrant Requirement"

In addition to the Warrant Preference, the Supreme Court has also created (and reaffirmed in many decisions) a Warrant Requirement. The Court has explained the Warrant Requirement as follows: "In a long line of cases, this Court has stressed that 'searches conducted outside the judicial process, without prior approval by judge or magistrate, are per se unreasonable under the Fourth Amendment—subject only to a few specifically established and well delineated exceptions.' . . . [I]n all cases outside the exceptions to the warrant requirement the Fourth Amendment requires the interposition of a neutral and detached magistrate between the police and the 'persons, houses, papers and effects' of the citizen." *Thompson v. Louisiana*, 469 U.S. 17, 19–20 (1984), quoting *Katz v. United States*, 389 U.S. 347, 357 (1967).

The rationale for the Warrant Requirement is the same as the rationale for the Warrant Preference, namely the Supreme Court's desire and attempt to maximize the number of occasions in which individual privacy is protected because law enforcement searches or seizures are reviewed—*prior* to the time that they take place—by judicial officers.

As the Supreme Court has made the point directly, "[a]n essential purpose of a warrant requirement is to protect privacy interests by assuring citizens subject to a search or seizure that such intrusions are not the random or arbitrary acts of government agents. A warrant assures the citizen that the intrusion is authorized by law, and that it is narrowly limited in its objectives and scope. . . A warrant also provides the detached and neutral scrutiny of a neutral magistrate, and thus ensures an objective determination whether an intrusion is justified in any given case." *Skinner v. Railway Labor Executives' Ass'n*, 489 U.S. 602, 621–22 (1989).

However, it is important to bear in mind that, although the Supreme Court has often held that there are only "a few specifically established and well delineated exceptions" to the Warrant Requirement, in truth, these "few" and "exceptional" categories of lawful and permissible warrantless searches account for the *overwhelming majority* of all searches performed by law enforcement officers. These warrantless (and lawful) searches include: searches based upon a showing of generalized exigency; searches incident to arrest; consent searches; car searches; administrative searches; drug testing; inventory searches; and investigative (*Terry*) stops and frisks.

2. Probable Cause

a. Constitutional Requirement

The Fourth Amendment requires expressly that warrants be supported by "probable cause." The nature of the probable cause inquiry is, however, different for search warrants than it is for arrest warrants. The Supreme Court has explained this difference (and the reasons for the difference) as follows:

> An arrest warrant is issued by a magistrate upon a showing that probable cause exists to believe that the subject of the warrant has committed an offense and thus the warrant primarily serves to protect an individual from an unreasonable seizure. A search warrant, in contrast, is issued upon a showing of probable cause to believe that the legitimate object of a search is located in a particular place, and therefore safeguards an individual's interest in the privacy of his home and possessions against the unjustified intrusion of the police.

Steagald v. United States, 451 U.S. 204, 212–13 (1981).

b. Probable Cause Test

Establishing "probable cause" requires a showing of something more than "mere suspicion," but something less than "beyond a reasonable doubt," the standard of proof required for a criminal conviction. More specifically, the Supreme Court has concluded that probable cause requires a showing by the Government of "a fair probability" on each of the points that the prosecution must establish in order for a warrant to issue.

To demonstrate probable cause sufficient to obtain an arrest warrant, the Government must establish a fair probability that a crime has been committed *and that* the person to be arrested committed the crime. To demonstrate probable cause sufficient to obtain a search warrant, the Government must establish a fair probability that the specified items sought are evidence of criminal activity *and that* those items are presently located at the specified place described in the search warrant application.

Moreover, as the Supreme Court has cautioned, "[i]n dealing with probable cause, . . . as the very name implies, we deal with probabilities. These are not technical; they are the factual and practical considerations of everyday life on which reasonable and prudent men, not legal technicians, act." *Brinegar v. United States*, 338 U.S. 160, 175 (1949). Accordingly, in evaluating the presence or absence of probable cause sufficient to support issuance of a search warrant, "[t]he task of the issuing magistrate is simply to make a practical, commonsense decision whether, given all the circumstances set forth in the affidavit before him, . . . there is a fair probability that contraband or evidence of a crime will be found in a particular place." *Illinois v. Gates*, 462 U.S. 213, 238 (1983). *See also Safford Unified School Dist. No. 1 v. Redding*, 557 U.S. 364, 371 (2009) ("Perhaps the best that can be said generally about the required knowledge component of probable cause for a law enforcement officer's evidence search is that it raise a 'fair probability,' . . . or a 'substantial chance,' . . . of discovering evidence of criminal activity.").

Using these "commonsense" tests, the Supreme Court has concluded that probable cause existed to arrest a driver and both of his two passengers in a car where five baggies of cocaine and a rolled-up wad of cash had been discovered: "We think it an entirely reasonable inference from these facts that any or all three of the occupants had knowledge of, and exercised dominion and control over, the cocaine . . . [W]e think it was reasonable for the officer to infer a common enterprise among the three men. The quantity of drugs and cash in the car indicated the likelihood of drug dealing, an enterprise to which a dealer would be unlikely to admit an innocent person with the potential to furnish evidence against him." *Maryland v. Pringle*, 540 U.S. 366 (2003).

c. Informant Information & Probable Cause

Prior to 1983, the Supreme Court used the so-called *Aguilar-Spinelli* test to evaluate the existence of probable cause based upon information obtained from an informant. *Aguilar v. State of Texas*, 378 U.S. 108 (1964); *Spinelli v. United States*, 393 U.S. 410 (1969). Under *Aguilar-Spinelli*, when the Government presented informant information in affidavits as the basis for probable cause, it needed to meet a two-pronged test: (1) it needed to provide the magistrate with information that explained sufficiently how the informant obtained his or her information (the "underlying circumstances" prong); and (2) it needed to provide the magistrate with information that supported the informant's "veracity" and "reliability" (the "credibility" prong). For the magistrate to credit such informant information in determining probable cause, *both* of these prongs needed to be satisfied.

However, in 1983, in its decision in *Illinois v. Gates*, 462 U.S. 213, 238 (1983), the Supreme Court found the *Aguilar-Spinelli* two-pronged test "highly relevant" to the probable-cause determination, but rejected its two rigidly-constrained categories of proof as *necessary* elements to establish probable cause. In its place, the Court adopted in *Gates* a less mechanistic, "totality-of-the-circumstances" test by which issuing magistrates are to evaluate probable cause based upon informant information.

As the *Gates* Court explained: "[W]e conclude that it is wiser to abandon the 'two-pronged test' established by our decisions in *Aguilar* and *Spinelli*. In its place we reaffirm the totality-of-the-circumstances analysis that traditionally has informed probable cause determinations. . . This totality-of-the-circumstances approach is far more consistent with our prior treatment of probable cause than is any rigid demand that specific 'tests' be satisfied by every informant's tip. Perhaps the central teaching of our decisions bearing on the probable-cause standard is that it is a 'practical, nontechnical conception.' "

The Supreme Court's adoption in *Gates* of the totality-of-the-circumstances test does not mean that the two *Aguilar-Spinelli* prongs are no longer relevant to probable-cause determinations. They remain relevant; they are simply no longer necessary or dispositive. As the *Gates* Court pointed out, for example, "a deficiency in one [prong] may be compensated for, in determining the overall reliability of a tip, by a strong showing as to the other, or by some other indicia of reliability." Among other such "indicia of reliability" commonly used by courts is assessing informant information are corroboration of some of the informant's factual details (even if the specific facts that are corroborated demonstrate only otherwise innocent activity, e.g. the wearing of clothing of a particular color or style, the same color or style as a criminal suspect), and the informant's status as a "citizen" (as opposed to an informant from the criminal milieu).

d. Informer's Privilege

Often, out of fear for their safety and/or a desire to continue their future effectiveness as informants, the Government wishes to keep confidential the identities of informants who have provided information about criminal conduct. As a result, the Supreme Court has permitted such confidentiality—the "informer's privilege"—when defense counsel seeks to find out a confidential informant's actual identity in a suppression hearing. *McRay v. State of Ill.*, 386 U.S. 300 (1967). However, magistrates still retain the discretion (but not the obligation) to order the Government to reveal an informant's identity when there is some reason to believe that his or her information is not believable (or that the informant does not actually exist). Sometimes, the revelation of an informant's identity and/or the taking of additional testimony from him or her occurs in an *in camera* proceeding, out of the presence of the defendant and defense counsel.

e. Staleness

For probable cause information to properly support the issuance of a search warrant, "the proof must be of facts so closely related to the time of the issue of the warrant as to justify a finding of probable cause at that time." *Sgro v. United States*, 287 U.S. 206, 210 (1932). Probable-cause information that does not meet this test is said to be "stale" and cannot, accordingly, support the issuance of a warrant.

Whether probable-cause information is or is not stale, however, is *not* determined simply by the length of time between the observation, discovery, or reporting of the probable-cause information and the time that a warrant is sought. Some evidence of crime is likely to disappear rather quickly (e.g. a half-smoked marijuana cigarette); some evidence of crime is likely to persist for quite a long time (e.g. a corpse buried in a basement). As a result, in addition to the passage of time, courts have considered as relevant to the staleness inquiry such additional factors as: the nature of the criminal evidence sought (e.g. is it large or small, moveable or fixed?); the location of the evidence on the premises (e.g. is it in plain view or buried under concrete?); the state in which the evidence was observed (e.g. is it solid or liquid, easily disposable or permanent?); and the nature of the place to be searched (e.g. is it a readily moveable vehicle or a residential home?).

f. Anticipatory Warrants

In 2006, the Supreme Court for the first time expressly upheld the constitutionality of so-called "anticipatory warrants." *United States v. Grubbs*, 547 U.S. 90 (2006). An anticipatory warrant is a search warrant issued based only upon a showing of *prospective* probable cause, i.e. a showing that evidence of crime will be or is likely to be present on the premises sought to be searched at some specified time in the future subsequent to the occurrence of some specified triggering condition.

The *Grubbs* Court held that "for a conditioned anticipatory warrant to comply with the Fourth Amendment's requirement of probable cause, two prerequisites of probability must be satisfied. It must be true not only that if the triggering condition occurs 'there is a fair probability that contraband or evidence of a crime will be found in a particular place,' but also that there is probable cause to believe the triggering condition will occur. The supporting affidavit must provide the magistrate with sufficient information to evaluate both aspects of the probable-cause determination." However, the Court further held that the Fourth Amendment does not require that the triggering condition for an anticipatory search warrant be set forth in the warrant itself.

Many if not most anticipatory warrants involve informant information that narcotics will be delivered to a certain place at a certain time in the future (the "triggering condition"). Indeed, often, law enforcement agents know for a virtual certainty that such a delivery will be made—and when it will be made—as their own agents are making the delivery (or monitoring the delivery, e.g. by surveilling a delivery service). In these cases of "controlled deliveries," the narcotics can be said to be on a "sure course" to the designated search premises and anticipatory warrants are often issued (and upheld) on this basis. However, most lower courts approving such anticipatory warrants have further ruled that such anticipatory warrants become invalid and cannot be executed when and if the contingent event (e.g. the delivery of narcotics) that established prospective probable cause does *not* in fact occur (e.g. no delivery appears to have been made).

3. Obtaining Warrants

a. Affidavits

All of the information that the prosecution intends to use to support the issuance of a search warrant must be fully disclosed to the issuing magistrate at the time he or she is considering the application for a search warrant. Ordinarily, this information is presented to the court in the form of written affidavits, sworn to by the affiant under oath. And, as the Supreme Court has warned, "an otherwise insufficient affidavit cannot be rehabilitated by testimony concerning information possessed by the affiant when he sought the warrant but not disclosed to the issuing magistrate. . . A contrary rule would, of course, render the warrant requirements of the Fourth Amendment meaningless." *Whiteley v. Warden*, 401 U.S. 560, 565 n.8 (1971).

A majority of American jurisdictions go farther than this constitutional requirement, and further require that the issuing magistrate may consider *only* the information that is contained within "the four corners" of the affidavits before the magistrate in evaluating whether or not probable cause exists. In a minority of jurisdictions, however, the issuing magistrate may also consider—in determining whether or not probable cause exists—sworn oral statements made by affiants or other witnesses put forward as supplements to information contained in the affidavits themselves.

b. Challenging Affidavits

Affidavits offered as support for a probable-cause finding may be challenged by defense counsel in two different ways. First, they may be challenged "on their face," i.e. counsel may argue that the facts set out therein are simply insufficient to establish probable cause to search. Second, defense counsel may try to "go behind" an affidavit at a suppression hearing by establishing that some or all of the averments made in that affidavit were false. But the mere falsity of affidavit information is not enough—in and of itself—to render a warrant based thereon defective and unconstitutional. The Supreme Court, in *Franks v. Delaware*, concluded that search warrant affidavits are to be treated as presumptively valid, and that to successfully go behind an affidavit, "[t]here must be allegations of deliberate falsehood or of reckless disregard for the truth, and those allegations must be accompanied by an offer of proof. . . Allegations of negligence or innocent mistake are insufficient." *Franks v. Delaware*, 438 U.S. 154, 171 (1978).

The pretrial hearing at which defense counsel attempts to make such a showing (that the affiant deliberately lied or made an averment in reckless disregard for the truth) is called a "*Franks* hearing." If defense counsel is able to show at a *Franks* hearing that particular averments in an affidavit were in fact intentionally or recklessly made (and not merely false or simply negligently made) *or* that the affiant intentionally or recklessly *omitted* material information from the affidavit to the same effect, the offending averments are redacted from the affidavit (or the material omissions are included) and then the redacted (or amended) affidavit is re-evaluated to determine whether or not is still supports a finding of probable cause. In other words and importantly, even when an affiant has been determined to have intentionally lied in a search warrant affidavit, that affidavit may nonetheless still establish probable cause to search on the basis of the redacted averments.

c. Review of Probable–Cause Determinations

Unlike probable-cause determinations made by trial courts in cases involving warrantless searches by law-enforcement authorities, *see Ornelas v. United States*, 517 U.S. 690 (1996), probable-cause determinations in cases where an issuing magistrate has actually issued a search warrant are *not* reviewed *de novo* by appellate courts to determine whether or not the underlying affidavits established probable cause. Rather, the standard for review is much more deferential to the issuing magistrate. The Supreme Court has ruled that if "the [issuing] magistrate had a '*substantial basis* for. . . conclud[ing]' that a search would uncover evidence of wrongdoing, the Fourth Amendment requires no more." *Illinois v. Gates*, 462 U.S. 213, 236, 103 S.Ct. 2317, 76 L.Ed.2d 527 (1983), *quoting Jones v. United States*, 362 U.S. 257, 271 (1960) (emphasis added).

d. Issuing Magistrates

A judge authorized by a jurisdiction to issue a warrant—whatever his or her official title—is generically referred to as an "issuing magistrate." Issuing magistrates ordinarily may issue search warrants only for the search of places located within the issuing court's jurisdiction. A jurisdiction may lawfully make anyone an issuing magistrate, even if that person is neither a lawyer nor a judge.

However, the Supreme Court has made it clear that "an issuing magistrate must meet two tests. He must be neutral and detached and he must be capable of determining whether probable cause exists for the requested arrest or search." *Shadwick v. City of Tampa*, 407 U.S. 345, 350 (1972). A state Attorney General, for example, is not sufficiently neutral and detached to be empowered to issue warrants: "Prosecutors and policemen simply cannot be asked to maintain the requisite neutrality with regard to their own investigations." *Coolidge v. New Hampshire*, 403 U.S. 443, 450 (1971).

A defendant may also attack the validity of a search warrant by pointing to specific examples of partiality that demonstrate that the issuing magistrate who approved the warrant was not acting in a neutral and detached fashion in this particular case. The Supreme Court has ruled, for example, that Georgia magistrates who received a $5 payment each time they issued a search warrant (and received nothing each time that they declined to issue one) had a pecuniary interest that rendered such warrants defective and unconstitutional: "The situation . . . is one which offers 'a possible temptation to the average man as a judge . . . or which might lead him not to hold the balance nice, clear and true between the State and the accused.' " *Connally v. Georgia*, 429 U.S. 245, 250 (1977), *quoting Ward v. Village of Monroeville*, 409 U.S. 57, 59–60 (1972).

And the Supreme Court has further concluded that an issuing magistrate who became so caught up in the execution of the search warrant that he accompanied the executing officers to the scene and even helped to direct and to participate in the search was, as a result of that participation, not acting as a neutral and detached magistrate, but rather—impermissibly and unconstitutionally—as an "adjunct law enforcement officer." *Lo–Ji Sales, Inc. v. New York*, 442 U.S. 319, 327 (1979).

4. The Particularity Requirement

a. Constitutional Requirement

The Fourth Amendment prescribes that "no Warrants shall issue, but upon probable cause, supported by Oath or affirmation, *and particularly describing the place to be searched, and the persons or things to be seized.*" (Emphasis added.) As the Supreme Court has explained the rationale for the particularity requirement, "[b]y limiting the authorization to search to the specific areas and things for which there is probable cause to search, the requirement ensures that the search will be carefully tailored to its justifications, and will not take on the character of the wide-ranging exploratory searches the Framers intended to prohibit." *Maryland v. Garrison*, 480 U.S. 79, 84 (1987) (footnote omitted). Accordingly, "a search conducted pursuant to a warrant that fails to conform to the particularity requirement of the Fourth Amendment is unconstitutional." *Massachusetts v. Sheppard*, 468 U.S. 981, 988 n.5 (1984).

The Supreme Court has used the following test to determine whether the particularity requirement has been satisfied in the description contained in a search warrant of the place or places to be searched: "It is enough if the description is such that the officer with a search warrant can with reasonable effort ascertain and identify the place intended." *Steele v. United States*, 267 U.S. 498, 503 (1925).

With respect to the particularity requirement and the search warrant description of the things to be seized, the Supreme Court has added that "[t]he requirement that warrants shall particularly describe the things to be seized makes general searches under them impossible and prevents the seizure of one thing under a warrant describing another. As to what is to be taken, nothing is left to the discretion of the officer executing the warrant." *Marron v. United States*, 275 U.S. 192, 196 (1927).

Significantly, the Supreme Court has added that "[t]he Fourth Amendment . . . does not set forth some general 'particularity requirement.' It specifies only two matters that must be 'particularly describ[ed]' in the warrant: 'the place to be searched' and 'the persons or things to be seized.' " *United States v. Grubbs*, 547 U.S. 90 (2006).

b. Particularity & Search Premises

When describing search premises, there is no specific item of descriptive information that absolutely *must* be included in the warrant description. The important question to ask is whether the description is so specific that it identifies only one place, *only* the premises intended to be searched, and no other place. If the description fails this test, the warrant is constitutionally deficient. Typical forms of descriptive information included in the description of search premises are: street numbers; geographic indicators; apartment numbers; city, county, and state locations; legal property descriptions; plat map references; directions on a map (sometimes attached); descriptions of the house or building color, style, composition, or size; description of the neighborhood character (e.g. urban, suburban, rural); and the name of the owner and/or residents.

Moreover, where the warrant authorizes only a search of a part of a building, e.g. a single apartment in a multi-unit, residential building, that limitation must be indicated in the search warrant description in order for it to meet this constitutional test. Most courts are willing, furthermore, to evaluate the particularity of a warrant description (the place to be searched or things to be seized) on the basis of the description contained in the search warrant itself and in any physically attached affidavits or lists, assuming that there are appropriate words of reference to those documents included in the warrant itself.

c. Particularity & Things to Be Seized

In describing the things to be seized pursuant to execution of a search warrant, the description need be only as particular as the circumstances require. A description of contraband, like "narcotics" or "drugs," for example, is sufficiently specific. What more could be said? But the description of the fruits of a crime or tangible evidence must be more specific; the description must be particular enough that the items can be readily determined by the executing officers to be seizable pursuant to the warrant.

A reference to "stolen property" is, accordingly, too general and, hence, unconstitutionally deficient. A reference to stolen "jewelry," however, described by detailed reference to characteristics as to nature, appearance, dimensions and initialing is patently constitutional. Moreover, a less-detailed description may be constitutional as well where that is the most that can be said under the prevailing circumstances. The Indiana Court of Appeals, for example, has upheld as constitutional the description of the following items to be seized—"piglets of approximately six to eight (6 to 8) weeks in age, being a crossbreed of Yorkshire, Hampshire and Duroc"—where the owner of the stolen piglets identified them himself at close range, the court adding that "[a] more thorough description is difficult to imagine, as 6–8 week old piglets are not normally the subjects of detailed morphological identification." *Mann v. State*, 180 Ind.App. 510, 389 N.E.2d 352, 355–56 (Ind. Dist. Ct. App. 1979).

As previously noted, most courts are willing to evaluate the particularity of a warrant description (the place to be searched or things to be seized) on the basis of the description contained in the search warrant itself and in any physically attached affidavits or lists, assuming that there are appropriate words of reference to those documents included in the warrant itself.

d. Minor or Partial Errors Irrelevant

It is important to bear in mind that the fact that there may be a minor error in the search warrant description of the place to be searched does not automatically render the warrant constitutionally defective. It is not uncommon for warrant descriptions to include inadvertent typographical errors, e.g. "2958 N. 23rd Street" instead of "2958A N. 23rd Street." As long as it is nonetheless clear to the executing officers where precisely the search is to take place, e.g. from an otherwise accurate description (aside from the typographical error in the address number) of the home at 2958A N. 23rd Street, so accurate that the executing officers could not inadvertently search the wrong place, the warrant is constitutional, despite the descriptive error. *See, e.g., United States v. Johnson*, 26 F.3d 669, 694 (7th Cir. 1994) ("2958" instead of "2958A" N. 23rd Street).

The same is true of minor errors in the description of the things to be seized contained in a search warrant. For example, an incorrect description of a stolen Bendix–Westinghouse motor compressor, described (erroneously) as containing the identifying numbers "CH49OTA–9–2085, Serial #AAOO–2002" instead of the correct numbers "CH49OTA–9–A2085, Serial #A9O–2002," was held not to render a warrant constitutionally defective where "there was only one air conditioning unit located at the described premises, and, further, only one Bendix compressor installed in said unit. The warrant cannot be described as sanctioning a general exploratory search." *United States v. Rytman*, 475 F.2d 192, 192–93 (5th Cir. 1973).

Moreover, even if some items seized pursuant to a search warrant were not described with particularity (or were not even described at all), and must, as a result, be suppressed as seizures in violation of the particularity requirement, the search warrant itself remains constitutional as to any remaining items seized pursuant to that warrant that were described particularly. In other words, the defective items are "severed" from the other, lawfully-seized items under the warrant. There is an exception to this "severance" rule, however, in the highly unusual situation where executing officers "grossly exceed the scope of a search warrant in seizing property, [as, in that event,] the particularity requirement is undermined and a valid warrant is transformed into a general warrant thereby requiring suppression of all evidence seized under that warrant." *United States v. Medlin*, 842 F.2d 1194, 1199 (10th Cir. 1988).

e. "All Persons" Warrants

Some law enforcement agencies have obtained search warrants listing as search targets "all persons on the [search target] premises." The question has arisen whether such "all persons" warrants violate the particularity requirement. Normally, if a person is a search target of a search warrant, he or she must be described particularly (although not necessarily by name), just as is the case with any other non-human search target, e.g. a residence, a business, or a vehicle. The theory offered to justify such "all persons" warrants is that they are proper in those situations when the search premises are being used for such clearly criminal purposes, e.g. a "crack house," that everyone present must necessarily be involved with criminal activity.

The Supreme Court has expressly reserved judgment on the constitutionality of such "all persons on the premises" warrants, *Ybarra v. Illinois*, 444 U.S. 85, 92 n.4 (1979), and the lower courts are split on the question. Some courts have found "all persons" warrants unconstitutional, arguing that innocent "[p]ersons may visit even suspect premises for valid reasons," *Beeler v. State*, 677 P.2d 653, 656 (Okla. Crim. Ct. App. 1984), and that innocent "[p]ersons who might reasonably be expected to be found approaching the front door of a residence include a uniformed mail carrier or package delivery person, a volunteer seeking donations for charitable purposes, or a neighbor seeking to borrow a cup of sugar," *State v. Reid*, 319 Or. 65, 872 P.2d 416, 419 (1994).

However, other courts have found such "all persons" warrants to be constitutional, provided that they are closely scrutinized by the issuing magistrate who then makes the determination that probable cause indeed exists to search all the persons present on the search premises. As one Florida court made the point, "[t]he search-all-persons-present warrant is unobjectionable if the evidence tendered to the issuing magistrate supports the conclusion that it is probable anyone in the described place when the warrant is executed is involved in the criminal activity in such a way as to have evidence of the criminal activity on his person." *Bergeron v. State*, 583 So.2d 790, 791 (Fla. Dist. Ct. App. 1991).

5. *Execution of Search Warrants*

a. *Who May Execute?*

Officers executing a search warrant are deemed to be "executing officers." A search warrant may lawfully be executed by the specific law enforcement officers directed in the warrant itself or by any other law enforcement officers authorized by applicable statutes in that jurisdiction. In either event, the executing officers must be acting within their own jurisdiction. In carrying out the search, the executing officers may, however, also use the services of officers from other law enforcement agencies or, where necessary, private citizens.

But the Supreme Court ruled in 1999 that executing officers may *not* permit media representatives to tag along—in so-called "media ride-alongs"—while they are executing a search warrant. *Wilson v. Layne*, 526 U.S. 603 (1999). Since these reporters and photographers are not actually assisting in the execution of the warrant, the Court held, "[s]urely the possibility of good public relations for the police is simply not enough, standing alone, to justify the ride-along intrusion into a private home." *Id.*, 526 U.S. at 613.

b. *Time Limits*

Search warrants must be executed both within the jurisdiction's maximum time limit for execution (usually established by court rule) and also prior to the time the probable-cause information supporting the warrant grows stale. Such prescribed maximum time limits on search warrants vary widely, from two to sixty days. After, the time limit passes, the warrant is "dead." Unless it is renewed with a fresh showing of probable cause prior to its execution (including probable-cause evidence offered previously which is not stale), evidence seized pursuant to the execution of such a dead warrant will be suppressed.

c. *Nighttime Searches*

In 1974, three justices—a minority of the Court—concluded that there was a federal constitutional requirement that a special showing of need had to be made to the issuing magistrate if a search warrant was to be executed at night. *Gooding v. United States*, 416 U.S. 430 (1974). But this opinion has never commanded a majority of the Supreme Court. However, most jurisdictions (including the federal courts) require—by statute or court rule—that a special showing of need be made if a search warrant is to be executed at night. The rationale for this restriction is the feeling that searches made at night are more intrusive of individuals' privacy, e.g. search premises' occupants are often undressed and asleep at night, and nighttime entries raise a greater risk of a violent response from the search premises occupants who may not realize immediately who is forcing their way onto the premises.

Accordingly, in most jurisdictions, officers seeking to obtain a nighttime warrant must specify exactly why they *need* to search at night. The most common explanations for the necessity of a nighttime search include: evidence of prior nighttime drug sales; evidence of easily-destructible evidence on the search premises that is likely to be moved; and the presence of fugitives or individuals who are likely to disappear in the night. It is important to add, however, that even though most jurisdictions have rules requiring such special showings in order to justify issuance and execution of a nighttime warrant, only about half of those same jurisdictions apply an exclusionary rule to remedy breach of this particular rule.

d. Knock-and-Announce Doctrine

In 1995, the Supreme Court unanimously ruled that the common-law "knock-and-announce" doctrine is part of the Fourth Amendment and, hence, applicable to all federal and state executing officers. *Wilson v. Arkansas*, 514 U.S. 927 (1995).

As previously discussed with respect to nighttime warrants, due to search premises' occupants' privacy interests and the desire to reduce the likelihood of violence directed against executing officers who may enter search premises without warning, the knock-and-announce doctrine requires executing officers to do four things: (1) audibly "knock" (or otherwise make their presence known) at the outer door to search premises, thus giving notice to the occupants inside of the law enforcement presence; (2) "announce" the *identity* of the executing officers (e.g., "It's the Police!"); (3) "announce" the *purpose* of the executing officers (e.g., "We have a warrant!"); and (4) "delay" for a period of time sufficient to permit the occupants to reach and to open the door.

After a proper announcement has been made and the executing officers have properly delayed for a sufficient period of time, the officers may then enter the search premises forcibly, including breaking down doors and engaging in the destruction of other property, if so doing is necessary and reasonable in order to effect their entry. *United States v. Ramirez*, 523 U.S. 65, 118 S.Ct. 992, 140 L.Ed.2d 191 (1998). There is no need for executing officers to wait for someone to be home at the search premises before they may make a forcible entry. Nor do executing officers need to look for or obtain the cooperation of search premises' occupants before beginning their search.

Jurisdictions vary widely, however, in the amount of time they require executing officers to delay before making a forcible entry to search premises after the officers have announced their presence at an exterior door. In general, a delay of thirty-seconds has been treated as sufficient in virtually every jurisdiction to meet the Fourth Amendment delay requirement. The Supreme Court has upheld a delay of only 15 to 20 seconds, however, where the search premises occupant was suspected of selling cocaine from those premises as cocaine is the sort of evidence that can be quickly destroyed. *United States v. Banks*, 540 U.S. 31 (2003). In contrast, the Court noted, "[p]olice seeking a stolen piano [i.e., evidence that cannot be quickly destroyed] may be able to spend more time to make sure they really need the battering ram."

Violation of the knock-and-announce doctrine by executing officers renders the search warrant defective as a constitutional matter, but a 5–to–4 majority of the Supreme Court concluded in 2006 that the federal exclusionary rule nonetheless does not apply to law enforcement officers' knock-and-announce violations. *Hudson v. Michigan*, 547 U.S. 586 (2006). The Supreme Court majority concluded, in an opinion authored by Justice Scalia, that "the social costs of applying the exclusionary rule to knock-and-announce violations are considerable; the incentive to such violations is minimal to begin with, and the extant deterrences against them are substantial—incomparably greater than the factors deterring warrantless entries when *Mapp* was decided."

Additionally, there are also a number of permissible exceptions to the knock-and-announce doctrine. In many jurisdictions, for example, the rule has been held inapplicable to a nonviolent "entry by trick" (sometimes called a "ruse"). Various courts have upheld no-knock entries after search premises' occupants have peaceably opened the door in response to a law enforcement officer pretending to be, for example, a hotel desk clerk, a hotel security guard, a narcotics customer, a mail carrier, a package delivery service carrier, a real estate agent, a prostitute, a prostitution client, a pizza delivery person, and a meter reader.

Law enforcement agencies must, however, be very careful how they use this ploy. Where an entry by trick is attempted and results in the same sort of violent and unannounced entry that the Supreme Court has held is proscribed by the Fourth Amendment knock-and-announce doctrine, the warrant execution is unconstitutional. For example, the Arizona Supreme Court found the execution of a search warrant unconstitutional where an executing officer pretended to be someone else in order to get the occupant to open the door, but then broke the door in when his ruse failed. *State v. Bates*, 120 Ariz. 561, 587 P.2d 747 (1978).

Another commonly-applied exception to the knock-and-announce doctrine is the exigency exception. Executing officers may ignore any or all four of the elements of the knock-and-announce doctrine (and make a so-called "no-knock entry," sometimes an immediate entry using a battering ram) when they are faced with the prospect of the destruction of criminal evidence and/or danger to the executing officers upon entry. In 1997, the Supreme Court made it clear, however, that a showing of exigency sufficient to serve as an exception to the knock-and-announce doctrine must be specific to the particular search premises; it cannot be presumed in stereotypical fashion that exigency exists simply because the case at hand falls into a presumably dangerous category of cases, e.g. felony narcotics cases. *Richards v. Wisconsin*, 520 U.S. 385 (1997).

As the Supreme Court ruled, further, establishing a test to be used for the purpose of assessing the existence of exigency, "[i]n order to justify a 'no-knock' entry, the police must have a *reasonable suspicion* that knocking and announcing their presence, under the particular circumstances, would be dangerous or futile, or that it would inhibit the effective investigation of the crime by, for example, allowing the destruction of evidence. This standard—as opposed to a probable cause requirement—strikes the appropriate balance between the legitimate law enforcement concerns at issue in the execution of search warrants and the individual privacy interests affected by no-knock entries." *Id*. at 520 U.S. at 394.

Finally, no-knock entries have also been permitted (and the ordinary requirements of the knock-and-announce doctrine excused) when adherence to the knock-and-announce doctrine would be a "useless gesture" (sometimes called instead a "futile gesture" or an "idle act"). The Supreme Court, for example, has upheld the no-knock execution of a search warrant where the occupant of hotel room search premises saw through his open hotel room door a uniformed police officer standing in the hallway who was there with other officers to execute a search warrant for narcotics, and, in response, the occupant immediately slammed his hotel room door shut. The officers responded by making an immediate no-knock entry. The Supreme Court concluded that the occupant's "apparent recognition of the officers combined with the easily disposable nature of the drugs[] justified the officers' ultimate decision to enter without first announcing their presence and authority." *Id*. at 520 U.S. at 396.

In numerous other cases, courts have held that requiring executing officers who have already been spotted by search premises' occupants to follow all of the requirements of the knock-and-announce doctrine is a "useless gesture" and, accordingly, it is not required as a matter of Fourth Amendment law.

Where individuals obtaining a search warrant from an issuing magistrate can establish that the conditions that would excuse compliance with the knock-and-announce doctrine at the scene will be present at the search premises (generally exigency established through danger to the officers or the destructibility of evidence), the Supreme Court has ruled, albeit in *obiter dicta*, that "[t]he practice of allowing magistrates to issue no-knock warrants seems entirely reasonable when sufficient cause to do so can be demonstrated ahead of time." Accordingly, executing officers may be authorized to obtain a no-knock warrant, just as, in many jurisdictions, they may obtain a nighttime search warrant.

However, practically, there is no real value to law enforcement officers to obtain a no-knock warrant. Executing officers may make a no-knock entry in any event—whether or not they possess a no-knock warrant—where reasonable suspicion that exigent circumstances exist can be established at the scene. Moreover, a no-knock warrant will *not* actually support a no-knock entry where the circumstances that justified its issuance before the issuing magistrate are clearly no longer present at the moment of execution (e.g. the attack dogs have been removed). As the Massachusetts Supreme Judicial Court has explained, where "the facts existing at the time the warrant is issued . . . no longer exist at the time the warrant is executed[,] . . . the officers would be required to knock and announce their purpose. The changed circumstances would render ineffective the magistrate's decision that a no knock entry was justified." *Commonwealth v. Scalise*, 387 Mass. 413, 439 N.E.2d 818 (1982).

e. Post–Execution Requirements

Most jurisdictions provide by court rule that executing officers must leave a copy of the search warrant and a receipt for items seized at the search premises, and that they must promptly file a "return" with the issuing court, noting when the warrant was executed and specifying precisely what was seized. However, most jurisdictions treat these notice and record-keeping requirements as non-constitutional (ministerial) in nature and, accordingly, do not remedy their breach with application of the exclusionary rule.

In addition, most jurisdictions have court rules or statutory provisions creating procedures for the return of property seized pursuant to a search warrant. However, the Supreme Court has ruled that governments are not constitutionally required to give detailed and specific instructions and advice to individuals seeking to obtain the return of their lawfully-seized property after the property is no longer needed for investigative or prosecutorial purposes. *City of West Covina v. Perkins*, 525 U.S. 234 (1999).

6. Seizures Pursuant to Warrant

a. What Can Be Seized?

Items that have been specified and particularly described in a search warrant as evidence of crime may be seized at the search premises under the authority of that warrant. But, in addition to those items, executing officers are also permitted to seize other, non-described items that the officers see in "plain view" while they are lawfully present at a place executing a search warrant, provided that it is immediately apparent to the officers that these items are connected with criminal activity and that the officers possess probable cause to believe that such items are evidence of crime. *Horton v. California*, 496 U.S. 128 (1990).

It does not matter that items seized by executing officers because they are in plain view are totally unconnected with the crime that is the subject of the search warrant being executed. The seizure of such plain-view items is nonetheless lawful. For example, the Eighth Circuit Court of Appeals has upheld the constitutionality of the plain-view seizure of chemicals used for manufacturing methamphetamine, seized while officers were executing a search warrant looking for weapons. *United States v. Murphy*, 69 F.3d 237 (8th Cir. 1995).

Or, the plain-view items may be connected to the crime that is the subject of the warrant, but not specified in the warrant itself. For example, the Georgia Court of Appeals has upheld the plain-view seizure of slips of paper with internet sites listed on them pursuant to execution of a search warrant for computerized images of child pornography. *Walsh v. State*, 236 Ga.App. 558, 512 S.E.2d 408 (1999).

b. Where Can Seizures Be Made?

The fact that items found in plain view may be seized by executing officers raises the further question of precisely *where* executing officers are permitted to look for such items. The answer is that executing officers may search anywhere on the search premises that the items particularly described in the search warrant may be hidden. As long as the officers are searching in such a place, e.g. a bathroom closet while looking for marijuana, they may lawfully seize items particularly described in the warrant and/or plain-view items, again provided that it is immediately apparent to the officers that these items are connected with criminal activity and that the officers possess probable cause to believe that such items are evidence of crime.

Although the Supreme Court has cautioned that "the Fourth Amendment confines an officer executing a search warrant strictly within the bounds set by the warrant," *Bivens v. Six Unknown Named Agents*, 403 U.S. 388, 394 n.7 (1971), most courts have held that where probable cause exists to search a particular room or location in a residence and where the warrant does not expressly limit the search to that room or location, the entire residence may be searched. Evidence may, of course, have been moved within the search premises. As the Pennsylvania Supreme Court has explained, "the scope of a search warrant is limited by the items to be seized and where they may be found and not to a particular location within those premises." *Commonwealth v. Waltson*, 555 Pa. 223, 724 A.2d 289 (1998).

Moreover, a search warrant description that authorizes a search not only of a particular home, building or place, but of "premises" as well (or a similar term, like "curtilage," "outbuildings," or "appurtenances"), generally is treated as permitting a search of the land immediately surrounding and associated with the search target, any and all buildings located thereon (e.g. a garage or a shed), and any vehicles found thereon. However, a search pursuant to a search warrant cannot extend—pursuant to the authority of the warrant itself—to neighboring areas outside of—or beyond—the search premises.

The exception to this otherwise common-sense rule is where a neighboring area reasonably appears to the executing officers to be part of the search premises covered by a warrant. The Supreme Court has, for example, upheld as constitutional a search of a third-floor apartment in a building where the executing officers reasonably did not realize that the third floor was divided into two separate apartments, and that they were searching the wrong one. *Maryland v. Garrison*, 480 U.S. 79 (1987). However, the Court warned that "the [executing] officers . . . were required to discontinue the search of [the wrong] apartment as soon as they discovered that there were two separate units on the third floor and therefore were put on notice of the risk that they might be in a unit erroneously included within the terms of the warrant."

c. Intensity of Search

When executing officers are searching at a location where they are entitled lawfully to search, the question still arises how intensely they may search within that area, e.g. may they force open a safe, pull up carpeting and/or remove wall coverings? The general rule is that the permissible intensity of a search is dictated and limited by the nature of the items being sought under the warrant. As the Supreme Court has made the point, "[a] lawful search of fixed premises generally extends to the entire area in which the object of the search may be found and is not limited by the possibility that separate acts of entry or opening may be required to complete the search." *United States v. Ross*, 456 U.S. 798 (1982).

The Supreme Court has also provided examples of the appropriate application of this rule:

[A] warrant that authorizes an officer to search a home for illegal weapons also provides authority to open closets, chests, drawers, and containers in which the weapon might be found. A warrant to open a footlocker to search for marihuana would also authorize the opening of packages found inside. A warrant to search a vehicle would support a search of every part of the vehicle that might contain the object of the search. When a legitimate search is under way, and when its purpose and its limits have been precisely defined, nice distinctions between closets, drawers, and containers, in the case of a home, or between glove compartments, upholstered seats, trunks, and wrapped packages in the case of a vehicle, must give way to the interest in the prompt and efficient completion of the task at hand.

Using this sort of approach, lower courts have, for example, concluded that a search warrant for drugs justified a search of a briefcase, but that a warrant for handguns did not justify a search of envelopes, a notebook, medicine vials, or other small containers.

d. Property Damage or Destruction

It is lawful for executing officers to damage or to destroy property in undertaking a search where such damage is reasonably necessary to effect the search. The Supreme Court has acknowledged generally that "officers executing search warrants on occasion must damage property in order to perform their duty." *Dalia v. United States*, 441 U.S. 238, 247 (1979). More specifically, the Court has added that "[a]n individual undoubtedly has a significant interest that the upholstery of his automobile will not be ripped or a hidden compartment within it opened. These interests must yield to the authority of a search, however." *United States v. Ross*, 456 U.S. 798, 823 (1982).

Nonetheless, there are limits to the permissible extent of property destruction in the execution of a warrant. The Supreme Court has recently warned that "[e]xcessive or unnecessary destruction of property in the course of a search may violate the Fourth Amendment, even though the entry itself is lawful and the fruits of the search not subject to suppression." *United States v. Ramirez*, 523 U.S. 65, 71 (1998). Such an excessive search may lead to a subsequent civil action for damages against the offending police officers and their police department.

e. Duration of Search

Searches are limited in duration by a similar rule of reasonable necessity. Searches of a home that last for several hours are not uncommon. However, once all of the objects particularly described and sought under a warrant have been found, no further searches are permissible under the authority of that warrant.

f. Persons & Their Property on or Near Search Premises

The Supreme Court has ruled that search premises' occupants can be detained (but not searched) under the authority of a search warrant for criminal evidence on the premises occupied as such detention may minimize violence and the potential destruction of evidence. In a 1981 decision, the Court held that "a warrant to search for contraband founded on probable cause implicitly carries with it the limited authority to detain the occupants of the premises while a proper search is conducted." *Michigan v. Summers*, 452 U.S. 692, 705 (1981); *see also Los Angeles County, California v. Rettele*, 550 U.S. 609, 613 (2007).

This limited detention authority outlined in *Summers* has been extended by lower courts to individuals not actually on the search premises, but close to it, often just departing from or arriving at the search premises. When and if, however, executing officers develop probable cause to arrest or search such a detained individual (or establish reasonable suspicion to frisk him or her), such a temporary detention may (and often does) mature into a more intrusive Fourth Amendment encounter.

When executing officers either know or reasonably should know that property found on search premises belongs to a non-suspect third-party, e.g. a purse belonging to a social guest, that property *cannot* be searched under the authority of the search warrant. This rule does not apply when the officers have no idea who owns the property in question. And this rule has also been held by the Supreme Court to be inapplicable to the search of property belonging to a non-suspect, third-party vehicle passenger subject to a lawful search of the car for contraband. As the Court ruled, "police officers with probable cause to search a car may inspect passengers' belongings found in the car that are capable of concealing the object of the search." *Wyoming v. Houghton*, 526 U.S. 295, 307 (1999).

The Supreme Court has also extended the *Summers* decision by concluding that executing officers executing a search warrant on a suspected gang clubhouse in which armed gang members were believed to reside acted reasonably when they detained one of the occupants in handcuffs for two to three hours while the search was in progress given the fact that the warrant was for weapons and there was evidence of gang membership. *Muehler v. Mena*, 544 U.S. 93 (2005). Chief Justice Rehnquist, writing for the majority, concluded that "[i]nherent in *Summers'* authorization to detain an occupant of the place to be searched is the authority to use reasonable force to effectuate the detention . . . The governmental interests in not only detaining, but using handcuffs, are at their maximum when, as here, a warrant authorizes a search for weapons and a wanted gang member resides on the premises. In such inherently dangerous situations, the use of handcuffs minimizes the risk of harm to both officers and occupants."

The Supreme Court has also concluded that it was not unreasonable for executing officers to hold search premises occupants at gunpoint for one to two minutes, standing and naked, even though they were not the same race as the suspects the officers mistakenly thought lived in the house, since the officers believed the real suspects might be armed: "When officers execute a valid warrant and act in a reasonable manner to protect themselves from harm, . . . the Fourth Amendment is not violated." *Los Angeles County, California v. Rettele*, 550 U.S. 609, 614-16 (2007).

POINTS TO REMEMBER

- The police are required to use a warrant to search unless an exception applies (which is much of the time).

- To search, police officers must establish probable cause—a fair probability—that evidence of a crime is presently at the place to be searched.

- Whether probable cause exists is assessed by considering the "totality of the circumstances."

- Probable cause to support a search can (only) be challenged in a *Franks* hearing by showing that erroneous information was included in a supporting affidavit intentionally or recklessly and that the information was necessary to a finding of probable cause.

- Search warrants must particularly describe the place to be searched and the evidence to be seized.

- In executing a search warrant, the executing officers must knock, announce their purpose and their identity, and delay a sufficient period of time to give the occupants a chance to answer the door and may make a "no-knock" entry when they possess a reasonable suspicion that evidence is being destroyed or that they or others are in danger, but the federal exclusionary rule does not apply to violations of these rules.

- Evidence not described in a warrant may nonetheless be seized by executing officers if the officers are lawfully in the place from which they see this evidence in "plain view" and it is immediately apparent to them that the evidence has a connection with (any) criminal activity.

Focal Points for Protected Fourth Amendment Interests

- Katz reasonable expectation of privacy test.

- Oliver: open fields & curtilage.

- Greenwood & Bond: conveyance to third parties & public access.

- Place: canine sniff is sui generis.

- Knotts and Karo: beepers substitute for visual surveillance.

- Riley & Dow Chemical: limits on aerial technology.

- Kyllo: heat in the home.

- *Quon*: text messages.

B. Protected Fourth Amendment Interests

The modern Fourth Amendment privacy definition was articulated in *Katz v. United States*, 389 U.S. 347, 360, 361 (1967) (Harlan, J., concurring) as follows: "[T]here is a twofold requirement, first that a person have exhibited an actual (subjective) expectation of privacy and, second, that the expectation be one that society is prepared to recognize as 'reasonable.' " Most of the Court's post-*Katz* cases address the second *Katz* issue concerning the reasonableness of a privacy expectation. When the Court determines that a particular expectation of privacy is unreasonable, the police may make a privacy intrusion without complying with the Fourth Amendment. Whenever the Court rules against a privacy claim, a particular intrusion is deemed to be neither a "search" nor a "seizure" that is regulated by the Fourth Amendment.

In the pre-*Katz* era, the Court's privacy doctrine reflected common law property concepts in its protection of the "curtilage," which is the land "immediately surrounding and associated with the home." "Open fields" were exempt from Fourth Amendment requirements and could be entered and searched without a warrant. *Hester v. United States*, 265 U.S. 57 (1924). The absence of a physical trespass to property provided a justification for rejecting Fourth Amendment protection for telephone conversations when police tapped a telephone wire on the outside of a home in *Olmstead v. United States*, 277 U.S. 438 (1928). This holding was abandoned in *Katz*, when the Court ruled that a person inside a public phone booth had a reasonable expectation of privacy in his conversations. Therefore, agents could not use an electronic listening and recording device attached to the outside of the booth unless they complied with the Fourth Amendment. The *Katz* Court declared that "the Fourth Amendment protects people, not places," and observed:

> [O]nce it is recognized that the Fourth Amendment protects people—and not simply "areas"—against unreasonable searches and seizures, it becomes clear that the reach of that Amendment cannot turn upon the presence or absence of a physical intrusion into any given enclosure.

Katz is an important precedent because of its guiding principles, as well as its emphasis that privacy rulings must be grounded in the particular context that surrounds the government intrusion. One enduring principle was articulated in *Katz* as follows:

> What a person knowingly exposes to the public, even in his own home or office, is not a subject of Fourth Amendment protection. But what he seeks to preserve as private, even in an area accessible to the public, may be constitutionally protected.

The rationales for the *Katz* holding also reflect a focus on the context of the *Katz* defendant's reliance on his expectation of freedom from police surveillance:

> One who occupies [a public phone booth], shuts the door behind him, and pays the toll that permits him to place a call is surely entitled to assume that the words he utters into the mouthpiece will not be broadcast to the world. To read the Constitution more narrowly is to ignore the vital role that the public telephone has come to play in private communication.

Thus, the "reasonableness" of the *Katz* defendant's expectation of privacy was based, in part, on the widespread public custom of treating telephone conversations as private, despite the technological access to such conversations that would be available to the phone company or the police. The Court's validation of the *Katz* defendant's privacy expectation also reflected its concern about the unlimited nature of the power sought by the government to gain access to the contents of that communication in any place at any time.

However, the Court did not extend the *Katz* holding to a case where government agents gained access to the contents of a conversation by means of a third party who was a trusted participant. In *United States v. White*, 401 U.S. 745 (1971), the Court held that defendants cannot reasonably expect that their companions are not "reporting to the police," nor can they expect that such companions are not recording their conversations for the purpose of such reporting. The Court has reached similar conclusions when defendants convey information to third parties, who then provide that information to the authorities. See *United States v. Jacobsen*, 466 U.S. 109 (1984) (freight carrier); *United States v. Miller*, 425 U.S. 435 (1976) (bank); *Smith v. Maryland*, 442 U.S. 735 (1979) (phone company).

In precedents after *Katz*, the Court recognized that multiple factors are relevant to the reasonableness inquiry, including common law property concepts that reflect a social consensus about privacy values. Thus, the Fourth Amendment does "protect places" as well as people when a reasonable expectation of privacy may be invoked concerning such places. The Court validated the "open fields" exception from the pre-*Katz* era by finding it to be consistent with the *Katz* privacy analysis in *Oliver v. United States*, 466 U.S. 170 (1984). The *Oliver* Court provided this guidance concerning the relevant variables in a reasonableness inquiry:

> In assessing the degree to which a search infringes upon individual privacy, the Court has given weight to such factors as the intention of the [Framers], the uses to which the individual has put a location, and our societal understanding that certain areas deserve the most scrupulous protection from government [invasion].

Oliver, 466 U.S. at 178. Each of these factors supported the Court's conclusion that a privacy interest should be recognized in the "curtilage," where intimate activities associated with the home may occur, but not recognized in the "open fields," where they typically do not occur. The status of a potential "curtilage" area is evaluated with reference to four factors: its proximity to the home, whether it is enclosed, the nature of its uses, and the steps taken to protect it from observation. See *United States v. Dunn*, 480 U.S. 294 (1987) (defining scope of curtilage).

The Court's post-*Katz* cases address issues of standard "human" surveillance and issues of "enhanced" surveillance using technologies that are as varied as canine sniffs, tracking beepers, helicopter "fly overs," aerial mapping cameras, and thermal-imaging devices. In a controversial decision that emphasized the theme of public access, the Court held that a defendant had no reasonable expectation of privacy in garbage that was placed in opaque trash bags, left on the curb and searched by police who procured the bags from the garbage collector. *California v. Greenwood*, 486 U.S. 35 (1988). The Court placed the *Greenwood* defendants in the unprotected *Katz* category of those who knowingly expose a private item to the public. The defendants not only conveyed access to their trash bags to the "third-party" garbage collector, but also knowingly exposed the bags to the access of "animals, children, scavengers, snoops, and other members of the public." The *Greenwood* dissenters treated the defendants as belonging in the protected *Katz* category of people who seek to preserve an effect "as private, even in an area accessible to the public." Emphasizing that the trash bag is a "common repository for one's personal effects," the *Greenwood* dissenters argued that the mere "possibility" that a "meddler" could obtain nonconsensual access to property should not negate a privacy interest that is "recognized and permitted by society."

The *Greenwood* logic did not carry the day in the context of carry-on luggage placed in an overhead bin by a bus passenger and squeezed by a police officer in *Bond v. United States*, 529 U.S. 334 (2000). Both *Greenwood* elements of "public access" and "conveyance to a third party" were present in *Bond*, because other passengers and bus employees could be expected to handle or touch the luggage. But the *Bond* Court recognized that public customs do not extend beyond mere "handling" to encompass the conduct of feeling a bag "in an exploratory manner." Thus, the police crossed a line that could be drawn between reasonably expected and unexpected behavior from the public and from third parties with access to the luggage. The *Bond* majority also emphasized that "tactile" observation is "more intrusive than purely visual inspection," and thereby distinguished post-*Greenwood* precedents that relied on the rationale of "public access" to reject privacy claims in various visual-surveillance contexts. The *Bond* dissenters protested that the Court was engaged in developing a "jurisprudence of 'squeezes,' " and they would have relied on *Greenwood*'s rationales to reject the privacy claim in *Bond*.

The *Bond* Court did not hold that luggage in a public area is protected *per se* from all intrusions. In a pre-*Bond* decision, the Court approved canine sniffs by narcotics-detection dogs of luggage in a public place, holding that such an intrusion does not violate a reasonable expectation of privacy in *United States v. Place*, 462 U.S. 696 (1983). The canine sniff was labeled as *sui generis* by the Court, which relied on two rationales to reject the privacy claim. First, the sniff is minimally intrusive because it does not involve the opening of luggage or the exposure of its contents. Second, the sniff "discloses only the presence of absence of narcotics," and this limited disclosure provides protection for innocent citizens from general police "rummaging" in their possessions. The Court later recognized in *City of Indianapolis v. Edmond*, 531 U.S. 32 (2000), that a canine sniff of the exterior of an automobile is not a "search" or a "seizure" under *Place*. Such a sniff is performed by walking the narcotics-detection dog around the exterior of a car. This event "does not require entry into the car and is not designed to disclose any information other than the presence or absence of narcotics." Therefore, the sniff in *Edmond* was justified by the rationales of *Place*. However, the Court has not held that a canine sniff can never violate a reasonable expectation of privacy. In *Illinois v. Caballes*, 543 U.S. 405 (2005) the Court similarly held that a canine sniff of a car exterior was not a search or seizure during a traffic stop.

Other forms of "enhanced" surveillance have presented the Court with the difficult task of establishing limits concerning police use of technology. With regard to "tracking beepers," the Court ruled in *United States v. Karo*, 468 U.S. 705 (1984), that police must not use these devices to obtain information that could not have been obtained through visual surveillance. In a pre-*Karo* decision, the Court approved of beepers as a substitute for visual surveillance in *United States v. Knotts*, 460 U.S. 276 (1983). In *Knotts*, the police attached a tracking beeper inside a container, and then followed the defendant's car in which the container was located. The police lost visual surveillance of the car, but the beeper allowed them to track the car to the area of the defendant's cabin. In rejecting the defendant's privacy argument, the *Knotts* Court reasoned as follows:

> A person traveling in an automobile on public thoroughfares has no reasonable expectation of privacy in his movements from one place to another. [No] expectation of privacy extended to the visual observation of [the defendant's] automobile arriving on his premises after leaving a public highway, nor to movements of objects such as the [container] outside the cabin in the "open fields." [Nothing] in the Fourth Amendment prohibited the police from augmenting [their] sensory facilities with such enhancement as science and technology afforded them [here].

The *Knotts* Court, however, limited its approval of "tracking beepers" to a situation where "there is no indication that the beeper was used in any way to reveal information as to the movement of the [container] inside the [defendant's premises]." The *Karo* Court found that a violation of a reasonable expectation of privacy did occur when police in *Karo* used a beeper in a container to discover "a critical fact about the interior of the premises" that the Government "would not have otherwise obtained without a warrant," namely that the container had been moved inside the premises in *Karo*. The *Karo* Court observed that the threat to privacy interests posed by indiscriminate "monitoring of property that has been withdrawn from public view would present far too serious a threat to privacy interests in the home to escape entirely some sort of Fourth Amendment oversight." By contrast, the threat to privacy interests posed by beeper surveillance as a substitute for visual surveillance was not a subject of concern to the *Knotts* Court. For, as that Court noted, if "dragnet type of law enforcement practices" should "eventually occur, there will be time enough then to determine whether different constitutional principles may be applicable."

The Court's aerial surveillance cases reveal that there is no reasonable expectation of privacy from some police "fly overs" of property; aerial surveillance of home curtilage from a helicopter flying as low as 400 feet has been approved, and the use of an aerial mapping camera is acceptable during "fly overs" of commercial property. *Florida v. Riley*, 488 U.S. 445 (1989); *Dow Chemical v. United States*, 476 U.S. 227 (1986). These cases rely on the "public access" rationale of *Greenwood*, as reflected in the findings that members of the "flying public" could make "naked eye" observations of the curtilage like the police in *Riley*, and could use a "conventional" mapping camera like the one in *Dow Chemical*. But both the *Riley* and *Dow Chemical* opinions emphasized the limits of the police intrusions in those cases, and thus implied that the Court may not be prepared to approve aerial surveillance in other contexts. The *Riley* Court noted that the police observed marijuana growing in a greenhouse, not "intimate details connected with the use of the home or the curtilage"; further, "there was no undue noise, and no wind, dust, or threat of injury" cause by the helicopter "fly over" in *Riley*. Likewise in *Dow Chemical*, the Court observed that the photographs were "not so revealing of intimate details as to raise constitutional concerns."

The *Dow Chemical* Court predicted that "an electronic device [used] to penetrate walls or windows" might violate a reasonable expectation of privacy, and in *Kyllo v. United States*, 533 U.S. 27 (2001), the Court was sharply divided concerning the nature of intrusion caused by a "thermal imaging device." The device in *Kyllo* was aimed at a private home from across the street, and the heat scan showed that the garage was hotter than the rest of the house and "substantially warmer than neighboring homes." This evidence was used to establish the probable cause required for the issuance of a warrant to search the home for an "indoor growing operation" using halide lights to grow marijuana. The *Kyllo* majority determined that the homeowner possessed a reasonable expectation of privacy from the use of the thermal imaging device, and ruled more broadly as follows:

> We think that obtaining by sense-enhancing technology any information regarding the interior of the home that could not otherwise have been obtained without physical "intrusion into a constitutionally protected area" constitutes a search—at least where (as here) the technology in question is not in general public use. This assures preservation of that degree of privacy against government that existed when the Fourth Amendment was adopted.

The *Kyllo* majority's rationales relied on *Katz*, *Karo*, and *Dow Chemical*. The Court rejected the government's argument that the heat device detected heat only from the external surface of the home, reasoning that such a "mechanical interpretation" of privacy was rejected in *Katz*. The *Kyllo* majority also noted that *Karo* implies that a homeowner should not be subject to police use of technology that may discern human activity inside the home. The *Kyllo* majority rejected the government's alternate argument that the heat device did not "detect private activities occurring in private areas," reasoning that "[i]n the home, all details are intimate details, because the entire area is held safe from prying government eyes." The *Kyllo* dissenters argued that the heat device was only a form of "off-the-wall surveillance." Therefore, the *Kyllo* dissenters rejected the privacy interest using the *Greenwood* "public access" rationale. They argued that since "the ordinary use of the senses" could enable members of the public to detect the "off-the-wall" heat loss, the police should be allowed to detect the same information from a distance using a device that discloses only limited information like the canine sniff in *Place*. It seems certain that future cases involving new technologies will provide further challenges to the Court's ability to develop a coherent body of privacy jurisprudence that will "conserve public interests as well as the interests and rights of individual citizens." *Kyllo*, 533 U.S. at 40.

When venturing into the field of "privacy in the electronic sphere" after *Kyllo*, the Court decided to assume *arguendo* that a government employee, a police officer, had a reasonable expectation of privacy in the text messages he sent on the pager provided to him by his government employer, the city police department, in *City of Ontario v. Quon*, 130 S. Ct. 2619 (2010). Based on this assumption, the Court went on to find that the examination of the text messages by the police chief, for the purpose of determining whether they were work-related, did not violate the Fourth Amendment because this warrantless intrusion satisfied the criteria for a reasonable "special needs" search of the workplace.

The *Quon* Court emphasized that its reluctance to address the expectation of privacy issue more directly was based on the concern that a broad holding "concerning employees' privacy expectations vis-à-vis employer-provided technological equipment" might have unpredictable implications. Given the uncertainty as to "how workplace norms" relating to the monitoring of electronic communications may evolve, the Court concluded that at present, it would have difficulty predicting not only how employees' expectations would be shaped by the current "rapid changes" in technology, but also "the degree to which society will be prepared to recognize those expectations as reasonable." For these reasons, the Court found that "prudence counsel[ed] caution" when faced with the facts in *Quon*, because as demonstrated in *Olmstead*, "the judiciary risks error by elaborating too fully on the Fourth Amendment implications of emerging technology before its role in society has become clear."

POINTS TO REMEMBER

- It is a violation of a person's reasonable expectation of privacy for the police to perform any of these intrusions without complying with Fourth Amendment requirements:

  — Squeeze luggage to determine its contents when the luggage has been placed in the overhead rack of a bus by a passenger;

  — Use a thermal imaging device to determine the amount of heat emanating from the exterior walls of a home;

  — Conduct an electronic intrusion that captures the substance of phone conversations, as by using a device affixed to the outside of a public phone booth to record the conversations of the person within the booth;

  — Place a tracking beeper in an object and use it to obtain information about the location of that object when the location is inside a person's premises;

  — Enter on to property and perform visual surveillance there when the property constitutes the "curtilage" around a home.

- It is *not* a violation of a person's reasonable expectation of privacy for the police to perform any of these intrusions without complying with Fourth Amendment requirements:

— Use a dog trained to detect contraband to perform a canine sniff of luggage in a public place or of the exterior of an automobile;

— Enter on to property and perform visual surveillance there when the property constitutes the "open fields";

— Obtain the substance of phone conversations from an undercover agent who records those conversations as a trusted participant;

— Obtain trash bags from a garbage collector, which bags were placed on the curb outside a house by the homeowner, and then search the garbage inside them;

— Conduct aerial surveillance of the "curtilage" surrounding a home at the height of 400 feet, or use an aerial mapping camera to take photographs of the areas surrounding commercial buildings;

— Place a tracking beeper in an object and use it to obtain information about the location of that object when the location is in the "open fields."

Focal Points for Warrantless Searches Section

- The Fourth Amendment and warrantless searches.

- The plain view exception.

- The search incident to legal arrest exception.

- Booking searches.

- The automobile exception.

- The inventory exception.

- The consent exception.

- Administrative inspections.

- Stop and Frisk.

- Other investigatory searches and seizures.

- Investigatory seizures of property.

- Exigent circumstances.

C. Warrantless Searches and Seizures

Although the Fourth Amendment prohibits "unreasonable" searches and seizures, it does not explicitly require that either searches or seizures be conducted pursuant to a warrant. Although the Court has articulated a "preference" for warrants, it has frequently found that warrantless searches are "reasonable."

The Court distinguishes between warrantless arrests and warrantless searches. Even though warrantless arrests are generally permissible, warrantless searches are disfavored and are "per se unreasonable subject only to a few specifically established and well-delineated exceptions." *Katz v. United States*, 389 U.S. 347, 357 (1967).

This chapter focuses on warrantless searches and seizures and includes a number of so-called "exceptions" to the warrant requirement. These exceptions constitute an important component of search and seizure jurisprudence.

1. Plain View Exception

"Plain view" is a frequently used exception to the warrant requirement. When the police are in a place where they have the right to be (as when they are conducting a lawful search), either pursuant to a warrant or pursuant to an exception to the warrant requirement, this exception allows them to seize items that they find in "plain view." While a seizure of property constitutes an invasion of the owner's possessory interest, the seizure is justified by the fact that the officer found it lying in "plain view."

The plain view exception only applies when the police are in a place where they have the right to be. For example, if the police see defendant rolling a marijuana cigarette in a public place, they may seize the cigarette (and any other marijuana that they find in plain view). They may also seize contraband they find while conducting a valid search of a private place. For example, if the police search defendant's house pursuant to a valid warrant (which gives them the right to be on the premises), and they find cocaine lying in plain view, they may seize the cocaine. Of course, if the police illegally entered the house, the exception would not apply even though the cocaine was lying in plain view.

In order for the plain view exception to apply, the contraband's incriminating character must be "immediately apparent." If the police see defendant carrying what appears to be an ordinary cigarette, they may not seize it simply because it "might" contain marijuana. Prior to the seizure, it must be "immediately apparent" that the cigarette contains marijuana rather than ordinary tobacco. In other words, the police must be able to ascertain the cigarette's incriminating character.

Several cases illustrate the "immediately apparent" requirement. In *Coolidge v. New Hampshire*, 403 U.S. 443 (1971), the police seized defendant's car from his driveway because they thought that it might contain microscopic fibers that would implicate him in a crime. The Court held that the seizure was invalid. The police were unable to ascertain the evidential value of the car until they made a microscopic examination of the interior, and therefore the incriminating character of the car was not "immediately apparent." Likewise, in *Arizona v. Hicks*, 480 U.S. 321 (1987), although the police validly entered an apartment to search for evidence relating to a shooting, they observed expensive stereo components which they moved to observe the serial numbers. The officers later confirmed (based on the serial numbers) that the components were stolen. The Court invalidated the search holding that the serial numbers were not "immediately apparent" before the police moved the components to observe the numbers. Justice Powell dissented: "[The majority's] distinction between 'looking' at a suspicious object in plain view and 'moving' it even a few inches trivializes the Fourth Amendment."

A further illustration of the "immediately apparent" requirement is provided by the holding in *Minnesota v. Dickerson*, 508 U.S. 366 (1993). In that case, a police officer stopped Dickerson and forced him to submit to a frisk for weapons. The search revealed no weapons, but the officer found a small "lump" in respondent's nylon jacket. The officer examined the lump with his fingers by sliding it back and forth until he was able to determine that it was crack cocaine. The officer then seized the cocaine. The Court held that the contraband was not in plain view and that the seizure was invalid. The Court held that the officer was unable to ascertain that the "lump" was contraband until he manipulated it. Such manipulation went beyond the scope of a frisk for weapons.

In determining that an object's character is "immediately apparent," officers may rely on their training and experience. For example, in *Texas v. Brown*, 460 U.S. 730 (1983), Brown was stopped at a driver's license checkpoint. At the time, he was holding an opaque green party balloon knotted about one-half inch from the tip. The Court concluded that the heroin was "immediately apparent": "The fact that Maples could not see through the opaque fabric of the balloon is all but irrelevant: the distinctive character of the balloon itself spoke volumes as to its contents—particularly to the trained eye of the officer."

The plain view exception also requires that the police have a right of lawful access to the thing itself. For example, suppose that a police officer is walking down a city street and observes marijuana laying on a table inside a nearby house. If the officer does not possess a warrant to enter the house, and cannot enter under one of the recognized exceptions to the warrant requirement, the officer cannot justify entry under the plain view exception. The officer's observation will give him probable cause to obtain a warrant to search the house for the marijuana.

Sometimes, even though the officer would not otherwise have the right to enter a building or apartment, "exigent circumstances" allow him to do so. In the prior example, suppose that the occupant of the apartment saw the officer observing the marijuana and immediately takes steps to destroy it (by flushing it down the toilet). By virtue of exigent circumstances, the officer might be free to enter the apartment to prevent the destruction.

The police may invoke the plain view exception even when their discovery of contraband was not "inadvertent." In *Horton v. California,* 496 U.S. 128 (1990), the Court rejected an argument that this exception should contain an "inadvertence" requirement. In that case, an officer had a warrant to search Horton's home for the proceeds of a robbery. During the search, he found other items (specifically, an Uzi machine gun, a .38 caliber revolver, two stun guns, a handcuff key, a San Jose Coin Club advertising brochure (the victim was the Treasurer of the Club), and a few items of clothing identified by the victim). The officer seized all of these things even though he admitted that he expected to find the weapon on the premises, and therefore the discovery of that item was not "inadvertent." The Court held that the seizure was nonetheless valid: "The fact that an officer is interested in an item of evidence and fully expects to find it in the course of a search should not invalidate its seizure if the search is confined in area and duration by the terms of a warrant or a valid exception to the warrant requirement."

POINTS TO REMEMBER

- The "plain view" exception justifies the seizure of evidence that the police find lying in plain view provided that the police are in a place where they have the right to be.

- Before contraband can be regarded as being in "plain view," its status as contraband must be immediately apparent.

- By itself, the plain view exception will not justify a warrantless entry into a residence even though the officer, standing in a public place, can see contraband lying in plain view.

- Under the plain view exception, the discovery of evidence need not be inadvertent.

2. Search Incident to Legal Arrest

The search incident to legal arrest exception is one of the most well-established exceptions to the warrant requirement. It provides that, when the police make a legal arrest, they have the right to make a search incident to that arrest.

What constitutes a "legal" arrest? A custodial arrest is the most serious form of seizure, and it occurs when the police take a suspect into custody in order to bring charges. Until 1976, there was uncertainty about the requirements for an arrest. Then, in *United States v. Watson,* 423 U.S. 411 (1976), the Court clarified the Fourth Amendment's meaning and application in this context. *Watson* held that the police may arrest without a warrant provided that they have reasonable cause to believe that the arrestee committed a felony. Essentially, the Court reaffirmed the common law rule which allowed peace officers to arrest without a warrant "for a misdemeanor or felony committed in his presence as well as for a felony not committed in his presence if there [are] reasonable ground for making the arrest." In reaching its decision, the Court emphasized that warrantless arrests had been historically permissible. Indeed, Congress passed a statute authorizing warrantless arrests as early as 1792 (shortly after the Fourth Amendment was adopted), as had several states. And the Court noted that warrantless arrests had "survived substantially intact" in every state.

Watson was qualified, as it pertained to arrests that occur at a person's home, in *Payton v. New York,* 445 U.S. 573 (1980). In that case, the Court held that the Fourth Amendment draws "a firm line at the entrance to the house. Absent exigent circumstances, that threshold may not reasonably be crossed without a warrant." In reaching its decision, the Court emphasized the importance of interjecting a magistrate's independent judgment "between the zealous officer and the citizen," but held that an arrest warrant would suffice because it "implicitly carries with it the limited authority to enter a dwelling in which the suspect lives when there is reason to believe the suspect is within." In *Steagald v. United States*, 451 U.S. 204 (1981), the Court extended *Payton* by holding that a law enforcement officer may not search for the subject of an arrest warrant in the home of a third party without first obtaining a search warrant. Of course, when a warrant is required, it must be supported by probable cause, oath and affirmation, and must particularly describe the place to be searched and the things to be seized.

Warrantless Misdemeanor Arrests

In *Atwater v. City of Lago Vista*, 532 U.S. 318 (2001), the Court extended the *Watson* rule (allowing warrantless arrests) to misdemeanor criminal offenses. In that case, Atwater was arrested for a minor offense (not wearing a seat belt) that could only be punished by a fine. Although the officer had the choice of whether to arrest Atwater or issue her a citation, he chose to arrest. Atwater's young children were "frightened, upset, and crying" as Atwater was handcuffed and placed in the back of a squad car. At the station, Atwater was subjected to a search and mug shots and eventually placed in a jail cell where she remained for an hour before being bailed out. Atwater pleaded no contest to the charge of driving without a seat belt (the other charges, driving without a license or insurance, were dropped), and sued for damages claiming an infringement of her "right to be free from unreasonable seizure." The Court, denied the suit because the arrest was constitutionally permissible, specifically rejecting Atwater's argument that warrantless misdemeanor arrests were historically permissible only when the offense was one "involving or tending toward violence." The Court found that the historical evidence was conflicting, but seemed to authorize warrantless arrests even for relatively minor offenses. The Court noted that, even when someone is arrested, there is an opportunity for prompt judicial review (within 48 hours). Justice O'Connor dissented, arguing that a custodial arrest is the "quintessential seizure." and that other means (i.e. citations) were available to vindicate the state's interest. As a result, she concluded that an arrest for a minor offense is "unreasonable."

In *Devenpeck v. Alford*, 543 U.S. 146 (2004), the Court refused to accept the proposition that the probable-cause inquiry is confined to the facts actually invoked at the time of arrest, or the proposition that the offense supported by these known facts must be "closely related" to the offense for which defendant was charged. In that case, a police officer possessed probable cause to believe that defendant had been impersonating a police officer. When the charges against defendant were dismissed, the officer brought a civil action under 42 U.S.C. § 1983. The Court emphasized that the officer had probable cause to arrest defendant for impersonating a police officer, and chose not to charge for that offense solely because of a departmental policy against "stacking" charges.

Arrests in Violation of State Law. In *Virginia v. Moore*, 553 U.S. 164 (2008), the Court held that an arrest (in that case, for driving with a suspended license) can be reasonable even though state law provides that police officers should issue a citation for that offense rather than make a custodial arrest. The Court held that an arrest is permissible under the Fourth Amendment as long as it is based on probable cause: "In a long line of cases, we have said that when an officer has probable cause to believe a person committed even a minor crime in his presence, the balancing of private and public interests is not in doubt. The arrest is constitutionally reasonable." The Court went on to note that the calculus does not change simply because "a State chooses to protect privacy beyond the level that the Fourth Amendment requires."

Material Witness Arrests. In *Ashcroft v. Al-Kidd*, 131 S.Ct. 2074 (2011), the Court dealt with allegations that Attorney General Ashcroft had misused a material-witness warrant to detain terrorism suspects. The plaintiffs claimed that he had detained them as suspects rather than for the intended purpose of securing material witnesses. Under federal law, a judge may order the arrest of a person whose testimony is regarded as "material in a criminal proceeding [if] it is shown that it may become impracticable to secure the presence of the person by subpoena." 18 U.S.C. § 3144. Abdullah al-Kidd (who was detained for 16 days and under supervised release for 14 months) sued, complaining that then-Attorney General John Ashcroft authorized federal prosecutors and law enforcement officials to use the material-witness statute to detain individuals with suspected ties to terrorist organizations. He contended that federal officials did not intend to call most of these individuals as witnesses, but that Ashcroft chose to detain them simply because he suspected them of supporting terrorism (although he lacked sufficient evidence to actually charge them with a crime). The Court held that "Fourth Amendment reasonableness 'is predominantly an objective inquiry,' and that the question is whether '"the circumstances, viewed objectively, justify [the challenged] action." If so, in the Court's view, the governmental actor's intent is irrelevant: "Since al-Kidd conceded that individualized suspicion supported the issuance of the material-witness arrest warrant, and did not assert that his arrest would have been unconstitutional absent the alleged pretextual use of the warrant, the Court found no Fourth Amendment violation, and concluded that there was no need to address the question of whether Ashcroft was entitled to qualified immunity."

Does it matter whether the arrest is a "sham" or "pretext" to allow the police to search a vehicle? In *Arkansas v. Sullivan*, 532 U.S. 769 (2001), the Court answered this question in the negative. In that case, Sullivan was stopped for speeding and for having an improperly tinted windshield. After seeing Sullivan's license, the officer realized that he was aware of intelligence suggesting that Sullivan was involved in narcotics. When the officer noticed a rusting roofing hatchet on the floorboard of Sullivan's car, he arrested Sullivan for speeding, driving without his registration and insurance documentation, carrying a weapon (the roofing hatchet), and improper window tinting. A subsequent search of the vehicle revealed methamphetamine. At trial, Sullivan moved to suppress the evidence because (or so he alleged) his arrest was merely a "pretext and sham to search" his vehicle. The Court rejected the argument noting that it was unwilling to "entertain Fourth Amendment challenges based on the actual motivations of individual officers" and that "[s]ubjective intentions play no role in ordinary, probable-cause Fourth Amendment analysis."

Although warrantless arrests are generally permissible, the Court has limited the ability of the police to use deadly force to effect an arrest. In *Tennessee v. Garner*, 471 U.S. 1 (1985), the Court held that the Constitution generally prohibits the use of deadly force because the use of such force "is a self-defeating way of apprehending a suspect and so setting the criminal justice mechanism in motion." The Court held that deadly force could be used when the suspect "poses a threat of serious physical harm either to the officer or to others." However, in analyzing the facts presented by the *Garner* case, the Court concluded that the police should not have used deadly force. The Court noted the suspect's youth, slightness, and lack of a weapon, and concluded that he did not pose a threat of physical danger to himself or others. Justice O'Connor dissented: "The public interest involved in the use of deadly force as a last resort to apprehend a fleeing burglary suspect relates primarily to the serious nature of the crime."

Garner was qualified in *Scott v. Harris*, 127 S.Ct. 1769 (2007). In *Scott*, when a policeman attempted to stop a fleeing motorist by ramming the motorist's vehicle from behind, the resulting accident left the motorist in a quadriplegic condition. The motorist sued under 42 U.S.C. § 1983, alleging, *inter alia*, a violation of his federal constitutional rights–use of excessive force resulting in an unreasonable seizure under the Fourth Amendment. The Court found no Fourth Amendment violation. Since the motorist was involved in "a Hollywood-style car chase of the most frightening sort, placing police officers and innocent bystanders alike at great risk of serious injury," the Court concluded that the decision to ram the vehicle was "objectively reasonable" under the circumstances. In addition, the Court concluded that the case was objectively distinguishable from *Garner*, which involved the shooting of a fleeing unarmed suspect, because the motorist posed "an actual and imminent threat to the lives of any pedestrians who might have been present, to other civilian motorists, and to the officers involved in the chase." Moreover, the motorist "intentionally placed himself and the public in danger by unlawfully engaging in the reckless, high-speed flight that ultimately produced the choice between two evils that Scott confronted." The Court noted that the the police were not required to desist and simply allow the motorist to escape: Justice Stevens, dissented, arguing that "In my judgment, jurors in Georgia should be allowed to evaluate the reasonableness of the decision to ram respondent's speeding vehicle in a manner that created an obvious risk of death and has in fact made him a quadriplegic at the age of 19."

POINTS TO REMEMBER

- When the police make a lawful arrest, they are entitled to make a search incident to arrest.

- In general, warrantless arrests are permissible provided that the officer has reasonable cause to believe that the suspect has committed a felony.

- Warrantless misdemeanor arrests are also permissible even for relatively minor offenses.

- Absent consent or some other exception, a suspect may not be arrested in his own home without an arrest warrant, or at a third party's home without a search warrant.

- The police may not used deadly force to effect an arrest unless the suspect presents a threat of serious physical harm to the officer or the public.

The Scope of a Search Incident to Arrest. Once a legal arrest occurs, the police are allowed to make a search incident to arrest. The seminal decision is *Chimel v. California*, 395 U.S. 752 (1969). In that case, Chimel was legally arrested at his home for the burglary of a coin shop, and the police searched the entire house including the attic, garage and a small workshop. The search took 45 minutes to an hour and the police seized various coins and other objects. Although the Court held that the police may conduct searches incident to arrest, it held that the police had exceeded the permissible scope of the search in that case.

The *Chimel* Court recognized that a search incident to legal arrest is "reasonable" for two reasons. First, the arrestee might have a weapon that he can use to endanger the police or to effect an escape. Second, the arrestee might have evidence in his possession that he might try to destroy.

The Court emphasized that the scope of a search incident to arrest must directly correlate to the justifications for that search, and therefore is limited to the arrestee's person and those areas "within his immediate control." In other words, the search extends only to "the area from within which he might gain possession of a weapon or destructible evidence." By searching all of Chimel's house—including the attic, garage and workshop—the police had gone significantly beyond the area of his "immediate control." A dissenting Justice White argued that a search of the entire house was proper because the police faced exigent circumstances (the presence of Chimel's wife who might have removed the coins after he was taken away).

Except in rare circumstances, the arrest must precede the search in order to fit within this exception. However, in *Rawlings v. Kentucky*, 448 U.S. 98 (1980), after petitioner admitted ownership of a sizeable quantity of drugs, the police searched his person (the search revealed money and a knife) and placed him under arrest. The Court viewed the search of Rawlings' person as "incident to arrest" even though it preceded the arrest: "Once petitioner admitted ownership of the sizable quantity of drugs found in Cox's purse, the police clearly had probable cause to place petitioner under arrest. Where the formal arrest followed quickly on the heels of the challenged search of petitioner's person, we do not believe it particularly important that the search preceded the arrest rather than vice versa."

The search incident to legal arrest exception applies even when the defendant is being arrested for a minor offense (i.e., a traffic offense), and even though the police have no proof that the arrestee is carrying a weapon or contraband. For example, in *United States v. Robinson*, 414 U.S. 218 (1973), a police officer stopped Robinson who was driving a car. Based on a stop that had occurred four days earlier, the officer had reason to believe that Robinson was driving without a driver's license (an offense punishable by a jail term, a fine, or both). The officer arrested Robinson for driving without a license, and subjected him to a "pat down" search which led to the discovery of heroin. Respondent was convicted of possession and facilitation of concealment of heroin. The Court held that a search incident to arrest was permissible even though the arrest was for a minor offense.

Search Incident to Arrest and the Automobile Exception. For many years, the search incident to legal arrest's application to individuals arrested while traveling in automobiles was governed by the holding in *New York v. Belton*, 453 U.S. 454 (1981). In that case, Belton and three passengers were arrested while riding in an automobile. Following the arrest, the officer searched the passengers and the passenger compartment of the car including a jacket that he found on the back seat (in which he found contraband). The Court upheld the search articulating a "bright line rule" that, when the police arrest the occupant of a vehicle, they can search the passenger compartment of the vehicle. Clarifying *Chimel's* "area of immediate control" standard, the Court held that "articles inside the relatively narrow compass of the passenger compartment of an automobile are in fact generally, even if not inevitably, within 'the area into which an arrestee might reach in order to grab a weapon or evidentiary ite[m].' " The search extends to items found in containers within the passenger compartment.

Belton was overruled in *Arizona v. Gant*, 556 U.S. 332 (2009). After arresting a man who had just exited his automobile, the police placed him in handcuffs in the back seat of a police car, and conducted a search incident to legal arrest of the vehicle. The search revealed narcotics and illegal weapons. Quoting *Chimel* v. *California*, the Court emphasized that a search incident to legal arrest is limited to "the arrestee's person and the area 'within his immediate control'-construing that phrase to mean the area from within which he might gain possession of a weapon or destructible evidence." The Court went on to note that, if "there is no possibility that an arrestee could reach into the area that law enforcement officers seek to search, both justifications for the search-incident-to-arrest exception are absent and the rule does not apply." Since Gant was handcuffed and locked in the back of a police car, the interior of his vehicle was not within the area of his "immediate control." The Court did suggest that the police might justifiably search the vehicle of an arrestee in several situations. For example, if an arrestee is unsecured, and within reaching distance of the passenger compartment, and there are not sufficient numbers of officers to restrain him/her, then a search might be permissible. Of course, under the automobile exception, if the police have reasonable cause to believe that the vehicle contains evidence related to the crime, a search may also be permissible.

Chimel is subject to temporal and spatial limitations. *Chimel* provides the "spatial limitation": the police can only search the area within the arrestee's "immediate control." Although the immediate control standard provides the police with some guidance regarding the scope of the search, the "immediate control" standard suffers from ambiguity. For example, in *Chimel*, although it was clear that the police could not search the entire house including the garage, the precise limits of the search were far from clear. Assuming that Chimel was arrested in his living room, it is perhaps reasonable to assume that the police may search that room, but it is unclear whether the police may search nearby rooms. Presumably, they can not search upstairs (if the house has a second floor). In addition, it is unclear whether the police may open locked containers in rooms that they are allowed to search. In *Coolidge v. New Hampshire*, 403

U.S. 443 (1971), the Court provided some insight. In that case, defendant was arrested inside his home and the police searched his car which was sitting outside on the driveway. The Court held that the car search did not fit within the scope of a permissible search incident to arrest. The Court limited its holding to "occupants" of a vehicle and "recent occupants."

The "temporal limitation" requires that the search incident to legal arrest be conducted relatively contemporaneously with the arrest. *Preston v. United States*, 376 U.S. 364 (1964), illustrates the point. In that case, petitioner and his companions were arrested while riding in an automobile and taken to the police station for booking. Afterwards, a police officer towed their car to a garage. After the men were booked, police officers searched the passenger compartment of the car and found two loaded revolvers. Soon thereafter, the officers conducted a search of the trunk and found evidence implicating defendants in a robbery. The Court invalidated the search as "too remote in time or place to have been made as incidental to the arrest." Of course, the search would now be illegal under *Gant* as well.

POINTS TO REMEMBER

- When the police make a lawful arrest, they are entitled to make a search incident to arrest.

- The search incident to legal arrest is justified by the need to remove weapons that the arrestee might use to effect escape.

- It is also justified by the need to remove evidence that the arrestee might destroy.

- The search extends to those areas within the arrestee's "immediate control."

- The search must be relatively contemporaneous with the arrest.

- When the arrestee is traveling in a an automobile, the search incident exception extends to the entire passenger compartment.

1. Booking Searches

Closely related to the search incident to legal arrest exception is the so-called "booking" or "detention" exception. After the police "book" a suspect, and before they place the suspect in jail, the police usually conduct a "booking" search. In *Illinois v. Lafayette*, 462 U.S. 640 (1983), the Court upheld this type of search noting that it is "is reasonable for police to search the personal effects of a person under lawful arrest as part of the routine administrative procedure at a police stationhouse incident to booking and jailing the suspect."

In *Lafayette*, the Court identified a number of governmental interests that justify booking searches. First, by removing valuables from someone who is being placed in the jail population, jail officials prevent those items from being stolen. Second, by removing and inventorying the items, jail officials help protect themselves against false claims of theft. Third, the search prevents the arrestee from introducing contraband, weapons, and other dangerous items into the jail that could be used by inmates to injure themselves or others. Finally, by inspecting an arrestee's personal property, jail officials are better able to ascertain and verify a suspect's identity.

Under the booking exception, jail officials have the right to remove both contraband and valuables. For many years, a number of jails routinely strip search anyone placed in a jail cell. In *Lafayette*, the Court gave limited support to strip searches noting that the governmental interests that justify a jail search "might even justify a strip search." However, there was much civil litigation over strip searches, especially strip searches of those arrested for minor offenses, and many jails discontinued the practice. However, in *Florence v. Board of Chosen Freeholders*, 132 S.Ct. 1510 (2012), the Court was deferential to the asserted security interests of jail officials, and upheld the constitutionality of routine strip searches.

Courts tend to loosely apply temporal limitations in this context. For example, in *United States v. Edwards*, 415 U.S. 800 (1974), the Court upheld a booking search which took place nearly 10 hours after a defendant's arrest: "searches and seizures that could be made on the spot at the time of arrest may legally be conducted later when the accused arrives at the place of detention."

Some have tried to limit the scope of booking searches by arguing that police should use the "least intrusive" alternative. Suppose, for example, that a backpacker is arrested and asks the police to simply put his backpack in a locker rather than search it. In *Lafayette*, the Court concluded that jail officials need not resort to the least intrusive alternative. In other words, in the case of the backpacker, they have the right to search the backpack.

POINTS TO REMEMBER

- Jail officials have the right to conduct "booking" or "detention" searches before they put individuals in jail.

- Booking searches protect the detainee's valuables, protect the jail against false claims, prevent the introduction of dangerous items and contraband into the jail, and help jail officials ascertain and verify a detainee's identity.

- The scope of a booking search is broad, extending even to a strip search, but strip searches are permissible although generally avoided for minor offenses.

- Booking searches are allowed even if the police have less intrusive alternatives available to them.

2. Automobile Exception

The automobile exception is one of the oldest exceptions to the warrant requirement. It provides that, when the police have probable cause to believe that an automobile contains the fruits, instrumentalities or evidence of crime, they may search the vehicle without a warrant.

The automobile exception was first recognized in *Carroll v. United States*, 267 U.S. 132 (1925). In that case the Court justified the exception by noting that, although owners or drivers have constitutionally protected privacy interests in their cars, they are given less protection than in a home because of the "ready mobility" of automobiles. The Court viewed this mobility as creating exigent circumstances which justify a warrantless search.

Why are the privacy interests associated with an automobile entitled to less protection? Initially, it was thought that this lesser protection interest was due to the fact that cars have windows and therefore it is possible to see inside them. In more recent cases, the Court has recognized that an automobile is subject to less rigorous warrant requirements "because the expectation of privacy with respect to one's automobile is significantly less than that relating to one's home or office" due to the "pervasive regulation" of vehicles on the highway. *See California v. Carney*, 471 U.S. 386 (1985). This regulation includes the possibility of periodic inspections as well as licensing requirements. "As an everyday occurrence, police stop and examine vehicles when license plates or inspection stickers have expired, or if other violations, such as exhaust fumes or excessive noise, are noted, or if headlights or other safety equipment are not in proper working order."

In light of these two factors (mobility and diminished expectation of privacy), the Court has held that the existence of probable cause justifies an immediate warrantless search of an automobile "before the vehicle and its occupants become unavailable." It does not matter whether the car is being driven at the time of the stop so long as it is capable of moving and therefore has "ready mobility."

One issue that has troubled the courts is how to treat special types of vehicles such as mobile homes. In *California v. Carney*, 471 U.S. 386 (1985), the Court treated a mobile home like an automobile because it had mobility similar to an automobile, and therefore was subject to the diminished expectation of privacy associated with automobiles. While recognizing that the mobile home has "some, if not many of the attributes of a home," the Court emphasized that this particular mobile home was "readily mobile." In addition, the home was subject to the pervasive regulation associated with vehicles: "[T]he vehicle was licensed to 'operate on public streets; [was] serviced in public places; [and was] subject to extensive regulation and inspection.' "And the vehicle was so situated that an objective observer would conclude that it was being used not as a residence, but as a vehicle. Justice Stevens dissented arguing that "When a motor home is parked in a location that is removed from the public highway, [society] is prepared to recognize that the expectations of privacy within it are not unlike the expectations one has in a fixed dwelling."

Like the search incident to legal arrest exception, the automobile exception is also subject to a contemporaneousness requirement. But there are few decisions in which that requirement has been strictly applied. One example of strict application is *Coolidge v. New Hampshire*, 403 U.S. 443 (1971). In that case, when Coolidge was arrested at home for murder, the police impounded Coolidge's car (which was sitting on the front driveway) and towed it to the police station. The car was searched two days later, as well as a year later. Even though the police had probable cause to search the vehicle, the Court held that a warrant was required noting that the police had known for some time that Coolidge was a suspect in the murder and had suspected that he had used this particular automobile. Concluding that the word "automobile" is "not a talisman in whose presence the Fourth Amendment fades away and disappears," the Court invalidated the search noting that there was "no alerted criminal bent on flight, no fleeting opportunity on an open highway after a hazardous chase, no contraband or stolen goods or weapons, no confederates waiting to move the evidence, not even the inconvenience of a special police detail to guard the immobilized automobile." Since it was quite possible for the police to obtain a warrant, the Court concluded that neither a search at the scene nor a search at the station was permissible.

Most other decisions have loosely applied the contemporaneousness requirement. For example, in *Chambers v. Maroney*, 399 U.S. 42 (1970), although petitioner was riding in an automobile at the time of his arrest, the vehicle was searched at the police station rather than at the scene. The court upheld the search even though the car had been immobilized and it would have been relatively easy to obtain a warrant. The Court saw no "difference between on the one hand seizing and holding a car before presenting the probable cause issue to a magistrate and on the other hand carrying out an immediate search without a warrant. Given probable cause to search, either course is reasonable under the Fourth Amendment." Likewise, in *United States v. Johns*, 469 U.S. 478 (1985), the police stopped and searched a vehicle based on probable cause. The police removed packages from the vehicle, and searched the packages several days later. The Court upheld the search noting that respondents failed to show "that the delay in the search of packages adversely affected legitimate interests protected by the Fourth Amendment." Justice Brennan dissented noting that "no exigency precluded reasonable efforts to obtain a warrant prior to the search of the packages in the warehouse."

For many years, the courts struggled with the question of whether the automobile exception should apply to items that were only "incidentally" in a vehicle. An early decision was *United States v. Chadwick*, 433 U.S. 1 (1977). In that case, federal narcotics agents had probable cause to believe that a 200–pound double-locked footlocker contained marijuana. The agents tracked the locker as it was moved across the country by train, and as it was carried through a train station to a waiting car. As soon as defendants lifted the locker into the trunk of a car, the agents arrested Chadwick and his companions, seized the locker, and searched it. In *Chadwick*, the government tried to justify the search under the automobile doctrine, noting that not only was the foot locker found in an automobile, but it was readily movable having just been transported across the country. The Court refused to apply the automobile exception noting that a person expects more privacy in his luggage and personal effects than he does in his automobile.

Chadwick was followed and extended by the Court's subsequent decision in *Arkansas v. Sanders*, 442 U.S. 753 (1979). In that case, the Court refused to apply the automobile exception to a suitcase that was being transported in the trunk of a car. In *Sanders*, the police had probable cause to believe that marijuana was being transported in the suitcase, and they watched defendant place the suitcase in the trunk of a taxi. After following the taxi for several blocks, the police stopped the taxi and searched the suitcase. The Court again held that the automobile exception did not apply. The Court reaffirmed the idea that a higher expectation of privacy is associated with luggage, and held that the presence of luggage in an automobile did not diminish the owner's expectation n of privacy in the suitcase.

Chadwick and *Sanders* were distinguished by the Court's later holding in *United States v. Ross*, 456 U.S. 798 (1982). In that case, the police searched Ross' car after receiving information that he had completed a drug transaction with drugs from the trunk of his car. In the trunk, the police found a brown paper bag containing illegal drugs. In upholding the search, the Court gave guidance regarding the scope of the automobile exception. The Court held that the "scope of a warrantless search based on probable cause is no narrower—and no broader—than the scope of a search authorized by a warrant supported by probable cause." Thus, "[i]f probable cause justifies the search of a lawfully stopped vehicle, it justifies the search of every part of the vehicle and its contents that may conceal the object of the search." Using this analysis, the *Ross* Court upheld the search of the trunk including a "probing search" of compartments and containers found in the automobile provided that the police have probable cause for the search.

Ross distinguished *Chadwick* and *Sanders* on the basis that the *Ross* rule (that the police may search any container found in a vehicle) applied when the police have probable cause to search an entire vehicle, but that *Chadwick* applies when the officers have probable cause to search only a container within the vehicle. Under *Ross*, the police could search closed containers found during a warrantless search. Even though closed containers might be protected by privacy interests, those interests "yielded to the broad scope of an automobile search."

In its later decision in *California v. Acevedo*, 500 U.S. 565 (1991), the Court flatly overruled both *Chadwick* and *Sanders*. In that case, based on a prior investigation, the police were aware that Daza had a package of marijuana in his apartment. Watching the apartment, the police saw Acevedo enter the apartment and leave with a paper bag (about the size of a marijuana package that Daza had recently received). Acevedo placed the bag in his car and began to drive away. Fearing that the bag contained marijuana, and that the evidence would be lost if Acevedo were allowed to leave, the police stopped him and immediately searched his trunk. The search revealed a bag that did in fact contain marijuana. In deciding the case, the Court flatly overruled *Chadwick*. The Court held that "a container found after a general search of the automobile and a container found in a car after a limited search for the container are equally easy for the police to store and for the suspect to hide or destroy." As a result, the Court was unable to find a "principled distinction in terms of either the privacy expectation or the exigent circumstances between the paper bag found by the police in *Ross* and the paper bag found by the police here." The Court refused to recognize a distinction "between a container for which the police are specifically searching and a container which they come across in a car."

The Court expressed other concerns about the *Chadwick* rule as well. First, the Court felt that the rule was subject to manipulation. "[If] the police know that they may open a bag only if they are actually searching the entire car, they may search more extensively than they otherwise would in order to establish the general probable cause required by *Ross*." In addition, the Court found that the *Chadwick* rule provided minimal privacy protection since it allowed the police to seize a container and hold it while they apply for a warrant, and the police might be able to search anyway under the search incident to legal arrest exception. Finally, the Court noted that the *Chadwick* rule had "confused courts and police officers and impeded effective law enforcement. . ." The Court felt that the rule simply did not provide "clear and unequivocal" guidelines to the law enforcement profession. As a result, *Acevedo* adopted a single rule governing automobile searches (the police may search containers without a warrant if their search is supported by probable cause) and flatly eliminated the warrant requirement for closed containers. In recent years, there has been considerable litigation regarding whether a cell phone is a "container" in the *Ross* sense so that police can search cell phone records without a warrant.

POINTS TO REMEMBER

- The automobile exception allows the police to make a warrantless search of a vehicle provided that they have probable cause to believe that the automobile contains the fruits, instrumentalities or evidence of crime.

- The automobile exception is justified by the "diminished expectation of privacy" associated with automobiles, as well as by the fact that cars are readily mobile.

- The courts have loosely applied the "contemporaneousness" requirement as applied to automobiles.

- The scope of the automobile search is tied to the probable cause that justifies it.

- In other words, the police can search parts of the car for which they have probable cause to believe that the fruits, instrumentalities or evidence of crime can be found.

- At one point, the automobile exception did not allow the police to search "closed containers" that were in a vehicle only "incidentally."

- Today, the exception has been broadened to include closed containers.

3. Inventory Exception

There is also an "inventory" exception to the warrant requirement. When the police impound vehicles, they routinely inventory the contents. The leading decision is *South Dakota v. Opperman,* 428 U.S. 364 (1976), a case that involved a warrantless search of an abandoned vehicle. In upholding the search, the Court emphasized that the inventory exception is justified by the need "to protect an owner's property while it is in the custody of the police, to insure against claims of lost, stolen, or vandalized property, and to guard the police from danger."

Before the police conduct an inventory search, they are not required to show reasonable cause to believe that the particular vehicle contains dangerous items. For example, in *Colorado v. Bertine*, 479 U.S. 367 (1987), after Bertine was arrested for driving under the influence of alcohol, his car was towed to an impoundment lot. While the police were waiting for a tow truck to arrive, they inventoried the contents of the car pursuant to police procedure. The search revealed controlled substances, a significant amount of cash, and drug paraphernalia. In upholding the search, the Court specifically rejected the argument that an inventory search must be premised on a specific danger to public safety. The Court found that "other considerations" were sufficient to uphold the search: "[T]he police were potentially responsible for the property taken into their custody. By securing the property, the police protected the property from unauthorized interference. Knowledge of the precise nature of the property helped guard against claims of theft, vandalism, or negligence. Such knowledge also helped to avert any danger to police or others that may have been posed by the property."

The Court specifically rejected the argument that the inventory was "unreasonable" because the van was towed to a "secure, lighted facility," and there was little chance of property being stolen from it. The Court held that the police could inventory the vehicle even in a secure facility: "the police may still wish to protect themselves or the owners of the lot against false claims of theft or dangerous instrumentalities."

Before an inventory search will be permitted, the vehicle must have been legally impounded. Rules vary regarding the circumstances under which impoundment is permissible. In some states and municipalities, a vehicle can be towed and impounded merely for illegal parking. In addition, when the driver of a car is arrested (i.e., for driving under the influence), the police might impound a vehicle rather than leave it by the side of the road. In *Bertine*, the Court rejected the claim that Bertine should have been "offered the opportunity to make other arrangements for the safekeeping of his property." While the officer could have allowed Bertine to make alternative arrangements, the Court held that the Fourth Amendment did not require the officer to do so. In the Court's view, "reasonable police regulations relating to inventory procedures administered in good faith satisfy the Fourth Amendment, even though courts might as a matter of hindsight be able to devise equally reasonable rules requiring a different procedure." The Court noted that police procedures mandated the search.

Once a vehicle is lawfully impounded, the scope of an inventory search is fairly broad. Not only may the police search the passenger compartment, they can also search the trunk. In addition, the police can open closed containers.

Courts will sometimes require that inventory searches be conducted pursuant to departmental regulation so that the discretion of individual police officers is minimized. For example, in *Florida v. Wells*, 495 U.S. 1 (1990), Wells was arrested and his car was impounded. An inventory search at the impoundment facility revealed two marijuana cigarettes, and a locked suitcase that was found to contain a considerable quantity of marijuana. Since the Florida Highway Patrol had no policy regarding the opening of closed containers during inventory searches, the Court upheld a lower court decision excluding the evidence. While the Court noted that the inventory exception could extend to closed containers, the Court was troubled by the fact that the Florida Highway Patrol "had no policy whatever with respect to the opening of closed containers encountered during an inventory search." Because of the absence of such a policy, the Court concluded that the search was "not sufficiently regulated to satisfy the Fourth Amendment."

The Court does not preclude individual police officers from exercising any discretion. For example, in *Bertine*, even though departmental regulations gave police discretion about whether to conduct an inventory search, the Court upheld the search of Bertine's vehicle. The Court held that police officers could exercise discretion provided that "discretion is exercised according to standard criteria and on the basis of something other than suspicion or evidence of criminal activity." The Court held that the city regulations involved in that case, which allowed the officer to decide whether the vehicle should be impounded or should be parked and locked (based on whether the vehicle was likely to be vandalized), were permissible. The Court concluded that the officer did not impound the vehicle simply to search it.

Some state supreme courts restrict the availability of inventory searches under their state constitutions. In *Wagner v. Commonwealth*, 581 S.W.2d 352 (Ky. 1979), the Kentucky Supreme Court held that a vehicle could be impounded without a warrant in Kentucky in only four situations:

> 1. The owner or permissive user consents to the impoundment;

> 2. The vehicle, if not removed, constitutes a danger to other persons or property or the public safety and the owner or permissive user cannot reasonably arrange for alternate means of removal;

> 3. The police have probable cause to believe both that the vehicle constitutes an instrumentality or fruit of a crime and that absent immediate impoundment the vehicle will be removed by a third party; or

> 4. The police have probable cause to believe both that the vehicle contains evidence of a crime and that absent immediate impoundment the evidence will be lost or destroyed.

The court went on to hold that, even when a vehicle is lawfully impounded, it cannot be routinely searched: "[S]uch an inventory is impermissible unless the owner or permissive user consents or substantial necessities grounded upon public safety justify the search." *Wagner* was clarified in *Cardwell v. Commonwealth*, 639 S.W.2d 549 (Ky. App. 1982), in which the court held that the police had properly towed a vehicle (because it protruded onto the road and constituted a hazard). The Court also upheld an inventory search because the trunk lock was broken and the officer was acting to preserve valuables.

POINTS TO REMEMBER

- The police may conduct routine inventory searches of lawfully impounded vehicles.

- The purpose of an inventory search is to protect valuables, protect the police against false claims, and remove items that may present a danger to the public.

- The scope of an inventory search is potentially broad extending to the passenger compartment, the trunk and closed containers.

- Inventory searches will sometimes be invalidated when department regulations fail to sufficiently limit the discretion of individual police officers (i.e., regarding the opening of closed containers).

- Some state supreme courts, using their state constitutions, have limited the power of the police to conduct inventory searches.

4. Consent

The consent exception is not really an "exception" to the warrant requirement. Any constitutional right can be waived, including the Fourth Amendment right to be free from unreasonable searches and seizures.

Schneckloth v. Bustamonte, 412 U.S. 218 (1973), provides insight into the meaning of the term "consent." That case involved six men who were traveling in an automobile. When the vehicle was stopped (because one headlight and a license plate light were burned out), and the driver could not produce a driver's license, the officer asked the driver and passengers to step out of the vehicle. The officer then asked Alcala, a passenger who claimed that his brother owned the car, if he could search the vehicle. Alcala replied, "Sure, go ahead." The officer testified that it "was all very congenial at this time." The officer testified that Alcala actually helped in the search of the car, by opening the trunk and glove compartment. In the driver's words: "[T]he police officer asked Joe (Alcala), he goes, 'Does the trunk open?' And Joe said, 'Yes.' Alcala obtained the keys and opened the trunk." In the car, the officer found three stolen checks which were introduced at Bustamonte's subsequent trial (at which he was convicted).

In upholding the search, the Court provided guidance regarding the meaning of the term "consent." The Court held that consent searches are permissible, but that the state bears the burden of showing "that the consent was, in fact, freely and voluntarily given." Consent would not exist when the suspect was "coerced." In determining whether consent was voluntary or coerced, the Court indicated that a "totality of the circumstances" test should be applied. A reviewing court should analyze a variety of factors, including factors peculiar to the suspect (i.e., if the suspect is particularly vulnerable because of lack of schooling or low intelligence), and factors that suggest coercion (i.e., the police had their guns drawn, they demanded the right to search, or they exercised other forms of subtle coercion).

One factor considered in the "totality" is whether the suspect knows that he has the right to refuse consent. However, absence of such knowledge is not determinative. In *Schneckloth*, the Court recognized that in some situations (i.e. when the police have evidence of illegal activity, but lack probable cause to arrest or search), a consent search may be the only way to solve a case. In addition, the Court felt that a knowledge requirement (knowledge of the right to refuse) might be difficult to apply. The Court acknowledged that there would be situations when a suspect knows of his right to refuse (as when a defendant tells the police that he is aware of his right or when his prior experience demonstrates knowledge), but that many cases would arise in which the state could not prove that a suspect knew that he had the right to refuse consent. The Court was concerned that a defendant could undermine consent simply by testifying that he did not know that he had the right to refuse. In addition, the Court declined to require the police to inform a suspect of his right to refuse:

> Consent searches are part of the standard investigatory techniques of law enforcement agencies. They normally occur on the highway, or in a person's home or office, and under informal and unstructured conditions. The circumstances that prompt the initial request to search may develop quickly or be a logical extension of investigative police questioning. The police may seek to investigate further suspicious circumstances or to follow up leads developed in questioning persons at the scene of a crime. These situations are a far cry from the structured atmosphere of a trial where, assisted by counsel if he chooses, a defendant is informed of his trial rights.

The Court also rejected the argument that consent to search must involve "an intentional relinquishment or abandonment of a known right or privilege," or that a waiver must be made "knowingly and intelligently." The Court held that the requirement of a knowing and intelligent waiver has only been applied to rights that are deemed necessary to "a fair trial," including the right to counsel at trial, guilty pleas, the right to confront witnesses, and the prohibition against double jeopardy. The Court regarded Fourth Amendment rights as different because they were designed to protect the "security of one's privacy against arbitrary intrusion by the [police]," rather than to guarantee a fair trial, and therefore the Court refused to hold that "every reasonable presumption ought to be indulged against voluntary relinquishment." In addition, the Court concluded that the community has an interest in encouraging consent because "the resulting search may yield necessary evidence for the solution and prosecution of crime, evidence that may insure that a wholly innocent person is not wrongly charged with a criminal offense." The Court expressed concern that a knowing and intelligent waiver standard could not be applied in the context of consent searches: "[It] would be unrealistic to expect that in the informal, unstructured context of a consent search, a policeman, upon pain of tainting the evidence obtained, could make the detailed type of examination demanded."

The Court rejected the argument that its *Miranda* decision required a finding "that knowledge of a right to refuse is an indispensable element of a valid consent." The Court viewed *Miranda* as focused on the highly coercive nature of custodial interrogation, and the court questioned whether consent searches were "necessarily accompanied by such coercion." Indeed, unlike interrogations which frequently take place at the stationhouse, most consent searches "took place on the suspect's turf" and the Court was unwilling to presume that the consent was coerced.

The Court suggested that a variety of factors might be relevant to the determination of whether consent was voluntary or coerced. Factors that might be considered included characteristics specific to the suspect, including "minimal schooling" and low intelligence. Other factors that are relevant include "the lack of any effective warnings to a person of his rights; and the voluntariness of any statement taken under those conditions has been carefully scrutinized to determine whether it was in fact voluntarily given."

Justice Brennan, dissenting, stated that it "wholly escapes me how our citizens can meaningfully be said to have waived something as precious as a constitutional guarantee without ever being aware of its existence." Justice Marshall also dissented arguing that the "Court has always scrutinized with great care claims that a person has foregone the opportunity to assert constitutional rights. . . In fact, I have difficulty in comprehending how a decision made without knowledge of available alternatives can be treated as a choice at all."

Schneckloth was followed and expanded in *Ohio v. Robinette*, 519 U.S. 33 (1996). In that case, defendant was lawfully stopped for speeding on an interstate highway and given a verbal warning. Before the officer released Robinette, he asked whether Robinette was carrying contraband. When Robinette answered in the negative, the officer asked for and obtained permission to search Robinette's car. The search revealed a small amount of marijuana and contraband drugs. The Court held that the officer was not required to tell Robinette that he was "free to go" before asking for consent to search the vehicle: "The Fourth Amendment test for a valid consent to search is that the consent be voluntary, and 'voluntariness is a question of fact to be determined from all the circumstances.' "

Not all state supreme courts, in their interpretations of their state constitutions, agree with the U.S. Supreme Court's holding in *Schneckloth* . In *State v. Johnson*, 68 N.J. 349, 346 A.2d 66 (1975), the New Jersey Supreme Court rejected *Schneckloth's* holding in interpreting and applying the New Jersey Constitution. The Court reached that conclusion even though New Jersey Constitution tracks the language of the Fourth Amendment ("(T)he right of the people to be secure in their persons, houses, papers and effects, against unreasonable searches and seizures shall not be violated. . ."). The Court explained:

> [W]here the State seeks to justify a search on the basis of consent it has the burden of showing that the consent was voluntary, an essential element of which is knowledge of the right to refuse consent. Many persons, perhaps most, would view the request of a police officer to make a search as having the force of law. Unless it is shown by the State that the person involved knew that he had the right to refuse to accede to such a request, his assenting to the search is not meaningful. One cannot be held to have waived a right if he was unaware of its existence. . . However, in a non-custodial situation, such as is here presented, the police would not necessarily be required to advise the person of his right to refuse to consent to the search. Our decision is only that in such a situation if the State seeks to rely on consent as the basis for a search, it has the burden of demonstrating knowledge on the part of the person involved that he had a choice in the matter. . .

See also State v. Carty, 170 N.J. 632, 790 A.2d 903 (2001) (New Jersey Supreme Court held that the police must have a "reasonable suspicion of criminal activity" before seeking a motorist's consent to search, and must also specifically inform the motorist of his right to refuse the consent).

The scope of a consent search is generally dictated by the scope of the consent, and can extend to closed containers. In *Florida v. Jimeno*, 500 U.S. 248 (1991), believing that respondent was carrying narcotics, a police officer asked for permission to search his car. Respondent consented stating that he had nothing to hide. When the search revealed cocaine in a paper bag on the floorboard, the Court held that the consent extended to the paper bag: "Respondent granted Officer Trujillo permission to search his car, and did not place any explicit limitation on the scope of the search. [I]t was objectively reasonable for the police to conclude that the general consent to search respondent's car included consent to search containers within that car which might bear drugs." Justice Marshall dissented: "[A]n individual has a heightened expectation of privacy in the contents of a closed container[, and] consent to a search of [a car's] interior [cannot] necessarily be understood as extending to containers in the car."

Even when consent is given, it may be vitiated by police assertions of authority and right. In *Bumper v. State of North Carolina,* 391 U.S. 543 (1968), the police went to an elderly widow and asked for permission to search her house (the police believed that her grandson had committed a crime). When they arrived, one officer stated "I have a search warrant to search your house." The grandmother responded, "Go ahead," and opened the door. The Court held that the consent was invalid noting that the state bears the burden of showing that the consent was "freely and voluntarily given" and that consent did not exist simply because the woman acquiesced to a "claim of lawful authority":

> When a law enforcement officer claims authority to search a home under a warrant, he announces in effect that the occupant has no right to resist the search. The situation is instinct with coercion—albeit colorably lawful coercion. Where there is coercion there cannot be consent.

Justice Black dissented: "[The] searching officers had valid permission to conduct their search" and she voluntarily consented when she stated: "I let them search, and it was all my own free will. Nobody forced me at all."

Consent may also be vitiated by misrepresentations, but the nature of the misrepresentation is important. In *Bumpers*, not only did the police make a show of authority, they misrepresented the fact that they had a warrant. The Court indicated that such a misrepresentation might also invalidate consent. In *Lewis v. United States,* 385 U.S. 206 (1966), an undercover narcotics agent misrepresented himself as a drug purchaser, and gained entry into a home to make a drug purchase. After the deal was consummated, the agent arrested the seller. The Court held that the consent to enter was valid because an undercover agent could enter on the same basis as any other prospective drug purchaser.

A number of cases have dealt with the question of whether a third party can consent to a search of property. In *United States v. Matlock,* 415 U.S. 164 (1974), a woman consented to the search of a house that she shared with Matlock, including their bedroom. In the bedroom, the police found evidence that they used against Matlock. The Court held that the woman could consent to a search of the room because she had "common authority" over the area. In the Court's view, "common authority" involves something more than a "mere property interest" and rests on "mutual use of the property by persons generally having joint access or control for most purposes, so that it is reasonable to recognize that any of the co-inhabitants has the right to permit the inspection in his own right and that the others have assumed the risk that one of their number might permit the common area to be searched." In *Coolidge v. New Hampshire*, 403 U.S. 443 (1971), the Court held that consent existed when a wife surrendered her husband's guns and clothing to the police. In *Frazier v. Cupp*, 394 U.S. 731, 740 (1969), defendant's cousin authorized the police to search defendant's duffel bag. The Court held that defendant had assumed the risk that his cousin would consent to the search since they shared the bag.

In *Georgia v. Randolph*, 126 S.Ct. 1515 (2006), the Court held that a wife's consent to search did not validate the search in the face of the husband's objections. The Court distinguished *Matlock* on the basis that that case involved consent by a co-tenant against an "absent, nonconsenting person with whom that authority is shared." The Court concluded that, unless there is some "recognized hierarchy" within a household (e.g., parent and child or barracks housing military personnel of different grades), "there is no societal understanding of superior and inferior" and "a physically present inhabitant's express refusal of consent to a police search is dispositive as to him, regardless of the consent of a fellow occupant." Chief Justice Roberts, joined by Justice Scalia, dissented, arguing that the Court's holding provides "random" protection because everything depends on the happenstance of whether a co-occupant is present at the door objecting. He went on to argue that if "an individual shares information, papers, *or places* with another, he assumes the risk that the other person will in turn share access to that information or those papers *or places* with the government." In addition, he expressed concern that the decision would have its "most serious consequence" in domestic abuse situations because it might forbid the "police from entering to assist with a domestic dispute if the abuser whose behavior prompted the request for police assistance objects." Justice Scalia also dissented, arguing that "[The issue] is what to do when there is a *conflict* between two equals. [It] does not follow that the spouse who *refuses* consent should be the winner of the contest."

The *Randolph* Court suggested that the right to consent might vary depending on the circumstances and the relationships between the parties. As a result, the Court reaffirmed prior decisions to that effect. For example, in *Chapman v. United States*, 365 U.S. 610 (1961), defendant's landlord notified the police that he smelled a strong "odor of whisky mash" at defendant's house, and he subsequently gave police permission to search the house. Although the search revealed a distillery and illegal mash, the court held that the landlord did not have authority to consent to the search and that the search was unlawful. In *Stoner v. California*, 376 U.S. 483 (1964), following a robbery, a police investigation focused on Stoner who was staying at the Mayfair Hotel. After explaining that petitioner was a suspect in an armed robbery, the front desk clerk offered to open petitioner's room stating that: "I will be more than happy to give you permission and I will take you directly to the room." The clerk then took the officers to the room, unlocked it, and said, "Be my guest." In the room, the officers found incriminating evidence. The court held that the clerk did not have the authority to permit the search. As for children, *Randolph* suggested that the authority to consent depends on circumstances. "[A] child of eight might well be considered to have the power to consent to the police crossing the threshold into that part of the house where any caller, such as a pollster or salesman, might well be admitted," but no one would "reasonably expect such a child to be in a position to authorize anyone to rummage through his parents' bedroom."

In *United States v. Diggs*, 544 F.2d 116 (3rd Cir. 1976), the police focused on Diggs as the principal suspect in a bank robbery. Previously, Diggs had given a small metal box to Mrs. Bradley stating that it contained "stocks and bonds and silver paper and important papers that he had saved up for his children" and asked her to keep it for them "so they wouldn't be tempted to spend it." Diggs did not provide the Bradleys with a key to the box, and did not provide them with instructions regarding its disposition. Following his arrest, Mrs. Bradley turned the box over to FBI agents who opened it and found the robbery proceeds. The Court held that Mrs. Bradley could consent to the search: "[T]he right of the custodian of the defendant's property who has been unwittingly involved by the defendant in his crime to exculpate himself promptly and voluntarily by disclosing the property and explaining his connection with it to government agents, must prevail over any claim of the defendant to have the privacy of his property maintained against a warrantless search by such agents." "Diggs, must be held to have assumed the risk that the Bradleys whom he had thus involved in criminal conduct as custodians of the box might, when they learned the facts which appeared to incriminate them, disclose its contents in order to exculpate themselves, as in fact they did."

Can someone who lacks "common authority" nonetheless consent to a search? In *Illinois v. Rodriguez*, 497 U.S. 177 (1990), police made a warrantless entry into Rodriguez's apartment with the consent of his girlfriend who had lived there for several months and who possessed a key. She referred to the apartment as "our apartment" and she claimed to have clothing and furniture there. In fact, although she had lived in the apartment with Rodriguez, she had moved out more than a month before, her name was not on the lease, she did not pay rent, and she had taken the key without Rodriguez's knowledge or consent (although she had not moved all of her furniture out yet). In addition, although she sometimes went to the apartment after she moved out, she never did so unless Rodriguez was there. Inside the apartment, the police found cocaine and seized the drugs and related paraphernalia.

In upholding the search, the Court affirmed the warrant preference, as well as the general rule that a warrantless search could be based on consent from the owner or from "a third party who possesses common authority over the premises." The Court stated that "common authority" refers to people who have "mutual use" of property with "joint access or control," and held that the state bears the burden of showing that common authority exists. Applying the consent exception, the Court concluded that the girlfriend did not possess "common authority" over the apartment because she did not have "joint access or control for most purposes." Nevertheless, the Court upheld the warrantless search. The Court focused on the touchstone of the Fourth Amendment, "reasonableness," and held that a search based on the consent of one with "apparent authority" might also be reasonable. The Court was reluctant to require the police to "exercise judgment regarding the facts" and to ensure that their judgment is "not only responsible but correct." The Court required only that the officers make a "reasonable" judgment regarding the facts before them. The Court noted that this approach would sanction a reasonable mistake: "Because many situations which confront officers in the course of executing their duties are more or less ambiguous, room must be allowed for some mistakes on their part. But the mistakes must be those of reasonable men, acting on facts leading sensibly to their conclusions of probability." In the Court's view, the police act "reasonably" when they enter a dwelling based on a reasonable but erroneous belief "that the person who has consented to their entry is a resident of the premises." The Court noted that the belief might not be reasonable if "the surrounding circumstances could conceivably be such that a reasonable person would doubt its truth and not act upon it without further inquiry." An objective standard applies: "would the facts available to the officer at the [moment] 'warrant a man of reasonable caution in the belief' that the consenting party had authority over the premises? If not, then warrantless entry without further inquiry is unlawful unless authority actually exists. But if so, the search is valid." In *Rodriguez*, the Court concluded that the officers reasonably believed that the girlfriend had authority over the apartment.

Justice Marshall dissented, focusing on the warrant requirement. "[Because] the sole law enforcement purpose underlying third-party consent searches is avoiding the inconvenience of securing a warrant, a departure from the warrant requirement is not justified simply because an officer reasonably believes a third party has consented to a search of the defendant's home."

POINTS TO REMEMBER

- Consent searches are permissible because Fourth Amendment rights, like all other rights, can be waived.

- In determining whether consent is valid, courts focus on whether the consent was voluntarily given or was coerced.

- Courts apply a "totality of the circumstances" test in determining the question of voluntariness.

- In the "totality," courts consider various factors including factors particular to the suspect including "evidence of minimal schooling" and low intelligence.

- While absence of knowledge of the right to refuse consent is a factor to be considered, consent can be valid even when the defendant is unaware of the right to refuse.

- Other relevant factors include the attitude and actions of the police (i.e., did they have guns drawn, did they request or demand permission to search).

- Third parties can sometimes consent to a search when they have common authority over the place or things to be searched.

- If the police reasonably believe that a person who gives them consent has the right to consent, then the court might uphold the search even though the person who gave the consent lacked common authority over the place or things to be searched.

5. Administrative Inspections

Administrative agencies regularly conduct various types of inspections. For example, health inspectors enter restaurants to determine whether food preparation and service areas are clean, as well as to make sure that food is being kept in healthy conditions. OSHA inspectors examine construction and factory sites to make sure that workers are employed in safe and healthy conditions. In some instances, administrative officials seek to enter people's homes or yards (e.g., child welfare officials enter a house looking for abused or neglected children).

Until the 1960s, there was doubt about whether the Fourth Amendment applied to administrative inspections. No one doubted that the Fourth Amendment applied when the police searched homes or businesses for evidence of criminal activity. However, many commentators argued that administrative inspections were fundamentally different than police searches, and were not therefore subject to Fourth Amendment requirements.

The Court resolved this doubt in *Camara v. Municipal Court*, 387 U.S. 523 (1967), by holding that administrative inspections are subject to the Fourth Amendment. The case involved a San Francisco ordinance that authorized city inspectors to enter buildings "to perform any duty imposed upon them by the Municipal Code." When Camara refused to allow inspectors to enter his apartment without a warrant, he was charged and ultimately convicted of violating that part of the ordinance which made it illegal to refuse to permit a lawful inspection. In overturning the conviction, the Court emphasized that the Fourth Amendment was designed to safeguard the privacy of individuals against "arbitrary invasions by governmental officials," and reiterated its long-standing preference for warrants.

Camara overruled the Court's prior decision in *Frank v. State of Maryland*, 359 U.S. 360 (1959). In that case, the Court upheld a municipal inspection system noting that such systems "touch at most upon the periphery" of the "protection against official intrusion." In *Franks*, the Court distinguished between searches for evidence of "criminal action" and inspections designed "merely to determine whether physical conditions exist which do not comply with minimum standards prescribed in local regulatory ordinances." While agreeing that administrative inspections are "less hostile" than other inspections, the *Camara* Court flatly rejected the idea that the Fourth Amendment interests were at the "periphery":

> [E]ven the most law-abiding citizen has a very tangible interest in limiting the circumstances under which the sanctity of his home may be broken by official authority, for the possibility of criminal entry under the guise of official sanction is a serious threat to personal and family security.

The Court noted that violations of many ordinances could lead to criminal charges, and that mere refusal to allow entry could lead to fines or imprisonment.

The *Camara* Court also rejected the argument that the warrant requirement could not effectively function in the administrative context. The government had argued that administrative inspections are not based on probable cause, but on broad factors such as an area's age and condition, and that the probable cause standard is difficult to apply in such contexts unless judges "rubber stamp" administrative decisions. The Court disagreed, noting that the purposes of the Fourth Amendment are served by requiring a warrant in this context. The warrant is important because it notifies the homeowner regarding the purpose of and authorization for the inspection and limits of the inspector's power. In addition, the warrant serves as a check on administrative discretion by requiring a neutral and disinterested magistrate to determine whether the inspection is warranted.

An important aspect of the *Camara* decision was the balancing of competing interests. In determining whether the search was "reasonable," and in deciding what procedural requirements should be imposed, the Court balanced the governmental interest against the private interest. The Court viewed the governmental interest in administrative inspections as one in ensuring "city-wide compliance with minimum physical standards for private property" and in preventing "the unintentional development of conditions which are hazardous to public health and safety." The Court noted that administrative inspections focus on avoiding such things as fire, epidemics and unsightly conditions. At the same time, the Court recognized that administrative searches involve "significant intrusions" on individual privacy, and held that warrants help protect individual security.

After balancing these interests, the Court held that the Fourth Amendment imposed a warrant requirement on administrative inspections. In addition, the Court held that administrative inspections should be based on probable cause. This latter aspect of the holding was striking given that the Court recognized that "the only effective way to seek universal compliance with the minimum standards required by municipal codes is through routine periodic inspections of all structures." Strict application of the probable cause requirement would make it very difficult for administrative officials to periodically inspect all structures. How, for example, would administrative officials be able to show that they had "probable cause" to believe that defective conditions existed at every property?

The Court solved this dilemma by altering the probable cause requirement. Historically, the probable cause requirement had been applied in a defendant specific/place specific way. In other words, even if the government could show that a particular area suffered from a high crime rate, the government could not search any particular person or building in that area without an adequate basis for believing that the particular person or building to be searched was involved in criminal activity or contained contraband. In *Camara*, the Court did not require a building specific showing of probable cause for building inspections. Instead, the Court held that the decision to inspect all buildings in a particular area could be based on an assessment of "conditions in the area as a whole, not on its knowledge of conditions in each particular building." In other words, even if a recently renovated building was in a run-down area, administrative officials might be free to inspect that building even though there was no indication or likelihood of a defective condition in that particular building.

Camara held that "area inspections" required reasonable legislative or administrative standards. Such standards need not focus on the condition of the building in question, but could focus on general criteria such as "the passage of time, the nature of the building (*e.g.*, a multifamily apartment house), or the condition of the entire area." In the Court's view, this revised probable cause standard served a valid purpose by guaranteeing "that a decision to search private property is justified by a reasonable governmental interest."

In altering the probable cause requirement, the Court resorted to the balancing test discussed earlier. The Court balanced the need to search "against the invasion which the search entails." The Court found that administrative inspections "have a long history of judicial and public acceptance," and the Court doubted that "any other canvassing technique would achieve acceptable results." The Court noted that many conditions (i.e., faulty wiring) "are not observable from outside the building and indeed may not be apparent to the inexpert occupant himself." In addition, the Court noted that administrative inspections are not focused on the discovery of evidence, and "involve a relatively limited invasion of the urban citizen's [privacy]."

Despite *Camara's* holding, most administrative inspections continue to take place without a warrant. Although homeowners and businessmen are free to insist upon a warrant, they rarely do. Instead, they consent to warrantless administrative inspections. Indeed, many industry groups encourage their members to give consent. By consenting, the business puts the inspector in a better mood and (hopefully) the inspector will find fewer violations.

The Court also recognized that there are a number of situations when warrantless inspections are constitutionally permissible. For example, a warrant is not required in "emergency situations" involving the seizure of unwholesome food, smallpox vaccinations, health quarantines, or the summary destruction of tubercular cattle.

In addition, the Court has established an exception to the warrant requirement for certain "closely regulated" businesses. As the Court stated in *Marshall v. Barlow's, Inc.*, 436 U.S. 307 (1978), "Certain industries have such a history of government oversight that no reasonable expectation of privacy could exist for a proprietor over the stock of such an enterprise." The closely regulated business exception was first recognized in *Colonnade Catering Corp. v. United States*, 397 U.S. 72 (1970), a case that involved the warrantless search of a catering business pursuant to several federal revenue statutes relating to liquor dealers. Although the Court invalidated the search on other grounds, it held that the liquor industry was "long subject to close supervision and inspection." In *Donovan v. Dewey*, 452 U.S. 594 (1981), the Court held that underground and surface mines qualified as closely regulated businesses. Likewise, in *United States v. Biswell*, 406 U.S. 311 (1972), a case that involved a warrantless inspection of the premises of a pawnshop operator who was federally licensed to sell sporting weapons, the Court upheld a warrantless inspection: "When a dealer chooses to engage in this pervasively regulated business and to accept a federal license, he does so with the knowledge that his business records, firearms, and ammunition will be subject to effective inspection." However, as the Court recognized in *Marshall v. Barlow's Inc.*, not all businesses can be regarded as "closely regulated." In that case, the Court refused to permit warrantless inspections of all businesses for Occupational Safety and Health Act purposes.

The Court has held that business owners who engage in closely regulated businesses have a "reduced expectation of privacy." As a result, in this "special needs" situation, the Court has upheld warrantless searches provided that certain criteria are met: there must be a "substantial government interest that informs the regulatory scheme pursuant to which the inspection is made"; the warrantless inspections must be "necessary to further [the] regulatory scheme," and the statute must provide certainty and regularity results in "a constitutionally adequate substitute for a warrant." In other words, "the regulatory statute must perform the two basic functions of a warrant: it must advise the owner of the commercial premises that the search is being made pursuant to the law and has a properly defined scope, and it must limit the discretion of the inspecting officers." In addition, the statute must limit the discretion of inspectors by time, place, and scope. For example, in *Dewey*, the Court held that forcing mine inspectors to obtain a warrant before every inspection "might alert mine owners or operators to the impending inspection, thereby frustrating the purposes of the Mine Safety and Health Act—to detect and thus to deter safety and health violations."

The outer limits of the "closely regulated" industry exception were established in *New York v. Burger*, 482 U.S. 691 (1987). That case involved a junkyard that was in the business of dismantling cars and selling car parts. Police officers from the New York City

Police Department sought to inspect the junkyard pursuant to a New York law that authorized warrantless inspections of junkyards. During the inspection of Burger's business, the officers copied down the vehicle identification numbers on a number of vehicles that were subsequently determined to be stolen. Based on this evidence, Burger was charged with possession of stolen property and operation of a junkyard in non-compliance with state law (requiring the maintenance of a "police book" etc.).

In upholding the search, the Court held that junkyards qualified as "closely regulated" businesses because, in addition to other requirements, junkyards were required to maintain a police book showing their acquisition and disposition of motor vehicles and vehicle parts, and they were required to make these records and inventory available for inspection by the police and other governmental agents. The Court concluded that junkyard businesses qualified as "closely regulated" even though junkyards and vehicle dismantlers had not been in existence very long and therefore did not have a long history of regulation. The Court viewed the industry as similar to secondhand shops and general junkyards which had "long have been subject to regulation." As a result, the Court found that junkyard owners engaged in dismantling have a reduced expectation of privacy.

After concluding that dismantling was a closely regulated business, the Court examined the New York statute to determine whether it met the three criteria for warrantless inspections of closely regulated businesses. The Court found a "substantial interest" in regulating the vehicle-dismantling and automobile-junkyard industry "because motor vehicle theft has increased in the State and because the problem of theft is associated with this industry." The Court held that the state could reasonably find that regulation of the vehicle-dismantling industry "reasonably serves" the substantial interest in eradicating automobile theft: "[S]tolen cars and parts often pass quickly through junkyards, and frequent, unannounced inspections 'are necessary in order to detect them' "In addition, the statute provided a "constitutionally adequate substitute for a warrant." The statute informed the operator of a vehicle dismantling business that inspections would be made on a regular basis and provided details regarding the scope of the inspections. Finally, the Court held that the "time, place, and scope" of the inspection was limited "to place appropriate restraints upon the discretion of the inspecting officers." Inspections were limited to regular business hours, and the scope of the search was narrowly defined: the inspectors could examine the records, as well as "any vehicles or parts of vehicles which are subject to the record keeping requirements of this section and which are on the premises."

The *Burger* decision was extraordinary because the search did not involve ordinary administrative inspections by administrative officials, but instead involved police searches for evidence of criminal activity. Nevertheless, the Court upheld the police search as an administrative inspection: "a State can address a major social problem both by way of an administrative scheme and through penal sanctions." "[S]o long as a regulatory scheme is properly administrative, it is not rendered illegal by the fact that the inspecting officer has the power to arrest individuals for violations other than those created by the scheme itself."

Justice Brennan, dissenting, questioned whether vehicle dismantlers really qualify as closely regulated businesses. He noted that the regulations governing their existence were not extensive:

[Few] substantive qualifications are required of an aspiring vehicle dismantler; no regulation governs the condition of the premises, the method of operation, the hours of operation, the equipment utilized, etc. This scheme stands in marked contrast to, *e.g.*, the mine safety regulations relevant in *Donovan v. Dewey*.

In addition, he questioned whether there was any assurance that inspections would be conducted on a regular basis, or at all. In other words, the statute provided no constitutionally adequate substitute for a warrant. Finally, he noted that the law authorized searches intended solely to uncover evidence of criminal acts: "[T]he State has used an administrative scheme as a pretext to search without probable cause for evidence of criminal violations."

In *United States v. Parker*, 583 F.3d 1049 (8th Cir. 2009), the court held that interstate trucking is a closely regulated industry so that state officials can stop truckers at checkpoints and conduct random inquiries regarding compliance with state truck regulation laws:

"[C]losely regulated' industr[ies have] a reduced expectation of privacy." Therefore, closely regulated industries may be subject to warrantless searches of property, if "the rules governing the search offer an adequate substitute for the fourth amendment warrant requirement." To qualify as a valid substitute, the rules governing the search must first provide adequate notice by being "sufficiently comprehensive and defined that the owner of commercial property cannot help but be aware that his property will be subject to periodic inspections undertaken for specific purposes." Second, the rules must limit the discretion of inspecting officers "in time, place, and scope." This court has held that commercial trucking is considered one of these "closely regulated" areas. . .

In *Parker*, a police officer made a random check of a truck that was pulling a trailer containing three vehicles: a 2001 Ford Excursion, a 1995 Nissan Quest, and a 2000 Chevrolet Silverado. The check was a "Level 1 inspection" under the North American Standard Inspection Program (NASIP) that involved a check of the driver's logbook, bills of lading, insurance, and license. During the stop, the officer determined that the driver did not have a commercial license, and that his logbook was not up-to-date, and ordered defendant not to proceed for the next 10 hours. Although the officer did not require defendant to remain with the truck, he did remain and ultimately consented to a search of vehicles that he was transporting (which were found to contain contraband drugs).

POINTS TO REMEMBER

- Administrative inspections are subject to the Fourth Amendment's prohibition against unreasonable searches and seizures.

- Before the government can compel a person or business to submit to an administrative inspection, the government must obtain a warrant based on probable cause.

- However, the definition of probable cause has been redefined in this area of the law to include "reasonable legislative or administrative standards" for periodic inspections.

- As in other areas of the law, warrants might not be required when an emergency situation is involved.

- Warrants are not required for inspections of "closely regulated" businesses.

6. Stop and Frisk

Although the "stop and frisk" exception is one of the more recent exceptions to the warrant requirement, it has reshaped Fourth Amendment law.

The exception was created in *Terry v. State of Ohio*, 392 U.S. 1 (1968). In that case, a police officer observed suspicious behavior (three men appeared to be casing a business) and became concerned that a robbery was about to take place. Since robbers carry guns, the officer believed that the men were armed. The officer approached the men and asked for their names. When the men gave only a "mumbled" response, the officer grabbed Terry, spun him around, and patted down the outside of his clothing revealing a revolver. The officer then "patted down" the other two men and found a second weapon. The officer arrested the men and charged them with carrying concealed weapons.

In upholding the officer's actions, the Court provided detailed guidance regarding police-citizen street encounters. At the outset, the Court emphasized that Terry was protected by the Fourth Amendment as he walked on public streets. It held that the "stop" involved a "seizure" and the "frisk" involved a "search." A seizure occurs when the police "accost an individual and restrain his freedom to walk away," and a search occurs when the police simply explore a person's outer clothing in an effort to discover weapons.

The Court then focused on whether the officer had acted "reasonably" as that term is defined in the Fourth Amendment. The Court concluded that a stop and frisk could not be regarded as a petty indignity, and in fact constituted a "serious intrusion . . . upon the sanctity of the person, which may inflict great indignity and arouse strong resentment." The stop and frisk was a procedure that was not to be "undertaken lightly." Although the Court reiterated its preference for a warrant, it recognized that there was an "entire rubric of police conduct—necessarily swift action predicated upon the on-the-spot observations of the officer on the beat—which historically has not been, and as a practical matter could not be, subjected to the warrant procedure." The Court held that the "stop" and "frisk" fell within this "rubric" of police action.

In reaching its conclusion, the Court applied the "need" versus "intrusion" balancing test which it had previously announced in *Camara*. In other words, the Court examined the "governmental interest which allegedly justifies official intrusion upon the constitutionally protected interests of the private citizen." In applying the test, the Court found a governmental interest in "effective crime prevention and detection." Since the officer believed that a "stick-up" might be in progress, and that the suspects might be armed and dangerous, the officer was justified in his perception that immediate action was needed. Since the officer did not have "probable cause" to arrest the suspects, he began with a limited intrusion as he approached Terry and his co-conspirators and asked them to identify themselves. Only when he received an unsatisfactory response did the officer seize Terry and pat him down. The Court concluded that these actions were justified by the circumstances. If the officer had waited until the group implemented their robbery plan, there was a serious risk that "the suspects might [have] endanger[ed] others or the police officer in the meantime." Accordingly, the officer was entitled to take steps "to assure himself that the person with whom he is dealing is not armed with a weapon that could unexpectedly and fatally be used against him [or others]."

The Court held that the officer's authority was limited. As with all exceptions to the warrant requirement, a stop and frisk must "be strictly circumscribed by the exigencies which justify its initiation." Since the stop and frisk exception is designed simply to allow the police to protect themselves and others from a suspect who might be armed and dangerous, the search must be confined to an intrusion designed to discover hidden weapons. The search in *Terry* was permissible because the officer only searched the outer clothing until he found a weapon, and therefore "confined his search strictly to what was minimally necessary to learn whether the men were armed and to disarm them once he discovered the weapons." In other words, he did "not conduct a general exploratory search for whatever evidence of criminal activity he might find."

Before the police can invoke the stop and frisk exception, they must be able to point to "specific and articulable facts which, taken together with rational inferences from those facts, reasonably warrant that intrusion." And, in deciding whether action is warranted, the courts apply an objective standard: "would the facts available to the officer at the moment of the seizure or the search 'warrant a man of reasonable caution in the belief' that the action taken was appropriate?" In other words, police cannot intrude on individual rights based only on "inarticulate hunches" or subjective good faith. In *Terry*, this standard was met because the officer observed the suspects walking up and down the street in a manner which suggested that they might be "casing" a store in preparation for an armed robbery.

The Court also recognized that different investigative scenarios might produce a different balancing of the interests. The Court distinguished a stop and frisk from an arrest. The Court viewed an arrest as a completely different form of intrusion than a limited search for weapons, and suggested that "the interests each is designed to serve are likewise quite different." An arrest is "the initial stage of a criminal prosecution" and one that "is inevitably accompanied by future interference with the individual's freedom of movement, whether or not trial or conviction ultimately follows." Accordingly, a higher standard of proof—probable cause—is required. By contrast, the Court regarded a "protective search for weapons" as "a brief, though far from inconsiderable, intrusion upon the sanctity of the person." Moreover, when a protective search is involved, the officer may be aware of danger long before there is probable cause for an arrest. The Court concluded that a protective search is permissible when the officer has reason to believe that he is "dealing with an armed and dangerous individual." Even if the officer is not certain, a protective search might be permissible if "a reasonably prudent man in the circumstances would be warranted in the belief that his safety or that of others was in danger" considering "the specific reasonable inferences which he is entitled to draw from the facts in light of his experience."

In subsequent cases, the Court has routinely required that police action be based on objective criteria rather than simply a "hunch." In *Florida v. J.L.*, 529 U.S. 266 (2000), the police received an anonymous tip that a young black male at a bus stop was wearing a plaid shirt and carrying a gun. Two officers responded, found three young black males at the stop, including one who was wearing a plaid shirt. Apart from the tip, the officers had no reason to believe that any of the males were engaged in illegal conduct. The officers immediately frisked defendant and found a gun in his pocket. The Court invalidated the search: "All the police had to go on in this case was the bare report of an unknown, unaccountable informant who neither explained how he knew about the gun nor supplied any basis for believing he had inside information about J.L." The Court also rejected the state's contention that *Terry* should encompass a "firearms exception" permitting police to stop and frisk individuals for firearms.

Likewise, in *Sibron v. New York*, 392 U.S. 40 (1968), a companion case to *Terry*, a police officer observed Sibron from 4:00 P.M. to midnight, and saw him converse with six or eight persons whom the officer knew to be narcotics addicts. Late in the evening, the officer saw Sibron enter a restaurant and speak with three known narcotics addicts. The officer could not hear any of the conversations, and did not see "anything pass between Sibron and any of the others." At that point, the officer asked Sibron to come outside and he stated "You know what I am after." Sibron then said something inaudible and reached into his pocket. Immediately, the officer thrust his hand into the pocket discovering heroin. The Court concluded that the officer had acted impermissibly:

> The suspect's mere act of talking with a number of known narcotics addicts over an eight-hour period no more gives rise to reasonable fear of life or limb on the part of the police officer than it justifies an arrest for committing a crime.

The Court concluded that, not only did the officer lack adequate grounds for the search, but the search went beyond the scope of a *Terry* search ("with no attempt at an initial limited exploration for arms, Patrolman Martin thrust his hand into Sibron's pocket and took from him envelopes of heroin."). Justice Black dissented: "It seems to me to be a reasonable inference that [Sibron] might well be reaching for a gun. A policeman under such circumstances has to act in a split second; delay may mean death for him."

In some cases, the Court has assumed that an armed suspect is "dangerous" based on the circumstances. In *Michigan v. Long*, 463 U.S. 1032 (1983), deputies saw Long's car traveling "erratically" at excessive speed. When the car turned into a side road and swerved into a ditch, the officers stopped to investigate. Long appeared to be "under the influence of something" and both officers observed a large hunting knife on the floorboard of the driver's side of the car. The officers then subjected Long to a *Terry* frisk which revealed no weapons, and they also searched his vehicle for weapons. In the car, they found marijuana. The Court upheld the search and Long's conviction for possession:

> [R]oadside encounters between police and suspects are especially hazardous, and . . . danger may arise from the possible presence of weapons in the area surrounding a suspect. These principles compel our conclusion that the search of the passenger compartment of an automobile, limited to those areas in which a weapon may be placed or hidden, is permissible if the police officer possesses a reasonable belief based on "specific and articulable facts which, taken together with the rational inferences from those facts, reasonably warrant" the officers in believing that the suspect is dangerous and the suspect may gain immediate control of weapons. "[T]he issue is whether a reasonably prudent man in the circumstances would be warranted in the belief that his safety or that of others was in danger." * * *

The Court concluded that the standard was met given the late hour, the rural nature of the area, the fact that Long was intoxicated, and the fact that he possessed a weapon.

The scope of a protective search is relatively limited. As *Sibron* illustrates, although an officer can "search" a suspect by patting down his outer clothing, the officer cannot reach inside the clothing or pockets unless and until the pat down reveals a weapon. Nevertheless, in *Adams v. Williams*, 407 U.S. 143 (1972), the Court upheld such an intrusion. In the middle of the night, a police officer was in a high crime area when he was informed that an individual seated in a nearby vehicle was carrying narcotics and had a gun at his waist. After calling for assistance, the officer approached the vehicle to investigate. The officer tapped on the car window and asked the driver to open the door. When the driver rolled down the window instead, the officer reached into the car and removed a fully loaded revolver from the driver's waistband. The gun had not been visible to the officer from outside the car, but it was in precisely the place indicated by the informant. The officer then arrested the driver for unlawful possession of the pistol. A search incident to arrest found substantial quantities of heroin on the driver's person and in the car, as well as a machete and a second revolver hidden in the automobile. The Court upheld the search and seizure noting that the informant's tip provided adequate cause. Although the officer exceeded the ordinary scope of a frisk, the Court upheld the officer's actions given the unique circumstances: "[T]he policeman's action in reaching to the spot where the gun was thought to be hidden constituted a limited intrusion designed to insure his safety, and we conclude that it was reasonable."

In *Illinois v. Wardlow*, 528 U.S. 119 (2000), while police officers were patrolling in a heavy narcotics trafficking area, the officers saw defendant flee when he saw them. After the officers caught defendant, they subjected him to a pat-down search for weapons. During the frisk, the officer squeezed a bag that defendant was carrying and felt a heavy, hard object similar to the shape of a gun. The officer then opened the bag and discovered a .38–caliber handgun with five live rounds of ammunition. Relying on *Terry*, the Court upheld the search: "[N]ervous, evasive behavior is a pertinent factor in determining reasonable suspicion. Headlong flight—wherever it occurs—is the consummate act of evasion: it is not necessarily indicative of wrongdoing, but it is certainly suggestive of such. [Officer] Nolan was justified in suspecting that Wardlow was involved in criminal activity, and, therefore, in investigating further."

POINTS TO REMEMBER

- Even though the Court has expressed a preference for warrants, it has upheld various warrantless searches and seizures under a "reasonableness" standard.

- In deciding whether a search or a seizure is "reasonable," the Court balances the "need" for the search against the "intrusion" caused thereby.

- Using the "need" versus "intrusion" test, the Court has upheld stop and frisks.

- The stop and frisk implicates the Fourth Amendment because a stop is a "seizure" and a pat down or frisk is a "search."

- A stop and frisk is permissible when a police officer reasonably believes that criminal activity is afoot and that the suspect is armed and dangerous.

- Before the police can conduct a stop and frisk, there must be an "objective" basis for believing that the stop and frisk is necessary.

a. Other Investigatory Searches and Seizures

In *Terry,* the Court recognized that there are many different types of seizures ranging from an investigatory stop to an arrest. Most seizures are investigative in nature and can be relatively brief. Roadside stops usually fit this description. But police also "seize" individuals for fingerprinting, lineups and interrogation purposes. These seizures are subject to differing constitutional requirements.

The definition of "seizure." The first task in any case is to determine whether a "seizure" has occurred. In *California v. Hodari D.,* 499 U.S. 621 (1991), the Court provided guidance on this issue. In that case, police officers were on patrol in a high crime area when they saw a group of youths near a car. When the youth saw the officers, they panicked and ran. Hodari D. was among the youth and the officers chased him. As an officer came close to catching him, Hodari tossed away what turned out to be cocaine. A moment later, the officer tackled Hodari and handcuffed him. The Court concluded that Hodari had not been seized when he abandoned the cocaine (and, therefore, that the Court need not determine whether the seizure was reasonable or whether the evidence should be excluded under the "fruit of the poisonous tree" doctrine). The Court suggested that the word "seizure" has always been defined to mean a "taking possession." To constitute an arrest, "the mere grasping or application of physical force with lawful authority, whether or not it succeeded in subduing the arrestee, was sufficient." The difficulty for Hodari was that, at the time he threw away the cocaine, he had not been grasped or subjected to any physical force, but had simply been subjected to a "show of authority." The Court concluded that there was no seizure when Hodari refused to yield to that show of authority. In the Court's view, an arrest required either "physical force" or "submission to the assertion of authority." Justice Stevens dissented. "[T]he same issue would arise if the show of force took the form of a command to 'freeze,' a warning shot, or the sound of sirens accompanied by a patrol car's flashing lights. . . [T]he constitutionality of a police officer's show of force should be measured by the conditions that exist at the time of the officer's action. [The] character of the citizen's response should not govern the constitutionality of the officer's conduct."

Hodari D.'s logic has been applied in other cases as well. In *Michigan v. Chesternut,* 486 U.S. 567 (1988), when Chesternut saw a patrol car nearing the corner where he stood, he turned and began to run. The officers followed respondent around the corner "to see where he was going" and drove alongside him for a short distance. During this time, the officers saw Chesternut discard a number of packets that were found to contain illegal narcotics. The Court concluded that Chesternut had not been seized when he threw away the narcotics:

> [T]he police conduct involved here would not have communicated to the reasonable person an attempt to capture or otherwise intrude upon respondent's freedom of movement. The record does not reflect that the police activated a siren or flashers; or that they commanded respondent to halt, or displayed any weapons; or that they operated the car in an aggressive manner to block respondent's course or otherwise control the direction or speed of his movement. While the very presence of a police car driving parallel to a running pedestrian could be somewhat intimidating, this kind of police presence does not, standing alone, constitute a seizure. . .

The Court has distinguished the *Hodari D.* and *Chesternut* situations from the slightly different situation found in *United States v. Mendenhall*, 446 U.S. 544 (1980). In *Mendenhall*, two Drug Enforcement Agency (DEA) agents observed Mendenhall disembarking from an airplane. Believing that her conduct was characteristic of persons unlawfully carrying narcotics, the agents approached her, identified themselves, and asked to see her identification and airline ticket. She produced her driver's license, which bore the name of Sylvia Mendenhall, and stated that she resided at the address appearing on the license. Because her airline ticket was issued in a different name, the agent inquired about the discrepancy between the license and the ticket, and Mendenhall stated that she "just felt like using that name." When one of the agents stated that he was a federal narcotics agent, Mendenhall "became quite shaken, extremely nervous. She had a hard time speaking." At that point, the agent asked Mendenhall to accompany him to the airport DEA office for further questions. She made no verbal response to the request, but went with the officer. The issue was whether Mendenhall had been seized or whether she went to the office voluntarily. At the office, she consented to a strip search even though she had illegal narcotics in her possession.

The Court found that there was no seizure (had she been seized, that fact would have been relevant to the question of whether her consent was voluntary). In deciding the case, the Court held that a seizure occurs only when the police "by means of physical force or show of authority," have in some way restrained the liberty of a citizen. There is no seizure when the individual "remains free to disregard the questions and walk away." The question is whether "in view of all of the circumstances surrounding the incident, a reasonable person would have believed that he was not free to leave." This determination should be made under a "totality of the circumstances" test with the government bearing the burden of proof. Relevant factors include "the threatening presence of several officers, the display of a weapon by an officer, some physical touching of the person of the citizen, or the use of language or tone of voice indicating that compliance with the officer's request might be compelled." Absent some evidence of coercion, there is no seizure.

The Court concluded that Mendenhall had not been seized. The Court noted that the encounter occurred in a public area, that the agents were not wearing uniforms, did not display weapons, and did not "summon" Mendenhall but instead approached her and identified themselves as federal agents. In addition, the agents "requested" rather than demanded to see Mendenhall's identification and ticket. As a result, the Court concluded that Mendenhall had no reason to believe "that she was not free to end the conversation in the concourse and proceed on her way," and so she had not been seized. Even though Mendenhall's actions appeared to be inconsistent with her self interest (since she agreed to a strip search when she had contraband secreted in her clothes), the Court concluded that this fact was not enough to indicate a seizure. "It may happen that a person makes statements to law enforcement officials that he later regrets, but the issue in such cases is not whether the statement was self-protective, but rather whether it was made voluntarily." The fact that Mendenhall was not explicitly told that she was free to leave was not determinative.

The Court also held that the movement from the public area to the DEA office did not change the encounter to a seizure. In the Court's view, the agents simply "asked" Mendenhall to accompany them, and did not demand or use threats or a show of force. The Court rejected the argument that factors specific to Mendenhall suggested that the movement to the office involved a seizure. The facts showed that Mendenhall was 22 years old, female, black, had not graduated from high school, and was being confronted by white male officers. Mendenhall argued that, given her characteristics, the events would have appeared more coercive to someone like her. The Court disagreed concluding that none of these factors was "decisive," and that "the totality of the evidence" suggested that Mendenhall had voluntarily agreed to accompany the officers to the DEA office. Since the Court concluded that Mendenhall had not been seized, the Court found it unnecessary to determine whether her consent to the search was tainted by an unlawful detention. Justice White dissented. He argued that, although Mendenhall "was not told that she was under arrest, she in fact was not free to refuse to go to the DEA office . . . [T]he Government [cannot] rely solely on acquiescence to the officers' wishes to establish the requisite consent."

Florida v. Royer, 460 U.S. 491 (1983), was very similar to *Mendenhall*, but the Court distinguished the two cases. In *Royer*, a man was approached by the police who asked to see his license and airplane ticket, but did not return them to him. When the officer realized that Royer was traveling under an assumed name, they asked him to go with them to the DEA office at the airport. In addition, they removed Royer's luggage from the airplane and brought it to the office. There, Royer consented to a search of his suitcases. The Court held that Royer had been seized because the officers had kept his license and plane ticket and removed his luggage from the plane.

The Court has applied *Hodari D.* and *Mendenhall* to police interrogations that take place on buses. In *Florida v. Bostick*, 501 U.S. 429 (1991), two police officers boarded a bus during a stopover. The officers picked out Bostick (a passenger) and asked for permission to inspect his ticket and identification. The ticket matched Bostick's identification and both were given back to him. The officers then explained that they were narcotics agents looking for illegal drugs, and requested permission to search Bostick's luggage. The police specifically advised Bostick that he had the right to refuse consent, and they did not threaten him with a weapon. The Court concluded that Bostick had not been seized and that his consent was valid: "[When a] person is seated on a bus and has no desire to leave, the degree to which a reasonable person would feel that he or she could leave is not an accurate measure of the coercive effect of the encounter." Justice Marshall dissented:

> [A] passenger unadvised of his rights and otherwise unversed in constitutional law has no reason to know that the police cannot hold his refusal to cooperate against him. [O]fficers who conduct suspicionless, dragnet-style sweeps put passengers to the choice of cooperating or of exiting their buses and possibly being stranded in unfamiliar locations. It is exactly because this 'choice' is no 'choice' at all that police engage this technique. [The police may] continue to confront passengers without suspicion so long as they [take] simple steps, like advising the passengers confronted of their right to decline to be questioned, to dispel the aura of coercion and intimidation that pervades such encounters.

Bostick was followed by the holding in *United States v. Drayton*, 536 U.S. 194 (2002). The two cases were factually similar.

However, in *Drayton*, one officer positioned himself on the driver's seat (leaving the aisle and bus door open), and two officers went to the rear of the bus and began working their way towards the front speaking with passengers. The two officers positioned themselves behind the passengers to whom they were speaking (in an effort to avoid blocking the aisle). The officers did not tell the passengers that they were free to exit the bus even if they declined to coope-rate, and did not tell them that they could refuse to cooperate. In fact, some passengers did leave the bus to smoke a cigarette or ob-tain a snack. When the officers approached Drayton, they identified themselves, asked whether he had any bags, and asked for permis-sion to search them. Drayton gave consent and handed the bag to an officer. The officer then asked for permission to check Brown's person, and Brown responded "sure." Brown leaned forward, pulled a cell phone out of his pocket, and opened his jacket. One officer patted Brown down and "detected hard objects similar to drug packages detected on other occasions." The officer then arrested and handcuffed Brown, and removed him from the bus. The officer asked for permission to check Drayton, and Drayton lifted his hands apart from his legs. The officer patted Drayton down, and arrested him when the search revealed drugs. A subsequent search of both Brown and Drayton revealed that the hard objects were co-caine. When Drayton was prosecuted for conspiracy to distribute cocaine, Drayton argued that the consent was invalid because he had been seized. The Court disagreed.

The Court began by noting that police officers are free to ap-proach individuals and ask them questions without creating a "sei-zure." Applying a totality of the circumstances test, the Court reaf-firmed *Bostick's* conclusion that the proper focus should be on "whether a reasonable person would feel free to decline the officers' requests or otherwise terminate the encounter." The Court also held that officers do not have to advise suspects that they can refuse to cooperate or that they can refuse consent. The fact that the officer showed his badge was not enough, in and of itself, to convert this incident into a seizure. Even if the officers carried holstered fire-arms, this fact alone was insufficient to transform the incident into a seizure. Likewise, the officer's position at the front of the bus did not create a seizure because the officer "did nothing to intimidate passengers, and he said nothing to suggest that people could not exit and indeed he left the aisle clear."

The Court then addressed whether, after Brown was arrested, Drayton was seized when the officers approached him. Drayton ar-gued that, following Brown's arrest, "no reasonable person would feel free to terminate the encounter." The Court disagreed empha-sizing that the officer was polite to Drayton and did not indicate that Drayton was required to answer his questions. Indeed, the Court concluded that "Brown's arrest should have put Drayton on notice of the consequences of continuing the encounter by answering the officers' questions."

Justice Souter dissented. In his view, the police took control of the entire passenger compartment, and accosted passengers in extremely close quarters. "The reasonable inference was that the 'interdiction' was not a consensual exercise, but one the police would carry out whatever the circumstances; that they would prefer 'cooperation' but would not let the lack of it stand in their way." He went on to note that it "is very hard to imagine that either Brown or Drayton would have believed that he stood to lose nothing if he refused to cooperate with the police, or that he had any free choice to ignore the police altogether."

The Court has applied similar rules to immigration "sweeps" of factories. In *Immigration and Naturalization Service v. Delgado*, 466 U.S. 210 (1984), the INS surveyed the work force at a factory in search of illegal aliens. Although the survey was conducted pursuant to a warrant, some agents positioned themselves near the building exits while other agents fanned out through the factory to question employees at their work stations. The agents displayed badges, carried walkie-talkies, and wore holstered arms. The agents approached employees, identified themselves, and asked questions relating to their citizenship. If an employee's answers suggested that he was a United States citizen, the questioning ended. If the employee gave an uncredible response or admitted that he was an alien, the employee was asked to produce his immigration papers. During the survey, employees continued with their work and were free to walk around within the factory.

The Court rejected the employees' claim that they had been "seized" at the time of the questioning, concluding that, since the employees were at work, their freedom of movement was restricted "by the workers' voluntary obligations to their employers." Even though the INS posted agents at the doors, the Court concluded that this did not transform the situation into a seizure. In the court's view, the agents were there to insure that all employees were questioned, and the Court noted that, if "mere questioning does not constitute a seizure when it occurs inside the factory, it is no more a seizure when it occurs at the exits." The Court also rejected the argument that the way in which the surveys were conducted "created a psychological environment which made [employees] reasonably afraid they were not free to leave." Agents were only questioning employees and no employees were actually detained who did not flee or try to evade the agents. Even though the latter group was detained, the Court regarded them as distinguishable from those who did not. "[T]he encounters with the INS agents [were] classic consensual encounters rather than Fourth Amendment seizures." Justice Brennan concurred in part and dissented in part:

> "[It is] fantastic to conclude that a reasonable person could ignore all that was occurring throughout the factory and, when the INS agents reached him, have the temerity to believe that he was at liberty to refuse to answer their questions and walk away."

In *Brendlin v. California*, 551 U.S. 249 (2007), the Court held that a passenger in an automobile is "seized" when the police stop the automobile with lights and siren. In finding that a seizure occurred, the Court noted that an "officer who orders one particular car to pull over acts with an implicit claim of right based on fault of some sort, and a sensible person would not expect a police officer to allow people to come and go freely from the physical focal point of an investigation into faulty behavior or wrongdoing." It is "reasonable for passengers to expect that a police officer at the scene of a crime, arrest, or investigation will not let people move around in ways that could jeopardize his safety."

Whether a seizure has, or has not occurred, is important for a variety of reasons. In cases like *Mendenhall*, when a suspect has consented to a subsequent search, the existence of a "seizure" is relevant to the question of whether the consent was voluntary or coerced. If the seizure is illegal, that factor suggests coercion. In cases like *Hodari D.*, the question of whether there has been a seizure is also important. If Hodari D. had been seized when he abandoned the cocaine, the Court would have been forced to determine whether the seizure was legal or illegal. If the seizure was illegal, and discovery of the contraband was directly attributable to the seizure, then the evidence might be deemed "fruit of the poisonous tree" of the illegal seizure. As a result, the evidence might be subject to exclusion.

POINTS TO REMEMBER

- A "seizure" occurs when the police take "physical possession" of an individual.

- A seizure can also occur when a suspect voluntarily submits to a show of police authority.

- In the show of authority situation, the beginning of a seizure can be traced to the point when a reasonable person in the suspect's position would not feel free to leave.

- The determination of whether there is a "seizure" is determined by reference to the totality of circumstances.

- When INS agents "sweep" through a factory, there may or may not be a seizure depending on how the sweep is conducted.

- When the police enter a bus to question the occupants, there may or may not be a seizure depending on how the incident is handled.

Constitutional Requirements for Various Types of Seizures. As the foregoing discussion suggests, police-citizen encounters can take a variety of forms. Some of these interactions involve "seizures" while others do not. As we shall see, even when police conduct a seizure, the seizure can take many different forms. The task in this section is to examine the various types of seizures, and to determine the rules that apply to each type of seizure.

Arrests. The quintessential form of seizure is the "custodial arrest" which results in the individual being taken to the police station for booking. From *Watson*, we know that this most severe and intrusive form of seizure requires probable cause. Probable cause requires a showing of "reasonable cause" to believe that a crime has been committed and that the person to be arrested committed it.

Investigative Stops. At the other end of the spectrum, the least intrusive form of seizure is the so-called "investigative stop." An investigative stop occurs when the police "stop" an individual for questioning (or, perhaps, to issue a citation). By definition, an investigative stop is necessarily brief. Of course, the critical question in many situations is whether the suspect has been "seized" at all. If a police officer simply approaches an individual on the street to ask a few questions (or, in an airport, as occurred in *Mendenhall*), there may be no seizure if a reasonable person in the suspect's position would feel free to leave. As *Mendenhall* suggests, something more than a police-citizen interaction is required to constitute a seizure.

What is required for an "investigative stop?" *Mendenhall* tells us that this most minimal form of seizure need be justified by nothing more than a "reasonable suspicion" that defendant is involved in criminal activity. *Terry* supports *Mendenhall* and suggests that, if in addition to suspecting that an individual is engaged in criminal activity, the officer also has reason to believe that the suspect is "armed and dangerous," the officer can conduct a frisk.

"Reasonable suspicion" is determined using a totality of the circumstances standard: "Based upon [the] whole picture the detaining officers must have a particularized and objective basis for suspecting the particular person stopped of criminal activity." In *United States v. Sokolow*, 490 U.S. 1 (1989), the Court held that the "reasonable suspicion" standard involves "something more than an 'inchoate and unparticularized suspicion or hunch,' " but "considerably less than proof of wrongdoing by a preponderance of the evidence."

Delaware v. Prouse, 440 U.S. 648 (1979), provides guidance regarding the limits of vehicle stops. In that case, the officer admitted that he stopped Prouse merely to check his driver's license and registration. He also admitted that he did not have probable cause, and that he had not witnessed any evidence of suspicious activity. The Court invalidated the search balancing the governmental interest in the stop against the motorist's interest in privacy. The Court specifically rejected the state's argument that automobile stops could be justified as a means of promoting public safety on the roads. Although the Court recognized that vehicular traffic can present a "danger to life and property," and even though the Court agreed that the states have a "vital interest" in ensuring that drivers are licensed and that that vehicles are "fit for safe operation," the Court held that the state could use alternative mechanisms for ensuring these ends (e.g., the police could stop motorists for "observed violations" and could check licenses and registrations at that time). The Court also concluded that "the incremental contribution" of random stops was insufficient to justify giving police the "unbridled discretion" to stop motorists. Automobile travel is a "basic, pervasive, and often necessary mode of transportation to and from one's home, workplace, and leisure activities," and "many find a greater sense of security and privacy in traveling in an automobile than they do in exposing themselves by pedestrian or other modes of travel." The Court concluded that citizens should not be subjected to the possibility of "unfettered governmental intrusion" every time they enter an automobile.

In dicta, *Prouse* sanctioned some other warrantless, suspicionless, types of vehicle stops. For example, it concluded that states could maintain truck weigh-stations and inspection checkpoints without violating the Fourth Amendment. The Court recognized that some vehicles may be subjected to longer detention and more intrusive inspections than others.

Applying the Reasonable Suspicion Standard. In *Alabama v. White*, 496 U.S. 325 (1990), the Court held that police could rely on an anonymous tip in developing "reasonable suspicion." The Court suggested that "reasonable suspicion" depends on both the "quantity and quality" of the evidence. When an informant's tip is involved, "if a tip has a relatively low degree of reliability, more information will be required to establish the requisite quantum of suspicion than would be required if the tip were more reliable."

In *United States v. Sokolow*, 490 U.S. 1 (1989), the Court found a "reasonable suspicion of criminal activity" when a suspect (1) paid $2,100 for two airplane tickets from a roll of $20 bills; (2) traveled under a name that did not match the name under which his telephone number was listed; (3) his original destination was Miami, a source city for illicit drugs; (4) he stayed in Miami for only 48 hours, even though a round-trip flight from Honolulu to Miami takes 20 hours; (5) he appeared nervous during his trip; and (6) he checked none of his luggage.

In *Whren v. United States*, 517 U.S. 806 (1996), two undercover police officers were patrolling in a "high drug area." When they witnessed respondent driving in an unusual manner (he sat for an unusually long time at a stop sign, and then took off at a high rate of speed), they stopped him. Although respondents conceded that the officers had probable cause to stop them for traffic violations, they argued that it was a pretextual stop designed to search for drugs. The Court upheld the stop: "[Prior] cases foreclose any argument that the constitutional reasonableness of traffic stops depends on the actual motivations of the individual officers involved. [T]he Constitution prohibits selective enforcement [based] on considerations such as race. But the constitutional basis for objecting to intentionally discriminatory application of laws is the [Equal Protection Clause]. Subjective intentions play no role in ordinary, probable-cause Fourth Amendment analysis."

Vehicle Stops. Should investigative stops of individuals be treated differently than investigative stops of those who are found walking down public streets? Arguably, a stop of an automobile is more severe because the police usually stop a vehicle by turning on their lights (and, sometimes, their siren). From an individual standpoint, this stop is potentially more unsettling. On the other hand, the police may have a greater need for an investigative stop in this context. For example, if the police see someone driving erratically, or they believe that a suspect is involved in criminal activity, there may be a strong need for immediate action.

Questioning and Fingerprinting. Between an arrest and an investigative stop, there are many other types of seizures. In a number of cases, the Court has provided guidance regarding the rules applicable to these seizures. For example, in *Dunaway v. New York*,

442 U.S. 200 (1979), the Court held that, if the police want to pick up a suspect and take him to the station for questioning, they must have probable cause. The Court regarded this type of seizure as tantamount to an arrest. In *Davis v. Mississippi*, 394 U.S. 721 (1969), the Court held that probable cause is also required when the police want to pick up a suspect and take him to the station for fingerprinting. However, in *Hayes v. Florida*, 470 U.S. 811 (1985), in *dicta*, the Court suggested that when fingerprinting is done in the field, as part of a brief detention, it might be justified based on only a reasonable suspicion of criminal activity.

Requests for identification. When can the police request identification from a suspect? For a number of years, the Court's decisions limited the authority of police to demand identification from a suspect. Many of these cases were decided on vagueness grounds. For example, in *Kolender v. Lawson*, 461 U.S. 352 (1983), the Court struck down a criminal statute which required persons "who loiter or wander on the streets to provide a 'credible and reliable' identification and to account for their presence when requested by a peace officer under circumstances that would justify a stop under the standards of *Terry v. Ohio*." The Court concluded that the statute was unconstitutionally vague by "failing to clarify what is contemplated by the requirement that a suspect provide a 'credible and reliable' identification."

Brown v. Texas, 443 U.S. 47 (1979), also involved the identification issue. In that case, two officers were cruising in a patrol car when they observed appellant and another man walking in opposite directions away from one another in an alley. Although the two men were a few feet apart, the officers believed that the two had been together or were about to meet before the patrol car appeared. The officers stopped one of the men, and asked him to identify himself and explain what he was doing. The officer testified that he stopped the man because the situation "looked suspicious and we had never seen that subject in that area before." The area where appellant was stopped had a high incidence of drug traffic. However, the officers did not suspect appellant of any specific misconduct, nor did they have any reason to believe that he was armed. Appellant refused to identify himself and angrily asserted that the officers had no right to stop him. One officer then "frisked" the man, but found nothing. The man was then arrested under a state law which made it a crime for a person to refuse to give his name and address to an officer "who has lawfully stopped him and requested the information." The Court reversed his conviction finding that the officer did not have "a reasonable suspicion that he was involved in criminal conduct." Absent a reasonable suspicion, the individual interest in privacy outweighs the governmental interest in crime prevention.

However, in *Hiibel v. Sixth Judicial District Court*, 542 U.S. 177 (2004), the Court held that the police could demand identification from a suspect, and upheld an officer's decision to arrest for a refusal to comply with the demand. The Court noted that the Nevada law involved in that case was in the tradition of so-called "stop and identify" statutes which permit an officer to ask or require a suspect to disclose his identity. In addition, the Court distinguished the Nevada statute from the stop and identify laws struck down on vagueness grounds in prior cases such as *Papachristou v. Jacksonville*, 405 U.S. 156 (1972), *Brown v. Texas,* 443 U.S. 47 (1979), and *Kolender v. Lawson*, 461 U.S. 352 (1983). The Court upheld the request because it avoided vagueness problems in only requiring a suspect to reveal his name and in not requiring any particular form of identification. The Court relied on the *Terry* balancing test, and concluded that an "officer's reasonable suspicion that a person may be involved in criminal activity permits the officer to stop the person for a brief time and take additional steps to investigate further." The Court emphasized that questioning a suspect about his identity is routine, is accepted and serves important governmental interests of alerting an officer to whether a "suspect is wanted for another offense, or has a record of violence or mental disorder," and "may help clear a suspect and allow the police to concentrate their efforts elsewhere." The threat of criminal sanction helps ensure that the request for identity is complied with. In addition, the Court concluded that the request for identification did not change the nature of the stop itself: it does not change its duration or its location. The Court rejected the contention that the required disclosure of identity violated the Fifth Amendment privilege against compelled self-incrimination: "Answering a request to disclose a name is likely to be so insignificant in the scheme of things as to be incriminating only in unusual circumstances." The Court left open the possibility that "a case may arise where there is a substantial allegation that furnishing identity at the time of a stop would have given the police a link in the chain of evidence needed to convict the individual of a separate offense." Justice Stevens and Justice Breyer both dissented, arguing that the disclosure was incriminating.

Passenger Stop and Frisks. In *Arizona v. Johnson*, 555 U.S. 323 (2009), the question was whether a police officer, who made a valid stop of a motor vehicle, could frisk the passengers for weapons. The Court focused on the two *Terry* requirements: the officer must reasonably suspect that the person apprehended is committing or has committed a criminal offense, as well as that the suspect is armed and dangerous. The Court held that, in a traffic-stop situation, "a lawful investigatory stop-is met whenever it is lawful for police to detain an automobile and its occupants pending inquiry into a vehicular violation." In other words, there need not be evidence that the occupants were involved in other criminal activity. However, in order to justify a patdown of an individual driver or passenger during a traffic stop, "the police must harbor reasonable suspicion that the person subjected to the frisk is armed and dangerous."

POINTS TO REMEMBER

- Investigative "stops" or "seizures" that do not involve a frisk require only a reasonable suspicion that the person being stopped is engaged in criminal activity.

- Motorists cannot be randomly stopped to check their license and registration, but can only be stopped when there is a "reasonable suspicion" that they are involved in criminal activity.

- "Reasonable suspicion" is determined under a "totality of the circumstances" test.

- As a result, each case must be judged on its own facts.

- A suspect may not be forced to go to the police station for questioning or fingerprinting absent probable cause.

- However, if the fingerprinting is done in the field rather than at the station, it might be justified based on a "reasonable suspicion."

- The police may not stop individuals to demand identification absent a reasonable suspicion of criminal activity.

Scope and Length of Seizures. Even if an investigatory seizure is permissible, it must be appropriately limited. As we have seen, seizures take a variety of forms ranging from an investigative stop to a custodial arrest. In general, although the Court has upheld various types of stops, it has held that the length of the stop must be correlated to the nature of the stop. In other words, the length and scope of a seizure can vary depending on the circumstances.

As noted, an investigate stop must be "temporary and no longer than necessary to effectuate the purpose of the stop." The state bears the burden of proof on this issue. In *United States v. Sharpe*, 470 U.S. 675 (1985), the Court rejected a court of appeals decision holding that investigative stops could not last longer than twenty minutes. The Court concluded that there is "no rigid time" limit on *Terry* stops. In each case, the courts must consider, not only the length and intrusiveness of the stop, but also "the law enforcement purposes to be served by the stop as well as the time reasonably needed to effectuate those purposes." In light of this analysis, the question is whether the police "diligently pursued a means of investigation that was likely to confirm or dispel their suspicions quickly, during which time it was necessary to detain the defendant." "[The] question is not simply whether some other alternative was available, but whether the police acted unreasonably in failing to recognize or to pursue it."

In *Royer*, the officer's decision to remove him to the detective office rendered the seizure unreasonable. The Court suggested that "the investigative methods employed should be the least intrusive means reasonably available to verify or dispel the officer's suspicion in a short period of time," and the Court suggested that removal to an office was too intrusive. The Court suggested that the police could have confirmed or denied their suspicions through the use of a trained dog.

In *United States v. Sokolow*, 490 U.S. 1 (1989), believing that Sokolow was a drug courier, DEA agents approached him during a stopover in Los Angeles. Sokolow "appeared to be very nervous and was looking all around the waiting area." Later that day, when Sokolow arrived in Honolulu, he proceeded to the street and tried to hail a cab (he did not stop for luggage because he had none), four DEA agents approached him, displayed credentials, and moved Sokolow back onto the sidewalk. One asked Sokolow for his airline ticket and identification, and Sokolow said that he had neither. Sokolow was escorted to the DEA office at the airport. There, his luggage was examined by a narcotics detection dog, which alerted on Sokolow's brown shoulder bag. The agents arrested respondent and obtained a warrant to search the shoulder bag. They found no illicit drugs, but the bag did contain several suspicious documents indicating respondent's involvement in drug trafficking. The agents had the dog reexamine the remaining luggage, and this time the dog alerted on a larger bag. By now, it was late evening and the police could not obtain a second warrant. They allowed respondent to leave for the night, but kept his luggage. The next morning, the agents obtained a warrant and found 1,063 grams of cocaine inside the bag.

Respondent challenged the search on the basis that the police failed to use "the least intrusive means available to verify or dispel their suspicions that he was smuggling narcotics." The Court rejected the challenge and qualified *Royer's* statement about using the least intrusive means available: "That statement, however, was directed at the length of the investigative stop, not at whether the police had a less intrusive means to verify their suspicions before stopping Royer. The reasonableness of the officer's decision to stop a suspect does not turn on the availability of less intrusive investigatory techniques. Such a rule would unduly hamper the police's ability to make swift, on-the-spot decisions—here, respondent was about to get into a taxicab—and it would require courts to indulge in 'unrealistic second-guessing.' "

A number of cases have involved the use of so-called drug courier profiles. In both *Royer* and *Mendenhall*, these profiles provided the basis for the stop. In *United States v. Sokolow*, 490 U.S. 1 (1989), the Court upheld the use of so-called "drug courier profiles" like the one used in *Royer*: "A court sitting to determine the existence of reasonable suspicion must require the agent to articulate the factors leading to that conclusion, but the fact that these factors may be set forth in a 'profile' does not somehow detract from their evidentiary significance as seen by a trained agent."

POINTS TO REMEMBER

- Although there is "no rigid time" limit on *Terry* stops, an investigate stop must be "temporary and no longer than necessary to effectuate the purpose of the stop."

- In deciding whether a stop is excessive, the courts must consider, not only the length and intrusiveness of the stop, but also "the law enforcement purposes to be served by the stop as well as the time reasonably needed to effectuate those purposes."

- The ultimate question is whether the police "diligently pursued a means of investigation that was likely to confirm or dispel their suspicions quickly, during which time it was necessary to detain the defendant."

- In *Royer*, the officer's decision to remove him to the DEA office rendered the seizure unreasonable.

Special Rules for Special Situations. The Court has also created a number of special rules that apply to searches and seizures that occur in the home or other special contexts. From earlier readings, you know that the police cannot arrest an individual at home, or at the home of another, without a warrant. But, even if the police have a warrant, a number of other questions arise. Can the police "seize" the owner of the home when they execute a search warrant? Can they "seize" others who are present on the premises? Can the police search the premises to protect themselves against potential threats?

In a number of cases, the Court has answered these questions. For example, in *Michigan v. Summers*, 452 U.S. 692 (1981), the occupant of a house was detained while a search warrant for the house was being executed. The Court held that the warrant made the occupant sufficiently suspect to justify his temporary seizure: the "limited intrusion on the personal security" of the person detained was justified "by such substantial law enforcement interests" that the seizure could be made on articulable suspicion not amounting to probable cause.

Sometimes, when the police execute a warrant, they find others present on the scene, or they fear the presence of others. Can the police conduct a protective sweep to protect themselves? In *Maryland v. Buie*, 494 U.S. 325 (1990), the police arrested Buie as he emerged from the basement of his home, and an officer went down the basement to make sure that no one else was there. In the basement, the officer found a red running suit that implicated Buie lying in plain view. The Court held that the officer acted properly in entering the basement. Referencing *Terry*, the Court upheld the search noting that the "interest of the officers in taking steps to assure themselves that the house in which a suspect is being, or has just been, arrested is not harboring other persons who are dangerous and who could unexpectedly launch an attack." The Court placed particular emphasis on the fact that the police are on the suspect's "turf," noting that "an ambush in a confined setting of unknown configuration is more to be feared than it is in open, more familiar surroundings." The Court did not regard the protective sweep as a "*de minimis* intrusion," but the Court concluded that the police are entitled "in such circumstances to take reasonable steps to ensure their safety after, and while making, the arrest," and that this "interest is sufficient to outweigh the intrusion such procedures may entail."

The Court went on to hold that "as an incident to the arrest the officers could, as a precautionary matter and without probable cause or reasonable suspicion, look in closets and other spaces immediately adjoining the place of arrest from which an attack could be immediately launched." To search farther afield, there must "be articulable facts which, taken together with the rational inferences from those facts, would warrant a reasonably prudent officer in believing that the area to be swept harbors an individual posing a danger to those on the arrest scene." The Court held that the protective sweep involved nothing more than a cursory inspection, and should last "no longer than is necessary to dispel the reasonable suspicion of danger and in any event no longer than it takes to complete the arrest and depart the premises."

Justice Stevens, concurring, questioned whether an officer who is worried about his safety, would risk entering the basement at all. Justice Brennan, dissenting, argued that there has been an "emerging tendency on the part of the Court to convert the *Terry* decision" from a narrow exception into one that " 'swallow[s] the general rule that [searches] are "reasonable" only if based on probable cause.' "

He felt that, given the "special sanctity of a private residence and the highly intrusive nature of a protective sweep," police must have probable cause before they conduct a protective sweep.

May the police detain innocent suspects in a degrading (naked) fashion? In *Los Angeles County v. Rettele*, 550 U.S. 609 (2007), the police entered a house with a warrant, barged into the bedroom, rousted the plaintiffs from bed (even though they were naked), and made them stand naked for a few minutes. Plaintiffs sued under 42 U.S.C. § 1983, claiming that the police should have terminated the search upon discovering that respondents were of a different race than the suspects, and should not have ordered respondents from their bed while naked. The Court disagreed, noting that there was evidence that the suspects resided at the address (even though unknown to the police the house had recently been sold to the plaintiffs) and that they would be armed. When the officers realized they had made a mistake, they apologized and left within five minutes. The Court balanced the intrusion against the governmental interests, and concluded that the officers had acted permissibly. The Court emphasized that, although plaintiffs were of a different race than the suspects, it was possible that the suspects lived in the house as well. In addition, the police were entitled to "ensure their own safety and the efficacy of the search." Thus, even though the plaintiffs were naked, the police were not required to turn their backs: "Blankets and bedding can conceal a weapon, and one of the suspects was known to own a firearm, factors which underscore this point. . . Deputies were not required to turn their backs to allow Rettele and Sadler to retrieve clothing or to cover themselves with the sheets. Rather, '[t]he risk of harm to both the police and the occupants is minimized if the officers routinely exercise unquestioned command of the situation.' " However, the Court emphasized that the duration of the seizure was relatively short.

Temporary detentions while seeking warrant. In *Illinois v. McArthur*, 531 U.S. 326 (2001), the Court held that the police could temporarily detain a man while seeking a warrant to search his home. In that case, a woman asked police to accompany her to her trailer so that she could remove her belongings. Although her husband was inside, the officers remained outside. When the woman emerged, she told police that her husband "had dope in there" hidden under the couch. The officer then asked the husband for permission to search the trailer, but the husband refused. One of the officers then remained at the trailer while the other went with the woman to obtain a search warrant. The remaining officer prevented the man from re-entering his trailer without a police officer. A subsequent search pursuant to warrant revealed marijuana and drug paraphernalia. McArthur moved to suppress the pipe, box, and marijuana on the ground that they were the "fruit" of an unlawful police seizure, namely, the refusal to let him reenter the trailer unaccompanied, which would have permitted him, he said, to "have destroyed the marijuana." The Court balanced the "privacy-related and law-enforcement-related concerns" and held that the police acted properly in temporarily seizing McArthur. The Court concluded that exigent circumstances existed, and that the restraint was "reasonable" given that it "was tailored to that need, being limited in time and scope, and avoiding significant intrusion into the home itself." The Court emphasized that the police had probable cause to believe that the trailer contained contraband, that the contraband would be destroyed before they could obtain a warrant, and that the police imposed only a limited restraint by preventing McArthur from re-entering his trailer while a search warrant was sought. The search did not occur until the warrant was obtained. Justice Stevens dissented noting that possession of marijuana was a class C misdemeanor with a maximum sentence of 30 days in jail, and arguing that possession is not a law enforcement priority. He argued that the Court should have placed a higher value on the sanctity of the home.

A similar decision was rendered in *Segura v. United States*, 468 U.S. 796 (1984), in which the police unlawfully entered and occupied an apartment for 19 hours before searching it. During this period, they were waiting for a warrant. The Court held that it would have been permissible for the police to seal the apartment from the outside and restrict entry while a warrant was obtained, and that the occupation was also permissible.

Can an Officer Order the Driver and Passengers to Exit a Lawfully–Stopped Vehicle? In *Pennsylvania v. Mimms*, 434 U.S. 106 (1977), the Court held that a police officer may, as a matter of course, order the driver of a lawfully stopped car to exit the vehicle. In *Maryland v. Wilson*, 519 U.S. 408 (1997), the Court extended this rule to passengers. In *Wilson*, an officer attempted to stop a speeding vehicle, but the driver refused to stop. During the ensuing pursuit, the officer observed the three occupants repeatedly turn to look at the officer and repeatedly duck. After the car was stopped, and the officer approached the car, a trembling and nervous driver exited and met him halfway. After the driver produced a valid driver's license, the officer asked for rental documents and the driver returned to his car. At this point, the officer noticed that one of the passengers was sweating and nervous, and the officer ordered him to exit the car. When he did, some cocaine dropped to the ground. The Court held that the officer validly ordered Wilson to exit the vehicle, citing the interest in officer safety, and noting the fact that there was more than one person in the vehicle increased the "possible sources of harm to the officer." The Court concluded that the intrusion on passengers was minimal, and that the motivation of a passenger to use violence to prevent detection and apprehension for a crime is great.

Justice Stevens dissented: "[I]f a police officer [has] an articulable suspicion of possible danger, the officer may order passengers to exit the vehicle as a defensive tactic without running afoul of the Fourth Amendment. [But] the Court's ruling [applies] equally to traffic stops in which there is not even a scintilla of evidence of any potential risk to the police officer."

POINTS TO REMEMBER

- When the police make a lawful search of a house, they may detain occupants of the house that they find on site.

- When the police arrest an individual at home, they can conduct a limited protective sweep designed to ensure their own safety.

- The police can ask the driver and passengers of a lawfully stopped vehicle to exit the vehicle.

- While a warrant is being sought, the police may temporarily detain the owner of a home to prevent him from destroying evidence inside the home.

- Police can enter and hold an apartment to prevent the destruction of evidence while a warrant is sought.

Traffic Roadblocks and Checkpoints. The police sometimes establish roadblocks or traffic checkpoints to look for drunk drivers, and to check licenses and registrations. For many years, there was doubt regarding the validity of these roadblocks because the police were stopping drivers as to which they did not have probable cause, or even a reasonable suspicion that the drivers were drunk or that they were not carrying proper license and registration.

Despite the absence of suspect specific information, the Court has upheld some types of checkpoints. As will be discussed more fully below, in *United States v. Martinez–Fuerte*, 428 U.S. 543 (1976), the Court upheld immigration checkpoints established close to the U.S. border. The purpose of these stops was to detect the presence of illegal aliens in automobiles.

Likewise, in *Michigan Department of State Police v. Sitz*, 496 U.S. 444 (1990), the Court upheld sobriety checkpoints. In that case, the police stopped all vehicles to briefly examine drivers for signs of intoxication. If there was no evidence of intoxication, drivers were immediately allowed to pass the checkpoint. If intoxication was detected, the motorist was directed to a nearby location where another officer would do a number of things (check the motorist's driver's license and car registration and conduct a sobriety test). Drivers who were found to be intoxicated were arrested. During the 75 minute checkpoint, 126 vehicles passed through and each vehicle was delayed for approximately 25 seconds. Two drivers were detained for field sobriety testing, and one of the two was arrested for driving under the influence of alcohol. A third driver who drove through without stopping was pulled over and ultimately arrested for driving under the influence. Despite recognizing that the checkpoints constituted Fourth Amendment seizures, the Court upheld the checkpoints because of the strong governmental interest in preventing drunk driving, and the slight intrusion caused by the brief stops. Justice Brennan dissented: "Some level of individualized suspicion is a core component of the protection the Fourth Amendment provides against arbitrary government action."

Despite the holdings in *Martinez-Fuerte* and *Sitz*, the Court refused to uphold the validity of drug interdiction checkpoints. In *City of Indianapolis v. Edmond*, 531 U.S. 32 (2000), the police set-up drug checkpoints (similar to the drunk driving checkpoints) designed to detect illegal narcotics. There were six such roadblocks that stopped a total of 1,161 vehicles and led to 104 arrests (55 of which were for drug-related crimes). At the checkpoints, 30 police officers participated and the police stopped a predetermined number of vehicles in sequence. An officer would approach each stopped vehicle, advise the driver of the purpose of the stop, and ask the driver to produce a license and registration. In addition, the officer would look for signs of impairment, conduct a plain view examination of the vehicle from the outside, and walk a narcotics-detection dog around the outside of the vehicle. Officers were instructed that they could search further only with consent or based on a particularized suspicion. The police tried to conduct the stops so that they lasted no more than five minutes. Checkpoint locations were selected in advance based on crime statistics and traffic flow, were generally set-up during daylight hours, and were accompanied by signs which read "NARCOTICS CHECKPOINT ___ MILE AHEAD, NARCOTICS K–9 IN USE, BE PREPARED TO STOP." Once a group of cars had been stopped, other traffic was allowed to pass without interruption until all the stopped cars had been processed or diverted for further processing.

In invalidating the searches, the Court emphasized that suspicionless searches and seizures are generally regarded as unreasonable. The Court recognized that it had upheld exceptions for situations involving so-called "special needs" which the Court regarded as "beyond the normal need for law enforcement." Included within these "special needs" situations were cases involving random drug testing of student-athletes, drug tests for Customs Service employees seeking transfer or promotion to certain positions, drug and alcohol tests for railway employees involved in train accidents or found to be in violation of particular safety regulations, and for administrative inspections of closely regulated businesses. The Court noted that it had also upheld brief suspicionless seizures at fixed border checkpoints designed to intercept illegal aliens, and at sobriety checkpoints designed to remove drunk drivers from the road. Finally, the Court indicated that it would probably uphold checkpoints designed to verify drivers' licenses and vehicle registrations.

The Court distinguished these "special needs" situations from drug interdiction checkpoints on the basis that none of them involved a "checkpoint program whose primary purpose was to detect evidence of ordinary criminal wrongdoing." For example, sobriety checkpoints were "clearly aimed at reducing the immediate hazard posed by the presence of drunk drivers on the highways, and there was an obvious connection between the imperative of highway safety and the law enforcement practice at issue." The Court placed great emphasis on the "gravity of the drunk driving problem and the magnitude of the State's interest in getting drunk drivers off the road." In suggesting that license and registration checkpoints would be valid, the Court focused on the states' "vital interest in ensuring that only those qualified to do so are permitted to operate motor vehicles, that these vehicles are fit for safe operation, and hence that licensing, registration, and vehicle inspection requirements are being observed."

The Court viewed drug interdiction checkpoints differently. Like the other stops, a drug interdiction checkpoint constitutes a seizure even though use of the drug detection dogs did not constitute a search (for this latter holding the Court relied on its prior decision in *Place*). Nevertheless, the Court regarded the primary purpose of the stops—to interdict illegal narcotics—as determinative. It stated:

> We have never approved a checkpoint program whose primary purpose was to detect evidence of ordinary criminal wrongdoing. Rather, our checkpoint cases have recognized only limited exceptions to the general rule that a seizure must be accompanied by some measure of individualized suspicion. We suggested in *Prouse* that we would not credit the "general interest in crime control" as justification for a regime of suspicionless stops. Consistent with this suggestion, each of the checkpoint programs that we have approved was designed pri-

marily to serve purposes closely related to the problems of policing the border or the necessity of ensuring roadway safety. Because the primary purpose of the Indianapolis narcotics checkpoint program is to uncover evidence of ordinary criminal wrongdoing, the program contravenes the Fourth Amendment.

Even though the Court recognized that other types of roadblocks might result in arrests for crime, the Court viewed them as different because they were not "designed primarily to serve the general interest in crime control", and the Court was reluctant "to recognize exceptions to the general rule of individualized suspicion where governmental authorities primarily pursue their general crime control ends." The Court saw drug interdiction as different from alcohol in terms of highway safety: "The detection and punishment of almost any criminal offense serves broadly the safety of the community, and our streets would no doubt be safer but for the scourge of illegal drugs. Only with respect to a smaller class of offenses, however, is society confronted with the type of immediate, vehicle-bound threat to life and limb that the sobriety checkpoint . . . was designed to eliminate."

The Court did indicate that there might be situations when it would be appropriate to set-up a roadblock to deal with crime control issues on an emergency basis. For example, when there is the threat of an imminent terrorist attack, or when the police are pursuing a fleeing dangerous criminal, a roadblock might be appropriate.

Chief Justice Rehnquist, joined by Justice Thomas, dissented. He concluded that the checkpoints served the state's interest in preventing drunk driving and checking driver's licenses and vehicle registrations, and that the dog sniffs did not lengthen these legitimate seizures. He would have engaged in a balancing test under which he weighed the "gravity of the public concerns served by the seizure, the degree to which the seizure advances the public interest, and the severity of the interference with individual liberty." Balancing these interests, he concluded that drug interdiction checkpoints follow "naturally from *Martinez-Fuerte* and *Sitz*": "These stops effectively serve the State's legitimate interests; they are executed in a regularized and neutral manner; and they only minimally intrude upon the privacy of the motorists. They should therefore be constitutional."

However, in *Illinois v. Lidster*, 540 U.S. 419 (2004), the Court upheld a roadblock designed to elicit information from the motoring public regarding an elderly bicyclist who was struck and killed by a hit and run motorist. The roadblock was established about one week after the accident at about the same time of night and at about the same place as the accident. Police cars with flashing lights partially blocked the eastbound lanes of the highway forcing traffic to slow down. As each vehicle drew up to the checkpoint, an officer would stop it for 10 to 15 seconds, ask the occupants whether they had seen anything happen there the previous weekend, and hand each driver a flyer. The flyer said "ALERT . . . FATAL HIT & RUN ACCIDENT" and requested "assistance in identifying the vehicle and driver in this accident which killed a 70 year old bicyclist." Lidster was apprehended at the checkpoint for driving under the influence of alcohol, and he challenged the roadblock as an illegal stop.

In upholding the roadblock, the Court distinguished its prior holding in *Indianapolis v. Edmond,* on the basis that "special law enforcement" concerns will sometimes justify highway stops without individualized suspicion: "Like certain other forms of police activity, say, crowd control or public safety, an information-seeking stop is not the kind of event that involves suspicion, or lack of suspicion, of the relevant individual." In addition, the Court suggested that information-seeking highway stops are less objectionable because they are less "likely to provoke anxiety or to prove intrusive because they are brief and do not involve questions designed to elicit self-incriminating information." Although such stops are potentially intrusive, in that motorists are forced to pull over, the Court analogized to other situations where the police seek the voluntary cooperation of the public in their efforts to solve crimes. Using a *Terry*-like analysis, the Court suggested that the motorist stops would likely be "brief" and should "prove no more onerous than many that typically accompany normal traffic congestion." In addition, the Court doubted that a prohibition was needed to prevent a proliferation of such stops. Moreover, the Court suggested that "practical considerations" (e.g., limited police resources and community hostility to related traffic tie-ups) are likely to prevent the proliferation of such stops. Nevertheless, the Court indicated that it would evaluate each such roadblocks on their own terms focusing on "the gravity of the public concerns served by the seizure, the degree to which the seizure advances the public interest, and the severity of the interference with individual liberty." In the facts before it, the Court emphasized the importance of the public concern (investigation of a crime that had resulted in a human death), the purpose of the stop (to help find the perpetrator of a specific and known crime), the fact that the roadblock advanced this objective, and the fact that the roadblock was "appropriately tailored . . . to fit important criminal investigatory needs," and "took place about one week after the hit-and-run accident, on the same highway near the location of the accident, and at about the same time of night."

Moreover, the roadblock "required only a brief wait in line—a very few minutes at most" and was designed to produce "little reason for anxiety or alarm" because the police stopped all vehicles "systematically."

Justice Stevens, joined by justices Souter and Ginsburg, concurred in part and dissented in part. He noted that "motorists who confront a roadblock are required to stop, and to remain stopped for as long as the officers choose to detain them. [Some] drivers may find an unpublicized roadblock at midnight on a Saturday somewhat alarming. On the other side of the equation, the likelihood that questioning a random sample of drivers will yield useful information about a hit-and-run accident that occurred a week earlier is speculative at best."

POINTS TO REMEMBER

- Near-border checkpoints can be established at which INS agents stop cars to check for illegal aliens.

- The police may also establish sobriety checkpoints provided that they stop motorists according to a pre-conceived plan (i.e., every third motorist) rather than randomly.

- Sobriety checkpoints are designed to serve the broader interest in road safety that is implicated by drunk drivers.

- The police might also be free to establish license and registration checkpoints or roadblocks (even though they cannot randomly stop motorists to check licenses and registrations)

- The police may not establish drug interdiction roadblocks or checkpoints designed to serve the general interest in crime control.

- Roadblocks might be permissible to prevent an imminent terrorist attack or to apprehend a fleeing felon.

Probationers and Parolees. Inside prisons, inmates have few Fourth Amendment rights. The need for prison security is deemed to be more important than prisoners' reduced privacy interests. Even after their release from prison, inmates who become probationers and parolees are subject to special rules. In *Griffin v. Wisconsin,* 483 U.S. 868 (1987), the Court held that a State's operation of its probation system presented a "special need" for the "exercise of supervision to assure that [probation] restrictions are in fact observed." As a result, warrantless searches of probationers were deemed to be reasonable.

In *United States v. Knights*, 534 U.S. 112 (2001), the Court held that warrantless searches might be permissible of one who is on probation, and whose condition of parole obligated him to submit to warrantless searches. The condition required Knights to submit to "search at anytime, with or without a search warrant, warrant of arrest or reasonable cause by any probation officer or law enforcement officer." Knights signed the probation order. Three days later, a fire occurred at a nearby electric power transformer and police officers suspected that Knights was one of the culprits (along with a friend of his named Simoneau). An officer conducted an initial investigation which revealed additional evidence that Knights and his friend were involved. The officer, who was aware of the condition of Knights' probation, then made a warrantless search of Knights' apartment. The search revealed evidence that incriminated Knights in the fire. In subsequent criminal proceedings, Knights moved to suppress on grounds that the probationary condition only applied to searches for "probationary" rather than "investigatory" purposes. The Court disagreed and upheld the search.

In evaluating the case, the Court concluded that the probation condition served "the two primary goals of probation— rehabilitation and protecting society from future criminal violations." The Court emphasized that the probation order clearly stated the condition, and "Knights was unambiguously informed of it." As a result, the condition diminished Knights' reasonable expectation of privacy. In assessing the governmental interest, the Court emphasized that "the very assumption" of probation is that the probationer "is more likely than the ordinary citizen to violate the law." As a result, the Court held "that the balance of these considerations requires no more than reasonable suspicion to conduct a search of this probationer's house." Once reasonable suspicion exists "that criminal conduct is occurring that an intrusion on the probationer's significantly diminished privacy interests is reasonable." In addition, a warrant is unnecessary. The Court concluded that the police had the necessary reasonable suspicion to search Knight's home.

In *Samson v. California*, 126 S.Ct. 2193 (2006), the Court upheld a California statute providing that parolees, as a condition of their release, could be searched "at any time of the day or night, with or without a search warrant and with or without cause." In determining that the search was "reasonable," the Court balanced a parolee's expectation of privacy against the degree to which the search is needed "for the promotion of legitimate governmental interests." Relying on *Knights*, the Court noted that "parolees have fewer expectations of privacy than probationers," and that "parole is more akin to imprisonment than probation is to imprisonment." "The essence of parole is release from prison, before the completion of sentence, on the condition that the prisoner abides by certain rules during the balance of the sentence." Since these conditions had been clearly expressed to the parolee, the Court found that petitioner did not have an expectation of privacy that society would recognize as legitimate. In addition, the Court concluded that the State has an "overwhelming interest" in supervising parolees because "parolees . . . are more likely to commit future criminal offenses." Justice Stevens, joined by justices Souter and Breyer, dissented, arguing that "neither *Knights* nor *Griffin* supports a regime of suspicionless searches, conducted pursuant to a blanket grant of discretion untethered by any procedural safeguards, by law enforcement personnel who have no special interest in the welfare of the parolee or probationer." "The suspicionless search is the very evil the Fourth Amendment was intended to stamp out."

POINTS TO REMEMBER

- Inmates in jails and prisons do not have the same Fourth Amendment rights as ordinary citizens.

- Outside prisons and jails, probationers and parolees still have reduced rights vis-a-vis other citizens.

Border Searches. Special rules have always applied to searches conducted at or near the United States border. At the border itself, customs and immigration officials have the right to "stop" those who seek to enter the United States, and to force them to prove their right to enter (by presenting their passport and relevant immigration documents).

Customs officials have usually enjoyed the right to conduct limited searches of those who enter the United States. These searches are designed to accomplish a variety of objectives: to make sure that entrants are not carrying contraband, that they do not have dutiable items that they have failed to declare, and that they are not carrying harmful or dangerous items (i.e., agricultural products with dangerous parasites).

However, even at the border, there are limits on the scope of governmental power. For example, customs officials do not have the automatic right to conduct body cavity searches. However, when customs officials reasonably believe that an entrant has swallowed contraband and is carrying it inside his body, customs officials are entitled to hold the individual until he performs normal excretory functions. Likewise, in *United States v. Flores–Montano*, 541 U.S. 149 (2004), the Court upheld the actions of customs officials who dismantled a gasoline tank at the United States border in a successful search for marijuana hidden in the tank. The dismantlement required a 20 to 30 minute delay to obtain a mechanic, and an additional 15 to25 minutes to dismantle the tank. The Court upheld the search, refusing to make fine distinctions between "routine" searches and more "intrusive" searches at international borders. The Court noted a long history of routine border searches conducted without probable cause or a warrant "in order to regulate the collection of duties and to prevent the introduction of contraband into this country," and concluded that the "Government's interest in preventing the entry of unwanted persons and effects is at its zenith at the international border" so that "searches made at the border, pursuant to the longstanding right of the sovereign to protect itself by stopping and examining persons and property crossing into this country, are reasonable simply by virtue of the fact that they occur at the border." As for the fact that the fuel tank was dismantled, the Court emphasized that "since fuel tanks are designed to contain only fuel, it is doubtful how there could be more of an invasion of privacy than the search of the automobile's passenger compartment." Although respondent expressed concern that the disassembly and reassembly of his gas tank might constitute a significant deprivation in that it could damage the vehicle, the Court noted that few instances of damage had been reported, and that the possibility of damage was in any event justified by "the Government's paramount interest in protecting the border."

Inside the United States, the rules regarding searches and seizures are somewhat more complicated and tend to parallel the ordinary search and seizure rules. Sometimes, for example, the police seek to stop a vehicle because they believe that it contains illegal aliens. In *United States v. Brignoni–Ponce*, 422 U.S. 873 (1975), the Court held that such stops could only be justified by a "reasonable suspicion" of criminal activity. In that case, the Court stated: "Except at the border and its functional equivalents, officers on roving patrol may stop vehicles only if they are aware of specific articulable facts, together with rational inferences from those facts, that reasonably warrant suspicion that the vehicles contain aliens who may be illegally in the country."

Illustration of the reasonable suspicion standard is provided by the holding in *United States v. Arvizu*, 534 U.S. 266 (2002). In that case, a border patrol agent was conducting a checkpoint near the Mexican border when a magnetic sensor indicated the presence of traffic that might be consistent with smuggling on a nearby road. An officer investigated and found a vehicle that slowed dramatically when it saw the officer. Inside the vehicle were five people including three children. The driver appeared stiff and tried to act as if the officer was not there (rather than waving as the locals generally did in that area). In addition, it appeared that the kids legs were high (as if there was something on the floor). As the officer followed the vehicle, all of the children began to wave in an "odd" way. The vehicle then turned at the last place that it could turn before it reached an immigration checkpoint. Radio communication with the station revealed that the vehicle was registered to a place near the Mexican border that was "notorious for alien and narcotics smuggling." At that point, the officer stopped the vehicle and the driver consented to a search that revealed the existence of marijuana. Based on these facts, the Court concluded that a reasonable suspicion existed:

> When discussing how reviewing courts should make reasonable-suspicion determinations, we have said repeatedly that they must look at the "totality of the circumstances" of each case to see whether the detaining officer has a "particularized and objective basis" for suspecting legal wrongdoing. This process allows officers to draw on their own experience and specialized training to make inferences from and deductions about the cumulative information available to them that "might well elude an untrained person." Although an officer's reliance on a mere " 'hunch' "is insufficient to justify a stop, the likelihood of criminal activity need not rise to the level required for probable cause, and it falls considerably short of satisfying a preponderance of the evidence standard.

> Our cases have recognized that the concept of reasonable suspicion is somewhat abstract. But we have deliberately avoided reducing it to " 'a neat set of legal rules.' " In Sokolow, for example, we rejected a holding by the Court of Appeals that distinguished between evidence of ongoing criminal behavior and probabilistic evidence because it "create[d] unnecessary difficulty in dealing with one of the relatively simple concepts embodied in the Fourth Amendment." . . .

> [W]e hold that [the officer] had reasonable suspicion to believe that respondent was engaged in illegal activity. It was reasonable for [the officer] to infer from his observations, his registration check, and his experience as a border patrol agent that respondent had set out from Douglas along a little-traveled route used by smugglers to avoid the 191 checkpoint. [The officer's] knowledge further supported a commonsense inference that respondent intended to pass through the area at a time when officers would be leaving their backroads patrols to change shifts. The likelihood that respondent and his family were on a picnic outing was diminished by the fact that the minivan had turned away from the known recreational areas accessible to the east on Rucker Canyon Road. Corroborating this inference was the fact that recreational areas farther to the north would have been easier to reach by taking 191, as

opposed to the 40–to–50–mile trip on unpaved and primitive roads. The children's elevated knees suggested the existence of concealed cargo in the passenger compartment. Finally, for the reasons we have given, Stoddard's assessment of respondent's reactions upon seeing him and the children's mechanical-like waving, which continued for a full four to five minutes, were entitled to some weight.

Despite the general rules regarding automobile stops (requiring reasonable suspicion), the Court has established special rules for near border roadblocks or checkpoints. *United States v. Martinez–Fuerte*, 428 U.S. 543 (1976), involved a near-border checkpoint at which agents slowed all traffic "to a virtual, if not a complete, halt" at a highway roadblock, and referr[ed] vehicles chosen at the discretion of Border Patrol agents to an area for "secondary inspection." The Court upheld the checkpoint noting that: "[The] objective intrusion—the stop itself, the questioning, and the visual inspection—also existed in roving-patrol stops. But we view checkpoint stops in a different light because the subjective intrusion—the generating of concern or even fright on the part of lawful travelers—is appreciably less in the case of a checkpoint stop."

POINTS TO REMEMBER

- Border searches have always been treated differently than searches that occur inside the borders of the United States.

- Customs officials have an automatic right to stop individuals who seek to enter the United States, and to force those individuals to prove their right to enter.

- Customs officials also have the right to conduct limited searches at the border to make sure that the entering individual is not carrying contraband or other items that may be harmful to the United States, its economy and people (i.e., customs officials routinely search for agricultural products which may contain harmful parasites).

- Customs officials cannot routinely conduct body cavity searches.

- Customs officials may, if they reasonably suspect that an individual is carrying contraband inside his body, hold the individual until he excretes.

- Immigration stops can be made inside the United States based on a reasonable suspicion that a vehicle contains aliens.

- Immigration "checkpoints" or "roadblocks" can be established within the United States close to the border.

b. Investigatory Seizures of Property

The Court has extended Terry's analysis to investigative seizures of property. In *United States v. Place*, 462 U.S. 696 (1983), Place's behavior aroused the suspicions of police at the Miami airport. The officers approached him and, after questioning him for awhile, were very suspicious about his conduct. After Place was allowed to depart for New York, Miami agents contacted Drug Enforcement Administration (DEA) authorities in New York to relay their suspicions. In New York, after Place called a limousine, two agents approached him and stated their belief that he was carrying narcotics. When Place refused to consent to a search of his luggage, the agents decided to hold it while they sought a warrant from a judge. The agents provided Place with a phone number at which one of them could be reached, and then subjected the bags to a "sniff test" by a trained narcotics detection dog. The dog reacted positively to one bag. Although the sniff was conducted within a 90 minute period, the agents kept the bags until Monday morning (the sniff took place late on a Friday afternoon) when they obtained a search warrant from a judge. In the subsequent search, they found cocaine in the bag.

In invalidating the search, the Court began by reiterating the warrant preference but noting that containers can be seized based on probable cause while the police seek a warrant. This temporary seizure is permissible because "the risk of the item's disappearance or use for its intended purpose before a warrant may be obtained outweighs the interest in possession." Especially when the police "possess specific and articulable facts warranting a reasonable belief that a traveler's luggage contains narcotics, the governmental interest in seizing the luggage briefly to pursue further investigation is substantial." Indeed, the Court concluded that the police had a "compelling interest in detecting those who would traffic in deadly drugs for personal profit."

The Court then recognized that an intrusion on possessory interests could vary "both in its nature and extent" ranging from an "on the spot" inquiry (as with the use of a dog to sniff the luggage) to the relinquishment of custody and control. The Court suggested that some brief seizures were so minimally intrusive that they could be justified based "only on specific articulable facts that the property contains contraband or evidence of a crime." For example, based on a reasonable conclusion that a traveler's luggage contains narcotics, the police could briefly detain the luggage for investigative purposes "provided that the investigative detention is properly limited in scope." Although a canine sniff does not qualify as a search, but only a seizure, the Court concluded that "the police conduct intrudes on both the suspect's possessory interest in his luggage as well as his liberty interest in proceeding with his itinerary." "Such a seizure can effectively restrain the person since he is subjected to the possible disruption of his travel plans in order to remain with his luggage or to arrange for its return."

Applying these rules, the Court concluded that the seizure of Place's luggage went too far. "The length of the detention of respondent's luggage alone precludes the conclusion that the seizure was reasonable in the absence of probable cause." The Court noted that "the brevity of the invasion of the individual's Fourth Amendment interests is an important factor in determining whether the seizure is so minimally intrusive as to be justifiable on reasonable suspicion." The Court concluded that the 90 minute detention of Place's luggage was too long, especially given that the agents had advance notice of Place's arrival and could have prepared for the additional investigation. "In short, we hold that the detention of respondent's luggage in this case went beyond the narrow authority possessed by police to detain briefly luggage reasonably suspected to contain narcotics." The additional step, of holding the bags over the weekend, was also deemed to be unreasonable.

The Court has also upheld the seizure of mailed packages. In *United States v. Van Leeuwen*, 397 U.S. 249 (1970), respondent mailed two 12–pound packages at a post office near the Canadian border. One package was addressed to a post office box in California, and the other to a post office box in Tennessee. Respondent declared that they contained coins. Each package was sent airmail registered and insured for $10,000, a type of mailing that did not subject them to discretionary inspection. When the postal clerk told a policeman that he was suspicious of the packages, the policeman noticed that the return address on the packages was a vacant housing area, and that the license plates of respondent's car were Canadian. The policeman called the Canadian police who in turn called customs officials in Seattle. Customs officials in Seattle called both California and Tennessee and learned that both of the addressees were under investigation for trafficking in illegal coins. A customs official thereupon obtained a search warrant, and the packages were opened and inspected. Respondent was tried for illegally importing gold coins. The Court upheld the seizure:

> No interest protected by the Fourth Amendment was invaded by forwarding the packages the following day rather than the day when they were deposited. The significant Fourth Amendment interest was in the privacy of this first-class mail; and that privacy was not disturbed or invaded until the approval of the magistrate was obtained. [O]n the facts of this

case—the nature of the mailings, their suspicious character, the fact that there were two packages going to separate destinations, the unavoidable delay in contacting the more distant of the two destinations, the distance between Mt. Vernon and Seattle—a 29–hour delay between the mailings and the service of the warrant cannot be said to be "unreasonable" within the meaning of the Fourth Amendment. Detention for this limited time was, indeed, the prudent act rather than letting the packages enter the mails and then, in case the initial suspicions were confirmed, trying to locate them en route and enlisting the help of distant federal officials in serving the warrant.

POINTS TO REMEMBER

- Despite the warrant preference, containers can be seized based on probable cause while the police seek a warrant.

- This temporary seizure is permissible because "the risk of the item's disappearance or use for its intended purpose before a warrant may be obtained outweighs the interest in possession."

- Based on a reasonable conclusion that a traveler's luggage contains narcotics, the police may briefly detain the luggage for investigative purposes "provided that the investigative detention is properly limited in scope."

- Although a canine sniff does not qualify as a search, it can intrude on the suspect's possessory interest in his luggage as well as his liberty interest in proceeding with his itinerary.

- A 90 minute detention of luggage to effectuate a canine sniff is excessive when the police have ample advance notice and could have arranged the sniff more efficiently.

- When customs officials have reason to believe that mailed packages contain contraband, they can cause a limited delay (1 day) in the mailing of a package to give them time to obtain a warrant.

7. Exigent Circumstances

The police can also dispense with a warrant when they are faced with "exigent circumstances." For example, when a police officer hears gun shots followed by cries for help from a nearby apartment, the officer can enter the apartment to render emergency help and assistance. *See McDonald v. United States*, 335 U.S. 451 (1948). Likewise, "a warrant is not required to break down a door to enter a burning home to rescue occupants or extinguish a fire, [or] to bring emergency aid to an injured person." *See Wayne v. United States*, 318 F.2d 205 (D.C. Cir. 1963).

In *Brigham City v. Stuart*, 126 S.Ct. 1943 (2006), the Court discussed and elaborated on the scope of the "emergency" or "exigent circumstances" exception. In that case, police officers responded to a call regarding a loud party at a residence at three o'clock in the morning. On arriving, they heard shouting from inside, proceeded to investigate, and saw-through a screen door and windows-an altercation taking place in the kitchen of the home. At this point, an officer opened the screen door and announced his presence. Nobody noticed. The officer entered, again cried out, and as the occupants slowly became aware that the police were on the scene, the altercation ceased. The officers subsequently arrested respondents and charged them with contributing to the delinquency of a minor, disorderly conduct, and intoxication.

In a unanimous opinion by Chief Justice Roberts, the Court upheld the entry into the house. Although the Court recognized that warrantless searches of homes are presumptively unreasonable, the Court acknowledged that the "ultimate touchstone of the Fourth Amendment is 'reasonableness,' " and held that warrantless searches might be permissible when exigent circumstances exist. The Court concluded that the exigent circumstances exception includes a need to enter "to assist persons who are seriously injured or threatened with such injury." The Court rejected the argument that the situation involved in this case was not serious enough to justify the officers' intrusion into the home, noting that "the officers were confronted with *ongoing* violence occurring *within* the home" and that "the officers had an objectively reasonable basis for believing both that the injured adult might need help and that the violence in the kitchen was just beginning." The Court concluded that the Fourth Amendment did not require the police to delay until someone was unconscious or semi-conscious before entering: "The role of a peace officer includes preventing violence and restoring order, not simply rendering first aid to casualties; an officer is not like a boxing (or hockey) referee, poised to stop a bout only if it becomes too one-sided. The manner of the officers' entry was also reasonable. [O]nce the announcement was made, the officers were free to enter; it would serve no purpose to require them to stand dumbly at the door awaiting a response while those within brawled on, oblivious to their presence."

Warden v. Hayden, 387 U.S. 294 (1967), the case that articulated the so-called "hot pursuit" exception to the warrant requirement, presents another example of exigent circumstances. In that case, following an armed robbery, two cab drivers provided the police with a description of the robbers and followed them to a nearby house. When the police arrived at the house moments later, a search revealed Hayden in a bedroom. Other officers, searching other parts of the house, found weapons and clothing used in the robbery. The Court held that the warrantless search of the entire house was valid because of "the exigencies of the situation":

> The Fourth Amendment does not require police officers to delay in the course of an investigation if to do so would gravely endanger their lives or the lives of others. Speed here was essential, and only a thorough search of the house for persons and weapons could have insured that Hayden was the only man present and that the police had control of all weapons which could be used against them or to effect an escape.

Hayden was followed and affirmed in *United States v. Santana*, 427 U.S. 38 (1976). In that case, after an undercover drug buy, the police went to "Mom" Santana's home to arrest her (Santana provided the drugs to the seller). They found Santana standing in the doorway with a brown paper bag in her hand. As the police exited their van, they shouted "police" and displayed their identification. When Santana retreated into the vestibule of her house, the officers followed through the open door and caught her. As she tried to pull away, the bag tilted and "two bundles of glazed paper packets with a white powder" fell to the floor. The Court upheld the entry into the house applying the "hot pursuit" exception: "[T]he need to act quickly here is even greater than in [*Hayden*]." The fact that the pursuit here ended almost as soon as it began did not render it any the less a "hot pursuit" sufficient to justify the warrantless entry into Santana's house. "Once Santana saw the police, there was [a] realistic expectation that any delay would result in destruction of evidence. Once she had been arrested the search, incident to that arrest, which produced the drugs and money was clearly justified."

In *Kentucky v. King*, 131 S.Ct. 1849 (2011), the Court further defined the exigent circumstances exception. In that case, the question was whether the exigent circumstances exception applied when the police knocked on a door, thereby announcing their presence, and thus caused the occupants of an apartment to attempt to destroy evidence. The Court answered that question in the affirmative: "Where, as here, the police did not create the exigency by engaging or threatening to engage in conduct that violates the Fourth Amendment, warrantless entry to prevent the destruction of evidence is reasonable and thus allowed."

In reaching its conclusion, the Court rejected various limitations that had been imposed on the exigent circumstances doctrine by lower courts. For example, the Court rejected the idea that the exception did not apply when the police "deliberately created the exigent circumstances with the bad faith intent to avoid the warrant requirement." The Court held that it was unwilling to engage in a subjective analysis regarding the intentions of police officers: "Legal tests based on reasonableness are generally objective, and this Court has long taken the view that 'evenhanded law enforcement is best achieved by the application of objective standards of conduct, rather than standards that depend upon the subjective state of mind of the officer.'" The Court also rejected a "reasonable foreseeability" test which would have asked whether it "was reasonably foreseeable that the investigative tactics employed by the police would create the exigent circumstances." The Court noted that it had "rejected the notion that police may seize evidence without a warrant only when they come across the evidence by happenstance," noting that "whenever law enforcement officers knock on the door of premises occupied by a person who may be involved in the drug trade, there is *some* possibility that the occupants may possess drugs and may seek to destroy them." Finally, the Court rejected the idea that, if thee police have probable cause and the time to obtain a warrant, they must do so. The Court concluded that such an approach "unjustifiably interferes with legitimate law enforcement strategies":

> There are many entirely proper reasons why police may not want to seek a search warrant as soon as the bare minimum of evidence needed to establish probable cause is acquired... First, the police may wish to speak with the occupants of a dwelling before deciding whether it is worthwhile to seek authorization for a search. They may think that a short and simple conversation may obviate the need to apply for and execute a warrant. See *Schneckloth v. Bustamonte,* 412 U.S. 218, 228 (1973). Second, the police may want to ask an occupant of the premises for consent to search because doing so is simpler, faster, and less burdensome than applying for a warrant. A consensual search also "may result in considerably less inconvenience" and embarrassment to the occupants than a search conducted pursuant to a warrant. Third, law enforcement officers may wish to obtain more evidence before submitting what might otherwise be considered a marginal warrant application. Fourth, prosecutors may wish to wait until they acquire evidence that can justify a search that is broader in scope than the search that a judicial officer is likely to authorize based on the evidence then available. And finally, in many cases, law enforcement may not want to execute a search that will disclose the existence of an investigation because doing so may interfere with the acquisition of additional evidence against those already under suspicion or evidence about additional but as yet unknown participants in a criminal scheme.

As a result, the Court held that: "[l]aw enforcement officers are under no constitutional duty to call a halt to criminal investigation the moment they have the minimum evidence to establish probable cause." The Court also rejected the idea that the exigent circumstances exception did not apply when the police had acted "contrary to standard or good law enforcement practices (or to the policies or practices of their jurisdictions)." The Court concluded that such an approach "fails to provide clear guidance for law enforcement officers and authorizes courts to make judgments on matters that are the province of" the police.

The Court noted that the exception should not turn on whether the police had taken actions which suggested that entry to the apartment was "imminent and inevitable." The Court concluded that "the ability of law enforcement officers to respond to an exigency cannot turn on such subtleties[.] A forceful knock may be necessary to alert the occupants that someone is at the door. Furthermore, unless police officers identify themselves loudly enough, occupants may not know who is at their doorstep." The Court concluded that the occupant of a residence has no obligation to open the door or to converse with the police, and need not consent to allow the police to enter or respond to questions. However, if the occupants respond by trying to destroy evidence, they "have only themselves to blame for the warrantless exigent-circumstances search that may ensue." However, the Court remanded for consideration of the question of whether exigent circumstances actually existed in that case.

Justice Ginsburg dissented, arguing that there was "little risk [in this case] that drug-related evidence would have been destroyed had the police delayed the search pending a magistrate's authorization." In other words, prior to the knock, there was no evidence of exigency. In her view, the "existence of a genuine emergency depends not only on the state of necessity at the time of the warrantless search; it depends, first and foremost, on 'actions taken by the police *preceding* the warrantless search.' *United States v. Coles,* 437 F.3d 361, 367 (C.A.3 2006)." In her view, the police should have posted officers on the premises and sought a warrant.

Not all "exigent circumstances" cases involve hot pursuit. Some involve simply a situation where there is a need to act quickly. In *Michigan v. Fisher,* 130 S.Ct. 546 (2009), the Court applied the exigent circumstances exception to the entry of a house. In that case, when police responded to a disturbance, they were directed to a house where a man was purportedly "going crazy." When they arrived, they found the household in considerable chaos: a pickup truck with its front smashed, damaged fenceposts, three broken house windows (with the glass still on the ground outside). In addition, the officers noticed blood on the hood of the pickup, on clothes inside of it, as well as on one of the doors to the house. Through a window of the house, the officers could see Fisher screaming and throwing things. The back door was locked, and a couch had been placed to block the front door. The officers knocked, but Fisher refused to answer. However, they could see that Fisher had a cut on his hand, and they asked him whether he needed medical attention. Fisher ignored these questions and profanely demanded that the officers obtain a search warrant. When one of the officers entered the house, Fisher pointed a gun at him and the officer retreated. Fisher was charged with assault with a dangerous weapon and possession of a firearm during the commission of a felony.

Relying on *Brigham City v. Stuart,* 547 U.S. 398 (2006), the *Fisher* Court upheld the entry into the house relying on the "emergency aid exception," and noting that the police "may enter a home without a warrant to render emergency assistance to an injured occupant or to protect an occupant from imminent injury." The Court went on to note that the "emergency aid exception" does not "depend on the officers' subjective intent or the seriousness of any crime they are investigating when the emergency arises," but rather requires only "an objectively reasonable basis for believing, that "a person within [the house] is in need of immediate aid."

Applying those principles to the case before it, the Court found that the circumstances were such as to justify application of the exception:

> [The] police were responding to a report of a disturbance [and] encountered a tumultuous situation in the house-and here they also found signs of a recent injury, perhaps from a car accident, outside. [The] officers could see violent behavior inside [and saw] Fisher screaming and throwing things. It would be objectively reasonable to believe that Fisher's projectiles might have a human target (perhaps a spouse or a child), or that Fisher would hurt himself in the course of his rage. [W]e find [that] the officer's entry was reasonable under the Fourth Amendment. [Officers] do not need ironclad proof of "a likely serious, life-threatening" injury to invoke the emergency aid exception[.] Only when an apparent threat has become an actual harm can officers rule out innocuous explanations for ominous circumstances. But "[t]he role of a peace officer includes preventing violence and restoring order, not simply rendering first aid to casualties." It sufficed to invoke the emergency aid exception that it was reasonable to believe that Fisher had hurt himself (albeit nonfatally) and needed treatment that in his

rage he was unable to provide, or that Fisher was about to hurt, or had already hurt, someone else.

Justice Stevens, joined by Justice Sotomayor, dissented, arguing that "the factual question was whether [the police officer] had 'an objectively reasonable basis for believing that [Fisher was] seriously injured or imminently threatened with such injury.' " Justice Stevens would have answered that question in the negative. He found the police decision to leave the scene and not return for several hours-without resolving any potentially dangerous situation and without calling for medical assistance-inconsistent with a reasonable belief that Fisher was in need of immediate aid.

A good example of the emergency aid exception is provided by the holding in *People v. Sirhan*, 7 Cal.3d 710, 102 Cal.Rptr. 385, 497 P.2d 1121 (1972), a lower court decision. After Senator Robert Kennedy was murdered, the police took Sirhan Sirhan into custody. Shortly thereafter, the police searched Sirhan's home where they found several items that were ultimately used against him (several pages from two of his notebooks and an envelope). The government justified the search based on exigent circumstances: "there was a pressing emergency to ascertain the existence of a possible conspiracy to assassinate presidential candidates or high government officials. . ." The court upheld the search:

> [The] officers believed that there might be a conspiracy [to] assassinate political leaders in this country. It also may be inferred [that] they believed that an emergency existed and that prompt action on their part was necessary. [Their] beliefs were entirely reasonable. The crime was one of enormous gravity. . . The victim was a major presidential candidate, and a crime of violence had already been committed against him. The crime thus involved far more than possibly idle threats. Although the officers did not have reasonable cause to believe that the house contained evidence of a conspiracy to assassinate prominent political leaders, we believe that the mere possibility that there might be such evidence in the house fully warranted the officers' actions. It is not difficult to envisage what would have been the effect on this nation if several more political assassinations had followed that of Senator Kennedy. Today when assassinations of persons of prominence have repeatedly been committed in this country, it is essential that law enforcement officers be allowed to take fast action in their endeavors to combat such crimes.

But the "exigent circumstances" label does not always or automatically cause the warrant requirement to disappear. In a number of cases, the Court has held that the circumstances were not sufficiently exigent to justify a warrantless search. For example, in *Minnesota v. Olson*, 495 U.S. 91 (1990), the police had probable cause to believe that Olson was involved in an armed robbery that resulted in the death of a gas station attendant. The next morning, after a woman called the police and said that Olson admitted his participation in the robbery to two other women, a "probable cause arrest bulletin" was issued for Olson's arrest. When the police learned that Olson had gone to the home of the two women, police surrounded the home. A detective then telephoned Julie (one of the two women) and told her that Olson should come out of the house. The detective heard a male voice say, "tell them I left." Julie stated that Olson had left. Thereafter, the detective ordered the police to enter the house. Without seeking permission and with weapons drawn, the police entered and found Olson hiding in a closet. Subsequently, Olson made an inculpatory statement at police headquarters. In evaluating these facts, the Court declined to hold that there were exigent circumstances that justified the warrantless entry into the home. The Court began by downplaying Olson's role noting that he was the driver of the getaway car and was not the one who pulled the trigger. The Court noted that the murder weapon had already been recovered, and there was no suggestion that either of the women were in danger, or that Olson could escape (the house was surrounded).

Another case in which the Court refused to apply the exigent circumstances exception is *Vale v. Louisiana*, 399 U.S. 30 (1970). In that case, police officers went to Vale's home with a warrant for his arrest. While observing the house, officers saw a car drive up. Vale, who was known to the officers, came out of the house and conversed with the driver. After looking up and down the street, he returned to the house, but reappeared shortly. After looking up and down the street again, Vale went back to the car. By that point, the police had become convinced that a narcotics sale was taking place and converged. Vale turned and walked quickly towards the house. The officers subdued Vale on the front steps of his house, and told him that they were going to search the house. The search produced illegal narcotics. The Court held that the search could not be justified under the "exigent circumstances" exception:

> [The] officers were not responding to an emergency. They were not in hot pursuit of a fleeing felon. The goods ultimately seized were not in the process of destruction. Nor were they about to be removed from the jurisdiction. The officers were able to procure two warrants for Vale's arrest. They also had information that he was residing at the address where they found him. There is thus no reason [to] suppose that it was im-

practicable for them to obtain a search warrant as well. We decline to hold that an arrest on the street can provide its own 'exigent circumstance' so as to justify a warrantless search of the arrestee's house.

Mr. Justice Black dissented: "[Vale's] arrest took place near the house, and anyone observing from inside would surely have been alerted to destroy the stocks of contraband which the police believed Vale had left there. [T]he police were faced with the choice of risking the immediate destruction of evidence or entering the house and conducting a search. I cannot say that their decision to search was unreasonable."

Welsh v. Wisconsin, 466 U.S. 740 (1984), provides yet another example of a situation when the exception did not apply. In that case, police received eyewitness reports indicating that Welsh had been driving under the influence of alcohol. The police went to Welsh's home, and, when Welsh's stepdaughter answered the door, the police entered and proceeded to Welsh's bedroom where they found him lying in bed. The police arrested Welsh and took him to the police station where he refused to submit to a breathalyzer test. Emphasizing the sanctity of the home, the Court concluded that the police acted improperly since they were unable to show that exigent circumstances existed. The Court found that there was no hot pursuit. It also found that there was no continuing threat to "public safety" because Welsh had abandoned his car and returned home. The only need for immediate action stemmed from the fact there was "evanescent" evidence in the sense that police wanted to test Welsh's blood-alcohol level before the level of alcohol dissipated. However, the Court concluded that the state's interest in the evidence was minimal given that the state had chosen to classify the offense as "noncriminal." "[Given] this expression of the State's interest, a warrantless home arrest cannot be upheld simply because evidence of the petitioner's blood-alcohol level might have dissipated while the police obtained a warrant." Justice White dissented: "[T]his Court has long recognized the compelling state interest in highway safety."

Other exigent circumstances cases have dealt with police attempts to gather evidence from the body of a suspect. Like *Welsh*, these cases usually involve "evanescent evidence"—evidence that is likely to disappear absent prompt or immediate action. For example, in *Cupp v. Murphy*, 412 U.S. 291 (1973), Murphy's wife died by strangulation at her home, and there was no evidence of a break-in or robbery. During questioning, the police noticed a dark spot on Murphy's finger. Suspecting that the spot might be dried blood, and aware that strangulation often leaves evidence under the assailant's fingernails, the police requested permission to take a sample of the spot. When Murphy refused, and was seen trying to remove the blood, the police took the sample without a warrant. Tests revealed that the samples included traces from the victim's skin and blood. The Court upheld the search: "[C]onsidering the existence of probable cause, the very limited intrusion undertaken incident to the station house detention, and the ready destructibility of the evidence, we cannot say that this search violated the Fourth and Fourteenth Amendments." Mr. Justice Douglas dissented in part: "[Scraping] a man's fingernails is an invasion [of] privacy and it is tolerable, constitutionally speaking, only if there is a warrant for a search or seizure issued by a magistrate on a showing of 'probable cause' that the suspect had committed the crime. [Murphy] could have been detained while one was sought; and that detention would have preserved the perishable evidence the police sought."

In *Rochin v. California*, 342 U.S. 165 (1952), the police, who believed that Rochin was selling narcotics, went to his home and found two capsules which might have been narcotics. When the officers inquired about the capsules, Rochin immediately swallowed them. Rochin was handcuffed and taken to a hospital where the police instructed doctors to force an emetic solution into Rochin's stomach through a tube despite his objections. The solution caused Rochin to vomit and the police recovered the capsules which were found to contain morphine. In concluding that the police had violated Rochin's rights, the Court referred to the Due Process Clause which it characterized as focusing on whether the police actions had offended "canons of decency and fairness" which apply even to those "charged with the most heinous offenses." The Court viewed the "canons of decency and fairness" as "so rooted in the traditions and conscience of our people as to be ranked as fundamental" or as "implicit in the concept of ordered liberty." The Court concluded that the officer's conduct shocked the conscience of the court:

> Illegally breaking into the privacy of the petitioner, the struggle to open his mouth and remove what was there, the forcible extraction of his stomach's contents—this course of proceeding by agents of government to obtain evidence is bound to offend even hardened sensibilities. They are methods too close to the rack and the screw to permit of constitutional differentiation.

Rochin was followed by *Schmerber v. California*, 384 U.S. 757 (1966) where Schmerber was arrested at a hospital while receiving treatment for injuries suffered in an automobile accident. A police officer, who believed that Schmereber's intoxication caused the accident, directed a physician to take a blood sample from him. Chemical analysis of the sample revealed that Schmereber was legally intoxicated, and the analysis was used to convict him. The Court upheld the blood sample extraction even though it involved an intrusion into Schmerber's body. Although the Court rejected a Fifth Amendment privilege against self-incrimination challenge (because the withdrawal of blood is "non-testimonial" in nature), the court noted that the officer had probable cause to arrest Schmerber, when he "arrived at the scene shortly after the accident smelled liquor on petitioner's breath, [and] petitioner's eyes were 'bloodshot, watery, sort of a glassy appearance.' " The officer also observed Schmerber at the hospital and witnessed similar evidence of intoxication. The Court noted that search warrants are ordinarily required for searches of homes, and should also be required for bodily intrusions. Nevertheless, the Court upheld the search on the basis that was an "emergency" which would have led to the destruction of evidence. The Court relied on evidence suggesting that "the percentage of alcohol in the blood begins to diminish shortly after drinking stops, as the body functions to eliminate it from the systems' " and therefore there was insufficient time to seek a warrant. Accordingly, the Court held that withdrawal of the blood was appropriate as incident to petitioner's arrest. The Court emphasized that the test used was "reasonable," was highly effective in determining whether an individual is intoxicated, is commonly used in routine physical examinations, the quantity of blood extracted was minimal, and the procedure involves virtually no risk, trauma, or pain. The Court emphasized that the test was performed in a reasonable manner: "by a physician in a hospital environment according to accepted medical practices."

8. Special needs cases

A number of cases have created exceptions to the warrant requirement for so-called "special needs" situations. For example, *Skinner v. Railway Labor Executives' Association*, 489 U.S. 602 (1989) involved a challenge to Federal Railroad Administration (FRA) regulations mandating blood and urine tests of railroad employees involved in "major" train accidents, and authorizing railroads to administer breath and urine tests to employees who violate certain safety rules. The regulations were designed to combine the problem of drug and controlled substance abuse by such employees. The Court upheld the regulations emphasizing the governmental interest ("in ensuring the safety of the traveling public and of the employees themselves"), and noting the need to exercise supervision to make sure that restrictions on drug and alcohol use are being observed. The Court noted the evanescent nature of drugs and alcohol in the bloodstream, and the need to act quickly to take samples after an accident: "[T]he delay necessary to procure a warrant nevertheless may result in the destruction of valuable evidence." Indeed, the Court held that the tests could be based on "reasonable suspicion" rather than "probable cause" because the "privacy interests implicated by the search are minimal," and delay could jeopardize "an important governmental interest."

The Court also found that the intrusion on privacy was limited. In part, this was due to the fact the movement of railroad employees was already restricted by their work, and any "additional interference with . . . freedom of movement that occurs in the time it takes to procure a blood, breath, or urine sample for testing cannot, by itself, be said to infringe significant privacy interests." The Court also found that railroad employees suffered from a diminished expectation of privacy due to the fact that they worked "in an industry that is regulated pervasively to ensure safety, a goal dependent, in substantial part, on the health and fitness of covered employees."

To the extent that breath tests were involved, the Court found that they were not intrusive, could be conducted safely outside a hospital environment, and "with a minimum of inconvenience or embarrassment." Also, "breath tests reveal the level of alcohol in the employee's bloodstream and nothing more." The Court was more concerned about urine tests which the Court refused to characterize as "minimal." But the Court found them less intrusive here because they were not collected under the direct observance of a monitor. In addition, the sample was collected in a medical environment.

The Court held that drug testing could be required even in the absence of a reasonable suspicion. The Court emphasized that the employees' jobs involved them in "duties fraught with such risks of injury to others that even a momentary lapse of attention can have disastrous consequences." In addition, the testing helped railroads gain "invaluable information about the causes of major accidents" and allowed them "to take appropriate measures to safeguard the general public." Testing would help railroads determine, not only whether an accident was caused by alcohol or drug impairment, but whether impairment aggravated an accident caused by other considerations. "[A] requirement of particularized suspicion of drug or alcohol use would seriously impede an employer's ability to obtain this information, despite its obvious importance. Experience confirms the FRA's judgment that the scene of a serious rail accident is chaotic."

Justice Marshall dissented arguing that probable cause is an "indispensable prerequisite for a full-scale search." He found this testing program objectionable because it allowed testing even "if every member of this group gives every indication of sobriety and attentiveness." In addition, to the extent that the test involved the drawing of blood, he found a significant intrusion from the fact that a hypodermic needle could be used to pierce the employee's skin. He also objected to a urine test because it "intrudes deeply on privacy and bodily integrity. Urination is among the most private of activities. It is generally forbidden in public, eschewed as a matter of conversation, and performed in places designed to preserve this tradition of personal seclusion." Finally, he viewed the testing itself as a further intrusion because it might detect not only drugs or alcohol but also "medical disorders such as epilepsy, diabetes, and clinical depression." He felt that the benefits of suspicionless blood and urine testing were outweighed by the costs.

Drug tests for pregnant women. In *Ferguson v. City of Charleston*, 532 U.S. 67 (2001), the Medical University of South Carolina (MUSC) became concerned about cocaine use by pregnant women. In an effort to cooperate with state officials who were prosecuting pregnant users of cocaine, MUSC developed a policy of testing pregnant women for cocaine use if they met any of nine diagnostic criteria (no prenatal care, late prenatal care after 24 weeks gestation, incomplete prenatal care, abruptio placentae, intrauterine fetal death, preterm labor "of no obvious cause," IUGR [intrauterine growth retardation] "of no obvious cause," previously known drug or alcohol abuse, unexplained congenital anomalies). Once the urine tests were executed, MUSC developed a "chain of custody" designed to make sure that the results could be used in criminal proceedings. The policy also included education and referral to a substance abuse clinic, but used the threat of criminal sanctions to coerce cooperation. If the women cooperated, they were not prosecuted. The issue was whether the hospital's decision to perform a diagnostic test without consent and without a warrant constituted an unreasonable search.

The Court concluded that this case differed from its prior holdings in *Skinner, Von Raab, Vernonia,* and *Chandler.* The Court again resorted to balancing by focusing on "the individual's interest in privacy against the 'special needs' that supported the program." The Court regarded the invasion that occurred from a drug test as "far more substantial" than the invasion involved in other cases. Unlike the prior "special needs" cases, the Court noted that the typical medical patient expects that the results of diagnostic tests will not be released to third parties. The Court noted that its prior special needs cases had involved programs that were "divorced from the State's general interest in law enforcement." In this case, the purpose of the program was to use "law enforcement to coerce the patients into substance abuse treatment." The Court indicated that it would uphold laws requiring medical personnel to report when "in the course of ordinary medical procedures aimed at helping the patient herself, come across information that under rules of law or ethics is subject to reporting requirements."

The Court then focused on the state interest in protecting the health of the mother and child. The Court found that the purpose was "ultimately indistinguishable from the general interest in crime control." The hospital's policy focused on compliance with police department guidelines for the preservation of evidence. Thus, it considered such factors as "the chain of custody, the range of possible criminal charges, and the logistics of police notification and arrests." The policy did not focus on medical treatment for the mother or the infant although it did provide for treatment of the mother's addiction. In addition, the police were extensively involved in development and administration of the policy. So, the goal was to generate evidence for law enforcement purposes. "The threat of law enforcement may ultimately have been intended as a means to an end, but the direct and primary purpose of MUSC's policy was to ensure the use of those means." "Given the primary purpose of the Charleston program, which was to use the threat of arrest and prosecution in order to force women into treatment, and given the extensive involvement of law enforcement officials at every stage of the policy, this case simply does not fit within the closely guarded category of 'special needs.' "

While medical officials had an obligation "to provide the police with evidence of criminal conduct that they inadvertently acquire in the course of routine treatment, when they could not undertake to obtain such evidence from their patients *for the specific purpose of incriminating those patients,* without making sure that the patients are fully informed about their constitutional rights, as standards of knowing waiver require."

Justice Scalia, joined by two other justices, dissented. He argued that MUSC was ministering not only to the mother, but also to the children. "[What] petitioners, the Court, and to a lesser extent the concurrence really object to is not the urine testing, but the hospital's reporting of positive drug-test results to police. But the latter is obviously not a search." He concluded that extraction of the drug sample was with consent, and that there was no evidence that the consent was invalid. "Until today, we have *never* held—or even suggested—that material which a person voluntarily entrusts to someone else cannot be given by that person to the police, and used for whatever evidence it may contain."

In *Samson v. California*, 126 S.Ct. 2193 (2006), the Court upheld a California statute providing that parolees, as a condition of their release, could be searched "at any time of the day or night, with or without a search warrant and with or without cause." In determining that the search was "reasonable," the Court balanced a parolee's expectation of privacy against the degree to which the search is needed "for the promotion of legitimate governmental interests." Relying on *Knights*, the Court noted that "parolees have fewer expectations of privacy than probationers," and that "parole is more akin to imprisonment than probation is to imprisonment." "The essence of parole is release from prison, before the completion of sentence, on the condition that the prisoner abides by certain rules during the balance of the sentence." Since these conditions had been clearly expressed to the parolee, the Court found that petitioner did not have an expectation of privacy that society would recognize as legitimate. In addition, the Court concluded that the State has an "overwhelming interest" in supervising parolees because "parolees . . . are more likely to commit future criminal offenses." Justice Stevens, joined by justices Souter and Breyer, dissented, arguing that "neither *Knights* nor *Griffin* supports a regime of suspicionless searches, conducted pursuant to a blanket grant of discretion untethered by any procedural safeguards, by law enforcement personnel who have no special interest in the welfare of the parolee or probationer." "The suspicionless search is the very evil the Fourth Amendment was intended to stamp out."

POINTS TO REMEMBER

- The police can dispense with a warrant when they are faced with "exigent circumstances."

- Examples of exigent circumstances include situations in which a police officer hears shots from a nearby apartment followed by cries for help, when a fireman breaks down the door of a burning house to rescue occupants, or when a police officer is hot pursuit of a dangerous fleeing felon.

- The exigent circumstances exception is frequently invoked when police act quickly to prevent the destruction of evidence.

- Even though the police arrest a suspect outside his home, the police may not ordinarily enter and search the home without a warrant absent some indication that evidence inside the house is about to be destroyed.

- In limited circumstances, the police may remove evidence from the body of a suspect without a warrant (i.e., a suspect, who was thought to have strangled his wife, was seen scraping blood from his fingernails).

- Generally, the justification for this type of extraction focuses on "evanescent" or disappearing evidence. In other words, if the police do not act quickly, the evidence will be lost.

- Intrusions into a suspect's body are limited by the "canons of decency and fairness" implicit in the "concept of ordered liberty" found in the due process clause.

- Under these "canons," the police may not force emetic solution into a suspect's stomach and force him to regurgitate evidence.

- Assuming that the procedure used presents little risk to the suspect, and is conducted under appropriate medical conditions, the police might be permitted to make a warrantless extraction of a blood sample from a person who they reasonably believe was driving under the influence of alcohol.

- The Court struck down drug testing programs for pregnant women.

- The Court found that this type of testing did not fall within the Court's prior precedents governing drug testing.

9. Special rules for school-age children

In a number of cases, the Court has applied special rules to searches of school-age children. In *New Jersey v. T.L.O.*, 469 U.S. 325 (1985), the Court upheld a limited search of a high school student. In that case, a teacher found two girls smoking in a lavatory, and took both girls to the assistant vice principal, Mr. Choplick. When T.L.O. denied that she had been smoking, Choplick demanded to see her purse where he found cigarettes, as well as rolling papers, marijuana and a substantial number of one-dollar bills. At that point, T.L.O. confessed to the crime of selling marijuana. The Court upheld the search. Although the Court held that the Fourth Amendment applies to searches by public school officials, the Court balanced the child's interest in privacy against "the substantial interest of teachers and administrators in maintaining discipline in the classroom and on school grounds."

Noting that public schools had been the scene of drug use and violent crimes, the Court held that the "school setting requires some easing of the restrictions to which searches by public authorities are ordinarily subject." The Court declined to impose the warrant requirement, and held that searches should be evaluated under a two-part test that focuses on the "reasonableness" of the school's action. The question is whether the search was "justified at its inception" by virtue of the fact that the search was "reasonably related in scope to the circumstances which justified the interference in the first place." A search would be upheld if the school official had "reasonable grounds for suspecting that the search [would] turn up evidence that the student has violated or is violating either the law or the rules of the school." In addition, the search must be "reasonably related to the objectives of the search and not excessively intrusive in light of the age and sex of the student and the nature of the infraction."

Applying these criteria, the Court upheld Choplick's action. Since a teacher had reported that she saw T.L.O. smoking in a lavatory, Choplick had reason to believe that she was carrying cigarettes in her purse. Although the search extended to a zippered compartment in the purse, the Court held that Choplick acted reasonably because he had already found rolling papers and marijuana. When the zippered compartment revealed an index card with a notation of "people who owe me money," Choplick acted appropriately in reading two letters that he found in the compartment to see whether T.L.O. was involved in drug trafficking.

The Court has also rendered two "special needs" decisions relating to drug testing of public school students. In *Vernonia School Dist. 47J v. Acton,* 515 U.S. 646 (1995), the Court upheld a school policy providing for the suspicionless drug testing of school athletes. While the Court agreed that the testing implicated Fourth Amendment interests (the collection and analysis of drug samples involved a search), the Court concluded that a warrant and probable cause might be inappropriate in this context because such requirements " 'would unduly interfere with the maintenance of the swift and informal disciplinary procedures [that are] needed.' "The Court did not condone all school drug testing, but rather conducted a fact-specific balancing of the children's Fourth Amendment rights and legitimate governmental interests. In analyzing the privacy interest, the Court placed great emphasis on the fact that the testing took place in a school environment, noting that a "student's privacy interest is limited that environment where the State is responsible for maintaining discipline, health, and safety. Schoolchildren are routinely required to submit to physical examinations and vaccinations against disease." In addition, the Court found that the need to secure "order in the school environment sometimes requires that students be subjected to greater controls than those appropriate for adults."

In *Board of Education of Independent School District v. Earls,* 536 U.S. 822 (2002), the Court upheld drug tests for all students involved in extracurricular activities. In that case, a rural school district adopted a student drug testing policy that required all middle and high school students to participate in drug testing as a condition of participating in a variety of competitive extracurricular activities. The policy required students to take a drug test before participating, to submit to random drug testing while participating in that activity, and to agree to be tested at any time upon reasonable suspicion. The tests were conducted by urinalysis and were designed to detect illegal drugs (i.e., amphetamines, marijuana, cocaine, opiates, and barbiturates), but not to detect medical conditions or prescription medications. The testing policy was challenged by participants in the show choir, the marching band, the Academic Team, and the National Honor Society.

Once again the Court applied a balancing test and weighed "the nature of the intrusion on the individual's privacy against the promotion of legitimate governmental interests." The Court refused to hold that the Fourth Amendment imposes an "irreducible requirement of [individualized] suspicion." Indeed, the Court held that it might be impractical to apply a probable cause standard in the school environment. The Court noted that "special needs" are involved in the public school context, and that "Fourth Amendment rights . . . are different in public schools" because schools have custodial and tutelary responsibility for children.

In analyzing the testing policy, the Court did not regard as critical the fact that children participating in nonathletic extracurricular activities are not subject to physicals and communal undress to which athletes are subject. In any event, the Court found that students who participate in competitive extracurricular activities voluntarily subject themselves to many of the same intrusions on their privacy as do athletes with occasional off-campus travel and communal undress, and all have special rules for participation imposed by the school and state associations. As a result, the Court found that students had a diminished expectation of privacy. The Court emphasized that the urine samples were collected in a less intrusive way because the faculty monitor waited outside the door to collect the sample, and did not observe the act of urination, and the Court held this method of collection to be a "negligible" intrusion.

The Court also emphasized that the policy required the school to keep test results confidential in a file separate from a student's other educational records, and provided that results could only be released to school personnel on a "need to know" basis. In addition, test results could not be turned over to the police and could not lead to discipline or academic consequences. Test results might be used to limit participation in extracurricular activities if a student tested positive twice. However, the first positive test would result only in a meeting between school officials and the student's parent or guardian, and the student could continue to participate in extracurricular activities if he received drug counseling and had a second test within two weeks. A second positive test could result in a 14 day suspension and a requirement of monthly tests. A third positive test could result in a suspension for 88 days or the remainder of the academic year, whichever was longer. As a result, the Court concluded that the "the invasion of students' privacy is not significant."

In analyzing the governmental interest, and "the efficacy of the Policy in meeting them," the Court emphasized "the importance of the governmental concern in preventing drug use by schoolchildren," and it acknowledged that the drug abuse problem has gotten worse. The Court noted that schools have a "special responsibility" for children for whom they have "undertaken a special responsibility of care and direction," and that the school district presented evidence of drug use in its schools.

The Court noted that it has not required "a particularized or pervasive drug problem before allowing the government to conduct suspicionless drug testing." In part, this was due to the need to "prevent and deter the substantial harm of childhood drug use." The school need not wait until the problem is out of hand. In addition, the Court found that the school had an interest in testing both athletes and non-athletes engaged in extracurricular activities, and that "the safety interest furthered by drug testing is undoubtedly substantial for all children, athletes and non-athletes alike." The Court concluded that an "individualized reasonable suspicion of wrongdoing" was not required because it would place various burdens on schools and might subject them to suits, thereby rendering the overall program less effective. The Court concluded that "testing students who participate in extracurricular activities is a reasonably effective means of addressing the School District's legitimate concerns in preventing, deterring, and detecting drug use."

Justice Ginsburg, joined by three other justices, dissented. She argued that the testing program was "capricious, even perverse": "Petitioners' policy targets for testing a student population least likely to be at risk from illicit drugs and their damaging effects." She also argued that "invasive and suspicionless drug testing" could not be justified solely based on a showing that "drugs jeopardize the life and health of those who use them." She also argued that "[i]nterscholastic athletics similarly require close safety and health regulation; a school's choir, band, and academic team do not."

Strip Searches of Students. In *Safford v. Unified School District # 1 v. Redding*, 129 S.Ct. 2633 (2009), when school officials developed reason to believe that a 13 year-old female student had concealed prescription and over-the-counter drugs in her clothes, they searched her bra and underpants. The incident began when the assistant principal of the school (Kerry Wilson) came into the room and asked Savana (the girl in question) to go to his office. There, he showed her a day planner, unzipped, in which there were several knives, lighters, a permanent marker, and a cigarette. Wilson asked Savana whether the planner was hers. Although Savana admitted that it was hers, she said claimed that she had lent it to a friend, Marissa Glines, a few days before, and that none of the items in the planner belonged to her. Wilson then showed Savana four white prescription-strength ibuprofen 400-mg pills, and one over-the-counter blue naproxen 200-mg pill, all used for pain and inflammation, but banned under school rules without advance permission. He asked Savana if she knew anything about the pills. Savana answered that she did not. Wilson then told Savana that he had received a report that she was giving these pills to fellow students; Savana denied it and agreed to let Wilson search her belongings. Helen Romero, an administrative assistant, came into the office, and together with Wilson searched Savana's backpack, finding nothing. At that point, Wilson instructed Romero to take Savana to the school nurse's office to search her clothes for pills. Romero and the nurse asked Savana to remove her jacket, socks, and shoes, leaving her in stretch pants and a T-shirt (both without pockets), which she was then asked to remove. Finally, Savana was told to pull her bra out and to the side and shake it, and to pull out the elastic on her underpants, thus exposing her breasts and pelvic area to some degree. No pills were found.

In *Safford*, the Court held that school officials had conducted an unreasonable search in violation of the Fourth Amendment. The Court noted that a standard of reasonable suspicion applied to a school administrator's search of a student, and that a school search "will be permissible in its scope when the measures adopted are reasonably related to the objectives of the search and not excessively intrusive in light of the age and sex of the student and the nature of the infraction." While the Court concluded that school officials had sufficient cause to justify searching Savanna's backpack and outer clothing, it regarded the strip search as too intrusive: "The very fact of Savana's pulling her underwear away from her body in the presence of the two officials who were able to see her necessarily exposed breasts and pelvic area to some degree, and both subjective and reasonable societal expectations of personal privacy support the treatment of such a search as categorically distinct, requiring distinct elements of justification on the part of school authorities for going beyond a search of outer clothing and belongings." For Savanna, it was potentially "embarrassing, frightening, and humiliating." Although the Court did not suggest that strip searches of students would never be allowed, it did hold that there were insufficient indications of danger in this case (in regard to the nature of the suspected drugs and the quantity), and insufficient reason to believe that Savanna was carrying the pills in her underwear. The court concluded that the "combination of these deficiencies was fatal to finding the search reasonable." Nevertheless, the Court held that school officials were entitled to qualified immunity against liability because there was a lack of clarity in the law at the time that they acted.

POINTS TO REMEMBER

- Special rules apply to searches of school-age children.

- School officials can conduct a limited search of high school students based on only a showing of "reasonable grounds for suspecting that the search [would] turn up evidence that the student has violated or is violating either the law or the rules of the school."

- In addition, school officials must show that the search is "reasonably related to the objectives of the search and not excessively intrusive in light of the age and sex of the student and the nature of the infraction."

- Suspicionless drug testing of student athletes has been upheld.

- Also upheld have been suspicionless drug testing of all students involved in extracurricular activities.

Chapter 5

POLICE INTERROGATIONS & CONFESSIONS

Focal Points for Police Interrogations and Confessions

- Pre-Miranda Due Process.

- McNabb-Mallory Rule.

- Pre-Miranda Sixth Amendment Massiah Right to Counsel.

- Fifth Amendment and Miranda.

- Miranda Custody.

- Miranda Interrogation.

- Adequate Miranda Warnings.

- Waiver of Miranda Rights.

- Invocation of Miranda Rights.

- Uses of Miranda-Defective Evidence.

- Post-Miranda Sixth Amendment Massiah Right to Counsel.

- Massiah Reliance on Counsel and Waiver.

- Massiah Deliberate Elicitation.

- Massiah Warnings and Waivers.

- Post-Miranda Due Process.

A. Pre–*Miranda* Doctrines

The most famous confession case of the 20th century is undoubtedly *Miranda v. Arizona*, 384 U.S. 436 (1966), holding that the Fifth Amendment requires "*Miranda* warnings" to be given to all persons during custodial interrogation. During the 30 years before *Miranda*, the Supreme Court relied on other doctrinal sources for judicial regulation of police interrogation. The Court created rules based on the Fourteenth Amendment right to Due Process, on the Sixth Amendment right to counsel, and on the Court's supervisory power over the federal courts. Both Due Process and Sixth Amendment doctrines continue to play an important role in legal challenges to police interrogation procedures. The post-*Miranda* versions of each of these doctrines have been influenced by the permutations of Fifth Amendment interpretations that have evolved in the decades since *Miranda* was decided.

1. Pre–Miranda Due Process

In *Brown v. Mississippi*, 297 U.S. 278 (1936), the Court issued its first decision holding that the admission into evidence of an involuntary confession by a state court violated Due Process. Earlier decisions concerning the admissibility of confessions in federal courts had relied on the common law of evidence or the Fifth Amendment privilege. But these grounds were not available in cases involving state defendants. The Supreme Court has no authority to revise the state common law rules of evidence, and the Fifth Amendment privilege did not apply to the states at the time of *Brown*. The *Brown* Court was forced to rely on the few precedents where state trial procedures had been condemned because of Due Process violations—where both court and jury were deceived by the prosecutor's deliberate use of perjured testimony, where indigent and illiterate defendants lacked defense counsel in a capital case, and where a defendant was "hurried to conviction under mob domination." See *Mooney v. Holohan*, 294 U.S. 103 (1935); *Powell v. Alabama*, 287 U.S. 45 (1932); *Moore v. Dempsey*, 261 U.S. 86 (1923). Like these trials, the *Brown* trial was labeled as a "mere pretense." *Brown* held that the police interrogation "method" of physical torture caused any confession to be "involuntary" and that the admission of such a statement into evidence violated Due Process. The Court reasoned that the use of such coerced confessions at trial "offends some principle of justice so rooted in the traditions and conscience of our people as to be ranked fundamental."

The facts of *Brown* presented an extreme example of police violence, and the Court declared that it was "difficult to conceive of methods more revolting to the sense of justice" than those used by the police in *Brown*. Three defendants were told that they would be physically tortured until they confessed. One was hanged three times from a tree and suffered two bouts of severe whipping. The other two defendants were whipped with a strap until their bare backs were cut to pieces. The police officers admitted that they had committed these acts. No evidence supported the capital convictions other than the confessions, and the Court assumed that the confessions were false. In the Court's view, the state had substituted "the rack and torture chamber" for the witness stand, and "contrived a conviction resting solely upon confessions obtained by violence."

Soon, however, more difficult Due Process cases arose to test the scope of the *Brown* prohibition on violent interrogations. The constitutional rhetoric of "involuntariness" derived from common law evidence concepts that banned the use of confessions produced by "inducements, promises, threats, violence, or any form of coercion." This Due Process prohibition came to be justified both by the need to prevent the use of "presumptively false evidence" in court, and by the need to prevent unfairness "in the use of evidence whether true or false." *Lisenba v. California*, 314 U.S. 219, 234–236 (1941). However, the concepts of "coercion" and "unfairness" were inherently subjective and difficult to define. In the ensuing years, the Court sometimes ruled that a confession was admissible as an act of "free will," despite the potentially coercive aspects of an interrogation. Yet over time, the Court expanded the definition of coercion to include physical and psychological treatment that fell short of the police brutality in *Brown*, and moved closer to a ruling that custodial interrogation was inherently coercive. Such a Due Process ruling never arrived, however. When *Miranda* was decided in 1966, the Court chose to shift the grounds for that ruling to the Fifth Amendment, soon after the privilege was applied to the states. See *Malloy v. Hogan*, 378 U.S. 1 (1964) (incorporating the Fifth Amendment privilege into Due Process as a fundamental right).

The first step toward an expanded definition of coercion was taken in *Ashcraft v. Tennessee*, 322 U.S. 143 (1944), where the defendant was interrogated *incommunicado* for thirty-six hours, without sleep or rest, by relays of officials. The *Ashcraft* confession was found to be involuntary *per se* because of an "inherently coercive" interrogation. Later cases illustrated three different approaches to finding Due Process violations by relying on a totality of circumstances. The first approach focused primarily on the traditional police methods of coercion, such as threats of violence, promises of incentives, use of false statements, or some combination of these methods. See *Malinski v. New York*, 324 U.S. 401 (1945) (a defendant is stripped to his underwear and promised "a good shellacking"); *Leyra v. Denno*, 347 U.S. 556 (1954) (police psychiatrist pretends to be regular doctor and promises relief from pain). Other cases also relied on the defendant's peculiar susceptibility to police coercion. This second approach relied on judicial scrutiny of a large number of factors that related to the police conduct, the surrounding circumstances, and the defendant's character and life experiences. See *Spano v. New York*, 360 U.S. 315 (1959) (defendant was foreign-born, only a junior high school graduate, had a history of emotional instability, was questioned in relays by many officers for eight hours, and was repeatedly told falsely that his failure to confess would cause his childhood friend to lose his job as a police cadet). Finally, the Due Process cases decided on the eve of *Miranda* exhibited a third type of totality analysis that focused on the characteristics of *incommunicado* interrogation rather than on the defendant's peculiar vulnerability. One example of this approach is provided by *Haynes v. Washington*, 373 U.S. 503 (1963).

The *Haynes* Court held that the defendant's confession was involuntary because his "will was overborne at the time he confessed" by the police refusal to allow the defendant to "call his wife to see about legal counsel," and by the police promise that he would be allowed to make such a call later if he confessed. This promise was false, as the police did not allow Haynes to call his wife until some days after his arrest and confession. The Court interpreted the police conduct in *Haynes* as an implicit threat to continue the defendant's *incommunicado* interrogation as long as necessary until a confession was obtained. Thus, one element of the *Haynes* reasoning relied on the traditional Due Process intolerance for a police threat, inducement, or trick.

However, a second element of the *Haynes* reasoning emphasized a different point, namely that the "context" of the Due Process violation involved the "basic techniques" of "secret and *incommunicado* detention and interrogation," including the withholding of any warnings about the rights to remain silent or consult counsel, and about the dangers that any "answers might be used against" the defendant. None of these warnings were Due Process requirements *per se*, although soon they would be required by *Miranda*. However, the police failure to provide these warnings was treated as evidence of coercion in *Haynes*, where the only other evidence of coercion was the false promise of access to counsel in exchange for a confession. No special vulnerability of the defendant to coercion was noted by the Court, and the interrogation by two officers lasted only one and a half hours. *Haynes* made it clear that a large, *Spano*-like accumulation of coercive circumstances was not necessary for a Due Process violation. Moreover, the *Haynes* Court's focus on the inherent coerciveness of custodial interrogation reveals a concern that transcends the scrutiny of the coercive particulars of police questioning of a given defendant. In the Court's words:

Official overzealousness of the type [in Haynes] has only deleterious effects. [I]t is the deprivation of the protected rights themselves which is fundamental and the most regrettable, not only because of the effect on the individual defendant, but because of the effect on our system of law and justice. Whether there is involved the brutal "third degree," or the more subtle, but no less offensive, methods here obtaining, official misconduct cannot but breed disrespect for law, as well as for those charged with its enforcement.

The post-*Brown* cases expressed a variety of rationales for the invalidation of confessions on Due Process grounds. The *Brown* Court condemned sham trials and revolting interrogation methods, but as the Court's definitions of coercion grew in scope, the rationales for those definitions grew in spirit. Post-*Brown* opinions expressed a desire for Due Process "procedural safeguards" that would protect members of "political, religious, or racial minorities" who might be the victim of "dictatorial" and "secret inquisitorial processes." *Chambers v. Florida*, 309 U.S. 227, 238 (1940). The standard police practice of *incommunicado* interrogation was criticized as being "subversive of the accusatorial system." *Watts v. Indiana*, 338 U.S. 49, 55 (1949). The focus on the "inquisitorial" aspects of interrogations led the Court to note the similarity between police "coercion" that violates Due Process and the "compulsion" that violates the Fifth Amendment. *Gallegos v. Colorado*, 370 U.S. 49, 51–52 (1962). In summarizing the rationales of its Due Process precedents in *Rogers v. Richmond*, 365 U.S. 534, 540–41 (1961), the Court explained that coerced confessions must be inadmissible because:

> the methods used to extract them offend an underlying principle in the enforcement of our criminal law: that ours is an accusatorial and not an inquisitorial system—a system in which the State must establish guilt by evidence independently and freely secured and may not by coercion prove its charge against an accused out of his own mouth.

Despite the Court's characterization of uncontrolled police interrogation as "the inquisitorial system without its safeguards" (namely the presence of counsel and a judge), a majority of the Court never created Due Process safeguards in the sense of concrete, positive requirements for police conduct during interrogations. *Watts*, 338 U.S. at 55. Instead, the Due Process decisions in the pre-*Miranda* era typically created case-by-case blueprints for police interrogations "gone wrong." Only a plurality of the Court was prepared to endorse a proposed Due Process requirement that a defendant should be entitled to consult with counsel any time after indictment on a capital charge. See *Spano v. New York*, 360 U.S. 315, 327 (1959) (Justice Douglas, concurring). Even in *Haynes*, the Court reiterated its traditional position that police interrogation "is undoubtedly an essential tool in effective law enforcement," and emphasized the need for case-by-case scrutiny:

The line between proper and permissible police conduct and techniques and methods offensive to due process is, at best, a difficult one to draw, particularly in cases such as this where it is necessary to make fine judgments as to the effect of psychologically coercive pressures and inducements on the mind and will of an accused. But we cannot escape the demands of judging or of making the difficult appraisals inherent in determining whether constitutional rights have been violated.

In post-*Miranda* Due Process decisions, the Court would retain this case-by-case approach. See *Arizona v. Fulminante*, 499 U.S. 279 (1991). However, the new element of police disregard of *Miranda* requirements became relevant in measuring coercion using the totality of the circumstances in Due Process inquiries. See *Mincey v. Arizona*, 437 U.S. 385 (1978). The Court also relied on *Miranda* policy concerns to reinterpret Due Process theory. See *Colorado v. Connelly*, 479 U.S. 157 (1986). For further discussion of post-*Miranda* Due Process doctrine, see part E of this chapter, *infra*.

2. The McNabb–Mallory Rule

The Supreme Court expanded its regulation of the admissibility of confessions in federal courts by creating new rules based on its historic supervisory power in *McNabb v. United States*, 318 U.S. 332 (1943). In the years before *Brown*, the Court relied on the common law of evidence in federal cases to bar the admission of confessions obtained by inducements, promises and threats. See *Hopt v. Utah*, 110 U.S. 574 (1884). See also *Bram v. United States*, 168 U.S. 532 (1897) (excluding involuntary confession based on common law of evidence and Fifth Amendment privilege). After the Fourteenth Amendment's Due Process doctrine emerged in *Brown* as the source of confession law for state courts, this doctrine became the model for Fifth Amendment Due Process law that applied to confession cases in federal courts. In *McNabb*, however, the Court decided to exercise its duty to establish and maintain "civilized standards of procedure and evidence" that go beyond "those minimal historic safeguards" which are required by "due process of law."

In its first use of this supervisory power in a confession case, the *McNabb* Court created an exclusionary rule for confessions obtained during the improper detention of arrestees who were not taken promptly to a federal judicial officer upon arrest. This rule was adopted as an enforcement mechanism for the statutory mandate that required federal agents to bring an arrested person to "the nearest judicial officer" for a "hearing, commitment, or taking bail for [trial]." See 18 U.S.C. § 5951. The Court reasoned that Congress intended that arrestees should be brought to a magistrate with "reasonable promptness." The Court also inferred that federal agents were not meant to assume the "function" of interrogation through subjecting "the accused to the pressures of a procedure which is wholly incompatible with the [very] restricted duties of the investigating and arresting officers of the [Government.]" The implicit purpose of the statute was held to be its role as a "safeguard" to guarantee that detentions of arrestees were based on "legal cause" and "to avoid all the evil implications of secret interrogations of persons accused of crime."

In fact, the interrogations in *McNabb* might have been found to violate Due Process, as two of the defendants were subjected "to unremitting questioning by numerous officers" for two days, and a third defendant was subjected to five or six hours of continuous questioning. All three defendants were without the "aid of friends or benefit of counsel." Had they been brought promptly to a judicial officer after arrest, they would have been informed about their right to counsel. However, the Court found it unnecessary to decide the Due Process issue in *McNabb*. In explaining the propriety of a "double standard" for confessions in state and federal courts, the Court declared that Due Process cases required the exercise of "appropriate respect for the deliberative judgments" of state officials, and that such federalism concerns were "wholly irrelevant to the formulation and application of proper standards for the enforcement of the federal criminal law in the federal courts."

When Congress incorporated the substance of the *McNabb* statute into Rule 5(a) of the Federal Rules of Criminal Procedure in 1946, the new rule explicitly required that arrested persons must be presented to a judicial officer "without unnecessary delay." In *Mallory v. United States*, 354 U.S. 449, 453 (1957), the Court interpreted this term as allowing arresting officers only a "brief delay" for such purposes as "quick verification through third parties" of an arrestee's statements. The Court repeatedly warned against the practice of pre-appearance questioning at "police headquarters" that "lends itself, even if not so designed, to eliciting damaging statements" from the arrestee. The six-hour delay in *Mallory* was held to be unnecessary, because a magistrate was readily available in the same building where the defendant was questioned for two hours and even given a lie detector test. As in *Haynes*, the *Mallory* Court criticized the federal agents' failure to tell the defendant about rights that soon would be described in *Miranda*'s required warnings.

The *McNabb–Mallory* rule never was incorporated into Due Process doctrine and applied to the states, despite repeated requests by state defendants for this federal remedy during the years between *McNabb* and *Miranda*. In theory, the rule created a virtual ban on custodial interrogation during the time after arrest and before a first appearance. When the rule was first created in *McNabb*, the Court saw no need to impose the rule on the states in lieu of the less demanding Due Process doctrine. Later, in the years after *Mallory*, the Court moved in the direction of creating more demanding Due Process standards, and experimented in cases such as *Massiah* and *Escobedo* with the idea of a Sixth Amendment ban on interrogation without the presence of counsel. Once *Miranda*'s Fifth Amendment safeguards were established in 1966, it was not clear whether the Court would continue to regard the *McNabb-Mallory* standard as a necessary extra safeguard for federal interrogations. This issue became moot in 1968 when Congress enacted legislation that effectively superceded the *McNabb-Mallory* rule in the Omnibus Crime Control and Safe Streets Act. The rule survives now only in states where it was codified or adopted as state law. Ultimately, the *McNabb-Mallory* rule became a museum piece of confession doctrine that lost its statutory legitimacy in the post-*Miranda* world.

3. The Pre–Miranda Sixth Amendment Massiah Right to Counsel

In *Massiah v. United States*, 377 U.S. 201 (1964), the Supreme Court held that an indicted defendant's surreptitious questioning by an undercover police agent violated the Sixth Amendment right to counsel. Years later, the Court declared that *Massiah* clearly established "that once adversary proceedings have commenced against an individual, he has a right to legal representation when the government interrogates him." *Brewer v. Williams*, 430 U.S. 387, 388 (1977). Yet the implications of *Massiah*'s holding were not so easy to discern at the time of the decision. Massiah was indicted for narcotics crimes, retained a lawyer, and was released on bail. His co-defendant agreed to allow the police to install a radio transmitter in his car, so the police could overhear his conversations with Massiah, which produced incriminating, inadmissible statements. A narrow formulation of *Massiah*'s holding would be as follows: If federal agents deliberately elicit incriminating statements from an indicted defendant, through surreptitious interrogation by an undercover agent, those statements may not be used against the defendant at his or her trial upon the charge for which he or she was indicted.

The *Massiah* Court began its analysis by citing with approval the *Spano* plurality's Due Process proposal that a *per se* right to consult with counsel during police questioning should be recognized for indicted defendants who possess the right to appointed counsel at trial. Only defendants charged with capital crimes would have benefited from this proposal in state courts at the time of *Spano*, because only those defendants had a *per se* Due Process right to appointed counsel at trial under the Court's modern interpretation of *Powell v. Alabama*, 287 U.S. 45 (1932). However, by adopting the *Spano* plurality's proposal as a matter of Sixth Amendment doctrine, the *Massiah* Court established a *per se* right to consult with counsel during police questioning for all federal defendants, because all such defendants qualified for appointed counsel at trial under the Sixth Amendment doctrine of *Johnson v. Zerbst*, 304 U.S. 458 (1938). The new Sixth Amendment *Massiah* right to consult counsel also applied implicitly to indicted state felony defendants, who now qualified for appointed counsel at trial according to *Gideon v. Wainwright*, 372 U.S. 335 (1963) (incorporating the Sixth Amendment right to counsel into Due Process as a fundamental right). Once this right to consult counsel was recognized in *Massiah*, it was evident that the scope of this right in the *Massiah* context had not been resolved by the *Spano* plurality. The defendant in *Spano* had been interrogated openly by police officers, not questioned surreptitiously by an undercover agent; the *Spano* defendant also explicitly asked for his attorney and had been denied any consultation with him. So the *Massiah* Court was required to explain what the "right to consult counsel" should entail in the context of an undercover interrogation where the defendant never realized that he needed to ask for counsel to protect his interests at trial.

The *Massiah* Court relied on three arguments to support its holding that the simple act of surreptitious, "deliberate elicitation" of incriminating statements was sufficient to violate the Sixth Amendment. First, the Court borrowed the reasoning of the *Spano* plurality in noting that the aid of counsel during interrogation was as important as the aid of counsel at trial. A lack of access to counsel during questioning "might deny a defendant 'effective representation by counsel at the only stage when legal aid and advice would help him.' " Second, the Court borrowed the reasoning of *Powell* in declaring that the period "from the time of arraignment until the beginning of [trial]" is the "most critical period of the proceedings." Counsel's investigation and preparation are "vitally important," and so defendants are "as much entitled to [the] aid of counsel during that period as at the trial itself." Finally, the *Massiah* Court recognized that if the Sixth Amendment right to consult counsel were to be meaningful, "it must apply to indirect and surreptitious interrogations as well as those conducted in the jailhouse." Otherwise, the police could evade the duty to allow consultation with counsel by relying instead on interrogations by undercover agents who would be immune from Sixth Amendment requirements. As a closing aside, the Court acknowledged that it was proper for the police and their agents to continue their investigation of the defendant, in order to discover the identities of the intended buyer of the narcotics and of other criminal associates. The Court thereby implied that the defendant's incriminating statements might be admissible in proceedings other than his trial on the narcotics offenses.

Massiah left open a number of questions that were not answered by the Court until the post-*Miranda* era. These questions included the following: When does the Sixth Amendment right to counsel attach? Is there a Sixth Amendment right to be informed of the *Massiah* right during interrogation? After the *Massiah* right attaches, must it be invoked through a request for counsel in the context of police interrogation? How may the right be waived? Does the ban on "deliberate elicitation" extend to conduct that does not involve actual questioning of the defendant? Ultimately, the Court chose to provide answers to these questions after many *Miranda* precedents addressed the same questions in the Fifth Amendment context. Thus, the Court's interpretations of *Massiah* reflect the influence of many elements of *Miranda* doctrine. For further discussion of *Massiah* doctrine in the post-*Miranda* era, see part D of this chapter, *infra*.

Soon after *Massiah*, the Court took a step in the direction of expanding the Sixth Amendment right to consult counsel into the pre-indictment phase of a criminal proceeding in *Escobedo v. Illinois*, 378 U.S. 478 (1964). Ultimately, however, the rights created in *Escobedo* would become redundant after *Miranda*. The arrested defendant in *Escobedo* had not been indicted, and the police had denied his requests to consult his counsel during his interrogation. The prosecutor argued that if pre-indictment defendants were to be granted *Massiah* rights, this would cause a significant reduction in the number of confessions obtained from them. The *Escobedo* Court rejected this argument as a reason for limiting the Sixth Amendment to the post-indictment phase of a criminal proceeding. The scope of the new *Escobedo* right was defined as follows:

[We] hold, therefore, that where, as here, the investigation is no longer a general inquiry into an unsolved crime but has begun to focus on a particular suspect, the suspect has been taken into police custody, the police carry out a process of interrogations that lends itself to eliciting incriminating statements, the suspect has requested and been denied an opportunity to consult with his lawyer, and the police have not effectively warned him of his absolute constitutional right to remain silent, the accused has been denied "The Assistance of Counsel" in violation of the Sixth Amendment. . .

Notably, the *Escobedo* Court's rationale for its expansion of the *Massiah* right was broad enough to encompass the provision of

Sixth Amendment rights to all arrested defendants. For example, the Court reasoned that the right to counsel at trial "would be a very hollow thing" if defendants were denied counsel at the "critical" arrest stage "when legal aid and advice are surely needed." In heated terms, the Court criticized the prosecution's plea for a restriction of the *Massiah* right to the post-indictment context, declaring that "[t]he rule sought by the State here [would] make the trial no more than an appeal from the interrogation." However, the *Escobedo's* Court's limited holding suggested that the Court was reluctant to create a right to consult counsel during all interrogations. It appeared that the *Escobedo* Court meant to extend the *Massiah* right only to pre-indictment defendants who asked for counsel, and gave such defendants only the right not to be interrogated in the absence of counsel. *Escobedo* did not give these defendants the literal right to consult with counsel.

Only two years after *Escobedo*, the Court created new Fifth Amendment rights in *Miranda* that gave all interrogated arrestees, including those protected by *Escobedo*, the express right to be warned about the right to remain silent. *Miranda* also went further than *Escobedo* by giving defendants a right to additional warnings concerning the dangers of self-incrimination and the guarantee of appointed counsel for indigents. But like *Escobedo*, *Miranda* did not provide a right of actual consultation with counsel. Instead, *Miranda* provided the right to be informed about the right to consult counsel, and the right not to be interrogated in the absence of counsel once the right to consult counsel is invoked. In retrospect, *Escobedo* was a doctrinal stepping stone to *Miranda*. This is revealed both by the similarity of the holdings in these cases, and by the *Miranda* Court's recognition that the Fifth Amendment concept of "custodial interrogation" was meant to replace *Escobedo's* concept of a "focus" on the defendant.

Having served as a stepping stone to *Miranda*, *Escobedo* rights effectively became redundant once *Miranda* rights were created. At first, subsequent cases limited *Escobedo* to its facts, and later the Court repudiated the *Escobedo* rationale that extended the Sixth Amendment right to counsel to the pre-indictment phase of a criminal investigation. This was because the Court became committed to the rule that the right to counsel attaches only at "critical stages" that occur after "the initiation of adversary judicial criminal proceedings—whether by way of formal charge, preliminary hearing, indictment, information, or arraignment." *Kirby v. Illinois*, 406 U.S. 682, 689 (1972) (no Sixth Amendment right to counsel at a pre-indictment lineup). Only the initiation of adversary judicial proceedings now marks the commencement of a "criminal prosecution" under the Sixth Amendment. In the end, *Escobedo's* Sixth Amendment grounding was formally rejected altogether, and its now redundant ruling was reinterpreted as a Fifth Amendment precedent in *Moran v. Burbine*, 475 U.S. 412 (1986).

B. The Fifth Amendment and *Miranda*

In *Miranda v. Arizona*, 384 U.S. 436, 479 (1966), the Supreme Court found the practice of *incommunicado* interrogation to be "at odds with" the Fifth Amendment privilege, and decided that unless "adequate protective devices" are "employed to dispel the compulsion inherent in custodial surroundings, no statement obtained from a defendant can truly be the product of his free choice." The "Fifth Amendment safeguards" proposed by the Court included the following:

> [An interrogated person in custody] must be warned prior to any questioning that he has the right to remain silent, that anything he says can be used against him in a court of law, that he has the right to the presence of an attorney, and that if he cannot afford an attorney one will be appointed for him prior to any questioning if he so desires. Opportunity to exercise these rights must be afforded to him throughout the interrogation. After such warnings have been given, and such opportunity afforded him, the individual may knowingly and intelligently waive these rights and agree to answer questions or make a statement. But unless and until such warnings and waiver are demonstrated by the prosecution at trial, no evidence obtained as a result of interrogation can be used against him.

In addition to imposing a duty to give "*Miranda* warnings" before seeking a waiver, the Court also required police to honor the defendant's invocations of the Fifth Amendment rights to silence or counsel:

> Once warnings have been given, the subsequent procedure is clear. If the individual indicates in any manner, at any time prior to or during questioning, that he wishes to remain silent, the interrogation must cease. [If] the individual states that he wants an attorney, the interrogation must cease until an attorney is present. At that time, the individual must have an opportunity to confer with the attorney and to have him present during any subsequent questioning. If the individual cannot obtain an attorney and he indicates that he wants one before speaking to police, they must respect his decision to remain silent.

> [If] authorities conclude that they will not provide counsel during a reasonable period of time in which investigation in the field is carried out, they may refrain from doing so without violating the

person's Fifth Amendment privilege so long as they do not question him during that time.

The bar to admissibility of confessions obtained in violation of these rules extends to all statements made during custodial interrogation, for "no distinction may be drawn between inculpatory statements and statements alleged to be merely 'exculpatory.' "

The *Miranda* rules can be seen as an outgrowth of the Court's concern in Due Process cases with police failure to give warnings concerning the rights to silence and counsel, and with police refusal to honor the requests to consult counsel made by persons undergoing interrogation. The FBI used the four "*Miranda* warnings" before *Miranda* made them Fifth Amendment requirements. Therefore, the Court predicted that the FBI practice "can readily be emulated by state and local enforcement agencies," and opined that the new practices would not create "an undue interference with a proper system of law enforcement." Yet these new rules were quite controversial, as revealed in the harsh criticisms of the four *Miranda* dissenters. Justice Harlan noted that at least thirty states had argued against further limitations on interrogation in their briefs before the Court, and he argued that the Court's ruling was a "heavy-handed," "one-sided," "precipitous" form of "hazardous experimentation" that would present a "real risk" to "society's welfare" because it would "markedly decrease" the number of confessions. Justice White argued that the goal of the *Miranda* majority was to forbid interrogation without counsel "for all practical purposes," and predicted that the new rules would cause a decrease in convictions and "have a corrosive effect" on the deterrence of crime. While the worst fears of the dissenters turned out to be unfounded, the sharp disagreements evidenced in the *Miranda* opinion continue to characterize many divided decisions interpreting the *Miranda* rules in later decades.

The core of the *Miranda* Court's reasoning consisted of two findings. The first finding was that all custodial interrogation creates a "potentiality for compulsion." The second was that the "human dignity" value of the Fifth Amendment would be protected only if new rules were created to limit this inherent compulsion so that confessions may be found to be "truly [the] product of [a person's] free choice." The Court's first finding was based on its review of police manual instructions for interrogation techniques; the substance of these manuals was summarized in the *Miranda* opinion, in order to illustrate the "atmosphere of domination" and manipulation that the Court found to be characteristic of modern interrogation practice. The Court's second finding was based on the conviction that a "full opportunity to exercise the privilege" could be provided at the station house if the accused were to be "adequately and effectively apprised of his rights and the exercise of those rights [fully] honored."

Thus, the Due Process goal of protecting a defendant's "free will" was also a Fifth Amendment goal in *Miranda*. But *Miranda* articulated this goal as a mandate to protect the privilege, and created a Fifth Amendment right to counsel for the purpose of protecting a defendant's access to the privilege during the interrogation process. Further, *Miranda* spelled out a positive blueprint for police conduct that was not supplied in Due Process cases. Police officers benefitted from the *Miranda* regime, because if they gave warnings and honored invocations, they gained the authority to seek *Miranda* waivers that would make confessions admissible. The willingness of interrogated persons to waive their rights was a phenomenon that the *Miranda* dissenters did not take into account in their criticisms of the majority opinion. Justice White's dissent, for example, predicted that requiring "an express waiver [and] an express end to questioning whenever [an interrogated person] demurs must heavily handicap questioning," and that "to suggest or provide" counsel "simply invites the end of the interrogation." But numerous post-*Miranda* precedents reveal that the mere provision of warnings does not discourage some defendants from waiving their rights, nor does the cut off of questioning put an end to the prospect of later waivers being obtained from defendants who change their minds about their invocations.

The *Miranda* Court left many questions open for resolution in later cases, especially definitional questions. The Court provided little guidance on the meaning of two key concepts, namely "custodial interrogation" and "knowing and intelligent waiver." The custody concept was described broadly as the status of being "deprived [of] freedom of action in any significant way," while "interrogation" was described simply as being "subjected to questioning." A waiver was recognized as not being "voluntary" if an accused is "threatened, tricked, or cajoled." But otherwise the Court appeared to assume that case-by-case scrutiny of the totality of the circumstances would be necessary to assess the validity of a waiver. Other less obvious questions were left open, such as the definition of adequate warnings, adequate invocations, and adequate retractions of invocations.

Miranda is also noteworthy for the rights it does not provide. There is no right to be informed that if a defendant invokes silence or counsel rights, a cut off of questioning will follow. A "station house lawyer" does not have to be "present at all times to advise prisoners." Therefore, any invoking defendant who seeks counsel may be denied access to counsel. Such a defendant has no right to be informed why counsel is being denied, as long as police honor the invocation by ending the interrogation. *Miranda* provides no right to make contact with people in the world outside the interrogation room, and the case does not speak to the question whether defense counsel may obtain access to a client during interrogation. Finally, despite the critical tone of the Court's litany of interrogation procedures, none of these techniques of psychological "domination" is declared to be a *Miranda* violation *per se*. So traditional ploys such as Mutt and Jeff routines or false identifications in phony lineups are events that have no independent significance, except as they may affect the character and validity of warnings, waivers, or invocations.

As the Court explained, the *Miranda* rules are not intended to be a "constitutional straightjacket," and the states courts and legislatures are free to create different ones to protect the privilege, as long as they are "equally effective." Despite this concession, the Court has not recognized any alternate rules as adequate *Miranda* substitutes, and has invalidated a Congressional attempt to overrule *Miranda* by legislation. See *Dickerson v. United States*, 530 U.S. 428 (2000) (Congress cannot supercede Fifth Amendment safeguards with statutory "voluntariness" standard to govern the admissibility of confessions in federal court). The meaning of the *Miranda* Court's labeling of *Miranda* rights as "prophylactic safeguards" has occasioned much debate, but unlike Fourth Amendment claims, *Miranda* claims are not barred from federal habeas review. *Withrow v. Williams*, 507 U.S. 680 (1993). *Compare Chavez v. Martinez*, 538 U.S. 760 (2003) (explaining how *Miranda* violation may not give rise to a Fifth Amendment claim to create a cause of action under § 1983).

The Court has, however, created some significant exceptions to *Miranda*. For example, the rules do not apply to questioning conducted by undercover police agents, to "routine booking questions," or to police questioning about a weapon under the "public safety exception." *Illinois v. Perkins*, 496 U.S. 292 (1990); *Pennsylvania v. Muniz*, 496 U.S. 582 (1990); *New York v. Quarles*, 467 U.S. 649 (1984). Statements taken in violation of *Miranda* may be used to impeach the defendant if he or she chooses to testify. *Harris v. New York*, 401 U.S. 222 (1971). *Miranda* does not bar a prosecutor's commentary on a defendant's decision to remain silent after warnings, although such commentary violates Due Process. *Doyle v. Ohio*, 426 U.S. 610 (1976). In other less dramatic ways, some post-*Miranda* precedents have interpreted *Miranda*'s dictates narrowly or amended its limits in order to expand the range of constitutionally acceptable police conduct. Only rarely have *Miranda*'s contours been expanded. Yet its basic substance and framework has proved to be durable enough to contain the Court's continuing debates about the best way to balance the "traditional investigatory functions" of the police with "the rights of the individual when confronted with the power of government" during police interrogations.

C. *Miranda*'s Application

1. Miranda Custody

Only the simultaneous existence of "custody" and "interrogation" triggers the duty to give *Miranda* warnings. All the defendants whose cases were consolidated for review in *Miranda* were in "custody" by any definition because they were under formal arrest. But the *Miranda* Court did not limit the Fifth Amendment definition of "custody" to this narrow concept. Had the Court done so, it might have created an incentive for police officers to delay the moment of arrest so as to be able to interrogate without giving the warnings. As the Court declared, *Miranda* applies to any person "deprived of freedom of action in any significant way." A narrower formula emerged in post-*Miranda* cases, but even that formula preserves judicial discretion to make custody findings based on a variety of factors. The modern custody inquiry is whether there is a formal arrest or "restraint on freedom of movement" of "the degree associated with a formal arrest." The inquiry requires case-by-case scrutiny of "all of the circumstances surrounding an interrogation," in order to determine whether a reasonable person would have felt that "he or she was not at liberty to terminate the interrogation and leave." *Thompson v. Keohane*, 516 U.S. 99 (1995).

Some of the earliest post-*Miranda* cases held that custody could exist outside the station house. For example, in *Mathis v. United States*, 391 U.S. 1 (1968), the defendant was confined in state prison. He was incarcerated on a charge that was unrelated to the subject of the interrogating officer's investigation, and the Court held that his incarceration qualified as Fifth Amendment custody. The reason for his custody was held to be irrelevant to his need for *Miranda*'s protection. Likewise in *Orozco v. Texas*, 394 U.S. 324 (1969), the defendant was held to be in custody in his own home when he was awakened in his bedroom at 4:00 a.m. by four police officers. He was not informed that he was under arrest, but he was questioned about his presence at the scene of a homicide and about the location of his gun. In both *Mathis* and *Orozco*, the prosecutor argued unsuccessfully that custody did not exist because of the lack of inherent compulsion in the defendants' "familiar surroundings." However, in *Beckwith v. United States*, 425 U.S. 341 (1976), this argument was successful in defeating a finding of custody for a defendant who was interviewed at his home for three hours by Internal Revenue Service agents. The *Beckwith* defendant had not been "detained against his will" in the manner of *Orozco* or *Mathis*. His claim of "psychological restraint" was weaker because he had consented to the interview, and he had been told that the agents were entitled to investigate criminal tax fraud as well as his civil tax liability. Moreover, he had been warned that his answers could be used against him and that he could consult counsel before answering questions.

Not every station house encounter between a defendant and a police officer qualifies as a "custodial" one. The *Miranda* Court noted that the duty to give warnings is not triggered by certain types of questioning:

> When an individual is in custody on probable cause, the police may, of course, seek out evidence in the field to be used at trial against him. Such investigation may include inquiry of persons not under restraint. General on-the-scene questioning as to facts surrounding a crime or other general questioning of citizens in the fact-finding process is not affected by our holding. [In] such situations the compelling atmosphere inherent in the process of in-custody interrogation is not necessarily present.

In *Oregon v. Mathiason* 429 U.S. 492 (1977), the Court relied on three factors to hold that a defendant could be interviewed at the station house without *Miranda* warnings. First, the defendant was a parolee who was "invited" by police to come to the station house and so his presence there was "voluntary." Second, he was told during his interview that he was "not under arrest." Third, after making incriminating statements, he was released as promised, although he was arrested later. The *Mathiason* Court reasoned that any interview with the police could have coercive aspects, and that police should not be required to administer warnings to all interviewees. The *Mathiason* defendant was told that he was a suspect, which was true, and that his fingerprints had been found at the crime scene, which was false. These statements were deemed to be irrelevant to the custody inquiry. Thus, *Mathiason* demonstrated that coercive statements may not supply proof of the type of restraint needed for a finding of custody. Lower courts have extended *Mathiason* to permit witness interviews without *Miranda* warnings even when the defendant is questioned in a secure area of a jail. See *People v. Stansbury*, 9 Cal.4th 824, 38 Cal.Rptr.2d 394, 889 P.2d 588 (Ca. 1995) (defendant had to pass through a locked parking structure and locked entrance to the jail to reach the interview room).

The Court has determined that certain situations are non-custodial *per se*, absent unusual circumstances. For example, in *Minnesota v. Murphy*, 465 U.S. 420 (1984), a probationer's interview with a probation officer was held to be a non-custodial event. The Court rejected the argument that sufficient restraint was established by the obligations of probationers to report to their probation officers and to be truthful with them "in all matters," upon penalty of probation revocation. The Court found that these obligations create no more compulsion than is faced by a witness called before a grand jury, who is not entitled to *Miranda* warnings under *United States v. Mandujano*, 425 U.S. 564 (1976). The Court reasoned that the "compulsion" felt by the probationer-interviewee in *Murphy* is not comparable to the compulsion felt by anyone being interrogated by police at the station house. By contrast, that paradigm "custodial" defendant is typically thrust into unfamiliar surroundings where he or she is unable to "escape a persistent examiner" who creates the impression that the police interrogation will "continue until a confession [is obtained]."

The Court provided further guidance concerning non-custodial situations in *Berkemer v. McCarty*, 468 U.S. 420 (1984). In determining that the typical "traffic stop" does not qualify as "custody," the Court explained that a temporary detention for purposes of receiving a traffic citation does not compare to the "police-dominated" atmosphere of a station house interrogation. In the typical traffic stop, a driver expects to be detained only briefly, and to be questioned by no more than one or two police officers in the comparative safety of the public eye. The *Berkemer* Court also expressed concern that requiring *Miranda* warnings during all traffic stops would "substantially impede the enforcement" of traffic laws. However, the Court recognized that some traffic stops may not fit the typical non-custodial pattern, and that *Miranda* warnings will be needed in these circumstances. The traffic stop in *Berekemer* did fit the criteria for a typical non-custodial stop, because the time between the stop and arrest was short, the police officer asked only a "modest" number of questions, and the driver was initially not informed that the stop might not be temporary.

The Court uses an objective standard to determine custody and "the only relevant inquiry is how a reasonable [person] in the suspect's shoes would have understood [the] situation." Or as the Court explained, "initial determination of custody depends on the objective circumstances of the interrogation, not on the subjective views harbored by either the interrogating officers or the person being questioned." *Stansbury*, 511 U.S. at 324. This means that an individual defendant's idiosyncratic reaction to an encounter with police will not dictate a finding of custody. More importantly, it also means that a police officer's opinion about the custodial status of the interrogated person is irrelevant to the custody inquiry, as long as this opinion is not revealed to that person. The *Stansbury* Court articulated this rule as follows:

An officer's knowledge or beliefs may bear upon the custody issue if they are conveyed, by word or deed, to the individual being questioned. Those beliefs are relevant only to the extent they would affect how a reasonable person in the position of the individual being questioned would gauge the breadth of his or her "freedom of action." Even a clear statement from an officer that the person under interrogation is a prime suspect is not, in itself, dispositive of the custody issue, for some suspects are free to come and go until the police decide to make an arrest. The weight and pertinence of any communications regarding the officer's degree of suspicion will depend upon the facts and circumstances of the particular case.

Although the perspective of a "reasonable person in the suspect's shoes" is an ambiguous concept, the Court views "objective facts" about an interrogated person as being relevant to custody, by contrast with a person's "subjective experience," which should not be taken into account as part of the custody inquiry for policy reasons. As explained in *Yarborough v. Alvarado*, 541 U.S. 652 (2004), the purpose of using an objective standard for custody is to insure that police officers will not have to "make guesses" about the existence of particular circumstances "before deciding how they may interrogate" a person. For example, the *Yarborough* Court held that a person's "law enforcement history" and "interrogation history" are subjective experiences rather than objective facts. Officers often will not know this history, and even when they do, any conclusions they might draw about its relevance to custody are likely to be speculative. Familiarity with police procedures might contribute to an interrogated person's feeling free to leave, or might cause the person "to view past as prologue and expect another in a string of arrests."

In contrast, in *J.D.B. v. North Carolina*, 131 S. Ct. 2394 (2011), the Court held that consideration of a child's age is consistent with the "objective nature" of custody analysis. Unlike prior experience with a law enforcement, which may influence a person's sense of freedom of action in different ways and is contingent on the psychology of an individual suspect, a child's age has an "objectively discernible relationship" to a youth's understanding of freedom of action. Therefore, if a child's age would have been "objectively apparent to a reasonable officer," then its inclusion in the custody analysis is appropriate, even though the age factor will not necessarily be "a determinative, or even a significant, factor in every case."

Thanks to the Court's use of the "totality of the circumstances" approach to custody, lower courts have identified a large number of factors that may be relevant to the custody inquiry. These factors include: the purpose of the investigation, the location and length of the interrogation, the interrogated person's awareness of his or her freedom to leave the scene, the person's actual freedom from a variety of forms of physical restraint, the use of coercive interrogation methods, and other factors.

2. Miranda Interrogation

The *Miranda* opinion's litany of police techniques revealed the Court's concern that a broad array of potentially coercive conduct during interrogations could be used to elicit incriminating statements. The definition of "interrogation" was a crucial concept for determining police compliance with the three *Miranda* duties: to give warnings before interrogating persons in custody, to refrain from interrogating after warnings in the absence of waiver, and to refrain from interrogating after an invocation of rights. More than a decade after *Miranda*, the Court finally established an all-purpose test in *Rhode Island v. Innis*, 446 U.S. 291 (1980), for assessing whether a particular police comment or action would qualify as "interrogation." The *Innis* Court began its analysis by noting that not all statements obtained from persons in custody "are to be considered the product of interrogation." Volunteered statements are admissible evidence, and "interrogation" must "reflect a measure of compulsion above and beyond that inherent in custody itself." Therefore, *Miranda* safeguards "come into play whenever a person in custody is subjected to either express questioning or its functional equivalent," defined as follows:

> [T]he term "interrogation" [refers] to any words or actions on the part of the police (other than those normally attendant to arrest and custody) that the police should know are reasonably likely to elicit an incriminating response from the suspect. The latter portion of this definition focuses primarily upon the perceptions of the suspect, rather than the intent of the police.

The Court explained that *Miranda* was meant to protect defendants against "coercive police practices," and therefore "objective proof of the underlying intent of the police" is not a necessary element of a finding of "interrogation." In this respect the *Innis* definition of interrogation is consistent with the *Stansbury* definition of custody, as both rules eschew a focus on police intent or state of mind.

The *Innis* definition of "interrogation" provoked a split on the Court as it was applied to the facts of *Innis*. This split reveals that difficult subjective judgments must be made when interpreting police conduct. The *Innis* defendant was arrested at 4:30 a.m. because he had been identified from a photo array by the victim of a midnight robbery, in which the perpetrator used a sawed off shot gun. The defendant was also suspected of a shotgun murder that occurred five days earlier. He was arrested and invoked his right to counsel after being given three sets of *Miranda* warnings; he was then placed in the rear seat of a police car for transport to the station house, and three police officers traveled with him. Innis overheard two of the officers talking to each other about how they should "continue to search for the weapon" because "a school for handicapped children [was] located nearby," and because "God forbid" that a little girl might "pick up the gun, maybe kill herself." Innis then immediately stated that he would show the officers the location of the gun, and led them to that location.

The *Innis* majority emphasized five aspects of the police dialogue that justified its conclusion that interrogation did not occur. The police conversation was "brief," it was not "evocative," and it was not directed to Innis but merely overheard by him. Further, the police had no knowledge of any "peculiar" susceptibility of Innis to an appeal for the safety of handicapped children, or of any disorientation or upset suffered by Innis at the time of arrest. By contrast, the *Innis* dissenters argued that, "One can scarcely imagine a stronger appeal to the conscience" of "any suspect." In their view, the police dialogue resembled the classic interrogation technique of an "appeal to a suspect to confess for the sake of others," in order to "display some evidence of decency and honor." The evocative aspect of the dialogue sufficed to justify a finding of interrogation. For the *Innis* majority, the incriminating response of the defendant was "unforeseeable," and the police dialogue consisted of a "few off hand remarks." This conversation constituted an "understandable" sharing of law enforcement concerns that just happened to "strike a responsive chord" in the defendant. For the dissenters, the police comments seemed like a ploy, only "nominally addressed" to another police officer, and uttered not coincidentally at the very time when the police officers drove past "the very place where they believed the weapon was located."

The Court applied the *Innis* test in more unusual circumstances in *Arizona v. Mauro*, 481 U.S. 520 (1987), and determined that police officers did not indirectly "interrogate" an arrestee when they allowed his wife to speak to him and recorded the incriminating statements made during this encounter. The Court declined to hold that it was reasonably foreseeable that the police "use" of the wife as a "substitute interrogator" would produce a confession. Instead, the *Mauro* majority emphasized that the officers merely yielded to the wife's demands, and that the defendant was fully aware of the police witness and the tape recorder, which measures were justified by security concerns. For the *Mauro* majority, the police conduct did not rise to the level of using "the coercive nature of confinement to extract confessions"; for the *Mauro* dissenters, the police "control" of this incrimination opportunity constituted a form of "exploitation" that should have qualified as interrogation under *Innis*.

Three important *Miranda* exceptions allow police to engage in conduct that would constitute "interrogation" under *Innis* without honoring the duty to give *Miranda* warnings. The common doctrinal thread for these exceptions is the Court's recognition of a particular police need to gather information that might not be provided by an arrestee if the warnings were given. In considering the justifications for these exceptions, the Court decided that each one could be squared with the policies espoused in *Miranda*.

The origin of the "routine booking question" exception is the *Innis* Court's recognition that any questions "normally attendant to arrest and custody" should not count as "interrogation" under *Miranda*. In *Pennsylvania v. Muniz*, 496 U.S. 582 (1990), the Court held that "routine booking questions" should be treated as an exception to *Miranda*'s mandate that warnings must be provided before questioning occurs. This exception allows police to gather the biographical data needed to complete the booking process and arrange for pretrial services. The rationale for this exception is that the answers to questions about a defendant's name, address, age, and like subjects, are "reasonably related to administrative concerns." These questions are not related to the quest for incriminating statements that is meant to be limited by the *Miranda* safeguards. Therefore, a question will not qualify for the "routine booking question" exception if it is "designed to elicit incriminatory admissions." For example, the prosecutor in *Muniz* did not try to argue that an appropriate booking question was, "What is the date of your sixth birthday?" The purpose of that question was to determine whether the defendant was so intoxicated that he could not remember or calculate that date. The *Muniz* Court held that the "sixth birthday" question called for a testimonial response, and so it qualified for the application of the privilege. The failure to give Muniz the *Miranda* warnings before asking him that question was therefore held to violate the Fifth Amendment. *Muniz* also held that when police give "carefully scripted police instructions" as to how to perform physical sobriety tests after the booking process, such instructions are "attendant to" a legitimate police procedure and do not qualify as interrogation under *Innis*.

In *Illinois v. Perkins*, 496 U.S. 292 (1990), the Court created a second interrogation exception in its ruling that *Miranda* warnings are not required if a person "is unaware that [he or she] is speaking to a law enforcement officer." This exception allows police to use undercover agents to pose as prison inmates in order to obtain incriminating statements from an incarcerated defendant. In *Perkins*, two informants played this role, and after offering to help the defendant plan a jail break, they persuaded him to provide details about his involvement in a murder. The *Perkins* Court emphasized that according to the *Innis* interpretation of *Miranda*, "interrogation" must "reflect a measure of compulsion above and beyond that inherent in custody itself." The type of compulsion caused by a police interrogation was held to be absent when a person in custody believes that a conversation partner is a fellow prisoner. Thus, the *Perkins* interrogation did not "implicate the concerns underlying *Miranda*," which relate to the risks of self-incrimination that are inherent in a "police-dominated atmosphere." The *Perkins* rule is consistent with some precedents that require a person to assume the risk that a companion may be an undercover agent or police informant. See, e.g., *Hoffa v. United States*, 385 U.S. 293 (1966) and *United States v. White*, 401 U.S. 745 (1971) (assumption of risk in Fourth Amendment context). Notably, however, *Perkins* is inconsistent with *Massiah*'s Sixth Amendment rule that prohibits the use of undercover agents to "deliberately elicit" of incriminating statements from defendants who have been indicted, regardless of whether such defendants are in custody. *Massiah v. United States*, 377 U.S. 201 (1964).

The "public safety exception" in *New York v. Quarles*, 467 U.S. 649 (1984), allows police to ask an arrestee a question about the location of a weapon that the arrestee may have abandoned or hidden in a public area near the scene of arrest. These questions may be asked without first providing *Miranda* warnings that could prompt the arrestee to refuse to disclose any information about the weapon. The scope of the police power to ask a "public safety" question is illustrated by the factors enumerated in *Quarles*. The police officers were confronted with the "immediate necessity" of ascertaining the whereabouts of a gun, as they had reliable information that the arrestee had recently discarded the gun somewhere in the supermarket where they arrested him. If the gun were not located, it posed several dangers to public safety, because it could be used by a customer, an employee, or a hypothetical accomplice. Moreover, the police asked "only the question necessary to locate the missing gun" before providing the defendant with *Miranda* warnings. Notably, the Court decided that the actual "motivation of the individual officers" for asking the question about the gun was not relevant. This is because the "kaleidoscopic situation" of making arrests requires police "spontaneity," and because officers often act out of a "host of different, instinctive, and largely unverifiable motives." As long as a question about a weapon was "reasonably prompted by a concern for public safety" under the circumstances of the arrest, the arrestee's answer to the question is admissible evidence, as well as any weapon that is located thanks to that answer.

The Court's debate in *Quarles* focused both on question whether a danger to "public safety" actually existed on the facts of *Quarles*, and on the question whether the *Miranda* Court's reasoning implicitly allowed for the creation of such an exception. The *Quarles* dissenters argued that the police "could easily have cordoned off the store" and searched for the gun, without asking the defendant about its whereabouts. They also argued that there was no danger to public safety because the store was deserted at midnight, except for a few employees at the checkout counter. The defendant had been handcuffed, and the police had put away their guns, suggesting that they did not fear either the defendant or a hypothetical accomplice. The dissenters conceded that in a "dire emergency," such as imminent peril created by a bomb threat, it would be appropriate for police to violate the duty to give *Miranda* warnings in order to protect the public safety. But they disapproved of the breadth of the *Quarles* exception. Justices Marshall and Brennan deemed the exception "an unwise and unprincipled departure" from *Miranda* precedents. Justice O'Connor viewed the exception as a doctrine that would blur "the clear strictures" of *Miranda*, and noted that the Court had "repeatedly refused to bend the literal terms" of *Miranda* in order to make enforcement of *Miranda* rules easier for police officers and courts. The *Quarles* majority, however, declared that the "doctrinal underpinnings" of *Miranda* did not require a strict application of the warnings requirement in *Quarles*, and that the "need for answers" to police questions related to the public safety outweighed the "need" for *Miranda*'s protection of the privilege.

3. Adequate Miranda Warnings

The Court requires the prosecution to bear the burden of proving that the *Miranda* warnings were given. For example, if the defendant claims that the warnings were never given, and the arresting officer is unable to recite the warnings at a suppression hearing, the prosecution has failed to meet its burden. *See Tague v. Louisiana*, 444 U.S. 469 (1980). The Court does not require the prosecution to provide any particular form of proof that the warnings were administered. It is common for police departments to provide written as well as oral warnings, and to ask arrestees to sign a form to acknowledge that they received and understood them. The receipt of the warnings is the first layer in the foundation for all government arguments that a valid *Miranda* waiver was obtained.

a. Warnings that Convey Rights

Some years after *Miranda*, the Court decided to establish guidelines concerning the types of ambiguity that are tolerable in the language of the *Miranda* warnings. In *California v. Prysock*, 453 U.S. 355 (1981), the juvenile defendant argued that the third and fourth warnings provided to him violated *Miranda* because they did not state expressly that he had a right to consult an appointed lawyer free of charge, both before and during interrogation. The Court rejected this claim, ruling that separate references to the right to consult counsel before questioning and the abstract right to appointed counsel were sufficient to convey the meaning of the *Miranda* rights. The police officer's language in *Prysock* was as follows:

> You have the right to talk to a lawyer before you are questioned, have him present with you while you are being questioned, and all during the questioning. Do you understand this? . . . You also, being a juvenile, you have the right to have your parents present, which they are. Do you understand this? . . . You have the right to have a lawyer appointed to represent you at no cost to yourself. Do you understand this?

The defendant's argument rested on the idea that there was a crucial gap in the warnings, namely the failure to connect the right to consult counsel before questioning with the right to appointed counsel. Having failed to see this connection, the defendant did not realize that the "lawyer appointed to represent" him "at no cost" would be appointed before any questioning began. The defendant assumed instead that any "appointed lawyer" would be appointed after the interrogation, presumably by a judge at some proceeding in the future.

The *Prysock* problem arose because three different descriptions of the right-to-counsel warnings appear in the *Miranda* opinion, and each description explains only one aspect of the right. The Fifth Amendment right to counsel is quite complex, and yet the *Miranda* opinion contains no helpful summary of all of its relevant features. (By contrast, the rights explained in the first and second *Miranda* warnings are described repeatedly in consistent terms: "You have the right to remain silent. Anything you say may be used against you in a court of law.") Moreover, the *Miranda* opinion nowhere states that a particular text of the warnings must be used by police. So lower courts concluded that valid warnings might differ in form from the warnings in the *Miranda*. This conclusion was supported by *Miranda*'s observation that, "[t]he warnings required and the waiver necessary in accordance with our opinion [are], in the absence of a fully effective equivalent, prerequisites to the admissibility of any statement made by a defendant." This comment suggested that different "equivalent" versions of each of the four warnings would be valid, as long as these versions conveyed the essential features of the rights provided by the *Miranda* opinion.

The strongest argument for the *Prysock* defendant was that one of the *Miranda* Court's descriptions of the right-to-counsel warnings closely resembled the defendant's requested warning about the "right to have an appointed lawyer free of charge, before and during interrogation." The *Miranda* opinion states that a defendant "has the right to the presence of an attorney, and [if] he cannot afford an attorney, one will be appointed for him prior to any questioning." This language is part of a four-warning package that is described as a "summary" of the holding. Yet this textual pedigree did not impress the *Prysock* majority. The Court held that the language of the *Prysock* warnings was adequate to "fully convey" the defendant's *Miranda* rights. What saved the *Prysock* warnings was the clarity with which the right to consult counsel was attached to the time period "prior to and during interrogation." The defendant was expected to be capable of drawing the inference that the description of the right to "appointed counsel" referred back to the earlier description of the right to consult counsel before questioning. The existence of ambiguity in the warnings was not deemed to be significant.

The *Prysock* Court did recognize, however, that the "right-to-counsel" warnings would be constitutionally inadequate if they expressly suggested "any limitation on the right to the presence of appointed counsel" that was different from the "rights to a lawyer in general." Specifically, "if the reference to the right to appointed counsel was linked with some future point in time after the police interrogation," then the text of the warning would "not fully advise the suspect of his right to appointed counsel before" an interrogation. The *Prysock* dissenters argued that close scrutiny of the record showed that the *Prysock* warnings were "sufficiently ambiguous" to merit invalidation. In particular, the dissenters were critical of the police officer for breaking off the *Miranda* warnings after the third warning and inserting the "extra warning" about the juvenile defendant's state law right to have his parents present. But the *Prysock* majority ignored the dissenters' argument that this interruption might have confused the defendant. Perhaps the Court was concerned that the phrasing of the right-to-counsel warnings used in *Prysock* was common enough that a ruling in the defendant's favor would cast doubt upon the validity of many waivers.

The Court was called upon in *Duckworth v. Eagan*, 492 U.S. 195 (1989), to interpret the *Prysock* ban on references that "linked" the appointment of counsel to a post-interrogation event. In a controversial opinion, the *Duckworth* majority held that *Prysock* was not violated when the warnings were accompanied by an extra warning that an attorney would be provided "if and when you go to court." The language of the printed warning in *Duckworth* was as follows:

> You have the right to talk to a lawyer for advice before we ask you any questions, and to have him with you during questioning. You have this right to the advice and presence of a lawyer even if you cannot afford to hire one. We have no way of giving you a lawyer, but one will be appointed for you, if you wish, if and when you go to court. If you wish to answer questions now without a lawyer present, you have the right to stop answering questions at any time. You also have the right to stop answering at any time until you've talked to a lawyer.

The *Duckworth* defendant argued that the "if and when" language linked the appointment of counsel to the post-interrogation event of "going to court," and thereby allowed an arrestee to infer that no lawyers will be available for indigents before interrogations occur. The gap in these warnings was the absence of a statement that questioning would be delayed, if the defendant asked for appointed counsel, until after a lawyer was appointed and consulted with the defendant. As in *Prysock*, however, the *Duckworth* majority found that the existence of ambiguity in the warnings was not fatal to their constitutional validity.

The *Duckworth* majority relied on four rationales to uphold the use of the extra "if and when" warning that was embedded in the right-to-counsel warnings. First, the extra warning accurately described the procedure for appointment of counsel in state court. Second, the extra warning could be justified on the grounds that it provided an answer to a question that arrestees might ask, namely, "When will counsel be appointed?" Third, the extra warning described a police practice that is permissible under *Miranda*, as police do not have to provide counsel for invoking defendants. Finally, the "totality" of the warnings adequately conveyed the meaning of the *Miranda* rights. The linguistic link between appointment of counsel and the future trip to court was nullified by the language about the right to consult counsel "before" questioning and the right to stop answering "until" consulting counsel. After *Duckworth*, the *Prysock* ban on improper "linkages" operates only under unpredictable conditions. Presumably, the ban may remain in effect if one or more of the four *Duckworth* rationales is inapplicable in a particular case.

The *Duckworth* dissenters criticized the Court for ignoring the impact of the extra warning on "frightened" suspects, "unlettered in the law," who cannot hope to interpret the "if and when" language like "lawyers or judges schooled in interpreting legal or semantic nuance." The dissenters argued that it posed "no great burden on law enforcement officers to eradicate the confusion stemming from the 'if and when' caveat" by simply deleting it. Otherwise, some arrestees may interpret the *Duckworth* warning as implying that indigents cannot receive appointed lawyers until after questioning. Or worse, some may interpret it as meaning, "talk now or remain in custody for an indeterminate length of time." That interpretation is based on the possible implication that an arrestee may never be taken to trial, may therefore never receive an appointed lawyer, and may therefore be held in custody without a lawyer until such time as a decision about going to trial is made.

Both *Prysock* and *Duckworth* illustrate three important features of the *Miranda* warnings. First, even the right-to-counsel warnings described in *Miranda* do not provide a thorough articulation of the substance of that right. Thus, any police warning about the right to counsel must be a "shorthand" description that requires the listener to draw a variety of inferences. Second, *Miranda* does not require police to provide answers to the questions that may be asked by an arrestee who does not understand the implications of the shorthand warnings. The Court's *Miranda* precedents reveal that police often resort to repeating the warnings more than once, in the hopes that the warnings will provide safe, all-purpose answers to dispel any potential confusion that could invalidate a waiver. The *Duckworth* decision reveals how difficult it may be for police to attempt to improve upon the standard warnings without creating further confusion. Finally, the right-to-counsel warnings are hard to understand because the *Miranda* Court chose to express them in the language of the "right to have" instead of the more accurate language of the "right to ask" to consult counsel, which is not the same thing as the right to receive an immediate consultation.

The Court extended the reasoning of *Prysock* and *Duckworth* in *Florida v. Powell*, 130 S. Ct. 1195 (2010), holding that warnings reasonably conveyed the *Miranda* rights even though they did not describe the right to have counsel present during interrogation. The Court concluded that a "commonsense reading" of two other warnings implied the existence of the missing right. After the usual first two warnings ("you have the right to remain silent" and "if you give up the right to remain silent, anything you say can be used against you in court"), the remaining *Powell* warnings read as follows: "You have the right to talk to a lawyer *before* answering any [police] questions," and "You have the right to use any of these rights at any time you want during this interview."

As in *Prysock*, the Court found that nothing in the *Powell* warnings indicated that counsel's presence would be restricted, and as in *Duckworth*, the warnings were held to satisfy *Miranda* "in their totality." The final "catchall" warning was viewed as confirmation that an arrestee could exercise the right to talk to a lawyer "while the interrogation was underway," and the preceding warning "merely conveyed when [the arrestee's] right to an attorney became effective." The *Powell* dissenters argued that the more natural reading of the warnings not only conveyed a temporal time limit on the right to consult counsel, but also "entirely omitted an essential element" of the *Miranda* rights, namely the right to consult counsel during questioning, unlike the warnings in *Prysock* and *Duckworth*.

b. Midstream Warnings

Properly phrased warnings may be inadequate because they cannot effectively perform their function of communicating the *Miranda* rights and protecting a person's Fifth Amendment privilege during custodial interrogation. In *Missouri v. Seibert*, 542 U.S. 600 (2004), the Court held that when police "question first and warn later," the warnings that are given "midstream" between two interrogations that are "close in time and similar in content" do not "reasonably convey" the *Miranda* rights as required by *Duckworth*. Instead, such warnings are likely to mislead the interrogated person and to deny him the necessary understanding of "the nature of his rights and the consequences of abandoning them." The *Seibert* Court recognized that the technique of "question first" had become popular with some police departments, despite the fact that prewarning statements would be inadmissible under *Miranda*, on the theory that the post-warning statement would be admissible:

> [The] manifest purpose [of the strategy is] to get a confession the suspect would not make if he understood his rights at the outset; the sensible underlying assumption is that with one confession in hand before the warnings, the interrogation can count on getting [a second one]. Upon hearing warnings only in the aftermath of an interrogation [and confession], a suspect would hardly think he had a genuine right to remain silent, let alone persist in so believing once the police began to lead him over the same ground again.

Therefore, the *Seibert* Court interpreted the "adequate warnings" doctrine to establish the "inadequacy" of warnings that are inserted as a formalistic litany in the midst of "integrated and proximately conducted questioning."

Yet the *Seibert* Court noted that midstream warnings may be adequate in some circumstances, such as those in *Oregon v. Elstad*, 470 U.S. 298 (1985), where police made a "good faith" mistake in failing to give warnings before a single comment by an officer prompted an unwarned admission by Elstad during his arrest in his home. The warnings given later at the station were "adequate," according to the *Seibert* Court, because the station house interrogation was deemed to be a "new and distinct experience" for Elstad, and thus his station house confession was admissible. The *Seibert* dissenters argued that the Court misinterpreted *Elstad* as an adequate warnings precedent, and ignored *Elstad*'s view that the psychological effects of unwarned interrogation and initial confession upon a post-midstream-warning confession could be ignored for *Miranda* purposes in the absence of "actual coercion." However, the *Seibert* Court sidestepped this criticism by noting that *Elstad*'s definition of a voluntary waiver following a midstream warning was not at issue in *Seibert*, and that if midstream warnings qualify as "inadequate" under *Seibert*'s criteria, then the post-warning confession will be inadmissible and the voluntary waiver issue will not need to be addressed. In the wake of *Seibert*, lower courts must examine the circumstances of midstream warning cases in order to determine whether they more closely resemble the *Seibert* or the *Elstad* interrogations. The *Seibert* Court noted that the "deliberate" use of the "question first" strategy is not necessary for a *Seibert* violation, and even if police officers tell a person that her pre-warning statement cannot be used as evidence, this does not necessarily "change the character" of the question first procedure sufficiently to make the warnings "adequate" under *Seibert*.

4. Waiver of Miranda Rights

Miranda requires the prosecution to prove that an arrestee waived his or her *Miranda* rights in order for any statement obtained during interrogation to be admitted at trial. The *Miranda* opinion provided only one example of a hypothetical case where a waiver could be found—an express statement that an arrestee "is willing" to talk and "does not want an attorney," followed closely by an incriminating statement. Three caveats implied that waivers might be difficult to obtain: a waiver may not be presumed from silence after warnings or from the "fact that a confession was in fact eventually obtained"; a waiver is invalid unless there is evidence that an arrestee "understandingly rejected the offer" of counsel; a waiver may be negated based on a "lengthy interrogation or *incommunicado* incarceration," or on evidence that an arrestee was "threatened, tricked or cajoled." Yet these few observations did not provide much guidance to lower courts or police who must assess the validity of a large variety of waivers on a case-by-case basis.

Miranda requires that waivers must be "voluntary, knowing and intelligent." Three procedural rulings explain the proof process for this concept, as distinguished from its substantive definition. First, the state must prove waiver by a preponderance of the evidence. *Colorado v. Connelly*, 479 U.S. 157 (1986) (rejecting "clear and convincing evidence" standard, despite *Miranda*'s language that state has a "heavy burden" for meeting the "high standard" for proving waiver). Second, a waiver may be demonstrated through oral statements and conduct, and does not have to be in writing. An "express" waiver is not required, as waiver may be inferred from the circumstances of a case. *North Carolina v. Butler*, 441 U.S. 369 (1979). Finally, proof of valid waiver must include proof that an arrestee understood the *Miranda* warnings, and therefore a court may not rely on a presumption that such an understanding exists. *Tague v. Louisiana*, 444 U.S. 469 (1980). In order to satisfy the *Tague* burden, police sometimes choose to administer the *Miranda* warnings with an accompanying query whether the arrestee understands his or her rights, and seek a written acknowledgment of this understanding.

In *Moran v. Burbine*, 475 U.S. 412 (1986), the Court summarized the ideas in post-*Miranda* precedents defining "voluntary, knowing, and intelligent" waiver as follows:

> The inquiry has two distinct dimensions. First, the relinquishment of the right must have been voluntary in the sense that it was the product of a free and deliberate choice rather than intimidation, coercion, or deception. Second, the waiver must have been made with a full awareness of both the nature of the right being abandoned and the consequences of the decision to abandon it. Only if the "totality of the circumstances surrounding the interrogation" reveals both an uncoerced choice and the requisite level of comprehension may a court properly conclude that the *Miranda* rights have been waived.

Most of the Court's waiver cases have involved requests for extra warnings by defendants who claim they were misled by some police failure to provide information about the consequences of waiver. In each of these cases, the defendants argued that the *Miranda* warnings were inadequate to provide the information they needed. In only a few cases, the defendants have argued that their behavior and statements should not be interpreted as evidence of waiver. In virtually every waiver case, the Court has chosen to uphold waivers and rebuffed arguments that the *Miranda* warnings need to be improved.

The first key component of a waiver is its "voluntary" quality. It is difficult for an arrestee to argue that a waiver is not "voluntary" on the facts of a case. This is because the standard for "involuntariness" is the same as the Due Process standard. *Oregon v. Elstad*, 470 U.S. 298 (1985). A defendant needs to demonstrate that coercive police conduct caused his or her waiver to be the product of intimidation, coercion, or deception under the *Moran* test. *Elstad* holds that there must be evidence that the "will [was] overborne and [the] capacity for self-determination critically impaired." Coercive police conduct is broadly defined, and it includes physical violence "or other deliberate means calculated to break" the arrestee's will. A totality of the circumstances test is employed, so that the "traditional indicia of coercion" are relevant: "the duration and conditions of [detention]," the "manifest attitude of the police" toward the defendant, the "physical and mental state" of the defendant, [and] the "diverse pressures which sap or sustain" the defendant's "powers of resistance and self-control." *Colorado v. Spring*, 479 U.S. 564, 574 (1987).

The Court has rejected claims of involuntary waivers in a variety of contexts. In particular, the Court has been unsympathetic to claims that police silence constitutes a form of coercion. In *Colorado v. Spring*, 479 U.S. 564 (1987), the Court held that "mere silence" as to "the subject matter of an interrogation" is not the kind of "trickery" that invalidates a waiver as involuntary. The police in *Spring* failed to tell the defendant, before his waiver, that they planned to ask him questions about an old murder crime as well as about the unrelated crime for which had been arrested. The defendant made admissions about the murder, and claimed that his waiver was involuntary because it was coerced by the psychological ploy of the police. The *Spring* majority decided that the defendant had been affirmatively warned that anything he said could be used against him, and so he should have inferred that he was giving the police an all-purpose, unlimited waiver of rights for interrogation about all his crimes. The *Spring* Court reserved the question whether sufficient "coercion" would exist to invalidate a waiver in a case where police affirmatively misrepresented the scope of the interrogation. The *Spring* dissenters agreed with the defendant that the deliberate police silence was a trick that made the waiver involuntary, as it rose "to a level of deception" that should not be tolerated under *Miranda*.

In a waiver ruling concerning the sufficiency of voluntariness evidence, the Court rejected the argument that a mentally ill defendant is incapable of voluntarily waiving his *Miranda* rights. In *Colorado v. Connelly*, 479 U.S. 157 (1986), the defendant approached an off-duty police officer on the street and confessed to murder. The officer responded by reciting the *Miranda* warnings, and the warnings were repeated by a second officer who was summoned to question him. The defendant told the officers that he had been a patient in several mental hospitals in the past, but he displayed no signs of mental illness during interrogation. The next day, during his interview with appointed counsel, the defendant revealed that auditory hallucinations led him to confess. The *Connelly* majority held that the psychological pressure to confess emanated from the defendant himself and not from any "government coercion," and therefore no involuntary waiver claim could be made under *Miranda*. At the time of his waiver, the defendant "appeared to understand fully the nature of his acts." Even though the impromptu confession to murder might appear to be odd, the defendant's waiver was voluntary because there was no "police overreaching." The *Connelly* dissenters lost their bid to have the definition of "coercion" expanded to include the defendant's inner psychological state.

The second vital component of a waiver is its "knowing and intelligent" quality. In *Spring*, the defendant argued that they needed more information in order to make a knowing waiver. This claim was rejected for two reasons. First, the Court concluded that the *Miranda* warnings supplied all the information necessary for a "knowing and intelligent" waiver. As the Court explained: "[We] have never read the Constitution to require that the police supply a suspect with a flow of information to help him calibrate his self-interest in deciding whether to speak or stand by his rights." Second, the Court emphasized that it would be difficult to craft an appropriate extra warning to satisfy the defendant's request. An extra "*Spring* warning" about the subject matter of an interrogation would require an "extension of *Miranda* [that] would spawn numerous problems of interpretation because any number of factors could affect a suspect's decision to waive *Miranda* rights." However, the *Spring* dissenters favored the creation of the requested extra warnings in order to enhance the knowing quality of the waivers sought from the defendants in each case.

The same rationales that defeated the defendant's waiver arguments in *Spring* also defeated the claim in *Moran v. Burbine*, 475 U.S. 412 (1986). The *Moran* defendant claimed a need to know that a lawyer had contacted the police on his behalf, asking that he not be interrogated and seeking contact with him. The Court assumed that the police had knowingly or recklessly ignored the lawyer's request in interrogating the defendant after his waiver in the absence of the lawyer. However, the Court reasoned that, "Events occurring outside the presence of the suspect and entirely unknown to him surely can have no bearing on the capacity to comprehend and knowingly relinquish a constitutional right." The *Miranda* warnings provided "all the information *Miranda* requires the police to convey," and any attempt to create an extra "*Moran* warning" would muddy "*Miranda*'s relatively clear waters," and "spawn" a host of difficult legal questions. The Court also feared the consequences of "reading *Miranda* to require the police [to] inform a suspect of an attorney's efforts to reach him." This new warning "would work a substantial [and] inappropriate shift in the subtle balance struck in [*Miranda*]," and would "come at a substantial cost to society's legitimate and substantial interest in securing admissions of guilt." The *Moran* dissenters were sharply critical of the *Moran* majority's willingness to tolerate "police deception of the shabbiest kind." They favored the proposed "*Moran* warning," and noted that the *Moran* holding "seems to suggest that police may deny counsel all access to a client who is being held," contrary to the prevailing view of the A.B.A. and most state courts at the time.

In a difficult case concerning the sufficiency of evidence of a "knowing and intelligent" waiver, the Court decided that an arrestee could simultaneously invoke the right to counsel and waive the right to silence through a "conditional" waiver. In *Connecticut v. Barrett*, 479 U.S. 523 (1987), the arrestee told police three times, after three sets of warnings, that he was willing to talk but would not make a written statement without a lawyer. He then made oral admissions and police refrained from asking him for a written statement. The *Barrett* defendant's statements did not match the examples of waiver provided in *Miranda*; he neither made express statements that he "was willing" to talk and did "not want an attorney," nor did he make statements that he "understandingly rejected the offer" of counsel. The defendant argued that the illogical distinction he made between oral and written statements showed his incomplete "understanding of the consequences" of his waiver, and therefore that his "limited" invocation of counsel should have been treated as an "all-purpose" invocation by police. However, the defendant had told the police repeatedly that he understood his rights, and testified that he knew he did not have to talk to police without a lawyer present. The *Barrett* Court noted that the defendant's decision to talk may have been "illogical," but decided that this should not disable police from obtaining a valid waiver. The defendant "made clear his intentions, and they were honored by police." Under these circumstances, the *Barrett* defendant was deemed to understand the *Miranda* warning that "anything you say may be used against you," and his "conditional waiver" of the right to silence was held to be voluntary, knowing and intelligent.

The Court provided further guidance about the evidence necessary to demonstrate an implicit waiver in *Berghuis v. Thompkins*, 130 S. Ct. 2250 (2010). The Court relied initially on *Butler*'s formula that waiver may be implied through "the defendant's silence, coupled with an understanding of his rights and a course of conduct indicating waiver." But the Court also chose to restate that formula more broadly, in declaring that "an accused's uncoerced statement establishes an implied waiver of the right to remain silent" when the prosecution shows that the *Miranda* warnings were given and "understood by the accused." The evidence showed that the defendant could read the warnings that the officer gave him in writing and then recited aloud. No evidence supported a claim of "coercion" based on threats or injuries. Thus the Court's broadly phrased interpretation of *Butler* was satisfied because the warnings were understood, the defendant's single incriminating statement was uncoerced, and that same statement constituted the implicit waiver of silence. The Court also concluded that the defendant's single incriminating statement was "sufficient to show a course of conduct indicting waiver." The Court found confirmation for this conclusion in the defendant's conduct of remaining largely silent during the almost three-hour interrogation that preceded the incriminating statement, and in his conduct of failing to invoke his rights.

The *Berghuis* dissenters argued that the defendant's "course of conduct" did not support a waiver finding, pointing to his refusal to sign an acknowledgment that he understood his rights, and to his prolonged unresponsiveness. The dissenters emphasized that evidence of waiver is needed beyond an inculpatory statement itself, given the inherently coercive nature of custodial interrogation. Ultimately, the dissenters not only disagreed with the *Berghuis* majority's finding of waiver on the facts, but also viewed the Court's broad interpretation of *Butler* as a "substantial retreat" from *Miranda* and from waiver precedents.

5. Invocation of Miranda Rights

Miranda requires that police officers must honor an arrestee's invocations of the right to silence, the right to counsel, or both, by "cutting off" the interrogation. In post-*Miranda* cases, the Court has resolved three questions about invocation rights. First, the Court's decisions treat an invocation of counsel differently from an invocation of silence; police are barred from initiating discussions and seeking waiver after the former but not after the latter invocation. Second, the Court allows police to seek a waiver after either type of invocation when it is the arrestee who initiates a generalized discussion of the investigation with the police. Finally, the Court requires that an invocation of counsel must be "unambiguous," and lower courts apply the same requirement to an invocation of silence. If an arrestee's invocation does not satisfy this standard, police may ignore the invocation.

The Court decided in *Michigan v. Mosley*, 423 U.S. 96 (1975), that the invocation of silence does not require a permanent cessation of interrogation, as long as the police "scrupulously honor" the invocation. The defendant in *Mosley* told police that he did not want to answer questions about the robberies for which he was arrested, and two hours later he was contacted by a different police officer who was investigating a murder crime. After receiving a second set of warnings during questioning in a different part of the station house, the defendant waived his rights and made incriminating statements. The *Mosley* Court began its analysis by noting the text of the governing *Miranda* rule and its policy justifications:

> Once warnings have been given, the subsequent procedure is clear. If the individual indicates in any manner, at any time prior to or during questioning that he wishes to remain silent, the interrogation must cease. At this point he has shown that he intends to exercise his Fifth Amendment privilege; any statement taken after the person invokes his privilege cannot be other than the product of compulsion, subtle or otherwise. Without the right to cut off questioning, the setting of in-custody interrogation operates on the individual to overcome free choice in producing a statement after the privilege has been once invoked.

The *Mosley* Court chose to view this passage as leaving open the question whether, and under what circumstances, "a resumption of questioning is permissible."

The *Mosley* Court answered this question by declaring that it would be "absurd" to interpret *Miranda* as establishing "a blanket prohibition" against questioning after invocation of the right to silence. The Court's first rationale was that the prohibition would create "wholly irrational obstacles" to police investigations and "deprive suspects" of the opportunity to make "informed and intelligent assessments" of their interests. The second rationale was that *Miranda*'s purpose for the "cut off questioning" rule was to give an arrestee "control" over the timing, subject and duration of an interrogation, in order to counteract "the coercive pressures of the custodial setting." Therefore, a resumption of questioning after some time lapse did not necessarily undermine such a purpose.

The *Mosley* Court posited two types of re-interrogation at opposite ends of a spectrum of constitutionality. The improper type was re-interrogation "after a momentary cessation" following the invocation of silence. This type of questioning would undermine the will of the arrestee and "frustrate the purposes of *Miranda*." The proper type of re-interrogation was illustrated by the facts of *Mosley*, where the defendant's first invocation was "scrupulously honored." This concept was explained as a combination of several factors: the invocation appeared to be limited to the robbery crimes, the subject of questioning was an "unrelated" crime, a two-hour time lapse occurred before the re-interrogation, the defendant received a second set of *Miranda* warnings, and the second interrogation was conducted by a different police officer. However, the scope of the *Mosley* Court's multi-factor holding was unclear, and the Court has not shed further light on Mosley's application to other scenarios.

The *Mosley* dissent criticized the *Mosley* majority's lack of adequate safeguards to protect the arrestee's invocation of the privilege, finding the requirements of a time lapse and a new set of *Miranda* warnings to be "vague and ineffective." As an alternate safeguard, the *Mosley* dissent proposed that any re-interrogation should be delayed until after arraignment or that "resumption of questioning should await appointment and arrival of counsel." But the defendant in *Mosley* had not invoked the right to counsel, and so the *Mosley* majority rebutted the dissent's argument as follows:

> The dissenting opinion asserts that Miranda established a requirement that once a person has indicated a desire to remain silent, questioning may be resumed only when counsel is present. But clearly the Court in Miranda imposed no such requirement, for it distinguished between the procedural safeguards triggered by a request to remain silent and a request for an attorney and directed that "the interrogation must cease until an attorney is present" only "[i]f the individual states that he wants an attorney."

Soon after *Mosley*, the Court refused to allow a defendant to be re-interrogated following an invocation of the right to counsel in *Edwards v. Arizona*, 451 U.S. 477 (1981). The *Miranda* instructions for police conduct following such an invocation were as follows:

> If the individual states that he wants an attorney, the interrogation must cease until an attorney is present. At that time, the individual must have an opportunity to confer with the attorney and to have him present during any subsequent questioning. If the individual cannot obtain an attorney and he indicates that he wants one before speaking to police, they must respect his decision to remain silent.

The *Edwards* Court held that a defendant cannot give a valid waiver if police initiate a re-interrogation after the invocation of counsel. In effect, the Court accepted *Miranda*'s blanket prohibition against questioning after invocation of the right to counsel. The defendant in *Edwards* had declared, "I want an attorney before making a deal." The police had cut off questioning but then returned the next morning for a second round of questioning about the same offenses, and the defendant had been told that he "had to" talk to them. After providing a second set of warnings, the police had obtained a waiver and a confession. They had emulated at least two of the *Mosley* factors, by delaying their re-interrogation for some time after the invocation, and by providing the second set of warnings. But these factors were ignored in *Edwards* and *Mosley* was deemed irrelevant. The Court determined that the *Edwards* waiver was invalid because the police initiated the second interrogation. The only proper scenario for the procurement of such a waiver was held to be one where the arrestee "initiates further communication, exchanges, or conversations with the police" after invocation of the right to counsel.

In distinguishing *Edwards* from *Mosley*, the *Edwards* Court emphasized that *Miranda* recognized the assertion of the right to counsel as "a significant event," different in kind from the invocation of the right to silence. The *Edwards* Court also cited *Mosley*'s recognition of the different "procedural safeguards" that were "triggered" by the two different invocations. The defendant in *Edwards* had "expressed his desire to deal with the police only through counsel," and therefore the Court determined that he should not be "subject to further interrogation by the authorities until counsel has been made available to him." However, the *Edwards* opinion did not speak directly to the question whether the ban on re-interrogation after the invocation of counsel should apply to a re-interrogation concerning a different crime. Nor did the *Edwards* Court address the propriety of re-interrogation following an arrestee's actual consultation with counsel.

The Court ruled that the *Edwards* rule bars re-interrogation about different crimes in *Arizona v. Roberson*, 486 U.S. 675 (1988). After invoking his right to counsel during questioning about a burglary, the *Roberson* defendant spent three days in custody without any sign of counsel, and then was re-interrogated about a different burglary. Under *Edwards*, his statements made after waiver during the second interrogation were required to be suppressed. The *Roberson* Court relied on several rationales to justify its use of the *Edwards* rule to govern re-interrogations on all subjects. The Court emphasized the virtue of a bright line-rule barring all re-interrogations after invocation of counsel; such a rule would be easy for police, prosecutors, and lower courts to interpret and apply. Also, the Court cited the *Edwards* theory that a request for counsel raises the presumption that an arrestee "is not competent to deal with the authorities without legal advice." Any invocation of counsel may be presumed, therefore, to be an all-purpose invocation, seeking the advice of counsel concerning questioning about any crime. The *Roberson* Court cited *Spring*'s holding by analogy and reasoned that if a waiver is presumed to be unqualified, then any invocation should be similarly treated.

The *Roberson* dissenters objected to the Court's extension of *Edwards*, and preferred the *Mosley* doctrine as the controlling rule solution for re-interrogations about different crimes. The dissenters argued that re-interrogations like the one in *Roberson* present less of a danger of police badgering of arrestees, compared to *Edwards* re-interrogations about the same crime. They also reasoned that re-interrogations would provide helpful information to arrestees, but this idea was given short shrift by the *Roberson* majority, which declared that counsel could easily help the defendant to acquire such information. The *Roberson* dissenters also noted that police "routinely" solve "major crimes" by checking the fingerprints of persons in custody and thereby discovering that certain arrestees are wanted for questioning about other offenses. But the *Roberson* majority ignored the dissenters' argument that the guarantee of the *Edwards* right to all arrestees who invoke the right to counsel would deprive the police of a vital law enforcement tool.

The Court's final extension of *Edwards* came in a case where re-interrogation followed the defendant's consultation with counsel in *Minnick v. Mississippi*, 498 U.S. 146 (1990). The defendant in *Minnick* invoked his right to counsel after his arrest in California for a crime in Mississippi, and the arresting FBI agents allowed him to meet with counsel several times. His lawyer told him not to talk to anyone or to sign any waivers. But when the Mississippi sheriff arrived at the San Diego jail, Minnick was told that he "had" to talk to him. Even though Minnick refused to sign a waiver, his conversation with the sheriff about the folks back home led to a discussion of the crime. The *Minnick* Court held that the *Edwards* rule bars re-interrogation of any kind unless counsel is present. This holding was built on *Miranda*'s recognition that "even preliminary advice given to the accused by his own attorney can be swiftly overcome" by the inherent coercion of the interrogation setting. The *Minnick* Court rejected the argument that the *Edwards* bar should end once consultation occurred, noting that "consultation" is too imprecise a concept for lower courts to define and police to interpret. As in *Roberson*, the *Minnick* Court valued the "clarity and certainty" of a "bright-line rule" application of *Edwards*, and concluded that the presence of counsel was the only "protective device" after invocation that could provide adequate protection for an arrestee's Fifth Amendment right to counsel. The *Minnick* dissenters viewed *Edwards* as inconsistent with the Court's precedents on waiver issues, and reasoned that after "any discussion" with an attorney, an arrestee would no longer need the protection of *Edwards* because the arrestee would be less "likely to be ignorant of [his or her] rights and to feel isolated in a hostile environment."

In rejecting the idea that an *Edwards* invocation creates an "eternal" prohibition on subsequent waiver seeking and interrogation, the Court held in *Maryland v. Shatzer*, 130 S. Ct. 1213 (2010), that the protection of an *Edwards* invocation should expire after a "break in custody" for 14 days. At that point, the Court concluded that it is "farfetched to think" that an officer's "asking the suspect whether he would like to waive his *Miranda* rights" will "wear down the accused" through the type of police "badgering" that the *Edwards* "cut off" rule was designed to prevent. The *Shatzer* Court chose to endorse the 14-day rule in order to provide certainty for law enforcement officers who need to know when renewed interrogation is lawful, and to provide "plenty of time" for the suspect to "shake off any residual coercive effects of his prior custody" by getting "reacclimated to his normal life" and "consulting with friends and counsel." The *Shatzer* Court also held that when an inmate is "released back into the general prison population" for 14 days, after being subjected to an episode of "interrogative custody" to which *Miranda* applies, that release constitutes the equivalent of a "break in custody" that will mark the expiration of the inmate's *Edwards* invocation that occurred during interrogative custody.

The *Edwards* ban on re-interrogation after invocation of counsel only protects arrestees who do not falter in their invocations. The *Edwards* opinion specifically noted that the ban on re-interrogation after the invocation of counsel does not apply if the defendant "initiates further communication, exchanges, or conversations with the police." The rationale for this exception is that the defendant should be left alone after invocation and not "badgered" by police officers, but if the defendant "initiates" a discussion, then he or she has demonstrated a lack of desire to deal with the police only through counsel. In essence, the "initiation" exception operates as a presumption that a defendant has retracted an invocation of counsel. Soon after *Edwards*, the Court reached a consensus that initiation is not *per se* proof of waiver. Therefore, assuming that a post-invocation "initiation" has occurred, the police must proceed to seek a valid waiver under the totality of the circumstances. *Oregon v. Bradshaw*, 462 U.S. 1039 (1983).

The definition of "initiation," however, proved to be a controversial question for the Court, which split into two camps on this point. The *Bradshaw* plurality decided that an "initiation" would be found whenever an arrestee engages in a "generalized discussion" of the investigation. Compare *Wyrick v. Fields*, 459 U.S. 42 (1982) (when defendant requested a polygraph examination, he thereby initiates dialogue with the authorities). The *Bradshaw* dissenters proposed that an "initiation" should be found only when an arrestee communicates explicitly about "the subject matter of the criminal investigation" in a way that invites "further interrogation." Both sides agreed that questions "relating to routine incidents of the custodial relationship," such as a request for a drink of water or requests to use the telephone, were "bare inquiries" that should not qualify as "initiation."

The *Bradshaw* plurality concluded that the defendant asked a question after invocation that evinced "a willingness and a desire for a generalized discussion of the investigation." Shortly after he invoked his right to counsel, while he was being transferred from the police station to the jail, the defendant asked the escorting officer, "Well, what is going to happen to me now?" The officer did not immediately answer his question, but instead gave an incomplete version of the *Miranda* warnings:

> You do not have to talk to me. You have requested an attorney and I don't want you talking to me unless you so desire because anything you say—because—since you have requested an attorney, you know, it has to be at your own free will.

Only after the defendant said that "he understood," did the officer proceed to discuss where the defendant "was being taken and the offense with which [the defendant] would be charged." The officer suggested the defendant should take a polygraph, and the defendant's waiver was obtained the next day after new warnings were given. The *Bradshaw* plurality held that the police officer had not violated *Edwards* by resuming the waiver seeking process. The Court acknowledged that the defendant's question was "ambiguous." But the Court emphasized that the police officer's response showed that the officer understood the question as "relating generally to the investigation." As the question "could reasonably have been so interpreted," the officer's resumption of waiver seeking was valid under *Edwards*. The *Bradshaw* dissenters argued that, taken in context, the defendant's question was "a normal reaction to [being] placed in a police car, obviously for transport to some destination." Thus, even under the plurality's definition of "initiation," the dissenters would have ruled that Bradshaw's question did not suggest that he had "opened a dialogue with the authorities" but only responded to his custodial surroundings.

While an ambiguous initiation is sufficient for an arrestee to lose the *Edwards* right, an ambiguous invocation is not sufficient to acquire that right. In *Davis v. United States*, 512 U.S. 452 (1994), the Court determined that the standard for an adequate invocation after waiver should be "that a reasonable police officer in the circumstances would understand the statement to be a request for an attorney." The *Davis* standard resembles the *Bradshaw* and *Innis* standards, as it is an "objective inquiry" that focuses on a reasonable police officer's understanding. Under *Davis*, an arrestee must make "some statement that can reasonably be construed to be an expression of a desire for the assistance of an attorney." If an invocation is "ambiguous or equivocal in that a reasonable officer in light of the circumstances would have understood only that the suspect *might* be invoking the right to counsel," then the invocation may be ignored. The defendant in *Davis* had waived his rights and answered questions for one and a half hours before pausing to utter these words: "Maybe I should talk to a lawyer." After being asked to clarify his request, Davis replied that he was "not asking for a lawyer," and then added, "No, I don't want a lawyer." On these facts, the *Davis* Court held that the initial "maybe" request for counsel did not "meet the requisite level of clarity," and so the *Edwards* right did not attach and the police did not have to cut off questioning.

Some state courts before *Davis* required police to stop a post-waiver interrogation and ask for clarification of an ambiguous invocation. The *Davis* concurrence approved of this requirement, fearing that whenever an arrestee thinks that an invocation of counsel has been ignored, the arrestee "may well see further objection as futile and confession (true or not) as the only way to end the interrogation." The *Davis* majority rejected the imposition of a "duty to clarify" upon the police, although noting that "clarification" is a good police practice. Hence, the officers in *Davis* would have been entitled to ignore the defendant's ambiguous comment about talking to a lawyer, and to continue their interrogation without asking for clarification. The *Davis* majority acknowledged that its holding would disadvantage those suspects who "because of fear, intimidation, lack of linguistic skills, or a variety of other reasons" do not clearly articulate their invocations of the right to counsel. But the benefit of requiring an "unambiguous" invocation was that police officers would not "be forced to make difficult judgment calls" about ambiguous invocations, and not be faced with "the threat of suppression if they guess wrong." In order to preserve the "bright-line" quality of the *Edwards* rule, the *Davis* Court declined to create "a third layer of prophylaxis to prevent police questioning when the suspect *might* want a lawyer."

As for the definition of an adequate invocation before waiver, in the pre-*Davis* era the Court held that it was "neither indecisive nor ambiguous" for an arrestee to invoke counsel by immediately responding to the warning about the right to consult counsel in these words: "Uh, yeah, I'd like to do that." *Smith v. Illinois*, 469 U.S. 91, 93 (1984). The *Smith* Court also held that even though the defendant's invocation interrupted the police officer before all the warnings had been administered, the officer should have stopped the interrogation as soon as the invocation was uttered. By continuing to read the last warning about appointed counsel to the defendant, and then continuing to seek a waiver, the police officer violated the "bright-line" rule of *Edwards* that "all questioning must cease." The *Smith* Court rejected the prosecution's argument that the *Smith* defendant's post-invocation responses to continued questioning could be used "to cast doubt on the clarity of his initial request for counsel." The rationale for this rejection is that the police should not be allowed to ignore unambiguous invocations "as if the defendant had requested nothing," in the hope that later statements might create some retrospective ambiguity in the invocation. The *Smith* Court did not address the question of how an ambiguous invocation would be defined or what consequences should follow from such an invocation, and *Davis* provided answers to both questions.

The Court extended the unambiguous invocation requirement to invocations of the right to silence in *Berghuis v. Thompkins*, 130 S. Ct. 2250 (2010), reasoning that there is "no principled reason" to adopt a different standard from that approved in *Davis* for invocations of the right to counsel. The Court emphasized that the *Davis* standard "results in an objective inquiry," whereas if ambiguous invocations of silence must be honored by officers, then they must make "difficult decisions about an accused's unclear intent" and risk suppression of incriminating statements if they guess wrong and do not cut off questioning. On the facts, the *Berghuis* Court concluded that no unambiguous invocation of silence had occurred because the defendant made only a few limited verbal responses during a three-hour interrogation, and never said that "he wanted to remain silent" or that "he did not want to talk to the police."

The *Berghuis* dissenters argued that the *Davis* rule is a "poor fit for the right to silence," because the information that a suspect has "the right to remain silent" is "unlikely to convey that he must speak," and speak unambiguously, "in order "to ensure the right will be protected." As an alternative, the dissenters proposed that officers should honor ambiguous invocations that are not so equivocal as to suggest, for example, only a willingness to listen before deciding whether to respond. The dissenters predicted that because "differentiating 'clear' from 'ambiguous' statements" under *Davis* "is often a subjective inquiry," and because suspects often use "equivocal or colloquial language" when attempting to invoke the right to silence, the application of *Davis* to such invocations will "significantly burden the exercise of the right."

6. Uses of Miranda-Defective Evidence

a. When Defective Evidence Leads Police to Other Evidence

If the police violate the *Miranda* rules and obtain a statement during custodial interrogation, that statement will be inadmissible, but no *Miranda* "fruits doctrine" requires the police to show that subsequently obtained evidence was not "tainted" by the *Miranda* violation. In *Oregon v. Elstad*, 470 U.S. 298 (1985), the Court rejected the need for using the Fourth Amendment "fruit of the poisonous tree" doctrine in the *Miranda* context. Later precedents continue to recognize the inapplicability of *Wong Sun v. United States*, 371 U.S. 471 (1963) to *Miranda* violations. See *United States v. Patane*, 542 U.S. 630 (2004); *Missouri v. Seibert*, 542 U.S. 600 (2004). For example, the *Elstad* Court determined that the failure to give warnings before obtaining an initial confession does not require a second confession, obtained after warnings, to be treated an inadmissible fruit of the initial Miranda violation. However, even though the *Elstad* Court declared that police ordinarily may remedy an initial failure to warn by the subsequent giving of warnings, which will suffice to make a post-warning waiver valid, the *Seibert* decision later qualified Elstad's generalization by holding that "midstream" warnings may be inadequate to convey the *Miranda* rights in some circumstances. See the topic of Adequate Warnings, supra.

The rejection of the *Wong Sun* "fruits" doctrine in the *Miranda* context is justified by various precedents on the theory that the exclusion of all non-attenuated fruits of *Miranda* violations is not necessary in order to provide adequate deterrence of such violations by police officers. For example, the Court held in *Michigan v. Tucker*, 417 U.S. 433 (1974), that if police discover the identity of a witness named in defendant's unwarned statement, which is *Miranda*-defective because of a "good faith" police failure to warn, the testimony of that witness is admissible in the prosecution's case-in-chief. The Court assumed also that police will not subject a non-suspect witness to the inherently coercive process of custodial interrogation, and therefore assumed that the exclusion of the testimony is not necessary in order to deter police more effectively from failing to warn suspects. Similarly, in *United States v. Patane*, 542 U.S. 630

(2004), the Court held that if police discover physical evidence based on information provided in a defendant's unwarned statement, that evidence is admissible as long as the statement was not procured by "actual coercion." The concurring justices in *Patane* emphasized the important probative value and reliable nature of physical evidence, as well as the unlikely need for excluding such evidence in order to enhance deterrence of *Miranda* violations. The *Patane* plurality perceived that "the exclusion of unwarned statements [is] a complete and sufficient remedy" for the failure to warn; the plurality also noted that while the "exclusion of the physical fruit of actually coerced statements" is required, *Miranda*-defective statements should not be treated the same way because they are only "presumed to have been coerced."

b. Impeachment Based on Defective Statements or Silence During Interrogation

The "impeachment exception" to *Miranda* was established in *Harris v. New York*, 401 U.S. 222 (1971), where the Court ruled that an unwarned statement could be admitted during cross-examination to impeach the credibility of the defendant's testimony. The *Harris* Court reasoned that sufficient deterrence of *Miranda* violations by police could be obtained from the exclusion of *Miranda*-defective statements from the prosecution's case-in-chief. The Court also viewed an impeachment exception as necessary to prevent the *Miranda* doctrine from being used as a "shield" for the commission of perjury by defendants who could contradict their statements to police without fear of those statements being admitted to impeach them. The *Harris* dissenters feared that the impeachment exception would create an incentive for police officers to violate *Miranda* in order to obtain impeachment evidence, but the *Harris* majority was skeptical that such exploitation of the *Harris* rule would be likely to occur.

A prosecutor who wishes to offer a defendant's post-warning silence as a form of impeachment evidence will encounter the Due Process bar created in *Doyle v. Ohio*, 426 U.S. 610 (1976). The *Doyle* Court recognized that the exercise of the "right to remain silent" as described in the *Miranda* warnings would be penalized at trial if a prosecutor were allowed to ask a defendant during cross-examination why she refrained, after being arrested and receiving warnings, from telling the police some aspect of the story that she has communicated to the jury in her testimony. Therefore, the Court held that questions about such a defendant's silence or comments about silence during closing argument constitute Due Process violations. However, the *Doyle* bar is limited to cases where a defendant is silent following both the event of arrest and the delivery of *Miranda* warnings. The bar does not apply when a defendant makes a statement instead of remaining silent as in *Anderson v. Charles*, 447 U.S. 404 (1980). Nor does the bar apply to pre-arrest silence or to post-arrest silence before warnings are delivered. See *Jenkins v. Anderson*, 447 U.S. 231 (1980); *Fletcher v. Weir*, 455 U.S. 603 (1982). In some circumstances, when defense counsel objects to a *Doyle* violation, it may be sufficient for the trial judge to caution the jury to disregard the impermissible question by the prosecutor in order to satisfy Due Process. See *Greer v. Miller*, 483 U.S. 756 (1987).

D. Post–*Miranda* Sixth Amendment *Massiah* Right to Counsel

After the *Miranda* decision, the Court did not rely on *Massiah*'s Sixth Amendment right to counsel doctrine in a confession case until *Brewer v. Williams*, 430 U.S. 387 (1977). The *Brewer* case was argued on Fifth Amendment grounds, but the Court avoided making law on difficult *Miranda* issues by relying on the *Massiah* doctrine to resolve the case. By the time *Brewer* was decided, the Court had abandoned *Escobedo*'s position that pre-indictment defendants in custody were entitled to the Sixth Amendment right to counsel, holding in *Kirby v. Illinois*, 406 U.S. 682, 689 (1972) that the right attaches only at "critical stages" that occur after "the initiation of adversary judicial criminal proceedings—whether by way of formal charge, preliminary hearing, indictment, information, or arraignment." The *Brewer* Court did make law on a clean slate with regard to other unresolved *Massiah* issues, including these: Does the *Massiah* ban on undercover agent interrogation extend to police interrogation? May the *Massiah* right be waived? After the *Massiah* right attaches, may police "deliberately elicit" incriminating statements if there has been no explicit "invocation" of the *Massiah* right by a defendant? If such a request is made, must police "cut off" questioning? Does "deliberate elicitation" include words or actions that do not involve express questioning? Is there a Sixth Amendment right to be informed of the *Massiah* right before an interrogation? The doctrines created for answers to these questions reflect the influence of the *Miranda* doctrines, despite the different doctrinal origins of the Fifth and Sixth Amendment rights to counsel.

1. Massiah Reliance on Counsel and Waiver

The Court held that police violated the Sixth Amendment right of an arraigned defendant in custody when an officer deliberately elicited incriminating statements from him without a waiver in *Brewer v. Williams*, 430 U.S. 387 (1977). *Brewer* was an especially controversial case because it involved the suppression of evidence relating to the homicide of a child on Christmas Eve. The *Brewer* Court issued multiple rulings concerning the scope of *Massiah* and its ramifications. First, the Court appeared to hold implicitly that there is no *per se* ban under *Massiah* on police questioning of defendants, although *Massiah* does ban the deliberate elicitation of statements by undercover police agents. Second, in order to conduct questioning, the police must obtain a Sixth Amendment waiver. Third, if police officers do not obtain such a waiver, then they may not engage in "deliberate elicitation" of incriminating statements. Such "elicitation" includes not only express questioning, but also other kinds of police statements that are "tantamount to interrogation." There was agreement on the Court that the *Massiah* waiver standard should be the same as the Sixth Amendment waiver standard established in *Johnson v. Zerbst*, 304 U.S. 458, 464 (1938): "an intentional relinquishment or abandonment of a known right or privilege." However, the Court split over the questions whether "deliberate elicitation" and waiver occurred on the facts of *Brewer*.

On the advice of his Des Moines lawyer, Williams surrendered to the police and was arraigned on an abduction charge in Davenport, while two officers traveled by car from Des Moines to retrieve Williams and escort him back for "booking" in Des Moines. Williams was suspected of murdering the victim of the abduction. His lawyer obtained the agreement of police officials that he would not be questioned in transit, and would be allowed to consult with the lawyer in Des Moines before questioning. During his arraignment in Davenport, Williams conferred with another lawyer. When the Des Moines detective and his partner arrived on the scene, the Davenport lawyer reminded the detective about the police agreement not to interrogate Williams. The detective refused to allow the Davenport lawyer to accompany Williams on the 160–mile car trip. Williams received *Miranda* warnings from the Davenport police, the Davenport magistrate, and the Des Moines detective. Both his lawyers also warned him against making any statements. Soon after the police car left Davenport, the detective delivered the so-called "Christian burial speech." He told Williams that he expected that they would be driving past the area where the victim's body was hidden, and that Williams might be unable to find it because "[t]hey are predicting several inches of snow for tonight." The detective reminded Williams that, "you yourself are the only person that knows where this little girl's body is." The detective opined, "that the parents of this little girl should be entitled to a Christian burial for the little girl who was snatched away from them on Christmas Eve and murdered." He added that, "I feel we should stop and locate [the body] on the way [to Des Moines] rather than waiting until morning and trying to come back out after a snow storm and possibly not being able to find it at all." Finally the detective said, "I do not want you to answer me. I don't want to discuss it any further. Just think about it as we're riding down the road." After thinking about it for 100 miles, Williams made incriminating statements and ultimately led the police to the body.

In order to exclude the confession on Sixth Amendment grounds, the *Brewer* majority appeared to rely silently on the *Miranda* model. According to this model, the violation of a *Massiah* right on the facts of *Brewer* would require three elements: the attachment of the *Massiah* right to counsel, the failure of police to obtain a waiver of *Massiah* rights, and finally, the prohibited act of "deliberate elicitation" (as equivalent to improper "interrogation") by police that produced incriminating statements. First, the *Brewer* majority held that the Sixth Amendment right to counsel attached to Williams because the arraignment qualified as the commencement of "adversarial judicial proceedings." Next, the *Brewer* majority held that the detective engaged in "deliberate elicitation" by making the "Christian burial speech," which was viewed as "tantamount to interrogation." The Court noted that the detective "purposely sought during Williams' isolation from his lawyers to obtain as much incriminating information as possible." Given the format of the speech and the detective's admonition "not to answer" him but just to "think about it," the *Brewer* majority's holding implicitly recognized that express questioning was unnecessary for a finding of "deliberate elicitation." Finally, the *Brewer* majority concluded that Williams did not waive his *Massiah* right before the "deliberate elicitation" occurred, as there was no affirmative evidence of waiver before the "Christian burial speech" was delivered. The Court noted that, "At no time during the trip did Williams express a willingness to be interrogated in the absence of an attorney." Instead, he stated several times that he would talk to police after seeing his lawyer in Des Moines. There was also evidence that negated waiver, namely the defendant's "consistent reliance on the advice of counsel in dealing with the authorities," and his "express and implicit assertions of his right to counsel."

The *Brewer* dissenters would have defined the concepts of "deliberate elicitation" and "waiver" differently under *Massiah*. The dissenters argued that the detective's speech was merely a "statement," and the defendant's "implied waiver" was valid because his free will was "not overborne" for three reasons. The detective's speech occurred two hours before the confession, it was not "coercive," and it was "accompanied by a request" that the defendant "not respond to it." The *Brewer* dissenters acknowledged that the detective's speech may have "influenced" the defendant's decision to make incriminating statements. But they argued that this influence was not sufficient to invalidate the waiver. The evidence of the defendant's understanding of his *Massiah* rights was supplied by the three sets of *Miranda* warnings and the two warnings from counsel. Therefore, the defendant's statements before and after the detective's speech exhibited a "knowing and intentional" relinquishment of the right to counsel when he made incriminating statements.

The *Brewer* majority's opinion left four important *Massiah* issues unresolved, and post-*Brewer* decisions have filled in the analytical gaps in *Brewer*'s portrait of *Massiah*'s requirements. First, the *Brewer* majority did not explain whether police must provide a *Massiah* defendant with a "*Massiah* warning." The Court noted that the detective did not "preface" his "Christian burial speech" with a warning to Williams "that he had the right to the presence of a lawyer." But the Court also made no finding that Williams failed to receive adequate notice of his *Massiah* rights. If the Court assumed that the repeated *Miranda* warnings had supplied such notice, this assumption went unmentioned as well. Second, the *Brewer* majority did not explain whether the Sixth Amendment waiver standard was more demanding than *Miranda*'s Fifth Amendment standard of "voluntary, knowing and intelligent" waiver. Ultimately, the Court provided clear answers on both points, by holding that the waiver standards for *Miranda* and *Massiah* rights are so similar that the *Miranda* warnings serve as an adequate method for informing a defendant of *Massiah* rights in *Patterson v. Illinois*, 487 U.S. 285 (1988).

Third, the *Brewer* majority did not explain whether the defendant's "reliance" on counsel or his "assertions" of the *Massiah* right were an essential prerequisite for the exercise of those rights during post-arraignment questioning by police. Instead, the Court treated the defendant's reliance and assertions only as evidence that logically negated waiver. Ultimately, the Court made it clear that *Massiah*'s ban on "deliberate elicitation" without waiver arises when the *Massiah* right attaches at the initiation of "adversary judicial proceedings." However, the police may seek a *Massiah* waiver from a defendant who invokes his *Massiah* right, as long as their "deliberate elicitation" of statements is limited to crimes other than the charged offense to which the Sixth Amendment has attached.

Finally, the *Brewer* majority did not make it clear whether the *Massiah* concept of "deliberate elicitation" was equivalent to the *Miranda* concept of "interrogation." It was not until after *Brewer* that the Court settled upon a definition for *Miranda* "interrogation" in *Rhode Island v. Innis*, 446 U.S. 291 (1980). The *Innis* Court observed that the concepts of "deliberate elicitation" under the Sixth Amendment and "interrogation" under the Fifth Amendment are "not necessarily interchangeable, since the policies underlying the two constitutional protections are quire distinct." *Innis*, 446 U.S. at 300 n.4. Similarly, in *Fellers v. United States*, 540 U.S. 519 (2004), the Court held that the defendant's *Massiah* right was violated because deliberate elicitation occurred, and treated the *Miranda* interrogation concept as irrelevant to the *Massiah* analysis. It is also notable that the *Perkins* exception to *Miranda* allows the "interrogation" by undercover agents of persons in custody, whereas *Massiah* does not allow the "deliberate elicitation" of incriminating statements by undercover agents from persons who possess Sixth Amendment rights, regardless of their custodial status. Compare *Illinois v. Perkins*, 496 U.S. 292 (1990) with *Massiah v. United States*, 377 U.S. 201 (1964).

2. Massiah Deliberate Elicitation

Not all types of contact by undercover agents with *Massiah* defendants are prohibited by post-*Massiah* precedents. The Court held that "deliberate elicitation" did not occur in *Kuhlmann v. Wilson*, 477 U.S. 436 (1986), when a police informant was placed in the defendant's cell and told to "keep his ears open," in case the defendant provided incriminating information. The *Kuhlmann* Court identified the purpose underlying *Massiah*'s ban on "deliberate elicitation" as the prohibition of secret interrogation through "investigatory techniques that are the equivalent of direct police interrogation." Therefore, when an undercover informant-cellmate merely listens to a defendant's statements, without making comments to stimulate incriminating conversations, this behavior does not resemble police interrogation and does not need to be barred by the Sixth Amendment.

In a pre-*Kuhlmann* decision, the Court held that "deliberate elicitation" existed when an undercover informant-cellmate was not a "passive listener" and joined as an active participant in conversations with the defendant despite instructions "not to initiate any conversation with [the defendant] about the crime." *United States v. Henry*, 447 U.S. 264 (1980). The *Henry* Court reserved the question addressed in *Kuhlmann*, whether "deliberate elicitation" would occur under *Massiah* if "an informant is placed in close proximity" to a defendant, but "makes no effort to stimulate conversations about the crime charged." In *Henry*, the Court did resolve two issues that established the foundation for the *Kuhlmann* holding. *Henry* held that *Massiah* applied when a jail inmate acted "under instructions as a paid informant" and pretended to be nothing more than a "fellow inmate." Such an informant's conduct was viewed as "attributable to the government," even if the informant had been warned not to ask questions or initiate conversations with the defendant. The *Henry* Court also held that the same definition for "deliberate elicitation" should be used for all cases involving undercover police agents, regardless of whether the defendant is in custody.

The *Kuhlmann* majority found that the informant-cellmate was a "passive listener," as the majority interpreted the record in the case. The record showed that the *Kuhlmann* informant made one remark that deviated from the role of "passive listener." This occurred when the informant listened to the defendant's story that he was present at the robbery but didn't know the robbers, and then responded with the comment that his story, "didn't sound too good." However, this critical remark did not elicit further statements from the defendant immediately. It was only some days later, after a visit from his brother, that the defendant changed his story and made incriminating statements to the informant. The trial judge found that the informant followed his instructions to ask no "questions with respect to the crime," and that the defendant's incriminating statements were "spontaneous and unsolicited." Therefore, the *Kuhlmann* majority decided that the defendant failed to prove that "the police and their informant took some action, beyond merely listening, that was designed deliberately to elicit incriminating remarks."

The *Kuhlmann* dissenters viewed the *Kuhlmann* informant as no different from the one in *Henry*, who had engaged in "deliberate elicitation" by "encouraging" the defendant to talk about the crime, and "conversing with him on the subject." It was irrelevant to the dissenters whether the informant had asked questions. The dissenters concluded that the government "intentionally created a situation in which it was foreseeable that [the defendant] would make incriminating statements without the assistance of counsel." They preferred this standard to the test used by the *Kuhlmann* majority that required "some action, beyond merely listening." The dissenters also criticized the police conduct in giving the defendant a cell that "overlook[ed] the scene of the crime"; the *Kuhlmann* majority held this fact to be irrelevant to the issue of "deliberate elicitation," because, "for all the record shows, that fact was sheer coincidence."

The Court rejected a proposed expansion of the powers of undercover police agents to "deliberately elicit" statements in *Maine v. Moulton*, 474 U.S. 159 (1985). The prosecutor in *Moulton* argued that *Massiah* exclusionary rule should be limited to situations where the motive for an investigation was to gather information concerning the charge to which the Sixth Amendment attached at indictment. The *Moulton* investigation was prompted by a different concern; the defendant, who had been indicted for theft crimes, was believed to be planning to kill a witness. The undercover agent in *Moulton* obtained statements about a variety of crime through "deliberate elicitation," and the prosecution wished to use these statements in the trial for the theft crimes. However, the *Moulton* Court decided that even a weighty reason for the investigation did not justify the creation of an exception to *Massiah*'s exclusionary rule, because it would create a risk of "evisceration" of *Massiah* rights. The *Moulton* majority noted that a variety of weighty reasons could be proposed for undercover investigations, and that *Massiah* exceptions ought not be created "whenever the police assert an alternative, legitimate reason for their surveillance" of a defendant, aside from the purpose of gathering evidence for trial on a charged offense. The *Moulton* dissenters wanted to allow statements to be admissible at a trial for any crime if the goal of an undercover investigation was to "deliberately elicit" statements for "legitimate purposes not related to the gathering of evidence" concerning the charged offense. The dissenters viewed the costs of excluding such evidence as outweighing the benefits, and therefore argued that *Massiah*'s exclusionary rule should not be applied in the context of the *Moulton* type of undercover investigation.

The *Moulton* Court affirmed one important limitation of *Massiah*, however, which is that statements obtained through "deliberate elicitation" by undercover agents are admissible at a trial on offenses other than the crime to which the Sixth Amendment right has attached. The *Moulton* majority described this scope limitation as a "sensible solution" to the problem of the government's need to continue to investigate "the suspected criminal activities" of indicted defendants. Therefore, if the defendant in *Moulton* had been charged subsequently with conspiracy to commit homicide or other crimes, any statements obtained during the undercover investigation before the defendant was charged with those new crimes would be admissible at a trial on those new charges. The *Moulton* Court explained the *Massiah* Court's limitation of the *Massiah* exclusionary rule as follows:

> [T]o exclude evidence pertaining to charges as to which the Sixth Amendment right to counsel has not attached at the time the evidence was obtained, simply because other charges were pending at that time, would unnecessarily frustrate the public's interest in the investigation of criminal activities.

The *Moulton* Court also clarified the scope of *Massiah*'s prohibition of "deliberate elicitation" by holding that it applies to situations where the defendant initiates a meeting with an undercover police agent as well as to situations where the agent initiates a meeting with the defendant. The informant in *Massiah* was a co-defendant who initiated a meeting with the defendant and allowed the government to listen to their conversations via radio transmitter. In *Moulton* it was the defendant who proposed to meet the co-defendant informant "for the express purpose of discussing the pending charges and planning a defense for the trial," and the co-defendant came to the meeting wearing a body wire transmitter to record what was said. The *Moulton* majority noted that while the state may obtain incriminating statements from a charged defendant "by luck or happenstance," *Massiah*'s rationale supports this conclusion:

> [K]nowing exploitation by the State of an opportunity to confront the accused without counsel being present is as much a breach of the State's obligation not to circumvent the right to the assistance of counsel as is the intentional creation of such an opportunity.

3. Massiah Warnings, Waivers, and Invocations

The Court held that the waiver standards for *Miranda* and *Massiah* rights are so similar that the *Miranda* warnings serve as an adequate method for informing a defendant of *Massiah* rights in *Patterson v. Illinois*, 487 U.S. 285 (1988). The *Patterson* majority began its analysis by comparing the language of the *Massiah* and *Miranda* waiver standards. Compare *Johnson v. Zerbst*, 304 U.S. 458, 464 (1938) ("an intentional relinquishment or abandonment of a known right or privilege") with *Moran v. Burbine*, 475 U.S. 412, 421 (1986) ("full awareness of both the nature of the right being abandoned and the consequences of the decision to abandon it"). The Court then interpreted the "key inquiry" in both "formulations" of waiver to be the following:

> Was the accused, who waived his Sixth Amendment rights during postindictment questioning, made sufficiently aware of his right to have counsel present during the questioning, and of the possible consequences of a decision to forgo the aid of counsel?

The Court next examined the language of the *Miranda* warnings to determine whether they provided adequate notice of the *Massiah* right described in the hybrid waiver formulation, and concluded that they did. The defendant in *Patterson* had received *Miranda* warnings after arrest and had not invoked the Fifth Amendment right to counsel. He was then informed of his indictment and given another set of *Miranda* warnings; he then signed a waiver and made statements that were held to be admissible. His post-indictment *Miranda* warnings adequately informed him of both his *Miranda* and *Massiah* rights, and his *Miranda* waiver adequately established a *Massiah* waiver as well.

The Court determined that the third and fourth *Miranda* "right-to-counsel" warnings satisfy the first component of the *Patterson* waiver formulation, to make the defendant "sufficiently aware of his right to have counsel present during the questioning." Next, the *Patterson* majority determined that the second *Miranda* warning about the consequences of waiving the privilege described implicitly "the possible consequences of a decision to forgo the aid of counsel such consequences." In *Miranda* cases like *Prysock* and *Duckworth*, which analyze the "adequacy" of particular versions of the warnings, the Court determined that arrestees could be expected to draw appropriate inferences from the text of the warnings. The *Patterson* majority similarly expected that a *Massiah* defendant could listen to the warning that "anything you say may be used against you in a court of law," followed by the right-to-counsel warnings, and draw suitable inferences as follows:

> This [second *Miranda*] warning sufficed [to] let [the defendant] know what a lawyer could "do for him" during the postindictment questioning: namely, advise [the defendant] to refrain from making [any] statements. By knowing what could be done with any statements he might make, and therefore, what benefit could be obtained by having the aid of counsel while making such statements, [the defendant] was essentially informed of the possible consequences of going without counsel during questioning.

The *Patterson* majority recognized that different Sixth Amendment waiver standards should be used at different stages of a case, following the initiation of "adversary judicial proceedings." The waiver standard should take into account "a pragmatic assessment of the usefulness of counsel to the accused" at a particular proceeding. Therefore, the waiver standard for a defendant seeking to waive the right to counsel at trial requires "rigorous restrictions on the information that must be conveyed to a defendant" because of the "enormous importance and role that an attorney plays at a criminal trial." But for a *Massiah* defendant, "the role of counsel" at questioning is "relatively simple and limited." Given the lack of "a substantial difference between the usefulness of a lawyer to a suspect during custodial interrogation, and his value to an accused at postindictment questioning," the Court concluded that the waiver procedure at the latter stage should be "simple and limited" in the manner of the *Miranda* waiver procedure. Finally, the *Patterson* majority also observed that post-*Brewer* precedents did not support the creation of a more rigorous waiver standard for *Massiah* defendants compared to *Miranda* defendants, reasoning as follows:

While our cases have recognized a "difference" between the Fifth Amendment and Sixth Amendment rights to counsel, and the "policies" behind these constitutional guarantees, we have never suggested that one right is "superior" or "greater" than the other, nor is there any support in our cases for the notion that because a Sixth Amendment right may be involved, it is more difficult to waive than the Fifth Amendment counterpart.

The *Patterson* dissenters argued that once *Massiah* rights attach, it should be "impermissible" for a prosecutor or "his or her agents" to conduct "an evidence-gathering interview" with the defendant. Unlike *Miranda* interrogations, the purpose of interrogating a *Massiah* defendant is to "buttress the government's case," not to solve a crime. Additionally, the *Patterson* dissenters argued that the *Miranda* warnings do not adequately inform a *Massiah* defendant of the "dangers and disadvantages of self-representation." As an alternative to the warnings, the dissenters cited with approval the "comprehensive inquiry" required by *Faretta v. California*, 422 U.S. 806 (1975), for a defendant seeking to waive the right to counsel at trial.

After *Patterson*, there remained few distinctions between *Miranda* and *Massiah* protections for *Massiah* defendants in custody. Notably, *Massiah* defendants who are *not* in custody may not be subjected to "deliberate elicitation" without a waiver, after the initiation of "adversary judicial proceedings," whereas uncharged defendants must depend on *Miranda*'s protections that attach only at the initiation of "custody" and "interrogation." When *Massiah* defendants are taken into custody, they will possess both *Massiah* and *Miranda* rights, whereas uncharged defendants in custody possess only *Miranda* rights. But as a practical matter, the *Massiah* defendants in custody must exercise both rights through the *Miranda* procedure when questioned by officers. They will receive *Miranda* warnings to notify them of both rights, and they will be asked for *Miranda* waivers that serve as waivers of both rights. When *Massiah* defendants in custody invoke the right to counsel, they will argue that they made unambiguous *Miranda* invocations under *Davis*, and thereby triggered the *Miranda* duty to "cut off" of questioning about all crimes under *Edwards* and *Roberson*. These *Massiah* defendants in custody are unlikely to litigate the question whether a *Miranda* invocation of counsel counted as a "*Massiah* invocation," because *Massiah*'s protection extends only to "deliberate elicitation" questioning about the charged offense, not to questioning about all crimes.

For more than 20 years, however, the Court recognized a unique type of "*Massiah* invocation" protection that was established in *Michigan v. Jackson*, 475 U.S. 625 (1986), but was later abolished when *Jackson* was overruled in *Montejo v. Louisiana*, 129 S. Ct. 2079 (2009). In *Jackson*, the Court endorsed the rule that a *Massiah* defendant's request during arraignment for appointed counsel constituted a *de facto* "*Massiah* invocation" of the Sixth Amendment right to counsel, which triggered a Sixth Amendment prohibition on subsequent waiver seeking and reinterrogation by police officers. This rule provided *Massiah* defendants in custody with greater protections than uncharged defendants who must invoke the *Miranda* right to counsel explicitly during custodial interrogation in order to trigger the Fifth Amendment prohibition on waiver seeking and reinterrogation.

The *Jackson* majority reasoned that the typical *Massiah* defendant cannot "be expected to articulate exactly why or for what purpose he is seeking counsel." Therefore, the request for counsel at arraignment should be treated as an implicit request for a "lawyer's services at every critical stage of the prosecution." The Court recognized that the purpose of *Massiah*'s protection was to give defendants the right to rely on counsel as the exclusive "medium" for communication with the police. Therefore, the Court concluded that the "additional safeguard" of the prohibition on post-invocation waiver seeking was necessary to protect the Sixth Amendment right to counsel. Based on the "offense specific" nature of *Massiah*'s protection, however, the Court later held that *Jackson*'s prohibition did not encompass waiver seeking and reinterrogation about uncharged offenses. *See McNeil v. Wisconsin*, 501 U.S. 171 (1991). Such offenses were defined broadly to include all crimes that require proof of a fact that the charged crime does not require. *See Texas v. Cobb*, 532 U.S. 162 (2001).

The *Jackson* dissenters saw no "perceived widespread problem" that police would engage in traditional *Miranda* interrogations in order to "badger" *Massiah* defendants after arraignment into abandoning their earlier requests for the assistance of counsel. Given their view that the potential badgering problem was the only possible justification for the *Jackson* prohibition, the dissenters also saw no reason to relieve *Massiah* defendants from the burden of uttering express invocations of the right to counsel, in order to earn the right to cut off questioning during post-arraignment interrogations. These arguments of the *Jackson* dissenters won the support of the Court majority in *Montejo*, which case initially presented only the narrow question whether the *Jackson* prohibition should be applied when a defendant receives court-appointed counsel without being required under state law to make a request for counsel on the record at an arraignment or other hearing. The *Montejo* Court not only rejected *Jackson*'s applicability to the latter scenario, but also decided to overrule *Jackson* entirely by relying on factors that justify departures from the principle of *stare decisis*.

The *Montejo* Court first noted that *Jackson*'s ruling fit the factor of being "unworkable" in the majority of states in which appointed counsel need not be requested on the record, because "a defendant who never asked for counsel" at a hearing "has not yet made up his mind in the first instance," and does not need anti-badgering protection. Then the Court noted that *Jackson* also fit two other factors because it was "only two decades old and eliminating it would not upset expectations." Finally, the Court emphasized that *Jackson*'s reasoning was flawed, so its holding deserved to be overruled because the *Jackson* Court failed to recognize that the "prophylactic" prohibition against post-arraignment waiver seeking would produce only "marginal benefits." The Court opined that "few, if any" involuntary waivers would be erroneously admitted at trial if *Jackson* were overruled, because the *Miranda* warnings and waiver requirement would weed out such waivers. Therefore, the *Jackson* rule could not "pay its way" because its marginal benefits were "dwarfed" by its "substantial costs to the truth-seeking process and the criminal justice system."

The *Montejo* dissenters argued that *Jackson*'s reasoning was not based on the anti-badgering rationale but was "firmly rooted in the unique protections afforded to the attorney-client relationship by the Sixth Amendment." The dissenters also argued that even assuming the *Miranda* warnings are adequate under *Patterson* to inform an "unrepresented" defendant of *Massiah* rights, they are not adequate to inform a "represented" defendant of "the Sixth Amendment right he is being asked to surrender." Therefore, the dissenters argued that the police in *Montejo* violated *Massiah* by "knowingly circumventing" the defendant's right to have counsel present, when they questioned him and obtained a *Miranda* waiver after counsel was appointed at the defendant's preliminary hearing.

E. Post–*Miranda* Due Process

Due Process doctrine continues to play a role in the judicial regulation of police interrogation, in part because the *Miranda* and *Massiah* doctrines contain gaps that can be filled only by reference to Due Process rules. *Miranda* does not apply to undercover investigations, to impeachment evidence, or to defendants who have waived the *Miranda* rights. *Massiah* is relevant only when a defendant has been charged with crimes to which the Sixth Amendment right has attached. The three most significant Due Process decisions in the post-*Miranda* era involve defendants who fall between these cracks of the *Miranda* and *Massiah* doctrines. These defendants include an inmate being questioned before indictment by an undercover agent, a mentally ill arrestee who waived his *Miranda* rights, and a defendant whose statements were taken in violation of the *Edwards* rule and used to impeach him under *Harris* when he testified at trial. *Mincey v. Arizona*, 437 U.S. 385 (1978) (impeached defendant); *Colorado v. Connelly*, 479 U.S. 157 (1986) (arrestee who waived *Miranda* rights); *Arizona v. Fulminante*, 499 U.S. 279 (1991) (pre-indictment inmate).

In the post-*Miranda* era, the Court affirmed its pre-*Miranda* Due Process rules and also established new holdings that reveal the influence of *Miranda* jurisprudence upon Due Process analysis. The affirmations of old holdings appear in *Fulminante*, where the Court used the totality of the circumstances approach to hold that a "credible threat of violence" was a Due Process violation. The new Due Process holdings appear in *Mincey*, where the Court ruled that police cannot take advantage of coercion created by external forces, and in *Connelly*, which held that some police "overreaching" is needed for a finding of coercion. In *Mincey*, the influence of *Miranda* is revealed by the Court's decision to treat *Miranda* violations as coercive elements in the Due Process totality of circumstances. In *Connelly*, police compliance with *Miranda* influenced the Court to find that the police did not take advantage of a mentally ill defendant's inner compulsion to confess. Finally, in two other new holdings, the Court addressed proof questions relating to Due Process. In *Lego v. Twomey*, 404 U.S. 477 (1972), the Court held that the prosecution should have to prove to a judge that a confession was "voluntary" under Due Process standards by a "preponderance of the evidence," in order for the confession to be admissible in evidence. If an involuntary confession is erroneously admitted into evidence, then the prosecution must prove to an appellate court that its admission was "harmless beyond a reasonable doubt" under *Chapman v. California*, 386 U.S. 18 (1967). See *Arizona v. Fulminante*, 499 U.S. 279 (1991).

The Court followed a traditional case-by-case approach to reach its finding of involuntariness in *Mincey v. Arizona*, 437 U.S. 385 (1978), where a police officer questioned a wounded arrestee for three hours while he was hospitalized in intensive care. The *Mincey* defendant's suffering was described in extreme terms. He was "debilitated and helpless," in "unbearable pain," "encumbered by tubes, needles, and breathing apparatus," and "confused and unable to think clearly." What was new about *Mincey*'s Due Process holding was that the police officer was not the chief external cause of the physical and psychological coercion from which the *Mincey* defendant suffered. Rather, the officer took advantage of Mincey's physical trauma by interrogating him in his vulnerable state, and also repeatedly violated *Miranda* by ignoring Mincey's three invocations of his right to counsel. The officer "ceased the interrogation only during intervals when Mincey lost consciousness or received medical treatment, and after each such interruption returned relentlessly to his task." Thus, the evidence of involuntariness consisted of police "relentlessness," of *Miranda* violations, and of Mincey's condition. The *Mincey* ruling affirmed *Spano*'s holding that a defendant's personal vulnerabilities could provide the foundation for a Due Process violation, and in Mincey's case, his condition was the main reason for the "involuntariness" of his confession.

The Court narrowed the focus of Due Process doctrine in *Colorado v. Connelly*, 479 U.S. 157 (1986), by declaring that the purpose of the Due Process exclusionary rule is "to substantially deter future violations" of Due Process. The Court concluded that "coercive police activity is a necessary predicate to a finding of involuntariness," and held that if a defendant's free will is "overborne" by his mental illness, this does not make his confession involuntary in the absence of police coercion. The *Connelly* defendant's confession was deemed voluntary because the police were not aware of the severity of his mental illness and did not exploit it during interrogation. The *Connelly* Court distinguished *Blackburn v. Alabama*, 361 U.S. 199 (1960), which held that Due Process is violated when police learn of a defendant's history of mental problems and exploit them with coercive tactics. The *Connelly* police knew only that the defendant had been a patient in several mental hospitals in the past, and knew nothing of the auditory hallucinations that led him to confess; his symptoms of mental illness were manifested only the day after his confession during an interview with appointed counsel. At the time of his unsolicited confession to an officer on the streets of Denver, the *Connelly* defendant was given *Miranda* warnings, and he "appeared to understand fully the nature of his acts" when he waived his rights. The *Connelly* dissenters argued that minimum Due Process standards should require substantial indicia of reliability of a confession based on extrinsic evidence, which was lacking in *Connelly*. They also argued that the police awareness of the arrestee's multiple hospitalizations was enough to show that they exploited his vulnerabilities under *Blackburn*.

The defendant in *Arizona v. Fulminante*, 499 U.S. 279 (1991) needed to rely on Due Process because his questioning by an undercover informant-inmate was not "interrogation" under *Miranda*, according to *Illinois v. Perkins*, 496 U.S. 292 (1990). Nor was the defendant questioned concerning a charged crime, so *Massiah* provided no bar to "deliberate elicitation" of his confession. The *Fulminante* majority viewed the defendant's situation as a match for *Payne v. Arkansas*, 356 U.S. 560 (1958), where a sheriff promised protection to an inmate from the angry mob outside the jailhouse door, in exchange for his confession. The equivalent of the "angry mob" in *Fulminante* was the group of inmates who had threatened the defendant with violence because of rumors that he had killed a child. The informant-inmate played the role of sheriff, bargaining for Fulminante's confession with a promise to provide protection from the other inmates. This promise carried weight, in the Court's implicit view, because the informant-inmate was pretending to be an organized crime figure. The *Fulminante* majority treated this promise as a "credible threat of violence," and viewed the defendant's situation as a frightening one. His failure to confess to the informant would result in his vulnerability to attacks by the threatening inmates. The *Fulminante* majority affirmed the legitimacy of the totality-of-the-circumstances analysis for Due Process issues, and treated the defendant's individual frailties as relevant to its finding that the confession was involuntary. The *Fulminante* dissenters shared a sharply different view of the record, viewing the evidence of the informant's bargain and the defendant's circumstances in prison as inadequate to justify the Court's result.

POINTS TO REMEMBER

- A confession is deemed to be involuntary and inadmissible according to Due Process requirements when it is procured by means of coercion, and there must be some government "overreaching" for a finding of coercion to be made.

- A "totality of the circumstances" approach is used to measure the voluntariness of a confession, and relevant variables include the police conduct, the surrounding circumstances and the characteristics and experiences of the defendant.

- A "credible threat of violence" will violate Due Process, as well as other forms of physical or psychological coercion.

- Police do not violate Due Process by obtaining the confession of a mentally ill arrestee, if they are not aware of the mental illness and if they comply with *Miranda*.

- *Miranda* protections include the right to receive warnings during custodial interrogation, the right not to be interrogated without making a "voluntary, knowing and intelligent" waiver, and the right to have the police cut off questioning if the rights to silence, to counsel, or to both are invoked.

- "Custody" exists during a formal arrest or when a person is restrained to the degree associated with a formal arrest.

- "Interrogation" occurs when police reasonably should know that their words or conduct are likely to elicit an incriminating response.

- Police may not initiate questioning or seek a waiver from a person who has invoked the right to counsel, as long as the arrestee does not "initiate" a generalized discussion of the investigation with the police after such invocation.

- Police may initiate questioning about a different crime and seek a waiver from an arrestee who has invoked only the right to silence, as long as the police "scrupulously honor" the invocation and provide new *Miranda* warnings and allow some significant period of time to pass before initiating contact.

- Police do not need to warn an arrestee about the following matters:

    — The subject matter of the questioning;

    — The fact that a lawyer wishes to speak to the arrestee and provide assistance during the interrogation;

    — The fact that a prior interrogation by police may be inadmissible at trial because of a *Miranda* violation.

- If police use an undercover agent to "deliberately elicit" statements from a defendant who has been charged with a crime to which the Sixth Amendment has attached, any statements obtained are not admissible at the trial on the charged offense.

- An undercover agent does not "deliberately elicit" statements by merely listening to a charged defendant.

- Police may seek a Sixth Amendment waiver from a defendant who has been charged with a crime to which the Sixth Amendment has attached. But police may not "deliberately elicit" statements from the defendant in the absence of the waiver.

- Police may use *Miranda* warnings to notify a defendant of the Sixth Amendment right to counsel, and may obtain a *Miranda* waiver to serve as an adequate waiver of Sixth Amendment rights.

Chapter 6

ENTRAPMENT

Focal Points for Entrapment Chapter

- Entrapment Defense: Sherman's Two–Part Subjective Test.

- Inducement and Predisposition.

- Objective Test—Predisposition is Irrelevant.

- Jacobson's Modern Subjective Test.

- Due Process Claims for Predisposed Defendants: Russell & Hampton

---

The entrapment defense has been part of state and federal criminal law for many years. The defense was created as a means for courts to regulate the participation by government agents in criminal acts during undercover investigations. The entrapment defense developed before modern Due Process law established limits on police conduct during interrogations, searches, and seizures. Therefore, Due Process concerns in this earlier era were incorporated into doctrinal elements that took the form of criminal law rules. Defendants who cannot satisfy the requirements of the modern entrapment defense now seek to use Due Process as a source of protection from "outrageous government conduct." The Supreme Court has acknowledged that Due Process standards may ban certain types of police entrapment activities, but the Court has yet to uphold a Due Process claim of this kind. Lower courts recognize the need for constitutional rules regarding undercover investigations and have created some Due Process limitations in this field.

A. The Entrapment Defense

The Court recognized the entrapment defense in federal criminal law in *Sorrells v. United States*, 287 U.S. 435 (1932). The Court initially endorsed the "subjective" test for entrapment, and modern decisions maintain this tradition. See *Sherman v. United States*, 356 U.S. 369 (1958); *Jacobson v. United States*, 503 U.S. 540 (1992). The example set by the Supreme Court is followed by most state courts. However, about one third of the state courts use some version of an "objective" test, endorsed by a plurality of the Court. See *Sherman*, 356 U.S. at 378–385 (Frankfurter, J., concurring). The "subjective" test requires a defendant to prove a sufficient "inducement" and the prosecution to rebut this proof with evidence of the defendant's "predisposition" to commit the crime beyond a reasonable doubt. The "objective" test, by contrast, does not consider the element of "predisposition," but instead focuses solely on inducement, as illustrated by the Model Penal Code's definition: "employing methods of persuasion or inducement which create a substantial risk that such an offense will be committed by persons other than those who are ready to commit it." Due Process concerns are expressed in the rationales and formulas used for both tests.

1. Subjective Test v. Objective Test

The Supreme Court's use of a "subjective" test for entrapment is illustrated by the holding in *Sherman v. United States*, 356 U.S. 369 (1958), that the defendant was entrapped as a matter of law. The *Sherman* defendant's proof of inducement was clear, and the government's proof of predisposition was found to be inadequate. The *Sherman* majority declared that the goal of the defense is to recognize that government officials should not "implant in the mind of an innocent person the disposition to commit the alleged offense and induce its commission in order that they may prosecute." *Sherman*, 356 U.S. at 372, citing *Sorrells*, 287 U.S. at 442. The *Sherman* majority also noted that the purpose of the twin inquiries into "inducement" and "disposition" is to distinguish those non-entrapment situations where government agents "merely afford opportunities" for crime from entrapment situations where crime occurs as "the product of the creative activity" of those agents.

The inducement proof in *Sherman* showed that the defendant met the government informant while seeking treatment for addiction, and that the informant feigned an addiction and repeatedly pleaded with the defendant to help him to obtain drugs to ameliorate his suffering as an addict. The *Sherman* defendant initially refused to help the informant, but ultimately acquiesced, and while sharing drugs with the informant, the defendant returned to his own addiction. The government's evidence of predisposition consisted only of "a nine-year old sales conviction and a five-year-old possession conviction." No evidence of the defendant's "readiness" to commit the crime of selling narcotics was produced; his apartment contained no narcotics and he made no profit on the sale of drugs to the informant. The *Sherman* Court declared that, "[t]he Government's characterization of [the defendant's] hesitancy to [the informant's] request as the natural wariness of the criminal cannot fill the evidentiary void" concerning predisposition.

The *Sherman* plurality criticized the *Sherman* majority's use of the "subjective" test for entrapment, and advocated an "objective" test that would treat predisposition as an irrelevant consideration. The plurality's proposed test was as follows:

> [I]n holding out inducements [police agents] should act in such a manner as is likely to induce to the commission of crime only those persons and not others who would normally avoid crime and through self-struggle resist ordinary temptations.

This test requires a case-by-case analysis, and relevant factors include, "the setting in which the inducement took place," the "nature of the crime involved," and "the manner in which the actual criminal business is usually carried on."

The *Sherman* majority's application of the "subjective" test for entrapment did not provide much guidance concerning the appropriate result in a case where the inducement evidence is weaker and the predisposition evidence stronger than in *Sherman*. Lower courts after *Sherman* were willing to affirm convictions based on inferences about predisposition that could be drawn from a defendant's prior record or from a "ready response" to a particular inducement. However, several decades after *Sherman*, the Court signaled a new readiness to scrutinize predisposition evidence in *Jacobson v. United States*, 503 U.S. 540 (1992).

2. The Modern Subjective Test

The Court now requires that as part of its burden of proof of predisposition, the government must show that the defendant was predisposed to commit the crime "before being approached by government agents." *Jacobson v. United States*, 503 U.S. 540 (1992). The *Jacobson* Court noted that two kinds of evidence of predisposition may be used to make this showing: evidence developed prior to the first government contact, and evidence developed during the course of the investigation before the commission of the crime. The proof of the *Jacobson* defendant's predisposition was held to be insufficient because he became predisposed only after two and a half years of repeated mailings from fictitious government entities in a child pornography sting operation. Based on the evidence of his inducement, his entrapment defense was upheld as a matter of law.

The *Jacobson* majority couched its holding in terms that were consistent with *Sorrells* and *Sherman*. The new element in its interpretation of the "subjective" test was the requirement that the government must prove that predisposition is "independent and not the product of the attention that the Government [directs] at" a target defendant during an undercover investigation. The *Jacobson* dissenters argued that the government should be required to prove only that the defendant's predisposition existed before inducements were offered. The inducements in *Jacobson* were preceded by contacts that the dissenters found to be a necessary part of a pornography sting operation. The government's mailings from "five fictitious organizations and a bogus pen pal" included a membership application, a sexual attitude questionnaire, two consumer research surveys, a list of potential pen pals, and invitations to receive brochures and catalogues. The *Jacobson* dissenters saw these contacts as reasonable tactics to determine the defendant's sexual interests, opining that, "a 'cold call' in such a business would not only risk rebuff and suspicion but might also shock and offend the uninitiated." But the *Jacobson* majority concluded that the new proof requirement for predisposition evidence was necessary to protect people like the defendant, who was "an otherwise law-abiding citizen who, if left to his own devices, likely would never run afoul of the law."

However, the *Jacobson* majority did emphasize that its new rule was not intended to alter the settled doctrine that "the ready commission of the criminal act amply demonstrates" a defendant's predisposition. Nor did the *Jacobson* majority explicitly impose a requirement that the government must have a reasonable suspicion of criminal activity before making contact with a target defendant. What *Jacobson* requires, which *Sherman* did not, is careful judicial scrutiny of the conduct of government agents from the moment of first contact with a defendant until the moment the defendant commits the crime. Thus, *Jacobson* moves the Court closer to the values, if not the rhetoric, of the "objective" test. The *Jacobson* majority was concerned that a particular pattern of repeated government contacts should not be tolerated. The majority's solution was to treat such contacts as foreclosing the ability of the government to prove predisposition, and thereby to deny the government the power to prosecute defendants whose predisposition was "created" by the government.

B. Due Process and "Outrageous Government Conduct"

The Court has observed that "due process principles" may prohibit some "outrageous" entrapment-style conduct of government officials. *United States v. Russell*, 411 U.S. 423 (1973). But the Court has not chosen to elucidate specific rules concerning Due Process limits on such conduct. The Court has rejected two opportunities to vindicate Due Process claims in cases where predisposition evidence would have made it difficult for the defendants to present a successful entrapment defense under the "subjective" test.

These defendants sought "to expand the traditional notion of entrapment" by seeking to prove that the conduct of government agents showed "an intolerable degree of government participation in the criminal enterprise," and thereby violated Due Process. *Russell*, 411 U.S. at 427. See also *Hampton v. United States*, 425 U.S. 484 (1976). Both cases involved drug crime prosecutions, and in each case the Court declined to find the conduct of government agents to be sufficiently "extreme" to justify a dismissal of the prosecutions on Due Process grounds.

The defendant in *United States v. Russell*, 411 U.S. 423 (1973), argued that the "criminal conduct would not have been possible" if the undercover agent had not "supplied an indispensable means to the commission of the crime that could not have been obtained otherwise through legal or illegal channels." Specifically, the agent supplied bottles of the chemical phenyl–2–propanone to defendants manufacturing methamphetamine, in return for the right to purchase part of the finished product. The *Russell* Court relied on three alternate rationales for rejecting the defendant's argument. First, the special ingredient was not impossible to obtain, and the defendant, in fact, obtained it from other sources. Second, the ingredient was a harmless and legal substance. Third, during the process of "infiltration" of drug "rings" by government agents, "the supply of some item of value that the drug ring requires" must be permissible in order for an agent to be "taken into the confidence of the illegal entrepreneurs." Therefore, the law enforcement tactic used in *Russell* was not be deemed to be fundamentally unfair or "shocking to the universal sense of justice" under Due Process precedents.

The Court created a further barrier to Due Process claims in *Hampton v. United States*, 425 U.S. 484, 490 (1976), observing that Due Process limitations "come into play only when the Government activity in question violates some protected right of the defendant." A plurality of the Court conceded that the agents "played a more significant role" in *Hampton* than in *Russell*. According to the defendant's evidence, one agent supplied him with the illegal drug while another agent acted as the buyer. However, the *Hampton* plurality held that these differences were not sufficient to justify a finding of a Due Process violation because the defendant acted "in concert" with the agents and was predisposed. The *Hampton* dissenters did not agree that predisposed defendants should be denied a Due Process claim. Instead, the dissenters would have found a Due Process violation in *Hampton* because the government was "buying contraband from itself and jailing the intermediary." Thus, the crime was "the product of the creative activity of its own officials." The *Hampton* dissent has inspired lower courts to develop a case-by-case approach for the evaluation of Due Process claims, focusing on such factors as the following:

> Whether the police conduct instigated a crime or merely infiltrated ongoing criminal activity, whether the defendant's reluctance to commit a crime was overcome by pleas of sympathy, promises of excessive profits, or persistent solicitation, whether the government controls the criminal activity or simply allows for the criminal activity to occur, whether the police motive was to prevent crime or protect the public; and whether the government conduct itself amounted to criminal activity or conduct "repugnant to a sense of justice."

State v. Lively, 130 Wash.2d 1, 921 P.2d 1035, 1046 (1996).

POINTS TO REMEMBER

- In a jurisdiction using the "subjective" test for entrapment, the defendant must prove sufficient "inducement" and then the prosecution must prove the defendant's "predisposition" beyond a reasonable doubt.

- In a jurisdiction using the "objective" test for entrapment, the defendant's predisposition is irrelevant. The defendant should prove that the police created an inducement that creates a substantial risk that such an offense will be committed by persons other than those who are ready to commit it.

- When proving predisposition in a "subjective" test jurisdiction, the prosecution must show that the defendant was predisposed to commit the crime "before being approached by government agents."

- It is not a violation of Due Process for the government to supply an ingredient that is difficult to obtain to defendants engaged in the manufacture of an illegal drug, in exchange for the right to purchase some of that manufactured illegal substance.

- It is not a violation of Due Process for one government agent to supply the illegal drug to a defendant and arrange for another government agent to buy the same drug from the defendant.

Chapter 7

IDENTIFICATION PROCEDURES

Focal Points for Identification Procedures

- Types of identification procedures (i.e lineups, blind lineups, confrontations and showups).

- The inapplicability of the privilege against self-incrimination
and privacy concepts to identification procedures.

- The problems with identification procedures: suggestiveness and the potential for "irreparable mistaken identification."

- Applicability of the Sixth Amendment right to counsel to identification procedures.

- The distinction between lineups that occur prior to the commencement of adversarial proceedings, and those that occur afterwards.

- Special rules that apply to photographic displays.

- Applicability of due process principles to all identification procedures.

- The distinction between "suggestiveness" and "reliability."

A. Constitutional Issues With Lineups and Other Identification Processes

Identification procedures can take many different forms. Most people are familiar with the so-called "lineup" (a/k/a "identification parade") in which a defendant is placed in a line with several others, and the eyewitness is asked to identify the perpetrator of the crime. But police also use a procedure called a "confrontation" or "showup" in which a suspect is confronted by an eyewitness and asked whether the suspect committed the crime. They also use a "blind lineup" in which two or more lineups are held, and the eyewitness is told that the suspect will not participate in one or more of the lineups. Finally, the police also conduct "photographic lineups" in which they display pictures of the suspect and others (in a format

261

that is similar to a lineup) and ask the witness whether one of the pictures depicts the criminal.

The United States Supreme Court has consistently refused to apply the privilege against self-incrimination to identification procedures. Although the goal of such procedures is to produce incriminating information, the Court has held that such procedures do not implicate the Fifth Amendment privilege against self-incrimination. The Court construes the privilege as protecting defendants only against "testimonial" self-incrimination (i.e., forcing the defendant to "testify" whether or not he committed the crime). Identification procedures are regarded as different and non-testimonial because, although the accused is forced to display his characteristics, he is not forced to testify against himself.

In *Gilbert v. California*, 388 U.S. 263 (1967), the Court held that a defendant could be required to provide a handwriting exemplar because it was "nontestimonial." The Court stated:

> One's voice and handwriting are, of course, means of communications. It by no means follows, however, that every compulsion of an accused to use his voice or write (compel) a communication within the cover of the privilege. A mere handwriting exemplar, in contrast to the content of what is written, like the voice or body itself, is an identifying physical characteristic outside its protection.

In *United States v. Wade*, 388 U.S. 218 (1967), the Court treated lineups as nontestimonial as well: "Neither the lineup itself nor anything shown by this record that [the accused] was required to do in the lineup violated his privilege against self-incrimination. [T]he privilege protects an accused only from being compelled to testify against himself, or otherwise provide the State with evidence of a testimonial or communicative [nature]." The Court also reinforced *Gilbert's* holding that accused could be required to utter the words used by the criminal. The Court has construed this utterance as involving nothing more than the exhibition of the characteristics of the suspect's voice.

The Court has also rejected the argument that lineups (and other identification procedures) violate a suspect's "privacy" interests. In *United States v. Dionisio*, 410 U.S. 1 (1973), the Court stated that:

> [t]he physical characteristics of a person's voice, its tone and manner, as opposed to the content of a specific conversation, are constantly exposed to the public. Like a man's facial characteristics, or handwriting, his voice is repeatedly produced

for others to hear. No person can have a reasonable expectation that others will not know the sound of his voice any more than he can reasonably expect that his face will be a mystery to the world.

As a result, the two primary constitutional challenges focus on due process and the right to counsel. These challenges are discussed more fully below.

B. The Sixth Amendment

One argument that has successfully been used to challenge identifications is the Sixth Amendment right to counsel. The leading case is *United States v. Wade,* 388 U.S. 218 (1967), in which Wade was charged with bank robbery. Following his arrest and the appointment of counsel, Wade was forced to participate in a lineup. Along with others, he was forced to wear strips of tape on his face (just as the robber had done) and was forced to say the words spoken by the robber ("put the money in the bag"). Both witnesses who viewed the lineup identified Wade as the robber. At his subsequent trial, the witnesses were asked whether the robber was in the courtroom and both identified Wade. They also testified regarding the lineup identification. Based in part on their testimony, Wade was convicted of the crime.

The Court held that the lineup implicated Wade's Sixth Amendment right to counsel. The Court began by rejecting the state's argument that the lineup involved "a mere preparatory step in the gathering of the prosecution's evidence" similar to the gathering of fingerprints, blood samples, clothing, and hair. Had a lineup been similar to these "preparatory steps," the Court held that counsel could have used scientific techniques to "meaningfully confront the government's case through cross-examination," and that the absence of counsel would not have precluded a fair trial. The Court viewed lineups as fundamentally different because of the potential for mistaken identification, and the possibility of suggestion "inherent in the manner in which the prosecution presents the suspect to witnesses for pretrial identification."

The *Wade* Court recognized the powerful nature of eyewitness evidence. When a victim or witness to a crime emphatically identifies someone as the perpetrator of a crime, a jury tends to place great weight on the identification. The Court also recognized that identification testimony can be unreliable. A witness' ability to accurately identify the perpetrator of a crime depends on a variety of factors including the witness' ability to accurately perceive at the time of the crime, and the witness' ability to accurately recall the perception. A number of factors can interfere with a witness' ability to accurately perceive including the fact that the witness may have limited time to observe the perpetrator, and may be forced to observe under unfavorable conditions (including stress and anxiety). Even if the witness accurately perceived at the time of the crime, the witness' memory can be distorted over time because memory can decay and shift.

The Court suggested several ways in which a lineup could be suggestive. For example, suggestiveness exists when the physical characteristics of the lineup participants are disparate (i.e., the suspect is tall and thin, but all other lineup participants are short and fat), as well as when the suspect is dressed in clothes like those worn by the perpetrator, but all other lineup participants are dressed quite differently. Suggestiveness can also be created by conditions in the lineup room (i.e. a spotlight is focused directly on the suspect), or by the actions of those conducting the lineup (i.e. the police focus on the suspect and ask the witness "He's the one who committed the crime, isn't he?").

In *Wade*, the Court found that a number of factors resulted in a suggestive identification. In that case, the eyewitnesses were taken to the courthouse to await the lineup. While they were waiting, Wade was standing nearby next to an FBI agent. Later, the other lineup participants appeared in a group. The Court felt that these circumstances suggested to the eyewitness that Wade was the suspect. In *Stovall v. Denno*, 388 U.S. 293 (1967), the Court also referred to the potential for suggestiveness created by a confrontation at which the accused was presented to the eyewitness without the presence of other possible suspects.

The Court is concerned about suggestiveness because it fears that witnesses' recollections could be influenced by police suggestions, and the Court recognized that suggestiveness could be created both intentionally and unintentionally. The result is the potential for mistaken identification, especially when "the witness' opportunity for observation was insubstantial, and thus his susceptibility to suggestion the greatest." Of course, once mistaken identification occurs, the witness will rarely recant so that "in practice the issue of identity may (in the absence of other relevant evidence) for all practical purposes be determined there and then, before the trial."

Once suggestiveness has led a witness to make a mistaken identification, it may be difficult or impossible for defense counsel to overcome any mistake. For one thing, defense counsel may find it difficult to reconstruct what really happened, or to conduct a meaningful cross-examination. At the lineup itself, neither the defendant nor the witnesses may have been aware of the many ways in which an identification could be tainted by suggestiveness. Moreover, the suspect will have been under emotional stress at the lineup, may not have been in a position to view everything that occurred, and may not have been able to object without drawing attention to himself. Finally, even if the defendant observed suggestiveness, he might be reluctant to take the stand if he has prior criminal convictions. As a result, it may be difficult for the accused "meaningfully to attack the credibility of the witness' courtroom identification." If the out-of-court identification was conducted under suggestive circumstances leading to irreparable mistaken identification, the "trial which might determine the accused's fate may well not be that in the courtroom but that at the pretrial confrontation. . ."

Because of the possibility for irreparable mistaken identification, the Court concluded that the post-indictment lineup was a critical stage at which Wade was entitled to counsel absent an "intelligent waiver." Since counsel was not provided to Wade, he was entitled to a new trial. At that trial, the eyewitness testimony must be excluded unless the state is able to show by "clear and convincing evidence" that the in-court identifications were based upon non-lineup observations. In other words, the issue was "[w]hether, granting establishment of the primary illegality, the evidence to which instant objection is made has been come at by exploitation of that illegality." If not, the in-court identification would not be allowed.

Whether the in-court identification was independent would be determined by a number of factors. Included were:

> the prior opportunity to observe the alleged criminal act, the existence of any discrepancy between any pre-lineup description and the defendant's actual description, any identification prior to lineup of another person, the identification by picture of the defendant prior to the lineup, failure to identify the defendant on a prior occasion, and the lapse of time between the alleged act and the lineup identification. It is also relevant to consider those facts which, despite the absence of counsel, are disclosed concerning the conduct of the lineup.

Since the Court could not determine whether Wades' in-court identification was the result of prior illegality, it reversed the conviction and remanded for further proceedings.

It is important to emphasize that Wade only applies to lineups (and other identification procedures) that take place after the commencement of adversary proceedings. In *Kirby v. Illinois*, 406 U.S. 682 (1972), the Court refused to extend *Wade* to identification testimony (a showup) that took place *before* the defendant had been indicted or otherwise formally charged with any criminal offense:

> [A] person's Sixth and Fourteenth Amendment right to counsel attaches only at or after the time that adversary judicial proceedings have been initiated against him. [The] initiation of judicial criminal proceedings is far from a mere formalism. It is the starting point of our whole system of adversary criminal justice. For it is only then that the government has committed itself to prosecute, and only then that the adverse positions of government and defendant have solidified. It is then that a defendant finds himself faced with the prosecutorial forces of organized society, and immersed in the intricacies of substantive and procedural criminal law. * * *

Justice Brennan dissented, arguing that "the dangers inherent in eyewitness identification and the suggestibility inherent in the context of the pretrial identification" are present in pre-indictment identification procedures. "[T]here inhere in a confrontation for identification conducted after arrest the identical hazards to a fair trial that inhere in such a confrontation conducted 'after the onset of formal prosecutional proceedings.' "As a result, he concluded that it was irrelevant whether the state had commenced adversary proceedings.

In *Moore v. Illinois*, 434 U.S. 220, 224–25 (1977), the Court reiterated the basic premise that the right to counsel extends only to post-charging procedures, but extended the right backward to the preliminary hearing. In the post-charging situation, the Court has applied the right not only to lineups, but also to "showups" and "confrontations."

In *Rothgery v. Gillespie County*, 554 U.S. 191 (2008), the Court reaffirmed the idea "that the right to counsel guaranteed by the Sixth Amendment applies only after adversary proceedings have commenced. The Court held that the adversary process can commence with "the initiation of adversary judicial criminal proceedings-whether by way of formal charge, preliminary hearing, indictment, information, or arraignment," as well as by "the first appearance before a judicial officer at which a defendant is told of the formal accusation against him and restrictions are imposed on his liberty." The Court relied on *Brewer v. Williams,* 430 U.S. 387, 398-399 (1977), and *Michigan v. Jackson,* 475 U.S. 625, 629 n. 3 (1986). The Court went on to hold that the right attaches whether or not a public prosecutor is aware of the initial proceeding.

Even if counsel is present at a lineup, counsel has a limited role. An attorney can "observe" and can object to suggestive conditions, but is not entitled to direct the lineup. Of course, if the eyewitness is in the room, the lawyer might not be able to object without being suggestive regarding the suspect. However, the attorney's observations can help him determine whether the lineup was unduly suggestive and likely to lead to irreparable mistaken identification. As a result, the observations can provide the basis for challenging admission of the identification (or any subsequent in-court identification) on due process grounds.

The Court has refused to apply the right to counsel to photographic displays. *United States v. Ash*, 413 U.S. 300 (1973), involved an armed robbery of a bank. When a government informer told police that Ash was involved in the crime, the police showed pictures of Ash and four other people to four witnesses. All made uncertain identifications of Ash. After Ash was indicted, the prosecutor arranged a second photographic display. Three witnesses selected Ash's picture (but not that of his co-defendant Bailey), but one witness was unable to make any selection. The Court held that Ash was not entitled to counsel at the photographic display. The Court emphasized that it was possible to adequately reconstruct the display, and therefore that any defects could be cured at trial. In addition, since Ash was not present at the display, the Court concluded that there was no chance that he "might be misled by his lack of familiarity with the law or overpowered by his professional adversary." The Court viewed the photographic display as comparable to the interviewing of witnesses, and the Court felt that the adversary mechanism could deal with any problems. Indeed, as the Court emphasized, the display was initially introduced by Bailey's attorney who pointed out that the witness was unable to identify him. "Although we do not suggest that equality of access to photographs removes all potential for abuse, it does remove any inequality in the adversary process itself and thereby fully satisfies the historical spirit of the Sixth Amendment's counsel guarantee."

The Court did recognize that photographic displays are subject to manipulation and suggestion:

"Evidence favorable to the accused may be withheld; testimony of witnesses may be manipulated; the results of laboratory tests may be contrived. In many ways the prosecutor, by accident or by design, may improperly subvert the trial. The primary safeguard against abuses of this kind is the ethical responsibility of the prosecutor, who, as so often has been said, may 'strike hard blows' but not 'foul ones.' If that safeguard fails, review remains available under due process standards."

But the "Court refused to hold that photographic displays were subject to such abuse that a new constitutional rule was required."

Justice Brennan dissented, arguing that photographic displays present the same potential for irreparable mistaken identification as lineups. In addition, since photographs present individuals in two dimensions rather than three, they are inferior to lineups and create a greater potential for misidentification. In any event, they are equally susceptible to suggestion from the choice of photographs or the manner in which the photographs are displayed. It is difficult to reconstruct what happened at trial. As a result, counsel needs to be present as a trained observer.

C. Due Process Considerations

Another argument that has been successfully raised against identification procedures is a due process challenge. Under the due process clause, review is available when a defendant can show that the identification methods used were "unnecessarily suggestive and conducive to mistaken identification." The due process clause applies to both pre-indictment and post-indictment identifications. Indeed, when a lineup is held prior to the commencement of adversarial proceedings, as well as when the defendant's attorney was present at the lineup, the due process defense might provide the only basis for challenging the identification.

One of the leading cases is *Stovall v. Denno*, 388 U.S. 293 (1967). In that case, an intruder stabbed a man to death in the kitchen of his home, and also stabbed the man's wife eleven times. While the wife was recovering in hospital, petitioner was brought to her hospital room for an identification. He was a black person, the only black in the room, and the wife was asked whether he was "the man" who committed the crime. The wife identified him and subsequently made an in-court identification. Although the Court recognized that an identification can be challenged on due process grounds, the Court upheld both identifications: "[A] claimed violation of due process of law in the conduct of a confrontation depends on the totality of the circumstances surrounding it, and the record in the present case reveals that the showing of Stovall to Mrs. Behrendt in an immediate hospital confrontation was imperative."

In evaluating the identification, the *Stovall* court relied on *Foster v. California*, 394 U.S. 440 (1969). In that case, Foster was charged with the armed robbery of a Western Union office. The witness, the office's night manager, was asked to view a lineup. In addition to Foster (a tall man of six feet in height), there were two short men (five feet, five or six inches in height). Foster was the only one who wore a leather jacket similar to the one worn by the robber. Despite these facts, the witness was unable to positively identify Foster as the robber. Although he "thought" that Foster was the man, he was not sure. The witness then asked to talk to Foster and the conversation was arranged in an office. Following this confrontation, the witness was still not sure whether Foster was the robber. Seven to 10 days later, the police arranged for the witness to view a second lineup. There were five participants in that lineup. Foster was the only person who appeared in both this and the prior lineup. At this lineup, the witness was "convinced" that Foster was the robber. At trial, the witness testified regarding the lineups and also made an in-court identification of Foster as the robber. The Court found that the case presented a "compelling example of unfair lineup procedures." "The suggestive elements in this identification procedure made it all but inevitable that the witness would identify petitioner whether or not he was in fact 'the man.' " "In effect, the police repeatedly said to the witness, 'This is the man.' This procedure so undermined the reliability of the eyewitness identification as to violate due process."

Despite *Foster's* holding, it can be difficult to prevail on a due process challenge. The mere existence of suggestiveness is not determinative of a due process violation, in and of itself. The Court will also focus on whether the identification was "reliable" (something which can occur even though the procedure was suggestive). For example, in *Neil v. Biggers*, 409 U.S. 188 (1972), respondent was convicted of rape based in part on a station-house "showup." Before conducting the showup, the police tried to arrange a lineup but were unable to find anyone who matched respondent's unusual physical description. During the showup, two police detectives walked respondent by the victim and directed him to say "shut up or I'll kill you." The victim testified that she had "no doubt" that respondent was the rapist. The Court upheld the use of the identification, noting that, although the showup was suggestive, the subsequent identification was "reliable" considering the "totality of the circumstances."

In *Biggers*, the Court identified factors to be considered in determining whether an identification is "reliable." These factors include the following:

> the opportunity of the witness to view the criminal at the time of the crime, the witness' degree of attention, the accuracy of the witness' prior description of the criminal, the level of certainty demonstrated by the witness at the confrontation, and the length of time between the crime and the confrontation.

In finding that the victim's identification was reliable, the *Biggers* Court noted that the victim had spent a "considerable period of time" with her attacker (up to half an hour), that there was adequate light in her house and a full moon outdoors, and she faced him "directly and intimately" at least twice. In addition, her description to the police, which included the assailant's approximate age, height, weight, complexion, skin texture, build, and voice, "was more than ordinarily thorough." In addition, she expressed "no doubt" regarding the identification and stated regarding his face that "I don't think I could ever forget." Finally, although seven months elapsed between the crime and the identification, she had viewed numerous lineups, showups and photographic displays without making an identification.

The Court reiterated its focus on "reliability" in *Manson v. Brathwaite,* 432 U.S. 98 (1977). In that case, an undercover narcotics officer went to an apartment to make a purchase. The door, which was illuminated by natural light, was opened part way and the transaction was consummated through this crack in the door. The transaction took 5 to 7 minutes. At the police station, the office described the seller as being "a colored man, approximately five feet eleven inches tall, dark complexion, black hair, short Afro style, and having high cheekbones, and of heavy build. He was wearing at the time blue pants and a plaid shirt." The officer was then shown a picture of respondent and identified him as the seller. At respondent's trial, the officer made a positive identification.

The Court upheld the in-court and pre-trial identifications against a due process challenge because they were deemed to be "reliable." "[R]eliability is the linchpin in determining the admissibility of identification testimony.." The Court referenced the *Biggers* criteria as the proper test for determining whether an identification is reliable. "Against these factors is to be weighed the corrupting effect of the suggestive identification itself." The Court emphasized that the officer was not a "casual observer" but instead was a trained police officer who specialized in dangerous duty who gave an accurate description of respondent, was certain of the identification, and gave it shortly after the crime. The Court concluded that these "reliability" factors were not outweighed by the "corrupting effect" of a suggestive identification. The Court concluded that there was insufficient likelihood of irreparable mistaken identification.

In *Perry v. New Hampshire,* 132 S.Ct. 716 (2012), the Court held that the reliability analysis would not apply to an identification procedure arranged by a private individual.

POINTS TO REMEMBER

- Although identification procedures can provide powerful evidence, they can also be unreliable.

- The principal problem with identification procedures is suggestiveness, which can be created both intentionally and unintentionally, and can lead to irreparable mistaken identification.

- The Sixth Amendment right to counsel applies to lineups that occur after the commencement of adversarial proceedings.

- The right to counsel does not apply to lineups that occur prior to the commencement of adversarial proceedings.

- The right to counsel also does not apply to photographic identifications.

- Even when the right to counsel applies, counsel's role is limited. Counsel does not have the right to "direct" the lineup, but only to appear, observe and object.

- Counsel may be reluctant to object for fear that the act of objection will itself be suggestive.

- By observing, counsel can determine whether the lineup is unduly suggestive and decide best how to challenge a resulting identification.

- Whether or not the right to counsel applies, the results of an identification procedure can be challenged on due process grounds.

- The presence of suggestiveness is an important factor in determining whether admission of the results of an identification violate due process.

- But suggestiveness is not always the determinative factor as the Court focuses on whether the identification is "reliable."

- An identification can result from suggestive procedures, but can still be reliable.

- Factors that bear on reliability include the opportunity of the witness to view the criminal at the time of the crime, the witness' degree of attention, the accuracy of the witness' prior description of the criminal, the level of certainty demonstrated by the witness at the confrontation, and the length of time between the crime and the confrontation.

- The reliability analysis is inapplicable to identifications arranged by private individuals.

Chapter 8

EXCLUSIONARY RULE

Focal Points for Chapter 8

- Constitutional remedy.

- Applies to federal and state court proceedings.

- Nothing else works.

- Incremental deterrence.

- Good-faith exception.

- Standing.

- Fruits doctrine.

- Inevitable discovery.

- Attenuation.

- Harmless error.

A. Suppression of Evidence as an Exclusionary Remedy

The exclusionary rule is a constitutional remedy that precludes the prosecution from introducing evidence in its case-in-chief seized by police officers or other government agents as a result of unconstitutional activity (often a search or seizure that violates the Fourth Amendment). This remedy does not apply automatically, but must be triggered by the defendant's successful argument of a motion to suppress at a suppression hearing, which usually takes place prior to trial. The exclusionary rule is principally intended to deter agents of the government from engaging in unconstitutional activity by removing the incentive to do so since it will result in no admissible evidence.

1. Constitutional Origins

The Supreme Court first adopted the exclusionary rule as a constitutional remedy in 1914, but it was initially deemed applicable only to *federal* criminal trials. *Weeks v. United States*, 232 U.S. 383 (1914). In *Weeks*, police officers searched defendant Weeks' room and seized papers and possessions to use against him at his subsequent criminal trial. Since the Court found that the search was undertaken without a search warrant or any other lawful justification, and was, accordingly, unconstitutional, it ruled that the evidence could not be admitted against Weeks;

> "[t]he tendency of those who execute the criminal laws of the country to obtain conviction by means of unlawful seizures and enforced confessions, the latter often obtained after subjecting accused persons to unwarranted practices destructive of rights secured by the Federal Constitution, should find no sanction in the judgments of the courts, which are charged at all times with the support of the Constitution, and to which people of all conditions have a right to appeal for the maintenance of such fundamental rights."

In 1961, in a landmark decision reversing *Wolf v. Colorado*, 338 U.S. 25 (1949), the United States Supreme Court extended the exclusionary rule to state proceedings. *Mapp v. Ohio*, 367 U.S. 643 (1961). In *Mapp*, three Cleveland police officers attempted to gain entrance to defendant Mapp's residence, the top floor of a two-family home, by claiming to have obtained information from a confidential informant that she was concealing a fugitive and was engaged in illegal gambling. After consulting by telephone with her attorney, Mapp refused to admit the police, but after a three-hour siege, the officers eventually forced their way into the house by breaking down a door. When Mapp's attorney arrived at the scene, he was not allowed to talk to Mapp and he was denied admission to the home. When Mapp demanded to see the officers' search warrant, after they had forcibly entered, one of the officers waved a piece of paper in the air. Mapp grabbed it and stuffed it inside her dress, and the officer reached in and removed the paper. (In fact, no warrant was ever offered into evidence and it is doubtful that a warrant ever existed.) Mapp was then handcuffed and forced to accompany the officers as they searched her house from top to bottom, purportedly looking for the fugitive and evidence of gambling. No fugitive nor gambling evidence was actually found, but the police did find some allegedly pornographic materials in Mapp's bedroom and Mapp was subsequently charged with—and convicted of—possession and control of that obscene material.

The *Mapp* Court, following the lead of a number of state courts which had concluded that the exclusionary rule was required under their own state constitutions, held that the same exclusionary rule recognized in *Weeks* applies in federal court to unconstitutional searches and seizures under the Fourth Amendment that produce evidence sought to be introduced by the government into state court criminal proceedings. Accordingly, in *Mapp*, the Court suppressed the evidence of obscenity seized by the Cleveland police officers and reversed Mapp's conviction.

The United States Supreme Court based its extension of the exclusionary rule to the states on a number of factors. Significantly, however, the Court found that the exclusionary rule was a constitutional requirement. Noting that "other remedies" for police misconduct "have been worthless and futile," the Court ruled that "all evidence obtained by searches and seizures in violation of the Constitution is, *by that same authority*, inadmissible in a state court." "Were it otherwise," the Court added,

> "then just as without the *Weeks* rule the assurance against unreasonable federal searches and seizures would be 'a form of words', valueless and undeserving of mention in a perpetual charter of inestimable human liberties, so too, without that rule the freedom from state invasions of privacy would be so ephemeral and so neatly severed from its conceptual nexus with the freedom from all brutish means of coercing evidence as not to merit this Court's high regard as a freedom 'implicit in' the concept of ordered liberty."

In recent decades, the Court has focused on deterrence in applying the exclusionary rule, and has applied a cost-benefit test in deciding whether to apply the rule. For example, in *Herring v. United States*, 129 S. Ct. 695 (2009), the Court refused to apply the exclusionary rule when a police officer reasonably believed that there was an outstanding warrant for an individual's arrest, but the belief was in error because of a bookkeeping error by a police official (the arrest warrant had been recalled, but the police official who maintained the logbook failed to note the recall). During the search incident to legal arrest, the police found contraband on the arrestee, and he moved to suppress. Relying on its prior precedent, suggesting that suppression is never "automatic," the Court focused on "the culpability of the police and the potential of exclusion to deter wrongful police conduct." Citing *Leon,* the Court suggested that "an assessment of the flagrancy of the police misconduct constitutes an important step in the calculus." In *Herring*, because the Court concluded that the error was the result of "isolated negligence attenuated from the arrest," the Court held that the evidence should be admitted. The Court stated that, to "trigger the exclusionary rule, police conduct must be sufficiently deliberate that exclusion can meaningfully deter it, and sufficiently culpable that such deterrence is worth the price paid by the justice system." Recordkeeping errors do not satisfy that standard unless the "the police have been shown to be reckless in maintaining a warrant system, or to have knowingly made false entries to lay the groundwork for future false arrests.

Justice Ginsburg dissented in *Herring*, arguing that the "exclusionary rule provides redress for Fourth Amendment violations by placing the government in the position it would have been in had there been no unconstitutional arrest and search." She found that the police had at least been negligent, noting that the Court's holding "underestimates the need for a forceful exclusionary rule and the gravity of recordkeeping errors in law enforcement." She went on to note that:

> [A] main objective of the rule "is to deter-to compel respect for the constitutional guaranty in the only effectively available way-by removing the incentive to disregard it." *Elkins v. United States,* 364 U.S. 206, 217 (1960). But the rule also serves other important purposes: It "enabl[es] the judiciary to avoid the taint of partnership in official lawlessness," and it "assur[es] the people-all potential victims of unlawful government conduct-that the government would not profit from its lawless behavior, thus minimizing the risk of seriously undermining popular trust in government." *United States v. Calandra,* 414 U.S. 338, 357 (1974) (Brennan, J., dissenting)[.] The exclusionary rule, it bears emphasis, is often the only remedy effective to redress a Fourth Amendment violation. . .

> Electronic databases form the nervous system of contemporary criminal justice operations[.] The risk of error stemming from these databases is not slim. Herring's *amici* warn that law enforcement databases are insufficiently monitored and often out of date. Government reports describe, for example, flaws in NCIC databases, terrorist watchlist databases, and databases associated with the Federal Government's employment eligibility verification system[.] Inaccuracies in expansive, interconnected collections of electronic information raise grave concerns for individual liberty. "The offense to the dignity of the citizen who is arrested, handcuffed, and searched on a public street simply because some bureaucrat has failed to maintain an accurate computer data base" is evocative of the use of general warrants that so outraged the authors of our Bill of Rights. *Evans,* 514 U.S., at 23 (STEVENS, J., dissenting)[.] Negligent recordkeeping errors by law enforcement threaten individual liberty, are susceptible to deterrence by the exclusionary rule, and cannot be remedied effectively through other means. . .

Justice Breyer, joined by Justice Souter, also dissented, arguing that "police recordkeeping errors should be treated differently than judicial ones," and that the exclusionary rule should apply.

The exclusionary rule applies not only to evidence seized as a result of Fourth Amendment (search and seizure) violations, but also to violations of other constitutional provisions. Just five years after *Mapp* was handed down, for example, in *Miranda v. Arizona*, 384 U.S. 436 (1966), the Supreme Court applied the exclusionary rule to protect an individual's Fifth Amendment right against self-incrimination when he or she is interrogated in police custody without having first received the *Miranda* warnings concerning his or her constitutional rights and entitlements.

2. State and Statutory Exclusionary Rules

As noted above, prior to the Supreme Court's landmark decision in *Mapp*, applying the exclusionary rule to the states, many state courts had already applied the exclusionary rule to unconstitutional law enforcement activity under their own state constitutions. Subsequent to the *Mapp* decision, many more state courts have reached the same conclusion. Accordingly, even were the Supreme Court to one day overrule *Mapp* (a prospect that does not seem likely at the present time), the exclusionary rule would not become mere constitutional history. Most states would continue to apply the exclusionary rule, albeit under their state constitutions, rather than under the federal constitution.

Moreover, any legislative body (state or federal) may enact statutes that contain an exclusionary rule to serve as a remedy for police (or even private) violations of criminal or civil prohibitions set out in the legislation. In such cases, whether or not the conduct at issue is unconstitutional and subject to application of the constitutional (federal and/or state) exclusionary rule, such a statutory exclusionary remedy would still apply as a matter of non-constitutional, statutory law.

3. Alternatives to the Exclusionary Rule

The application of an exclusionary rule, resulting in the suppression of often significant evidence of criminal activity, is a rather drastic remedy for responding to police misconduct. As the *Mapp* Court acknowledged, Justice (then Judge) Cardozo had previously made the (still) often-quoted criticism of the exclusionary rule that it is nonsensical that "under [the] constitutional exclusionary doctrine '[t]he criminal is to go free because the constable has blundered.' " *Mapp*, 367 U.S. at 659, *quoting People v. Defore*, 242 N.Y. 13, 21, 150 N.E. 585, 587 (1926).

The *Mapp* Court responded to Cardozo's criticism by conceding that "[i]n some cases this will undoubtedly be the result." But, the Court added pointedly, " 'there is another consideration—the imperative of judicial integrity.' The criminal goes free, if he must, but it is the law that sets him free. Nothing can destroy a government more quickly than its failure to observe its own laws, or worse, its disregard of the charter of its own existence. As Mr. Justice Brandeis, dissenting, said in *Olmstead v. United States*, 1928, 277 U.S. 438, 485: 'Our government is the potent, the omnipresent teacher. For good or for ill, it teaches the whole people by its example. * * * If the government becomes a lawbreaker, it breeds contempt for law; it invites every man to become a law unto himself; it invites anarchy.' Nor can it lightly be assumed that, as a practical matter, adoption of the exclusionary rule fetters law enforcement." *Mapp*, 367 U.S. at 659.

Nonetheless, despite political and academic criticisms, the exclusionary rule survives (although without the same strong *constitutional* grounding today as it had when *Mapp* was first decided) in large part because a majority of the Supreme Court continues to believe that "nothing else works" to deter police misconduct. Nothing else works. What else was there?

a. Public Opinion

In *Wolf v. Colorado*, the 1949 decision overruled by the Supreme Court in *Mapp*, Justice Frankfurter suggested that one of the reasons that it was unnecessary at that time to extend the application of the exclusionary rule to the states is that police misconduct can be prevented, *inter alia*, by "the eyes of an alert public opinion." *Wolf*, 338 U.S. at 31. Ultimately, reliance on public opinion to correct and remedy police misconduct has proved problematic for a number of reasons. One reason is that "the public" simply does not become aware of any significant percentage of cases in which such police misconduct occurs; it simply isn't newsworthy. Another reason is that since the cases with which the public does become familiar are ordinarily those in which the defendant clearly committed a criminal act (the headlines read, for example, "Murderer Seeks To Throw Out Confession" or "Drug Kingpin Tries to Suppress Mountain of Cocaine"), there is usually little sympathy on the public's part with the constitutional claims being presented for redress. Concerns about public safety in the short run typically trump concerns about the effect on society of such police misconduct.

b. Criminal Prosecution

Justice Murphy, concurring in the Supreme Court's 1949 *Wolf* decision, flatly dismissed the possibility of criminal prosecution of police officers who engage in constitutional misconduct is a potentially significant means of insuring the existence of an effective remedy for such misconduct. "Little need be said concerning the possibilities of criminal prosecution. . . Self-scrutiny is a lofty ideal, but its exaltation reaches new heights if we expect a District Attorney to prosecute himself or his associates for well-meaning violations of the search and seizure clause during a raid the District Attorney or his associates have ordered."

As Justice Murphy intimated, one of the reasons for such a dismissive attitude, which is shared widely today, is that—despite the occasional splashy prosecution—prosecutors rely upon police officers to do the bulk of the prosecutors' investigative work. Essentially, police officers "work for them." It is perhaps an understatement to point out that it does not create the best of working conditions if an employer regularly prosecutes his or her employees (and/or prosecutors in his or her own office who may have ordered or ratified the law enforcement misconduct).

Moreover, prosecutors do not and should not prosecute *every* case of criminal misconduct about which they become aware. Prosecutors possess substantial discretion—in the interests of separation of powers and justice—to choose who and when to prosecute . . . and who and when not to prosecute. As a result, short of an exceptionally blatant act of police misconduct, e.g. a patently unjustified shooting which has received widespread community attention, or a significant and recurring problem with a particular police officer or police department, prosecutors typically exercise their lawful discretion to prosecute by *not* prosecuting police officers whose conduct might nonetheless be (arguably) problematic as a matter of constitutional law.

In short, while the occasional criminal prosecution of police officers may well have some deterrent effect on subsequent police misconduct, the overall deterrent impact of such prosecutions is substantially diluted by the pronounced infrequency of their occurrence.

c. Disciplinary Proceedings and Review Boards

The majority in the Supreme Court's (since-overruled) 1949 *Wolf* decision mentioned the impact that administrative scrutiny might have on police misconduct, noting favorably the possible remedial impact of the "internal discipline of the police." 338 U.S. at 31. But internal police review proceedings suffer from the same difficulty that any *internal* review process in any profession possesses, namely the difficulty of individuals judging and sanctioning one's own peers ("There but for the grace of God, go I"). And *external* police review boards, when they have managed to overcome the political hurdles that impede their creation and operation, are often composed primarily or exclusively of civilian (i.e. non-law enforcement) members and, hence, suffer from the perceived lack of identity with the police officers whose conduct is under scrutiny ("Who are they to judge us? They don't know what police work is like.") In addition to these practical and political difficulties, such external civilian review boards often lack the statutory or legal power to put their recommendations relating to discipline of individual officers— or systemic police department improvements—into effect.

As a result of these sorts of problems, experience has demonstrated that disciplinary proceedings and review boards do not— and perhaps cannot—be expected to systematically or effectively prevent law enforcement officers from engaging in unconstitutional activity or remedy the consequences of such misconduct.

d. Civil Actions

It is possible for individuals to bring civil actions for damages—in state or federal court—against law enforcement officers who have allegedly violated such individuals' constitutional rights. In fact, many people do bring such lawsuits. Depending on the jurisdiction and the specific type of harm alleged, such actions may be brought, for example, as state-law tort actions, as federal civil rights actions (§ 1983), or as state or federal "constitutional torts." However, for a number of reasons, lawsuits of this sort do not provide a sufficient or an effective societal remedy for police misconduct. A successful or adequate recovery is unlikely, even where a police officer has in fact acted unlawfully. A police officer's reasonable "good faith" in undertaking policing activity is typically a complete defense to such actions. This is true despite the fact that the officer's conduct may nonetheless have been unconstitutional and resulted in damage to the plaintiff. And police officers are typically ill paid. Accordingly, even if such a lawsuit might be successful, overcoming the difficulties of getting by a "good faith" defense, the prospects of a damages recovery substantial enough even to subsidize good legal representation for the plaintiff is unlikely.

Of course, the likelihood of a more substantial damages recovery increases if an injured plaintiff can establish the additional responsibility of a "deep pocket," usually the governmental unit that employed a law enforcement officer alleged to have engaged in misconduct resulting in the plaintiff's damages. It is true that governmental units are not completely immune from such liability. However, recovery is available against such a governmental unit *only* to the extent that its "policy or custom, whether made by its lawmakers or by those whose edicts or acts may fairly be said to represent official policy, inflicts the injury . . ." *Monell v. Department of Social Services of the City of New York*, 436 U.S. 658, 694 (1978).

Nonetheless, a single decision by a prosecutor can satisfy the "policy or custom requirement." *Pembaur v. Cincinnati*, 475 U.S. 469 (1986). Moreover, municipalities are not entitled to qualified immunity from such liability in such lawsuits, even though their agents may have acted in good faith and possess, as a result, qualified immunity. *Owen v. City of Independence*, 445 U.S. 622, 638 (1980) ("there is no tradition of immunity for municipal corporations, and neither history nor policy supports a construction of § 1983 that would justify . . . qualified immunity . . .") Proving such a "policy or custom" is difficult. And this difficulty—coupled with the difficulties noted above with respect to successful litigation against the individual officers involved—make it extremely difficult to win these cases and, as a result, to obtain the legal support to even bring these cases in the first place.

In sum, although civil actions are sometimes available—and successful—as a remedy in damages for some specific instances of especially egregious police misconduct, experience has demonstrated that the such civil lawsuits are too sporadic and idiosyncratic to serve to effectively prevent law enforcement officers from engaging in unconstitutional activity or to otherwise remedy this problem.

e. Special Forums

Another theoretical substitute for the exclusionary rule might be the creation of some type of special administrative or judicial forum to handle exclusively complaints about police misconduct and to provide compensation for those individuals whose constitutional rights are determined or adjudicated to have been violated. *See, e.g., Bivens v. Six Unknown Named Agents*, 403 U.S. 388, 411, 422 (1971) (Burger, C.J. dissenting) ("Congress should develop an administrative or quasi-judicial remedy against the government itself to afford compensation and restitution for persons whose Fourth Amendment rights have been violated."). However, due in substantial part to the partisan and other political difficulties inherent in legislative creation of such a forum "policing the police," this remedial approach has not been adopted. Nor are such forums likely to be adopted in the foreseeable future. In any event, it has been argued persuasively that any forum of this sort would be doomed to failure, unlikely to be effective or workable in practice.

In *Lopez-Rodriguez v. Mukasey*, 536 F.3d 1012 (9th Cir. 2008), the court applied the exclusionary rule in a deportation proceeding on the basis that the Fourth Amendment violation was "egregious."

In that case, officers entered the suspects' home without a warrant, consent or exigent circumstances.

f. Exclusion and the Vienna Convention.

In *Sanchez-Llamas v. Oregon*, 548 U.S. 331 (2007), the Court refused to apply the exclusionary rule to a violation of Article 36 of the Vienna Convention on Consular Relations (Vienna Convention or Convention). Article 36 provides that, when a national of one country is detained by authorities in another, the authorities must notify the consular officers of the detainee's home country if the detainee so requests. In addition, the authorities must inform the detainee of his right to request consular assistance. Sanchez-Llamas was detained for shooting a police officer, and given a *Miranda* warning, but not informed of his right to consular assistance. He sought to suppress his statements because of non-compliance with Article 36. Another foreign national raised similar claims as well. After noting that Article 36 does not provide for the remedy of suppression, the Court held that United States law does not require suppression. The Court found that "where a treaty does not provide a particular remedy, either expressly or implicitly, it is not for the federal courts to impose one on the States through lawmaking of their own," and it went on to note that it has "applied the exclusionary rule primarily to deter constitutional violations." Moreover, the Court concluded that "the reasons we often require suppression for Fourth and Fifth Amendment violations are entirely absent from the consular notification context.. For example, although coerced confessions are excluded because they are unreliable, a failure to inform a defendant of his Article 36 rights is unlikely to render a confession involuntary. Justice Breyer, joined by justices Stevens and Souter, dissented, noting that the Convention insists upon "effective remedies" and sometimes suppression will be the only appropriate remedy. However, analysis of the circumstances is required.

B. Limits on the Exclusionary Rule's Application

1. Private Actors

The Fourth and Fifth Amendments do not apply to the acts of private—rather than governmental—actors. Hence, physical or testimonial evidence seized by private individuals is admissible in criminal proceedings, even if precisely the same actions producing precisely the same evidence would have been inadmissible if they had been undertaken by law enforcement officers. *Burdeau v. McDowell*, 256 U.S. 465 (1921). This is particularly significant because most policing work in the United States is done by private—not public—actors, e.g. security guards. In the absence of express statutory provisions to the contrary, the exclusionary rule does not apply to these actions of these private police.

However, the exclusionary rule *does* apply to the actions of private individuals who are acting with—or as the agents of—governmental actors. If, for example, the police search an employee's office along with a private employer and the search violates the Fourth Amendment, the exclusionary rule applies (even though a private actor, the employer, was involved) and all evidence seized as a product of that search is subject to suppression in a subsequent criminal proceeding.

2. Unconstitutional vs. Illegal Actions

Some problematic activity undertaken by government agents may not be unconstitutional, but is nonetheless illegal, e.g. it is prohibited by civil or criminal statutes or by administrative regulations. Nonetheless, absent the inclusion of an explicit exclusionary rule as a statutory remedy for such activity, the exclusionary rule is inapplicable to such misconduct. The exclusionary rule applies only to suppress the fruits of government agents' (usually but not always law enforcement officers) *unconstitutional* acts, not their (merely) illegal acts. *United States v. Caceres*, 440 U.S. 741 (1979).

For example, in many states, court rules prohibit the execution of search warrants during the nighttime unless the executing officers have made a special showing and obtained special permission from the magistrate issuing the warrant. However, this nighttime-search rule is not a federal constitutional requirement. Accordingly, the exclusionary rule is usually deemed not to apply to executing officers' violation of such search-warrant rules.

3. Non–Criminal Proceedings: Incremental Deterrence

Beginning in the 1970's until the present time, the Supreme Court has repeatedly stated that the Fourth Amendment exclusionary rule is not a constitutional requirement *per se* as was suggested in the Court's earlier *Mapp* decision. Rather, the Court has explained, the exclusionary rule is used as a remedy, albeit a required remedy, primarily if not exclusively in order to deter the future misconduct of law enforcement officials. As the Court made the point in 1974, the exclusionary "rule's prime purpose is to deter future unlawful police conduct and thereby effectuate the guarantee of the Fourth Amendment against unreasonable search and seizure." *United States v. Calandra*, 414 U.S. 338, 347 (1974).

The exclusionary rule's deterrent aim is furthered, the Supreme Court has indicated, when the exclusionary rule is applied to suppress unconstitutionally-seized evidence sought to be introduced by the government in the prosecution's case-in-chief at a criminal trial. But, the Court has added, given the substantial costs of the rule in suppressing otherwise relevant evidence of criminal activity, on balance, the exclusionary rule should *not* be applied in those settings where no additional, incremental deterrence of police misconduct is gained thereby. In other words, if police misconduct is not deterred by applying the exclusionary rule in a particular setting, it should not be used because the social costs of the rule's application (e.g. some criminals will go free) are so great.

a. Forfeiture Proceedings

Many American jurisdictions have enacted statutes that permit the government to seek the forfeiture to the government of instrumentalities used in the commission of specified criminal activity (e.g., commonly, cars, boats, or airplanes used to smuggle narcotics). Such "forfeiture proceedings" are civil rather than criminal in nature. However, in a decision handed down before the Supreme Court began limiting the application of the exclusionary rule to situations where incremental deterrence of police misconduct is achieved, the Court ruled that the exclusionary rule *does* apply with full force to suppress unconstitutionally-seized evidence sought to be introduced in such forfeiture proceedings because of the "quasi-criminal nature" of these proceedings. *One 1958 Plymouth Sedan v. Commonwealth of Pennsylvania*, 380 U.S. 693, 701 (1965) ("It would be anomalous indeed, under these circumstances, to hold that in the criminal proceeding the illegally seized evidence is excludable, while in the forfeiture proceeding, requiring the determination that the criminal law has been violated, the same evidence would be admissible. That the forfeiture is clearly a penalty for the criminal offense and can result in even greater punishment than the criminal prosecution has in fact been recognized . . .").

b. Grand Juries

In 1974, the Supreme Court ruled in *United States v. Calandra*, 414 U.S. 338, 347 (1974), that "[a]ny incremental deterrent effect which might be achieved by extending the [exclusionary] rule to grand jury proceedings is uncertain at best. Whatever deterrence of police misconduct may result from the exclusion of illegally seized evidence from criminal trials, it is unrealistic to assume that application of the rule to grand jury proceedings would significantly further that goal. Such an extension would deter only police investigation consciously directed toward the discovery of evidence solely for use in a grand jury investigation." As a result, the exclusionary rule was held inapplicable by the Court to the use of unconstitutionally-seized evidence sought to be presented to a grand jury.

c. Civil Proceedings

For similar reasons, the exclusionary rule does not apply ordinarily so as to permit the suppression of unconstitutionally-seized evidence in civil proceedings. *United States v. Janis*, 428 U.S. 433 (1976).

In *Janis*, the Supreme Court permitted evidence seized illegally by Los Angeles police officers to be introduced in the prosecution's case-in-chief in a federal, *civil* tax proceeding for back taxes brought by the Internal Revenue Service. As the *Janis* Court reasoned, "the additional marginal deterrence provided by forbidding a different sovereign from using the evidence in a civil proceeding surely does not outweigh the cost to society of extending the rule to that situation... [E]xclusion from federal civil proceedings of evidence unlawfully seized by a state criminal enforcement officer has not been shown to have a sufficient likelihood of deterring the conduct of the state police so that it outweighs the societal costs imposed by the exclusion. This Court, therefore, is not justified in so extending the exclusionary rule a sufficient likelihood of deterring the conduct of the state police so that it outweighs the societal costs imposed by the exclusion." *Id.* at 453–54, 454.

d. Different Sovereigns

The Supreme Court's decision in *Janis*, discussed above, holding that the exclusionary rule was inapplicable to the actions of the Los Angeles police in seizing unconstitutionally evidence subsequently admitted in a federal, civil (tax) proceeding, was premised not only on the civil nature of that proceeding, but also on the accompanying fact that "another sovereign" was involved, i.e. state law enforcement authorities turned over the evidence to federal authorities for their use in a federal proceeding.

However, there are significant limits to the permissibility of such inter-sovereign co-operation. In *Elkins v. United States*, 364 U.S. 206 (1960), the Supreme Court concluded that evidence seized illegally by state law enforcement officers cannot lawfully be introduced against a defendant in a *federal* criminal trial, i.e. the Court rejected the so-called "silver platter doctrine" which would have permitted the agents of one sovereign (the state) to turn unconstitutionally-seized evidence over to the agents of a different sovereign (the federal government) "on a silver platter." The *Janis* majority distinguished *Elkins*, however, by pointing out that *Elkins* applied to the use of unconstitutionally-seized evidence by another sovereign in a *criminal* proceeding. *Janis*, 428 U.S. at 457–58 ("common sense dictates that the deterrent effect of the exclusion of relevant evidence is highly attenuated when the 'punishment' imposed upon the offending criminal enforcement officer is the removal of that evidence from a civil suit by or against a different sovereign. In *Elkins* the Court indicated that the assumed interest of criminal law enforcement officers in the criminal proceedings of another sovereign counterbalanced this attenuation sufficiently to justify an exclusionary rule. Here, however, the attenuation is further augmented by the fact that the proceeding is one to enforce only the civil law of the other sovereign.").

Moreover, American courts do not apply the exclusionary rule where the improper law enforcement conduct that is the subject of complaint in a suppression motion is strictly that of law enforcement agents (or other foreign nationals) of another country as no incremental deterrence of American law enforcement officials would be effectuated in that manner.

e. Federal Habeas Corpus

The Supreme Court has ruled that the exclusionary rule does not apply to Fourth Amendment claims raised in federal habeas corpus proceedings where the petitioner had a full and fair opportunity to litigate these issues in his or her prior state court proceedings. *Stone v. Powell*, 428 U.S. 465 (1976).

As the Supreme Court reasoned in that decision, "the additional contribution, if any, of the consideration of search-and-seizure claims of state prisoners on collateral review is small in relation to the costs. To be sure, each case in which such claim is considered may add marginally to an awareness of the values protected by the Fourth Amendment. There is no reason to believe, however, that the overall educative effect of the exclusionary rule would be appreciably diminished if search-and-seizure claims could not be raised in federal habeas corpus review of state convictions. Nor is there reason to assume that any specific disincentive already created by the risk of exclusion of evidence at trial or the reversal of convictions on direct review would be enhanced if there were the further risk that a conviction obtained in state court and affirmed on direct review might be overturned in collateral proceedings often occurring years after the incarceration of the defendant. . . Even if one rationally could assume that some additional incremental deterrent effect would be presented in isolated cases, the resulting advance of the legitimate goal of furthering Fourth Amendment rights would be outweighed by the acknowledged costs to other values vital to a rational system of criminal justice." *Id.* at 493–94.

While it is not entirely clear what the Court meant by conditioning the inapplicability of the exclusionary rule on the federal habeas petitioner having previously had a "full and fair opportunity" to raise his or her Fourth Amendment claims in state-court proceedings, it is nonetheless clear that this condition is *not* satisfied by a state court's mere erroneous application of Fourth Amendment search-and-seizure law. *Williams v. Taylor*, 529 U.S. 362, 375 (2000).

f. Deportation Proceedings

The Supreme Court has ruled that the exclusionary rule does not apply in (civil) deportation proceedings. *Immigration & Naturalization Service v. Lopez–Mendoza*, 468 U.S. 1032 (1984). The Court concluded that "application of the rule in INS civil deportation proceedings . . . 'is unlikely to provide significant, much less substantial, additional deterrence.' Important as it is to protect the Fourth Amendment rights of all persons, there is no convincing indication that application of the exclusionary rule in civil deportation proceedings will contribute materially to that end." *Id.* at 1046, *quoting United States v. Janis*, 428 U.S. 433, 458 (1976).

g. Suppression of the Defendant

The "body" or identity of a defendant or respondent in a criminal or civil proceeding is never itself suppressible as a fruit of an unlawful or unconstitutional arrest. *Ker v. Illinois*, 119 U.S. 436 (1886); *Frisbie v. Collins*, 342 U.S. 519 (1952). This is sometimes called the "*Ker–Frisbie* Doctrine."

h. Violations of International Agreements

In *Sanchez-Llamas v. Oregon*, 126 S.Ct. 2669 (2007), the Court refused to apply the exclusionary rule to a violation of Article 36 of the Vienna Convention on Consular Relations (Vienna Convention or Convention). Article 36 provided that, when a national of one country is detained by authorities in another, the authorities must notify the consular officers of the detainee's home country if the detainee so requests. In addition, the authorities must inform the detainee of his right to request consular assistance. Sanchez–Llamas was detained for shooting a police officer, and given a *Miranda* warning, but not informed of his right to consular assistance. The Court concluded that the failure to inform did not require suppression of statements made by Sanchez–Llamas: "[W]here a treaty does not provide a particular remedy, either expressly or implicitly, it is not for the federal courts to impose one on the States through lawmaking of their own." Finding that the treaty did not mandate application of the exclusionary rule, the Court was reluctant to apply the rule noting that it imposed a "costly toll" upon "truth-seeking and law enforcement objectives" and therefore has been applied only to deter constitutional violations. Moreover, the Court found no basis for concluding that the confessions were coerced.

4. Good–Faith Exception

In 1984, the Supreme Court adopted an additional—and extremely significant—exception to the exclusionary rule, holding that it does not apply where a law enforcement officer has acted in reasonable "good faith" on the basis of an unconstitutional search warrant. *United States v. Leon*, 468 U.S. 897 (1984).

In large part, the Court adopted this exception because it concluded that police officers acting in good faith on the basis of what reasonably appears to them (albeit erroneously) to be a valid and lawful search warrant would not ordinarily be deterred by application of the rule. As the Court explained, "[w]e conclude that the marginal or nonexistent benefits produced by suppressing evidence obtained in objectively reasonable reliance on a subsequently invalidated search warrant cannot justify the substantial costs of exclusion." *Id.* at 922.

The *Leon* Court stressed repeatedly, however, as is evident in the quotation set out just above, that the "good-faith exception" to the exclusionary rule the Court adopted is an *objective* test, i.e. the police officer's reliance on the otherwise invalid search warrant must be reasonable. What does this mean? As the Court explained, "our good-faith inquiry is confined to the objectively ascertainable question whether a reasonably well trained officer would have known that the search was illegal despite the magistrate's authorization." *Id.* at 922 n.23.

Moreover, the Supreme Court added in *Leon* that the good-faith exception is always inapplicable in four different situations, namely where: "[(1)] the magistrate or judge in issuing a warrant was misled by information in an affidavit that the affiant knew was false or would have known was false except for his reckless disregard of the truth[; (2)] where the issuing magistrate wholly abandoned his judicial role[; (3) where] an officer . . . rel[ied] on a warrant based on an affidavit 'so lacking in indicia of probable cause as to render official belief in its existence entirely unreasonable'; [and (4) where], depending on the circumstances of the particular case, a warrant [was] so facially deficient—i.e., in failing to particularize the place to be searched or the things to be seized—that the executing officers cannot reasonably presume it to be valid." *Id.* at 923, *quoting Brown v. Illinois*, 422 U.S. 590, 610–611 (1975) (Powell, J., conc'g).

The good-faith exception to the exclusionary rule created by the Supreme Court was adopted as a matter of *federal* constitutional law. A number of state courts, disagreeing with the U.S. Supreme Court's deterrence—and/or its broader doctrinal—analysis, have concluded, directly to the contrary, that the good-faith exception to the exclusionary rule does not exist in their states under the authority of their own state constitutions. As a result, in such a state, the unconstitutional actions of a federal law enforcement agent (e.g. an FBI Special Agent) would be subject to application of the good-faith exception to the exclusionary rule, but the unconstitutional actions of a state law enforcement agent (e.g. a municipal police officer) would not be.

Additionally, it is important to emphasize that the good-faith exception adopted in *Leon* generally applies to searches pursuant to defective warrants and not to warrantless searches. There are several exceptions to this rule. For example, the Court has extended the good faith exception to warrantless searches based on existing judicial precedent. In *Davis v. United States,* 131 S.Ct. 2419 (2011), the question was whether the exclusionary rule should apply when police conducted an illegal search of an automobile, but judicial precedent (at the time of the search) suggested that the search was permissible. A number of lower courts had construed the Court's holding in *New York v. Belton,* 453 U.S. 454, 458–459 (1981), as authorizing a "search incident to legal arrest" of the passenger compartment of a vehicle when the arrestee was arrested while traveling in the vehicle. The search was authorized whether or not arrestee was within reaching distance of the vehicle at the time of the search. In *Petitioner v. Gant,* 556 U.S. 332 (2009), five justices (4 plus a concurring justice) agreed to limit such searches to situations when: (1) the arrestee is within reaching distance of the vehicle during the search, or (2) the police have reason to believe that the vehicle contains "evidence relevant to the crime of arrest." The search in *Davis* took place two years before the holding in *Gant* and would have been illegal under the broader interpretation of *Belton* adopted by some lower courts.

In refusing to apply the exclusionary evidence rule to the search, the Court emphasized that the rule is a "prudential" doctrine, which is not a "right." and is not designed to "redress the injury" occasioned by an unconstitutional search. Instead, the rule's sole purpose is to deter future Fourth Amendment violations, and the rule is subject to a cost-benefit test. As a result, when the police exhibit "deliberate," "reckless," or "grossly negligent" disregard for Fourth Amendment rights, "the deterrent value of exclusion is strong and tends to outweigh the resulting costs." However, a different calculus applies "when the police act with an objectively 'reasonable good-faith belief' that their conduct is lawful, or when their conduct involves only simple, 'isolated' negligence," there is less need for deterrence. Applying these principles to the case before it, the Court concluded that "the officers' conduct was in strict compliance with then-binding Circuit law and was not culpable in any way," and therefore the "officers who conducted the search did not violate Davis's Fourth Amendment rights deliberately, recklessly, or with gross negligence." As a result, the Court refused to apply the exclusionary evidence rule: "when binding appellate precedent specifically *authorizes* a particular police practice, well-trained officers will and should use that tool to fulfill their crime-detection and public-safety responsibilities. . . The deterrent effect of exclusion in such a case can only be to discourage the officer from 'do[ing] his duty.'" Justice Breyer, joined by Justice Ginsburg dissented, arguing that *Gant* should be retroactively applied to the police conduct involved in this case.

The Court has also extended the exception to other warrantless searches. For example, the Supreme Court has extended the good-faith exception to the exclusionary rule, however, to otherwise unconstitutional actions by law enforcement officers' based upon either: (1) a computerized police record erroneously indicating the existence of an outstanding arrest warrant, *Arizona v. Evans*, 514 U.S. 1 (1995); or (2) objectively-reasonable reliance upon a statute subsequently found to be unconstitutional. *Illinois v. Krull*, 480 U.S. 340, 349 (1987) ("The approach used in *Leon* is equally applicable to the present case. The application of the exclusionary rule to suppress evidence obtained by an officer acting in objectively reasonable reliance on a statute would have as little deterrent effect on the officer's actions as would the exclusion of evidence when an officer acts in objectively reasonable reliance on a warrant.").

In *Groh v. Ramirez*, 540 U.S. 551 (2004), the Court distinguished *Leon* and limited the Court's application of the good faith exception in the context of a civil suit. A peace officer applied for a search warrant, and supported it with a detailed affidavit, which set forth the basis for his belief that various contraband items were concealed on a ranch. Although the application particularly described the place to be searched and the contraband petitioner expected to find, the warrant (issued by a magistrate) failed to identify any of the items that petitioner intended to seize. Instead of a description of the "person or property" to be seized, petitioner typed a description of respondents' two-story blue house rather than the alleged stockpile of firearms. The warrant did not incorporate by reference the itemized list contained in the application, but did recite that the Magistrate was satisfied the affidavit established probable cause to believe that contraband was concealed on the premises, and that sufficient grounds existed for the warrant's issuance. The ensuring search revealed none of the anticipated contraband, and no criminal charges were filed. Subsequently, the Ramirezes sued petitioner and the other officers under *Bivens v. Six Unknown Fed. Narcotics Agents,* 403 U.S. 388 (1971), and Rev. Stat. § 1979, 42 U.S.C. § 1983, alleging, *inter alia,* violations of the Fourth Amendment.

The Court concluded that the warrant was plainly invalid because it failed to particularly describe the items to be seized. While the Court recognized that a warrant might cross-reference other documents (*e.g.,* the affidavit), the Court emphasized that no cross-reference had taken place in this case and the warrant simply stated that "the items to be seized" consisted of a "single dwelling residence ... blue in color." The Court concluded that petitioner was not entitled to qualified immunity, noting that the focus should be on whether the right that was transgressed was "clearly established." The Court noted that, because "the particularity requirement is set forth in the text of the Constitution, no reasonable officer could believe that a warrant that plainly did not comply with that requirement was valid." In addition, since petitioner prepared the invalid warrant, he could not rely on "the Magistrate's assurance that the warrant contained an adequate description of the things to be seized and was therefore valid." "[E]ven a cursory reading of the warrant in this case—perhaps just a simple glance—would have revealed a glaring deficiency that any reasonable police officer would have known was constitutionally fatal." The Court rejected the argument that the case involved simply a "lack of due care."

The Court has added, however, that the purpose of allowing the admission of such otherwise inadmissible evidence is *only* to impeach the defendant's credibility. The unconstitutionally-seized evidence is not permitted to be admitted (or considered by the factfinder) for the purpose of offering substantive evidence of the defendant's guilt. Admission of the evidence for that purpose would contravene the underlying deterrent aims of the exclusionary rule. *Oregon v. Hass,* 420 U.S. 714, 722 (1975) ("it does not follow ... that evidence inadmissible against Hass in the prosecution's case in chief is barred for all purposes. ... [T]he impeaching material would provide valuable aid to the jury in assessing the defendant's credibility; ... and again, making the deterrent-effect assumption, there is sufficient deterrence when the evidence in question is made unavailable to the prosecution in its case in chief.").

Although such impeaching evidence is usually testimonial in nature, e.g. some sort of confession or inculpatory statement (e.g. "I did it."; "I killed her."), the Supreme Court has extended the impeachment exception to the exclusionary rule to physical evidence as well. *United States v. Havens*, 446 U.S. 620 (1980).

In *Havens*, the defendant testified at trial that he did not own an incriminating item of clothing, a T-shirt. The Supreme Court ruled that this testimony by the defendant was impeached constitutionally by the prosecution when, in response to this statement, it introduced into evidence the T-shirt to which the statements pertained, even though the T-shirt had been seized unconstitutionally by the government. *Id.* at 627–28 ("a defendant's statements made in response to proper cross-examination reasonably suggested by the defendant's direct examination are subject to otherwise proper impeachment by the government, albeit by evidence that has been illegally obtained and that is inadmissible on the government's direct case, or otherwise, as substantive evidence of guilt.").

It is notable, however, that the impeachment exception to the ordinary application of the exclusionary rule applies only to impeachment of *the defendant's* testimony by the government, not to the attempted impeachment of other defense witnesses with unconstitutionally-seized evidence. *James v. Illinois*, 493 U.S. 307 (1990). Extension of this exception to *all* defense witnesses would compromise the deterrent effect of the exclusionary rule. *Id.* at 320 ("Our previous recognition of an impeachment exception limited to the testimony of defendants reflects a careful weighing of the competing values. Because expanding the exception to encompass the testimony of all defense witnesses would not further the truth-seeking value with equal force but would appreciably undermine the deterrent effect of the exclusionary rule, we adhere to the line drawn in our previous cases.").

Justice Kennedy, joined by Chief Justice Rehnquist, dissented, arguing that the warrant was invalid, but that the officer was entitled to qualified immunity because his mistaken belief was "reasonable." He argued that a "law enforcement officer charged with leading a team to execute a search warrant for illegal weapons must fulfill a number of serious responsibilities" which "demand the officer's full attention in the heat of an ongoing and often dangerous criminal investigation." He concluded that an "officer who complies fully with all of these duties can be excused for not being aware that he had made a clerical error in the course of filling out the proposed warrant," especially when the warrant is signed off on by a judge. Justice Thomas, joined by Justice Scalia and Chief Justice Rehnquist, also dissented: "The items to be seized were clearly specified in the warrant application and set forth in the affidavit, both of which were given to the Magistrate. . . It is clear that respondents here received the protection of the Warrant Clause. Under these circumstances, I would not hold that any ensuing search constitutes a presumptively unreasonable warrantless search."

5. "Knock and Announce" Violations

In *Hudson v. Michigan*, 126 S.Ct. 2159 (2006), the Court refused to apply the exclusionary evidence rule in the context of a violation of the "knock and announce" rule. In that case, although the police searched Hudson's house pursuant to a warrant, they waited only three to five seconds after knocking before entering. The Court held that the wait was insufficient and the question was whether the fruits of the search should be suppressed because of the premature entry. The Court answered that question in the negative, applying the cost-benefit test and noting that the exclusionary rule should not be indiscriminately applied, but rather should be reserved for situations "where its remedial objectives are thought most efficaciously served,"-that is, "where its deterrence benefits outweigh its 'substantial social costs.' " The Court held that the "interests protected by the knock-and—announce requirement are quite different—and do not include the shielding of potential evidence from the government's eyes". Those interests include the possibility of violence by a surprised resident, the protection of property (which could be damaged if the police make a forcible entry), and the protection of human dignity (so that the police do not break in on people in compromising positions). But the Court concluded that the does not protect "one's interest in preventing the government from seeing or taking evidence described in a warrant. Since the interests that *were* violated in this case have nothing to do with the seizure of the evidence, the exclusionary rule is inapplicable." The Court also concluded that the societal costs of exclusion would be significant because police might hesitate before entering, fearful of violating the knock and announce rule, and thereby endangering themselves and possibly losing evidence. In any event, violation of the knock and announce rule did not affect discovery of the evidence since the officers already possessed a warrant and would inevitably have gained entry to the property. In any event, the Court noted that other remedies, including civil rights actions, might be available for knock and announce violations. In addition, police forces have worked towards providing more education and enhancing professionalism. Justice Breyer, joined by justices Stevens, Souter and Ginsburg, dissented, arguing that "Although the police might have entered Hudson's home lawfully, they did not in fact do so." [W]e have described a failure to comply with the knock-and-announce rule, not as an independently unlawful event, but as a factor that renders the *search* "constitutionally defective."

C. Standing

1. Constitutional Limitation

A criminal defendant must have "standing" in order to possess the right even to raise the issue of unconstitutional law enforcement conduct pursuant to a motion to suppress evidence seized as a result of that unconstitutional conduct. Standing exists only where the defendant seeks to remedy a violation of his or her own *personal* constitutional rights, in contrast to a defendant's attempt to assert vicariously the violation of another person's constitutional rights. *Alderman v. United States*, 394 U.S. 165 (1969).

If, for example, the police arrest *A* unconstitutionally and then interrogate *A* without giving her *Miranda* warnings, any statement that *A* makes as a result of that unconstitutional conduct (arrest and custodial interrogation) could be suppressed by *A* in a criminal proceeding brought against her. But that very same statement could *not* be suppressed by *B*, even if the statement directly implicates him in the same (or different) criminal conduct (e.g. *A* said "*B* and I killed *C*."). *B* cannot suppress this statement because he lacks standing; he lacks standing because the unconstitutional conduct (illegal arrest; failure to give *Miranda* warnings) violated only *A's* constitutional rights, not *B's* constitutional rights.

An individual's personal constitutional rights are violated where the constitutional harm is done to that individual personally, or at a place (his or her home, for example) or to some thing (his or her car or backpack, for example) where and when he or she possessed a "reasonable expectation of privacy" (sometimes referred to by the Supreme Court as a "legitimate expectation of privacy"). *Rakas v. Illinois*, 439 U.S. 128 (1978). A defendant does not possess standing simply because evidence has been seized unconstitutionally from his or her co-defendant or co-conspirator.

The Supreme Court has further ruled that federal courts lack the authority to ignore the standing doctrine (which is a part of the substantive constitutional law) by excluding evidence on behalf of a defendant lacking standing on the basis of the court's inherent and non-constitutional "supervisory powers" over law enforcement. *United States v. Payner*, 447 U.S. 727 (1980).

a. Reasonable Expectation of Privacy

The concept of an individual's "reasonable expectation of privacy" is the same concept used to define which instances of questioned police conduct are subject to Fourth Amendment requirements and prohibitions.

In *Rakas v. Illinois*, 439 U.S. 128 (1978), however, the Supreme Court provided the following additional gloss on the meaning of a "legitimate" or "reasonable" expectation of privacy for purposes of entitling a defendant to raise the issue of unconstitutional police activity in a suppression motion: "[A] 'legitimate' expectation of privacy by definition means more than a subjective expectation of not being discovered. A burglar plying his trade in a summer cabin during the off season may have a thoroughly justified subjective expectation of privacy, but it is not one which the law recognizes as 'legitimate.' His presence, . . . is 'wrongful'; his expectation is not one that society is prepared to recognize as 'reasonable.' " 439 U.S. at 143 n.12, *quoting Jones v. United States*, 362 U.S. 257, 267 (1960), and *Katz v. United States*, 389 U.S. 347, 361 (1967).

The Supreme Court ruled in *Rakas* that a passenger in someone else's car does not—simply because of his or her status as a passenger standing alone—have standing to question the constitutionality of a search of the glove compartment and space under the front passenger seat of that car. The Supreme Court has also held that an individual does not have standing to complain about the constitutionality of the search of another person's purse (containing his drugs). *Rawlings v. Kentucky*, 448 U.S. 98 (1980). Nor does an individual have standing, in the Court's view, to challenge the constitutionality of evidence seized as a result of a police officer's peeping through a gap in a closed window blind into a ground floor apartment when the individual's presence in that apartment was strictly as part of a commercial transaction, and he was not present as a social guest or invitee. *Minnesota v. Carter*, 525 U.S. 83 (1998).

But the Supreme Court has concluded that an individual *does* have standing to challenge the constitutionality of a search of an apartment where he was present as an "overnight guest." *Minnesota v. Olson*, 495 U.S. 91, 98 (1990) ("To hold that an overnight guest has a legitimate expectation of privacy in his host's home merely recognizes the everyday expectations of privacy that we all share. Staying overnight in another's home is a longstanding social custom that serves functions recognized as valuable by society. [We] will all be hosts and we will all be guests many times in our lives. From either perspective, we think that society recognizes that a houseguest has a legitimate expectation of privacy in his host's home.").

b. Target Standing

The Supreme Court has on a number of occasions rejected the idea that an individual who is the "target" of law enforcement investigative activities should—by dint of that "target" status alone—possess standing to raise the issue of the constitutionality of police conduct directed at someone else, but intended to obtain evidence to be used against the target individual. Accordingly, if the police engage in unconstitutional activity directed against *A* in order to gain evidence to use against *B* (e.g. *A's* statement that *B* sold him cocaine), even though *B* was the target of the police misconduct, *B* lacks standing to raise the issue in a suppression hearing.

2. Automatic Standing

In *Jones v. United States*, 362 U.S. 257 (1960), the Supreme Court adopted an "automatic standing" rule that provided that defendants charged with possessory crimes (e.g. possession of narcotics) had standing "automatically" to challenge the constitutionality of the seizure of the items that are the subject of the possessory charge (whether or not these defendants would have had standing under the normal standing test). However, *Jones*—and the automatic standing rule—were subsequently overruled by the Supreme Court as a matter of federal constitutional law. *United States v. Salvucci*, 448 U.S. 83, 92 (1980) ("We simply decline to use possession of a seized good as a substitute for a factual finding that the owner of the good had a legitimate expectation of privacy in the area searched.").

The *Salvucci* Court ruled that the *Jones* automatic-standing rule was no longer needed to protect against a defendant's risk of self-incrimination (incurred by the defendant's claiming the possessory items for purposes of asserting standing to exclude them) since the Court had previously ruled that the testimony of defendants about their relationship to evidence sought to be suppressed in a suppression hearing cannot be used against them trial on the issue of their substantive guilt, at least over the defendant's objection. *Simmons v. United States*, 390 U.S. 377 (1968).

Some states, however, have retained the automatic standing rule under their own state constitutions.

D. Derivative Evidence: The "Fruits" Doctrine

Evidence derived from law enforcement agents' unconstitutional activity has been held to be inadmissible in criminal proceedings when it has been obtained as a direct result of that activity, but also when it has been derived only as an *indirect* result of such a constitutional breach. This point, applying the exclusionary rule to evidence seized as an indirect result of a constitutional breach, is formally referred to as the "derivative evidence rule." But, informally and far more commonly, it is called "the fruits doctrine." The fruits doctrine is itself a popular shorthand for the metaphor Justice Frankfurter used to describe the derivative evidence rule, namely as applying to "fruits of the poisonous tree." *Nardone v. United States*, 308 U.S. 338 (1939).

1. Constitutional Test

The Supreme Court has dictated that the fruits doctrine applies to both physical and testimonial evidence, and that the following test should be used to determine its application: "We need not hold that all evidence is 'fruit of the poisonous tree' simply because it would not have come to light but for the illegal actions of the police. Rather, the more apt question in such a case is 'whether, granting establishment of the primary illegality, the evidence to which instant objection is made has been come at by exploitation of that illegality or instead by means sufficiently distinguishable to be purged of the primary taint.' " *Wong Sun v. United States*, 371 U.S. 471, 487–88 (1963), *quoting Maguire, Evidence of Guilt*, 221 (1959).

The most important feature of this test is that the *Wong Sun* Court made clear (and the Court continues to hold) that the fruits doctrine is *not* applied by simply using a mechanistic "but for" type of causation test (e.g. "but for" the police officer's unconstitutional activity, the government would never have discovered the hidden marijuana). Rather, as the test indicates explicitly, some evidence that would satisfy a "but for" test will nonetheless be deemed admissible where it was either: (1) not acquired "by exploitation" of the officers' unconstitutional activity; and/or (2) because it was obtained "by means sufficiently distinguishable" from that unconstitutional activity to warrant such admission. These non-"but for" applications of the fruits doctrine are discussed immediately hereafter.

In *United States v. Patane*, 542 U.S. 630 (2004), the Court dealt with the question of whether a failure to give a suspect *Miranda* warnings necessitated suppression of the physical fruits of the suspect's unwarned but voluntary statements. Police arrested Patane for violating a temporary restraining order. The police who made the arrest were aware of information suggesting that Patane, a convicted felon, illegally possessed a .40 Glock pistol. During the arrest, the police tried to inform Patane of his *Miranda* rights, but he interrupted them, asserting that he knew his rights, and neither officer attempted to complete the warning. As a result, the *Miranda* warnings were never properly administered. Subsequent questioning revealed the whereabouts of the Glock which was seized and used to prosecute Patane. A plurality of the Court refused to suppress the gun noting that the *Miranda* rule protects against violations of the Self–Incrimination Clause, and that clause is not implicated by the introduction at trial of physical evidence resulting from voluntary statements. "[W]ith respect to mere failures to warn, nothing to deter" and there is no reason to apply the "fruit of the poisonous tree." Justice Kennedy, joined by Justice O'Connor, concurred, arguing that the admission of "nontestimonial physical fruits" (the Glock in this case) [does] not run the risk of admitting into trial an accused's coerced incriminating statements against himself. Justice Souter, joined by justices Stevens and Ginsburg, dissented, arguing that, in "closing their eyes to the consequences of giving an evidentiary advantage to those who ignore *Miranda,* the majority adds an important inducement for interrogators to ignore the rule in that case." He noted that *Miranda* emphasized "the inherently coercive character of custodial interrogation and the inherently difficult exercise of assessing the voluntariness of any confession resulting from it" so that "a *Miranda* violation raises a presumption of coercion and the Fifth Amendment privilege against compelled self-incrimination extends to the exclusion of derivative evidence." Justice Breyer also dissented, arguing for application of the "fruit of the poisonous tree" approach. Under his approach, courts should "exclude physical evidence derived from unwarned questioning unless the failure to provide *Miranda* warnings was in good faith."

2. Independent Source

The Supreme Court has long concluded that the fruits doctrine is inapplicable where law enforcement officers possessed an "independent source" for the information used to acquire evidence otherwise obtained unconstitutionally. *Silverthorne Lumber Co. v. United States,* 251 U.S. 385, 392 (1920) ("The essence of a provision forbidding the acquisition of evidence in a certain way is that not merely evidence so acquired shall not be used before the Court but that it shall not be used at all. Of course this does not mean that the facts thus obtained become sacred and inaccessible. If knowledge of them is gained from an independent source they may be proved like any others, but the knowledge gained by the Government's own wrong cannot be used by it. . .").

As the Court has explained the rationale for this independent source exception to the fruits doctrine, "[t]he independent source doctrine teaches us that the interest of society in deterring unlawful police conduct and the public interest in having juries receive all probative evidence of a crime are properly balanced by putting the police in the same, not a worse, position that they would have been in if no police error or misconduct had occurred. When the challenged evidence has an independent source, exclusion of such evidence would put the police in a worse position than they would have been in absent any error or violation." *Nix v. Williams*, 467 U.S. 431, 443 (1984).

If, for example, police officers obtained a search warrant to search *A's* home for stolen jewelry and the basis for that search was a prior unconstitutional entry into *A's* home during which entry the jewelry was discovered, any evidence seized as a result of the execution of that search warrant would be inadmissible under the fruits doctrine as evidence derived from the earlier unconstitutional search, subject to standard application of the exclusionary rule. But, if the police also had information from a reliable confidential informant, *B*, that *A* was in possession of stolen jewelry in his home, and *B's* information had no connection whatever with the earlier unconstitutional entry (i.e. it is "independent") and *B's* information itself established probable cause to—and was used to— obtain a search warrant (with or without the tainted information based on the unconstitutional entry; and before, at the same time as, or after the execution of the problematic warrant), any evidence seized pursuant to the execution of this search warrant would *not* be suppressible under the exclusionary rule, due to application of the "independent source" exception to the fruits doctrine.

3. Inevitable Discovery

Similar to—but, at the same time, a substantial step beyond— the independent source exception to the fruits doctrine, the inevitable discovery exception is essentially a form of a "hypothesized independent source" exception to the rule. The Supreme Court held in 1984 that evidence seized by the government which is the fruits of unconstitutional law enforcement activity is nonetheless admissible into evidence (again, as another exception to the fruits doctrine) where the government can prove by a preponderance of the evidence that it would have discovered this same evidence "inevitably," absent the constitutional violation. *Nix v. Williams*, 467 U.S. 431 (1984).

The rationale for the inevitable discovery exception was likened by the Supreme Court to the rationale for the independent source doctrine noted above, the Court pointing out that "exclusion of evidence that would inevitably have been discovered would also put the government in a worse position, because the police would have obtained that evidence if no misconduct had taken place. Thus, while the independent source exception would not justify admission of evidence in this case, its rationale is wholly consistent with and justifies our adoption of the ultimate or inevitable discovery exception to the exclusionary rule." *Nix*, 467 U.S. at 444.

Not all states accept the United States Supreme Court's approach to this issue. For example, in *People v. Winterstein*, 167 Wash.2d 620, 220 P.3d 1226 (2009), the State of Washington's Supreme Court held that the inevitable discovery doctrine is incompatible with Washington's Constitution: "It is well-established that article I, section 7 provides greater protection of privacy rights than the Fourth Amendment. It differs from its federal counterpart in that article I, section 7 'clearly recognizes an individual's right to privacy with no express limitations.' Based on the intent of the framers of the Washington Constitution, we have held that the choice of their language "mandate[s] that the right of privacy shall not be diminished by the judicial gloss of a selectively applied exclusionary remedy." Because the intent was to protect personal rights rather than curb government actions, we recognized that "whenever the right is unreasonably violated, the remedy must follow." The constitutionally mandated exclusionary rule provides a remedy for individuals whose rights have been violated and protects the integrity of the judicial system by not tainting the proceedings with illegally obtained evidence. Because of textual differences, state action may be valid under the Fourth Amendment but violate article I, section 7."

4. Attenuation

Because the fruits doctrine is not an application of a pure "but for" type of causation test, as discussed above, the Supreme Court has made it clear that the relationship between unconstitutional police activity and evidence seized as an indirect result of that activity may be so "attenuated" that the fruits doctrine should not— and does not—apply. In *Wong Sun*, for example, the Supreme Court held that the fruits doctrine did not apply to defendant Wong Sun's inculpatory statement obtained after he was released and then voluntarily returned to the police station "several days" after his (unconstitutional) arrest as "the connection between the arrest and the statement had 'become so attenuated as to dissipate the taint.' " Wong Sun, 371 U.S. at 491, *quoting Nardone v. United States*, 308 U.S. 338, 341 (1939).

It was significant to the Supreme Court in *Wong Sun* both that Wong Sun returned to the police station on his own initiative (a factor that the Court often refers to as an exercise of the defendant's "free will"), and—related to, but separate from, that factor—that a number of days had passed since he had been released (a factor that the Court sometimes refers to as "temporal proximity," i.e. the farther a defendant gets from the time of the unconstitutional conduct, the greater the opportunity for a reassertion of free will). But the determination whether or not attenuation exists in a particular case cannot be reduced easily to a pat formula focused only on free will and temporal proximity. As the Supreme Court has subsequently observed, "[t]he question whether a confession is the product of a free will under *Wong Sun* must be answered on the facts of each case. No single fact is dispositive. The workings of the human mind are too complex, and the possibilities of misconduct too diverse, to permit protection of the Fourth Amendment to turn on such a talismanic test." *Brown v. Illinois*, 422 U.S. 590, 603 (1975).

Significantly, the Supreme Court in *Brown* made it clear that the fact the police had given defendant Brown *Miranda* warnings after his unconstitutional arrest but prior to his confession did not in and of itself, *ipso facto,* render the link between the bad arrest and the statement attenuated. As the Court explained, "[t]he *Miranda* warnings are an important factor, to be sure, in determining whether the confession is obtained by exploitation of an illegal arrest. But they are not the only factor to be considered. The temporal proximity of the arrest and the confession, the presence of intervening circumstances, and, particularly, the purpose and flagrancy of the official misconduct are all relevant." *Id.* at 603–04 (citations and footnotes omitted). *See also Taylor v. Alabama*, 457 U.S. 687, 690 (1982) ("the fact that the confession may be 'voluntary' for purposes of the Fifth Amendment, in the sense that *Miranda* warnings were given and understood, is not by itself sufficient to purge the taint of the illegal arrest").

The Supreme Court has further ruled that the live testimony of witnesses who are discovered as an indirect result of unconstitutional police activity may often be so attenuated as to permit an exception to the exclusionary rule, despite the triggering unconstitutional event that started the causal chain which led to the discovery of the witness. *United States v. Ceccolini*, 435 U.S. 268 (1978). As the Court explained this conclusion, "[e]valuating the standards for application of the exclusionary rule to live-witness testimony . . ., we are first impelled to conclude that the degree of free will exercised by the witness is not irrelevant in determining the extent to which the basic purpose of the exclusionary rule will be advanced by its application. [The] greater the willingness of the witness to freely testify, the greater the likelihood that he or she will be discovered by legal means and, concomitantly, the smaller the incentive to conduct an illegal search to discover the witness. Witnesses are not like guns or documents which remain hidden from view until one turns over a sofa or opens a filing cabinet. Witnesses can, and often do, come forward and offer evidence entirely of their own volition. And evaluated properly, the degree of free will necessary to dissipate the taint will very likely be found more often in the case of live-witness testimony than other kinds of evidence." 435 U.S. at 276–77.

The Supreme Court has also held that a victim's in-court iden- tification of her attacker (but not her prior photographic or lineup identifications of the same individual) was admissible even though it was based upon a photograph taken of the defendant after an il- legal arrest. *United States v. Crews*, 445 U.S. 463, 471 (1980) ("A victim's in-court identification of the accused has three distinct elements. First, the victim is present at trial to testify as to what transpired between her and the offender, and to identify the defen- dant as the culprit. Second, the victim possesses knowledge of and the ability to reconstruct the prior criminal occurrence and to iden- tify the defendant from her observations of him at the time of the crime. And third, the defendant is also physically present in the courtroom, so that the victim can observe him and compare his ap- pearance to that of the offender. In the present case, it is our con- clusion that none of these three elements 'has been come at by ex- ploitation' of the violation of the defendant's Fourth Amendment rights.").

And the Supreme Court has also held admissible (as an excep- tion to the fruits doctrine) a confession obtained from a defendant, Harris, who had been arrested unconstitutionally in his home in violation of the rule established in *Payton v. New York*, 445 U.S. 573 (1980), that a search or arrest warrant is needed to enter a de- fendant's home in order to arrest him or her. *New York v. Harris*, 495 U.S. 14 (1990). The *Harris* Court explained that "[b]ecause the officers had probable cause to arrest Harris for a crime, Harris was not unlawfully in custody when he was removed to the station house, given *Miranda* warnings, and allowed to talk. [The] station house statement in this case was admissible because Harris was in legal custody . . . and because the statement, while the product of an arrest and being in custody, was not the fruit of the fact that the arrest was made in the house rather than someplace else." 495 U.S. at 18, 20.

E. Harmless Error

The Supreme Court has "stressed on more than one occasion, [that] the Constitution entitles a criminal defendant to a fair trial, not a perfect one." *Delaware v. Van Arsdall*, 475 U.S. 673, 681 (1986).

1. Non–Constitutional Errors

Where an appellate court finds non-constitutional errors to have existed at trial, the Supreme Court has held that "[i]f, when all is said and done, the conviction is sure that the error did not in-fluence the jury, or had but very slight effect, the verdict and the judgment should stand. . . But if one cannot say, with fair assur-ance, after pondering all that happened without stripping the erro-neous action from the whole, that the judgment was not substan-tially swayed by the error, it is impossible to conclude that substan-tial rights were not affected. The inquiry cannot be merely whether there was enough to support the result, apart from the phase af-fected by the error. It is rather, even so, whether the error itself had substantial influence. If so, or if one is left in grave doubt, the con-viction cannot stand." *Kotteakos v. United States*, 328 U.S. 750, 764–765 (1946).

2. Constitutional Trial Errors

When an appellate court determines that a defendant's *consti-tutional* rights were violated at trial (or that the trial court erro-neously found a constitutional violation not to have existed), the "harmless error" rule dictates that the defendant's conviction will not be reversed automatically on the ground of constitutional error if the error was "harmless." But, unlike the test for non-constitutional error, the Supreme Court has held that "before a fed-eral constitutional error can be held harmless, the court must be able to declare a belief that it was harmless beyond a reasonable doubt." *Chapman v. California*, 386 U.S. 18, 24 (1967).

Subsequent to the *Chapman* decision, the Supreme Court has ruled that numerous sorts of constitutional errors were harmless on this basis, including, for example: unconstitutionally overbroad jury instructions at the sentencing stage of a capital case; the admission of evidence at the sentencing stage of a capital case in violation of the Sixth Amendment Counsel Clause; a jury instruction containing an erroneous conclusive presumption; a jury instruction misstating an element of the offense; a jury instruction containing an errone-ous rebuttable presumption; the erroneous exclusion of defendant's testimony regarding the circumstances of his confession; a restric-tion on a defendant's right to cross-examine a witness for bias in violation of the Sixth Amendment Confrontation Clause; the denial of a defendant's right to be present at trial; an improper comment on a defendant's silence at trial, in violation of the Fifth Amend-ment Self–Incrimination Clause; a statute improperly forbidding the trial court from giving a jury instruction on a lesser included offense in a capital case in violation of the Due Process Clause; fail-ure to instruct the jury on the presumption of innocence; admission of identification evidence in violation of the Sixth Amendment Counsel Clause; admission of the out-of-court statement of a non-testifying co-defendant in violation of the Sixth Amendment Counsel Clause; a confession obtained in violation of *Massiah v. United States,* 377 U.S. 201 (1964); admission of evidence obtained in violation of the Fourth Amendment; and denial of counsel at a preliminary hearing in violation of the Sixth Amendment Confrontation Clause.

In *Crawford v. Washington,* 541 U.S. 36 (2004), the prosecution sought to introduce defendant's wife's out-of-court statements against him. However, the wife was unable to testify at trial because of the marital privilege, and defendant objected on the basis that he was denied his Sixth Amendment right to confront the witnesses against him. Relying on the Court's prior decision in *Ohio v. Roberts,* 448 U.S. 56 (1980), the trial court held that the unavailability of a witness does not bar admission of a statement provided that the statement bears "adequate 'indicia of reliability.' " Under *Roberts,* such evidence must either fall within a "firmly rooted hearsay exception" or bear "particularized guarantees of trustworthiness." In *Crawford,* the Court overruled *Roberts:* "[T]he Framers would not have allowed admission of testimonial statements of a witness who did not appear at trial unless he was unavailable to testify, and the defendant had had a prior opportunity for cross-examination. . . Where testimonial statements are at issue, the only indicium of reliability sufficient to satisfy constitutional demands is the one the Constitution actually prescribes: confrontation." Chief Justice Rehnquist, joined by Justice O'Connor, concurred, but dissented from the Court's decision to overrule *Roberts* noting that "[e]xceptions to confrontation have always been derived from the experience that some out-of-court statements are just as reliable as cross-examined in-court testimony due to the circumstances under which they were made."

In *Michigan v. Bryant,* 131 S.Ct. 1143 (2011), the Court applied *Crawford v. Washington,* 541 U.S. 36 (2004), and *Davis v. Washington,* 547 U.S. 813 (2006), to a dying victim's declarations to the police. The Court rejected a confrontation clause challenge, concluding that "circumstances of the interaction" objectively indicate that the "primary purpose of the interrogation" was "to enable police assistance to meet an ongoing emergency," the Court concluded that the statements were non "testimonial," and therefore could be admitted at trial without violating the Confrontation Clause. The police had asked the dying man what had happened, who had shot him, and where the shooting had occurred." The dying man identified a man named "Rick" as the assailant, but suggested that he had had a conversation through a door with a man (who he recognized as defendant) who had shot him through the door. Shortly thereafter, the dying man expired. The Court distinguished between investigations by law enforcement officers "directed at establishing the facts of a past crime, in order to identify (or provide evidence to convict) the perpetrator," and statements to an officer when the "primary purpose of the interrogation is to enable police assistance to meet an ongoing emergency." While the former types of statements are excludible under the Confrontation Clause, the latter are not because of the lesser likelihood of fabrication. The Court concluded that the statements in this case fit within the exception because an "objective analysis of the circumstances" of the "encounter and the statements and actions of the parties" suggested that the police did not know whether the threat was limited to the victim, and they did not know the location of the shooter. The Court concluded that the primary purpose of the police was to obtain the information needed to deal with the emergency. Justice Ginsburg dissented: "I agree with Justice SCALIA that Covington's statements were testimonial and that '[t]he declarant's intent is what counts.'"

In *Bullcoming v. New Mexico*, 131 S. Ct. 2705 (2011), the Court confronted the question of whether the Confrontation Clause permits the prosecution to introduce a forensic laboratory report containing a testimonial certification—made for the purpose of proving a particular fact—through the in-court testimony of a scientist who did not sign the certification or perform or observe the test reported in the certification. The Court held that surrogate testimony of that order does not meet the constitutional requirement: "The accused's right is to be confronted with the analyst who made the certification, unless that analyst is unavailable at trial, and the accused had an opportunity, pretrial, to cross-examine that particular scientist."

3. Constitutional Structural Defects

Until 1991, the Supreme Court had concluded that the admission at a criminal trial of a defendant's confession coerced according to prevailing Fourteenth Amendment law could never be deemed to be harmless error. In 1991, a 5–to–4 majority of the Supreme Court ruled otherwise, holding that "[i]t is evident from a comparison of the constitutional violations which we have held subject to harmless error, and those which we have held not, that involuntary statements or confessions belong in the former category. The admission of an involuntary confession is a 'trial error,' similar in both degree and kind to the erroneous admission of other types of evidence. [When] reviewing the erroneous admission of an involuntary confession, the appellate court, as it does with the admission of other forms of improperly admitted evidence, simply reviews the remainder of the evidence against the defendant to determine whether the admission of the confession was harmless beyond a reasonable doubt." *Arizona v. Fulminante*, 499 U.S. 279, 310 (1991).

Some constitutional errors are so fundamental, however, to the inherent reliability and fairness of a criminal trial that they are deemed to involve "structural defects" in the criminal justice system. These sorts of errors are, accordingly, held not to be subject to the ordinary harmless error analysis dictated by *Chapman*. The *Fulminante* Court explained this difference (and provided examples of structural defects) as follows: "The admission of an involuntary confession—a classic 'trial error'—is markedly different from . . . constitutional violations . . . not . . . subject to harmless-error analysis. One of those violations [is] the total deprivation of the right to counsel at trial. [Another is trial with a trial] judge who [is] not impartial. These are structural defects in the constitution of the trial mechanism, which defy analysis by 'harmless-error' standards. The entire conduct of the trial from beginning to end is obviously affected by the absence of counsel for a criminal defendant, just as it is by the presence on the bench of a judge who is not impartial. Since our decision in *Chapman,* other cases have added to the category of constitutional errors which are not subject to harmless error the following: unlawful exclusion of members of the defendant's race from a grand jury; the right to self-representation at trial; and the right to public trial. Each of these constitutional deprivations is a similar structural defect affecting the framework within which the trial proceeds, rather than simply an error in the trial process itself." *Fulminante*, 499 U.S. at 309–10 (citations omitted).

In overturning the conviction in *State v. Jones*, 228 P.2d 394 (Kan. 2010), the court refused to apply harmless error analysis despite overwhelming evidence of Jones' guilt. The case involved Jones, who was charged with kidnaping and rape, and who was found to be suffering from schizoaffective disorder and bipolar disorder. Although the trial court concluded that he was competent to stand trial, the court denied his request to proceed *pro se* at the preliminary hearing on the basis that his knowledge of the law was insufficient The court concluded that Jones had a constitutional right to represent himself that could not have been denied because of his lack of legal competence. Of course, had the court (properly) concluded that Jones was not competent to represent himself, the judge could permissibly have denied him the right to self-representation.

4. Federal Habeas Corpus Proceedings

In 1993, the Supreme Court ruled that the *Kotteakos* standard for assessing the existence of harmless error when non-constitutional errors are alleged, described above, applies to claims of constitutional error in federal habeas corpus proceedings. *Brecht v. Abrahamson*, 507 U.S. 619, 623 (1993) ("The *Kotteakos* harmless-error standard is better tailored to the nature and purpose of collateral review than the *Chapman* standard, and application of a less onerous harmless-error standard on habeas promotes the considerations underlying our habeas jurisprudence."). The Kotteakos standard does not, however, apply to structural defects. *California v. Roy*, 519 U.S. 2, 5 (1996) ("the *Kotteakos* standard [does] not apply to 'structural defects in the constitution of the trial mechanism . . .' ").

POINTS TO REMEMBER

- The exclusionary rule precludes the prosecution in state and federal criminal trials from introducing evidence seized as a result of unconstitutional activity in its case-in-chief.

- The exclusionary rule does not apply to the actions of private actors.

- The exclusionary rule is now justified primarily because of its deterrent effect on possible future law enforcement unconstitutional activity.

- In settings where no incremental deterrence of unconstitutional law enforcement activity is obtained, the exclusionary rule does not apply.

- The exclusionary rule does not apply where police officers act in objectively-reasonable "good faith" in executing an otherwise defective search warrant.

- In order to raise issue relating to unconstitutional law enforcement activity in a motion to suppress, an individual needs to possess "standing," i.e., his or her own personal constitutional rights must have been violated.

- The exclusionary rule applies not only to evidence seized as a direct result of unconstitutional police activity, but also to additional evidence derived indirectly from—the so-called "fruits" of—that activity.

- The fruits doctrine does not apply where the government proves by a preponderance of the evidence that it would have discovered unconstitutionally-seized evidence anyway if there had been no constitutional violation.

- The relationship between unconstitutional police activity and evidence seized as a result of that activity may be so "attenuated" that the fruits doctrine does not apply.

Chapter 9

PRETRIAL RELEASE

Focal Points for Chapter 9

- Eighth Amendment prohibition of excessive bail.

- Types of Pretrial release.

- Pretrial release statutes.

- Preventive detention.

A. Introduction

A defendant's pretrial release from custody typically is in exchange for a pledge of something of value that the defendant will appear in court and will comply with the court's orders in a pending criminal case. Bail is the Anglo–American criminal justice system's answer to the issue of what is to be done with an accused, whose guilt has not been proven, during the time period between arrest and trial. Conceptually, the use of bail is to accommodate the defendant's interest in pretrial liberty (consistent with the presumption of innocence) and society's interest in assuring that the accused is present for trial. In each case a judge decides whether to grant pretrial release, and if so, what monetary amount and/or conditions of release will assure the defendant's presence. A judge's discretion to make pretrial release available is limited, however, because most state constitutions expressly guarantee pretrial release before conviction.

Constitutional concerns about pretrial release concentrate on whether there is a right to release and, if so, whether the conditions of release are excessive. The Eighth Amendment states that "[e]xcessive bail shall not be required." *United States Const. Amend. VIII.* While state constitutions at least implicitly recognize the fundamental nature of the right to bail by their express prohibition of excessive bail, *United States v. Salerno,* 481 U.S. 739 (1987) found that there is no federal constitutional right to bail, holding that the Eighth Amendment is not violated by the use of pretrial detention due to the dangerousness of the defendant.

Several limited legislative or judicial exceptions exist to the general right of pretrial release. First, in states which use capital punishment, the denial of bail occurs in capital cases if the prosecution can show that the proof is evident or the presumption is great that the defendant is guilty. Second, the denial of bail frequently is authorized in cases in which a prisoner has escaped and is recaptured. Third, denial of bail also may be authorized in cases of criminal contempt. Finally, in response to a growing problem of defendants committing crimes during the period of pretrial release, some state legislatures and the Congress have enacted laws prohibiting pretrial release due to a defendant's criminal history or to the nature of the pending charges. *See* 18 U.S.C. §§ 3141–3150 for the Bail Reform Act of 1984.

Bail becomes excessive when a court sets it higher than reasonably necessary to assure a defendant's appearance at trial. In *Stack v. Boyle*, 342 U.S. 1 (1951), the Court stated that bail set at a figure higher than an amount reasonably calculated to fulfill the purpose of assuring that the defendant will stand trial and, if found guilty, submit to sentence, is excessive under the Eighth Amendment. That prohibition is not directly applicable to the states, but a comparable standard may be required as a matter of due process of law and equal protection of the laws. The equal protection approach to the issue of excessive bail is that the defendant is being detained solely on account of the economic inability to afford the monetary bail set by the court. The due process argument is two-fold: 1) the defendant is being punished without a trial and in violation of the presumption of innocence; and 2) continued pretrial detention prevents adequate trial preparation and could result in ineffective assistance of counsel.

The traditional rationale for the use of money bail and/or conditions imposed upon defendants pending trial is to ensure their appearance at trial. During the 1960s and 1970s, "bail reform" meant that nonmonetary information increasingly became an important part of the pretrial release process, in order (1) to avoid discrimination against accused persons who could not afford the monetary amount imposed for their release; as well as (2) to reemphasize the rationale of appearing for trial. Instead of focusing on whether an accused could afford an amount imposed by the court, defense counsel emphasizes that the facts of the defendant's situation demonstrate that the likelihood of appearance at trial would be increased by the imposition of nonfinancial conditions of release, e.g., that the accused not commit another crime during release, or the use of a curfew.

By the 1980s, the nature of "bail reform" changed. Increasing numbers of persons released pending trial were committing crimes—either against specific witnesses in the pending case, or against others in the community, or both. The nature of reform began to focus not on whether an accused would appear in court, but on whether and under what circumstances an accused legally could be detained and not released at all pending trial in order to prevent the accused from committing crimes.

B. Types of Release

The types of release described below may be strategically important both to the defendant and to the outcome of the defendant's case. From the defendant's perspective, personal recognizance or an unsecured bond is the least intrusive because the defendant does not have to expend any funds which could be used for other purposes such as hiring defense counsel. Prosecutors are likely to consent to these types of release for defendants who are charged with minor property crimes and have extensive ties to the community. Otherwise, prosecutors will prefer that a defendant be required to post at least 10% of the cash bond that is set. Judges may want to emphasize the importance of the bail that is set by requiring the defendant to post the entire amount of the cash bond. Property bonds are often set when young defendants are arrested and their parents are willing to post the equity in their home as collateral.

If the defendant does not appear as scheduled for a court appearance, the defendant will be obligated to pay the full amount of the unsecured appearance bond, the cash bond, or the percentage bond. If the young defendant does not appear for court, the loyal parents face the possibility of losing their home (as well as their child).

Personal Recognizance. Release on personal recognizance may not fall within the technical definition of a bail bond. Upon acquiring control over the person of the defendant, the court merely allows the defendant to be at liberty in return for a written promise to return and to comply with the orders of the court throughout the case. Because the defendant has this duty anyway and the only thing the defendant pledges is the surrender of liberty which is already under the power of the court, a release on personal recognizance is not a contractual undertaking for a consideration in the classical sense.

Release on personal recognizance has long been a practice in the courts, and for good reason. If the defendant has ties to the community (e.g., time she has resided in the current place, with whom the defendant lives, full-time or part-time employment, economic dependence on another person or on governmental compensation, ownership of property in the area, possession of a telephone line, etc.) and will likely return to court without the imposition of liability or other conditions, the requirement of a monetary amount for release accomplishes none of the purposes of bail but rather imposes a substantial hardship upon persons of limited resources. Perhaps for this reason, the law not only acknowledges the power of the courts to release a defendant on recognizance but indeed entitles a defendant to release in this manner (as, for example, in the federal Bail Reform Act) unless the court finds that something more is required to insure the defendant's appearance in court.

Unsecured Bond. An unsecured bond is a pledge by the defendant alone to be liable for a specified sum if the defendant should breach a material condition of release. Unlike the release on personal recognizance, the unsecured bond is a contractual undertaking in the true sense. The unsecured bond undoubtedly has an advantage over the release on personal recognizance in the case of a defendant of means who has long term ties to the community. The bond gives the defendant a financial stake in obeying the orders of the court and thus helps insure the defendant's appearance. On the other hand, the theoretical civil liability of an indigent defendant upon an unsecured bond provides no real stake in the proceedings.

Release on Nonfinancial Conditions. Release on nonfinancial conditions may not technically be a separate kind of bail or undertaking. However, the court has the power to annex nonfinancial conditions to the basic bond agreement that the defendant will be responsive to the orders of the court. Courts should impose the least onerous conditions which will insure the presence of the defendant in court. Such conditions may include but are not limited to placing the defendant in the custody of a person or agency, placing restrictions upon travel, association or place of abode, or requiring confinement during specified hours.

Cash Bond. A defendant may be released from custody by depositing cash in the amount of the bail with the court. The money is deposited by the clerk in an escrow account, and is available for forfeiture or for application to indebtedness upon judgment in the case. A major advantage of the cash bond is that it gives the defendant an immediate stake in the court proceedings. The cash may be returned only if upon compliance with the terms of the bond. The defendant thus faces an immediate financial loss, rather than some sort of distant civil liability, as would be true under an unsecured bond. A further advantage of the cash bond is that it creates a visible asset which can be assigned to counsel for a fee. Thus, the money can do double duty, and the private bar is able to obtain employment in cases which are otherwise assigned to appointed counsel due to depletion of resources in order to obtain release on bail.

Percentage Bond. Instead of a total cash bond, a court may permit the defendant to deposit only a percentage of the total amount of the bond. The money deposited is generally handled in the same way as a full cash bond. However, a portion of the deposit is kept by the court for operating costs. The percentage bond can be used effectively to permit the release from custody of defendants of limited means and still provide adequate assurance that they will appear in court.

Property Bond. The pledging of real property or of stocks and bonds as security for a bail bond is permitted. The proposed pledge of security must be justified by a detailed statement filed with the court. If the pledge is of real estate, it is recorded as a lien. Upon the failure of the defendant to comply with the terms of the bond, security in the form of real property or of stocks or bonds may be forfeited in whole or in part. On the other hand, if the defendant is discharged from the obligations of the bond, the stocks or bonds are returned to their owner, and any lien on real estate is released.

Surety Bond. The court may require the bond of a defendant to be underwritten by one or more sureties. In this classic bonding situation, the surety is undertaking an indebtedness to insure the conduct of another. However, unlike the surety offering security for a property bond, the surety on a surety bond is not required to create an encumbrance on property, and enforcement of the obligation is essentially the same as any other civil action for debt. The officers before whom bail may be taken shall ascertain that the amount deposited is no less than the amount fixed by the court. In the case of a surety bond, the surety or sureties must demonstrate by affidavit a net worth at least equal to the amount of the undertaking. Surety bonds are still used in the federal system and in some state courts.

The use of "bail bondsmen" lost favor in the 1970s when it became apparent that bondsmen and some defense attorneys were swapping referrals in exchange for services and kickbacks. Moreover, some states began to prefer that the use of "bounty hunters" on behalf of bonding companies to assist in locating non-appearing defendants was too closely related to the Wild West. Instead, some states began to phase out the use of bonding companies and leave the task of finding absent defendants to law enforcement personnel.

Guaranteed Arrest Bond Certificate. A guaranteed arrest bond certificate is a printed card or certificate of an association obligating the association and a licensed surety to guarantee the appearance in court of the member whose signature appears on the certificate and to pay any fine or forfeiture imposed upon the member, not to exceed a certain amount of money, e.g., five hundred dollars. Such a certificate may not be accepted for certain violations, such as the laws regulating motor carriers or for the offense of driving under the influence of an intoxicant. Such a certificate may be accepted for any traffic offense in lieu of a cash bond not to exceed five hundred dollars.

C. Bail Statutes

In most criminal cases, the issue of pretrial release is the first important decision for a judge. Prior to the judge's involvement, a person accused of a minor offense may be released according to the terms of a release schedule providing for specific ranges of monetary bail for specific misdemeanors. If a defendant accused of a felony has been interviewed by a pretrial services official prior to the initial appearance in court, the official will have compiled a report to the judge about the defendant. Possibly, the official also may have recommended a form of pretrial release for the particular defendant. Most states rely upon statutes to define the circumstances under which an accused may obtain pretrial release.

The Bail Reform Act of 1984 governs release determinations in federal courts, and serves as a reference for defining various types of pretrial release. Assuming that the accused is not a flight or safety risk, the federal statute *mandates* a recognizance bond or an unsecured appearance bond. 18 U.S.C. § 3142(b). With a view toward whether either type of release is appropriate, the pretrial service agency's activities will provide the judge with a much better idea about the defendant's assets, ties to the community, and prior record of appearing in court in response to any previous criminal charges. The official's work also will save time for the judge who probably has scores of other cases awaiting decisions.

Pretrial services agencies reach a conclusion about the advisability of recommending a recognizance release by calculating points on the basis of several factors. No one is eligible for personal recognizance who has been charged with or convicted of escape from custody, has any outstanding bench warrant issued, or has a detainer filed. The total pretrial release points are computed by subtracting the negative points from the positive points. For example, suppose that a total of eight verified points is necessary. Positive points may be given for:

1. Residency—for more than a year (+5 points) or for 3–12 months (+3);

2. Personal ties—whether the defendant lives with a spouse, child, parent, guardian, some relative or guardian (+4), another relative (+3); a non-related roommate (+2), or lives alone (+1);

3. Economic ties of the defendant to the community—whether the accused currently is employed for more than one year (+5) or for 3–12 months (+3); whether the defendant is dependent on a spouse, parent, other relative or guardian (+3), or whether the defendant is dependent upon unemployment, disability, retirement, or welfare compensation (+2); or has held a job for less than three months (+1);

4. Miscellaneous matters such as whether the accused owns property in the area (+3); has a telephone (+1); or expects someone at the initial court appearance (+1); and

5. Previous criminal record—whether the defendant has any convictions (excluding traffic convictions) in the past two years (+3).

Negative points are given for:

1. Whether the accused has a felony conviction in the past two years (–5 points);

2. Whether the accused failed to appear on a traffic citation in the last two years (–5)

3. Whether the defendant failed to appear on a misdemeanor charge in the past five years (–10); and

4. Whether the accused failed to appear on a felony charge at any time (–15).

In a felony prosecution, if a judge decides that a recognizance or unsecured release will not reasonably assure the defendant's presence at trial, the judge must decide about releasing the accused based on the facts about the specific defendant and the charges that have been brought against the defendant. Specifically, the judge must consider several factors and impose many conditions on the release:

(1) the nature and circumstances of the offense, e.g., crime of violence, drug offense, family dispute;

(2) the weight of the evidence against the accused (at a very early point in the case);

(3) the history and characteristics of the defendant, including not only the information already discussed for a recognizance release but also the defendant's history of drug or alcohol abuse, criminal history, and physical and mental condition;

(4) whether the defendant was on some type of release such as parole, probation or appeal for some other offense at the time of the current offense or arrest, 18 U.S.C. § 3142(g)(1)–(3); and

(5) what condition(s) will reasonably assure the defendant's appearance. 18 U.S.C. § 3142(c).

The nature of the inquiry is fact-intensive. For example, multiple defendants charged with the same offense may receive different treatment from the court in its evaluation of the release conditions which can reasonably assure each defendant's appearance at the next proceeding. Or, a series of individual defendants each charged with the same offense may receive vastly different types of release conditions—some may be released on personal recognizance, others with cash bond, and still others may be released only if a bonding company is willing to "post bond" for the defendant. Moreover, the release conditions for each defendant may differ. As the fourteen conditions in the federal statute suggest, in addition to the boilerplate conditions of not committing additional offenses and avoiding contact with the victim or persons known to engage in criminal activities, a defendant may be instructed not to leave the jurisdiction, to find employment, comply with a curfew, contact a pretrial services official on a daily basis, etc.

Pretrial release decisions are rarely subject to appeal, because most courts regard the issue of release as moot following disposition of the case by a guilty verdict, a guilty plea or an acquittal.

D. Pretrial Detention

The Bail Reform Act of 1984 not only governs pretrial release decisions but also pretrial detention determinations. Detention is authorized if the prosecution persuades the court that the defendant poses either a danger to the community or to any other person *or* a danger of not appearing for trial. The statute authorizes a judicial officer to order the detention of a defendant pending trial if the prosecution demonstrates by clear and convincing evidence that no release conditions will reasonably assure the safety of the community. Pretrial (also known as preventive) detention is constitutional, violating neither due process nor the Eighth Amendment, as long as that detention (1) serves a compelling state interest; (2) does not impose punishment before an adjudication of guilt; and (3) is implemented in a fair, nonarbitrary manner. *United States v. Salerno*, 481 U.S. 739 (1987). Preventive detention does not violate due process, because it is a regulatory measure imposed to regulate the "pressing societal problem" of defendants on pretrial release endangering the community by continuing to engage in criminal activity. The Court has found that the Congress did not intend to punish individuals through preventive detention. The regulatory goal of preventing danger to the community outweighed a defendant's liberty interest. The legislation is limited to specific categories of individuals arrested for specific categories of serious crimes, both of which are likely to pose a danger to the community. Preventive detention due to dangerousness is not "excessive bail" under the Eighth Amendment. The Court found that excessive bail applies only to cases which qualify for bail where the traditional concern is prevention of flight. Detention, on the other hand, is constitutionally permitted when a different compelling interest (here, the protection of the community) exists.

Together with several statutory sections already discussed, the following is the scheme of the Bail Reform Act. The first issue addresses whether the defendant poses a flight or safety risk. If the answer is yes, the court must consider whether the risk can be minimized by conditions. If the answer is no, the statute mandates a recognizance or an unsecured appearance bond. As to the flight and safety risk issues, if the risk can be minimized, the court tailors conditions to the risks posed by the defendant. However, if the risk cannot be minimized, the court holds a detention hearing.

The issue at the detention hearing is whether, given the offense and offender factors already discussed, there nonetheless are conditions to minimize the particular risk, or whether instead the defendant should be detained prior to trial without an opportunity for pretrial release because the accused is a safety or flight risk. At the hearing, the government has the burden of proof by a preponderance of the evidence to show that the defendant is a flight risk. The burden of proof is on the Government to prove by clear and convincing evidence that the defendant should be detained prior to trial as a result of the defendant being a safety risk. The statutory standard for assuring appearance is a reasonable likelihood of appearance rather than a guarantee of appearance.

To aid the prosecution in sustaining its burden of proof at the detention hearing, the statute establishes two rebuttable presumptions upon which the prosecution may rely. A rebuttable presumption of dangerousness arises when a judge finds that a defendant is charged with a violent crime, capital offense, or a drug felony with a maximum term of ten years imprisonment *and* within five years of the finding, the defendant was convicted of or released from prison for a similar offense that he committed while on release pending trial. 18 U.S.C. § 3142 (e). A rebuttable presumption of both dangerousness and risk of flight occurs when a defendant is charged with a drug felony with a maximum term of ten years imprisonment *or* with the use or possession of a firearm during the commission of any violent crime, drug trafficking crime, or a crime involving a minor, *and* there is a finding of probable cause that the defendant committed the offense charged.

Points to Remember

- The Eighth Amendment prohibits excessive bail, but does not grant a right to bail.

- Bail becomes excessive when it is set higher than reasonably necessary to assure a defendant's appearance at trial.

- Pretrial release is usually disallowed for all defendants charged with capital crimes or escape.

- Recently, the primary concern of pretrial release decisions has focused on preventing the release of suspects who would commit more crimes.

- By federal statute, an individual defendant posing a flight or safety risk may be detained before trial.

Chapter 10

PROSECUTORIAL DISCRETION

<table>
<tr><td>

Focal Points for Chapter 10

- Selective prosecution.

- Vindictive prosecution.

</td></tr>
</table>

A. Generally

For two important reasons, courts recognize that prosecutors have broad discretion about when and whether to pursue criminal prosecutions. First, the separation of powers doctrine is said to require broad discretion because prosecutors act as the executive branch's delegate to help discharge a chief executive's constitutional responsibility to "take care that they laws be faithfully executed." *United States v. Armstrong*, 517 U.S. 456 (1996). Courts also have repeatedly noted that "the decision to prosecute is particularly ill-suited to judicial review." *Wayte v. United States*, 470 U.S. 598 (1985). Prosecutors possess *discretion* (rather than an obligation or duty) to investigate and to prosecute and are not, accordingly, legally bound to do either, i.e., they cannot be judicially ordered to investigate or prosecute anyone. Among the discretionary factors that are not readily susceptible to judicial analysis are "the strength of the case, the prosecution's general deterrence value, the Government's enforcement priorities, and the case's relationship to the Government's overall enforcement plan." As long as probable cause exists to believe that the defendant has committed an offense, the prosecutor has discretion about whether to investigate or prosecute, which charges to bring as well as when and where to bring them, and whether to seek immunity or a plea bargain.

In addition to a significant measure of discretion with respect to who and when to investigate and who, what, and whether to charge, prosecutors in many jurisdictions also possess substantial authority to divert accused persons into whatever pretrial intervention (PTI) programs that may have been established in their jurisdiction. Typically, the successful completion by an accused of the conditions set upon entry into the PTI program results in the dismissal of the whatever pending charges which led to the PTI diversion. Concomitantly, failure to meet those PTI requirements results in the prosecutor's office taking the charges to trial.

B. Selective Prosecution

As a result of the wide discretion prosecutors have in prosecuting criminal cases, the potential exists for abuse of that discretion. Misuse of that discretion especially occurs when a prosecutor, with the requisite amount of probable cause, purposefully chooses to pursue a case because of the defendant's race, religion, or some other arbitrary classification. Such prosecutorial conduct is known as selective prosecution and denies an accused equal protection of the law. In *Wayte*, the defendant refused to register for the military draft and also wrote letters to various officials indicating his intent to continue his course of conduct. The United States Department of Justice obtained the names of those who had either reported themselves or were reported by others for failing to comply with draft registration requirements. Following repeated attempts to persuade him to register, Wayte and a dozen others were prosecuted for willfully failing to register. Unlike Wayte, approximately 670,000 other nonregistrants were never indicted. The Supreme Court required a two-part showing for a successful selective prosecution challenge. First, a defendant must establish that others who broke the same law were not prosecuted. Second, the defendant must show that the prosecution's decision to prosecute was based on impermissible considerations, such as race, religion, political beliefs, or the desire to prevent the exercise of other constitutional rights. Because there is a presumption of good faith prosecution, a defendant challenging an indictment as selective prosecution generally bears a heavy burden of proving facts sufficient to satisfy these two requirements, even to obtain information from the government supportive of a selective prosecution challenge.

The summary reversal in *United States v. Bass*, 536 U.S. 862 (2002) illustrates the weight of that burden. The lower court had held that the defendant had made a credible showing that similarly situated persons of a different race were not prosecuted based on nationwide statistics showing that the "United States charges blacks with a death-eligible offense more than twice as often as it charges whites" and that the United States "enters into plea bargains more frequently with whites than it does with blacks." The Court's response was that

> Even assuming that the *Armstrong* requirement can be satisfied by a nationwide showing (as opposed to a showing regarding the record of the decisionmakers in respondent's case), raw statistics regarding overall charges say nothing about charges

brought against similarly situated defendants. And the statistics regarding plea bargains are even less relevant, since respondent was offered a plea bargain but declined it. Under *Armstrong*, therefore, because respondent failed to submit relevant evidence that similarly situated persons were treated differently, he was not entitled to discovery.

C. Vindictive Prosecution

Unlike selective prosecution, due process governs the analysis of vindictive prosecution allegations. A defendant demonstrates prosecutorial vindictiveness by showing that he or she was reindicted on more serious charges in retaliation for exercising constitutional or statutory rights. A claim that the defendant was indicted as a persistent felon will generally not support an allegation of vindictive prosecution even where he or she earlier refused to plead to the lesser charge. *Bordenkircher v. Hayes*, 434 U.S. 357 (1978). To establish vindictiveness, the defendant must prove objectively that the prosecutor's charging decision was motivated by a desire to punish him or her for exercising his rights. *United States v. Goodwin*, 457 U.S. 368 (1982).

Vindictive prosecution was demonstrated in *Thigpen v. Roberts*, 468 U.S. 27 (1984), where the defendant was convicted in a district court of several misdemeanors growing out of an automobile accident where a passenger was killed. The defendant took a de novo appeal but while this was pending he was indicted for manslaughter. Although a second prosecutor was responsible for the increased charge the Court had little trouble finding that such an increased charge was prohibited by the possibility of vindictive action by the state in response to the defendant's exercise of his right to appeal. *Thigpen* thus concluded there was a presumption of unconstitutional vindictiveness which had not been dispelled by the state.

POINTS TO REMEMBER

- A prosecutor has discretion about whether to investigate and charge criminal conduct.

- Equal protection prohibits selective prosecution of individuals.

- To show selective prosecution, a defendant must show that others who broke the same law were not prosecuted.

- A defendant also must prove that the prosecutor's decision to bring charges was based on impermissible considerations like race or religion.

- Due process prohibits vindictive prosecution.

- A defendant must show that more serious charges were brought in retaliation for exercising constitutional or statutory rights.

Chapter 11

PRELIMINARY PROCEEDINGS

Focal Points for Chapter 11

- Initial appearance.

- Gerstein hearing.

- Preliminary hearing.

Following the arrest and administrative "booking" procedures, the police take the accused to a judge for a proceeding called an "initial appearance" or "preliminary arraignment." The functions of an initial appearance include informing the accused of the charge, appointing counsel, setting conditions of release, and scheduling future proceedings. The judge may combine the initial appearance with a "*Gerstein* hearing" for defendants who were arrested without a warrant, in order to examine the validity of their detention. Within a short period after the initial appearance, the judge conducts a preliminary hearing to determine whether there is probable cause to hold the defendant to answer the charges in a court which has jurisdiction to conduct the trial of felony cases.

A. Initial Appearance

Most jurisdictions require that the arresting officer bring the accused before the nearest available judge without unnecessary delay. See, e.g., Fed.R.Crim.P. 5(a)(1)(A). The period of delay in federal courts usually is measured from the time the accused is arrested on federal charges. An unreasonable delay between arrest and the initial appearance may violate due process. In evaluating an allegation of unreasonable delay, courts analyze the amount of time that passes as well as how and why the delay occurred. Confessions which are obtained during periods of unnecessary delay *prior to* the initial appearance may be inadmissible. For example, under 18 U.S.C. § 3501, delay is one of several statutory factors considered to decide whether a confession was given voluntarily during the period of unreasonable delay.

Federal Rule of Criminal Procedure 5(d) is typical of most rules setting the procedures for the initial appearance in court. At the initial appearance, the judge must inform the accused about:

(1) The charges;

(2) The right to remain silent;

(3) The right to request or retain an attorney;

(4) The fact that any statement made may be used against the accused;

(5) The general circumstances under which the accused may secure pretrial release;

(6) The right to a preliminary hearing; and

(7) A reasonable time to consult with an attorney.

While the court is not required to conduct any preliminary inquiry, it is customary and desirable at the outset that the court determine that the correct person is before the court. The court should inquire whether the person is actually the person who is accused of committing the offense charged and that the defendant is actually before the court, either in person or by counsel.

The court must give the defendant notice of the charges by informing the defendant in open court, by either reading or stating the substance of the charge. A defendant who has counsel prior to the initial appearance normally waives a formal reading of the charge, because counsel has previously ascertained the charge.

After the court gives the accused notice of the charges, procedural rules may require that the court ask the accused to enter a plea to those charges. Most defendants enter a plea of not guilty to felony charges, in part because defense counsel knows little about the charges at the time. If a defendant chooses to stand mute, the court, by rule or its inherent authority, enters a not guilty plea on the defendant's behalf.

Under rules like Federal Rule of Criminal Procedure 44(a), the right of the accused to be represented by counsel begins at the initial appearance. However, the initial appearance is not regarded as a "critical stage" at which the Sixth Amendment grants a right to counsel. On the other hand, an accused's request for counsel at the initial appearance precludes subsequent police interrogation about the charged offense but does not prohibit police interrogation about other crimes.

B. Gerstein Hearing

In *Gerstein v. Pugh*, 420 U.S. 103 (1975), the Supreme Court held that "the Fourth Amendment requires a judicial determination of probable cause as a prerequisite to extended restraint of liberty following arrest." A *Gerstein* hearing is necessary prior to the continued detention of an accused who was arrested without either a prior judicial determination of probable cause such as an arrest warrant or the return of a grand jury indictment.

The only issue determined at a *Gerstein* hearing is whether there is probable cause to believe that the accused committed an offense. *Gerstein* requires a "fair and reliable determination of probable cause." The hearing is nonadversarial in nature, with the accused having no right to counsel, to be present, or to question witnesses. Hearsay and written testimony are admissible. When a court determines that there is no probable cause, release from custody is the proper remedy but that finding does not foreclose a later prosecution. Similarly, the absence of a prompt decision about further detention does not invalidate a later conviction.

The determination of probable cause ordinarily must occur within 48 hours of the warrantless arrest. *County of Riverside v. McLaughlin*, 500 U.S. 44 (1991). This is not to say that the probable cause determination in a particular case passes constitutional muster simply because it is provided within 48 hours. Such a hearing may nonetheless violate *Gerstein* if the arrested individual can prove that the probable cause determination was delayed unreasonably. Examples of unreasonable delay are delays for the purpose of gathering additional evidence to justify the arrest, a delay motivated by ill will against the arrested individual, or delay for delay's sake. In evaluating whether the delay in a particular case is unreasonable, however, courts allow a substantial degree of flexibility. Courts cannot ignore the often unavoidable delays in transporting arrested persons from one facility to another, handling late-night bookings where no magistrate is readily available, obtaining the presence of an arresting officer who may be busy processing other suspects or securing the premises of an arrest, and other practical realities. Because of the similarity between the timing of the initial appearance and the timing of a *Gerstein* hearing following a warrantless arrest, a judge may conduct both proceedings at the time of the initial appearance.

C. Preliminary Hearing

Although *Gerstein* held that there is no constitutional right to a preliminary hearing, court rules like Federal Rule of Criminal Procedure 5.1, statutory enactments and court decisions provide for preliminary proceedings involving felony charges. The traditional purpose of a preliminary hearing, or examining trial, is to determine whether there is probable cause for the defendant's charge to be presented to the grand jury. The required "probable cause" is that an offense was committed and that the accused committed it. Without a finding of probable cause, the accused is released from custody. The preliminary hearing occurs shortly after arrest. Unlike a *Gerstein* hearing or the initial appearance, state rules and statutes provide that the preliminary hearing is a formal, adversarial proceeding.

A preliminary hearing is important, not only because of the protections afforded the accused but also because of its strategic position in the criminal justice system. The preliminary hearing interrelates with other aspects of the criminal process—arrest, bail, prosecutorial discretion, the grand jury, and the trial itself. For example, information disclosed at the preliminary hearing may influence a judicial decision to set bail or some other condition for pretrial release. Or, it may serve as a review of a prosecutor's decision to charge the accused at all or with a particular offense.

1. Functions of the Preliminary Hearing

Once a state authorizes a preliminary hearing, the Sixth Amendment right to counsel applies. Counsel is necessary the Court said to try to rebut the showing of probable cause, discover the prosecution's case, build a record for later impeachment, preserve testimony of witnesses who are unavailable for trial, and make effective arguments on matters like the necessity for bail.

a. Screening

The primary function of a preliminary hearing is the screening of cases. The prosecutor must prove that there is probable cause to believe that a crime was committed and that the defendant committed the crime charged. Preliminary hearings save accused persons from the humiliation and anxiety involved in a public prosecution. Whether the screening function is successful depends upon: 1) the extent of screening by the prosecutor before the case reaches the preliminary hearing stage; 2) whether the prosecutor bypasses the preliminary hearing by first obtaining an indictment; 3) whether the prosecutor at the preliminary hearing presents all the key witnesses or relies largely on the testimony of the arresting officer; and 4) the practical impact of the judge's finding of no probable cause.

For the prosecution, the preliminary hearing provides an opportunity for the termination of weak or groundless charges without lengthy preparation and trial time. With the opportunity to discover the nature of its own evidence early in the prosecution, the government is able to conform the charge(s) to its proof before trial. In cases originating by a "private" complaint obtained by a citizen where no police investigation has occurred, the preliminary hearing provides an immediate forum for testing the strength of the case until further investigation can be conducted.

b. Pretrial Discovery

In practice, the preliminary hearing may provide defense counsel with a valuable discovery technique. In meeting the evidentiary standard for sending the case to the grand jury, the prosecutor necessarily provides the defense with some discovery of the prosecution's case. Defense counsel may obtain even more discovery by cross-examining the prosecution's witnesses at the hearing and by subpoenaing other potential trial witnesses to testify as defense witnesses at the hearing. The extent of the discovery depends upon whether: 1) the prosecution relies entirely upon hearsay reports and thereby limits the witnesses it presents; 2) the probable cause standard is satisfied by presenting a minimal amount of testimony on each element of the offense; 3) the prosecutor follows a general practice of presenting most or all of the government's case; and 4) the defense is limited, in both cross-examination of prosecution witnesses and in the presentation of its own witnesses, to direct rebuttal of material presented by the prosecution.

The importance to the defense of the limited discovery accessible through the preliminary hearing depends in large part on the availability of alternative discovery procedures. For example, if prior statements of prospective witnesses and the arresting officer's report are readily accessible, the hearing's discovery potential may be relatively unimportant. On the other hand, if state law and practice provide for little pretrial discovery, the preliminary hearing may serve as the primary discovery device. Similarly, if discovery does not occur until after the critical time for plea negotiations, the preliminary hearing may serve as the main discovery device for the large percentage of cases resolved by guilty pleas.

c. Future Impeachment

Extensive cross-examination of prosecution witnesses at the preliminary hearing may be of value to the defense even though there is little likelihood of successfully challenging the prosecution's showing of probable cause and little to be gained by way of discovery. The skilled interrogation of witnesses can be a vital impeachment tool for use in cross-examination later at trial. Witnesses are more likely to make damaging admissions or contradictory statements at the preliminary hearing because they are less thoroughly briefed for that proceeding than they are for trial. In addition, the more some witnesses say before trial, the more likely that there will be some inconsistency between their trial testimony and their previous statements.

Of course, cross-examination designed to lay the foundation for future impeachment carries certain dangers for the defense. By focusing on potential weaknesses in a witness's testimony, a witness may be rehabilitated for trial and state that at the preliminary hearing she was confused but now all is clear. Cross-examination may also harden a witness's position, making the witness less able to retreat to a more friendly position. Finally, if the witness becomes unavailable at trial, the perpetuated testimony may be more damaging than that which would have existed without the cross-examination.

d. Perpetuation of Testimony

Preliminary hearing testimony traditionally has been admissible at trial as substantive evidence under the "prior testimony" exception to the hearsay rule, where the witness is unavailable to testify. The preliminary hearing thus perpetuates the testimony of witnesses so that it may be used even if the witness dies, disappears or otherwise becomes unavailable to testify. The Sixth Amendment Confrontation Clause permits admission of testimonial (such as prior testimony from a preliminary hearing) hearsay. *Crawford v. Washington*, 541 U.S. 36 (2004). Preliminary hearing testimony is admissible as substantive evidence at trial if: 1) it was given under oath; 2) the declarant is unavailable to testify at trial; and 3) a reasonable opportunity, whether exercised or not, for cross-examination on substantially the same issues was afforded the opposing party at the preliminary hearing.

e. Pretrial Release

Where conditions of pretrial release are set at the initial appearance on the basis of sketchy facts, the preliminary hearing provides the judge with the first extensive examination of the facts of the individual case. The testimony may persuade the court to modify the terms of release, or impose other terms or conditions of pretrial release. The hearing also insures that an accused who has been unjustifiably charged will be promptly released from custody.

f. Plea Bargaining

A preliminary hearing may be an "educational experience" for the defendant who is unpersuaded by defense counsel's opinion that the prosecution has such a strong case that a negotiated plea is in the defendant's best interest. Conversely, the proof at the hearing may be insufficient on the charged offenses, and require reduction of excessive charges. It thereby serves as a check against the prosecutorial practice of "overcharging" (by the number of charges and/or the severity of charges) in anticipation of plea negotiations.

2. Procedural Issues at the Preliminary Hearing

a. Timing of Preliminary Hearing

The preliminary hearing must occur within a reasonable time. For example, Federal Rule of Criminal Procedure 5.1(c) requires the hearing to occur no later than ten days after the initial appearance if the accused is still in custody and no later than twenty days if the defendant has obtained pretrial release. In many cases, the issue is not when the examination is held but whether it must be held at all. Most courts have held that there is no necessity for a preliminary hearing after a grand jury first has returned an indictment. If the only purpose of the preliminary hearing is to determine whether there is probable cause for holding the accused to answer further, this is a logical rule because the grand jury has decided the issue of probable cause and there is no need to have a court duplicate that determination. Thus, where an accused is first arrested *after* indictment, rather than on an arrest warrant, the accused is not entitled to a preliminary hearing. To the extent that the preliminary hearing is of benefit to the accused as an instrument of discovery, the prosecution can deny that benefit by indicting the accused prior to the scheduled time of the preliminary hearing. For example, 18 U.S.C § 3060(e) provides that no preliminary hearing is required for an arrested person if at any time subsequent to the initial appearance of that person and prior to the date fixed for the preliminary examination, an indictment is returned.

b. Waiver of Preliminary Hearing

A defendant may waive a preliminary hearing. Waiver rates vary substantially among jurisdictions and sometimes exceed 50%, even in places which provide quite extensive hearings. Despite the aforementioned advantages of the hearing, defense counsel may consider a waiver where the hearing presents a substantial danger to the defense. Defense counsel considerations may include the following.

(1) An essential prosecution witness will testify at the preliminary hearing but may be unavailable at trial. Recall that the recorded preliminary hearing testimony may be used against the defendant as substantive evidence at trial.

(2) A complainant is likely to "mellow" with time if he is not required to put his testimony "on the record" at this point. By contrast, a complainant who testifies under oath at a preliminary hearing may be less likely either to change the version of what happened or to consent to an interview with the defense.

(3) The preliminary hearing may add to adverse publicity that will make it difficult to obtain a fair trial.

(4) The preliminary hearing will call the prosecutor's attention to a curable defect in the case that otherwise would not be noticed until trial.

(5) The preliminary hearing will alert the prosecutor to the fact that the defendant is undercharged, and should be charged with more serious or simply more offenses than those in the complaint.

See Anthony G.Amsterdam, Trial Manual 5 for the Defense of Criminal Cases (1988). Even if the defendant waives the hearing, a jurisdiction's criminal rules may provide that prior to indictment or information the prosecutor may be entitled to demand a preliminary hearing. The prosecutor will oppose a defense waiver and insist upon a hearing under special circumstances, e.g., where either there appears to be a need to perpetuate testimony because a particular witness is likely to become unavailable, or a particular witness's testimony is "shaky" and there would be some value in placing him under oath.

c. Dispositions Following Preliminary Hearing

At the close of the prosecution's case at a preliminary hearing, defense counsel should move to dismiss the charges, based upon the failure of the proof to establish (1) that an offense was committed; (2) that the accused committed an offense; and (3) where the offense took place, for jurisdictional purposes. Frequently, after the judge denies defense counsel's motion for a dismissal based upon the above grounds, counsel will move the court to reduce the original charge to a lesser offense, e.g., from a felony to a misdemeanor, have the accused plead guilty to the reduced charge, and thereby dispose of the case. If a court permits a guilty plea to an amended charge which is a lesser included offense of the original charge, double jeopardy probably will prevent the prosecution from later reinstituting the original charge against the accused.

If the evidence presented at the preliminary hearing establishes probable cause to believe that the defendant has committed the offense, the court refers the case to the grand jury for possible indictment or to the court for trial following the filing of an information on any charge supported by probable cause. If the court does not find probable cause to refer the charge, it may nevertheless find probable cause as to some other offense. In this situation, the court may permit the prosecution to amend the charge if substantial rights of the defendant are not prejudiced. If the evidence at the preliminary hearing fails to establish probable cause, the defendant is discharged from the jurisdiction of the court. However, dismissal of the charge due to the insufficiency of the evidence at a preliminary hearing does not bar a subsequent prosecution or indictment arising out of the same transaction.

POINTS TO REMEMBER

- An accused must be taken before a judge without unnecessary delay following arrest.

- The judge must advise the accused about the charges and several constitutional rights.

- A judge must conduct a *Gerstein* hearing when a defendant is arrested without a warrant.

- In felony prosecutions, a preliminary hearing determines whether there is probable cause for the defendant's charge to be presented to the grand jury.

- Whether a court finds probable cause has no effect on whether the proceedings against the defendant go forward.

- The return of an indictment preempts the requirement for a preliminary hearing.

Chapter 12

GRAND JURIES

Focal Points for Chapter 12

- Selection of the grand jury.

- Grand jury secrecy.

- Sufficiency of the evidence presented to the grand jury.

- Prosecutorial misconduct.

- Defendant's rights.

- Grand jury subpoenas.

A. Introduction

Both the preliminary hearings discussed in Chapter 11 and the grand jury review considered in the present chapter test the government's case for the quantum of proof required to go to trial, although each usually requires only proof of probable cause (as opposed to proof beyond a reasonable doubt) that a crime has been committed and that a particular defendant committed the crime. Preliminary hearings and grand jury proceedings differ, however, in important respects. For example, preliminary hearings are public, while grand jury proceedings are secret. Preliminary hearings are adversary proceedings in which the defense can challenge the prosecution's case, but grand juries normally hear only the prosecution's case, and prospective defendants and defense counsel are excluded from the grand jury proceedings. Judges preside over preliminary hearings, while grand jury proceedings occur without judicial participation. Finally, judges determine the sufficiency of the evidence in preliminary hearings, while grand jurors (citizens of the local community) make this determination in grand jury proceedings.

The grand jury is an ancient common law entity which originated as a body of local residents who helped look into possible crimes. This investigative function of a grand jury has been characterized as a **sword** to root out crime. By the time of the American Revolution, however, the grand jury assumed another function—as a **shield** to protect citizens against malicious and unfounded prosecutions. The dual functions of the grand jury are considered separately in this chapter.

In the federal system, the view that the grand jury acts as a "shield" or "screen" against improper prosecutions is embodied in the Fifth Amendment to the United States Constitution, which provides: "No person shall be held to answer for a capital, or otherwise infamous crime, unless on a presentment or indictment of a Grand Jury. . ." The Supreme Court, however, has held that the States are not required to abide by the grand jury requirement imposed on the federal courts. See *Hurtado v. California*, 110 U.S. 516 (1884). About half the States have their own constitutional provisions or statutory requirements for grand jury indictment. The other half have either eliminated grand juries and permit prosecution by a verified document known as an information, or allow the prosecutor to choose between grand jury indictment and information. Even the states which use grand juries may have rules comparable to the federal rules, permitting defendants to waive the right to indictment and proceed by information. Fed. R. Crim. P. 7(b). (An information is a charge drawn up by the prosecutor and not submitted to a grand jury, although it may or may not be screened by a judicial officer at a preliminary hearing).

B. Selection of the Grand Jury

Grand juries in individual jurisdictions differ greatly in their composition and selection processes. At common law, the grand jury was comprised of twenty-three persons, at least twelve of whom had to agree in order to hand down an indictment for a criminal offense. Today, federal grand juries consist of between sixteen and twenty-three jurors, twelve of whom must agree to indict the defendant for any charge. Fed. R. Crim. P. 6(a)(1). Other jurisdictions use smaller grand juries, although all grand jury jurisdictions require that an indictment be based on the concurrence of at least a majority (rather than a unanimous view) of the grand jurors empaneled to review the charges.

The process of selecting grand jurors begins with the court's summoning a number of persons qualified to serve as grand jurors. The qualifications for grand jury service are set out in each jurisdiction's statutes and normally include requirements that the prospective grand juror be a citizen of the jurisdiction; reside there; be over eighteen years of age; have no felony convictions; and be a person of honesty, intelligence, and good demeanor. Purging the grand jury is the process of narrowing the number of qualified grand jurors to the number of jurors who will actually serve. The process eliminates otherwise qualified grand jurors who have legitimate excuses for not serving, such as health problems, or family obligations.

Defense counsel does not participate in the selection of the grand jury. Thus, any deficiencies in the composition of the grand jury must be raised when the defendant is brought to trial (also, objections cannot be raised for the first time on appeal). A timely pretrial objection allows the trial court to void the indictment and compel the prosecutor to present the case to a lawfully constituted grand jury. Challenges to the composition of the grand jury are made by a motion to dismiss or quash the indictment returned by the grand jury. Generally, the courts have recognized only two proper grounds for objecting to the composition of the grand jury: (1) one or more of the grand jurors failed to meet the statutory qualifications for service; or (2) the process for selecting grand jurors violated constitutional standards.

Although the states are not required to use grand juries, if they choose to do so, the Fourteenth Amendment Equal Protection Clause requires that no state may deliberately and systematically exclude individuals because of race, gender, or national origin. *Taylor v. Louisiana*, 419 U.S. 522 (1975). The basic elements of an equal protection challenge to the grand jury are the same as required for challenges to the trial jury. (The Supreme Court has not determined whether the Sixth Amendment requirement that the jury be drawn from a "fair cross-section of the community" applies to grand juries). Constitutional infirmities in the composition of a grand jury may invalidate a conviction even though the trial jury was legally constituted and guilt was established beyond a reasonable doubt. *Vasquez v. Hillery*, 474 U.S. 254 (1986).

C. Scope of Grand Jury Investigation

Once the grand jury is selected and empaneled, the judge will charge the grand jury. This charge may range from the judge's statements about the general state of the Union, to suggestions about particular matters that will come before the grand jury. All judges, however, will caution the grand jury to maintain the secrecy of its proceedings. Once the judge has charged the grand jury, the grand jury independently conducts its investigation of alleged criminal offenses. Unlike preliminary hearings, the judge does not preside over grand jury proceedings.

In the absence of the judge, the prosecutor focuses the grand jury's attention on the task at hand by: (1) submitting an *indictment*, which is a written accusation of crime prepared by the prosecutor; and (2) suggesting what witnesses and evidence the grand jury should consider. If the grand jury agrees that the evidence indicates that a specific person has committed a crime, it will return a "true bill" of indictment upon which the accused will face trial. If the grand jury concludes that the evidence does not warrant a trial, it will return "no true bill." The grand jury's refusal to return a true bill does not preclude the prosecutor from resubmitting the indictment to another grand jury. Until the actual trial begins, double jeopardy generally does not protect the accused from undergoing successive grand jury investigations.

Although the prosecutor may direct the grand jury's attention to the submitted indictments, the prosecutor may not limit the scope of the grand jury's investigation of other crimes because grand juries are often charged to inquire into all felonies, misdemeanors and violations of penal laws committed within its jurisdiction. A grand jury which goes beyond the indictments prepared by the prosecutor and launches its own investigation is often referred to as a "run away" grand jury. The charges returned by such a grand jury are referred to as presentments rather than indictments. (Indictments are submitted to the grand jury by a prosecutor; presentments are drawn up at the grand jury's initiative). The information necessary to return a presentment can be obtained from additional witnesses called by the grand jury or from the personal knowledge of the grand jurors. In contrast to trial jurors, grand jurors need not be impartial in the case.

D. Grand Jury Secrecy

Unlike most stages of a criminal prosecution, grand jury proceedings are conducted in secret. The Supreme Court has explained that the secrecy requirement is designed to serve five important objectives:

(1) to prevent the escape of those whose indictment may be contemplated;

(2) to insure the utmost freedom to the grand jury in its deliberations, and to prevent persons subject to indictment or their friends from importuning the grand jurors;

(3) to prevent subornation of perjury or tampering with the witnesses who may testify before the grand jury and later appear at the trial of those indicted by it;

(4) to encourage free and untrammeled disclosures by persons who have information with respect to the commission of crimes;

(5) to protect the innocent accused who is exonerated from disclosure of the fact that he has been under investigation, and from the expense of standing trial where there was no probability of guilt.

United States v. Procter & Gamble Co., 356 U.S. 677 (1958).

Grand jury secrecy requirements vary among jurisdictions, but generally the prosecutor and the grand jurors are prohibited from disclosing grand jury testimony except when authorized by court order. Most jurisdictions do not impose an obligation of secrecy upon grand jury witnesses, and the Supreme Court has held that a state may not prohibit grand jury witnesses from disclosing their own testimony after the term of the grand jury has ended.

E. The Grand Jury as a Shield

1. Sufficiency of the Evidence

Wood v. Georgia, 370 U.S. 375 (1962) described the grand jury as

"a primary security to the innocent against hasty, malicious and oppressive persecution; it serves the invaluable function in our society of standing between the accuser and the accused, whether the latter be an individual, minority group, or other, to determine whether a charge is founded upon reason or was dictated by an intimidating power or by malice and personal ill will."

Despite this lofty view of the function of a grand jury, many states have either eliminated grand juries in favor of proceeding by information, or the state may utilize preliminary hearings as another method of screening charges brought by a prosecutor. The majority view is that the shielding function of the grand jury, while attractive rhetoric, is illusory in practice. Statistics show that grand juries rarely refuse to indict, an understandable result in light of the fact that grand jury proceedings are not adversarial.

When a properly constituted grand jury returns an indictment, courts will not review the adequacy of evidence presented to a grand jury. *Costello v. United States* 350 U.S. 359 (1956) allows a grand jury to rely exclusively on hearsay evidence as the basis for an indictment. The following arguments support the *Costello* result: 1) the grand jury's function is investigative and not adjudicative; 2) if the grand jurors believe that they had sufficient evidence to support the return of the indictment, any judicial interference with that conclusion would threaten the theoretical (from the judge yes, from the prosecutor no) independence of the grand jury; 3) evidentiary rules ensure fairness in adversary proceedings, but the grand jury is not adversarial; and 4) inadmissible evidence usually has some probative value. At least hearsay may appear in some admissible form at a trial, but an illegally seized weapon will not. Any misleading effect of inadmissible evidence like hearsay will be remedied at trial. Justice Burton's concurrence is often cited in circumstances where the defendant claims that *no* evidence was heard by the grand jury. *Costello*'s assumptions seem to be that prosecutors rarely seek indictments supported primarily by incompetent evidence, and that grand jurors can recognize where competent evidence for a trial of the charges is lacking.

In *United States v. Calandra*, 414 U.S. 338 (1974), the Supreme Court indicated that the *Costello* rationale also barred a challenge to an indictment issued on the basis of unconstitutionally obtained evidence. In *Calandra*, the district court held that the defendant "need not answer any of the grand jury's questions based on" evidence obtained from an unconstitutional search. The Supreme Court reversed stating:

It is evident that this extension of the exclusionary rule would seriously impede the grand jury. Because the grand jury does not finally adjudicate guilt or innocence, it has traditionally been allowed to pursue its investigative and accusatorial functions unimpeded by the evidentiary and procedural restrictions applicable to a criminal trial. Permitting witnesses to invoke the exclusionary rule before a grand jury would precipitate adjudication of issues hitherto reserved for the trial on the merits and would delay and disrupt grand jury proceedings. Suppression hearings would halt the orderly progress of an investigation and might necessitate extended litigation of issues only tangentially related to the grand jury's primary objective. The probable result would be protracted interruptions of grand jury proceedings. . .

2. Misconduct Challenges

Following *Costello*, some federal courts employed a "prosecutorial misconduct" rationale to exert control over the type of the evidence presented to the grand jury. These cases relied upon the courts' inherent authority "to preserve the integrity of the judicial process" by dismissing indictments that were the product of "flagrantly abusive prosecutorial conduct." Prosecutor misconduct was held to include the presentation of evidence in an unfair manner, e.g., the knowing presentation of false testimony; the presentation of hearsay disguised as if the witness was testifying based on personal observations; or failing to produce known exculpatory evidence that clearly was material. This use of the judiciary's supervisory power was rejected in *United States v. Williams*, 504 U.S. 36 (1992).

Williams held that under no circumstances could a federal court dismiss an indictment on the ground that the prosecutor failed to present exculpatory evidence to the grand jury. Requiring the grand jury to weigh inculpatory and exculpatory evidence would alter the grand jury's historical role. Besides, federal courts do not possess the authority to prescribe standards of prosecutorial conduct before the grand jury. Arguably, even prosecutors may have difficulty early in a case determining all the possible charges and defenses. The prosecutor has no duty to present the defendant's version of the facts in a non-adversarial setting, and such a procedure would threaten to alter the grand jury from an investigative proceeding to a mini-trial on the merits.

Despite the *Williams* decision, most state courts which have confronted the issue have imposed a duty on prosecutors to disclose exculpatory evidence to the grand jury in the unique cases where the prosecutor has evidence in her file of the target's guilt and also evidence negating guilt which is genuinely exculpatory. In order to reduce the circumstances in which a prosecutor's duty will arise, most courts rejecting the *Williams* approach have also ignored the standard which imposed a requirement on prosecutors to disclose evidence which "reasonably tends to negate the guilt of the accused." Instead, most state courts have imposed a limited duty on the prosecutor to inform the grand jury of evidence which *directly* negates the guilt of the accused and is clearly exculpatory.

F. The Grand Jury as a Sword

The Supreme Court has often emphasized that screening charges before a grand jury creates a shield to protect innocent citizens against unfounded prosecutions. In practice, however, the grand jury's potential to "shield" innocent citizens is often subordinate to its functioning as a "sword" to root out crime through use of its investigative authority. Rather than viewing grand jury indictment as an unnecessary burden, many prosecutors favor use of grand jury proceedings in hopes of uncovering additional evidence. They seek to use the grand jury's broad subpoena powers over witnesses and documents, and in the typical grand jury proceeding the prosecutor determines what witnesses and evidence will be subpoenaed by the grand jury as part of the investigation.

Simply on the basis of the prosecutor's speculation about possible criminal activity, the grand jury can call anyone to testify. Unlike suspects or witnesses who are questioned by the police, an individual subpoenaed to appear before the grand jury has no general right to remain silent or to refuse to cooperate. In the absence of a constitutional provision such as the Fifth Amendment privilege against self-incrimination or a common law communication privilege, the witness "must tell what he knows" or risk being punished for contempt. *Branzburg v. Hayes*, 408 U.S. 665 (1972). The contempt sanction makes the grand jury subpoena particularly useful in obtaining statements from persons who will not voluntarily furnish information to the police. Even when a witness invokes the privilege against self-incrimination, the grand jury may, if authorized by law, grant the witness immunity and thus force an answer.

The grand jury also may issue a *subpoena duces tecum*, which is a command to a person to produce writings or objects described in the subpoena. The only constitutional limitations on subpoenas duces tecum or other grand jury investigative powers are the constitutional rights of individual witnesses. The accused ultimately named in the indictment is not yet a "defendant," and thus enjoys no rights or protections beyond that afforded any witness called before the grand jury. Again, without proof of probable cause, people may be summoned to appear to bring documents or other tangible objects with them. The breadth of a grand jury inquest is indeed large: any aspect of a person's life that might shed light on some criminal activity by somebody is within the proper scope of a grand jury investigation.

The Fourth Amendment provides no protection to witnesses called to testify before a grand jury. Because the Fourth Amendment exclusionary rule is inapplicable at a grand jury proceeding, witnesses may be questioned based on evidence derived from illegal searches and seizures. *United States v. Dionisio*, 410 U.S. 1 (1973) held that voice exemplars and handwriting samples do not invade any privacy right, because they relate to physical characteristics "constantly exposed to the public." *Dionisio* also found that a grand jury subpoena to appear before a grand jury is not a seizure in the Fourth Amendment sense. The Court noted the distinction between an arrest or stop and the "compulsion exerted" by a subpoena. While compliance with a subpoena may be inconvenient and burdensome, every person has a "historically grounded obligation" to appear and give evidence before the grand jury. As such, the grand jury had no need to explain the basis for its subpoenas.

Fifth Amendment Rights Applicable to Testimony

Any witness appearing before a grand jury may assert the Fifth Amendment privilege against self-incrimination, but even a target of the investigation has no right to receive *Miranda* warnings. *United States v. Mandujano*, 425 U.S. 564 (1976). Even if *Miranda* warnings were required to be given to a grand jury witness, failing to give the warnings to a defendant accused of perjury based upon the witness' false grand jury testimony would not be a valid defense. *Miranda* warnings apply only to custodial interrogation, which differs from questioning before a grand jury. A subpoenaed grand jury witness, the plurality noted, does not face a hostile or isolated setting found in a police station.

> After being sworn, respondent was explicitly advised that he had a right to remain silent and that any statements he did make could be used to convict him of crime. It is inconceivable that such a warning would fail to alert him to his right to refuse to answer any questions which might incriminate him. Even in the presumed psychologically coercive atmosphere of police custodial interrogation, *Miranda* does not require that any additional warnings be given simply because the suspect is a potential defendant; indeed, such suspects are potential defendants more often than not. Respondent points out that unlike one subject to custodial interrogation, whose arrest should inform him only too clearly that he is a potential criminal defendant, a grand jury witness may well be unaware that he is targeted for possible prosecution. While this may be so in some situations, it is an overdrawn generalization. In any case, events here [prior questioning by the prosecutor] clearly put respondent on notice that he was a suspect in the motorcycle theft.

A witness who discloses any incriminating fact waives the Fifth Amendment privilege as to all details about that fact. In *Rogers v. United States*, 340 U.S. 367 (1951), a grand jury witness testified that she was the local Communist Party treasurer. She denied having custody of other records because she had turned them over to someone else but she refused to identify that person. The Supreme Court held that once the witness had disclosed incriminating information about her activities, she could not invoke the privilege against self-incrimination to avoid disclosure of the details. However, a witness can validly claim the privilege if the answer calls for information beyond the "subject" of the prior testimony. Defense attorneys must use extreme caution when advising their clients about what questions to answer during their grand jury testimony.

The Supreme Court has indicated, though never explicitly held, that a witness before a grand jury has no Sixth Amendment right to be represented by counsel. A grand jury witness' rights may be substantially prejudiced after answering grand jury questions, but the witness may not have an attorney. Even with retained counsel, the witness' attorney is not allowed in the grand jury room to help avoid prejudice to the client. A witness who is unfamiliar with the law or who is the target of a probe may be particularly in need of counsel when an investigation becomes accusatory. After a witness has received immunity, the witness risks contempt for refusing to answer questions and certainly could use the advise of counsel.

G. The Subpoena Duces Tecum

1. The Reasonableness Requirement

A grand jury subpoena duces tecum, which seeks documents or other tangible objects, is typically issued by a court clerk at the request of the prosecutor or the grand jury. Thus, a court does not ordinarily review the issuance of the subpoena unless a witness moves to have it quashed or modified. The subpoena is not a court order. However, unless the subpoena is withdrawn or quashed, failure to comply with a court's order to comply with a subpoena is punishable as contempt.

There is a distinction between challenges to a subpoena duces tecum for trial and a subpoena duces tecum in a grand jury proceeding. The distinction is grounded in how a grand jury operates compared with a trial court. Under *United States v. R. Enterprises*, 498 U.S. 292 (1991), the burden is on the recipient of the subpoena to show that there is "no reasonable possibility that the category of material the Government seeks will produce information relevant to the general subject of the grand jury's investigation." (By contrast, the trial standard places the burden on the prosecution to show that the material sought is relevant to the investigation, the things sought are described with particularity, and covers only a reasonable period of time.) With a grand jury subpoena, the prosecution does not have to make a threshold showing of relevancy. All that the prosecution needs to show (as a matter of sustaining a burden of production) in response to a motion to quash on reasonableness grounds is that there is a grand jury investigation, the general nature and subject matter of the investigation (without having to give, e.g., statutory citations), and that the subpoenaed documents bear a general relation to the subject matter of the investigation. The burden of proof then switches to the recipient. A blanket denial or assertion of unreasonableness by the recipient does not meet the burden of proof.

2. Self–Incrimination by Compliance With Subpoena Duces Tecum

The Fifth Amendment applies when three conditions are met: (1) the government seeks to "compel" compliance with its demand that the defendant produce documents or tangible items; (2) the compelled material is "testimonial" in nature; and (3) the material "incriminates" the person required to produce it. The first requirement of compulsion is clearly met when a subpoena duces tecum orders the defendant to produce documents. The third requirement of "personal self-incrimination" implicates the "collective entity rule."

Because the Fifth Amendment prohibits compelling a person to be a witness against himself, its protections are limited to "testimonial" evidence, which requires a communicative act. The creation of a document may be testimonial. The requirement that the compelled material be "testimonial" in nature has led the Court to distinguish between the *creation of* and *production* of a document. When the government seeks documents previously created by the defendant, the act of creation is deemed to have been voluntary, not compelled. The act of producing the voluntarily created documents, however, is deemed "testimonial" only if the act establishes incriminating aspects *unrelated* to the contents of the document. See *United States v. Doe*, 465 U.S. 605 (1984). For example, the act of production may establish the existence of the documents; the defendant's control over the documents; or may constitute authentication of the documents, i.e., that the documents are those described by the subpoena.

In *Fisher v. United States*, 425 U.S. 391 (1976), taxpayers under criminal and civil investigation transferred documents from their accountants to their attorneys from whom the documents were subpoenaed. While the Court held that the subpoena did not violate the Fifth Amendment because it was directed to the attorneys, it did acknowledge that the attorney-client privilege would protect the attorneys from complying with the subpoena *if* the Fifth Amendment protected their clients from compliance. In *Fisher*, the voluntary preparation of the documents preceded the issuance of the subpoena. Thus, while the documents incriminated the taxpayers, preparation of the papers was voluntary and did not contain *compelled* testimonial evidence. And, because the taxpayers had no Fifth Amendment privilege regarding the content of the pre-existing documents, they could not insulate their disclosure by passing them along to their attorneys who attempted to rely on the attorney-client privilege to resist disclosure.

United States v. Hubbell, 530 U.S. 27 (2000) provided another application of the act of production doctrine. As part of a plea agreement, the defendant promised to provide the government with information relevant to its investigation. The prosecutor served defendant with a grand jury subpoena for the production of eleven categories of documents. After defendant appeared before the grand jury and invoked his Fifth Amendment privilege, the prosecutor obtained an order granting him immunity. Defendant then produced the documents. The prosecutor used the documents' contents in an investigation that led to defendant's indictment for other offenses. The trial court dismissed the indictment on the ground that the prosecutor's use of the subpoenaed documents violated the law on immunity, because all of the evidence he would offer against defendant at trial was derived either directly or indirectly from the testimonial aspects of the immunized act of producing the documents. The court held that a grant of use/derivative use immunity, a prosecutor must prove that evidence proposed to be used against a defendant is derived from a legitimate source wholly independent of that testimony, unless he can show prior knowledge of the existence or location of the documents.

The Court noted, too, that the compelled testimony relevant in the case was not in the contents of the documents produced, but in the act of producing those documents. Even if the act of production would not be used as proof at trial, the prosecutor still had made "derivative use" of the testimonial aspect of the act of producing the documents in obtaining the indictment and preparing for trial. The defendant's production of existing documents within the subpoena categories could provide a prosecutor with a lead to incriminating evidence or a link in the chain of evidence needed to prosecute.

3. The Collective Entity Rule

Under what circumstances, if any, can a corporation or other collective entity claim the Fifth Amendment privilege to avoid producing potentially incriminating documents for a grand jury's investigation? The test for a collective entity is whether one can fairly say under all the circumstances that a particular type of organization has a character so impersonal in the scope of its membership and activities that it cannot be said to embody or represent the purely private or personal interests of its constituents, but rather to embody their common or group interests only. If so, the privilege cannot be invoked on behalf of the organization or its representatives in their official capacity.

The collective entity rule originated in a case where a corporate officer had been served with a subpoena ordering him to produce corporate records and to testify concerning certain corporate trans-actions. The Court found a distinction between an individual and a corporation, with the latter having no right to refuse to submit its books and papers for an examination. *Braswell v. United States*, 487 U.S. 99 (1988) shows the interplay of the act of production doc-trine and the collective entity rule, and exemplifies the idea that corporations and other entities have no Fifth Amendment privilege. The custodian of records of any collective entity such as a corpora-tion cannot claim the privilege on behalf of the corporation against a compelled act of production. Nor does the custodian have any pri-vilege as to the corporate records, even though the act of production may amount to personal incrimination. In an attempt to "protect" the custodian's Fifth Amendment rights, the Court stated that the prosecution cannot inform the jury about who produced the docu-ment (de facto use immunity). However, the prosecutor can still prove that the documents came from the custodian's organization, thereby allowing the trial jury to infer that the custodian knew about the documents.

POINTS TO REMEMBER

- Grand jurors must be selected without systematic exclusion of individ-uals based on race, gender, or national origin.

- The prosecutor and grand jurors are generally prohibited from disclos-ing grand jury testimony to others.

- Courts will not review the adequacy of evidence presented to a grand jury.

- Prosecutors have no constitutional duty to present exculpatory evi-dence to a grand jury.

- A prosecutor also has no duty to inform a grand jury witness or target about the privilege against self-incrimination.

- In response to a grand jury subpoena duces tecum, a person may claim that compliance with the subpoena would violate Fifth Amendment rights.

- A prosecutor must show that at the time the subpoena issued the gov-ernment knew that the material sought existed, knew who had the ma-terial, and that the material sought was that described by the subpoe-na.

Chapter 13

CHARGING INSTRUMENT

Focal Points for Chapter 13

- Indictment and information.

- Notice of the charge.

- Defects on the face of the charging instrument.

- Jurisdictional defects.

- Venue.

- Amended pleadings.

A. Functions of Pleadings in Criminal Cases

1. Indictment v. Information

An indictment is a written criminal charge made by a grand jury. An information is a similar charge made by the prosecutor. In most states, all felony criminal charges are brought by indictment or information, which is the jurisdictional document in the trial court. An indictable offense is any offense, felony or misdemeanor, for which the punishment at common law was infamous, *i.e.*, a crime punishable by imprisonment at hard labor in a penitentiary. *Hurtado v. California*, 110 U.S. 516 (1884) held that Fourteenth Amendment due process did not require the states to use indictments as formal charging instruments. Since then, more than half the states have given prosecutors the option of proceeding by information against defendants. The remaining states require that a grand jury return an indictment against a defendant, but permit an information to be filed under certain circumstances. Federal Rule of Criminal Procedure 7(b) is typical of the latter procedure and provides that the constitutional right to be indicted may be waived in open court by a defendant who consents to the filing of an information instead of an indictment. Frequently, defendants who intend to plead guilty to the charges which the prosecutor would present to the grand jury waive the right to be indicted as part of plea bargain agreement.

The indictment or information must comply with certain statutory and constitutional requirements. When failure to comport with some of those requirements is apparent by looking at the document, such errors are collectively referred to as technical defects which appear on the "face" of the indictment or information. A defense attorney, examining an indictment or information for the first time, should look for apparent physical errors in the document itself.

The indictment or information is brought in the name of the sovereign, and concludes that the offense was against the peace and dignity of the sovereign. A number of other formalities are required by rules of court. A prosecutor's failure to satisfy these requirements does not deprive a court of jurisdiction. These standards are for the purpose of: (1) giving the defendant adequate notice of the charge; and (2) protecting the defendant from surprise in the course of a criminal prosecution.

2. Notice of the Charge

An indictment or information generally contains a caption setting forth the name of the court and the names of the parties. While the requirement of a caption is not strictly jurisdictional, it is an acceptable way of indicating jurisdictional requirements. An indictment or information designates the parties to it. The sovereign is named as the party plaintiff. The defendant must be designated by name or other description which will permit his identification with reasonable certainty.

An indictment or information is sufficient if it contains a "plain, concise and definite written statement of the essential facts constituting the offense charged." Fed.R.Crim.P. 7(c)(1). The offense may be pleaded alternatively in successive counts. In the case of an information, the facts usually must be stated to be upon the knowledge, information and belief of the prosecuting attorney or to be based upon a verified complaint.

The purpose of an indictment or information is to give the defendant fair notice of the charge in order to prepare a defense and to invoke double jeopardy protections if appropriate. The validity of the charge does not depend upon whether a more satisfactorily framed or more detailed document could have been returned. The document must state an offense which is within the power of the court to adjudicate.

3. Defects on the Face of the Charging Instrument

Courts give charging instruments a "common sense" construction. States may permit the use of conclusory language. The omission of details or the absence of allegations of all of the elements of the offense may generally be overlooked, especially when the indictment includes a citation to the applicable statute that was violated. On the other hand, merely reciting statutory language will not save an indictment unless all the elements of the offense are subsumed in the language or when the case law requires specific allegation. Errors or variances often may be corrected by amendment at any time before verdict, and those which cannot be corrected may normally be overcome by a new indictment or information.

Russell v. United States, 369 U.S. 749 (1962), the indictment charged the defendant with refusing to answer questions submitted by a congressional subcommittee. However, it was not a crime to refuse to answer irrelevant questions and the charging document failed to identify the subject of the inquiry which was crucial in deciding whether the defendant was justified in refusing to answer. The Court held that the indictment's fatal defect could not be cured by providing information in a bill of particulars, because the defendant had a right to have an adequately informed grand jury return the indictment rather than have the indictment effectively rewritten by the prosecutor.

On the other hand, *United States v. Resendiz–Ponce*, 549 U.,S. 102 (2007) held that an indictment for attempted re-entry into the United States after being deported was sufficient when it identified the time and place of the defendant's criminal activity, as well as the criminal statute that was violated. Unlike *Russell*, guilt under the pertinent statute did not depend "crucially upon . . . a specific identification of fact." Because the indictment complied with Rule 7(c)(1), an allegation in the indictment of any overt act committed during the illegal re-entry was unnecessary.

Legal Citations. Some court rules require that an indictment or information contain a citation to the applicable provision of law which the defendant is charged with violating. However, an error or omission in the citation may not be grounds for relief unless the defendant has been misled to the defendant's prejudice.

Signature. Generally, an indictment must be signed by the foreperson of the grand jury. An information must be signed by the prosecuting attorney. However, the absence of a required signature is not a jurisdictional defect.

Witnesses. Court rules may require that the names of the witnesses supporting an indictment or information be listed thereon. In the case of an indictment, only the witnesses who testify before the grand jury need be recorded, while on an information all witnesses relied upon must be enumerated on an information. In any event, the failure to endorse the names of witnesses usually does not affect the validity of the pleading.

Surplusage. Unnecessary allegations in an indictment or information may be disregarded as surplusage. They need not be proved by the prosecutor to sustain a conviction. Upon motion by the defendant, surplusage frequently may be stricken from the indictment or information by the court.

Official Forms. Official forms for the bringing of an indictment or information have been adopted by many state courts. Naturally, courts regard an indictment in compliance with the official forms as a sufficient charging document.

Duplicity and Multiplicity. Despite the presence of official forms for indictments in many states, prosecutors may create problems for themselves by drafting their own indictments. Constitutional problems can arise from duplicitous or multiplicitous indictments. A duplicitous indictment charges two or more distinct offenses in a single count. Duplicity may prevent the jury from deciding guilt or innocence on each offense separately and may obscure the specific charges on which the jury convicted the defendant. Duplicitous indictments may also violate constitutional protections such as the defendant's right to notice of the charges, and the prevention of exposure to double jeopardy in a subsequent prosecution. The rule prohibiting duplicitous indictments is a rule of pleading, and the defect is therefore not fatal to the indictment, which may be corrected by requiring the prosecution to elect the basis upon which it will proceed or by making a corrective instruction to the jury. A court, however, may dismiss a duplicitous indictment that is prejudicial to the defendant.

A multiplicitous indictment charges a single offense in several counts. Multiplicity may violate constitutional double jeopardy provisions by resulting in multiple sentences for a single offense, or otherwise may prejudice the defendant by suggesting to the jury that the defendant committed more than one crime. If each count of the indictment requires proof of facts that the other counts do not require, the offenses are not the same, and the indictment is not multiplicitous. In determining whether an indictment is multiplicitous, courts must consider whether the legislature clearly intended to provide for the possibility of multiple convictions and punishments for the same act. For example, in *United States v. Woodward*, 469 U.S. 105 (1985), the Court held that an indictment was not multiplicitous because there was no indication that Congress intended not to allow separate punishments for the distinct offenses of making false statements to a federal agency and intentionally failing to report transporting over $5,000 into the country.

As with duplicitous indictments, the rule prohibiting multiplicity is a pleading rule which is not fatal to the indictment. A court, however, may require the prosecution to elect the count on which it will proceed if the multiplicity is apparent before trial. If the problem surfaces during trial, the court will instruct the jury on the proper charges and may order the prosecution to dismiss or consolidate multiplicitous counts.

4. Jurisdictional Defects

A defendant may move to dismiss an indictment or information because of lack of jurisdiction. Jurisdiction relates to several concepts. A court may lack jurisdiction over the subject matter. Examples include a felony tried in a court of inferior jurisdiction, a crime occurring outside the state, or a federal crime tried in state court. The court may also lack jurisdiction over the defendant.

a. Jurisdiction of the Sovereign Over the Offense

The jurisdiction of a state to define and punish offenses is limited only by the state and federal constitutions. Within its constitutional sphere of action, the federal government may assert exclusive jurisdiction over particular offenses and thereby deprive the state of jurisdiction. However, unless the federal government has clearly preempted state action in this manner, jurisdiction over offenses is presumed to be within the police powers reserved to the states. Unless federal legislation regulating a particular crime manifests a clear intention to preempt the field, the offense is considered to be within the concurrent power of both sovereignties.

In order for a state to have jurisdiction over an offense, some part of the criminal transaction must have occurred within its geographical boundaries. Some offenses committed within the state are not crimes because the crime is against the federal government and not against the state. However, some offenses committed in the state may be punished by both the state and federal government. Where the situs of the crime is within the state, exclusive jurisdiction over the land may be that of the federal government and thus preclude state prosecution of an act committed on federal land. It is within the power of the federal government to assimilate state criminal laws into the federal law governing such enclaves. On the other hand, the federal government may define and punish offenses committed in a federal enclave which are entirely at odds with the law of the state in which the enclave is situated.

b. Jurisdiction of the Sovereign Over the Situs of the Offense

A state only has jurisdiction of offenses committed within its borders. Some part of the criminal transaction must have occurred within the geographical boundaries of the state. This jurisdictional concept is often confused with venue which refers to the local jurisdiction of where an offense is tried. So long as a criminal act has been committed in the state, jurisdiction over the offense does not depend upon the physical presence of the actor at the time of its commission. Neither does the consummation elsewhere of a criminal act which was commenced in the state deprive that state of jurisdiction over the offense. Likewise, there is no requirement that the consequences of a criminal act occur in the state in order to give it jurisdiction over the offense. The one indispensable element necessary for jurisdiction over the offense is the commission of some portion of the criminal transaction within the physical boundaries of the state.

Lack of jurisdiction over the offense can be raised in a motion to dismiss. It may also be raised after trial since it relates to subject matter jurisdiction. Where a court acts without jurisdiction, its proceedings are void and cannot be raised as double jeopardy.

c. Jurisdiction Over the Person

Jurisdiction over a person is essentially the physical power of a sovereignty to subject the person to its will. The creation of personal jurisdiction by force or other illegal acts has been repeatedly upheld. In a few instances, a person may be within the physical reach of the sovereignty without creating personal jurisdiction. For example, the doctrine of federal supremacy might possibly preclude the assertion of personal jurisdiction over a person who is physically within reach of the sovereignty if he has diplomatic immunity.

As a general rule, however, personal jurisdiction exists whenever a person is found within the boundaries of the state or is otherwise within the reach of its judicial process. The person need not be a resident or a citizen to be subject to the personal jurisdiction of a sovereignty. So long as the person participated in the commission of some criminal act in the state, his physical absence from the state when it was committed does not preclude the exercise of personal jurisdiction over him thereafter.

d. Waiver of Jurisdiction

Personal jurisdiction is the physical power of the sovereign over a person, and thus may be conferred by waiver or consent. However, subject matter jurisdiction is the power of the court over the subject matter of the action and cannot be created or waived by parties to the action. Venue, or local jurisdiction, can be waived.

5. Venue

a. Jurisdiction and Vicinage Compared

Assuming that a court has jurisdiction over a certain class of cases, the prosecution must prove that the necessary elements of the crime charged were perpetrated in the place alleged to be the situs of the offense. This establishes local jurisdiction of the offense, and is called venue. Venue is said to be jurisdictional, but a lack of venue does not deprive a court of jurisdiction to adjudicate the case. Its judgments are merely voidable rather than void.

Art. III, § 2 of the United States Constitution provides that criminal trials "shall be held in the State where the said crimes shall have been committed." This safeguard is reinforced by the command of the Sixth Amendment vicinage clause which has been deemed to provide the defendant, at least in federal trials, with a right to venue before an impartial jury of "the State and district wherein the crime shall have been committed." *Johnston v. United States*, 351 U.S. 215 (1956). State constitutions sometimes provide parallel provisions.

b. Multi–Venue Problems

Ordinarily a crime is committed in one place. However, because some offenses may be committed in more than one place, venue may be proper in any location where the crime began, continued, or was completed. Some offenses are said to be continuing in nature because the elements of the offense repeat themselves, and the offense therefore recurs over a period of time in several different places. For example, the offense of kidnaping begins when the defendant takes the victim into custody, and the offense continues in each place where the victim is moved. Embezzlement requires both the conversion of the property and the duty to account for the property, which may occur in different places. Some statutes, such as 18 U.S.C. § 3237, permit venue in any place where the crime was begun or where criminal acts or the forbidden result occurred.

c. Proof of Venue

Venue is a matter to be proved during trial. The court has the obligation to decide as a matter of law whether the incidents which occurred in the place were sufficient to say that the crime was committed there. The factfinder must then decide whether those events actually did occur within that place. Circumstantial evidence may be relied upon to establish the place in which the offense was committed. If venue is in two or more places, the place in which process is first issued may have exclusive venue during the pendency of the prosecution.

As a practical matter, venue is seldom contested in a pretrial motion to dismiss unless the lack of venue is evident from the face of the indictment or information. The defendant normally raises lack of venue in a motion for a directed verdict or in a motion for a new trial, where the claim is that the prosecution failed to prove venue. Venue jurisdiction may be waived by the intentional or inadvertent failure to raise the issue.

B. Amended Pleadings

In federal courts, Rule 7(e) limits the amendment of formal charges to informations. Most states allow amendments for informations or indictments, but the charge may be amended only upon a proper motion with leave of court. The amendment may be made at any time before verdict or findings, or even after proof has been taken. The amendment may include elements originally omitted from the charge or may correct facts incorrectly stated in the original charge. However, the amendment may not charge a new or different offense, nor shall an amendment be permitted which would prejudice the substantial rights of the defendant. For example, in *Stirone v. United States*, 361 U.S. 212 (1960), a defective constructive amendment of the charge occurred when the prosecution indicted the defendant for one crime (obstructing sand importation) and the evidence showed another crime (interference with steel exportation).

Another way for a charge to be impermissibly amended is for the jury instructions to broaden the scope of the indictment by permitting conviction for an uncharged offense. In cases not curable by amendment, if jeopardy has not attached to the prosecution, the defendant may be reprosecuted.

C. Variances Between Proof and Charge

Unlike a constructive amendment, a variance occurs when the proof offered at trial differs from the allegations of the indictment or information. A variance is less likely to produce a conviction for a different crime from that charged in the indictment, and thus courts regard it as a less serious encroachment than an amendment on the right to be tried only upon the charging instrument. Variances may relate to differences in the time a crime occurred, the number of alleged conspiracies, or the number of individuals participating in a conspiracy. The defense may object to the variance either: 1) when the prosecutor introduces evidence which the defense claims is irrelevant to the charged offense; or 2) when the prosecutor requests a jury instruction grounded on a theory sustained only by evidence which diverges from the charging document. See *Berger v. United States*, 295 U.S. 78 (1935).

POINTS TO REMEMBER

- Felony criminal charges may be brought by indictment or information, depending on jurisdictional standards.

- Even when an indictment is required, a defendant may waive indictment and be charged by information.

- A defendant must be sufficiently notified about the charges.

- Each jurisdiction maintains standards relating to the requirement of a charging instrument.

- Charging defects include whether the sovereign has jurisdiction over the offense, the situs of the offense, and the accused.

- Venue establishes local jurisdiction over the offense.

- Amended charges are permitted, as long as they do not prejudice the rights of the accused.

Chapter 14

JOINDER AND SEVERANCE

Focal Points for Chapter 14

- Joinder of offenses under procedural rules.

- Double jeopardy implications for joinder of offenses.

- Collateral estoppel.

- Joinder of defendants under procedural rules.

- Admission of codefendant's pretrial confession in joint trial.

Joint trials have an important role in the criminal justice system by promoting efficiency and serving the interests of justice. They also save public funds, reduce inconvenience to witnesses and law enforcement authorities, and reduce delays in bringing defendants to trial. Most procedural rules allow a prosecutor to combine offenses or defendants simply by charging multiple offenses of defendants in the same indictment or information. In addition, if offenses or parties are charged separately but initially *could* have been joined in a single indictment or information, criminal rules permit a trial judge the discretion to consolidate the charges for trial in a single charging document.

Once multiple offenses or defendants are joined, either by charging document or by court order, the defense or prosecution may ask the court to sever them from one another. A motion for severance may be based upon misjoinder of either offenses or defendants because the joinder rules have not been followed. In federal courts, even if joinder is proper under the rules, a pretrial motion to sever under Federal Rule of Criminal Procedure 14 leaves the determination of risk of prejudice and any remedy that may be necessary to the discretion of the trial court. If prejudice develops at trial after a motion to sever has been overruled, the defendant should renew the motion and move for a mistrial.

In addition to joinder and severance issues arising from the application of the criminal rules, the exercise of prosecutorial discretion to join or not to join offenses or defendants may have constitutional consequences relating to Fifth Amendment Double Jeopardy and collateral estoppel issues, as well as Sixth Amendment Confrontation Clause problems.

A. Joinder and Severance of Offenses

1. Joinder and Severance of Offenses Under the Rules of Criminal Procedure

Where a defendant is charged with multiple offenses, rules of procedure usually govern the joinder and severance of the offenses to determine whether there can be a single trial or several trials. In general, the rules give the prosecution the discretion to charge, in a single prosecution, all those offenses which a defendant allegedly committed in a closely connected series of events and within the same time sequence. Conversely, the rules permit the defendant to seek a severance of offenses that have been joined in a common prosecution. Federal Rule of Criminal Procedure 8(a) is typical, allowing but not requiring joinder of offenses. It states that two or more offenses may be charged together against a defendant if they are based upon:

(1) the same act or transaction (e.g., a rape and assault); or

(2) a series of acts or transactions constituting a common scheme (e.g., armed robbery, auto theft, possession of weapon); or

(3) the offenses being of similar character (e.g., bank robberies in same neighborhood two months apart).

Because the rule is permissive rather than mandatory, a defendant has no right to have all alleged offenses tried together. However, a defendant's motion to consolidate charges under Federal Rule of Criminal Procedure 13 may succeed *if* the charges could have been brought together.

Joinder is usually upheld when the crimes are closely related in character, circumstances and time. One example of a common scheme or plan is when the offenses show a near identical modus operandi and the offenses occur within such a close proximity of time and location to each other that there can be little doubt that the offenses were committed by the same person. A second type of case is where the crimes are somewhat similar in nature but are closely related in an overall scheme.

The efficiency to be realized from joining "same act" offenses or "same series" offenses may vanish when the only basis for the joinder is similarity of charged offenses which were committed at different places, different times or in different ways. When evidence of one offense is not admissible at the trial of another offense, joinder is inefficient and separate trials are preferable. Case law suggests, however, that if evidence of each crime is simple and distinct, though not admissible in separate trials, joinder may be proper if the trial judge properly instructs the jury about the dangers of cumulating evidence. Evidence of one crime *may be* admissible at the trial of the other, when it is relevant to motive, intent, the absence of mistake or accident, a common scheme or plan, or the identity of the person charged. In any of those circumstances, the court may not deem the joinder of offenses to be prejudicial and determine that separate trials of the similar offenses are unnecessary.

Arguably, any joinder of offenses is prejudicial to some extent, but where joinder is otherwise proper under the rules of procedure, the defendant must prove prejudice to justify and obtain a severance. There are several general discretionary considerations which may persuade a court to grant a severance. First, the jury may consider the defendant a "bad person" or infer a criminal propensity by the defendant simply because he is charged with so many offenses. Second, proof on one charge may "spill over" and assist in conviction on another charge. Unless there is a high probability of an acquittal on one count, courts will usually deny a severance on this ground. Third, the defendant may wish to testify about one offense, but not about another offense. The defendant must convince the trial court both that he has important testimony to give concerning one count but that there is a strong need to assert the Fifth Amendment privilege against self-incrimination and refrain from testifying on the other counts. Otherwise, the defendant must choose between defending himself, a fair trial, and the privilege against self-incrimination. Finally, the defendant may wish to assert antagonistic defenses to the joinable charges. For example, if he is charged with two assaults, he may want to claim an alibi as to one assault and insanity as to the other. Because one of the defenses is likely to diminish the credibility of the other, prejudice may be asserted in support of a motion for a severance.

2. Double Jeopardy Implications for the Joinder of Offenses

When the prosecution charges a defendant with multiple offenses, either in simultaneous or successive prosecutions, a constitutional issue may arise. The Double Jeopardy Clause of the Fifth Amendment shields a defendant from even the risk of being punished twice for the same offense. Double jeopardy protections depend on whether two offenses are considered to be the "same offense." That decision is important not only in the traditional double jeopardy scenario involving successive prosecutions for related acts, but also in a single prosecution involving multiple offenses and punishments.

A constitutional violation does not occur if the legislature intended to impose cumulative punishments for a single act which constitutes more than one crime. In *Missouri v. Hunter*, 459 U.S. 359 (1983), the Supreme Court held that "[w]here [a] legislature specifically authorizes cumulative punishment under two statutes, . . . the prosecutor may seek and the trial court or jury may impose cumulative punishment under such statutes in a single trial." *Hunter* held that in order to show legislative intent, the statutes defining the two offenses must require: 1) a "clearly expressed legislative intent" that supports the imposition of cumulative punishments; or 2) proof of different elements. Either the legislative history of the statute or the language or organization of a statute may reveal the legislative intent. If the offenses are set forth in different statutes or in distinct sections of a statute, and each provision or section unambiguously sets forth punishment for its violation, courts generally infer a legislative intent to authorize multiple punishments.

In most cases, the issue of legislative intent to impose multiple charges or punishments is ambiguous. Then, the Supreme Court test from *Blockburger v. United States*, 284 U.S. 299 (1932) governs whether multiple offenses and punishments in a single or successive prosecutions are constitutionally permissible. *Blockburger* held that two offenses do not constitute the same offense when *each* offense requires proof of elements that the other offense does not. The test may be satisfied despite substantial overlap in the evidence used to prove the offenses. In *United States v. Felix*, 503 U.S. 378 (1992) the Supreme Court held that an attempt to commit a substantive offense and a conspiracy to commit that offense are not the same offense for double jeopardy purposes even if they are based upon the same underlying facts. When a single act affects multiple victims, different offenses are committed. If one person is killed and another is wounded by the same bullet, multiple criminal offenses have been committed.

On the other hand, two offenses *do* constitute the same offense when only *one* of the offenses requires proof that the other offense does not. A lesser included offense is the same as the greater offense because by definition the greater offense includes all the elements of the lesser. Thus, multiple punishments following a single prosecution for both offenses are barred, in the absence of a clearly expressed legislative intent to the contrary. For example, in *Whalen v. United States*, 445 U.S. 684 (1980), the Supreme Court held because rape is a lesser included offense of felony-murder in the course of that rape, double jeopardy prohibited convictions in the same trial for both offenses. Only the felony-murder required evidence that proof of the rape did not: killing the same victim in the perpetration of the crime of rape. By contrast, proving that a rape had been committed by the defendant did not require the prosecutor to show anything different than what was necessary to prove the rape as to the felony-murder charge. Therefore, because rape and the felony-murder were the "same offense," cumulative punishments could not be imposed absent clear legislative intent.

United States v. Dixon, 509 U.S. 688 (1993) is the Court's most recent example of *Blockburger*'s application, but the factual contexts are unusual. Defendants were prosecuted for criminal offenses after they had been convicted of criminal contempt based upon the same conduct. Dixon was released on bond on a murder charge. One of his conditions for release was that he not commit any crime during his pretrial release. He was arrested for a drug offense, which the court that had released him determined that he had committed and held him in criminal contempt of its release order. The government then tried to prosecute Dixon for the drug offense. In the other case of the consolidated appeal, Foster's wife obtained a civil protection order that he not assault her. After she alleged that he had assaulted and threatened her, Foster was convicted of criminal contempt for violating the court's order. The government then charged Foster with several counts of assault. The Court found that Dixon's drug offense was effectively a lesser included offense of criminal contempt, as was Foster's assault charge.

The lesson for prosecutors from the *Blockburger* line of cases is to be careful not to trigger double jeopardy by *not* charging multiple offenses permitted by the joinder rules. For example, if a lesser offense is tried separately from a greater included offense, double jeopardy will probably prevent the prosecutor from being able to try the defendant on the greater offense. In the context of *Dixon*, a prosecutor must choose whether to pursue a contempt conviction and jeopardize not being able to charge the defendant with the substantive offense.

Despite the "same offense" principle from *Blockburger*, multiple prosecutions may be permitted in some circumstances. In *Brown v. Ohio*, 432 U.S. 161 (1977), the Court suggested that the legislature may divide a continuous course of conduct into separate offenses, even for conduct which occurs within a very short period of time. For example, when the defendant fires six gunshots at police during a chase, the result is six different counts of reckless endangerment.

Recently, the Supreme Court also has begun to consider another effect of charging a defendant with related offenses. As noted, double jeopardy may preclude multiple punishments for essentially the same conduct. Double jeopardy regarding punishments assumes that there is a dual "punishment." Most double jeopardy cases involve the prohibition of two criminal prosecutions. Double jeopardy also may apply to a criminal charge and another type of proceeding. In *Hudson v. United States*, 522 U.S. 93 (1997), the Court examined whether a civil penalty can be characterized as criminal and therefore subject to the double jeopardy concern. Bank officers were indicted for misapplication of bank funds, following imposition of monetary penalties by the Office of Comptroller of Currency (OCC). The Supreme Court held that:

> whether a particular punishment is criminal or civil is, at least initially, a matter of statutory construction. A court must first ask whether the legislature, "in establishing the penalizing mechanism, indicated either expressly or impliedly a preference for one label or the other." Even in those cases where the legislature "has indicated an intention to establish a civil penalty, we have inquired further whether the statutory scheme was so punitive either in purpose or effect," as to "transfor[m] what was clearly intended as a civil remedy into a criminal penalty." In making this latter determination, the factors listed in *Kennedy v. Mendoza–Martinez*, 372 U.S. 144, 168–169 (1963), provide useful guideposts, including: (1) "[w]hether the sanction involves an affirmative disability or restraint"; (2) "whether it has historically been regarded as a punishment"; (3) "whether it comes into play only on a finding of scienter"; (4) "whether its operation will promote the traditional aims of punishment-retribution and deterrence"; (5) "whether the behavior to which it applies is already a crime"; (6) "whether an alternative purpose to which it may rationally be connected is assignable for it"; and (7) "whether it appears excessive in relation to the alternative purpose assigned." It is important to note, however, that "these factors must be considered in relation to the statute on its face," and "only the clearest proof" will suffice to override legislative intent and transform what has been denominated a civil remedy into a criminal penalty.

When the Court applied the *Kennedy* factors to *Hudson*, it concluded that the OCC penalties had been civil rather than criminal In cases considering the question whether confinement is criminal or civil, the Supreme Court has looked to the actual conditions of confinement. For example, because involuntary confinement pursuant to a civil commitment statute is not punitive, that statute's operation does not raise double jeopardy concerns when it follows completion of a sentence for a criminal conviction.

3. Collateral Estoppel Implications for Joinder of Offenses

As previously discussed, a single criminal transaction or activity may be divided into multiple statutory crimes. If the prosecution chooses to divide the offenses into separate prosecutions or decides to bring the charges successively rather than simultaneously, an acquittal on one offense may preclude a trial on the other offense under the doctrine of collateral estoppel. This doctrine provides that determination of a factual issue in a defendant's favor at one proceeding may estop the prosecution from disputing the fact in another proceeding against the same defendant. Thus, when different offenses are charged and double jeopardy would normally not bar a second prosecution, collateral estoppel may, in effect, bar the second trial when a fact previously found in the defendant's favor is necessary to the second conviction.

For collateral estoppel to apply, the defendant must be contesting relitigation of an issue of ultimate fact previously determined in that defendant's favor by a valid and final judgment. First, the second prosecution must involve the same parties as the first trial. A defendant cannot estop the prosecution from relitigating a fact found against the prosecution in a proceeding against a different defendant. In *Standefer v. United States*, 447 U.S. 10 (1980), a unanimous Court held that one defendant's acquittal on a bribery charge did not preclude a later prosecution of another defendant for aiding and abetting the same bribery. Second, the factfinder must have "actually and certainly" determined the issue of fact in the earlier proceeding. For example, in *Schiro v. Farley*, 510 U.S. 222 (1994), in a homicide case, the jury was given ten possible verdicts and returned a verdict on only one of the verdict sheets, convicting the defendant for rape felony murder. Defendant claimed that the state was collaterally estopped from showing intentional killing (one of the other verdict sheet possibilities) as an aggravated factor supporting a death sentence. The Court held that "failure to return a verdict does not have collateral estoppel effect . . . unless the record establishes that the issue was actually and necessarily decided in the defendant's favor."

The most difficult problem in applying collateral estoppel is ascertaining what facts were established in the earlier case. Because juries render general rather than special verdicts in most criminal cases, a determination of which facts support the verdict requires careful analysis of the trial record. Only those fact determinations essential to the first decision are conclusive in later proceedings.

Not only must a court be able to determine that the fact issue was litigated in defendant's first trial, but also the nature of the reason for acquitting defendant in the earlier trial determines whether collateral estoppel applies in the current case. For example, assume that Defendant is charged with assaults against two victims at the same time and place, but the offenses are not joined. If she is acquitted at the first trial for assaulting Victim #1 because there is doubt as to whether she was present at the time of the assaults, her acquittal acts as a collateral estoppel defense to the second assault charge. On the other hand, if the acquittal at the first trial resulted from doubt about whether Defendant actually assaulted Victim #1, the prosecutor can still try to prove that she assaulted Victim #2.

In the Supreme Court's leading case of *Ashe v. Swenson*, 397 U.S. 436 (1970), the defendant allegedly robbed six participants in a poker game. At his first trial, however, the charge related to only one of the alleged robberies. Because there was no doubt that a robbery had occurred and that Knight had been a victim, the only issue at the first trial was whether defendant had robbed Knight. After defendant's acquittal for robbing Knight, the prosecution charged defendant was robbing Roberts, another participant in the poker game. In reversing a conviction on the second robbery charge, the Court believed that it was possible to identify why the first robbery trial had resulted in an acquittal. The resolution of the first trial's only issue established that the defendant had not been present to rob either Knight or anyone else at the poker game.

In limited circumstances, it may be easier to identify the basis for a criminal trial verdict under statutes effectively requiring the use of special verdicts to clarify the reason for an acquittal in a first trial. For example, in cases where the defendant has tried to prove a mental defect or mental retardation, the jury may be ordered to make a specific finding that the defendant was mentally defective or retarded. And in cases where the prosecution seeks the death penalty, the jury may need to designate in writing which aggravating circumstance it found to be applicable before the court can sentence the defendant to capital punishment.

Evidence of a crime for which the defendant was acquitted may be introduced at a later trial involving the same circumstances. In *Dowling v. United States*, 493 U.S. 342 (1990), while prosecuting a defendant for bank robbery, the Court held that the prosecution may introduce evidence of a burglary for which the defendant had been acquitted. The Court reasoned that the evidence was admissible at the robbery trial because the acquittal did not prove that the defendant was innocent but only that there was a reasonable doubt about the defendant's guilt. The difference in burdens of proof was the key distinction for the Court: in the first trial, the government failed to show beyond a reasonable doubt that Dowling had committed the act; to introduce evidence of the same act in another trial, the government need show only that a jury could reasonably conclude that the defendant committed the first act.

B. Joinder and Severance of Defendants

1. Joinder of Defendants Under the Rules

The rules of criminal procedure address joinder and severance procedures where multiple defendants are jointly alleged to have committed one or more crimes. The policy behind this type of rule is improved judicial economy and efficiency, since one trial is faster and less expensive than two. The joinder of defendants is permissive and severance is discretionary with the court. When multiple defendants are jointly charged, a severance may be available based upon specific allegations of prejudice. A more general request for severance may be grounded on the proposition that the defendants should not have been joined in the first place. This is similar to misjoinder of unrelated offenses.

In most jurisdictions, joinder of defendants is permitted where the defendants allegedly participated either in the same act or transaction or in the same series of acts or transactions. Unlike the rules on joinder of offenses, in order to be joined defendants must have committed offenses which are part of the same series of acts rather than being of a similar character. Joinder of defendants looks to the factual connecting link. Where the link is part of some larger plan, or there is some commonality of proof, joinder is permitted. Even where the connecting link is absent and joinder is not permitted under the rules, such a misjoinder is subject to harmless error analysis. Most rules also provide that defendants may be charged in one or more counts together or separately, but each defendant does not have to be charged in each count. *See, e.g.,* Federal Rule of Criminal Procedure 8(b).

Assuming that joinder is proper under the applicable rules, severance of defendants may be based upon specific allegations of prejudice in a joint trial. The prejudicial aspects of a joint trial are commonly considered as (1) the "spill over" effect of one defendant's heinous conduct affecting the jury's view of the others charged with that defendant; and (2) the dangers of any one attorney not having total control over the defense. While the prosecution is unified, the defense is fragmented because each defendant has an attorney and each attorney's view of the case may differ. Specific grounds for severance of defendants for factual prejudice relate to (1) the weight or type of proof as to one defendant, (2) antagonistic defenses or positions, (3) the desire to call the codefendant as a witness; and (4) the confession of a codefendant.

Where there is a great disparity in the weight or type of the evidence against the defendants, with the evidence against one or more defendants far more damaging than the evidence against the moving defendant, a severance may be appropriate. Otherwise, the guilt of others may "rub off" on the moving defendant. For example, a defendant being tried for a single offense may seek a severance from being jointly tried with a defendant who is charged with both the same offense as the other defendant and with being a recidivist.

If antagonistic defenses are alleged as the basis for a motion for separate trials, the moving defendant must show that the antagonism with a codefendant will mislead or confuse the jury, thereby rendering his defense ineffective. In *Zafiro v. United States*, 506 U.S. 534 (1993), the Court rejected a bright line test that severance is required whenever defendants have mutually antagonistic defenses. The four *Zafiro* defendants did not articulate any specific instances of prejudice but merely argued that the "very nature of their defenses, without more, prejudiced them." The Court responded that "it is well settled that defendants are not entitled to a severance merely because they may have a better chance of acquittal in separate trials." A court

> should grant a severance [only] if there is a serious risk that a joint trial would compromise a specific right of one of the defendants, or prevent the jury from making a reliable judgment about guilt or innocence. Such a risk might occur when evidence that the jury should not consider against a defendant and that would not be admissible if a defendant were tried alone is admitted against a codefendant. For example, evidence of a codefendant's wrongdoing in some circumstances erroneously could lead a jury to conclude that a defendant was guilty. When many defendants are tried together in a complex case and they have markedly different degrees of culpability, this risk of prejudice is heightened. Evidence that is probative of a defendant's guilt but technically admissible only against a codefendant also might present a risk of prejudice. Conversely, a defendant might suffer prejudice if essential exculpatory evi-

dence that would be available to a defendant tried alone were unavailable in a joint trial.

Even if there is some risk of prejudice, it may be curable with proper instructions. The Court noted that the trial court instructed the jury to give separate consideration to each defendant, and that each defendant was entitled to have his or her case judged only on the basis of the evidence applicable to the individual defendant. Thus, the instructions "sufficed to cure any possibility of prejudice."

The problem of calling a codefendant as a witness may conflict with the codefendant's privilege against self-incrimination. Obviously, a severance where the codefendant's trial is held first might eliminate the self-incrimination problem by virtue of a conviction or acquittal. Courts faced with severance motions based on the prospect of calling a codefendant often require specific statements of what the proposed testimony would contain as well as factors which would lead the court to believe that the testimony would truly be exculpatory. Where the allegations are vague, only partially helpful, or where there is doubt that the witness would testify and not claim the self-incrimination privilege, there is a tendency to deny the motion to sever.

2. Constitutional Implications for the Joinder of Defendants

When a codefendant already has confessed but may not testify at a joint trial, the prosecution could consider several strategic alternatives. The first alternative is to grant a severance to the non-confessing defendant. In this way, the codefendant's confession will not be used against the defendant. In ruling on a motion for separate trials, the trial judge may order the prosecutor to deliver to the court for *in camera* inspection any statements or confessions made by defendants which the prosecutor intends to introduce in evidence at a joint trial. The prosecution may also desire a severance where the other evidence against the codefendant is weak and a full unredacted confession is necessary to convict the codefendant.

A second alternative is that the prosecution not use the codefendant's confession in its case-in-chief in a joint trial. If the confessing codefendant testifies, the prosecution could then impeach the codefendant with the statements made in the confession. This would not constitute a denial of confrontation even if the codefendant denied making the statement. However, it is risky to hope the codefendant testifies in initially denying a severance and allowing introduction of the statement into evidence during the prosecution's case-in-chief.

A third alternative is a procedure called redaction, where all references to the moving, nonconfessing defendant are deleted. This may be accomplished by removing parts of or retyping the confession or requiring the witness to paraphrase the confession in such a manner as to avoid any references that might directly implicate other defendants. To be effective, the deletion must not call attention to the fact that the statement implicates other persons who are obviously at trial.

Bruton v. United States, 391 U.S. 123 (1968) held that in a joint trial the admission of a codefendant's extrajudicial confession incriminating the defendant violates the defendant's Sixth Amendment right to confrontation when the codefendant does not testify at trial. Incriminating out-of-court statements may be introduced before the confessing codefendant testifies. Where the codefendant does testify, there is no confrontation issue because the codefendant is subject to cross-examination.

In *Gray v. Maryland*, 523 U.S. 185 (1998), the prosecution erroneously redacted the codefendant's confession by substituting for the defendant's name in the confession a blank space or the word "deleted." The Court held that when the confession incriminates the defendant *directly*, no redaction which merely substitutes a blank space, "delete," a neutral pronoun, or symbol is permitted. Such substitutions do not make a significant legal difference and "*Bruton*'s protective rule applies." All references to the person's existence must be removed, even if that falsely suggests sole culpability by the confessor. *Richardson v. Marsh*, 481 U.S. 200 (1987) requires redaction which does not lead to an inference that a specific person was named (e.g., "me and some other guys committed the crime") and the redaction protects the identity of the person named, even though it probably invites the jury to fill in the blank with the name of the non-confessing defendant.

The major practical problem associated with the introduction of codefendant confessions is that, when the prosecutor wants to use the confession during the state's case-in-chief, it is unknown whether the codefendant will testify. As a result, during the joint trial of codefendants where one defendant has confessed and also implicated a codefendant, the prosecutor will submit for admission into evidence an edited version of the confession. If the confessing defendant does testify, the prosecutor tenders the unedited version of the confession during its rebuttal which follows the defense's presentation of its testimony.

POINTS TO REMEMBER

- Generally, a defendant may be charged with multiple offenses arising from the same act, series of acts, or from conduct of a similar character.

- Permissive joinder of offenses is subject to discretionary severance of charges due to prejudice.

- A legislature may explicitly authorize cumulative punishments without violating double jeopardy principles.

- Without such explicit authorization, a defendant cannot be convicted of the same offense in simultaneous or successive prosecutions.

- Two criminal offenses do not constitute the same offense when each offense requires proof of elements that the other offense does not.

- Double jeopardy does not preclude both criminal and civil punishments for the same conduct.

- Collateral estoppel may preclude relitigation of a fact issue previously decided in the defendant's favor.

- Multiple defendants may be joined for trial when they participated in the same act or series of acts.

- Permissive joinder of defendants is subject to discretionary severance for prejudice.

- Admission of a codefendant's pretrial confession incriminating the defendant violates the Sixth Amendment right of confrontation when the codefendant does not testify at trial.

Chapter 15

SPEEDY TRIAL

Focal Points for Chapter 15

- Delay in bringing the charge.

- Delay in bringing defendant to trial.

- Statutory prompt disposition provisions.

In any jurisdiction, there are frequently three sources of speedy trial rights: court rules for docket control, statutes specifying time periods especially in pretrial stages, and constitutional guarantees of a speedy trial. Depending on the legal source, the issues in pre-charge delay and post-charge delay cases may vary. The issues addressed in a discussion about speedy disposition of charges include the following.

(1) When does the right attach, e.g, at the time of the crime, arrest, formal charge?

(2) To whom does the right apply, e.g., all defendants, only defendants who have been unable to obtain pretrial release?

(3) How much time must elapse for a violation? Is that lapse of time dispositive of the issue or does it serve merely as a triggering mechanism which requires inquiry into other issues?

(4) Are some types of delay excusable, e.g., delay attributable to defense motions or the defendant's unavailability?

(5) To assert the right to a speedy disposition, must the defendant demand that disposition? If so, does that demand trigger the running of the time period or is it merely one of several factors for analysis?

(6) To obtain relief, must the defendant show prejudice to the defense case?

(7) What sanctions are available for a violation, e.g., dismissal with or without prejudice to the charges being brought again?

A. Delay in Bringing the Charge

Many jurisdictions do not apply a statute of limitations to felony prosecutions, but most use them for misdemeanor charges. However, constitutional due process rights may protect a defendant from delay between commission of the crime and the earlier of the arrest, indictment or information. However, proving a constitutional violation is difficult. In *United States v. Lovasco*, 431 U.S. 783 (1977), the defendant tried to invoke the Fifth Amendment due process right when the indictment was filed seventeen months after the investigator's report. The Court held that there was no due process violation even if the defendant is somewhat prejudiced, if the delay in obtaining the indictment ensures that the correct charges are brought against the appropriate defendants.

To establish a federal constitutional due process violation based on pre-charge delay, a defendant must show that (1) the delay resulted in actual prejudice to the ability of the defense to present its case; and (2) the prosecution's conduct was intentional and motivated by an intent to harass the defendant or to gain a tactical advantage over the defendant. In each case, the reasons for the delay and the prospective impact on a trial are relevant. The burden of establishing actual prejudice is a heavy one, with the defendant having to provide proof that the delay substantially prejudiced the defense. The defendant must show how any evidence or witnesses now unavailable would have assisted the defense or what exculpatory evidence would have been offered. Prejudice is not established merely by a claim of faded memory, inability to locate a witness, or a witness's refusal to testify. Moreover, the mere passage of time is insufficient. In addition, even if the defendant is able to show actual prejudice, there must be evidence that the delay was used deliberately by the prosecution to gain a tactical advantage. The requirement of purposeful delay reflects a judicial reluctance to interfere with prosecutorial discretion.

B. Delay in Bringing Defendant to Trial

An accused's right to a speedy trial is guaranteed by both the United States and state constitutions. The constitutional right to a speedy trial includes the right to speedy sentencing and a speedy appeal. The Sixth Amendment states in part that "[i]n all criminal prosecutions, the accused shall enjoy the right to a speedy . . . trial . . ." In *Barker v. Wingo,* 407 U.S. 514 (1972), the Court noted that the right to a speedy trial "is generically different from any of the other rights enshrined in the Constitution for the protection of the accused." First, society has an interest in a speedy trial for all accused that exists separate from and at times in opposition to the rights of the accused. Courts unable to provide prompt trials contribute to a backlog of cases enabling defendants to negotiate more effectively for guilty pleas and otherwise manipulate the system. Released persons awaiting trial for long periods have an opportunity to commit other crimes, especially the offense of bail jumping. For defendants confined to the deplorable conditions in some local jails because they cannot obtain pretrial release, delay can also have a detrimental effect on prospects for rehabilitation.

Second, the constitutional right, which has been applied to the states through the Fourteenth Amendment, probably is the only part of the Bill of Rights that most defendants are willing to ignore. After all, a decision by the prosecution to delay or drop criminal charges would satisfy most defendants, because no conviction may result. From the defendant's perspective, although delay is a often a common defense tactic, there is a concern that as the delay lengthens, witnesses may become unavailable or their memories may fade. The defendant's concern is that the prosecutor will not drop the charges, and that the delay of the trial will leave the accused in jail, without the ability to either provide for family or assist in the preparation of the defense case. However, unlike the right to counsel or the privilege against self-incrimination, the right to a speedy trial does not per se prejudice a defendant's ability to defend himself.

The right to a speedy trial attaches from the earlier of the date of the indictment or information, or the date of the arrest, *i.e.*, when the person becomes "accused." Similarly, the right to a speedy trial attaches when a detainer is lodged against an accused who is serving a sentence on other charges. Once the right to a speedy trial attaches, it continues until the charges are dismissed. The time between the dismissal and a new related charge does not count for purposes of the right to a speedy trial, i.e., once charges are dismissed, the person is no longer a subject of public accusation and has no restraints on liberty. Similarly, the time during which a prosecution's interlocutory appeal of a dismissal, while the defendant is not incarcerated and not subject to bail, does not count. However, due process may afford some protection if the defendant can identify prejudice from the delay.

In *Barker*, the Court held that any inquiry into a constitutional speedy trial claim requires a balancing of at least four factors: (1) the length of the delay; (2) the reasons for the delay; (3) whether and how the defendant asserted the speedy trial right; and (4) the amount of prejudice from the delay suffered by the defendant. Because of this balancing approach, it is impossible to determine with precision when the constitutional right has been denied. The Court thus rejected two alternate approaches: that a defendant must be tried within a specific time period, and a defendant's demand for a speedy trial right is a necessary precondition to judicial consideration of a constitutional violation. The first approach was rejected because there is no constitutional basis for quantifying the right as a function of a specific number of days or months. The latter approach was disapproved as inconsistent with the Court's pronouncements about the waiver of constitutional rights as an "intentional relinquishment or abandonment of a known right or privilege."

Barker held that the length of the delay serves as a threshold requirement or "triggering mechanism" for finding a violation of the speedy trial right. Although the length of the delay alone does not establish a constitutional violation, a court need not inquire into the other factors unless it finds the delay to be presumptively prejudicial. Later decisions have suggested that a delay of at least twelve months triggers further analysis under *Barker* because that delay was presumptively prejudicial.

Courts weigh delays intended to gain a trial advantage more heavily against the prosecution than unintentional delays resulting from institutional dysfunction. In the absence of a showing of bad faith or dilatory motive, the prosecution is not responsible for delays attributable to its own acts. Neutral reasons such as negligence and overcrowded calendars weigh less heavily, but are still considered because responsibility for such conditions rests with the prosecution. A period of delay attributable to tactics by the defendant is deemed a waiver of the right to a speedy trial for that period of delay.

Despite the view that a defendant does not have the duty to bring himself to trial, the defendant's failure to demand a speedy trial undercuts the defendant's constitutional argument. By contrast, a vigorous and timely assertion of the right provides strong evidence that the defendant is interested in a speedy disposition. A court will not treat a claim seriously that a trial started too late unless the defendant continuously has sought a speedy trial.

Barker stated that a court must weigh any prejudice to the defendant in light of the interests protected by the speedy trial guarantee: preventing oppressive pretrial incarceration, minimizing anxiety of the accused, and limiting impairment to the defense. Courts typically do not take the first two types of allegations very seriously. The third allegation is serious, and if demonstrated usually will result in a finding of prejudice. In *Reed v. Farley*, 512 U.S. 339 (1994), the Court, citing *Barker*, asserted that a "showing of prejudice is required to establish a violation of the Sixth Amendment Speedy Trial Clause, and that necessary ingredient is entirely missing here." *Reed* suggests a modification of the balancing test announced in *Barker*.

Doggett v. United States, 505 U.S. 647 (1992) also signaled a change in the *Barker* test by suggesting a relationship between the reason for the delay and the allocation of the burden of proof on the prejudice issue. On the one hand, when the reason for the delay is attributable to reasonable diligence by the prosecution, the defendant must show specific prejudice. At the other extreme, when the reason for the delay is intentional misconduct by the prosecution, a presumption of prejudice is "virtually automatic," with the burden of proof on the government to overcome the presumption. It is uncertain which party has the burden of proof when the reason for the delay is governmental negligence.

Barker expressly stated that dismissal with prejudice is the only possible remedy for a violation of the Sixth Amendment speedy trial right. Trial courts therefore cannot devise less extreme remedies such as a sentence reduction. The reprosecution prohibition probably results in fewer decisions finding constitutional violations. An alternative disposition is to find a violation of the relevant speedy trial statute (e.g., 18 U.S.C. § 3161 et seq) or the relevant docket control rule (*e.g.*, Federal Rule of Criminal Procedure 48(b)), both of which may prescribe dismissal without prejudice as an available method of enforcement. Still another remedy is to provide a writ of mandamus to compel a trial court to set a trial date for the defendant's case.

C. Statutory Prompt Disposition Provisions

An inmate in one jurisdiction has a Sixth Amendment right to a speedy trial on charges pending in another jurisdiction. A prosecutor must make a good faith and diligent effort to speedily prosecute inmates confined in other jurisdictions. Congress and most state legislatures are signatories to the Interstate Agreement on Detainers, which is intended to enable an inmate in one state to force the expeditious disposition of outstanding charges in other states. Prosecutors also can obtain prisoners for trial under the compact. The interstate compact is enacted in 48 states, Puerto Rico, the Virgin Islands, the District of Columbia, and the United States. As a congressionally sanctioned compact, it is a federal law subject to federal construction. When there is a pending charge in another county of the same state, separate intrastate statutes often permit the inmate to request a speedy disposition of the untried charge. *See, e.g.,* the Uniform Mandatory Disposition of Detainers Act.

In addition to the constitutional speedy trial standard and interstate compacts, many state legislatures and the Congress have enacted speedy trial legislation which establishes specific time limits for completing stages of a criminal prosecution. For example, the federal Speedy Trial Act (18 U.S.C. § 3161 et seq.) requires that an arrested defendant be formally charged within thirty days after the arrest and that the defendant's trial begin within seventy days after the formal charge is filed. In addition, the trial cannot begin earlier than thirty days from the date the defendant first appears before the court unless the defendant consents in writing to an earlier trial. Unlike the constitutional standard which makes the passage of time a "triggering mechanism," the statute makes the passage of time dispositive of whether there is a violation. Most speedy trial statutes, like the federal Act, do not require a defendant to show either that he demanded a speedy trial or that the effect of the delay was prejudicial.

Certain types of pretrial delays are automatically excluded from the computation of legislative time limits, e.g., periods of delay like the absence or unavailability of the defendant or an essential witness, delays resulting from the joinder of a codefendant, and delays resulting from other proceedings involving the defendant. The "other proceedings" provision requires exclusion of all delays attributable to pendency of pretrial motions regardless of whether the delays are reasonably necessary. Indeed, some courts have held that time for *preparation* of pretrial motions is properly excludable.

Continuances granted when the "ends of justice" outweigh the interest of the public and the defendant in a speedy trial give trial judges the flexibility to address complex or unusual cases. By contrast, a court cannot grant a continuance for delays caused by general congestion of the court calendar, or by the prosecution's failure to prepare diligently or obtain available witnesses.

To compute whether there has been a statutory violation, the court calculates the gross elapsed days and subtracts the number of days attributable to excludable time, leaving the net elapsed days. If the Act's time limits are not met, the charges against a defendant must be dismissed. The key determination for the trial judge is whether the dismissal must be with or without prejudice. The judge considers three factors in exercising discretion to dismiss charges with or without prejudice: 1) the seriousness of the offense; 2) the circumstances leading to dismissal; and 3) the effect of reprosecution on the administration of justice and the legislation. 18 U.S.C. § 3162(a)(1)–(2). It is an abuse of discretion if the trial judge fails to consider each statutory factor and explain other factors relied upon in deciding whether to dismiss charges.

A defendant cannot prospectively execute a written waiver of statutory speedy trial rights. In *Zedner v. United States*, 126 S.Ct. 1976 (2006), the Supreme Court stated that, under § 3162(a)(2), a waiver of the right to dismissal for a past statutory violation occurs when a defendant fails to filed a motion for dismissal before trial or entering a guilty plea. However, that provision does not indicate the Congress intended to permit prospective waivers, i.e., a defendant cannot opt out of the Act's requirements prior to a violation.

POINTS TO REMEMBER

- Due process may protect an accused from delay between the crime and the earlier of an arrest, indictment or information.

- A defendant must prove that the prosecutor's delay in charging was intentional and resulted in actual prejudice to the defendant's ability to present a case.

- The Sixth Amendment speedy trial right protects a defendant from delay from the earlier of the arrest or formal charge to the trial.

- A balancing of the length of the delay, reasons for the delay, assertion of the speedy trial right, and any prejudice from the delay determines whether there is a speedy trial violation.

- Several jurisdictions have speedy trial statutes which measure a violation only by the lapse of a specific length of time, after subtracting time attributable to specific types of excludable delay.

Chapter 16

DISCOVERY AND DISCLOSURE

Focal Points for Chapter 16

- Constitutional duty of prosecution to disclose exculpatory evidence.

- Defense discovery under rules or statutes.

- Prosecutorial discovery under rules of statutes.

- Discovery sanctions.

Pretrial discovery is the process of exchanging information between the prosecution and the defense. Prior to using the discovery rules, the defense may utilize informal methods for obtaining information from the prosecution. Prosecutors primarily look to police departments and grand jury investigations to uncover relevant facts. The grand jury offers prosecutors many of the advantages that civil litigants obtain through discovery depositions. The grand jury has the power to compel testimony and documents from many sources, and, unlike a civil deposition, the whole process occurs ex parte and in secret. The prosecutor proceeds unhampered by objections. The witness testifies without the presence of counsel.

Defendants, on the other hand, have no control over the grand jury process and in many cases are unaware of the grand jury's investigation until it results in an indictment. Once the investigation is complete, as a general rule defendants are not even entitled to the transcribed record of grand jury proceedings unless and until a grand jury witness later testifies for the government at trial.

Defendants, however, have many other avenues for discovery. A motion for a bill of particulars requests more specific information about the charge described in the indictment or information upon which the accused will stand trial. The charging instrument often sets forth the "bare bones" of the crime in conclusory language such as "the defendant did murder the victim at such a time and place." In order to prepare a meaningful trial defense, a bill of particulars might ask for a description of the particular form of murder (e.g., premeditated murder or felony murder) and the specific method by which the alleged murder was committed (e.g., with a gun, knife, or chain saw). In contrast to rules which mandate certain forms of discovery, the granting of a bill of particulars is largely discretionary with the judge; the important issue in each case is whether the information claimed to be omitted from the indictment has deprived the defendant of a substantial right and subjects him to being tried for a charge for which he has not been indicted.

As discussed previously, a preliminary hearing often yields important information about the nature of the prosecution's case. Although discovery is not an avowed purpose of preliminary hearings, discovery is an inherent byproduct of the requirement that the prosecution present at least a prima facie case to a judicial officer. Prosecutors, however, often limit the defense opportunity for discovery at the preliminary hearing by presenting the minimum evidence required to certify the case for trial, and some jurisdictions have been particularly hostile to defense counsel's efforts to expand the preliminary hearing into a discovery vehicle.

Outside the confines of judicial proceedings, discovery may occur as part of the give and take of plea bargaining between defense counsel and the prosecutor. Some prosecutors subscribe to an "open office" philosophy where the prosecutor voluntarily discusses the nature of the government's case and makes documentary and real evidence available for inspection by the defense.

In the absence of voluntary disclosure, the parties either must ask the court to order pretrial discovery or conduct discovery outside the purview of the court by making informal requests of each other. When granting a motion for discovery the court will specify the time, place, and manner of making the discovery, and may prescribe such additional terms and conditions as are required to prevent confusion or misunderstandings between defense counsel and the prosecutor. Since the rise of concern for "victim's rights," statutes and court rules often authorize the court to issue protective orders barring or limiting disclosures that would otherwise be required. If the court orders discovery, the parties have a continuing duty to disclose, as it becomes available, any additional evidence or material covered by the discovery order. The party seeking discovery is entitled to a reasonable opportunity to examine the discovery material and prepare for its use at trial. If counsel fails to provide adequate discovery, the court may order counsel to make further disclosure, grant a continuance of the trial to allow for additional discovery, or prohibit counsel from introducing at trial any undisclosed evidence.

At early common law, courts lacked any inherent authority to require pretrial discovery. During the 1940's, however, discovery in civil cases was dramatically expanded to give each side pretrial access to almost all relevant information possessed by the other side. The success of this liberalized civil discovery generated proposals to similarly expand pretrial discovery in criminal cases. Proponents of expanded discovery conceded that surprising the opponent at trial created exciting drama, but insisted that a criminal trial should emphasize the quest for truth rather than the gamesmanship of opposing counsel.

Opponents of expansive discovery contended that liberal discovery in criminal cases would give an unfair advantage to the defense because the defendant's privilege against self-incrimination would prohibit the prosecution from discovering defense evidence. The issues raised in the discovery debate have been resolved in each jurisdiction by court rules or statutes which detail what discovery must or may be granted to each side. Although the specific rules of each jurisdiction vary, most jurisdictions require the government to disclose: (1) prior statements of the defendant that are in the possession of the prosecution or other government agencies such as the police department; (2) a copy of the defendant's prior criminal record; (3) documents and tangible objects the prosecution intends to use at trial; and (4) scientific reports and tests such as autopsy reports and fingerprint analysis. In return, many jurisdictions require the defense to inform the prosecution of the defendant's intent to raise certain defenses such as alibi, insanity, self-defense or entrapment.

A. Constitutional Discovery

Although most discovery occurs under the authority of local statutes and court rules, the United States Constitution requires disclosure of certain information possessed by the government. Beginning with *Brady v. Maryland*, 373 U.S. 83 (1963), the Court has held that intentional or inadvertent suppression by the prosecution of evidence favorable to an accused upon request violates due process where the evidence is material either to guilt or punishment. *Cone v. Bell*, 129 S.Ct. 1769 (2009). Whether the prosecution was acting in good faith at the time of nondisclosure is not relevant to constitutional analysis; a showing of materiality, which is interchangeable with prejudice to the defendant, is critical.

United States v. Bagley, 473 U.S. 667 (1985) and *Kyles v. Whitley*, 514 U.S. 419 (1995) altered the scope and nature of earlier tests. First, the Court stated that impeachment evidence as well as exculpatory evidence is part of a prosecutor's constitutional duty to disclose. Second, a reversal for failure to disclose is to be determined by one standard regardless of whether there is no request, a general request, or a specific request for information: whether there was "a reasonable probability that, had the evidence been disclosed to the defense, the result of the proceeding would have been different." In *Kyles*, the Court noted that "[t]he question is not whether the defendant would be more likely than not have received a different verdict with the evidence, but whether in its absence he received a fair trial, understood as a trial resulting in a verdict worthy of confidence. [A] defendant need not demonstrate that after discounting the inculpatory evidence in light of the undisclosed evidence, there would not have been enough left to convict." Despite the comprehensive nature of the new standards, it is probably just as important under *Bagley* to make the request for information as specific as possible. *Bagley* noted the greater potential for prejudice in a specific request case, where an incomplete response by the prosecution might cause the defense to abandon lines of investigation, defenses or trial strategies that it otherwise would have pursued.

The constitutional determination of materiality for suppressed evidence is made collectively, not item-by-item. The cumulative standard of materiality requires the prosecutor to inquire in every case what, if any, evidence is undisclosed and to disclose when she believes that the materiality standard is satisfied. That duty includes a duty to learn about any favorable evidence known to the police or anyone else acting on behalf of the government in connection with the case.

The prosecution can refuse to disclose evidence before trial or try to save a conviction after trial by reasoning that the evidence against the defendant was overwhelming. Less than one year after *Kyles* announced that "*Bagley* error . . . cannot subsequently be found harmless," the Court retreated. After pointing out that it was not " 'reasonably likely' that disclosure of polygraph results . . . would have resulted in a different outcome at trial," the Court stated that even without the pertinent witness's testimony, the case against the defendant was "overwhelming."

The cases refer to favorable evidence as a method of describing material evidence. Helpful evidence is not necessarily favorable. For example, knowledge of evidence incriminating to the defendant may be helpful but it is not regarded as favorable. Negative test results are favorable, but inconclusive test results are not. The prosecutor's initial responsibility is to ascertain whether any evidence in the government's possession qualifies as favorable. If the evidence qualifies as favorable, the prosecutor must decide if it is material.

Lower courts have differed as to whether *Brady* applies to information that may be favorable to the defense, but which is inadmissible at trial, *e.g.*, inadmissible hearsay that the crime was committed by another person. Some courts limit *Brady* to material that would be admissible at trial, while others apply *Brady* to any information that might be useful in preparing a defense strategy.

Besides failure to disclose, another prohibited situation described by the Supreme Court is the prosecution's knowing failure to disclose perjured testimony. The defendant must prove that the witness committed perjury and that the prosecutor knew or should have known about it. The standard of materiality in these cases is whether "there is any reasonable likelihood that the false testimony could have affected the judgment of the jury."

Despite the motion for extensive disclosure, the right to discover potentially exculpatory evidence is not unlimited, nor will discovery be ordered upon pure speculation as to the possibly exculpatory nature of the requested materials. The defendant is entitled to inspect documents or other objects only upon a "plausible" showing that it might have exculpatory relevance. Even if discovery is ordered, the defendant has no constitutional right to search through the government's files free of court supervision. In *Pennsylvania v. Ritchie*, 480 U.S. 39 (1987), the Supreme Court held that the defendant's right to discovery could be fully protected by requiring that the requested files be submitted to the trial court for *in camera* review. The trial court could then determine whether the files contain information that probably would change the outcome of the trial, and thus must be disclosed to the defendant.

Recent case law has addressed whether a defendant who is considering a guilty plea has a constitutional right to disclosure of material evidence that the defendant could use at trial on the issue of guilty or for impeachment. In *United States v. Ruiz*, 536 U.S. 622 (2002), the Court held that a defendant has no constitutional right to disclosure of impeachment information prior to a guilty plea. Impeachment evidence's value to a defendant depends on how much he already knows about the case against him, and there is a small risk that innocent defendants would plead guilty without impeachment information. The Court left open whether pre-guilty plea disclosure of other types of *Brady* material is required.

The constitutional right to discovery of exculpatory evidence does not require the government to *preserve* all potentially exculpatory evidence for possible discovery by defendants. For example, police may be unable to recall all other investigative "leads" they pursued before arresting the suspect. In *California v. Trombetta*,

467 U.S. 479 (1984) though, the Court held that evidence must be preserved when its exculpatory value was apparent before the evidence was destroyed and when the evidence was of such a nature that the defendant would be unable to obtain comparable evidence by other reasonably available means. Unless a criminal defendant can show bad faith on the part of the police, failure to preserve potentially useful evidence does not constitute a denial of due process.

B. Discovery Under Rules and Statutes

Brady's due process obligation to disclose exculpatory evidence overrides any limitations on discovery provided by a jurisdiction's discovery statutes or rules. Regardless of whether *Brady* is applicable, each state is free to set discovery requirements as broadly or narrowly as it pleases. The only constitutional limitation on the state's choice is that the state must be even handed in its treatment of the prosecution and the defense. In *Wardius v. Oregon*, 412 U.S. 470 (1973), the state required the defendant to disclose his intent to present an alibi defense, but the defendant had no right of discovery against the prosecution. The Supreme Court stated:

> Although the Due Process Clause has little to say regarding the amount of discovery which the parties must be afforded, it does speak to the balance of forces between the accused and his accuser. . .In the absence of a strong showing of state interests to the contrary, discovery must be a two-way street. The State may not insist that trials be run as a "search for truth" so far as defense witnesses are concerned, while maintaining "poker game" secrecy for its own witnesses. It is fundamentally unfair to require a defendant to divulge the details of his own case while at the same time subjecting him to the hazard of surprise covering refutation of the very pieces of evidence which he disclosed to the State.

Given the limited holding of *Wardius*, it is not surprising to find broad variations among the states' discovery provisions. While some jurisdictions provide for broad discovery, others place severe limitations on the government's obligation to disclose portions of its case. Rule 16 of the Federal Rules of Criminal Procedure serves as a model for discovery rules in many jurisdictions.

Discovery provisions commonly extend only to those discoverable items within the prosecutor's possession, custody or control. This concept reflects an extension of discovery beyond information that the prosecution intends to use at trial. It clearly encompasses the files of the police department working with the prosecutor in a particular case, but there may be a question about whether "control" extends to any prosecutorial or law enforcement officer to which the prosecution might have access. Federal Rule 16 states that discovery may be had of information 1) within the possession, custody or control of the government, and 2) which the prosecutor knows or by the exercise of due diligence could know of its existence.

Discovery provisions commonly include an exemption from discovery that will exempt some form of prosecution work product. Federal Rule 16 states that, except as provided in the subsections authorizing discovery of the defendant's own statements, prior records, and reports of examinations and scientific tests, the rule "does not authorize the discovery or inspection of reports, memoranda, or other internal government documents made by an attorney for the government or other government agent investigating or prosecuting the case." The provision encompasses non-opinion as well as opinion work product, but unlike civil discovery it does not provide for disclosure of the non-opinion portions upon a showing of substantial need and undue hardship.

Where discovery provisions provide for mandatory defense discovery, the discovery is always subject to possible restriction through judicial issuance of a protective order. For example, Federal Rule 16 notes that upon a sufficient showing, the court may at any time order that discovery or inspection be denied, restricted, or deferred, or make such other order that is appropriate.

Federal Rule 16(a)(1)(B) requires the prosecution to disclose to the defense all relevant written or recorded statements of the defendant within the prosecution's possession or control. (While the defendant can obtain his own grand jury testimony, pretrial discovery under the federal rules prohibits access to other grand jury testimony.) Strong support for discovery of these statements is based on four considerations. First, the precise wording of the defendant's statement is especially important to defense counsel in preparing for trial or in determining whether a guilty plea is advisable. Second, disclosure does not pose a substantial threat of successful perjury since the defendant may be impeached effectively by reference to his own statement. Third, the disclosure of the defendant's statement does not create a reciprocity problem, because the state gained discovery from the defendant in obtaining the statement from him. Finally, if disclosure were not granted directly by the rule, the defendant would simply use a motion to suppress as an indirect discovery device.

In addition to defense discovery of written or recorded statements, Rule 16(a)(1)(A) permits discovery of the substance of any relevant oral statement made by the defendant whether before or after arrest in response to any interrogation by any person then known to the defendant to be a government agent. The rule's language requires no discovery of the defendant's blurted statements or of statements made by the defendant to someone he did not know was an agent for the government.

Only about one-third of the states have provisions requiring pretrial disclosure of a codefendant's statement, although some states grant discretion to the trial court to order disclosure where it would not conflict with any exemptions or prohibitions contained in the discovery provisions. If the codefendant will testify as a prosecution witness, disclosure is likely to be required where the statements of trial witnesses are discoverable before trial.

In addition to statements from the defendant, defense discovery rules like Federal Rule 16(a)(1)(F) commonly require pretrial disclosure of reports on physical and mental examinations and about scientific tests or experiments that are within the prosecution's possession or control. Pretrial disclosure is justified because once a report is prepared a scientific expert's position is not readily influenced and disclosure presents little danger of encouraging perjury or witness intimidation.

As with physical and mental examinations results and scientific reports, Federal Rule 16(a)(1)(E) allows a defendant to inspect and copy books, papers, documents, photographs, tangible objects, buildings or places which are within the possession, custody or control of the government under certain circumstances. Such objects must be either material to the preparation of the defendant's defense, intended for use at trial by the government as evidence during its case in chief, or were obtained from or belong to the defendant. However, the discovery rules are not intended to enable a defendant to examine documents which are material to the preparation of a constitutional defense such as selective prosecution. *United States v. Armstrong*, 517 U.S. 456 (1996).

C. Discovery by the Prosecution

Prosecutorial discovery may occur by operation of the general discovery rules, such as Federal Rule 16, or by subject specific rules like Federal Rules 12.1 and 12.2. By the general discovery rule, the prosecution's right to discovery is conditioned upon whether the defense has been granted discovery. Thus if the defendant files no motion or request to discover the prosecution's evidence, the prosecution will have no right to discover defense evidence. If, however, the defendant has been granted discovery, the prosecution may be granted a reciprocal right to discovery. For example, prosecutorial discovery under Federal Rule 16(b) is dependent upon prior defense discovery.

Many jurisdictions also give the prosecution an unconditional right to be notified prior to trial that the defendant intends to raise the defense of insanity and to present expert testimony to support this claim. Such provisions allow the prosecution the time to prepare its own expert witnesses to rebut the claim of insanity. Federal Rule 12.2 embodies the approach used by a majority of states. The Federal Rules also mandate the disclosure of defendant's intent to raise the defense of alibi under Rule 12.1, or an actual or believed exercise of public authority on behalf of a law enforcement or Federal intelligence agency under Federal Rule 12.3.

At least with respect to an alibi defense, *Williams v. Florida*, 399 U.S. 78 (1970) held that such disclosure rules do not violate the Fifth Amendment. In *Williams*, the defendant sought to be excused from Florida's notice-of-alibi rule that required him to give notice in advance of trial if he intended to claim an alibi and to furnish the prosecutor with information about the place he claimed to have been and the names of witnesses he intended to call in support of his alibi. The Court concluded that the privilege against self-incrimination is not violated by a requirement that the defendant give pretrial notice of an alibi defense and disclose his alibi witnesses. At most, the Court found that the rule compelled the defendant merely to accelerate the timing of his disclosure.

The federal notice-of-alibi rule requires a prosecutor to initiate a request to the defendant for written notice about his intent to rely on an alibi defense. The notice by the defendant must state the place at which the defendant claims to have been at the time of the offense, along with the same type of information required by the Florida rule. In the spirit of *Wardius*'s call for reciprocity, the prosecution must supply information establishing the defendant's presence at the crime and rebutting the alibi defense. If the defendant later withdraws the alibi defense, the fact of the withdrawal is not admissible against him.

Most states and the federal rules also require a defendant to give advance notice about the intent to rely on a defense of insanity, or the intent to introduce expert testimony that he lacked the mental state for the offense. The scope of the rule is broader than first appears, because it addresses issues far beyond insanity issues. The defendant must notify the prosecutor in writing of such intent, without waiting for the prosecutor to initiate the process. The prosecutor has no reciprocal duty under most rules. The trial judge may order the defendant to submit to a mental examination, but any statements to the examiner by the defendant are inadmissible on any issue other than his mental condition. As with the alibi notice rule, a withdrawn defense by the defendant is inadmissible. When Federal Rule 12.2 is used to address the issue of the defendant's mental condition, the federal rules address both parties' obligation to disclose a written summary of expert testimony that the party intends to use during its case-in-chief, describing the witnesses' opinions, the bases and reasons for those opinions, and the witnesses' qualifications. Federal Rule of Criminal Procedure 16(a)(1)(G); 16(b)(1)(C).

Generally, the federal rules do not authorize pretrial discovery of the identities of prosecution or defense witnesses. However, Federal Rule 26.2 permits *both* the defense and prosecution on motion to obtain any pretrial statement of any prosecution or defense witness in the possession of the opposition, after the witness testifies on direct examination. The key to understanding Rule 26.2 is the definition of a "statement" in Rule 26.2(f), which can be a written statement made and signed or adopted or approved by the witness, or a substantially verbatim recital of an oral statement that is recorded contemporaneously and contained in a recording or transcription of a recording.

D. Regulation of Discovery

The criminal defendant's right to pretrial discovery may come in conflict with the privacy rights of victims or other third parties. All jurisdictions empower the court to issue protective orders or limit the scope and terms of discovery, subject of course to constitutional limitations. If either party fails to comply with the court's discovery orders the court generally has a number of options for dealing with the violation. The remedies depend on the degree of the alleged violation as well as the prejudice which the offended party can establish. Possible sanctions authorized in various states include: an instruction to the jury to assume the accuracy of certain facts that might have been established through the nondisclosed material, holding the offending party in contempt of court; declaration of a mistrial, or in the case of a violation by the government, dismissal of the prosecution. The least drastic and preferred remedy for violations of discovery orders is to order immediate disclosure and offer a continuance for the party to examine the material.

In appropriate cases, *Taylor v. Illinois*, 484 U.S. 400 (1988) recognized that more drastic remedies are constitutionally permissible. In that case, the Court held that no violation of the Sixth Amendment Compulsory Process Clause occurred when the trial judge refused to allow a defense witness to testify because defense counsel engaged in wilful misconduct by ignoring the discovery rules to gain a tactical advantage. While other sanctions are usually adequate, in some instances preclusion of testimony or other evidence is the only effective remedy for what the court perceives to be a deliberate violation of the court's rules. In deciding what sanction to apply, *Taylor* noted that the judge balances the defendant's right to offer testimony against the (1) integrity of the adversary process, (2) the interest in the fair and efficient administration of justice, (3) the potential prejudice to the truth-determining function of the trial process, (4) the nature of the explanation given for the party's failure seasonably to comply with discovery requests, (5) the wilfulness of the violation, the simplicity of compliance, and (6) whether an unfair tactical advantage was being sought. Because the fault in violating the discovery rules usually belongs to the defense counsel rather than the defendant, a frequent concern may be that the exclusion sanction visits the blatant sins of the lawyer upon the client. Worse, the potential exists that a permissible sanction may be to preclude the defendant from testifying.

POINTS TO REMEMBER

- A prosecutor must disclose to the defendant exculpatory and impeachment evidence that is material to the defendant's guilt or punishment.

- The evidence must be disclosed regardless of whether the defendant requests the evidence.

- Evidence is material if there is a reasonable probability that the result of the trial would have been different if the evidence had been disclosed.

- The evidence must be favorable to the defendant, not merely neutral.

- Procedural rules provide for the defendant to request information from the prosecution about defendant's statements, reports of scientific tests, and documents and tangible objects.

- If a defendant requests and obtains information from the prosecution, the prosecution may obtain reports of scientific tests as well as documents and objects from the defendant.

- Some jurisdictions permit the prosecution pretrial discovery about a defendant's alibi or a defendant's mental condition.

- A court has the discretion to refuse to allow a party to introduce evidence at trial which was not produced pursuant to a pretrial discovery rules.

Chapter 17

GUILTY PLEAS

Focal Points for Chapter 17

- Plea alternatives.

- Plea negotiations.

- Legality and enforcement of plea agreements.

- Judicial role in plea agreements.

- Withdrawing a guilty plea.

Public perception to the contrary, most criminal cases are disposed of other than by a full trial by jury. It has been estimated that guilty pleas account for the disposition of as many as 95% of all criminal cases. This figure is probably correct when one considers that a guilty plea to one charge may dispose of multiple other cases by way of dismissal as part of a "package deal." While an attorney must obviously render competent services where the defendant's guilt is contested, it is probably also true that an attorney should explore the possibility that a case may be resolved in some manner other than a jury trial. This does not necessarily mean pleading to the charge and throwing one's client upon the mercy of the court. A host of procedural alternatives almost always exists.

A. Plea Alternatives

After an indictment or criminal information has been filed, the defendant is typically arraigned on that charging document and is asked to enter a plea in open court. The criminal rules contemplate that a defendant may plead not guilty, which, in any event, is a constitutional right. A plea of not guilty generally is regarded as a denial of every material allegation in the indictment. A defendant may plead not guilty and rely on all defenses, even those which are deemed to be affirmative in nature.

In many jurisdictions—if permitted by the procedural rules or by the court in the interests of justice—the accused may enter a plea of nolo contendere, *i.e.* indicating that he or she is simply not contesting the charges. Generally a "nolo plea" (as it is commonly called) is identical to a guilty plea except that, unlike a guilty plea (that has not been withdrawn), a nolo plea cannot be used as an admission of guilt against the defendant in a subsequent civil or administrative proceeding.

In addition, in most jurisdictions, instead of pleading guilty or not guilty (or entering a nolo plea), the defendant can invoke a psychological condition by pleading not guilty by reason of mental illness or mental retardation or, in some jurisdictions, guilty but mentally ill. A defendant may enter a plea of guilty but mentally ill if the court finds the defendant was mentally ill at the time of the offense. A defendant may be found guilty but mentally ill at a trial if the prosecution proves guilt beyond a reasonable doubt, and the defendant proves by a preponderance of the evidence that he was mentally ill at the time of the offense. In either case, the court may appoint at least one psychologist or psychiatrist to examine, treat and report on the defendant's mental condition at the time of sentencing. If the defendant is found guilty but mentally ill at the time of sentencing, treatment is provided for the defendant until the treating professional determines that such treatment is no longer necessary or until expiration of the sentence, whichever occurs first. Such treatment must be a condition of probation, shock probation, conditional discharge, parole or conditional release as long as the defendant requires treatment for the mental illness in the opinion of the treating professional.

A defendant may also plead guilty to the charges. A guilty plea is a defendant's admission in open court about committing the charges in the indictment. A plea of guilty differs in purpose and effect from a mere admission or an extrajudicial confession in that it is a conviction which is conclusive. A proper guilty plea dispenses with requirements of evidence of guilt. Once a guilty plea is entered, the court has nothing to do but impose sentence. A guilty plea constitutes a waiver of numerous constitutional rights, including the privilege against self-incrimination, a right to a trial by jury, and the right to confront one's accusers. While there are exceptions, a guilty plea constitutes an admission of all facts alleged and a waiver of all non-jurisdictional and procedural defects and constitutional infirmities in any prior stage of the proceeding. In addition, a guilty plea is a waiver of the right to appeal the conviction.

A defendant may wish to accept a plea bargain and plead guilty but continue to protest his or her innocence, because the defendant may desire to "take the plea bargain" and avoid the risk of going to trial where a higher sentence may be imposed. Nevertheless, since the trial court usually must find a factual basis for a guilty plea and insure that the plea is otherwise voluntary, the validity of such a plea is suspect. In *North Carolina v. Alford*, 400 U.S. 25 (1970), the Court allowed the use of a "best interest" guilty plea, and held that where a defendant is represented by competent counsel, and there is a record that strongly evinces guilt, an accused may voluntarily, knowingly, and understandingly consent to the imposition of a prison sentence even though the defendant is unwilling to admit participation in the crime, or even if the guilty plea contains a protestation of innocence.

In a number of jurisdictions, a defendant may, with the approval of the court, enter a conditional plea of guilty. In so doing, the defendant reserves in writing the right to appellate review of the adverse determination of any specified pretrial or trial motion. The conditional guilty plea avoids the necessity of a full trial for a defendant who wants appellate review of a claim but who heretofore had to go to trial to preserve the issue for appeal. Conditional pleas require that the court and the prosecutor approve the conditional guilty plea, and any defendant who prevails on appeal may later withdraw the conditional plea.

B. Plea Negotiation

Plea bargaining is one of the realities of the criminal justice system. Not only is plea bargaining enforceable, but the practice is sanctioned and encouraged. In *Blackledge v. Allison*, 431 U.S. 63 (1977) the Court held that:

Whatever might be the situation in an ideal world, the fact is that the guilty plea and the often concomitant plea bargain are important components of this country's criminal justice system. Properly administered, they can benefit all concerned. The defendant avoids extended pretrial incarceration and the anxieties and uncertainties of a trial; he gains a speedy disposition of his case, the chance to acknowledge his guilt, and a prompt start in realizing whatever potential there may be for rehabilitation. Judges and prosecutors conserve vital and scarce resources. The public is protected from the risks posed by those charged with criminal offenses who are at large on bail while awaiting completion of criminal proceedings.

The prosecutor frequently attempts to resolve a case by negotiations with the defense attorney. While the prosecutor may decide to negotiate with the defense attorney, the prosecutor is not compelled to do so. When the prosecutor does decide to negotiate, the system "presuppose[s] fairness." While a prosecutor cannot engage in vindictive conduct and must usually honor plea agreements, there are few legal sanctions which may be imposed on the prosecutor. Under the guise of allowing leniency in plea situations, the courts permit the prosecutor to engage in not so subtle threats. Thus, in *Bordenkircher v. Hayes*, 434 U.S. 357 (1978), the Court found that a prosecutor may carry out threats of increased charges made during plea negotiations if the defendant refuses to plead guilty to the original charge. While threats may be so severe as to set aside a later plea of guilty, in general, a plea is not involuntary because of fears of higher punishment.

The scope of the plea bargaining authority is very broad. A prosecutor may offer one defendant a "deal" and decline to negotiate with codefendants. In addition, the prosecutor may offer a "package deal" whereby all defendants in a single case must accept the terms or else the deal applies to none. The number of alternative plea options is almost limitless. Prosecutors nevertheless cannot base the decision to plea bargain upon unjustifiable standards such as race, religion or other arbitrary classification.

The reason defense lawyers continue to negotiate plea agreements is because of the fear that their clients may face uncertain punishment at trial. Indeed, the entire criminal justice system is geared toward encouraging guilty pleas. For example, in *Corbitt v. New Jersey*, 439 U.S. 212 (1978), the Court upheld a statute that allowed for a possibly lesser sentence for those who plead guilty but which was not available for those who went to trial. The practice of plea negotiations similarly encourages defendants to plead guilty rather than go to trial.

Obviously, an attorney must render competent service to the client during the plea bargaining process. The competency of counsel is frequently raised in post-conviction proceedings, since, absent rather narrow other factors, a defendant may not challenge a guilty plea unless the lawyer was incompetent. In general, mistaken tactical judgments about legal issues will not result in an invalid guilty plea. In *Brady v. United States*, 397 U.S. 742 (1970), the Court explained that the decision to

> plead guilty is heavily influenced by the defendant's appraisal of the prosecution's case . . . and by the apparent likelihood of securing leniency should a guilty plea be offered and accepted. Considerations like these frequently present imponderable questions for which there are no certain answers; judgments may be made that in the light of later events seem improvident, although they were perfectly sensible at the time. The rule that a plea must be intelligently made to be valid does not require that a plea be vulnerable to later attack if the defen-

dant did not correctly assess every relevant factor entering into his decision. A defendant is not entitled to withdraw his plea merely because he discovers long after the plea has been accepted that [he] misapprehended the quality of the State's case or the likely penalties attached to alternative courses of action. More particularly, absent misrepresentation or other impermissible conduct by state agents, a voluntary plea of guilty intelligently made in the light of the then applicable law does not become vulnerable because later judicial decisions indicate that the plea rested on a faulty premise. A plea of guilty triggered by the expectations of a competently counseled defendant that the State will have a strong case . . . is not subject to later attack because the defendant's lawyer correctly advised . . . as to possible penalties but later pronouncements of the courts, as in this case, hold that the maximum penalty for the crime in question was less than was reasonably assumed at the time the plea was entered.

In contrast to purely tactical recommendations, defense counsel must advise the defendant of the alternatives to a guilty plea. However, a defendant who does receive erroneous advice must have relied on it to the point that the plea would be otherwise involuntary. Assuming that the defense lawyer can obtain a plea offer from the prosecutor, the subsequent discussions with the client are of grave importance. Prior to trial a defendant is entitled to rely upon the lawyer to make an independent examination of the facts, circumstances, pleadings and laws involved and then to offer an informed opinion as to what plea should be entered. However, that assessment by counsel may be frustrated by the Court's refusal to require that the prosecution disclose to a defendant the same type of information constitutionally required for a defendant who is going to trial.

In making recommendations to plead guilty the defense attorney can be forceful through suggestion, but this cannot venture into deceit. If the defendant desires to plead guilty this can be done even if contrary to counsel's advice. After rendering competent legal advice, the final determination of a course of action should be that of the client and not the lawyer.

Implementation of a policy encouraging plea bargaining also requires encouraging frank communication between the defendant, counsel and the prosecution. No defendant or counsel will pursue such an effort if the fact of plea bargaining or statements made during the negotiations. Likewise, references by the defendant to the fact of plea bargaining or sentence negotiation are inadmissible. Notwithstanding the general prohibition on the admissibility of plea statements, a defendant can agree prior to plea discussions that any statement he made during those discussions could be used to impeach any contradictory statement if the case was tried. Waiver is not inconsistent with the rule's goal of encouraging voluntary settlement, because it "makes no sense to conclude that mutual settlement will be encouraged by precluding negotiation over an issue that may be particularly important to one of the parties to the transaction." *United States v. Mezzanatto*, 513 U.S. 196 (1995). Federal Rule 11(f) may apply (1) even though a guilty plea does not result or a guilty plea is entered but is later withdrawn, or (2) even though formal charges have not been filed at the time the statement is made.

The Federal Rules contain an elaborate structure of procedures for judicial consideration of plea agreements reached by parties. In *United States v. Hyde*, 520 U.S. 670 (1997), the Court observed that the Federal Rules:

> explicitly envision a situation in which the defendant performs his side of the bargain (the guilty plea) before the Government is required to perform its side (here, the motion to dismiss four counts). If the court accepts the agreement and thus the Government's promised performance, then the contemplated agreement is complete and the defendant gets the benefit of his bargain. But if the court rejects the Government's promised performance, then the agreement is terminated and the defendant has the right to back out of his promised performance (the guilty plea), just as a binding contractual duty may be extinguished by the nonoccurrence of a condition subsequent.

Not every criminal charge against a defendant ends in either a conviction or an acquittal. Sometimes, the charges are "dismissed" or other actions are taken. Federal Rule of Criminal Procedure 11(b)–(g) illustrate the different types of "plea agreements" which may be reached between a defendant and the government, and the procedure used to implement and safeguard such agreements. One type of plea agreement (sometimes referred to as an "A" agreement) recognized by the federal rules is that, in return for a guilty plea, the prosecutor will not bring, or will move to dismiss, other charges against the defendant. As part of a plea bargain agreement, the prosecutor may seek dismissal of the case with the court's permission. If the dismissal is granted before jeopardy attaches, subsequent reprosecution of the defendant may occur. A *nolle prosequi*, or nolle, is a formal declaration of record by the prosecution that it will not prosecute the case further either as to some of the counts of the indictment or as to some of the defendants. The prosecution thus may selectively "nolle" parts of the indictment, although it is not recognized by many courts.

As part of any plea agreement, especially an A agreement, the prosecution may reduce or amend a criminal charge on motion with leave of court. The reduction or amendment of charges is one of the most common elements in bargained pleas. The charge to which the plea is ultimately entered in such cases tends to reflect the severity of the defendant's conduct and the strength or weakness of the prosecutor's case, but it may bear little relationship to the charge initially brought in the case.

A second plea agreement (sometimes referred to as a "C" agreement) addressed in the federal rules is that the parties agree that a specific sentence or sentence range is the appropriate disposition of the case. The third type of plea agreement recognized by the federal rules (and sometimes referred to as a "B" agreement) is that the prosecutor will recommend, or agree not to oppose the defendant's request, that a specific sentence or sentence range is appropriate. The distinction between the an A or C agreement and a B agreement is that the court must accept or reject an A or C agreement, or may defer its decision until it has considered the presentence report. The necessity of an acceptance or rejection ensures that the defendant will either receive from the court the bargained for concessions or instead be given the opportunity to withdraw the plea.

Like an A agreement, under a B agreement the prosecutor is supposed to live up to the promise about the recommendation. However, the court is not bound in any way by the recommendation under a B agreement. In a B agreement, the court must advise the defendant that the opportunity to withdraw the plea does not exist if it decides not to follow the recommendation or request, because the recommendation or request by the prosecutor was all that the defendant was entitled to under the agreement. The court's advice to the defendant thus precludes the application of the acceptance provisions of Rule 11(c)(4) or a need for rejection of the agreement with the opportunity to withdraw under Rule 11(c)(5).

The three types of agreements specified in the federal rules are not mutually exclusive. Thus, if a defendant faces several charges, a B agreement may be reached to recommend a particular sentence on one count, and the prosecutor may move for dismissal of another count under an A agreement.

C. Legality and Enforcement of Plea Agreements

"[W]hen a plea rests in any significant degree on a promise or agreement of the prosecutor, so that it can be said to be part of the inducement or consideration, such promise must be fulfilled." *Santobello v. New York*, 404 U.S. 257 (1971). The threshold question relates to whether there was an agreement between the prosecutor and defendant. The agreement requires an offer and acceptance by both parties. Another important issue in the interpretation and application of a plea agreement is whether the parties intended that the agreement apply to a specific situation arising later. When a trial judge becomes involved in plea negotiations, the judge may be the source of a promise which induces the plea.

Assuming that a plea agreement exists between a defendant and the prosecution, who is bound by that agreement? In *Santobello*, the successor of the prosecutor who made a promise about sentencing to the defendant was bound by that promise. Generally, a plea agreement in a state prosecution is not binding on prosecutors in other jurisdictions or on officials in other parts of the same jurisdiction if they are not parties to the agreement.

If there is an agreement, did the prosecutor or defendant break the promise he made? A prosecutor is held to a high ethical standard, but that standard is not a constitutional requirement. A plea bargain standing alone has no constitutional significance since it is a mere executory agreement which, until embodied in the judgment of a court, does not deprive an accused of any constitutionally protected interest.

Although the prosecutor may make a pretrial agreement, the agreement is subject to the approval of the court. Some decisions indicate that the prosecution may unilaterally decide whether the defendant has broken the agreement. In *Ricketts v. Adamson*, 483 U.S. 1 (1987), the Court found that if a defendant refuses to provide the testimony he promised against a codefendant, in exchange for a reduction of charges, the guilty plea can be vacated because the defendant has breached his agreement. To avoid unilateral rescission of a plea agreement by the prosecution, a plea agreement should explicitly state that questions about the construction of the terms of the plea agreement must be decided by the court and not by the parties.

An agreement is not broken where the defendant receives what he or she bargained for. Alleged violations of plea agreements often focus on whether the prosecutor kept an agreement to recommend a particular sentence or at least not to oppose a desired disposition like probation. A prosecutor who keeps a promise to recommend a particular disposition need not do so enthusiastically or state the reasons for the recommendation.

What remedies are available for the unfulfilled agreement? In *Santobello*, the Supreme Court left to the discretion of the trial court whether a guilty plea should be set aside or specific performance of the prosecutor's promise should be granted.

D. The Judge's Role in Plea Bargaining and Considering Plea Agreements

Federal Rule 11(c)(1) prohibits the judge from participating in plea negotiations. There are valid reasons for a judge to avoid involvement in plea discussions. It might lead the defendant to believe that he would not receive a fair trial at a trial before the same judge. The risk of not going along with the disposition apparently desired by the judge might induce the defendant to plead guilty even if innocent. Such involvement makes it difficult for a judge to objectively assess the voluntariness of a plea. There are also several reasons in support of judicial participation in plea discussions. The plea itself becomes a more meaningful and informed plea, because it (1) causes the prosecutor to discuss freely the strength of the case, and (2) involves someone with a working knowledge of the wide array of sentencing possibilities.

A judge who considers a plea of guilty from a defendant must address the defendant personally in open court and determine that the plea is voluntary. The issue of voluntariness includes whether the defendant is capable of pleading guilty as well as whether the plea is the result of force, threats or promises that are not part of a plea agreement. In addition, the federal rules and many decisions suggest that a plea must be intelligently made, i.e., the defendant must have a sufficient amount of information about the charge to which he is pleading as well as the consequences of the plea.

While a defendant's guilty plea will be set aside if it is taken without the physical presence of the defendant, a defendant also must be mentally present, i.e., competent to stand trial. There is no higher mental standard required to enter a guilty plea than there is to stand trial. *Godinez v. Moran*, 509 U.S. 389 (1993).

A criminal defendant may not be tried unless he is competent and he may not waive his right to counsel or plead guilty unless he does so "competently and intelligently." In *Dusky v. United States*, 362 U.S. 402 (1960) (*per curiam*), we held that the standard for competence to stand trial is whether the de-

fendant has "sufficient present ability to consult with his lawyer with a reasonable degree of rational understanding" and
has "a rational as well as factual understanding of the proceedings against him." [W]hile we have described the standard for
competence to stand trial, however, we have never expressly
articulated a standard for competence to plead guilty or to
waive the right to the assistance of counsel. * * *

[E]ven assuming that there is some meaningful distinction between the capacity for "reasoned choice" and a "rational understanding" of the proceedings, we reject the notion that competence
to plead guilty or to waive the right to counsel must be measured by
a standard that is higher than (or even different from) the Dusky
standard.

We begin with the guilty plea. A defendant who stands trial is
likely to be presented with choices that entail relinquishment of the
same rights that are relinquished by a defendant who pleads guilty:
He will ordinarily have to decide whether to waive his "privilege
against compulsory self-incrimination" by taking the witness stand;
if the option is available, he may have to decide whether to waive
his "right to trial by jury"; and, in consultation with counsel, he may
have to decide whether to waive his "right to confront [his] accusers" by declining to cross-examine witnesses for the prosecution. A
defendant who pleads not guilty, moreover, faces still other strategic choices: In consultation with his attorney, he may be called upon
to decide, among other things, whether (and how) to put on a defense and whether to raise one or more affirmative defenses. In
sum, all criminal defendants—not merely those who plead guilty—
may be required to make important decisions once criminal proceedings have been initiated. And while the decision to plead guilty
is undeniably a profound one, it is no more complicated than the
sum total of decisions that a defendant may be called upon to make
during the course of a trial. (The decision to plead guilty is also
made over a shorter period of time, without the distraction and
burden of a trial.) This being so, we can conceive of no basis for demanding a higher level of competence for those defendants who
choose to plead guilty. If the Dusky standard is adequate for defendants who plead not guilty, it is necessarily adequate for those who
plead guilty. * * *

Requiring that a criminal defendant be competent has a modest aim: It seeks to ensure that he has the capacity to understand
the proceedings and to assist counsel. While psychiatrists and scho-
lars may find it useful to classify the various kinds and degrees of
competence, and while States are free to adopt competency stan-

dards that are more elaborate than the Dusky formulation, the Due Process Clause does not impose these additional requirements.

Prior drug use or addiction will not always make a plea involuntary unless the defendant is under the influence of drugs at the time he or she enters the plea. Where drugs are present at the time of the plea, the intoxication must be such as to render the defendant incompetent so as to lack an understanding of the plea.

The record of the trial court must affirmatively show that the defendant 1) waived the constitutional rights to silence, to a trial by jury, and to confront his accusers; and 2) both voluntarily waived those rights and understood the rights that he was waiving. *Boykin v. Alabama*, 395 U.S. 238 (1969). If a defendant testifies that the judge accepted a plea without explaining the rights or that the defendant did not understand the rights, the prosecution has the burden of proof that the judgment was entered in a way which fully protected the defendant's constitutional rights. A silent record does not suffice. In a recidivist proceeding, however, a presumption of regularity of the judgment exists. *Parke v. Raley*, 506 U.S. 20 (1992).

A waiver of counsel is "satisfied when the trial court informs the accused of the nature of the charges against him, of his right to be counseled regarding the plea, and of the range of allowable punishments attendant upon the entry of a guilty plea." However, prior to a guilty plea, a knowing and intelligent waiver of counsel does not constitutionally require warnings that the absence of counsel 1) raises the possibility that a viable defense would be overlooked, or 2) deprives a defendant of the opportunity for an independent opinion about the wisdom of pleading guilty. *Iowa v. Tovar*, 541 U.S. 77 (2004).

Prior to accepting a guilty plea, a trial court under the federal rules must inform the defendant of several sentencing consequences—the maximum aggregate sentence which could be imposed for the crimes to which the defendant is pleading guilty, any mandatory minimum penalty, any applicable forfeiture, order of restitution, or special assessment, the court's obligation to apply the federal Sentencing Guidelines, and the terms of any provision in the plea agreement waiving the defendant's right to appeal or collaterally attack the sentence.

The trial judge also should ensure that either it or defense counsel has informed the defendant of the nature of the charge to which the plea is offered. The defendant must understand the legal charge, not just the facts supporting the charge. A guilty plea is involuntary if the defendant is unaware of the essential elements of the offense to which he is pleading. In *Henderson v. Morgan*, 426 U.S. 637 (1976), the Court held that a plea was involuntary when neither defense counsel nor the trial court explained that intent was an element of second-degree murder.

> We assume, as petitioner argues, that the prosecutor had overwhelming evidence of guilt available. We also accept petitioner's characterization of the competence of respondent's counsel and of the wisdom of their advice to plead guilty to a charge of second-degree murder. Nevertheless, such a plea cannot support a judgment of guilt unless it was voluntary in a constitutional sense. And clearly the plea could not be voluntary in the sense that it constituted an intelligent admission that he committed the offense unless the defendant received "real notice of the true nature of the charge against him, the first and most universally recognized requirement of due process." There is nothing in this record that can serve as a substitute for either a finding after trial, or a voluntary admission, that respondent had the requisite intent.

The Court later retreated from its suggestion that the record should reflect the defendant's understanding of the essential elements of the criminal charge. "Where a defendant is represented by competent counsel, the court usually may rely on that counsel's assurance that the defendant has been properly informed of the nature and elements of the charge to which he is pleading guilty." *Bradshaw v. Stumpf*, 545 U.S. 175 (2005).

In *Bousley v. United States*, 523 U.S. 614 (1998), the defendant "claimed that his guilty plea was unintelligent because the District Court subsequently misinformed him as to the elements of [the] offense," and also argued that "the record reveals that neither he, nor his counsel, nor the court correctly understood the essential elements of the crime with which he was charged." The Court stated that he was not barred from pursuing his habeas corpus claim, because other cases rejecting a similar claim "involved a criminal defendant who pleaded guilty after being correctly informed as to the essential nature of the charge against him."

The court may decide not to accept a guilty plea unless there is a factual basis for the plea. The purpose of a factual basis is to ensure that the defendant does not mistakenly plead guilty when his actual conduct does not violate all the elements of the crime. A factual basis for the plea may be accomplished by having the prosecutor recite the facts or by having the defendant describe the conduct that gave rise to the charge, or a combination. Most courts recog-

nize that the evidence for the factual basis, whether from the prosecutor or from the defendant, need only be enough from which a
court can reasonably find that the defendant is guilty of the particular offense.

E. Withdrawing a Guilty Plea

It is not uncommon for a defendant who has previously tendered a guilty plea to subsequently seek to withdraw that plea,
whether it is days, months, or even years later. In "broken" plea
agreement cases, *i.e.* situations where the defendant believes that
he or she has not received the "deal" he or she bargained for, courts
generally permit such withdrawal if they agree that the deal was in
fact broken. However, where the bargained-for deal is simply to be a
"recommendation" or where the prosecutor has agreed simply not to
oppose a defense recommendation, and where the prosecutor has
not reneged on this particular deal, a defendant cannot count on
being able to withdraw a guilty plea if he or she is displeased with
the ultimate sentencing outcome. For example, Federal Rule of
Criminal Procedure 11(c)(3) states that under a B agreement the
court must advise the defendant that if the court does not follow the
recommendation or request the defendant has no right to withdraw
the plea.

Besides the broken plea agreement cases, there are innumera-
ble reasons why a defendant might later seek to withdraw his or
her guilty plea. Such reasons range from mere second thoughts
about the strategic thinking (defendant's and/or defense counsel's)
that resulted in a guilty plea, to dissatisfaction with or surprise at
the severity of the sentence received, to the emergence of new evidence or new witnesses (or the disappearance of evidence or witnesses).

Once properly tendered, in many states a defendant does not
generally have the right to withdraw a guilty plea. The attitude of
many courts was expressed in *United States v. Hyde*, 520 U.S. 670
(1997), where the Court reversed a case in which the trial court
permitted the defendant to withdraw a guilty plea after acceptance
of a plea but before acceptance of the plea agreement by the court,
without offering any justification. The Court observed:

After the defendant has sworn in open court that he actually
committed the crimes, after he has stated that he is pleading guilty
because he is guilty, after the court has found a factual basis for the
plea, and after the court has explicitly announced that it accepts the
plea, the Court of Appeals would allow the defendant to withdraw
his guilty plea simply on a lark. The Advisory Committee, in adding

the "fair and just reason" standard to Rule 32(e) in 1983, explained why this cannot be so: "Given the great care with which pleas are taken under [the] revised Rule 11, there is no reason to view pleas so taken as merely 'tentative,' subject to withdrawal before sentence whenever the government cannot establish prejudice. 'Were withdrawal automatic in every case where the defendant decided to alter his tactics and present his theory of the case to the jury, the guilty plea would become a mere gesture, a temporary and meaningless formality reversible at the defendant's whim. In fact, however, a guilty plea is no such trifle, but a "grave and solemn act," which is "accepted only with care and discernment." ' " [We] think the Court of Appeals' holding would degrade the otherwise serious act of pleading guilty into something akin to a move in a game of chess.

Nevertheless, prior to acceptance of a plea, the federal rules now permit such withdrawal for any reason or no reason. After acceptance of a plea agreement, but before imposition of sentence, the court may permit the defendant to withdraw the plea if the defendant presents "any fair and just reason" to do so. After the imposition of sentence, withdrawal is rarely permitted absent a finding of manifest injustice or a miscarriage of justice.

If the reason a defendant pleaded guilty was that he or she relied on the incompetent legal or tactical advice of defense counsel, where he or she can demonstrate that "there is a reasonable probability that, but for counsel's errors, [defendant] would not have pleaded guilty and would have insisted on going to trial," the guilty plea may be withdrawn as a result of ineffective assistance of counsel.

POINTS TO REMEMBER

- In many jurisdictions, a defendant may enter either a plea of not guilty, nolo contendere, guilty, guilty but mentally ill, not guilty by reason of insanity, an *Alford* plea, or a conditional guilty plea.

- Plea bargaining is an acceptable method of disposing of criminal cases.

- Procedural rules provide for plea agreements to dismiss charges, to provide for a specific sentence or sentence range, or to have the prosecutor recommend (or not to oppose) a specific sentence.

- Promises or agreements that form the basis of a plea must be fulfilled.

- A trial court has discretion to decide the appropriate remedy for a broken plea agreement.

- A judge must address a defendant personally in open court to determine if a plea is voluntary and if the defendant understands the rights being waived by the plea.

- Procedural rules may allow to defendant to withdraw a guilty plea under specified circumstances.

Chapter 18

JURY TRIALS

Focal Points for Chapter 18

- Sixth Amendment right to jury trial.

- Jury size and unanimity requirements.

- Fair cross section requirement.

- Challenges for cause.

- Peremptory challenges.

A. Right to Jury Trial

The Sixth Amendment provides in part that in all criminal prosecutions an "accused shall enjoy the right to a public trial, by an impartial jury of the State and district wherein the crime shall have been committed . . ." Further, Article III of the Constitution states that "[t]he trial of all crimes . . . shall be by jury; and such trial shall be held in the state where the said crimes shall have been committed . . ."

Only recently did the Supreme Court make the Sixth Amendment jury trial right applicable to the states through the Fourteenth Amendment Due Process Clause. In *Duncan v. Louisiana*, 391 U.S. 145 (1968), the defendant was convicted of simple battery, a misdemeanor under Louisiana law, and punishable by a maximum of two years' imprisonment and a $300 fine. He sought a trial by jury, but the trial judge denied the request because the state constitution granted jury trials only when capital punishment or imprisonment at hard labor could be imposed. Duncan was convicted and sentenced to serve 60 days in the parish prison and pay a fine of $150. Justice White upheld the defendant's right to a jury trial, and made the following comments.

The guarantees of jury trial in the Federal and State Constitutions reflect a profound judgment about the way in which law should be enforced and justice administered. A right to jury trial is granted to criminal defendants in order to prevent oppression by the Government. Those who wrote our constitutions knew from history and experience that it was necessary to protect against unfounded criminal charges brought to eliminate enemies and against judges too responsive to the voice of higher authority. The framers of the constitutions strove to create an independent judiciary but insisted upon further protection against arbitrary action. Providing an accused with the right to be tried by a jury of his peers gave him an inestimable safeguard against the corrupt or overzealous prosecutor and against the compliant, biased, or eccentric judge. If the defendant preferred the common-sense judgment of a jury to the more tutored but perhaps less sympathetic reaction of the single judge, he was to have it. Beyond this, the jury trial provisions in the Federal and State Constitutions reflect a fundamental decision about the exercise of official power—a reluctance to entrust plenary powers over the life and liberty of the citizen to one judge or to a group of judges. Fear of unchecked power, so typical of our State and Federal Governments in other respects, found expression in the criminal law in this insistence upon community participation in the determination of guilt or innocence. The deep commitment of the Nation to the right of jury trial in serious criminal cases as a defense against arbitrary law enforcement qualifies for protection under the Due Process Clause of the Fourteenth Amendment, and must therefore be respected by the States.

[In] determining whether the length of the authorized prison term or the seriousness of other punishment is enough in itself to require a jury trial, [we] refer to objective criteria, chiefly the existing laws and practices in the Nation. In the federal system, petty offenses are defined as those punishable by no more than six months in prison and a $500 fine. In 49 of the 50 States crimes subject to trial without a jury, which occasionally include simple battery, are punishable by no more than one year in jail. We need not, however, settle in this case the exact location of the line between petty offenses and serious crimes. It is sufficient for our purposes to hold that a crime punishable by two years in prison is, based on past and contemporary standards in this country, a serious crime and not a petty offense. Consequently, appellant was entitled to a jury trial and it was error to deny it. * * *

A jury trial, then, is constitutionally mandated for any offense that carries an authorized sentence of more than six months, regardless of whether the actual sentence imposed in the case is six months or less. In *Blanton v. City of North Las Vegas*, 489 U.S. 538 (1989), the Court theoretically expanded the jury trial guarantee when it held that a defendant is entitled to a jury trial when an offense requires less than six months punishment if additional statutory penalties are so severe that the penalties together indicate that the legislature considers the offense to be "serious."

Later decisions applying *Blanton* have not generously construed its holding in favor of a jury trial. In *United States v. Nachtigal*, 507 U.S. 1 (1993), the Court held that a DUI charge with a maximum penalty of six months' imprisonment, a $5,000 fine, a five-year term of probation, and other penalties was not constitutionally serious enough for a jury trial. The Court reiterated *Blanton's* presumption that offenses are presumptively "petty" for which the maximum authorized period of incarceration is six months. The scope of the federal jury trial right

> does not change where a defendant faces a potential aggregate prison term in excess of six months for petty offenses charged. [B]y setting the maximum authorized prison term at six months, the legislature categorized the offense . . . as petty. The fact that the defendant was charged with two counts of a petty offense does not revise the legislative judgment as to the gravity of the particular offense, nor does it transform the petty offense into a serious one.

Lewis v. United States, 518 U.S. 322 (1996).

In contempt proceedings, which have no legislatively authorized sentence, a jury must be afforded before an *actual* (as opposed to authorized) sentence of confinement for more than six months may be imposed for a post-verdict finding of contempt. In *Codispoti v. Pennsylvania*, 418 U.S. 506 (1974), the Court held that a contemnor has a right to a jury trial if multiple contempt sentences aggregate to more than six months.

A jury trial is also required when a court imposes serious fines for criminal contempt. In *International Union, United Mine Workers of Am. v. Bagwell*, 512 U.S. 821 (1994), the court held that contempt fines of $52 million for violation of a labor injunction were criminal and were subject to the jury trial right. However, the Court reiterated the long-accepted idea that direct contempts in the presence of the court are subject to immediate summary adjudication *without* jury trial.

The constitutional right to a jury trial may be waived by the defendant in favor of a bench trial, but a defendant does not have a right to a bench trial. Because a jury trial is the preferable mode of disposing of factual issues in criminal cases and society has an interest in the disposition of those cases, the prosecution and the court must concur in a waiver which is unaccompanied by a guilty plea. In *Singer v. United States*, 380 U.S. 24 (1965), the Court left open the possibility that the right to waive could belong to the defendant alone: "We need not determine in this case whether there might be some circumstances where a defendant's reasons for wanting to be tried by a judge alone are so compelling that the Government's insistence on trial by jury would result in the denial to a defendant of an impartial trial." A determination that the waiver is made voluntarily and with a full understanding of its consequences must precede the acceptance by the court of a waiver.

B. Aspects of the Jury Trial Right

While the federal rules states that a federal jury should consist of twelve jurors, the Supreme Court has upheld state rules requiring fewer than twelve jurors. For example, in *Williams v. Florida*, 399 U.S. 78 (1970), the Court held that a jury consisting of six jurors was constitutionally permissible. Later, the Court used empirical data to establish a constitutional minimum of six-person juries and to reject a jury of only five persons as violative of the Sixth and Fourteenth Amendments. *Ballew v. Georgia*, 435 U.S. 223 (1978).

First, recent empirical data suggest that progressively smaller juries are less likely to foster effective group deliberation. [At] some point, this decline leads to inaccurate fact-finding and incorrect application of the common sense of the community to the facts. Generally, a positive correlation exists between group size and the quality of both group performance and group productivity. A variety of explanations have been offered for this conclusion. Several are particularly applicable in the jury setting. The smaller the group, the less likely are members to make critical contributions necessary for the solution of a given problem. Because most juries are not permitted to take notes, memory is important for accurate jury deliberations. As juries decrease in size, then, they are less likely to have members who remember each of the important pieces of evidence or argument. Furthermore, the smaller the group, the less likely it is to overcome the biases of its members to obtain an accurate result. * * *

Second, the data now raise doubts about the accuracy of the results achieved by smaller and smaller panels. [Third,] the data suggest that the verdicts of jury deliberation in criminal cases will vary as juries become smaller, and that the variance amounts to an imbalance to the detriment of one side, the defense. [Fourth,] what has just been said about the presence of minority viewpoint as juries decrease in size foretells problems not only for jury decisionmaking, but also for the representation of minority groups in the community. * * *

[We] readily admit that we do not pretend to discern a clear line between six members and five. But the assembled data raise substantial doubt about the reliability and appropriate representation of panels smaller than six. Because of the fundamental importance of the jury trial to the American system of criminal justice, any further reduction that promotes inaccurate and possibly biased decisionmaking, that causes untoward differences in verdicts, and that prevents juries from truly representing their communities, attains constitutional significance.

Despite the *Williams* holding that the federal constitution does not require that a jury be composed of twelve members, many state constitutions require a twelve-person jury for all felony prosecutions and a six-person jury for misdemeanor prosecutions.

While federal courts and most state courts require a twelve-person jury verdict to be unanimous, there is no constitutional requirement of unanimity. *Apodaca v. Oregon*, 406 U.S. 404 (1972). Only Louisiana and Oregon allow juries to convict on less than unanimous votes such as 11–1 or 10–2 in felony cases. The Court also has upheld a conviction based upon a 9–3 vote. *Burch v. Louisiana*, 441 U.S. 130 (1979), later held that a unanimous verdict *is* required of a jury consisting of six members. In federal cases unanimous jury verdicts are *required* by the Federal Rules unless the parties stipulate otherwise.

Since those cases were decided, unanimity issues addressed by the courts have been more complex. For example, in *Schad v. Arizona*, 501 U.S. 624 (1991), the defendant was convicted of first-degree murder which included both premeditated and felony-murder theories. The prosecution offered proof on both. With a general verdict, it was uncertain whether the jury had been unanimous about premeditated murder. A plurality of the Court characterized the issue as whether alternative actions and mental states could constitute the basis for one crime. Indeed, the Court said that the issue "is one of the permissible limits in defining criminal conduct, [not] one of jury unanimity," and held that Schad's due process rights had not been violated when the trial court grouped felony murder and premeditated murder as alternative ways of committing the single crime of first-degree murder.

Later, in *Richardson v. United States*, 526 U.S. 813 (1999), a federal statute prohibited engaging in a continuing criminal enterprise (CCE), which is defined as a violation of the drug statutes where the "violation is part of a continuing series of violations." The Court had to decide whether the phrase "series of violations" refers to one element—a "series"—or whether it creates several elements, or violations, each of which requires unanimity. The Court held that a jury must agree unanimously not only that a defendant committed a "continuing series of violations" but also which specific violations made up that "continuing series of violations."

In some instances the jury will report that it is unable to reach a unanimous verdict. Where the jury reports that it is unable to reach a verdict and the trial court determines that further deliberations may be useful, the court may deliver a limited number of instructions to the jury before considering whether to declare a mistrial. The court may instruct the jury that, in order to return a verdict, each juror must agree to that verdict; jurors must consult with each other and deliberate to achieve an agreement, without harming individual judgment; each juror must decide the case after impartial appraisal of the evidence with other jurors; during deliberations, a juror may reexamine his or her views and change his or her opinion if persuaded that it is erroneous; and no juror should relinquish his or her honest beliefs about the evidence solely due to the opinion of the other jurors, or merely to return a verdict. *Lowenfield v. Phelps*, 484 U.S. 231 (1988), held that a supplemental instruction, which does not speak specifically to minority jurors but does serve the purpose of avoiding a retrial, is permissible after consideration of the context and circumstances in which it is given. When a jury has been kept together until it appears that there is no probability of agreement upon a verdict, the court then may discharge the jury without a verdict.

In criminal trials on multiple charges, the jury may convict on one count and acquit on another. On occasion such an action may seem wholly inconsistent. In some states, inconsistent verdicts as between separate counts are permissible unless there is a logical inconsistency resulting in more severe punishment. For example, it is inconsistent for the jury to return verdicts on two wanton crimes and one reckless crime when all three crimes occurred simultaneously. On the other hand, verdicts on three assault charges are not inconsistent when the injuries occurred as a result of three independent acts which produced the charges. By contrast, consistency among verdicts is not necessary when a *federal* defendant is convicted on one or more counts and acquitted on others. Convictions of different degrees of a crime like burglary for different *defendants* are not regarded as inconsistent.

C. Selecting Prospective Jurors

In most states, the master list for prospective jurors is drawn from such sources as all voter registration lists and/or a list of persons over the age of eighteen holding valid drivers' licenses. A computer periodically may generate a randomized jury list of prospective jurors. The jury panel in a court consists of as many names as are necessary for impaneling of the number of jurors required.

Each person drawn for jury service may be served with a summons directing him or her to report at a specified time and place and to be available for jury service for a period of time. Often, the summons is accompanied by a jury qualification form which must be completed and returned. The form may seek information about the person's address, date of birth, level of education, employer, and immediate family members. The form also may seek prior litigation information, as well as information which could disqualify the person under statutes from serving as jurors, e.g., United States citizenship, inability to speak and understand English, physical or mental disabilities which may prevent effective jury service, a current indictment or a past felony conviction against the prospective juror, or recent jury service. Unless the court determines in a particular case that the information contained on the form must be kept confidential or its use restricted in the interest of justice, the form is made available to the parties or their attorneys.

1. The Fair Cross–Section Requirement

The Sixth Amendment grants to criminal defendants the right to a "jury of the state and district wherein the crime shall have been committed." From this language has evolved the concept that the petit jury in a criminal case must be selected from a fair cross-section of the community where the crime occurred. This requirement applies only to the jury *panel* (also known as the jury array or jury venire) from which the petit jury is selected. The jury which actually decides the case does not have to reflect a cross-section of the community. The Equal Protection Clause of the Fourteenth Amendment also dictates restrictions on the composition of the petit jury.

The purposes of the cross-section requirement are: (1) avoiding "the possibility that the composition of juries would be arbitrarily skewed in such a way as to deny criminal defendants the benefit of the common-sense judgment of the community;" (2) avoiding an "appearance of unfairness," and (3) ensuring against deprivation of "often historically disadvantaged groups of their right as citizens to serve on juries in criminal cases." *Lockhart v. McCree*, 476 U.S. 162 (1986). Most of the early fair cross-section cases concerned the systematic exclusion of racial or ethnic groups from the jury panel. Later cases recognized violations of the fair cross-section requirement on the basis of gender. *Taylor v. Louisiana*, 419 U.S. 522

(1975) held that a male defendant had standing to challenge the constitutionality of a state law excluding women from jury service unless they had filed a written declaration. The Court also found that a petit jury must be selected from a representative cross-section of the community, because it is a fundamental aspect of the jury trial guarantee in the Sixth Amendment. A cross-section of the community is composed of "large, distinctive groups" which play "major roles in the community."

A jury panel from which a cognizable class of citizens has been systematically excluded is not a representative jury. It is difficult to identify all of the classes of citizens whose exclusion will be held to have impermissibly distorted a jury panel. Any identifiable racial minority would constitute such a class. On the other hand, the exclusive use of property tax lists has been said not to present a constitutional infirmity in the jury panel. Young adults and college students are not a distinctive group; jurors excluded from jury duty for cause as a result of their beliefs on capital sentencing are not a distinctive group. Likewise, the exclusion of young people which results from the intermittent recompiling of the jury lists has been justified in the interest of judicial economy.

2. Jury Selection Process

One way in which a jury may be selected begins with the clerk drawing the number of jurors required for a jury trial from a container holding the names of all members of the jury panel remaining after preliminary proceedings affecting jury qualifications and exemptions. In order to minimize the risk of a mistrial due to the excuse of jurors during the course of the trial, the trial court may direct the clerk to empanel one or two additional jurors. As their names are called, the jurors are tentatively seated in the jury box to be examined under oath concerning their qualifications. If jurors are excused from service following their examination, the clerk draws additional names until they are replaced.

The basis for challenging individual jurors may be contained in information concerning their qualifications which has been made available before trial. Independent investigation may also have disclosed the basis for challenging certain jurors. In most instances, however, individual jurors are not challenged until they have been examined under oath concerning their qualifications.

In most jurisdictions, the court initiates the examination and then permits counsel for the parties to conduct further examination. Even if the court conducts the examination, the parties are often entitled to submit supplemental inquiries. Moreover, the initial responses of individual jurors to questions propounded to the jury as a whole may require further inquiry.

Except for capital cases which may require individual voir dire, the examination of individual jurors may be restricted by the court. However, on matters requiring individual responses, the separate examination of individual jurors has been strongly encouraged. For example, the separate examination of jurors concerning pretrial publicity may be desirable in order to avoid the incidental exposure of other members of the panel to affirmative responses.

The purpose of voir dire examination is to determine any possible basis for challenging jurors for cause and to develop background information to be considered in the intelligent exercise of peremptory challenges. Another function of the voir dire examination is to learn about prejudices and attitudes in order to minimize their effect on the outcome of the case. Because of its central role in the selection of a fair and impartial jury, the voir dire examination is one of the most important parts of the trial. Its importance is augmented by the fact that it is the first opportunity afforded to counsel to address the jury in connection with the case. The impressions which the jurors have about the case and about counsel at the conclusion of the examination may last throughout the entire trial.

Voir dire examination may be used to develop the basis for exercising peremptory challenges as well as challenges for cause. *Mu'Min v. Virginia*, 500 U.S. 415 (1991). Therefore, the examiner may properly explore all matters which may relate to the case to be tried—the prospective jurors' knowledge and opinions, their relationships and associations, and their attitudes and prejudices. The potential of anything disclosed on voir dire examination to affect the outcome of the case may also be explored. If there are reasonable grounds to believe that a juror cannot render a fair and impartial verdict, the juror must be excused for cause. However, disqualification is not required merely because a juror does not understand or immediately accept every legal concept (such as mitigation of punishment when a defendant is under the influence of drugs or alcohol) presented during voir dire. The general test is not whether a juror agrees with the law when it is presented; it is whether, after hearing all of the evidence, the prospective juror can adjust his views to the requirements of the law and render a fair and impartial verdict.

The court may exercise considerable discretion in deciding whether to excuse an individual juror for cause. To show prejudice from this abuse of discretion, the party challenging the juror must use all peremptory challenges. *Ross v. Oklahoma*, 487 U.S. 81

(1988). Even if the parties fail to make a challenge for cause, the court has an affirmative duty to explore undisclosed information of which it is aware affecting the qualification of an individual juror.

The Supreme Court has reacted to lower courts' decisions on challenges for cause in a variety of contexts. For example, exposure to pretrial publicity does not alone result in the disqualification of jurors for cause. Likewise, potential jurors do not have to be asked about the specific content of news reports to which they have been exposed. *Mu'Min v. Virginia*, 500 U.S. 415 (1991). By contrast, the formation of an opinion prior to trial creates an inference that the juror cannot be fair and impartial.

The Court has frequently expressed its views on the relation between capital cases and challenges for cause. For example, questions about racial prejudice may be matters of constitutional right, as whether a capital defendant accused of an interracial crime is entitled to have prospective jurors informed of the race of the victim. There is no constitutional prohibition on removing jurors whose opposition to the death penalty is so strong that it would prevent or substantially impair the performance of their duties as jurors, even if death qualified juries are more conviction prone. *Lockhart v. McCree*, 476 U.S. 162 (1986). Even a single misapplication of that standard invalidates a death sentence. *Gray v. Mississippi*, 481 U.S. 648 (1987).

3. Exercising Peremptory Challenges

By rule in most jurisdictions, both parties can challenge a number of jurors without giving any reason whatsoever. Peremptory challenges, though, are not of constitutional dimension. If multiple defendants are being tried, each defendant usually is entitled to additional peremptory challenges to be exercised jointly with or independently of any other defendant. Procedural rules grant trial courts discretion to grant additional peremptory challenges when considering the facts of a particular case.

Under *Batson v. Kentucky*, 476 U.S. 79 (1986), "a defendant may establish a prima facie case of purposeful discrimination in selection of the petit jury solely on evidence concerning the prosecutor's exercise of peremptory challenges at the defendant's trial." The Equal Protection Clause prohibits intentional discrimination in jury selection on the basis of race and gender. *J.E.B. v. Alabama ex rel. T.B.*, 511 U.S. 127 (1994). A criminal defendant also cannot engage in purposeful discrimination in the exercise of peremptory challenges. Either the defendant or the prosecutor may object to race-based or gender-based exclusion of jurors through peremptory challenges, regardless of whether the defendant and the excluded jurors share the same race or gender.

Under *Batson*, the complaining party, who may rely on the fact that peremptory challenges provide an opportunity for discrimination, "must show that these facts and other relevant circumstances raise an inference that the [other party] used that practice to exclude veniremen from the petit jury" on account of their race or gender, which is an "inference of purposeful discrimination." It is then for the trial court, considering "all relevant circumstances," such as a pattern of exercising strikes from the venire on the basis of race or gender and the nature of the prosecutor's questions and statements on voir dire, to decide if the showing creates a prima facie case of discrimination.

If a prima facie case is shown, "the burden shifts to the [alleged offending party] to come forward with a neutral explanation for challenging jurors," which requires more than a denial of a discriminatory motive. If the chosen neutral reasons for the strikes "are so far at odds with the evidence that pretext is the fair conclusion," those explanations may indicate "the very discrimination the explanations were meant to deny." In *Miller-El v. Dretke*, 545 U.S. 231 (2005), the Court found reversible error when the trial court accepted offered race-neutral explanation which were pretextual. Peremptory challenges were used to strike ten of eleven qualified black venire panel members, when at last two of them were "ostensibly acceptable" to a prosecutor seeking the death penalty, and there were strong similarities between struck black venire members and retained white venire members.

Batson does not require the neutral explanation for peremptorily striking a potential juror to be derived from voir dire. Nor does the neutral explanation have to rise to a level sufficient to satisfy a strike for cause. A prosecutor may use her own personal knowledge concerning a juror and information supplied from outside sources. The test is not whether the information is true or false; it is whether she has a good-faith belief in the information and whether she can articulate the reason to the trial court in a race-neutral or gender-neutral way which does not violate the defendant's constitutional rights. The trial court then decides whether the prosecutor has acted with a prohibited intent. In his *Miller-El* concurrence, Justice Breyer repeated an earlier call from Justice Marshall in *Batson* and called for the elimination of peremptory challenges as the best solution to discrimination problems in jury selection.

Points to Remember

- A defendant has a Sixth Amendment right to a jury trial when the authorized punishment for a charge exceeds six months.

- For offenses with shorter authorized sentences, no jury trial right exists unless the statutory penalties are so severe as to render the offense "serious."

- A jury may be composed of as few as six persons.

- Most jurisdictions require a jury verdict to be unanimous.

- Prospective jurors must be selected from a fair cross-section of the place where the crime was committed.

- Prospective trial jurors may be questioned during voir dire to determine whether they can be excluded from the jury for cause.

- Neither party can exercise peremptory challenges to exclude jurors based on race or gender, unless there is a neutral explanation for the challenge.

Chapter 19

FREEDOM OF THE PRESS AND FAIR TRIALS

Focal Points for Chapter 19

- Pretrial publicity and change of venue.

- Due process and pretrial publicity.

- Press access to judicial proceedings.

- Broadcasting legal proceedings.

Guarantees of expressive freedom and a fair trial are fundamental to our society, but these guarantees do not always coexist harmoniously. In the context of the criminal justice process, freedom of the press may promote or undermine significant societal interests. Unfettered expression promotes self-government by exposing judicial or prosecutorial corruption or incompetence. In addition, it serves as a catalyst for reform by heightening the public's political awareness and understanding of the criminal process. Thus, the media's presence and influence avoid proceedings akin to the star chamber and practices inimical to fundamental fairness. While the press can serve many useful functions, its presence can be disruptive and can undermine the fairness of the trial process.

A. Failing to Control the Press

A trial judge can impose restraints upon the conduct of newsmen who are in or near the courtroom. The failure of the judge to take steps to restrict such behavior may deprive the defendant of the due process right to a fair trial. *Sheppard v. Maxwell*, 384 U.S. 333 (1966) involved a murder trial in which there was massive media coverage. During the nine weeks of trial, the courtroom was crowded with representatives of the news media whose movements in and out of the courtroom "often caused so much confusion that, despite the loud speaker system installed in the courtroom, it was difficult for the witnesses and counsel to be heard." Reporters were seated inside the bar, making "confidential talk among Sheppard and his counsel almost impossible during the proceedings." During recesses, pictures were taken in the courtroom, and newsmen even handled and photographed trial exhibits on the counsel table. Photographers and TV cameramen took pictures of the defendant, counsel, witnesses and jurors as they entered and left the courtroom.

The Court viewed the totality of circumstances, and concluded the defendant had been denied a fair trial. The trial judge had failed to take many steps which could have ensured courtroom decorum:

The carnival atmosphere at trial could easily have been avoided since the courtroom and courthouse premises are subject to the control of the court. * * * [T]he presence of the press at judicial proceedings must be limited when it is apparent that the accused might otherwise be prejudiced or disadvantaged. Bearing in mind the massive pretrial publicity, the judge should have adopted strict rules governing the use of the courtroom by newsmen * * *. The number of reporters in the courtroom itself could have been limited at the first sign that their presence would disrupt the trial. * * * Furthermore, the judge should have more closely regulated the conduct of newsmen in the courtroom.

The trial court could have exercised its "power to control the publicity about the trial." It should have made some effort to control the release of leads, information, and gossip to the press by police officers, witnesses, and the counsel for both sides. Much of the information thus disclosed was inaccurate, leading to groundless rumors and confusion. * * *

The fact that many of the prejudicial news items can be traced to the prosecution, as well as the defense, aggravates the judge's failure to take any action. * * * Effective control of these sources concededly within the court's power might well have prevented the divulgence of inaccurate information, rumors, and accusations that made up much of the inflammatory publicity, at least after Sheppard's indictment.

More specifically, the trial court might well have proscribed extrajudicial statements by any lawyer, party, witness, or court official which divulged prejudicial matters, such as the refusal of Sheppard to submit to interrogation or take any lie detector tests; any statement made by Sheppard to officials; the identity of prospective witnesses or their probable testimony; any belief in guilt or innocence; or like statements concerning the merits of the case. * * * Being advised of the great public interest in the case, the mass coverage of the press, and the potential prejudicial impact of publicity, the court could also have requested the appropriate city and county officials to promulgate a regulation with respect to dissemination of information about the case by their employees.

B. Pretrial Publicity and Defendant's Right to a Fair Trial

1. Change of Venue

When potential jurors have read or heard prejudicial publicity, a trial judge should inquire into the nature and extent of the exposure. To prove juror partiality, a defendant must show that the publicity either actually prejudiced a juror or so pervaded the proceedings that it raised a presumption of inherent prejudice. In *Sheppard*, the Court noted that "where there is a reasonable likelihood that prejudicial news prior to trial will prevent a fair trial, the judge should continue the case until the threat abates, or transfer it to another county not so permeated with publicity." During trial, a judge also has broad discretion to sequester the jury and caution the jurors to avoid media accounts of the proceedings.

While a defendant has a right to a criminal trial in the place of the crime, the defendant may desire a trial in another place and may file a motion for a change of venue. The right to request a change of venue belongs to either the defendant or the prosecution. Since venue is largely a creature of statute or rule, those procedures should be followed before relief may be granted.

Courts are reluctant to grant a change of venue due to expense and convenience, and it has the potential of being used as a dilatory tactic. Of course, it also runs counter to the tradition that the administration of criminal justice is primarily the concern of the community in which the crime was committed. On the other hand, a change of venue is a federally protected right which may require the court to overlook statutory procedures in some instances. Most jurisdictions require that the application for a change of venue be timely made or it may be waived.

After an application has been made, the court must determine whether the application establishes a prima facie case for granting a change of venue. If it does not, the application may be denied. If a prima facie showing has been made, the opposing party must then controvert the allegations or the change of venue must be granted. In making its determination the trial court has wide discretion which will not be disturbed if it is supported by sufficient evidence. In many instances the trial judge will defer a decision about the motion until voir dire has indicated whether there is a valid prospect of a fair trial for the defendant. Once in a while, however, circumstances suggest the need to grant the change of venue without the necessity of weighing the nature and extent of awareness about the defendant and the charge.

While a change of venue is frequently thought of as a contested matter because there is a concern about obtaining a fair trial, the parties may agree to a change where the defendant desires to plead guilty. A somewhat different procedure may exist to transfer the venue to another county for purposes of a plea. Federal Rule 20 and many corresponding state rules allow a defendant physically located in one place to plead guilty to charges pending in another place. As the late Professor Wright indicates, the federal rule

> is of benefit to the defendant. It permits a speedy disposition of his case if he desires to plead guilty without whatever hardship may be involved in transporting him back to the district in which he is charged. This may be especially important to a defendant who is arrested at his residence for a crime he committed elsewhere. There is an incidental benefit to the government, since it is spared the expense of transporting the defendant, and persons to escort him, back to the place of the crime.

Charles A. Wright, Federal Practice and Procedure: Criminal 3d § 321.

While the federal rule deals with avoiding transportation problems, there is an added benefit in that a defendant can dispose of multiple cases in a single court. For example, defendants are sometimes charged with multiple crimes, such as bad checks, that occur in several adjacent counties. By appropriate plea negotiations with the various prosecutors involved, the defendant may get a "package deal" on all of his pending charges. A single judge may take the plea and impose sentence in consideration of all the charges.

2. Due Process and Pretrial Publicity

Pretrial publicity can prejudice jurors and violate a defendant's right to an impartial jury. If jurors have potentially been exposed to prejudicial publicity, the court should make an inquiry to determine the existence of actual exposure. Under *Sheppard*, to establish juror partiality, the defendant must show that publicity either actually prejudiced an individual juror or so pervaded the proceedings that it raised a presumption of inherent prejudice. *Skilling v. United States*, 130 S.Ct. 2896 (2010). When there exists a "reasonable likelihood that prejudicial news prior to trial will prevent a fair trial," the judge should grant a continuance until the threat abates or allow a change of venue to another area where publicity about the case is less pervasive. The judge may also sequester the jury and provide cautionary instructions to safeguard against prejudice.

Skilling v. United States, 130 S.Ct. 2896 (2010) identified several factors which may lead to application of a presumption of prejudice: 1) the nature of the pretrial publicity, (2) the size and character of the community, (3) the length of time between the dissemination of the publicity and the trial, (4) whether the defendant was acquitted on any of the charges, and (5) actions by the trial court which reduced the risk that the defendant would not receive a fair trial. While the Court in *Skilling* stated that there is no "hard and fast formula" to satisfy the actual prejudice test, an inference of actual prejudice is shown in the particular case from examining the totality of circumstances: (1) the nature of the pretrial publicity, (2) the community atmosphere as reflected in the media at the time of trial, and (3) whether the *voir dire* testimony revealed pervasive hostility within the community.

Despite concerns about pretrial publicity and juror impartiality, jurors need not be completely ignorant of the facts and issues. A trial judge must assess the jurors' opinions to determine whether the jurors can impartially decide the case. In *Irvin v. Dowd*, 366 U.S. 717 (1961), petitioner was convicted of murder following a trial that was "extensively covered" by the news media and aroused "great excitement and indignation." The trial court granted a change of venue to an adjoining county. The court refused an additional request for change of venue on the basis that state law provided for only a single change of venue. The Court reversed:

Here the "pattern of deep and bitter prejudice" shown to be present throughout the community was clearly reflected in the sum total of the voir dire examination of a majority of the jurors finally placed in the jury box. Eight out of the 12 thought petitioner was guilty. With such an opinion permeating their minds, it would be difficult to say that each could exclude this preconception of guilt from his deliberations. The influence that lurks in an opinion once formed is so persistent that it unconsciously fights detachment from the mental processes of the average man. Where one's life is at stake—and accounting for the frailties of human nature—we can only say that in the light of the circumstances here the finding of impartiality does not meet constitutional standards. Two-thirds of the jurors had an opinion that petitioner was guilty and were familiar with the material facts and circumstances involved, including the fact that other murders were attributed to him, some going so far as to say that it would take evidence to overcome their belief. One said that he "could [not] give the defendant the benefit of the doubt that he is innocent." Another stated that he had a "somewhat" certain fixed opinion as to petitioner's guilt. No doubt each juror was sincere when he said that he would be fair and impartial to petitioner, but psychological impact requiring such a declaration before one's fellows is often its father. Where so many, so many times, admitted prejudice, such a statement of impartiality can be given little weight. As one of the jurors put it, "You can't forget what you hear and see." With his life at stake, it is not requiring too much that petitioner be tried in an atmosphere undisturbed by so huge a wave of public passion and by a jury other than one in which two-thirds of the members admit, before hearing any testimony, to possessing a belief in his guilt.

In essence, the right to a jury trial guarantees to the accused a fair trial by a panel of impartial jurors, i.e., a juror who has formed an opinion cannot be impartial. The Court's test is whether the nature and strength of the juror's opinion formed necessarily raises a presumption of partiality. Unless the defendant shows the actual existence of such an opinion in the mind of the juror as will raise a presumption of partiality, the juror need not necessarily be challenged for cause.

While deciding that the voir dire failed to establish hostility toward the defendant, *Murphy v. Florida*, 421 U.S. 794 (1975), emphasized that *Irvin* does not stand for the proposition that *any* jury exposure to information about the defendant's prior criminal record or to news accounts about the instant crime necessarily means that the defendant will be denied due process because of the jurors' partiality. The court in *Irvin,* had stated:

Although this Court has said that the Fourteenth Amendment does not demand the use of jury trials in a State's criminal procedure, every State has constitutionally provided trial by jury. In essence, the right to jury trial guarantees to the criminally accused a fair trial by a panel of impartial, "indifferent" jurors. The failure to accord an accused a fair hearing violates even the minimal standards of due process. [In] the ultimate analysis, only the jury can strip a man of his liberty or his life. In the language of Lord Coke, a juror must be as "indifferent as he stands unsworne." His verdict must be based upon the evidence developed at the trial. This is true, regardless of the heinousness of the crime charged, the apparent guilt of the offender or the station in life which he [occupies]. "The theory of the law is that a juror who has formed an opinion cannot be impartial."

It is not required, however, that the jurors be totally ignorant of the facts and issues involved. In these days of swift, widespread and diverse methods of communication, an important case can be expected to arouse the interest of the public in the vicinity, and scarcely any of those best qualified to serve as jurors will not have formed some impression or opinion as to the merits of the case. This is particularly true in criminal cases. To hold that the mere existence of any preconceived notion as to the guilt or innocence of an accused, without more, is sufficient to rebut the presumption of a prospective juror's impartiality would be to establish an impossible standard. It is sufficient if the juror can lay aside his impression or opinion and render a verdict based on the evidence presented in court.

In *Patton v. Yount,* 467 U.S. 1025 (1984), jury selection did not occur until four years after prejudicial pretrial publicity had greatly diminished. The Court noted that the relevant issue was not whether the community remembered the case, but whether the jurors who decided the case had such fixed opinions prior to the start of the trial that they could not judge the defendant's guilt impartially. In addition, the Court deferred to the trial court's findings of impartiality by noting that it would reverse on appeal only for manifest error.

When pretrial publicity threatens to prejudice a trial, the trial judge has a duty to ensure that prospective jurors have not formed preconceptions of the defendant's guilt. In *Mu'Min v. Virginia*, 500 U.S. 415 (1991), 8 of the 12 persons sworn as jurors answered on voir dire that they had read or heard something about the case. The defendant argued that his Sixth Amendment right to an impartial jury and his right to due process under the Fourteenth Amendment were violated because the trial judge refused to question further prospective jurors about the specific content of the news reports to which they had been exposed. Citing *Patton* and *Irvin*, the Court found that it was sufficient for a trial judge to ask a panel of prospective jurors collectively and in groups of four whether they had formed opinions based on publicity.

C. Gagging the Press

When attorneys are afraid that pretrial publicity may interfere with the defendant's right to a fair trial, the trial court may be asked to issue a "gag order" to prohibit discussion or publication of information about the approaching trial. Restraining the press from reporting on judicial proceedings is a method for protecting the defendant's right to a fair trial. Gag orders implicate First Amendment interests. As a preemptive restriction upon expression, such methods trigger the "heavy presumption" that exists against the constitutionality of "any system of prior restraint." *New York Times Co. v. United States*, 403 U.S. 713 (1971). They also impose upon government "a heavy burden [of] justification." In *Sheppard*, the Court held that a trial court may restrict extrajudicial "statements by any lawyer, party, witness, or court official which divulged prejudicial matters."

Later, in *Nebraska Press Association v. Stuart*, 427 U.S. 539 (1976), the Court held that a prohibition on the media's publication of information possibly prejudicial to a defendant will seldom, if ever, be a permissible means for preventing prejudicial publicity from occurring. In *Stuart*, the trial court entered orders prior to trial which barred both the publication of "any testimony given or evidence adduced" in court and the reporting of any confessions or incriminating statements made by the defendant to the police or to anyone else other than the press or of other facts "strongly implicative" of the defendant. The Court concluded that the bar on reporting what happened at the preliminary hearing violated the settled principle that "once a public hearing had been held, what transpired there could not be subject to prior restraint." As for the prohibition on the publication of information from other sources, the Court concluded that the prosecution had not met the heavy burden imposed as a condition to securing a prior restraint. The Court examined the facts of the case to determine whether the danger was great enough to justify such an invasion of free speech, which requires examination of "the evidence before the trial judge when the order was entered to determine (a) the nature and extent of pretrial news coverage; (b) whether other measures would be likely to mitigate the effects of unrestrained pretrial publicity; and (c) how effectively a restraining order would operate to prevent the threatened danger."

D. Press Access to Judicial Proceedings

A defendant may believe that the right to a fair trial can be compromised by too much openness and publicity. However, openness assures that established procedures are being followed and that any deviations become known. It also enhances both the fairness of the trial and the appearance of fairness that is essential to public confidence in the criminal justice system. The problems attendant to closing a courtroom are complex because at issue are the defendant's right to a fair trial and a public trial, as well as the right of the press and public to attend the trial, perhaps over the defendant's objection. Questions of access have arisen in the context of pretrial proceedings and trials.

The Sixth Amendment right to a public trial is rooted in traditional distrust of secret trials. Its purposes are to safeguard against any attempt to use the courts as instruments of persecution and to inform the public about governmental actions against citizens. Trials themselves historically have been open to the press and public, and the Court has established a presumption in favor of access. In *Richmond Newspapers, Inc. v. Virginia*, 448 U.S. 555 (1980), the Court found a First Amendment right of the press and public to attend criminal trials, absent findings sufficient to overcome the presumption of openness. Subsequently, in *Globe Newspaper Company v. Superior Court*, 457 U.S. 596 (1982), the Court invalidated a statute which required the closure of the entire trial involving certain sex crimes. The Court indicated that under limited circumstances a portion of the trial might be closed as where a minor rape victim's testimony related certain sensitive details.

In *Press-Enterprise Co. v. Superior Court*, 464 U.S. 501 (1984), the Court held that a trial judge could not close almost six weeks of jury selection. The Court noted that limited portions of the selection process might be closed in the case of individual jurors:

To preserve fairness and at the same time protect legitimate privacy, a trial judge must at all times maintain control of the process of jury selection and should inform the array of prospective jurors, once the general nature of sensitive questions is made known to them, that those individuals believing public questioning will prove damaging because of embarrassment, may properly request an opportunity to present the problem to the judge in camera but with counsel present and on the record.

By requiring the prospective juror to make an affirmative request, the trial judge can ensure that there is in fact a valid basis for a belief that disclosure infringes a significant interest in privacy. This process will minimize the risk of unnecessary closure. The exercise of sound discretion by the court may lead to excusing such a person from jury service. When limited closure is ordered, the constitutional values sought to be protected by holding open proceedings may be satisfied later by making a transcript of the closed proceedings available within a reasonable time, if the judge determines that disclosure can be accomplished while safeguarding the juror's valid privacy interests. Even then a valid privacy right may rise to a level that part of the transcript should be sealed, or the name of a juror withheld, to protect the person from embarrassment.

Another case styled *Press-Enterprise Co. v. Superior Court*, 478 U.S. 1 (1986), emphasized the historical tradition of openness and the functional value of openness for application of the First Amendment right of access to *pretrial* proceedings. Is there is a tradition of accessibility to the pretrial proceeding? For example, because preliminary hearings are open to the public while grand jury proceedings are not, open preliminary hearings are accorded "the favorable judgment of experience." Second, is public access to the preliminary proceeding similar to a trial and "plays a particularly significant positive role in the actual functioning of" the criminal justice process? Preliminary hearings

> cannot be closed unless specific, on the record findings are made demonstrating that "closure is essential to preserve higher values and is narrowly tailored to serve that interest." If the interest asserted is the right of the accused to a fair trial, the preliminary hearing shall be closed only if specific findings are made demonstrating that, first, there is a substantial probability that the defendant's right to a fair trial will be prejudiced by publicity that closure would prevent and, second, reasonable alternatives to closure cannot adequately protect the defendant's fair trial rights.

At least when the nature and traditions of a preliminary hearing are congruent with a trial, it is predictable that First Amendment values of openness will be a dominant factor.

Tradition, however, has not always cut in favor of open preliminary proceedings. In *Gannett Co., Inc. v. DePasquale*, 443 U.S. 368 (1979), the Court upheld a trial judge's order closing a suppression hearing at the defendant's request. The outcome in *Gannett* reflected an understanding that the Sixth Amendment guarantee of a public trial accrued not to the press or public but to the defendants. The decision's bottom line was that the Sixth Amendment established no constitutional right for the press or public to attend a criminal trial. The determination rested on the premise that "that the public interest is fully protected by the participants in the litigation." But five years later, *Waller v. Georgia*, 467 U.S. 39 (1984) held that the Sixth Amendment right to a public trial did not justify the prosecutor's request to close an entire suppression hearing over the defendant's objection.

The teaching of these cases is that a totally closed trial is prohibited. However, under narrowly tailored circumstances, limited portions of pretrial hearings, jury selection or even the trial itself may be closed to the public.

E. Broadcasting Legal Proceedings

The right of access to trials and pretrial hearings does not incorporate any freedom for the media to use a particular technology to cover such proceedings. To the contrary, even as cameras and other electronic instrumentalities have become increasingly common in state courts, the judiciary still exercises considerable control over the extent (if any) to which they may be used. Cameras in the courtroom have become a staple in state courts but, except for some experimentation in the civil context, have been disallowed at the federal level. The United States Judicial Conference, after overseeing an experiment with cameras in six federal districts and two courts of appeals, voted to maintain a policy against their presence.

A plurality of the Court in *Estes v. Texas*, 381 U.S. 532 (1965) concluded that televised proceedings entail "such a probability that prejudice will result that it is deemed inherently lacking in due process." In a concurring opinion of significant durability, Justice Harlan stressed the need for adaptability in the event future circumstances warranted it. As he put it

[Permitting] television in the courtroom undeniably has mischievous potentialities for intruding upon the detached atmosphere which should always surround the judicial process. Forbidding this innovation, however, would doubtless impinge upon one of the valued attributes of our federalism by preventing the States from pursuing a novel course of procedural experimentation. My conclusion is that there is no constitutional requirement that television be allowed in the courtroom, and, at least as to a notorious criminal trial such as this one, the considerations against allowing television in the courtroom so far outweigh the countervailing factors advanced in its support as to require a holding that what was done in this case infringed the fundamental right to a fair trial assured by the Due Process Clause of the Fourteenth Amendment.

Some preliminary observations are in order: All would agree, I am sure, that at its worst, television is capable of distorting the trial process so as to deprive it of fundamental fairness. Cables, klieg lights, interviews with the principal participants, commentary on their performances, "commercials" at frequent intervals, special wearing apparel and makeup for the trial participants—certainly such things would not conduce to the sound administration of justice by any acceptable [standard].

As technology reinvented the electronic instrumentalities of trial coverage, so that intrusiveness and distraction were diminished, case law veered in the direction of Justice Harlan's concurring opinion. Responding to liberalized provisions for electronic coverage of judicial proceedings, the Court in *Chandler v. Florida*, 449 U.S. 560 (1981) repudiated the notion that cameras in the courtroom per se offended due process. *Chandler* upheld a regulated state practice allowing electronic media and still photography coverage of public criminal proceedings over the objection of the accused. The Court emphasized that "no one has been able to present empirical data sufficient to establish that the mere presence of the broadcast media inherently has an adverse impact on that process." It stressed that the televising had occurred pursuant to guidelines designed to assure that the excesses found in *Estes* were avoided. The guidelines included restrictions on the type and manner of equipment used, designed to keep the recording unobtrusive, and a prohibition against the filming of the jury itself. They also required the trial judge to protect the fundamental right of the defendant to a fair trial. A particular defendant could still show that the "coverage of his case . . . compromised the ability of the jury to judge him fairly" or to "show that broadcast coverage of his particular case had an adverse impact on the trial participants sufficient to constitute a denial of due process." However, prejudice is not established by merely showing "juror awareness that the trial is such as to attract the attention of broadcasters."

POINTS TO REMEMBER

- A change of venue may be granted to either party when a fair trial is unlikely.

- Voir dire questioning can indicate whether pretrial publicity requires either dismissal of the charge of a continuance.

- A criminal proceeding must be open to the press when it is historically open and public and press access has a significant positive role in the functioning of the proceeding.

- States may regulate the broadcast of judicial proceedings.

Chapter 20

CONFRONTATION AND COMPULSORY PROCESS RIGHTS

Focal Points for Chapter 20

- Confronting and cross-examining adverse witnesses.

- Defendant's right to be present at proceedings.

- Admission of out-of-court hearsay statements.

- Admissibility of codefendant's pretrial confession.

- Compulsory process to compel attendance of witnesses at trial.

In addition to familiar Sixth Amendment rights such as the right to counsel and the right to a jury trial, the Sixth Amendment also provides a defendant with the right to confront adverse witnesses against her, as well as compulsory process to offer the testimony of witnesses in her favor and compel their attendance at trial. Confrontation and compulsory process rights are discussed briefly, with references to longer discussions in other parts of this book. For example, as noted in Chapter 8, Confrontation Clause violations are subject to harmless error analysis. *Delaware v. Van Arsdall*, 475 U.S. 673 (1986).

A. Identification Procedures

As discussed in Chapter 7, the right to the presence of counsel at pretrial identification procedures established in *United States v. Wade*, 388 U.S. 218 (1967) enables counsel to be more effective in confronting and cross-examining trial witnesses who testify about pretrial lineup identifications.

B. Preliminary Hearing

As discussed in Chapter 11, preliminary hearing testimony may be used as substantive testimony at trial without violating the defendant's Confrontation rights, as long as the preliminary hearing witness is unavailable at trial and the defendant had an opportunity to cross-examine the witness at the preliminary hearing. *Crawford v. Washington*, 541 U.S. 36 (2004).

C. Confrontation Rights at Trial

If a prosecution witness testifies against the defendant, but invokes the Fifth Amendment on cross-examination, there is a conflict between the witness's Fifth Amendment privilege against self-incrimination and the defendant's Sixth Amendment right to confrontation and compulsory process. Usually, the witness's right to remain silent overrides the defendant's rights in this context. *Alford v. United States*, 282 U.S. 687 (1931). The trial court may strike all or part of the witness's direct testimony.

1. Confronting and Cross-Examining Adverse Witnesses

At trial, the Sixth Amendment Confrontation Clause enables a defendant the right to face adverse witnesses. *Maryland v. Craig*, 497 U.S. 836 (1990). The rationale is that such a "confrontation enhances the accuracy of factfinding by reducing the risk that a witness will wrongfully implicate an innocent person." The right to confront adverse witnesses also includes the right to cross-examine adverse witnesses, and the right to be present at any stage of the trial that would enable the defendant to effectively cross-examine adverse witnesses.

The right to face adverse witnesses, however, is not absolute. Under *Craig*, the defendant's right to face adverse witnesses may give way if "necessary to further an important public policy [if] the reliability of the testimony is otherwise assured." The assurance of testimony's reliability may occur through the combined effect of the witness's presence before the tribunal, testimony under oath, cross-examination, and the factfinder's ability to observe the witness's demeanor. Any limitation on the right to confront adverse witnesses is decided on a case-by-case basis.

The Confrontation Clause also protects a criminal defendant's right to cross-examine adverse witnesses. Because the Clause only provides for the "opportunity [to] cross examin[e]," *Delaware v. Fensterer*, 474 U.S. 15 (1985), it is not violated by a defendant's actual failure to cross-examine a witness. Cross-examination must permit the defendant to test both the witness's credibility and the witness's knowledge of the facts bearing on the defendant's guilt or innocence. See *Olden v. Kentucky*, 488 U.S. 227 (1988); *Davis v. Alaska*, 415 U.S. 308 (1974). When a witness has difficulty recalling information while testifying, the defendant is entitled to a full and fair opportunity to probe the nature and extent of the witness's memory problems through cross-examination. *United States v. Owens*, 484 U.S. 554 (1988).

2. Right to Be Present During Criminal Proceedings

The right of a criminal defendant to be present during criminal proceedings arises from the Confrontation Clause as well as from Due Process. The Confrontation Clause assures a defendant the right to be present at any stage of the proceeding that would strengthen the opportunity for effective cross-examination. *Kentucky v. Stincer*, 482 U.S. 730 (1987). (*Stincer* also states that Due Process provides a defendant the "right to be present at any stage of the proceeding that is critical to its outcome if [the defendant's] presence would contribute to the fairness of the procedure.")

A criminal defendant has a right to be present at trial, but has no right to be present at a: (1) pretrial hearing when the defendant does not indicate how his or her presence could have contributed to a more reliable determination and when there are no questions asked about substantive trial testimony, or (2) conference when the defendant could have done nothing by being present and would have gained nothing by attending. *United States v. Gagnon*, 470 U.S. 522, 526–27 (1985). A court may deem the defendant to have waived his right to be present either after he voluntaily absents himself from the courtroom, *Taylor v. United States*, 414 U.S. 17 (1973), or after he engages in continuous disruption of the proceedings after warnings from the court. *Illinois v. Allen*, 397 U.S. 337 (1970).

Absent a trial court's determination in the exercise of its discretion that there is a state interest specific to the defendant justifying the use of physical restraints, Due Process prohibits the routine use of restraints in a guilt or penalty phase of a criminal trial. *Deck v. Missouri*, 544 U.S. 622 (2005).

3. Out-of-Court Hearsay Statements

The admission of out-of-court statements does not violate the Confrontation Clause if the person testifies as a witness at trial and is subject to full and effective cross-examination concerning his or her prior statements. *California v. Green*, 399 U.S. 149 (1970). The admission of hearsay evidence against a criminal defendant can implicate the Sixth Amendment because the defendant is not afforded the opportunity to confront the person making the out-of-court statement. (An out-of-court statement constitutes hearsay only if it is offered to prove the truth of the matter asserted.) In *Crawford v. Washington*, 541 U.S. 36 (2004), the Supreme Court modified this traditional principle by distinguishing between "testimonial" and "nontestimonial" evidence.

> Statements are nontestimonial when made in the course of police interrogation under circumstances objectively indicating that the primary purpose of the interrogation is to enable police assistance to meet an ongoing emergency. They are testimonial when the circumstances objectively indicate that there is no such ongoing emergency, and that the primary purpose of the interrogation is to establish or prove past events potentially relevant to later criminal prosecution.

Davis v. Washington, 126 S.Ct. 2266 (2006). Thus, a testimonial out-of-court statement is admissible at trial even if the person making the statement does not appear at trial but there was a prior opportunity for cross-examining her. "[T]he existence and duration of an emergency depend on the type and scope of danger posed to the victim, the police, and the public." *Michigan v. Bryant*, 131 S.Ct. 1143 (2011). In *Bryant*, the Court held that, because the shooting victim's statements to police were made to assist police to meet an ongoing emergency, they were not testimonial hearsay and were admissible at trial.

A nontestimonial out-of-court statement is admissible at trial regardless of either the declarant's availability to testify at trial or any prior opportunity to cross-examine her. In *Davis*, the Court held that a victim's statements responding to a 911 operator's interrogation were not testimonial, while the *Crawford* interrogation of a domestic violence victim was directed solely at establishing a past crime and was held to be testimonial. *Crawford* noted that the concept of "testimonial" applies "at a minimum to prior testimony at a preliminary hearing, before a grand jury, or at a former trial; and to police interrogations."

As mentioned, admission of a "testimonial" hearsay statement violates the Confrontation Clause, unless the person making the out-of-court statement is unavailable. A witness is considered unavailable if the prosecution cannot obtain that witness's attendance at trial, and the defendant had a prior opportunity to cross-examine that person. If the hearsay statement is "nontestimonial," a trial court may admit the statement without violating the Confrontation Clause as long as the hearsay exception is considered "firmly rooted." For example, in *Idaho v. Wright*, 497 U.S. 805 (1990), the Court held that the admission of a statement under Idaho's residual hearsay exception violated the defendant's Confrontation Clause right because the residual hearsay exception is not firmly rooted.

4. Joint Trials and the Confrontation Clause

As discussed in Chapter 14, in a joint trial, the admission of a codefendant's extrajudicial confession incriminating the defendant violates the defendant's right to confrontation when the codefendant does not testify at trial. *Bruton v. United States*, 391 U.S. 123 (1968). The principle applies even when the trial judge instructs the jury not to consider the confession against the defendant but only against the codefendant. The codefendant's statement, as applied to the defendant, must directly and powerfully incriminate the defendant. Where the codefendant later testifies, there is no confrontation issue because the codefendant is subject to cross-examination. Normally, the codefendant's confession is not admissible even when the defendant has also confessed and even if the jury is instructed not to consider it against the defendant. *Cruz v. New York*, 481 U.S. 186 (1987). Chapter 14 also discusses several judicial alternatives for the prosecution to use when a codefendant has confessed but may not testify at trial.

5. Compulsory Process

A Sixth Amendment right related to the Confrontation Clause is the Compulsory Process Clause, which grants a defendant the right to offer the testimony of favorable witnesses and to compel their attendance at trial. The Sixth Amendment provides that "[i]n all criminal prosecutions, the accused shall enjoy the right . . . to have compulsory process for obtaining witnesses in his favor." To exercise this right, a defendant must show that the testimony she seeks would be material, favorable to her, and not merely cumulative. *United States v. Valenzuela–Bernal*, 458 U.S. 858 (1982).

Washington v. Texas, 388 U.S. 14 (1967) invalidated a statute preventing accomplices from testifying for one another but allowing them to testify for the prosecution. The statute violated the Compulsory Process Clause by arbitrarily denying the defendant the right to present a materially favorable witness.

The Compulsory Process Clause, however, does not require the prosecution to affirmatively obtain defense witnesses' testimony. As discussed in Chapter 16, the Due Process Clause provides an analytical structure for discovery of exculpatory evidence.

POINTS TO REMEMBER

- The right to confront adverse witnesses includes the right to face adverse witnesses as well as the opportunity to cross-examine them.

- A defendant has the right to be present at any stage of a criminal proceeding that would strengthen the opportunity for effective cross-examination.

- Admission of a "testimonial" hearsay statement violates the Confrontation Clause, when the person making the out-of-court statement is unavailable to testify at trial and there was no prior opportunity to cross-examine her.

- Admission of a codefendant's extrajudicial confession incriminating the defendant violates the defendant's right to confrontation when the codefendant does not testify at trial.

- The Compulsory Process Clause grants a defendant the right to offer the testimony of favorable witnesses and to compel their attendance at trial.

Chapter 21

SENTENCING

Focal Points for Chapter 21

- Noncapital sentencing alternatives.

- Death as a punishment.

- Proportionality of punishment.

- Sentencing procedures.

Ordinarily it is a relatively simple matter to ascertain a client's potential "exposure" to a given criminal provision. All crimes contain an express or implied penalty. In the vast majority of cases, the actual punishment is contained in the definition of the offense by reference to statutes defining ranges of imprisonment terms and fines. In some instances, a punishment for a violation of one statute is found by reference to the "class" of the crime.

The possible punishment for each particular offense can be ascertained with relative ease. Where certain enhanced punishments are being sought by the government, pretrial notice will afford knowledge of this possibility. Nevertheless, simply because a punishment is set forth in the statute does not mean that a defendant will always be subject to these penalties. There are certain statutory and constitutional limitations on sentencing which may tend to lessen a particular penalty. In general, these include limitations on resentencing, alterations in the punishment, and certain notice rules. While it is seldom successful, counsel may attack a sentence which constitutes cruel and unusual punishment, violates double jeopardy prohibitions, or violates concepts of equal protection. See, e.g., *Hodgson v. Vermont*, 168 U.S. 262 (1897).

A. Noncapital Sentencing Alternatives

Fines and Costs. The punishment for a violation of the law may include a fine in addition to or, in some cases, instead of imprisonment. Due to certain constitutional limitations, a person may not usually be confined for failure to pay the fine or costs.

The general authority for the imposition of fines for violations of the criminal statutes is found in the statutes themselves. The procedure for the collection of fines is governed largely by statute. The controlling question is whether the defendant may be incarcerated for failure to pay the fine. Fines cannot be imposed upon any person determined by the court to be statutorily indigent. While incarceration is still a possibility for an intentional refusal to pay, the court must explore alternative means of satisfaction of the fine. *Bearden v. Georgia*, 461 U.S. 660 (1983). In instances where the defendant desires to appeal a fine, the trial judge may grant a stay of the payment and require bail.

In some jurisdictions, the sentencing court may issue a criminal garnishment order for all fines, court costs, restitution, and reimbursement charges, combining them in a single order of garnishment. Any convicted person owing fines, court costs, restitution, or reimbursement before or after his or her release from incarceration is subject to a lien upon his or her interest, present or future, in any real property.

The costs associated with litigation are also governed by statute. It appears that the defendant is responsible for the payment of costs only upon conviction. However, the defendant cannot be incarcerated for failure to pay costs. *Bearden v. Georgia*, 461 U.S. 660 (1983). Moreover, court costs cannot be imposed upon an indigent defendant.

Recently, states have begun to provide that the sentencing court may order a person incarcerated to reimburse the state or local government for the costs of incarceration. The sentencing court determines the amount to be paid based on the actual per diem, per person, cost of incarceration, the cost of medical services provided to a prisoner less any copayment paid by the prisoner, and the prisoner's ability to pay all or part of the incarceration costs.

Restitution. By statute, a person convicted of certain types of crimes such as a crime involving the taking of, injury to, or destruction of property can be ordered to restore the property or its value to the victim. An order of restitution may defer payment until the person is released from custody. However, the decision by a trial judge not to use this remedy does not deprive the victim of a civil action for the injury sustained.

Forfeiture or Confiscation of Property. A person convicted of certain types of crimes such as controlled substances, intoxicating liquors, eavesdropping devices, deadly weapons, gambling devices, and obscene matter can be ordered to forfeit property used in connection with commission of the offense. Forfeitures, as payments in kind, are "fines" if they constitute punishment for an offense. *Austin v. United States*, 509 U.S. 602 (1993). Thus, forfeiture of vehicles and realty used to facilitate commission of drug trafficking is allowed, because it serves as a punishment under the Eighth Amendment's Excessive Fines Clause.

In *Alexander v. United States*, 509 U.S. 544 (1993), as part of his punishment for violating federal obscenity laws and RICO, the trial court ordered the defendant to forfeit his businesses and almost $9 million acquired through racketeering activity. The Court found that the forfeiture was a permissible criminal punishment, not a prior restraint on speech, because it merely prevented him from financing his activities with assets derived from his prior racketeering offenses. RICO is oblivious to the expressive or nonexpressive nature of the assets forfeited. Petitioner's assets were forfeited because they were directly related to past racketeering violations.

Generally, under the Due Process Clause, the Government must provide notice and a meaningful opportunity to be heard before seizing real property subject to civil forfeiture. *United States v. James Daniel Good Real Property*, 510 U.S. 43 (1993). However, due process does not preclude forfeiture of property used for unlawful purposes by a defendant but which belongs to another person. *Bennis v. Michigan*, 516 U.S. 442 (1996).

Probation and Conditional Discharge. Probation is granted when the sentencing court suspends the execution of a sentence of imprisonment conditionally and releases the defendant under the supervision of a probation officer. Some jurisdictions grant "conditional discharge" when a defendant is released without supervision. These forms of release are regarded as "legislative clemencies," not constitutional rights, granted as a matter of grace.

Eligibility for probation or conditional discharge usually prohibits their use after convictions for such offenses as a capital offense, recidivist status, serious felonies involving the use of a firearm or while the defendant was already on probation of conditional discharge from another felony conviction, or a sex-related offense against a minor. Otherwise, many states require that a defendant be considered for probation or conditional discharge unless the court finds imprisonment to be necessary to protect the public.

Conditions of release are usually stated in writing and furnished to the defendant. All defendant are required to refrain from committing another offense, as well as other conditions (such as restitution) which the court deems to be reasonably necessary to enable the defendant to lead a law-abiding life. In addition to reasonable conditions, a court may require a defendant to submit to a period of imprisonment in the local jail at times to be determined by the court. This is known as a "split sentence." The court may initiate proceedings to determine whether to revoke the release because of a violation of its conditions.

Home Incarceration. Many states now permit defendants convicted of minor offenses to serve all or part of a definite term of imprisonment under conditions of home incarceration. Some provisions prohibit home incarceration for minor offenders with outstanding charges or a recent violent crime conviction. The sentencing judge may have discretion to order home incarceration as another type of "split sentence" for the defendant to serve part of the sentence at home and part of it in the local jail. As with probation and conditional discharge, a defendant under home incarceration signs an agreement listing all of the conditions for confinement.

Continuous Confinement for a Definite Term or Indeterminate Term. An indeterminate sentence is set within statutory limits, with the parole board having responsibility for deciding precisely when the defendant is eligible for early release. About two-thirds of the states use indeterminate sentences. A determinate sentence (also known as "flat time,") is for a fixed period without the possibility of early release, but supervision often accompanies that release.

B. Death as a Punishment

1. The Problem of Fairness

The death penalty is currently in effect in about three fourths of the states and the federal system. Methods of execution include electrocution, firing squad, gas chamber, hanging, and lethal injection. In *Furman v. Georgia*, 408 U.S. 238 (1972), the Court found that Georgia had not applied the death penalty fairly. Statistics on executions showed that black males who committed murder were executed far more frequently than white males, even though black males were not committing most of the crimes. The Court stated that capital punishment cannot be used unless the states can prove that it is being applied fairly. Since *Furman*, even those supportive of the death penalty as an appropriate punishment have become concerned about the manner in which it is used. Responding to growing criticism about the administration of the death penalty, a dozen states have commissioned studies of their penalty system to examine racial and geographic disparities within states, as well as serious problems with court-appointed lawyers and the appeals process.

For example, Illinois Governor George H. Ryan appointed the Illinois Commission on Capital Punishment in March, 2000 after declaring a moratorium on the execution of death row inmates two months earlier. The Commission's report issued two years later recommended 85 reforms to the capital punishment system in Illinois. The report has fueled a nationwide debate on the death penalty. Before leaving office in January, 2003, Governor Ryan commuted the death sentences of 167 of the state's death row inmates, and pardon four inmates completely.

The commission's recommendations included: conducting a pretrial review of prosecutorial decisions to seek capital punishment; reducing the list of death eligibility factors; requiring that no person may be sentenced to death based solely on uncorroborated single eyewitness or accomplice testimony or the uncorroborated testimony of jail house informants; videotaping the entire interrogation of homicide suspects at a police station, and not merely the confession; allowing trial judges to concur or reverse a jury's death sentence verdict; review by the state Supreme Court of all death sentences; supporting a capital case trial bar and requiring judges to be pre-certified before presiding over capital cases; requiring that juries be instructed as to all the possible sentencing alternatives before they consider the appropriateness of imposing a death sentence; affording capital defendants opportunity to make a statement to those who will be deciding whether to impose the ultimate punishment allowed by the state, a sentence of death.

2. The Typical Capital Case

The procedure for the trial of capital cases has been fashioned in response to federal precedent on the issue. The government must establish at least one aggravating circumstance beyond a reasonable doubt in order to impose the death penalty. Current capital punishment provisions are the product of a lengthy series of statutes and court opinions. See, e.g., *Gregg v. Georgia*, 428 U.S. 153 (1976).

In *California v. Brown*, 479 U.S. 538 (1987), the Court stated that there are two prerequisites to a valid death sentence. First, "death penalty statutes [must] be structured so as to prevent the penalty from being administered in an arbitrary and unpredictable fashion. . .Second, . . . the capital defendant generally must be allowed to introduce any relevant mitigating evidence." Later cases have defined the potential for imposition of the death penalty. For example, in *Tison v. Arizona*, 481 U.S. 137 (1987), the Court stated that the death penalty is not disproportionate for a murder committed with wanton indifference. Further, the Eighth Amendment prohibits capital punishment upon a prisoner who either is insane or mentally retarded, or was under the age of 18 at the time they committed their crimes. *Atkins v. Virginia*, 536 U.S. 304 (2002); *Roper v. Simmons*, 543 U.S. 551 (2005).

The prosecution must give defense counsel adequate notice that it will seek the death penalty. The defendant's guilt is initially determined at a "guilt" phase, and if the defendant is found guilty, a second hearing (the "penalty" phase) is conducted to determine the punishment. If the guilt phase of the proceeding is tried without a jury, the judge alone presides over the penalty phase. Likewise, if a jury has found guilt, the penalty phase is conducted as soon as possible before the same jury. When a defendant pleads guilty to a capital offense, the defendant may demand that a jury be impanelled to determine punishment.

At a pretrial conference, the defendant may allege that a sentence of death is being sought on the basis of race. The defendant must state with particularity how the evidence supports a claim that racial considerations played a significant part in the decision to seek a death sentence in his or her case. Relevant evidence may include statistical evidence or other evidence that death sentences were sought significantly more frequently either upon persons of one race than upon persons of another race, or as punishment for capital offenses against persons of one race than as punishment for capital offenses against persons of another race. The defendant has the burden of proving by clear and convincing evidence that race was the basis of the decision to seek the death penalty. The prosecution may offer evidence in rebuttal of the claims or evidence of the defendant. If the court finds that race was the basis of the decision to seek the death sentence, the court orders that a death sentence cannot be sought in that case.

In *Zant v. Stephens*, 462 U.S. 862 (1983), the Court held that all evidence may be introduced in a capital sentencing hearing even beyond factors in aggravation and mitigation as long as it is relevant, reliable and not prejudicial. Evidence is relevant to punishment if it is relevant to a statutory aggravating circumstance or to a statutory mitigating circumstance later raised by the defendant. See *Bell v. Ohio*, 438 U.S. 637 (1978).

Each jurisdiction defines the aggravating circumstances which must be proved before the death penalty can be imposed. A common aggravating circumstance is that the defendant has been previously convicted of a capital offense. *Romano v. Oklahoma*, 512 U.S. 1 (1994). A prior conviction cannot be used as an aggravating circumstance, however, if an appeal of the conviction is pending.

A second typical aggravating circumstance is that the defendant committed murder or kidnaping while engaged in the commission of a serious form of a felony such as arson, robbery, burglary, rape, or sodomy. See *Schiro v. Farley*, 510 U.S. 222 (1994). The focus of this aggravating circumstance is the commission of one of the listed offenses, regardless of whether the defendant actually could be convicted of the offense. For example, suppose the defendant argued that first degree burglary could not be an aggravating circumstance because the defendant was a 16 year old child and statutorily could not be tried as an adult for that crime. The fact that the person charged is under a legal disability by reason of age which prevents his being convicted of an offense in no way suggests that the offense has not been committed, or that if the child did in fact commit the offense, it cannot be proved as an aggravating circumstance in conviction of another offense for which he can be tried, convicted and punished as an adult.

A third aggravating circumstance is that by committing murder or kidnaping, the defendant knowingly created a great risk of death to two or more persons in a public place by means of a destructive device or weapon normally hazardous to more than one person. This aggravator is not improper merely because it duplicates one of the elements of the homicide. See *Lowenfield v. Phelps*, 484 U.S. 231 (1988). Presumably, this circumstance applies only in multiple murders or threats to several persons at or shortly prior to or shortly after an act of murder or kidnapping.

Another aggravating circumstance may deal with defendants who either pay for or receive remuneration for a murder. This circumstance appears to apply to the purchaser as well as the perpetrator. Moreover, it applies to persons who commit murder and expect to profit from the victim's death. While many statutes contain no minimum level of profit, the proof may permit the jury to infer that it would be substantial thereby adding to the motive for the crime.

A fifth type of aggravating circumstance may apply to the murder of a prison employee by a defendant who was a prisoner at the time of the homicide. The murder must have occurred while the prison employee was engaged in the performance of duties. A sixth aggravating circumstance deals with the intentional murders of more than one person.

Recently added aggravating circumstances by some states include the intentional killing of a state or local public official or police officer, sheriff or deputy sheriff while the official was engaged in the lawful performance of duties, and a defendant who murdered the victim, either when an emergency protective order or a domestic violence order was in effect, or when any other order designed to protect the victim from the defendant (such as an order issued as a condition of a bond, conditional release, probation, parole, or pretrial diversion) was in effect.

Although there is no burden to do so, as a practical matter the defense may introduce proof of any mitigating circumstances for consideration by the jury. *California v. Brown*, 479 U.S. 538 (1987). The purpose of the mitigating factors appears to be avoidance of the death penalty. The listed circumstances relate generally to matters which were insufficiently persuasive for the factfinder on the issue of guilt. Typical statutory mitigating circumstances include: a lack of a significant history of prior criminal activity, the defendant was under extreme mental or emotional disturbance, the victim participated in the act, the defendant believed he had a moral justification for the conduct, the defendant was only an accomplice, the defendant acted under duress, the defendant suffered from some diminished capacity, or the youth of the defendant. Evidence of statutory mitigating circumstances should be admitted, regardless of its cumulative effect and how long the witness has known the defendant. However, exclusion of mitigating testimony may be harmless.

At the conclusion of all the proof the parties have the right of closing argument with the defense usually having the right of the final argument. Other than the order of argument, in general the rules regarding final jury argument are similar to those in the regular trial. Because of the nature of the hearing there are additional areas of defense objection not usually available in a regular trial. Of particular note is the prohibition of minimizing the jury's responsibility in assessing the death penalty. See *Romano v. Oklahoma*, 512 U.S. 1 (1994). For example, a prosecutor cannot argue to the jury that responsibility for determining the appropriateness of a death sentence rests not with the jury but with an appellate court. *Caldwell v. Mississippi*, 472 U.S. 320 (1985).

At the conclusion of the arguments the judge must instruct the jury in a manner similar to instructions in the guilt phase. Most states use the following format for instructions during the penalty phase. First, with regard to the statutory aggravating and mitigating circumstances, the judge must charge only those factors raised by the proof. *Delo v. Lashley*, 507 U.S. 272 (1993). Second, the judge must instruct the jury as to the authorized sentences. Third, the judge must instruct the jury that imposition of the death penalty is permitted only if it finds the existence of at least one aggravating circumstance beyond a reasonable doubt. Fourth, the judge should instruct the jury on the necessity of unanimity and the presumption of innocence. Finally, the court defines the meaning of "mitigating circumstances." See *Penry v. Lynaugh*, 492 U.S. 302 (1989).

In most states that retain the death penalty, if the jury finds at least one aggravating circumstance beyond a reasonable doubt, its recommendation as to punishment of death must include a written designation of the aggravating circumstance. If the jury does not find at least one aggravating circumstance, the judge cannot impose a sentence of death. In this situation, the judge can impose a sentence of life. The Court has also approved imposition of the death penalty when the jury finds that aggravating circumstances are either in equipoise with or not outweighed by mitigating circumstances. *Kansas v. Marsh*, 126 S.Ct. 2516 (2006).

When a sentence of death is not imposed, any error committed during the proceeding is subject to a harmless error analysis. An appeal usually is automatic in cases in which the death penalty is imposed. If a death sentence is set aside because of an error in the penalty phase only, a new trial applies to the issue of punishment only.

C. Proportionality of Punishment

On several occasions, the Supreme Court has grappled with the issue of whether certain sentences are disproportionately severe. The Eighth Amendment, which forbids cruel and unusual punishments, contains a "narrow proportionality principle" that "applies to noncapital sentences." In *Rummel v. Estelle*, 445 U.S. 263 (1980), the Court held that a state did not violate the Eighth Amendment when it sentenced a three-time offender to life in prison with the possibility of parole. Rummel was sentenced to a lengthy prison term under a recidivism statute, when his two prior offenses were a felony for fraudulent use of a credit card to obtain $80 worth of goods or services, and a second conviction for passing a forged check in the amount of $28.36. His triggering offense was a conviction for felony theft—obtaining $120.75 by false pretenses.

The Court ruled that "Texas was entitled to place upon Rummel the onus of one who is simply unable to bring his conduct within the social norms prescribed by the criminal law of the State." The recidivism statute "is nothing more than a societal decision that when such a person commits yet another felony, he should be subjected to the admittedly serious penalty of incarceration for life, subject only to the State's judgment as to whether to grant him parole." The Court observed that "[o]utside the context of capital punishment, successful challenges to the proportionality of particular sentences have been exceedingly rare." Although it noted that "the proportionality principle would apply to the extreme example if a legislature made overtime parking a felony punishable by life imprisonment," the mandatory life sentence imposed upon Rummel did not constitute cruel and unusual punishment.

Three years after *Rummel*, in *Solem v. Helm*, 463 U.S. 277 (1983), the Court held that the Eighth Amendment prohibited "a life sentence without possibility of parole for a seventh nonviolent felony." The triggering offense in Solem was "uttering a 'no account' check for $100." Three factors were relevant to a determination of whether a sentence is so disproportionate that it violates the Eighth Amendment: "(i) the gravity of the offense and the harshness of the penalty; (ii) the sentences imposed on other criminals in the same jurisdiction; and (iii) the sentences imposed for commission of the same crime in other jurisdictions." In *Rummel*, the defendant was eligible for parole.

Eight years after *Solem*, the Court addressed the proportionality issue again in *Harmelin v. Michigan*, 501 U.S. 957 (1991), which involved a first-time offender convicted of possessing 672 grams of cocaine and sentenced to life in prison without possibility of parole. A majority of the Court rejected the claim that the sentence was grossly disproportionate but it could not agree on why the argument failed. Justice Kennedy, joined by two other Members of the Court, concurred in part and concurred in the judgment and identified four principles of proportionality review—"the primacy of the legislature, the variety of legitimate penological schemes, the nature of our federal system, and the requirement that proportionality review be guided by objective factors"—that "inform the final one: The Eighth Amendment does not require strict proportionality between crime and sentence. Rather, it forbids only extreme sentences that are 'grossly disproportionate' to the crime." Justice Kennedy's concurrence also stated that *Solem* "did not mandate" comparative analysis "within and between jurisdictions."

The proportionality principles in Justice Kennedy's concurrence directed the Court's most recent application of the Eighth Amendment in *Ewing v. California*, 538 U.S. 11 (2003). The issue there was "whether the Eighth Amendment prohibits the State of California from sentencing a repeat felon to a prison term of 25 years to life under the State's 'Three Strikes and You're Out' law." Justice O'Connor found that the states had an interest "in dealing in a harsher manner with those who by repeated criminal acts have shown that they are simply incapable of conforming to the norms of society as established by its criminal law." The state's interest in public safety and deterrence supported application of the recidivism principle, in the absence of a grossly disproportionate sentence.

Proportionality limitations may apply to forfeitures as well. In *United States v. Bajakajian*, 524 U.S. 321 (1998), the defendant was arrested while trying to take $357,144 on a flight to Cyprus, because he had failed to report that he possessed or had control of more than $10,000. After a bench trial on a criminal forfeiture charge, the trial court found the entire amount subject to forfeiture under a criminal forfeiture statute. The court, however, ordered only $15,000 forfeited, reasoning that forfeiture of more than that amount would be "grossly disproportional" to Bajakajian's culpability and thus unconstitutional under the Excessive Fines Clause. The court expressly found that all of the money came from a lawful source and was to be used for a lawful purpose. The Supreme Court agreed that the forfeiture of currency permissible under the statute constituted punishment, because the forfeiture only became possible upon conviction of willfully violating the reporting statute. After concluding that the forfeiture qualified as a "fine," the Court turned to the question of excessiveness. Bajakajian's crime was "solely a reporting offense," and the harm Bajakajian's caused was "minimal" in the sense that the government would be deprived only of information that the $357,144 left the country. Thus, the gravity of the crime compared to the amount in forfeiture sought would be "grossly disproportional."

How do enhancing recidivism sentencing statutes work? Used by about half the states, a defendant may be sentenced to a maximum of life imprisonment upon proof of a requisite number of prior convictions where the defendant is convicted of certain classifications of felonies. A person cannot be convicted as a recidivist unless a term of imprisonment is imposed as punishment for the underlying charge. Recidivist provisions do not create an independent offense but merely serves to enhance the punishment for a crime committed by a person who qualifies as a recidivist. A conviction for a capital offense such as murder is not subject to enhancement.

A defendant is entitled to notice of being charged as a recidivist before the trial of the underlying substantive offense. A separate indictment meets this requirement just as does a separate count in the indictment charging the substantive offense to which it refers. It is common practice for the indictment to specify the nature, time and place of the prior conviction.

Assuming the defendant is properly charged as a recidivist, trial initially takes place on the underlying felony. During this initial trial, no mention is made of the prior convictions, except for impeachment. The determination of whether the defendant is a recidivist must occur in a separate proceeding from the trial on the underlying felony. This penalty phase usually is conducted with the same jury. The defendant is not entitled to separate juries for the guilt and penalty phases. The evidence at the hearing is very narrow. The only function of the jury is to hear proof of prior convictions and to determine if a defendant's record of recidivism warrants punishment. Accordingly, the courts have denied the defendant an opportunity to introduce evidence of mitigation. During the hearing, the prosecution must prove every element of the recidivist charge beyond a reasonable doubt. A defendant charged with being a recidivist may plead guilty to the charge.

In many jurisdictions, there are two degrees of recidivist status, the elements of which are indistinguishable except for the number of previous felony convictions required. For example, a recidivist in the second degree must have been convicted of one previous felony before committing the current felony. A recidivist in the first degree must have been convicted of two or more previous felonies prior to committing the current felony. Naturally the penalties for a recidivist in the first degree are more severe. Except for prior convictions, any fact increasing sentence beyond the statutory maximum for the crime of conviction must be proved beyond a reasonable doubt. *Apprendi v. New Jersey,* 530 U.S. 466 (2000).

For both degrees, the defendant's prior conviction must have occurred prior to the date of the commission of the current felony. Likewise, for first degree status, the second felony must have been committed after the conviction of the first felony. For example, if a defendant is convicted and paroled, then commits another felony and is again incarcerated and released, upon committing a third felony, he has two prior felony convictions and is a first-degree offender. However, if the defendant's second conviction did not occur until after commission of the third felony, he has one prior felony conviction for offender status. The prior conviction must be for a felony in the sentencing jurisdiction or conviction of a crime in any other jurisdiction. If the defendant has been convicted of a crime in another state which is a felony in the sentencing jurisdiction, the conviction counts as a prior felony conviction for purposes of the recidivist statute. The prior conviction must have included imposition of a sentence of one year or more or of death.

A defendant who is indicted as a recidivist may challenge the validity of any prior conviction. The defendant must file a motion to suppress any evidence of prior convictions before trial, alleging that a prior conviction was obtained by constitutionally impermissible means. At a hearing on the motion to suppress, the burden is on the prosecution to prove the judgments of conviction for each of the prior offenses. This burden is sustained by a duly authenticated record of a judgment and conviction. When a defendant is found to be a recidivist, the sentence for the principal crime is replaced and enhanced.

Typically, if a defendant is found to be a recidivist in the second degree, the sentence imposed is "for the next highest degree than the offense for which [he was] convicted." For example, if the principal conviction is for a Class B felony, the enhanced sentence may be for a Class A felony. The sentence ranges for a first degree recidivist may range from twenty to fifty years or life imprisonment for the principal conviction of a Class A or Class B felony, and ten to twenty years for a Class C or Class D felony.

Suppose the defendant is convicted of a felony and is sentenced to twenty years, but the defendant is successful in obtaining a new trial. Could the judge or jury then sentence the defendant to thirty years? The answer, in non-capital cases, depends on who is imposing the sentence. In *North Carolina v. Pearce*, 395 U.S. 711 (1969), the Court held that, absent other factors, a defendant could not be given a higher sentence on a retrial following reversal of a conviction. In the context of jury sentencing where a different jury imposes a higher sentence on retrial than the jury in the initial trial, the correlating control and the threat are both absent. The foregoing principle is not applicable to capital cases. When a defendant is sentenced to life and succeeds in obtaining a new trial, he or she is no longer subject to the death penalty on any retrial. *Bullington v. Missouri*, 451 U.S. 430 (1981). This proposition, grounded on double jeopardy, applies even if a jury is waived. However, if an appellate court corrects a mistaken legal interpretation of an aggravating factor which does not alter the validity of the punishment, a retrial after a reversal for the trial error can result again in a death sentence. *Poland v. Arizona*, 476 U.S. 147 (1986).

Pearce does not totally prohibit a greater sentence in another situation. Where the same judge imposes the sentence, a higher sentence may be fixed if the judge finds a "change of circumstances." In *Wasman v. United States*, 468 U.S. 559 (1984), the Court clarified the perception that an increased sentence could only be based on circumstances occurring after the original sentence. The defendant had been charged with another criminal offense at the time of the original sentence but had been convicted of this offense by the time of the higher sentence. The Court found that a conviction which took place after the original sentence could be considered even though the conduct took place prior to the initial sentence. The Court concluded that a judge may justify an increased sentence by affirmatively identifying relevant conduct or events that occurred subsequent to the original sentencing proceeding.

When the legislature increases the punishment the defendant gains the benefit of the prior lesser punishment. This result is mandated by the proposition that such an increase is a prohibited *ex post facto* law. *Lindsey v. Washington*, 301 U.S. 397 (1937).

D. Sentencing Procedures

Due process plays an important role in the procedures a judge should use before sentencing a defendant. *Williams v. New York*, 337 U.S. 241 (1949). Sentencing judges may consider information beyond the statutory elements of the offense, e.g., family history, education, employment, and health. In addition, the judge may consider the defendant's untruthfulness or refusal to cooperate with law enforcement authorities. The judge "must be permitted to consider any and all information that reasonably might bear on the proper sentence for the particular defendant, given the crime committed." *Wasman v. United States*, 468 U.S. 559 (1984). Most jurisdictions grant to defendants notice about the general information relied upon to impose a penalty and the defendant's opportunity to participate and present evidence relevant to the sentencing decision. Given the importance of a sentencing authority's need to know about the defendant, the rules of evidence are inapplicable to the sentencing process.

If the defendant has been convicted, the case should proceed to sentencing without unreasonable delay. However, it is customary to postpone sentencing for a short period of time to enable the court to obtain a presentence report. The report must be prepared by a probation officer, must include an analysis of the defendant's background and may include a victim impact statement under appropriate circumstances. *Payne v. Tennessee*, 501 U.S. 808 (1991). The report is reviewed by the court before sentencing. Before imposing sentence, the trial court must advise the defendant or counsel of the contents of any presentence report. If the defendant wishes to controvert the contents of any report, the court must afford a fair opportunity and a reasonable period of time to challenge them. However, the court need not disclose the sources of confidential information contained in the report.

Normally, the judge who presided at the trial conducts the sentencing. Following a felony or misdemeanor conviction, the judge considers whether the defendant is eligible for probation or conditional discharge as an alternative to imprisonment. If the record does not clearly reflect a consideration of sentencing alternatives, the case must be remanded for proper sentencing. In addition to considering the presentence report, sentencing alternatives if any, and evidence concerning the nature and characteristics of the criminal conduct, the court decides whether to run any multiple sentences concurrently or consecutively.

Formal sentencing consists of pronouncing sentence in accordance with the previous plea or adjudication of guilt. Any pending motions which may affect the need for sentencing should be decided before sentencing is pronounced. The defendant should be given the common law right of allocution, to identify any reason why the sentence should not be pronounced or why a particular sentence is appropriate. It thus affords regularity to the proceedings and reduces the likelihood of a subsequent attack on the judgment. If the sentence is predicated upon a contested adjudication, the defendant must be advised of rights regarding appeal.

Whenever any fact besides a prior conviction that increases the maximum penalty for a crime with regard to federal law, Fifth Amendment due process and the Sixth Amendment jury trial right require that the fact must be charged in the charging instrument, submitted to a jury, and proved beyond a reasonable doubt. That standard applies as well to the states through the Fourteenth Amendment. *Apprendi v. New Jersey*, 530 U.S. 466 (2000). Thus, a judge cannot increase a penalty beyond a statutory maximum by making a factual determination under a preponderance of evidence standard.

Soon after *Apprendi* was decided, scores of challengers attempted to take advantage of what Justice O'Connor had termed a "watershed change in constitutional law." *Harris v. United States*, 536 U.S. 545 (2002) held that *Apprendi* is inapplicable to mandatory minimum sentences. Under federal law, carrying a firearm in relation to a drug trafficking offense requires a mandatory minimum sentence of five years. The judge, rather than jury, in Harris's case found that he had flourished a gun and sentenced him to seven years. Justice Kennedy's opinion first decided that the mandatory minimum provision was a sentence enhancement provision rather than a separate offense. This view affirmed *McMillan v. Pennsylvania*, 477 U.S. 79 (1986), which permitted a legislature to specify a condition for a mandatory minimum without making the condition an element of the crime. *Apprendi* did not apply to the mandatory minimum concept at issue, because that decision required a jury determination beyond a reasonable doubt for any fact that increased the penalty for a crime above the prescribed statutory *maximum* sentence. A "judge may impose the minimum, the maximum, or any other sentence within the range without seeking further authorization from" a jury.

By contrast, the Court in *Ring v. Arizona*, 536 U.S. 584 (2002) concluded that it violated *Apprendi* for a sentencing judge sitting without a jury to find an aggravating circumstance necessary for imposition of the death penalty. When the judge made that finding, the defendant was exposed to a penalty greater than that authorized by the jury's verdict alone, in violation of *Apprendi*. *Ring* is not retroactive. *Schriro v. Summerlin*, 542 U.S. 348 (2004).

A federal indictment that fails to allege a drug quantity that was necessary for and could result in an enhanced statutory maximum sentence violates *Apprendi*. In *United States v. Cotton*, 535 U.S. 625 (2002), the defendants never objected to the error at trial, thereby requiring a plain error analysis. The parties on appeal agreed that the omission of the drug quantity was an error that affected the defendant's substantial rights. However, the Court found that the error did not seriously affect the fairness, integrity, or public reputation of judicial proceedings and therefore did not constitute plain error requiring a reversal of the conviction.

Blakely v. Washington, 542 U.S. 296 (2004) held that "the 'statutory maximum' for *Apprendi* purposes is the maximum sentence a judge may impose solely on the basis of the facts reflected in the jury verdict or admitted by the defendant." Blakely pleaded guilty to kidnaping, a crime which supported a maximum sentence of 53 months. After the trial judge, however, found that the defendant had acted with "deliberate cruelty," the sentence increased to 90 months.

* * * The application of Washington's sentencing scheme violated the defendant's right to have the jury find the existence of "any particular fact" that the law makes essential to his punishment. * * * [T]he "statutory maximum" for Apprendi purposes is the maximum sentence a judge may impose solely on the basis of the facts reflected in the jury verdict or admitted by the defendant. The determination that [Blakely] acted with deliberate cruelty, like the determination in Apprendi that the defendant acted with racial malice, increased the sentence that the defendant could have otherwise received. Since this fact was found by a judge using a preponderance of the evidence standard, the sentence violated Blakely's Sixth Amendment rights.

Likewise, the Court invalidated California's determinate sentencing law, which gave the judge the authority to elevate a sentence by finding the existence of "circumstances in aggravation." *Cunningham v. California*, 549 U.S. 270 (2007).

The Court subsequently applied the *Apprendi* and *Blakely* holdings to invalidate the mandatory nature of the Federal Sentencing Guidelines. *United States v. Booker*, 543 U.S. 220 (2005). The remedy from a majority of the *Booker* Court was to consider the mandatory federal standards as "effectively advisory." The appellate standard for reviewing federal sentences outside the Guidelines is whether the trial court abused its discretion in deviating from the Guidelines. *Gall v. United States*, 128 S.Ct. 586 (2007). For example, federal judges may base sentences on their disagreement with the Guidelines' disparity between sentences for crack and powder cocaine crimes. *Kimbrough v. United States*, 128 S.Ct. 558 (2007).

POINTS TO REMEMBER

- A variety of sentencing alternatives to incarceration is available for courts.

- The death penalty is frequently challenged for the arbitrary method in which it is administered.

- The prosecution must establish at least one aggravating circumstance beyond a reasonable doubt in order to impose the death penalty.

- A criminal sentence may be challenged as grossly disproportionate under the Eighth Amendment.

- Enhanced sentences for defendant with prior felony convictions may lead to a life sentence.

- Sentencing procedures must satisfy due process regarding judicial consideration of all information relating to the defendant.

- Any factual information besides a prior conviction that increases the maximum penalty for a crime must be charged in the charging instrument, submitted to a jury, and proved beyond a reasonable doubt.

Chapter 22

DOUBLE JEOPARDY

Focal Points for Chapter 22

- When jeopardy attaches.

- Mistrials.

- Prosecution appeals of dismissals and acquittals.

- Retrial following appellate reversal.

- Prosecutorial vindictiveness.

Chapter 13 addressed the double jeopardy implications associated with the joinder of offenses. To review the basic principle, a defendant has both federal and state constitutional protections against being placed in jeopardy twice for the same offense. The pertinent part of the Fifth Amendment states: "[N]or shall any person be subject for the same offense to be twice put in jeopardy of life or limb." The Fifth Amendment Double Jeopardy protection applies to the states through the Fourteenth Amendment. *Benton v. Maryland*, 395 U.S. 784 (1969).

Because the debates of the constitutional framers provided little indication of the intended scope of double jeopardy protection, the courts have interpreted the double jeopardy clause in light of their understanding of its underlying purposes. The essence of the prohibition against double jeopardy is not that a defendant may incur a greater risk of being found guilty in a second trial than in a first trial, or that a second trial may be conducted prejudicially, but rather that the defendant would risk conviction for an offense for which the defendant has already been placed on trial and in jeopardy.

A successful claim involving double jeopardy will bar a trial on the indictment or information. The objection may be raised by a motion to dismiss at any time before trial. Although a failure to raise the objection before the second adjudication may operate as a waiver, it may be raised for the first time in a reviewing court if the double jeopardy issue can be decided as a matter of law on the facts established by the record.

Double jeopardy bars a second prosecution only if jeopardy attached in the original proceeding. In a jury trial, jeopardy attaches when the jury is sworn. *Crist v. Bretz*, 437 U.S. 28 (1978). If a case is tried before a judge, after waiver of a jury, jeopardy attaches when the first witness is sworn. Jeopardy also attaches when the trial court accepts a guilty plea. Conversely, withdrawal of a guilty plea is a waiver of the double jeopardy protection against trial on the charge in the indictment or information. If a case is dismissed or terminated prior to the attachment of jeopardy, jeopardy has not attached and the defendant may have to respond to the same criminal charges in further proceedings.

One of the requirements for the attachment of jeopardy is that the court hearing the case have proper jurisdiction. When the court exceeds its jurisdiction, a conviction is void and there is no bar to a new trial. Absent a facial jurisdictional defect, the prior adjudication is presumed to have been within the court's jurisdiction. Likewise, a prior conviction or acquittal procured by the defendant to defraud the government of an opportunity to attain the proper sentence does not bar a new prosecution.

The doctrine of dual sovereignty does not prohibit multiple prosecutions for the same offense by courts of different sovereignties. See, e.g., *Heath v. Alabama*, 474 U.S. 82 (1985). So, a defendant may be tried for a bank robbery by both federal and state authorities. On the other hand, the dual sovereignty theory does not apply to state and municipal prosecutions for the same act because the state and the municipality are regarded as the same sovereign, regardless of how the state chooses to classify its governmental subunits: the subunits derive their power to exist from the sovereign.

A. Mistrials and the Possibility of a Retrial

After jeopardy attaches, a case cannot be terminated without an adjudication because the defendant has a right to have the case completed by a particular factfinder. A mistrial declaration is the most common exception to this double jeopardy concept. A mistrial is granted whenever an error has occurred in the trial that cannot be cured by any remedial action of the parties or the court. In most jurisdictions, there is an extensive amount of case law dealing with the types of error in the admission of evidence and the conduct of counsel, witnesses, the court, and jury that are "curable" by instructions or continuances, and which errors require a mistrial.

When circumstances suggest that the proceedings should be terminated, with the court declaring a mistrial prior to a formal verdict, the judge at that time need not decide whether a subsequent trial on the same charge would be permissible. The only question before the court is whether the first trial should be discontinued. If the trial judge terminates the proceedings by declaring a mistrial, the court's order reflects a belief that retrial on the same charges should be permitted. Although a double jeopardy claim will not arise until the charges are brought again, that later double jeopardy claim constitutes an attack on the propriety of the original mistrial declaration, *i.e.*, there was no manifest necessity for declaring the mistrial.

Mistrials can be broadly characterized in two areas: (1) where the defendant does not consent to the mistrial; and (2) where the defendant consents to the mistrial. Consent of the defendant appears to be the primary distinction in the treatment of mistrials. *Oregon v. Kennedy*, 456 U.S. 667 (1982). A retrial is permissible if the defendant actively sought or consented to premature termination of the earlier proceedings. The doctrine of manifest necessity is not applicable to double jeopardy where the defendant wants a mistrial. However, where a defendant seeks and obtains a mistrial, he or she may invoke the bar of double jeopardy to prevent a second trial only if the conduct provoking his or her motion was prosecutorial or judicial conduct intended to provoke the defendant into moving for a mistrial.

The declaration of a mistrial over the defendant's objection is improper unless the court finds termination of the trial to be manifestly necessary. A trial court is in the best position to determine whether to declare a mistrial or to choose an alternative remedy such as admonishing the jury. If manifest necessity for a mistrial is present, a retrial is permitted. The decision to grant a mistrial is within the trial court's discretion. Double jeopardy does not provide a guarantee to the defendant that the government will vindicate its societal interest in the enforcement of the criminal laws in one proceeding. *United States v. Jorn*, 400 U.S. 470 (1971).

Although the manifest necessity concept may provide an unpredictable test, the declaration of a mistrial at the request of anyone other than the defendant sets the stage for a strong double jeopardy claim. A defense objection to preserve the claim should be made when defense counsel does not believe that the client's interests are best served by acquiescence in a mistrial and a new trial. Federal Rule 26.3 requires that the court consider the views of all parties before ruling on a motion for mistrial: "Before ordering a mistrial, the court must give each defendant and the government an opportunity to comment on the propriety of the order, to state whether that party consents or objects, and to suggest alternatives."

In *Illinois v. Somerville*, 410 U.S. 458 (1973), after the jury was sworn the prosecutor noticed a negligent omission of a vital allegation from the indictment that would require reversal of any conviction on appeal. The Supreme Court found that there was manifest necessity for the trial court's mistrial declaration. The case is indicative of the clash of interests favoring and opposing reprosecution following a mistrial. The prosecution argues that it has a strong interest in obtaining one reasonable opportunity to establish the defendant's guilt. In addition, any error in declaring the mistrial confers on the defendant an immunity from punishment for the crimes charged. This factor explains the reluctance of courts to second-guess the initial mistrial ruling when considering double jeopardy claims. Defense counsel argue that reprosecution is undesirable because it subjects the defendant to serious burdens even if the defendant is acquitted at a retrial. For example, delay in scheduling the retrial may impede the preparation of the defendant's case and increase the personal strain of a retrial. Invariably, the defense arguments return to the defendant's interest in completing the trial before a jury that was favorably disposed to the defendant's case.

In *Arizona v. Washington*, 434 U.S. 497 (1978), the trial court granted defendant a new trial, but during the opening statements of the retrial, the defense attorney referred to the prosecution's prior misdeeds. The trial court granted the prosecution's motion for a mistrial because the evidence of the first trial would have been inadmissible and the judge feared that the jury had been biased by these comments. The trial judge made no explicit finding of manifest necessity for the mistrial and did not expressly consider alternatives to granting a mistrial. The Court stated that when a mistrial is justified by a "high degree" of necessity, the defendant's right to a particular tribunal is outweighed by society's right to have one complete opportunity to prosecute the accused. When mistrials are declared due to hung juries, trial judges have considerable discretion to gauge firsthand the amount of time a particular jury needs to reach a verdict. Likewise, when defense counsel makes prejudicial comments to the jury, the trial judge can observe the impact of the statements on the jury and select the appropriate remedy. The Court observed that if the trial judge lacked broad discretion to erase the effects of prejudicial statements, unscrupulous defense attorneys would take unfair advantage of their clients' double jeopardy rights by intentionally biasing the jury. Therefore, appellate courts should defer to a trial judge's decision to grant a mistrial, unless there is an abuse of that discretion.

In upholding the broad discretion of a trial judge to declare a mistrial, the Court did not require trial courts to make express findings of manifest necessity, or explicitly to consider alternatives to the mistrial declaration on the record. That fails to provide lower courts with guidance in addressing other sorts of mistrials. For example, should a trial judge have broad discretion in every instance of defense counsel misconduct, such as prejudicial statements made during *closing* arguments after a long trial?

B. Termination of the Case by Dismissal or Acquittal

In the previous section on mistrials, manifest necessity for the mistrial declaration was crucial in order for the prosecution to retry a defendant who did not want a mistrial. The assumption underlying the mistrial was that the reason for terminating the first trial was not a fatal defect to a second trial. By contrast, *prior* to the attachment of jeopardy, the reason for terminating a criminal proceeding has no double jeopardy significance. For example, the government may appeal the grant of *pretrial* motions to dismiss. Even though a successful government appeal can lead to a new prosecution, double jeopardy does not bar the appeal because jeopardy had not attached at the time the trial court dismissed the charges. The defendant is not running the gauntlet more than once, *i.e.*, a reprosecution does not provide a second chance for the prosecution because it has not yet had a first chance.

Once jeopardy *has* attached, the way in which a trial ends is relevant to double jeopardy principles. Whether the cessation of a trial is a dismissal or acquittal is important to resolving whether the government can appeal the adverse termination of the case and whether the defendant can be reprosecuted. All jurisdictions provide statutory authority for the government to appeal from an adverse termination. In the absence of a double jeopardy prohibition, the government can appeal under statutory authority and, if successful, can reprosecute the defendant.

An acquittal of the defendant bars further prosecution of the defendant on the same offense. What is an acquittal? It is a termination of the proceedings in favor of the defendant, *on the merits*. For example, if the court finds insufficient evidence and directs the jury to return a verdict of "not guilty," an acquittal occurs. Likewise, a ruling by the trial court prior to a verdict that amounts to an acquittal also bars retrial. A trial judge cannot reconsider a mid-trial acquittal after the parties have rested their cases. *Smith v. Massachusetts*, 543 U.S. 462 (2005).

A dismissal is not the same as an acquittal, because even though it is a termination of the proceedings it is not a termination on the merits of the case. Where the court dismisses the charge after hearing proof and finds that the facts cannot support a conviction on the offense charged, a new trial is not allowed. The "dismissal" was actually on the merits, and is regarded for double jeopardy as an acquittal. However, where the indictment is dismissed as legally defective, double jeopardy does not preclude an appeal by the prosecution and a retrial if the appeal is successful.

A trial court's judgment of acquittal because the proof was insufficient bars a retrial after a hung jury. In *United States v. Martin Linen Supply Co.*, 430 U.S. 564 (1977), following a mistrial declaration due to a hung jury, the trial court granted defense counsel's timely motion under Federal Rule 29(c) for a judgment of acquittal. The Court treated the disposition as an acquittal and therefore not appealable. However, if the charge is dismissed on legal grounds after a hung jury, a new trial is allowed. In *United States v. Sanford*, 429 U.S. 14 (1976), the trial judge declared a mistrial after the jury was unable to agree on a verdict. Four months later, the judge dismissed the charge because the government had consented to the conduct which formed the basis of the allegation. The Court held that the dismissal was appealable and was akin to a pretrial order when jeopardy has not attached. The distinction is that an acquittal, however wrong, is accorded special weight.

Even where the judge makes errors in the admission of evidence, a ruling that ends in a functional acquittal bars retrial. In *Sanabria v. United States*, 437 U.S. 54 (1978), the Court held that when a defendant is acquitted at trial, he cannot be retried for the same charge, even if the legal rulings underlying the acquittal were erroneous. However, if the judgment of acquittal follows a jury's verdict of conviction, the acquittal may be appealed by the government since the original verdict of guilt can be reinstated. See *United States v. Wilson*, 420 U.S. 332 (1975).

C. Termination of the Case by Conviction

When a trial ends in a conviction, there is no constitutional prohibition against the government retrying a defendant who has succeeded in having his or her conviction set aside on appeal. The exception to this rule is that retrial is prohibited where a reversal is mandated by the insufficiency of the evidence, even though the defendant is the moving party. *Burks v. United States*, 437 U.S. 1 (1978). The rule of insufficiency applies as well to motions for a new trial before the trial judge. A new trial is allowed, however, if the trial judge would have decided the case differently than the jury did, rather than the amount of proof simply being inadequate to convict.

Where the appellate court reverses because of trial errors or defects in the charging instrument, as opposed to insufficiency of evidence, the defendant can be retried. For example, in *Lockhart v. Nelson*, 488 U.S. 33 (1988), the Court permitted a retrial when the appellate reversal was for trial errors in the admissibility of evidence, even though without such evidence there was insufficient proof to support the conviction.

When a defendant is tried for an offense but is convicted of a lesser included version of that offense, on retrial following a successful appeal he or she cannot be convicted of the greater included crime. The first verdict operates as an implied acquittal on the greater included offense, thereby precluding a retrial for that crime. Only instructions on the lesser included offense can be given to the jury at the second proceeding. However, in the event that the defendant is tried and convicted of a jeopardy-barred offense, the conviction can be reduced to a lesser included offense which is not barred by double jeopardy. The defendant has the burden of showing a reasonable probability that he or she would not have been convicted of the lesser included offense absent the presence of the barred offense.

D. Double Jeopardy Regarding Punishment

The double jeopardy prohibition of multiple prosecutions for the same offense limits a court's ability to impose or alter sentences. Consideration of relevant conduct to determine a defendant's sentence is not punishment for that conduct in violation of double jeopardy and does not preclude a later indictment based upon the same relevant conduct.

A sentence imposed at a proceeding sufficiently similar to a trial may be sufficiently final to invoke the protection of the double jeopardy clause. For example, if a life sentence is imposed in a bifurcated sentencing proceeding for a capital offense that resembles a trial on guilt or innocence, the double jeopardy clause prohibits imposition of the death penalty following a successful appeal and retrial. *Bullington v. Missouri*, 451 U.S. 430 (1981). Without a finding of an aggravating circumstance at the first trial, the initial life sentence constitutes an acquittal of the death penalty and thus the double jeopardy clause prohibits the subsequent imposition of a death sentence. Even if the acquittal were the result of an erroneous evidentiary ruling or an erroneous interpretation of legal principles, the life sentence stands. However, if an appellate court corrects a mistaken legal interpretation of an aggravating factor which does not alter the validity of the punishment, a retrial after a reversal of the conviction for a trial error can result again in a death sentence. When a jury's verdict in a capital sentencing proceeding is merely advisory, a court may impose the death penalty despite the jury's verdict of life imprisonment.

When a defendant successfully appeals his conviction, the double jeopardy clause does not bar the imposition of a more severe sentence if he is convicted on retrial. *North Carolina v. Pearce*, 395 U.S. 711 (1969). A court that is sentencing after retrial can consider any event, such as a conviction for an offense committed before the original sentencing or conduct occurring after the first trial. When a jury imposes the second sentence, the jury's independence minimizes the possibility that prosecutorial vindictiveness will influence the sentence.

The availability of an appeal by the defendant does not prohibit a higher punishment on a trial de novo on the same charge. However, a higher offense cannot be charged in the de novo appeal. The prosecution may also appeal a sentence imposed by the judge without violation of double jeopardy.

POINTS TO REMEMBER

- Jeopardy attaches when the jury is sworn, or in a bench trial when the first witness is sworn.

- A defendant who consents to a mistrial can be retried, unless the prosecution goaded the defendant and provoked the defendant's consent.

- Otherwise, a defendant may be retried if the mistrial declaration was manifestly necessary.

- Regardless of when a dismissal of charges occurs, a defendant may be retried if the dismissal is reversed on appeal by the prosecution.

- After jeopardy attaches, the prosecution cannot appeal an acquittal.

- When a conviction is reversed due to insufficient evidence, the defendant cannot be retried.

- An appellate reversal for trial error does not preclude a retrial.

- After a successful appeal, a defendant may receive a longer sentence at a retrial if the court identifies new information about the defendant.

Chapter 23

APPEALS

Focal Points for Chapter 23

- Direct appeals.

- Harmless error and plain error.

- Right to appeal.

There are significant differences between the trial and appellate stages of a criminal proceeding. The purpose of the trial stage from the government's point of view is to convert a criminal defendant from a person presumed innocent to one found guilty beyond a reasonable doubt. By contrast, it is ordinarily the defendant, rather than the government, who initiates the appellate process, seeking not to fend off the efforts of the prosecutor but rather to overturn a finding of guilt made by a judge or a jury below.

Following conviction, the state defendant has several avenues of relief available and has access to a number of forums where he can obtain review of his conviction. Motions to set aside the verdict and motions for a new trial are addressed to the trial court. Direct appeal lies with the state appellate courts, while habeas corpus petitions can be filed in both state and federal court. This chapter addresses the forms of judicial review in the order in which they normally arise, and highlights substantive differences between the forms of judicial review, as well as distinct procedural requirements relating to time and form. Although post-conviction remedies require close attention to details and are addressed in the next chapter, two general themes run throughout the review process.

The complexity of courtroom procedure inevitably leads to some errors, even when attorneys and judges are at their best. The defendant is entitled to a fair trial, not a perfect trial free from all minor or technical defects. If the reviewing courts find error in the record, reversal of the conviction is not warranted if the outcome of the trial would have remained the same in the absence of the error, i.e., a harmless error does not affect the defendant's right to a fair trial, nor does it call into question the accuracy of the finding of guilt. Harmless error is assessed differently depending on the nature of the error and the proceeding in which the error is raised.

The contemporaneous objection rule provides that no ruling of the trial court will be considered as a basis for reversal unless the objection was stated together with the ground therefor at the time of the ruling, except for good cause shown. This requirement is designed to preclude trial counsel from "sandbagging" the trial court by not calling possible errors to its attention. Objections must be raised at trial in order to afford opposing counsel an opportunity to respond to the objection and to allow the trial court to rule in the first instance as to the propriety of the objection. Appellate courts, however, are authorized to grant relief from this rule, and may conduct a full review of the conviction when necessary to attain the ends of justice. For example, Federal Rule 52(b) provides that "[a] plain error that affects substantial rights may be considered even though it was not brought to the court's attention." A more stringent standard for reversal is applied when the defendant fails to object at trial, and on appeal cites plain error by the trial court.

Closely related to the contemporaneous objection rule are the concepts of curative admissibility and proffers of proof. Curative admissibility retroactively corrects a trial court's initial error in admitting evidence, i.e., when a defendant unsuccessfully objects to evidence which he considers improper and then on his own behalf introduces evidence of the same character, he thereby waives his objection and forfeits his right to contest the trial court's ruling on appeal. (Waiver is not made by the mere cross-examination of a witness or the introduction of rebuttal evidence.) A proffer of evidence requires that when the trial court sustains an objection and excludes evidence, counsel offering the evidence must ensure that the record reflects what the evidence would have been. Failure to make a proffer of evidence deprives the appellate court of the information necessary to rule upon the objection. The offer of proof may be in the form of a stipulation of testimony, or the witness may testify for the record in the absence of the jury.

A. Review by the Trial Court

In most appeals, a higher court is asked to scrutinize the trial record for errors that would require reversal of the conviction. Many misdemeanor cases, however, are tried in lower courts, such as police courts or magistrate's courts, from which no record or transcript of the proceedings is available for review by a higher court. These lower courts are sometimes referred to as courts-not-of-record and usually operate without a jury and without all of the procedural safeguards provided in the trial of felony cases. A defendant convicted in such a lower court is often granted an absolute right to a trial de novo in a superior court, sometimes called a court-of-record. Although occasionally referred to as an appeal, the granting of a trial de novo is normally automatic upon the defendant's request. Thus no error need be alleged as to the first trial, and a defendant who exercises his right to a trial de novo is not entitled to judicial review of the sufficiency of the evidence presented to the lower court. *Justices of Boston Municipal Court v. Lydon*, 466 U.S. 294 (1984).

The right to a trial de novo generally exists even when the defendant pled guilty in the lower court. Neither the defendant's plea nor the lower court's judgment is admissible evidence at the trial de novo, but the defendant's prior testimony is admissible at the trial in the higher court.

B. Direct Appeal in the State Courts

Most jurisdictions have created a two-tiered appellate structure in which the convicted defendant has a right of appeal to an intermediate appellate court, but any further appeal to a higher court, usually the state Supreme Court, is often discretionary. The distinction between a right of appeal and discretionary review by an appellate court is important because the United States Supreme Court has held that in felony cases, counsel must be provided to indigent persons exercising their right to appeal. *Douglas v. California*, 372 U.S. 353 (1963). However, counsel need not be provided to indigent defendants seeking discretionary review. The right to counsel on appeal stems from the due process and equal protection clauses of the Fourteenth Amendment, not from the Sixth Amendment. Thus although the Sixth Amendment guarantees the defendant's right to self-representation at trial, there is no such right at the appellate stage. *Martinez v. Court of Appeal*, 528 U.S. 152 (2000).

The appellate process begins with the defendant's filing a notice or petition of appeal. The notice informs the parties, the trial judge and the appellate court that the case is being appealed. All jurisdictions require that the notice of appeal be filed within a specified period of time. For example, in the federal system the notice of appeal must be filed within ten days of the date of judgment. At the time the notice of appeal is filed, or at a subsequent specified date, the parties must designate portions of the trial record that will be sent to the appellate court. The appellate court bases its review of the case on the trial record which commonly includes: (1) jury instructions given or refused by the trial judge; (2) exhibits offered in evidence; (3) any orders entered by the trial court; (4) any opinion or memorandum decision rendered by the trial judge; (5) any pretrial discovery material requested; and (6) portions of the trial transcript in which the judge ruled upon objections to the introduction of evidence.

Counsel also must alert the appellate court to the basis of appeal by filing a statement of issues that the appellate court is asked to resolve. These issues will be expanded upon in counsels' written briefs which summarize the factual background of the case and set forth relevant legal arguments. The appellate court, usually in its discretion, may hear oral arguments on the issues raised. Many of the issues that arise in the course of a trial are to be resolved according to the broad discretion of the trial court. On appeal, such rulings will not be disturbed in the absence of an abuse of discretion. The trial court's application of defined legal standards (such as probable cause to arrest) is reviewed *de novo*. The appellate court must accept the trial court's factual determinations, so long as there is evidence to support those findings.

As noted earlier, the contemporaneous objection rule requires counsel to clearly state the nature and basis of any objection. Many appellate courts also require opposing counsel to state the basis for opposing the objection, and require the trial judge to "state on the record" the grounds on which his ruling was based. This requirement may conflict with another appellate rule which allows the reviewing court to sustain the trial court's ruling "if there is any reasonable view of the evidence that will support it."

C. Harmless Error and Plain Error

A trial error that is not of constitutional dimension (for example, the trial judge erred in admitting some minor item of evidence) is harmless when it plainly appears from the facts and circumstances of the case that the error did not affect the verdict. Reversal is required for a non-constitutional error only if it "had substantial and injurious effect or influence in determining the jury's verdict." *United States v. Lane*, 474 U.S. 438 (1986).

Application of the harmless error doctrine to constitutional error depends upon the nature of the error. "Structural defects in the constitution of the trial mechanism" require automatic reversal and are not subject to harmless error analysis. The rationale for this rule of automatic reversal was set forth in *Sullivan v. Louisiana*, 508 U.S. 275 (1993), where the trial court gave a constitutionally inadequate jury instruction on reasonable doubt and the prosecution's burden of proof.

Harmless error review looks . . . to the basis on which the jury actually rested its verdict. The inquiry, in other words, is not whether, in a trial that occurred without error, a guilty verdict would surely have been rendered, but whether the guilty verdict actually rendered in *this* trial was surely unattributable to the error. This must be so, because to hypothesize a guilty verdict that was never in fact rendered [under a proper definition of reasonable doubt] would violate the jury trial guarantee. [The] Sixth Amendment requires more than appellate speculation about a hypothetical jury's action, or else directed verdicts for the State would be sustainable on appeal; it requires an actual jury verdict of guilty.

The Supreme Court has recognized a number of structural errors requiring automatic reversal: (1) unlawful exclusion of members of the defendant's race from a grand jury; (2) exclusion of a juror reluctant to impose the death penalty; (3) violation of the right to a public trial; (4) violation of the right of self-representation; (5) a trial presided over by a biased judge; (6) violation of the right to counsel; (7) a constitutionally inadequate jury instruction on reasonable doubt.

In contrast to structural errors, "trial errors" are subject to harmless error review. Trial errors occur during the presentation of the case to the jury. For example, the Court recently held that *Apprendi* violations are subject to harmless error analysis when the trial court fails to submit a sentencing factor. *Washington v. Recuenco*, 126 S.Ct. 2546 (2006). Such constitutional errors are treated differently depending on whether they are raised on direct appeal or collateral review. On collateral review, (e.g. habeas corpus petitions) trial errors require reversal of the conviction only if the defendant proves "actual prejudice," i.e., the error had a "substantial and injurious effect or influence in determining the jury's verdict." *Brecht v. Abrahamson*, 507 U.S. 619 (1993). That standard applies, regardless of whether the state courts recognized the constitutional error or applied the more deferential *Chapman* standard. *Fry v. Pliler*, 127 S.Ct. 2321 (2007). See Chapter 8, Section E. On direct review, however, trial errors require reversal of the conviction unless the reviewing court finds such errors to be harmless "beyond a reasonable doubt."

A more stringent standard of review for harmless error is applied when the defendant failed to object to a trial error, but now calls such "plain error" to the attention of the appellate court. In such situations the appellate court *may* review the record for plain error and *may* reverse the conviction to attain the ends of justice. But what is a plain error? The error must be clear or obvious; it must prejudicially affect substantial rights, and the error must seriously affect the fairness, integrity, or public reputation of judicial proceedings. *United States v. Olano*, 507 U.S. 725 (1993).

D. The Right to Appeal

There was no right to appeal in criminal cases at common law, and England did not permit appeals from a criminal conviction until 1907. Appeals as of right in federal courts were nonexistent for the first century of our Nation, and appellate review of any sort was rarely allowed. The states did not generally recognize an appeal as of right until 1889.

At least in dicta, the United States Supreme Court has noted that "a review by an appellate court of the final judgment in a criminal case, however grave the offense of which the accused is convicted, was not at common law and is not now a necessary element of due process." *McKane v. Durston*, 153 U.S. 684 (1894). Once a state provides for appellate review, the review process must not violate equal protection or due process rights. For example, *Douglas v. California*, 372 U.S. 353 (1963) held that indigent defendants are constitutionally entitled to assistance of counsel on a first appeal granted as a matter of right.

Whatever the nature and scope of a right to appellate review, *Ortega-Rodriguez v. United States*, 507 U.S. 234 (1993) demonstrates that the right can be waived or forfeited. An appeals court may dismiss the appeal of a defendant who is a fugitive during the appellate process. However, if the defendant flees and returns to custody before the appellate process begins, denial of the appeal is not automatic.

E. Appeals of Last Resort

A defendant who fails to obtain a reversal on direct appeal may make collateral attacks on the conviction, such as a petition for a writ of habeas corpus discussed in the next chapter. As a supplement to judicial review, all jurisdictions grant a convicted defendant an opportunity to appeal to executive authority for a pardon or grant of clemency. For example, Article 2, Section 2, Clause 1 of the U. S. Constitution gives the President "Power to grant Reprieves and Pardons for Offences against the United States, except in Cases of Impeachment." President Gerald Ford pardoned, prior to trial, former President Richard Nixon for his role in the Watergate scandal. Former President Nixon was given a "full pardon," but the President has the power to "forgive the convicted person in part or entirely, to reduce a penalty in terms of a specified number of years, or to alter it with conditions which are in themselves constitutionally unobjectionable." *Schick v. Reed*, 419 U.S. 256 (1974).

POINTS TO REMEMBER

- Most jurisdictions provide one appeal of a criminal conviction as a matter of right.

- A subsequent appeal may be heard only when the court exercises its discretion to accept the case.

- A trial error is harmless when the error did not affect the verdict.

- A conviction is reversible for plain error even when the defendant failed to preserve the error for appeal.

Chapter 24

COLLATERAL REMEDIES

Focal Points for Chapter 24

- Time considerations.

- Exhaustion of state remedies.

- Custody requirements.

- Evidentiary hearing.

- Cognizable issues.

- Successive petitions.

- Procedural defaults.

A. Introduction

A defendant who fails on direct appeal may file a collateral attack on the conviction, the most common form being a *habeas corpus* petition. Most states have habeas corpus-like proceedings that closely follow federal habeas corpus, discussed in the remainder of this chapter. Failure to prevail in state habeas proceedings will not bar a subsequent federal habeas action. In fact, the filing of a state petition is often a necessary component of the federal petition.

Habeas corpus, a Latin term meaning "you have the body," is a collateral attack because it is not a continuation of the criminal process, but a civil suit brought to challenge the legality of the restraint under which a person is held. The petitioner in this civil suit, having lost the presumption of innocence upon conviction, has the burden to prove by a preponderance of evidence that his confinement is illegal. The respondent in a habeas action is the prisoner's custodian—the warden or other prison official. Habeas corpus has been called "the most celebrated writ in the English law," and the United States Supreme Court paid homage to this "Great Writ of Liberty" in *Fay v. Noia*, 372 U.S. 391 (1963):

We do well to bear in mind the extraordinary prestige of the Great Writ [in] Anglo–American jurisprudence. Received into our own law in the colonial period, given explicit recognition in the Federal Constitution, Art. I, section 9, cl. 2, incorporated in the first grant of federal court jurisdiction, habeas corpus was early confirmed by Chief Justice Marshall to be a "great constitutional privilege."

Although in form the Great Writ is simply a mode of procedure, its history is inextricably intertwined with the growth of fundamental rights of personal liberty. For its function has been to provide a prompt and efficacious remedy for whatever society deems to be intolerable restraints. Its root principle is that in a civilized society, government must always be accountable to the judiciary for a man's imprisonment: if the imprisonment cannot be shown to conform with fundamental requirements of law, the individual is entitled to his immediate release. Thus, there is nothing novel in the fact that today habeas corpus in the federal courts provides a mode for the redress of denials of due process of law. Vindication of due process is precisely its historic office.

However great the scope and focus of the writ, merely filing a habeas corpus petition does not insure that a federal court will review the merits of the petitioner's claim. If the habeas corpus petition is patently frivolous, or if the court can determine the merits of the allegations by reference to records of previous state or federal judicial proceedings, the petition may be denied without a full evidentiary hearing.

1. Time Considerations

At common law any person illegally detained could use the writ of habeas corpus to make repeated efforts to gain his freedom. "Res judicata did not attach to a court's denial of habeas relief . . . [instead] a renewed application could be made to every other judge or court in the realm, and each court or judge was bound to consider the question of the prisoner's right to a discharge independently, and not to be influenced by the previous decisions refusing discharge." *McCleskey v. Zant*, 499 U.S. 467 (1991). The common law courts tolerated multiple petitions and petitions filed years after the initial trial because the writ of habeas corpus originally performed only the narrow function of testing either the jurisdiction of the sentencing court or the legality of Executive detention. The scope of the writ later expanded beyond its original narrow purview to encompass review of constitutional error that had occurred in the proceedings leading to conviction. The expanded coverage of the writ led the Supreme Court to formulate the doctrines of exhaustion and procedural default as means of limiting abusive and repetitive habeas petitions. The Antiterrorism and Effective Death Penalty Act of 1996 [AEDPA] incorporates and expands upon these doctrines.

Prior to enactment of AEDPA there was no time limitation on the filing of a writ of habeas corpus, although some courts applied the doctrine of laches on a case-by-case basis. The doctrine of laches did not operate as an effective statute of limitations because it required that the government prove actual prejudice from the delay, which cannot be presumed merely from the passage of time.

Tolling under 28 U.S.C. §2244(d)(2), is triggered by judicial review of a state prisoner's request that the trial court use its discretion to reduce his sentence. *Wall v. Kholi*, 131 S.Ct. 1278 (2011). In order to promote speedy punishment and the finality of criminal justice proceedings, AEPDA created a rigid one-year limitation for filing a petition for habeas corpus relief. The year runs from the latest date of the final judgment on direct review or "the expiration of the time for seeking such review"; removal of any state-imposed impediment that unconstitutionally prevented the filing of such a petition; the Supreme Court's recognition of a new, retroactively applicable constitutional right; or the emergence or recognition of any new facts supporting the petitioner's claim that "could have been discovered through the exercise of due diligence." 28 U.S.C. § 2244(d)(1)(A)–(D). An example of the last ground occurs when a prisoner collaterally attacks his federal sentence on the ground that a state conviction used to enhance that sentence has since been vacated. In that situation, the limitations period begins to run when the prisoner receives notice of the order vacating the state conviction, provided that he showed due diligence in seeking to vacate the state conviction. See *Johnson v. United States*, 544 U.S. 295 (2005).

The one-year limitation is tolled while an application for state post-conviction or other collateral review is pending, even if it contains procedurally-barred claims. *Artuz v. Bennett*, 531 U.S. 4 (2000). However, an application for federal habeas corpus review is not an "application for state post-conviction or other collateral review," and the limitation therefore will not be tolled. *Duncan v. Walker*, 533 U.S. 167 (2001).

2. Exhaustion of State Remedies

Before a federal court will review a constitutional claim in a habeas corpus proceeding that seeks review of a state conviction, the claim first must be fairly presented to the state court system by properly pursuing a claim throughout the entire appellate process of the state. 28 U.S.C. § 2254(b)(1)(A). Exhaustion of remedies includes the presentations of claims to the state supreme court even though its review is discretionary. *O'Sullivan v. Boerckel*, 526 U.S.

838 (1999). The state court need not actually address the claim in a written opinion to satisfy this requirement. Federalism considerations simply will not permit a state prisoner to bypass the state courts and initiate the first review of his conviction in the federal courts.

The exhaustion requirement does not preclude habeas review; it merely delays such review. For example, in *Rose v. Lundy*, 455 U.S. 509 (1982), the Court held that a federal district court must dismiss a petition that combines unexhausted and exhausted claims. Following dismissal, the petitioner must either return to state court to present the unexhausted claims or resubmit only the exhausted claims to the federal court. A state prisoner who submits such a "mixed petition" may either return to the state courts to exhaust all claims or amend the petition to present only exhausted claims to the federal district court. A federal district court has discretion to stay a "mixed" petition while unexhausted claims are presented to a state court, and to return to federal court for review of the perfected petition within the statute of limitations. *Rhines v. Weber*, 544 U.S. 269 (2005).

If the petitioner fails to exhaust his state remedies, the federal court may dismiss the petition until such time as the petitioner has exhausted the available state remedies. The only exceptions to the exhaustion of remedies doctrine are when there is an absence of available state remedies or special circumstances render such remedies ineffective to protect the rights of the petitioner. 28 U.S.C. § 2254(b)(1)(B). Because the exhaustion of state remedies doctrine is based on comity and is not a jurisdictional requirement, the government may waive the requirement. See *Strickland v. Washington*, 466 U.S. 668 (1984).

3. Custody

To apply for a writ of habeas corpus, a person must be in "custody," which is liberally construed by the courts to include significant restraints on personal liberty as well as physical incarceration. *Jones v. Cunningham*, 371 U.S. 236 (1963). The writ may not be used to attack a sentence that has been fully served, to attack a conviction that merely imposed a fine or collateral civil disability not resulting in incarceration, or to challenge a conviction after the sentence has expired, because there is no longer "custody" under that conviction. In *Peyton v. Rowe*, 391 U.S. 54 (1968), the Supreme Court ruled that a petitioner serving consecutive sentences is considered "in custody" under any one of the sentences for purposes of filing a habeas petition. A consecutive sentence that has not begun, is currently running, or has expired may be challenged until all of the sentences have been served.

Apart from custody considerations, "criminal convictions do in fact entail adverse collateral legal consequences." *Sibron v. New York*, 392 U.S. 40 (1968). As a remedy of last resort, a convicted person no longer subject to confinement may challenge his prior conviction. For example, in *Korematsu v. United States*, 323 U.S. 214 (1944), the Supreme Court upheld the conviction of an American citizen of Japanese ancestry for being in a location designated as off limits to all persons of Japanese ancestry. Forty years later, the conviction was reversed because the government had misled the courts as to the military necessity of wartime relocation and internment of civilians in 1944.

4. Evidentiary Hearings

Following the filing of a petition, the state's answer to the petition and the record of the state court proceedings, the habeas court must determine whether an evidentiary hearing is required. If the petitioner has failed to develop the factual basis of a claim in state court proceedings, the federal court can hold an evidentiary hearing only when the petitioner has shown that (1) either the claim relies on a new, retroactive rule of constitutional law that was previously unavailable, or the claim relies on a factual basis that could not have been previously discovered by an exercise of due diligence; and (2) the facts underlying the claim show by clear and convincing evidence that, but for the constitutional error, there would have been no conviction. In *Williams v. Taylor*, 529 U.S. 420 (2000), the Supreme Court held that the failure to develop a factual basis of a claim requires a "lack of diligence or some greater fault, attributable to the prisoner or to the prisoner's counsel." However, a claim pursued with diligence in state court could still be heard by a federal court if it was undeveloped due to government misconduct such as concealment of information.

If a federal district court grants a hearing on the habeas petition, both the petitioner and the government must be given the opportunity to present evidence. The federal court must apply a presumption of correctness to state court factual determinations, unless the petitioner shows by clear and convincing evidence that the findings were erroneous.

Upon denial of the petition, the petitioner is remanded to custody. If the court grants the petition, the petitioner is discharged from custody, but the court may suspend execution of its order to allow the government to appeal or to institute a new trial within a specified period of time. The court also has authority to admit the petitioner to bail, pending the government's appeal or initiation of a new trial. When deciding whether to grant release pending appeal to a state prisoner who has won habeas relief a federal court may consider: (1) the risk that the prisoner may flee; (2) the danger the prisoner may pose to the public; (3) the state's interest in continuing custody and rehabilitation; and (4) the prisoner's interest in release pending appeal. *Hilton v. Braunskill*, 481 U.S. 770 (1987).

B. Violations of Federal Law

Only federal issues are cognizable in federal habeas proceedings; state constitutional or statutory violations are not. The most common habeas corpus claims are ineffective assistance of counsel, incriminating statements obtained by illegal police interrogation, improper judicial or prosecutorial conduct, and insufficient evidence.

Federal habeas corpus relief does not lie for errors of state law. Although 28 U.S.C. § 2254 speaks of a "violation of the Constitution or laws or treaties of the United States," almost all federal habeas petitions allege a violation of the Constitution. A conviction obtained in violation of a federal statute does not warrant habeas review unless the statutory violation qualifies as a "fundamental defect which inherently results in a complete miscarriage of justice, or an omission inconsistent with the rudimentary demands of fair procedure." *Reed v. Farley*, 512 U.S. 339 (1994). Most statutory violations are simply not important enough to invoke the extraordinary habeas jurisdiction.

A defining characteristic of the Warren Court in the 1960's was its willingness to increase federal habeas review of state court convictions by "constitutionalizing" many aspects of criminal procedure.

> The writ of habeas corpus known to the Framers was quite different from that which exists today. . .[T]he first Congress made the writ of habeas corpus available only to prisoners confined under the authority of the United States, not under state authority. . . It was not until 1867 that Congress made the writ generally available in "all cases where any person may be restrained of his or her liberty in violation of the constitution, or of any treaty or law of the United States." And it was not until well into this century that this Court interpreted that provision to allow a final judgment of conviction in a state court to be collaterally attacked on habeas. *Felker v. Turpin*, 518 U.S. 651 (1996).

The Warren Court's approach to federal habeas corpus was partially premised on a belief that the state courts could not be trusted to protect the constitutional rights of criminal defendants. In the landmark case of *Gideon v. Wainwright*, 372 U.S. 335 (1963), Justice Harlan expressed dissatisfaction with many state courts' discharge of their "front-line responsibility for the enforcement of constitutional rights." The Burger and Rehnquist Courts, however, embraced the concept of a "new federalism" by resurrecting faith in the state courts as protectors of individual freedom. *Stone v. Powell*, 428 U.S. 465 (1976) altered the judicial availability of federal habeas relief in Fourth Amendment cases, and was the first step in the Supreme Court's efforts to rein in federal judges reared on the Warren Court's "judicial activism" and distrust of state courts.

In *Stone v. Powell*, the Supreme Court limited the scope of federal habeas corpus review of Fourth Amendment violations by holding that a state prisoner is not entitled to habeas corpus relief on the ground that evidence obtained in an unconstitutional search and seizure was introduced at trial if the state provided an opportunity for full and fair litigation of the Fourth Amendment claim. This limitation on federal habeas claims does not apply to Sixth Amendment claims of ineffective counsel based on deficient representation in litigating a Fourth Amendment issue. See *Kimmelman v. Morrison*, 477 U.S. 365 (1986).

Although the Court's opinion in *Stone v. Powell* led to speculation that defendants might be denied habeas corpus review of other constitutional claims, the Supreme Court refused to extend that limiting principle to legal issues which are guilt-related. For example, in *Jackson v. Virginia,* 443 U.S. 307 (1979), the Court held that a claim that a prisoner was convicted on insufficient evidence is cognizable on federal habeas corpus review as a violation of due process. Unlike the Fourth Amendment exclusionary rule, the reasonable doubt standard of proof was deemed to relate to the accuracy of fact-finding. A federal court can hear an insufficiency of evidence claim, even if it was already heard by the state court. *Jackson's* holding, however, limited habeas relief to a showing that no rational trier of fact, viewing the evidence in the light most favorable to the prosecution, "could have found the essential elements of the crime beyond a reasonable doubt."

In *Withrow v. Williams*, 507 U.S. 680 (1993), the Court declined an opportunity to apply *Stone v. Powell* to another favorite target of Court opinions—*Miranda v. Arizona*. *Miranda*'s exclusionary rule is similar to the Fourth Amendment rule—both are designed to deter police violations, and both arguably are unrelated to accurate fact-finding. Nevertheless, the *Withrow* Court found that a federal court can hear a petition concerning a *Miranda* violation even if the prisoner had an opportunity for a full and fair hearing of the issue in state court. In rejecting an extension of *Stone* v. *Powell,* the Court stated that "prophylactic though it may be," *Miranda* safeguards a fundamental trial right that is not "necessarily divorced from the correct ascertainment of guilt." The Court also noted that eliminating *Miranda* habeas claims simply would result in the substitution of due process voluntariness claims in their place.

In *Rose v. Mitchell,* 443 U.S. 545 (1979), the Court held that a claim of racial discrimination in the selection of a state grand jury is cognizable on federal habeas corpus, even though the claimed error did not affect the determination of guilt and had been heard by the state court. The Court distinguished *Stone* on three grounds. First, the Court was unwilling to assume that state judges could fairly consider claims of grand jury discrimination, since those claims required the state courts to review their own procedures rather than those of the police. Second, the right to a indictment by a grand jury free from discrimination in its selection process is a personal constitutional right rather than a judicially created remedy. Third, state courts could be expected to respond to a determination that their grand jury selection procedures failed to meet constitutional requirements, *i.e.,* deterrence is effective.

Under the AEPDA, habeas relief will not be granted for any claim adjudicated on the merits in state courts unless the decision was "contrary to, or involved an unreasonable application of" federal law clearly established by the Supreme Court. A state court denial of post-conviction relief without stating its reasons qualifies as a § 2254(d) "adjudication on the merits," deserving deference as a reasonable decision. *Harrington v. Richter,* 131 S.Ct. 770 (2011). In *Williams v. Taylor,* 529 U.S. 362 (2000), the Court defined the distinction between the "contrary to" category and the "unreasonable application" category. "Contrary to" means that a state court either has arrived at a conclusion on a question of law opposite to that reached by the Supreme Court, or when confronted with materially indistinguishable facts from a Supreme Court precedent, arrived at an opposite result. "Unreasonable application" means that a state court either identified the correct legal rule but unreasonably applied it to the facts of the case, or unreasonably extended the legal principle to a new context that should not apply or unreasonably refuses to extend the principle to a new context. Because unreasonably applying federal law differs from incorrectly applying it, a state court's decision applying federal law must be both erroneous and unreasonable. The determination that a state court's judgment was contrary to or involved an unreasonable application of clearly established federal law under 28 U.S.C. § 2254(d) must be based on the record that was before the state court that decided the claim. *Cullen v. Pinholster*, 131 S.Ct. 1388 (2011).

Occasionally, the Court has found that a decision denying habeas relief was "contrary to" and "involved an unreasonable application of clearly established Federal law, as determined by the Supreme Court of the United States." For example, in *Abdul-Kabir v. Quarterman*, 550 U.S. 233 (2007) and *Brewer v. Quarterman*, 550 U.S. 286 (2007), the trial court's jury instructions prevented the jury from giving meaningful consideration and effect to relevant mitigating evidence during a capital trial's penalty phase.

In *Yarborough v. Alvarado*, 541 U.S. 652 (2004), the Court elaborated on whether a state court decision was an unreasonable application of clearly established law under *Williams v. Taylor*. Whether a decision is "unreasonable" can depend in part on the specificity of the legal rule. The more general the rule, the longer it may take for its meaning to emerge. The more specific the rule, the narrower is the range of a reasonable judgment. In *Yarborough*, the state court's failure to consider a juvenile suspect's age and inexperience with police interrogation in deciding that he was not "in custody" for *Miranda* purposes did not result in an "unreasonable application" of federal law, § 2254(d)(1).

C. Abuse of the Writ and Procedural Default

1. Successive Petitions as an Abuse of the Writ

The AEPDA establishes procedures for the disposition of second or successive petitions. A second or successive petition must pass through a "gatekeeping" system requiring a petitioner to move for an authorization order from a three-judge panel in the appropriate court of appeals before a district court may hear the petition. 28 U.S.C. § 2244(b)(3). *Burton v. Stewart*, 549 U.S. 147 (2007). In order to obtain an authorization order at the gatekeeping stage, a petitioner must make a prima facie showing that (1) the claim was not presented in a previous federal habeas petition; (2) either this new claim relies on a new rule of constitutional law that was previously unavailable, or its factual basis "could not have been discovered previously through the exercise of due diligence;" and (3) the facts underlying the claim, if proven and viewed in light of the whole evidence, show by clear and convincing evidence that, but for the constitutional error, no reasonable juror would have found the petitioner guilty of the offense. The certification decision is not appealable and is not subject to rehearing.

In *Felker v. Turpin*, 518 U.S. 651 (1996), the Supreme Court upheld the limits on second or successive petitions as "a modified res judicata rule, a restraint on what is called in habeas corpus practice 'abuse of the writ.' " A problem arises when a petitioner returns to federal court with a second habeas corpus petition raising previously dismissed claims. The Court does not regard habeas petitions filed after a dismissal *without* prejudice of an earlier petition as second or successive petitions. *Slack v. McDaniel*, 529 U.S. 473 (2000).

Because collateral proceedings are governed by civil rather than criminal rules, a Civil Rule 60 motion may also constitute a successive petition (and is therefore subject to the AEPDA's gatekeeping provisions) when it contests the merits of the court's denial of relief or seeks to advance new grounds for relief. On the other hand, Rule 60(b) challenges to the integrity of the trial court proceeding do not implicate the AEPDA provision on successive petitions. *Gonzalez v. Crosby*, 543 U.S. 1086 (2005).

2. Procedural Default

The most common form of procedural default is the defendant's failure to present a federal constitutional claim to the trial court and thus preserve the issue for appellate review. The consequence of a procedural default is that the petitioner may be barred from judicial review of the forfeited claim in both state and federal courts. Unlike *Stone v. Powell* which bars federal habeas relief only when Fourth Amendment issues are given a full and fair hearing in the state courts, if there is a procedural bar, there is no hearing on the constitutional challenge in any state or federal court.

When a state court decision is based on independent and adequate state grounds, habeas corpus relief is available only to a prisoner who can show either cause for the procedural default and actual prejudice from a violation of federal law, or that the federal court's failure to review the claims will result in a fundamental miscarriage of justice. In *Murray v. Carrier*, 477 U.S. 478 (1986), the Court stated that the "existence of cause for procedural default must ordinarily turn on whether the prisoner can show that some objective factor external to the defense impeded counsel's efforts to comply with the State's procedural rule."

A lawyer's error is insufficient cause unless it amounts to a violation of the Sixth Amendment right to effective counsel. If defense counsel says that she did not raise an issue in the state court proceedings because the state court would have been unsympathetic to the claim, the apparent futility of making an objection does not constitute cause. *Engle v. Isaac*, 456 U.S. 107 (1982). The Court also rejected adoption of a rule requiring trial counsel to exercise "extraordinary vision" or to object to every aspect of the proceedings in the hope that some aspect might make a latent constitutional claim.

> We have long recognized that the Constitution guarantees criminal defendants only a fair trial and a competent attorney. It does not insure that defense counsel will recognize and raise every conceivable constitutional claim. Where the basis of a constitutional claim is available, and other defense counsel have perceived and litigated that claim, the demands of comity and finality counsel against labeling alleged unawareness of the objection as a cause for a procedural default.

Similarly, an allegation that an issue was not raised due to its novelty does not excuse a procedural default if the claim "had been percolating in the lower courts for years" at the time of the default. *Smith v. Murray*, 477 U.S. 527 (1986).

Cause may be proved by showing that the "factual or legal basis for a claim was not reasonably available to counsel" or that governmental interference rendered procedural compliance impracticable. For example, in *Amadeo v. Zant,* 486 U.S. 214 (1988), the Court held that governmental concealment of evidence that women and African Americans were intentionally underrepresented on jury lists constituted cause for the defendant's failure to raise a timely challenge to the jury panel.

Prejudice is a stricter standard than the "plain error" doctrine applicable on direct review because direct appeal is designed to afford a means for the prompt redress of miscarriages of justice. This standard is "out of place when a prisoner launches a collateral attack against a criminal conviction after society's legitimate interest in the finality of the judgment has been perfected by the expiration of the time allowed for direct review or by the affirmance of the conviction on appeal." Thus, in *United States v. Frady*, 456 U.S. 152 (1982) prejudice did not follow simply from the fact that a jury instruction was erroneous. The Court held that the petitioner failed to show that the error "worked to his actual and substantial disadvantage, infecting his entire trial with error of constitutional dimensions." In other words, prejudice must be evaluated by the effect of the error in the context of the whole trial.

D. Claims of Actual Innocence as "Gateways" to Federal Habeas Corpus Review

A common misperception, at least among the lay public, is that federal courts and ultimately the United States Supreme Court, sit as courts of last resort to correct any and all injustice done to American citizens.

> It would be marvelously inspiring to be able to boast that we have a criminal-justice system in which a claim of "actual innocence" will always be heard, no matter how late it is brought forward, and no matter how much the failure to bring it forward at the proper time is the defendant's own fault. But of course we do not have such a system, and no society unwilling to devote unlimited resources to repetitive criminal litigation ever could.

Bousley v. United States, 523 U.S. 614 (1998).

Herrera v. Collins, 506 U.S. 390 (1993) indicated that a claim of innocence is a vital component (a gateway) of attempts to gain habeas review otherwise barred by the procedural default rule. Innocence claims, however, must be based on actual innocence rather than mere legal insufficiency. *Schlup v. Delo*, 513 U.S. 298 (1995) characterized petitioner's claim based on ineffective assistance of counsel and the prosecution's failure to disclose evidence as *procedural*, in contrast to the *substantive* claim of innocence based on newly discovered evidence raised in *Herrera*. The Court characterized "actual innocence" cases as "extraordinary."

In *House v. Bell*, 126 S.Ct. 2064 (2006), the Court held that petitioner had satisfied the difficult showing required by the actual innocence exception to defaulted claims, and that his federal habeas proceeding therefore could go forward. DNA testing established that semen on the murder victim's clothing came from her husband rather than from House, the defendant; that evidence was the only forensic evidence linking House to the murder. In addition, House in his post-trial proceedings had presented evidence that the murder victim's husband had confessed to the murder. The Court found this to be the "rare" case where, if the jury had heard all the conflicting evidence, it likely would have viewed the record as a whole as creating reasonable doubt. House's proof cast doubt on his guilt to satisfy *Shlup*'s gateway standard for obtaining federal review, even though the Court found that he had not shown freestanding innocence under *Herrera*.

Before a federal court reviews allegations of actual innocence, it first must address the nondefaulted claims for comparable relief and other grounds for cause to excuse the procedural default. *Dretke v. Haley*, 541 U.S. 386 (2004)

POINTS TO REMEMBER

- The Antiterrorism and Effective Death Penalty Act of 1996 (AEDPA) severely limited the availability of federal habeas corpus relief.

- A collateral attack on a criminal conviction requires filing of a separate lawsuit, which is civil in nature.

- AEPDA has a one-year limitation for filing a petition for relief, and generally it prohibits the filing of successive petitions.

- Before filing a federal habeas petition, as a matter of comity a person must exhaust state remedies by presenting the claim to the state's highest court.

- A person may obtain federal habeas relief only if he is in custody, which includes significant restraints on personal liberty as well as physical incarceration.

- Federal habeas relief is available only for *federal* (not state) constitutional or statutory violations.

- If a person's Fourth Amendment claim was heard in state court, it cannot be considered by a federal court in a habeas proceeding.

- Failure to preserve an issue for appellate review precludes consideration in a habeas corpus proceeding unless there was cause for and actual prejudice from the failure to preserve the issue, or unless the petitioner can prove actual innocence.

Table of Cases

Table of Statutes

Table of Rules
